Systems Analysis and Design and the Transition to Objects

Sandra Donaldson Dewitz
San Jose State University

The McGraw-Hill Companies, Inc.
New York St. Louis San Francisco Aukland Bogotá
Caracas Lisbon London Madrid Mexico City Milan Montreal
New Delhi San Juan Singapore Sydney Tokyo Toronto

McGraw-Hill

A Division of The **McGraw·Hill** *Companies*

Systems Analysis and Design and the Transition to Objects

1 2 3 4 5 6 7 8 9 0   FGR FGR   9 0 9 8 7 6

ISBN 0-07-016763-X

Sponsoring editor: Frank Ruggirello
Editorial assistant: Kyle Thomes
Production supervisor: Natalie Durbin
Project manager: Cecelia G. Morales
Copyeditor: Maggie Jarpey
Interior design: Cecelia G. Morales
Cover design: John Edeen
Composition: Arizona Publication Service
Printer and binder: Quebecor Printing Fairfield, Inc.

Cover image courtesy of Quilt San Diego. Quilt artist: Carol Soderlund. Photographer: Carina Woolrich. The quilt is titled *Covenant*.

Library of Congress Catalog Card Number 95-81167

TABLE OF CONTENTS

6 ◆ Problem Definition and Feasibility Analysis   192

Case Illustration: A Problem Definition Report for ETG   221

7 ◆ Joint Application Development: A Technique for User-Driven Development   240

PREFACE

Systems Analysis and Design and the Transition to Objects is designed for use in a junior-level, one-semester systems analysis and design (SA&D) course intended to provide MIS students with a strong foundation in SA&D concepts, methodologies, techniques, and tools. Those who have the luxury of a two-semester SA&D course sequence will find that the text can be easily supplemented with additional readings or lectures on special topics suggested in the *Instructor's Manual*.

Although many SA&D texts adequately address traditional systems development, few or none provide a transition from the traditional structured and information engineering approaches to the object-oriented (OO) approaches used increasingly today, especially to develop small systems. Some SA&D texts pay lip service to the object-oriented paradigm, presenting a free-standing chapter or two describing its concepts and techniques. In contrast, *Systems Analysis and Design and the Transition to Objects* bridges the gap between these two paradigms, presenting both views of the systems world and integrating their approaches, when feasible. Its goal is to help instructors and students feel comfortable in either or both worlds. Consequently, it not only explains traditional SA&D concepts and techniques, such as the top-down approach, problem definition, feasibility analysis, enterprise analysis, and data flow diagrams; it also addresses fundamental object-oriented concepts and techniques, such as encapsulation, inheritance, polymorphism, use cases, and object communication.

MOTIVATION

This textbook was written to address three problems I see in many systems analysis and design (SA&D) texts:

1. Failure to incorporate object thinking and object-oriented development techniques as a central theme.
2. Omission or inadequate coverage of iterative, interactive development methodologies and strategies.
3. Excessive breadth with insufficient depth of topic coverage.

The first two problems are ones of omission. Most SA&D textbooks emphasize traditional structured development to the exclusion of more timely development approaches, such as object-oriented analysis and design, rapid application development (RAD), and joint application development (JAD). Although the traditional waterfall has not gone "dry," teaching it as though it is the only source of development wisdom is a disservice to today's students, who are bombarded by articles on OO, RAD, and JAD in the popular media and who will work in a world that is adopting these approaches.

The third problem is one of excess. Most systems analysis and design textbooks are weighty tomes that cover a broad range of topics, barely skimming the surface of most topics. Students are drowned in a deluge of concepts and techniques, few of which they fully assimilate because "there just isn't time!" Time—usually just fifteen weeks—is the enemy of every SA&D instructor trying to help his or her students acquire the myriad SA&D concepts and skills required of a systems analyst. For too many semesters, I have felt like the distraught child in D. H. Lawrence's "The Rocking-Horse Winner." Just as that child feverishly whipped his rocking horse to the finish line, all the while chanting "There must be more money. There must be more money!"—I have feverishly "whipped" myself and my students to semester's end, all the while droning "There must be more time. There must be more time!"

This textbook attempts to correct these problems in the following ways.

1. By making object thinking and object-oriented techniques central to the text.

2. By promoting an iterative, interactive development methodology and devoting two chapters to JAD and RAD.

3. By reducing the number of concepts covered but increasing the depth of coverage.

To achieve the third objective, I was determined not to present a technique or concept if I could not have students complete a related activity. For the most part, I have been consistent. This is especially evident in Part Three, which discusses analysis and design techniques. Here fewer techniques are presented, but each is related to the other so that, for example, students see how system design evolves from use cases or physical data flow diagrams that define system requirements, to the object relationship model and program structure charts or object models that define system data structures and behaviors, and on to the dialog flow diagram that defines the system's interfaces.

INSTRUCTIONAL APPROACH

The guiding instructional philosophies of this textbook are just-in-time learning, learning by example, and learning by doing. *Just-in-time learning* means that students learn a concept or technique at the time they need to use it. It also means that, instead of presenting exercises only at the end of each chapter, this text includes *exercises within each chapter* to help students assess their understanding immediately after reading about a concept or technique. Answers to these "Check Your Understanding" exercises are provided at the end of the text.

Learning by example means that students are provided numerous examples to facilitate learning. Illustrations of concepts and techniques take three forms:

1. Detailed, step-by-step problem-solving sections that demonstrate, for example, how to analyze a case problem to construct a DFD or how to analyze a source document to define system data structures.

2. Minicases that relate SA&D concepts to business practices.

3. A text-spanning case that illustrates development activities, techniques, and deliverables.

Parts One and Two include chapter minicases, derived from practitioner journals such as *Computerworld*, to illustrate fundamental systems development concepts as applied in the real world. Part One concludes by introducing the longer Entertainment To Go (ETG) case, which illustrates the systems development activities. Part Two presents a complete problem definition report based on the ETG case. For the past several semesters, I have used this problem definition report as a model to guide my students as they prepare this first major project deliverable, and I have seen the quality of student reports improve dramatically. Part Two also presents an ETG case installment that describes a JAD workshop held to define ETG's requirements and to begin analysis and design of ETG's new order processing system.

In Part Three, Chapters 9 through 12 each open with an ETG case installment that continues the JAD workshop and illustrates the analysis and design techniques discussed in each chapter. In addition, the ETG case is used as source material for the data, process, object, and interface modeling techniques presented in each chapter. Parts Three and Four conclude with brief ETG case installments to provide a unified view of these concepts and techniques. By studying the ETG case, students come to understand what a systems analyst does and are able to see how SA&D concepts and techniques are used to develop an information system.

Learning by doing means that mastering most concepts and techniques is achieved by an activity requiring students to apply what they have learned. The "activity" is not just a standalone exercise; instead, it is one of a series of project activities, each of which yields a system deliverable: for example, identification of system objectives, project constraints and scope, and leveled DFDs documenting the current system or specifying the functional requirements of the new system. I believe that students do not really understand a concept until they have successfully applied it. Omitting material that cannot be addressed in a related project activity allows deeper coverage of each concept; in addition, students have time to achieve a greater degree of understanding and to assimilate each concept more fully. Furthermore, students learn what a systems analyst really does by performing a series of analysis and design activities focused on a specific project.

TEXT STRUCTURE

The text material is presented in thirteen chapters and four technical modules divided into four parts. Each chapter

◆ Begins with learning objectives to guide students as they study the material.

◆ Contains Check Your Understanding exercises to help students gauge their understanding of the chapter's concepts and techniques.

◆ Concludes with a review of learning objectives summarizing what students have learned.

◆ Provides a list of key terms, discussion questions, and, where appropriate, practice exercises.

Each technical module explains an analysis and design technique (e.g., data flow diagrams or logical data modeling) and ends with key terms and practice exercises. Each part concludes with an installment of the Entertainment To Go case illustration described earlier.

Part One provides an overview of the systems development product and process. Chapter 1 defines an information system as being composed of people, procedures, data, software, and hardware (the PPDSH components) and as performing input, processing, output, storage, and control (IPOSC) functions. It also examines the catalysts for and goals of systems development. Chapter 2 describes system components and functions in more detail. Technical Modules A and B present two traditional techniques used to analyze and to document system functions and components: data flow diagrams and system flowcharts. Chapter 3 examines the traditional systems development (TSD) paradigm, discusses several problems with TSD, and presents a methodology (called the Bridge) that incorporates object-oriented techniques, JAD, and RAD to iteratively, interactively analyze and design an information system.

Object-oriented concepts are woven into the fabric of these chapters. Chapter 1 introduces terms such as object class, object instance, attribute, method, and inheritance. Chapter 2 compares the OO and traditional treatments of the data and software components. Chapter 3 discusses the benefits of OO systems development (e.g., reusability and interoperability).

Part Two grounds systems development in an organizational setting and describes the activities of preliminary investigation and analysis. Chapter 4 describes systems development as planned organizational change and introduces three trends that affect systems development: business process reengineering, interorganizational information systems, and the move from glasshouse to client/server systems. Chapters 5 and 6 examine the activities of the preliminary investigation and analysis stage of the Bridge methodology. Topics and techniques addressed include enterprise analysis (affinity diagrams), enterprise modeling (organization chart, workflow diagram, and enterprise object model—all of which are described in Technical Module C: Enterprise Modeling), and problem definition and feasibility analysis. Part Two ends with Chapter 7's discussion of joint application development workshops, roles, tools, and benefits.

Part Three contains the "meat" of the text, presenting system data structure, behavior, and interface analysis and design techniques. Chapter 8 explains two types of prototyping—requirements prototyping and evolutionary prototyping—and discusses the objectives, tools, and methodology of RAD. Technical Module D and Chapters 9 through 11 present the techniques of iterative analysis, design, preliminary construction, and review. The activities in this stage include more fully defining the requirements of the new system and designing and constructing a preliminary system (i.e., prototype) that fulfills these requirements. Concepts investigated here include logical data modeling, physical database design, traditional and OO behavior modeling, and human-computer interaction. Analysis and design techniques presented in Part Three include

◆ Use cases, an object-oriented technique for specifying system requirements, behaviors, and interfaces.

◆ Object relationship models, which define the system's business objects and their attributes, methods, and relationships.

◆ Physical DFDs, which specify how the functions of the new system will be implemented.

◆ Program structure charts, structured text, and formal use cases, which specify the system's automated and manual behaviors.

◆ Dialog flow diagrams, which define the flow of control between the system's interfaces.

Part Three concludes with Chapter 12's discussion of documenting design specifications and planning final construction, testing, and installation activities.

Part Four examines the activities of final construction, system test and installation, and post-implementation review. Here implementation activities are viewed from the systems analyst's perspective, focusing on those activities an analyst is most likely to perform: purchasing hardware and software, preparing system and user documentation, creating test data and test plans, training users, and conducting the post-implementation evaluation.

ANCILLARIES

Instructor's Manual and Disk

The instructor's manual provides a complete set of tools for developing your course. In addition to suggesting how to schedule course readings and activities and how to integrate cooperative learning exercises, it includes chapter outlines, teaching strategies, exercise answers, and transparency masters of many figures for each chapter. The Instructor's manual also provides discussion questions for each chapter opening case and ETG case installment and indicates additional readings on selected topics. Pointers on using the CASE Project Workbook (described below) are also given.

The instructor's disk contains exercise solutions created using a CASE tool or graphics program so that you may modify and print these DFDs and other models to use as handouts or transparencies. This disk also contains a document file (Microsoft Word 6.0 for IBM-compatibles) of Chapter 6's sample problem definition report so that you can modify the report organization and contents to suit your preferences. Also included are PowerPoint presentations on selected topics.

Test Bank

The test bank contains a variety of true/false, multiple-choice, matching, fill-in-the-blank, short-answer, and essay questions for each chapter. The computerized test bank is available in IBM-compatible format and runs in an easy-to-use Windows or DOS environment.

CASE Project Workbook

To help you assign relevant "hands-on" activities to support student learning, a CASE project workbook is available to supplement the textbook. This workbook explains fundamental CASE tool features and functions and includes several business cases to be used in semester-long projects. Each case provides an overview of the organization, describes the organization's existing information system (including sample source documents and reports), and provides transcripts of user interviews. The workbook also contains a set of tear-out project exercise forms.

Some of the exercises encourage students to use CASE and other tools (e.g., the tools provided in popular DBMS packages such as Access and Paradox, spreadsheets, graphics programs, presentation tools, and so on); these exercises include pointers on using the tool effectively. Other exercises can be completed "by hand." Contact your local McGraw-Hill representative for CASE tools available with the workbook.

ACKNOWLEDGMENTS

Although only one person appears as the author of this text, numerous reviewers, students, friends, colleagues, and McGraw-Hill staff contributed to its completion. First and foremost, I thank Eleanor Jordan at The University of Texas, who has been—perhaps without her knowledge!—my benevolent spirit-guide and silent partner in this undertaking. Her confidence in me, as a graduate student writing parts of her systems development textbook, gave me the self-confidence to write my own. Eleanor's "take" on systems development permeates this textbook; she has inspired my love of and enduring interest in SA&D.

I have benefited greatly from "test driving" earlier drafts of this text in my SA&D classes. A heart-felt "Thanks!" to all the Bus 93 students at San Jose State University who endured learning from a work-in-progress and who offered innumerable and invaluable suggestions for improving the clarity of the text. A special word of appreciation to Man-Wa Yeung, who compiled the glossary, and to Lisa Emmett, who prepared solutions to many exercises. Thanks also to my colleague, Dr. William Nance, for providing valuable feedback and for writing most of the section on affinity diagrams.

Appreciation is also extended to the reviewers whose constructive criticisms helped me evolve the text:

Charles Billbrey
James Madison University

Joseph Brady
University of Delaware

Robert Bretz
Western Kentucky University

Robert Cerreny
Florida Atlantic University

Anthony Hendrickson
University of Nevada, Las Vegas

Ellen Hoadley
Loyola College, Maryland

Christopher Jones
Brigham-Young University, Hawaii

Peeter Kirs
University of Texas, El Paso

Robert Kleim
Arizona State University

Constance Knapp
Pace University

Charles Lutz
Utah State

Peter Markulis
SUNY Geneseo

John Rettenmayer
Northeast Louisiana University

T. W. Usowicz
San Francisco State

Michael Varano
Villanova University

Clinton White
University of Deleware

The editorial and production staff at McGraw-Hill have also shaped this final product. Three people deserve special mention. First, my editor, Frank Ruggirello. Frank has been a "task master" whose encouragement (and occasional whip-cracking!) have spurred me to accomplish more than I thought possible. His confidence in my ability and judgment are greatly appreciated. Second, my project manager, Cecelia Morales of Arizona Publication Service. Cecelia has brought joy to the process. Her patience and good humor in dealing with my missed deadlines eased the stress of bringing this work to completion; her many small touches in refining the text and catching omissions have significantly improved the text. Third, the series editor, Peter Keen. Peter's lavish compliments kept me going during my "this book stinks!" episodes; his insightful criticisms helped sharpen the text's focus.

Finally, an "I promise it won't happen again!" to my family, who have missed many meals, much attention, and *me,* during the past year. Yes, Mike, I do have time to play Scrabble or to spend the afternoon golfing. And Missy, no, you don't have to make do with those poor excuses for walks; we can roam the woods again! Cinnamon and Smokey—I promise to bring fresh veggies once a day and to plant white clover ASAP. Casey . . . . You're a cat! What do you care?

PART ONE

An Overview of
Systems Development

You have come to the study of systems analysis and design at an interesting, but confusing time for novices and experts alike. The practice of systems development is in flux as we undergo a paradigm shift in the way we view the software and data components of an information system. Throughout the 1970s and 1980s, the accepted development paradigm was embodied in two methodologies[1]: Yourdon's and DeMarco's Structured Systems Analysis and Design (SSA&D) and Martin's Information Engineering (IE). Both of these methodologies, to varying degrees, advocate analyzing and designing software through functional decomposition—that is, examining an information system in terms of the functions it performs and the data it maintains. Most CASE (computer-aided systems engineering) tools currently on the market embody one of these methodologies, which we refer to as *traditional systems development* (TSD).

Today the software and data components of an information system are increasingly being viewed as a collection of related objects. In this paradigm, called Object-Oriented Analysis and Design (OOA&D), or more simply, *object-oriented systems development* (OOSD), the emphasis is on the "things" that comprise the system. These things are described by their attributes and behaviors. Several methodologies are arising to guide systems development under this new paradigm: especially noteworthy are Rumbaugh's Object Modeling Technique [Rumbaugh et al. 1991] and the Booch Method [1993]. Although most organizations are at least thinking about making the shift to OOSD or have begun to use this methodology in a few isolated projects, less than 10 percent are actively practicing it as their primary development approach in critical projects.

What does this mean to you? It means that you will be among the generation of information systems professionals to bridge the gap between these two paradigms. It means that you must have not only a strong foundation in structured

---

[1] A methodology is a structured problem-solving process accompanied by a set of tools and techniques.

methodologies, but also a clear understanding of the concepts, tools, and techniques of the OOSD methodologies. However, because these paradigms put forth fundamentally divergent system views and require very different ways of thinking about systems, spanning the chasm between them can be difficult.

This text attempts to make bridging the gap easier by integrating, where feasible, the concepts and techniques of both paradigms. Instead of focusing on TSD and paying lip service to the new paradigm (i.e., by presenting OOSD concepts in isolated chapters), this text is designed to teach both approaches to the systems world thoroughly enough that you will feel comfortable developing systems with either. Learning to view information systems from both perspectives should deepen your systems understanding in general.

Part One provides an overview of systems development, introducing the terms, concepts, and techniques that will be discussed in greater detail later in this text. Chapter 1 discusses the product, process, impetus, and goals of systems development. It defines what a system is and explains the systems approach to analysis and design. This chapter also introduces you to the concept of system decomposition, both in terms of processes and data (the traditional development paradigm) and in terms of objects (the object-oriented development paradigm). Finally, Chapter 1 discusses the impetus for and the goals of systems development.

Chapter 2 describes the product of systems development in terms of information system functions and components. Whether you develop an information system using a traditional or an object-oriented methodology, the product of your efforts is the same: *technology* (software and hardware) to be used by *people* within an *organization* (procedures and data).

Chapter 3 describes the process of systems development, presenting a concise overview of both the traditional and the object-oriented development methodologies. In addition, this chapter discusses the limitations of the traditional paradigm and the benefits of the object-oriented paradigm. Part One ends with the first installment of the Entertainment To Go case, which provides an overview of the development methodology used in this text.

Each of these chapters introduces a great number of terms. You need to become conversant in these terms because they will appear again in later chapters. In addition, a major step in becoming a member of a professional group is learning its jargon, the sometimes arcane language that is unique to that group. Learning the terms listed at the end of each chapter will prepare you for your career as an information systems professional.

1

SYSTEMS DEVELOPMENT
Product and Process

SYSTEMS DEVELOPMENT IS CHILD'S PLAY AT HASBRO

Cabbage Patch dolls, a big seller for Hasbro, Inc., begin their lives in China and then are shipped to Seattle, eventually finding homes in the adoring arms of little girls throughout the U.S. The first step in this "adoption" process—importation to the U.S.—requires Hasbro to track shipments and deliveries and to comply with U.S. customs laws.

Formerly, this tracking process was performed by a paper-intensive system that involved faxing shipment documents from Hong Kong and customs information from Seattle to Hasbro's headquarters in Pawtucket, Rhode Island. Often the same documents would have to be faxed between these sites three or four times to verify that shipments had been received and to determine the import tax owed the federal government.

Today this process is performed using electronic forms and *electronic data interchange*: the computer-to-computer transmission of standard business documents in electronic form. To begin the transformation from paper to electronic forms, Hasbro's systems developers created electronic forms screens that duplicated the format and content of the paper forms. Critical data collected on these screens, such as pricing information and the amount of the duty on each product, were incorporated into Hasbro's database. Thus, as forms were created in Hong Kong or in Seattle, the data on these forms were immediately available to users at the Pawtucket headquarters. In addition, Hasbro set up electronic links with U.S. Customs so that duty payments could be made electronically.

In its first electronic incarnation, Hasbro's system ran on an IBM 3090 mainframe. But shortly after the mainframe-based import tracking system was completed, Hasbro management decided that mainframe processing was too expensive. Furthermore, users were frustrated by the typical four-hour turnaround time for printing reports from mainframe-controlled data. The tracking system's infrequent transaction-processing activity made inefficient use of the mainframe, which, moreover, involved cumbersome procedures and job queues. So, having barely completed implementation of the mainframe system, Hasbro's systems developers began migrating the tracking system to a client/server architecture.

Hasbro's developers began the second project by analyzing the shipment tracking and duty payment processes and then designing a PC-based local area network (LAN) system running in a Windows environment. Tracking data were still stored on the mainframe but could be accessed, analyzed, and reported on the user's PC. Implementation of the client/server system was facilitated because COBOL applications running on the mainframe could be ported directly to the Windows environment with few modifications.

The move to client/server consumed just three months and yielded substantial benefits, including better reporting, reduced turnaround time, and more timely information about product status.

Adapted from M. Ballou, "Client/Server Turns to Kids' Stuff," *Computerworld*, May 30, 1994, pp. 73, 77. Copyright 1995 by Computerworld, Inc., Framingham MA 01701. Reprinted from Computerworld.

The chapter opening case, "Systems Development Is Child's Play at Hasbro," describes an information system developed to support an organization's business processes. Inspired by organizational needs and technological advances, Hasbro adopted a systems approach to produce an information system that improved its effectiveness and efficiency.

In this chapter, we present an overview of systems development. First, we look at the *product* of systems development: an information system. We define the term "system" and describe how an information system conforms to this definition. We also define the term "object" and explain how this term provides a somewhat different view of information systems components. Next, we examine the *process* of systems development, defining the system life cycle and the systems approach to problem solving. Two systems development paradigms are briefly described: traditional systems development and object-oriented systems development.

This chapter also examines the catalysts and the goals of systems development, which are sometimes overlooked when developers become enmeshed in the details of systems analysis and design. *Catalysts* are factors that create the need to initiate a systems development project. Systems development *goals* state the criteria by which development projects are judged: system quality, project management, and organizational relevance. After completing this chapter, you should be able to

1. Define "system" and explain how an information system conforms to this definition.
2. Explain the object-oriented concepts of object class, object instance, and inheritance.
3. Describe the phases of the system life cycle.
4. Explain the systems approach to problem solving.
5. Define "system decomposition" and explain several ways of decomposing an information system;
6. Describe the catalysts for systems development.
7. List and discuss the goals of systems development.

1.1 ◈ SYSTEMS DEVELOPMENT PRODUCT: AN INFORMATION SYSTEM

A **system** is a set of *related components* that *work together* in a particular *environment* to perform whatever *functions* are required to achieve the system's *objective*. Notice that several words in this definition are italicized; these five italicized words or phrases are key to understanding what a system is and what a system does. The phrase *related components* emphasizes that a system consists of several elements that interrelate in predefined ways. These "pieces and things" must *work together*; that is, each of the related elements is critical to the makeup of the system, which will work poorly—if at all—if one of its elements is missing or malfunctioning. All of the components of the system must be integrated effectively to produce a synergistic effect; *synergy* is achieved when the components cooperate or interact to perform system functions. For a system to perform these functions, the whole must be far greater than the sum of its parts. That is, no matter how well designed each component is, if they are not assembled properly, the system will not be a high-quality, effective system.

We will examine a particular kind of system, an open system that interacts with and is affected by its environment. Thus, the word *environment* in our definition of a system draws our attention to the effect of internal and external entities and factors on the system. These factors may support or constrain the system's ability to perform its basic *functions*: accept inputs from its environment, process these inputs in some fashion, and then generate outputs to the system's environment. Another basic system function is to monitor its own status. That is, a system should be self-regulating. Finally, the word *objective* in our definition indicates that a system exists to achieve some purpose.

Consider this example: In the human respiratory system, the related components include the lungs and the circulatory system (i.e., the heart and the veins that carry blood throughout the body). These system components work together to oxygenate the blood, the system's objective. The respiratory system is contained within a particular human body—the system's internal environment—and interacts with the external environment: the lungs inhale oxygen (input) and exhale carbon dioxide (output). The respiratory system is self-regulating in that, when the body needs more oxygen to perform a strenuous task, the breathing rate and the heart rate increase.

The human respiratory system's ability to achieve its objective is affected by its internal environment; for example, people with emphysema, heart disease, or cystic fibrosis often have trouble processing sufficient quantities of oxygen, thereby impairing their ability to perform strenuous activities. This system is also affected by its external environment, as anyone who has tried to jog on a smog-alert day can attest!

WHAT IS AN INFORMATION SYSTEM?

The human respiratory system just described is an example of a physical system. However, the same concepts apply to an **information system**: a system that accepts data from its environment (input) and manipulates the data (processing) to produce information (output). For example, in the chapter-opening case, Hasbro's import tracking system accepts inputs (shipment and delivery data) from its environment and processes this data to produce outputs (duty payments to U.S. customs). This description of Hasbro's system is represented graphically in Figure 1.1. **Information system functions** include *input, processing, output, storage,* and *control*. We use the acronym **IPOSC** as a shorthand method of indicating system functions.

Information systems can be manual or automated. A manual information system relies on human intelligence to manipulate data to produce information. For example, as you read this text, you are probably using a manual information system to process the concepts it contains. You use your eyes and your ability to read to gather inputs; you use your critical-thinking skills to process this data and to select the most important concepts as the "output" of this processing. Then you use a pen or pencil to take notes, thus storing your outputs in your notebook. In addition, the data used in this learning process is stored in the textbook itself.

In this text, we are interested primarily in automated information systems. An automated information system performs the same functions as a manual system but by means of information technology. Thus, in an automated system, the **information system components** include *people, procedures, data, software,* and *hardware* [Kroenke 1992]. We use the acronym **PPDSH** as a shorthand method of indicating system components. The components of Hasbro's import tracking system include, among others, shippers, customs officers, and users at headquarters (people); faxing shipping documents and verifying shipment receipt (procedures); shipping and delivery documents (data); COBOL programs (software); and PCs (hardware). These components work together to perform business functions and to produce information for management decision making.

In an information system, the internal and external aspects of **system environment** are as follows: The internal environment, or *organizational context*, is the users, organization structure, and policies and procedures. The external environment consists of all factors outside

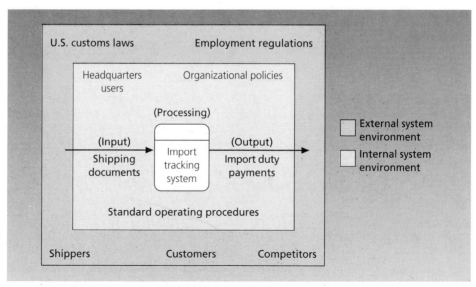

FIGURE 1.1   Hasbro's Import Tracking System

the organization that affect the system, including the external entities with which it interacts. In the Hasbro case, the organizational context includes users at headquarters, organizational policies, and standard operating procedures; the external environment includes U.S. customs law and external entities such as shippers. These aspects of Hasbro's import tracking system's environment are also illustrated in Figure 1.1.

✓ Check Your Understanding 1-1

Match each of the following aspects of the human respiratory system to the related aspect of an information system.

____ 1.	inhale oxygen (input)	a.	external factors and entities
____ 2.	human body (internal environment)	b.	generate reports
____ 3.	air pollution (external environment)	c.	improve efficiency or effectiveness
____ 4.	oxygenate the blood (system objective)	d.	accept transaction data
____ 5.	exhale carbon dioxide (output)	e.	organizational context

WHAT IS AN OBJECT?

The preceding discussion of "What Is a System?" is based on the traditional systems view, describing an information system in terms of its functions and components. Subsequent chapters reflect the fact that this traditional systems view is evolving as object-oriented concepts gain support among systems developers. This section introduces you to some of these concepts, using a fable to present an intuitive look into the object-oriented world.

An OO Fable

Once upon a time there were two unhappy people, a dog, and a ball. One person, Fred, was very lonely. The other person, Cathy, was unemployed. Fred had heard that dog owners are seldom lonely, so Fred went to a pet store and bought a dog, a male German Shepherd puppy that he named Fido. Cathy heard that vets are in high demand, so she earned a veterinary medicine degree from Tufts University and opened an animal clinic so that she would be happy and have a steady, well-paying job.

Fred, though no longer lonely, was still unhappy because he worried that his dog, Fido, was very bored. So Fred went back to the pet store and bought a small red ball. Fred taught Fido how to retrieve the ball. Fred would throw the ball, and Fido would fetch it. Now that Fido had a ball to play with, he was no longer bored; in fact, Fido was very happy, and Fred was no longer worried; he was very happy.

One day, when Fred threw the ball, Fido swallowed it. Fido became very sick; Fred became very worried. Fred took Fido to Cathy's animal clinic. Cathy treated Fido (you don't want to know the details), and Fred paid Cathy. Fido was no longer sick. Fred, although no longer worried, was a little bit poorer, whereas Cathy was a little bit richer.

No, you have not been demoted to grade school and assigned to read stories on the order of "See Dick. See Dick run. Run, Dick, run. Run, run, run." The purpose of this fable is to make a point: if you understand the characters, actions, and relationships in this story, you already understand many object-oriented concepts.

You may not realize it, but, from the time you were a child, you have been learning the concepts of the object-oriented (abbreviated OO) paradigm. Very early in your life, you learned to recognize objects and to distinguish one kind of object (e.g., a rattle) from another object (e.g., your mother) on the basis of what it looked like and what it could do. You also learned how objects are related (e.g., your mother gives you a rattle), how one object affects or interacts with another object (e.g., your mother smiles when you play and frowns when you cry). As you became more cognitively mature, you began to classify objects as being subtypes and supertypes of other objects; for example, you realized that rattles are a subtype of the general class of toys and that you and your mother are humans, a subtype of the general class of mammals.

As these examples demonstrate, OO concepts are intuitive and closely parallel your knowledge of the real world. Unfortunately, the way in which these concepts are discussed in much of the OO literature tends to obscure and complicate what should be transparent and simple. This text attempts to lift the veil of complexity in which OO concepts are cloaked by simplifying the vocabulary used to describe these concepts.

Object Classes, Attributes, and Methods

An **object class** (or simply, class) is a set of people, places, things, or transactions that share common attributes and perform common functions. An object can be the building block of almost any data or software component. For example, the icons used in a graphical user interface are objects that contain not only information about their current status but also program codes that allow them to execute their assigned functions. In this text, we are most concerned with **business objects**: the people, places, things, and transactions that perform functions to help an organization reach its goals. They share common attributes in the sense that similar types of data must be maintained about them. Employees, vendors, and customers are examples of people-type classes that are of interest to an organization; in the fable, the people classes are DOG-OWNER, VET, and PERSON. Warehouses, branch offices, and shipping docks are examples of place-type classes; the place classes in the fable are PET-STORE and ANIMAL-CLINIC. Examples of thing-type classes include products, office equipment, and supplies; thing classes in the fable include BALL and, for lack of a better classification, DOG. Finally, transaction-type classes include purchases, sales, returns, and payments. The fable's transaction classes include PAYMENT and TREATMENT.

In object thinking, each object class is an abstraction or model of a real concept. As illustrated in Figure 1.2, a real-world concept, such as "dog," can be modeled as a DOG object class that has attributes (i.e., data) and performs functions (i.e., software processes). Notice that classes are modeled as segmented boxes, with the class name in all uppercase letters in the top segment, attributes shown in mixed-case letters in the middle segment, and functions shown in mixed-case letters in the bottom segment. Notice also that, in this text, the class names are always indicated in uppercase letters.

Attributes describe the class features of interest; for example, in the fable, the DOG attributes of interest are Name, Breed, and Sex; BALL has the attributes Size and Color. We can

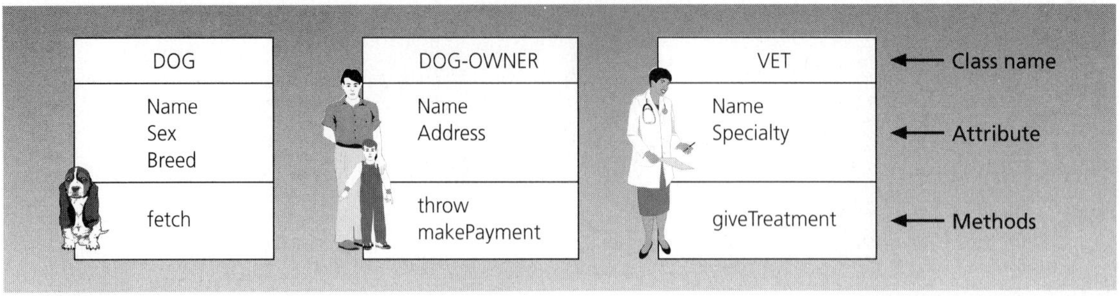

FIGURE 1.2   Object classes as abstractions of real-world people, places, things, and transactions

think of attributes as descriptions of the data to be maintained about each object. In addition, each class may have one or more functions that it performs. These functions are variously called *methods, behaviors, operations,* or *services* in the OO literature. In this text, we will use the term **methods** to indicate the actions an object can perform. A method may be a mathematical operation, an If-Then rule, or any of the IPOSC functions. For example, methods of DOG-OWNER may be throw and makePayment; a method of DOG may be fetch, sit, or come. Thus, an OO model describes how a real-world thing "looks" by detailing its attributes and how it behaves by detailing its methods.

Object Instances and Inheritance

So far, we have dealt only with the abstract concept of an object class. An **object instance** (or simply, instance) is a *particular* person, place, thing, or transaction. In other words, an object instance is one member of an object class. Each object instance is described by specific values for the attributes of its object class and can perform all the methods of its object class. For example, an instance of DOG is Fido (Name), a male (Sex) German Shepherd (Breed). An instance of VET is Cathy, and an instance of DOG-OWNER is Fred. Cathy and Fred are also instances of PERSON.

The instances of VET, DOG-OWNER, and PERSON bring us to a concept that is integral to the OO systems view: **inheritance**—an object instance "inherits" the attributes and methods of its superclass (PERSON), in addition to having all the attributes and methods of its subclass (DOG-OWNER and/or VET). Figure 1.3 uses a *Venn diagram,* a modeling technique used in set theory, to model the PERSON, VET, and DOG-OWNER classes as superclasses and subclasses and to show where the members of these classes—Cathy and Fred—fit.

In a Venn diagram, each class is modeled as a circle; a subclass is modeled as a circle within another circle or as a circle overlapping another circle. In the left-hand Venn diagram in Figure 1.3, both Fred and Cathy are members of the superclass PERSON. In addition, each is the member of a subclass: Fred is a DOG-OWNER, and Cathy is a VET. Both Fred and Cathy "inherit" all the attributes and methods of the PERSON superclass, but each also has other attributes and methods, Fred being an instance of a DOG-OWNER and Cathy of a VET subclass.

The right-hand Venn diagram in Figure 1.3 illustrates the case where a VET may also be a DOG-OWNER, for example, in the very likely situation that Cathy owns a dog. Here the subclasses of PERSON are somewhat more complex, including three subclasses: DOG-OWNER

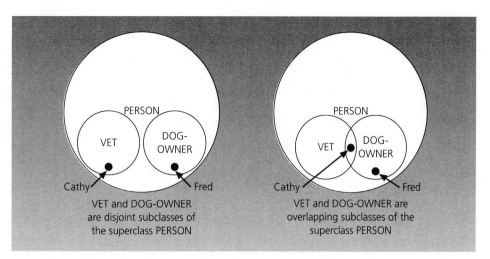

FIGURE 1.3   Object classes and subclasses

(persons who own a dog but who are not a vet), VET (persons who are a vet but who do not own a dog), and DOG-OWNER/VET (persons who both own a dog and are a vet).

Inheritance sets up a one-way identity between two object instances. (*Identity* is the quality of being the same in form or function.) The identity is one-way in that a VET instance is a PERSON instance and a DOG-OWNER instance is a PERSON instance, but a PERSON instance is not necessarily a VET instance or a DOG-OWNER instance (otherwise, to be people, we would all have to own dogs and be vets!). What is most important here is that we can define specialized subclasses that inherit all the attributes and methods of their more generalized superclass. Thus, inheritance allows us to model business objects in accordance with our view of the world; inheritance also provides the flexibility and reusability that are hallmarks of the OO systems view.

Why should you be interested in these concepts? Because, increasingly, the OO systems view is being used to develop systems.

1.2 ◆ THE PROCESS OF SYSTEMS DEVELOPMENT

As illustrated in Figure 1.4, the **system life cycle** divides the life of an information system into two phases: development and production. During the **development phase**, an information system is analyzed, designed, and implemented; during the **production phase**, it is used to perform business functions. The point at which a system moves from the development phase into the production phase is called **conversion**.

Although the life cycle model in Figure 1.4 shows the phases as being equal, you should realize that the ratio of time-in-production to time-in-development varies with every system. Most systems are repeatedly returned to development for upgrades and modifications. Thus, the phases are cyclic in that an existing production system is returned to the development phase to provide new functionality or to exploit new technologies. For example,

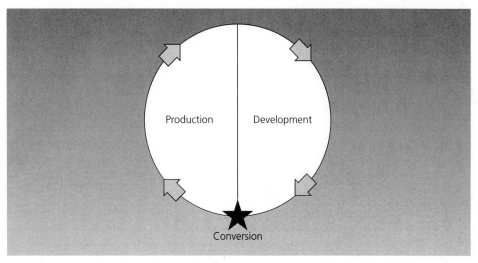

FIGURE 1.4   System life cycle

in the chapter opening case, Hasbro's mainframe-based import tracking system was put back into development to take advantage of a client/server system's more timely processing and data-access capabilities.

Most systems are highly complex structures, consisting of numerous elements that interact in numerous ways. If you know anything about the human respiratory system, you realize that the description given in Section 1.1 was a gross simplification of how the heart and lungs work together to provide oxygen to the body. Understanding this system took years of medical research, and its explication would consume several chapters in an anatomy textbook. Similarly, most information systems are also very complex structures. When trying to understand a complex system, the "divide and conquer" strategy of the systems approach is quite useful.

THE SYSTEMS APPROACH

The **systems approach** is a problem-solving method that breaks a complex problem into pieces, designs a solution for each piece, and then integrates the solutions into a complete system. In so doing, we reduce complexity and increase the likelihood that each aspect of the problem will be fully considered. As applied to information systems, the systems approach decomposes a system into subsystems and then analyzes each subsystem and the ways it interacts with other subsystems and with its environment. For example, in the Hasbro case, developers may have decomposed the import tracking system into two subsystems: one for shipment tracking and one for import duty processing.

The systems approach recognizes two major activities: analysis and design. **Systems analysis** is the process of studying an existing system—whether manual or automated—and its environment. The purposes of analysis are to understand the components and functions of the current system, to identify the organization's information and processing needs, and to determine the characteristics of a new system to meet these needs. **Systems design** is the process of synthesizing or reassembling the components and functions identified during analysis. The purpose of design is to specify the components and functions of a system that will be most efficient and effective in meeting the organization's information needs. During design, one or more alternative solutions are outlined and presented for evaluation. Then the chosen solution is designed in detail. These design specifications become the "blueprint" used to construct the system.

A major activity in systems analysis is **system decomposition**: taking apart the system to gain a full understanding of its parts. Three traditional ways of decomposing a system are (1) by its functions—input, processing, output, storage, and control; (2) by its components — people, procedures, data, software, and hardware; and (3) by its subsystems—for example, decomposing an accounting system into payroll, sales order processing, accounts receivable, inventory control, and accounts payable subsystems. Today another way of decomposing a system has gained acceptance; this technique analyzes a system in terms of the objects that comprise it. In this textbook, we will consider both the traditional and the object-oriented systems approaches, each of which is the basis for a systems development paradigm.

TWO SYSTEMS DEVELOPMENT PARADIGMS

The **traditional systems development (TSD)** paradigm analyzes a system to identify the functions it must perform. **Functional decomposition** is the process of identifying the major activities of a system (for example, "Process duty payments") and then breaking each activity into its composite steps (for example, "Verify shipment receipt," "Determine shipment product category," "Calculate import duty," and "Generate duty payment"). Emphasizing the processes or functions that a system performs, functional decomposition is the underlying framework of the TSD paradigm. This paradigm is embodied in Yourdon's [1979] and DeMarco's [1979] **Structured Systems Analysis and Design (SSA&D)** and Martin's [1990] **Information Engineering (IE)**.

In contrast, in **object structure and behavior analysis (OS&BA)** a system is decomposed into objects. This paradigm emphasizes the things that comprise the system and how these things act and interrelate. First, the business objects that comprise the system are identified. Next, an object model is created, describing each class in terms of its attributes, methods, and relationships to other classes. This specification of object classes is the foundation of the **object-oriented systems development (OOSD)** paradigm. Booch [1993], Coad and Yourdon [1990, 1991], Martin and Odell [1992], Rumbaugh [1991], and Schlaer and Mellor [1988], among others, have all proposed methods to guide systems development under this new paradigm.

These two development paradigms adopt different perspectives to decompose a system. TSD focuses on what a system does, that is, on the *verbs* that describe the system; OOSD focuses on what a system is made of, that is, on the *nouns* that describe the system. Simply stated, TSD is concerned with *functions performed on data*; OOSD is concerned with *objects performing functions*. Although one paradigm seems to be the inverse of the other, they are similar in that both are concerned with software and data. Whereas TSD separates the software and data components, OOSD combines data and software into a single construct, an object class.

These development paradigms are also similar in that they both propose a problem-solving methodology and a set of techniques and tools to help you analyze and design a system. A **methodology** is a systematic description of the sequence of activities required to solve a problem. A methodology also provides a set of **techniques** that can be used to perform specific activities. These techniques are often formal graphical languages used to model a system. A **model** is a simplified representation of some aspect of the real world, which is used to help us analyze the real world and to communicate our understanding to others. Just as an architect prepares a blueprint and a building plan before a house is constructed, a systems designer must prepare various models of an information system before the system is implemented.

In this text, you will learn about four major categories of models: enterprise, process, data, and object.

1. An *enterprise model* graphically represents organizational entities and the relationships between entities; popular enterprise modeling techniques include affinity diagrams, which are matrices that map data to processes and organizational entities to data, and workflow diagrams, which model relationships as flows of data.

2. A *process model* provides a graphical representation of a system's functions; examples of process models include data flow diagrams and program structure charts.

3. A *data model* provides a graphical representation of a system's data and the relationships between data elements; the most widely used data model is the entity-relationship diagram.

4. An *object model* graphically represents a system's classes, including attributes, methods, and relationships.

A **tool** is software that supports one or more techniques. A **computer-aided systems engineering (CASE) tool** enforces a methodology and provides tools to support various techniques. For example, Texas Instruments' Information Engineering Facility (IEF) enforces the sequence of steps in Martin's IE methodology and the techniques used in that methodology. CASE tools such as Computer Systems Advisers' Silverrun and Intersolv's Excelerator support the SSA&D methodology of Yourdon and DeMarco. Object-oriented CASE tools are beginning to appear—for example, ParcPlace's Visual Works, KnowledgeWare's ObjectView, Martin Marietta's OMTool, and IBM's Visual Age. In addition, a number of traditional systems development CASE tools have begun to support OO techniques.

 Check Your Understanding 1-2

1. The following statements describe activities performed by the Hasbro systems development team. Classify each activity as an analysis activity (AA) or as a design activity (DA).

_____ a. Studying the paper-based import tracking system.

_____ b. Creating electronic forms screens.

_____ c. Describing the shipment tracking and duty payment processes of the mainframe system.

_____ d.   Specifying the hardware and software of a PC-based local area network.

_____ e.   Deciding how to port COBOL applications from the mainframe to a Windows environment.

2.   Indicate whether each of the following statements describes the traditional systems development (TSD) paradigm or the object-oriented systems development (OOSD) paradigm or both.

_____ a.   Encapsulates data and software into a single construct.

_____ b.   Emphasizes verbs that describe the system, i.e., functions performed on data.

_____ c.   Identifies a system's major processes and then decomposes each process into its subprocesses.

_____ d.   Focuses on nouns that describe the system, i.e., objects performing functions.

_____ e.   Supported by problem-solving methodologies, techniques, and tools.

1.3 ◈ SYSTEMS DEVELOPMENT CATALYSTS AND GOALS

So far this chapter has provided a rudimentary description of what an information system is and how it is developed. These topics will be discussed at great length in the remainder of this text. However, before you plunge into the details of systems analysis and design, it is important that you understand *why* information systems are developed. Information systems do not exist in a vacuum, nor are they created simply because technological advances have made their development possible. Every information system exists within an organization and was developed to help that organization perform its activities more efficiently or effectively. Because organizations, like individuals, must operate with limited resources, one may assume that these organizations invest in information systems because they expect to profit from the investment —"profit" in the sense of becoming more productive, reducing costs, improving decision making, or gaining an advantage over competitors. In the remainder of this chapter, we examine why organizations develop information systems and how they evaluate the success of a systems development effort.

SYSTEMS DEVELOPMENT CATALYSTS

The impetus for a systems development project comes from three catalysts: user demand, technology push, and strategic pull. As shown in Figure 1.5, these catalysts need to be recognized by someone with the authority to initiate a development project.

User demand arises out of problems users have with the current system—system errors, system efficiency, system compatibility, or system enhancements. *System errors* are related to system reliability; the system may generate incorrect output, or its hardware and software components may be subject to frequent failures. For example, an application program may frequently "bomb," causing users to lose data, or the hardware may be "down" too often (that is, it has a short mean-time-to-failure), causing users to sit by idly waiting for the system to come "up" again. These problems plagued the Social Security Administration (SSA) throughout the

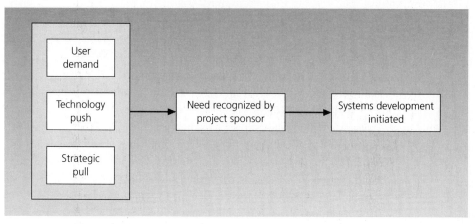

FIGURE 1.5   Catalysts for systems development

1970s and 1980s, causing it to launch a number of systems development projects [Laudon & Laudon 1994]. For example, the SSA's telecommunications network was down about 10 percent of the time, and 25 percent of its processing runs terminated abnormally (abended) before completion.

System efficiency problems are related to issues such as turnaround time, processing capacity, ease of use, redundant data entry, and inefficient data access. Again, the SSA is a case in point. Many of the SSA's fundamental business operations (detecting overpayments, computing benefits, notifying employers of errors) had backlogs of several months; a few operations were burdened by a three-year backlog. The SSA's database was stored on more than 500,000 reels of magnetic tape (many of which were disintegrating!), requiring hundreds of computer operators to retrieve, load, and replace tapes as applications were run. And the database was poorly designed and controlled; each of the SSA's 1,300 programs required its own data set, each data set containing redundant, inconsistent data. In addition, the SSA's hardware was outdated—so much so that several of its mainframes were no longer supported by the manufacturer—and provided insufficient processing capacity. The telecommunications network could not provide the network capacity the SSA needed. These system inefficiencies made even basic tasks of the SSA workers very difficult and frustrating, leading to a high level of job dissatisfaction and high turnover.

System compatibility problems stem from changes in one system component that necessitate changes in another component. For example, if an organization decides to move from a mainframe-based system to a client/server system employing a network of minicomputers and personal computers, it will need to acquire new software, redesign its procedures, and train its personnel. Similarly, if an organization upgrades its desktop computers, it may find that existing software no longer runs quite the same on the new hardware. A more insidious compatibility problem arises when an organization modifies its data component and then must expend tremendous resources to modify its software component. For example, when the California Department of Motor Vehicles needed to add a social security number field to its vehicle registration and driver's license files, it required 18 programmer-years of effort to revise the programs to reflect this addition [Bozeman 1994]. System compatibility problems also arise when an organization merges with or acquires another organization, thus also gaining responsibility for its information systems.

The need for *system enhancements* represents the most common user-inspired impetus for systems development. Most organizations exist in a dynamic environment in which the only constant is change. And changes in an organization's environment require changes in the information systems that support its existence in that environment. These changes may arise from internal factors, such as organizational growth or the need to provide better management decision-support tools; or they may arise from external factors, such as regulatory agencies requiring the organization to provide reports on its employment practices or its use and disposal of hazardous chemicals. As the organization's environment changes, its information needs change, thus necessitating system enhancements.

Technology push describes how new technology can be a catalyst in systems development. As new technologies make possible new, more effective and efficient ways of doing business, many organizations fund development projects to exploit these opportunities. Perhaps the most significant technological catalyst over the past decade has been the availability and affordability of desktop computers, database management systems, and telecommunications. The advent of desktop computers has not only transformed organizations but has also created systems development backlogs as developers work overtime to provide users desktop access to an organization's information resources. The move from traditional file processing to relational and distributed database management systems spawned a huge number of development projects; organizations redesigned their data component to facilitate data access and report generation. Similarly, the availability and falling costs of telecommunications networks unleashed a pent-up demand for greater connectivity, not only within an organization but also between organizations. Exploiting these technological advances continues to "push" many systems development efforts today.

Strategic pull describes how an organization's objectives and strategies can be an impetus for systems development. Changing strategies "pull" an organization into developing systems that support these strategies and help the organization stay competitive. For example, a change in marketing strategy may require new information systems to implement the strategy and to track measures of the strategy's success. Similarly, if a manufacturer decides to market its products globally, it will need to develop information systems to support global communications. In many cases, organizations develop information systems to help them overcome competitive threats. UPS and Federal Express are prime examples of competitors who have expended tremendous resources as each attempts to claim supremacy in the highly competitive package-delivery business.

Today many organizations recognize that information technology enables new ways of performing business processes. Consequently, many organizations are launching systems development projects that redesign fundamental business processes in an attempt to improve efficiency, effectiveness, and competitiveness. Thus, process redesign is a major strategic catalyst for systems development.

User demand, technology push, and strategic pull—knowing which of these catalysts is the primary impetus for a development project helps you understand the problem or opportunity to be addressed, the people who sponsor the project or will benefit from the system, and the objectives the system is supposed to help the business achieve. This knowledge is invaluable as you strive to meet the system development goals described in the next section.

Check Your Understanding 1-3

Analyze the chapter opening case, "Systems Development Is Child's Play at Hasbro," to determine the catalysts for developing the import tracking system (both mainframe and client/server projects). Categorize each factor as user demand, technology push, or strategic pull. Feel free to infer more than the case states, but be sure to justify whatever inferences you make.

SYSTEM DEVELOPMENT GOALS

In this section, we consider the goals of systems development. What are the criteria by which a systems development effort can be judged? These criteria define your goals as a systems developer and are the standards against which your contribution to the organization is measured.

As you develop an information system, three **system development goals** should guide your efforts. First, you want to deliver a high-quality system that efficiently and effectively performs or supports business processes. Second, you want to manage the development project so that time and resources are not wasted and so that the system's users support and participate in your efforts. Third, you want to focus your efforts on systems that support the goals and strategies of your organization. Simply stated, then, the goals of systems development are system quality, project management, and organizational relevance [Jordan & Machesky 1990], as illustrated in Figure 1.6.

System Quality

System quality is a product goal; it describes the quality criteria used to evaluate the PPDSH product of systems development. A high-quality information system addresses all five

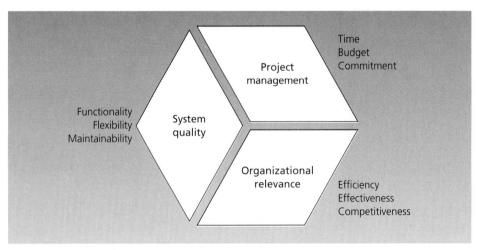

FIGURE 1.6   Goals of systems development. Reproduced from *Systems Development: Requirements, Evaluation, Design, and Implementation,* by E. Jordan and J. Machesky, pp. 33–46. Boston, MA: PWS-Kent, 1990. Copyright 1990 by boyd & fraser publishing company. All rights reserved.

components, effectively integrating people, procedures, data, software, and hardware to achieve synergy. As a systems developer, you strive to create information systems that satisfy the organization's information needs, are easy to maintain, and can adapt to the changing environment of your organization. Thus, the subgoals of the system quality goal are functionality, maintainability, and flexibility.

A high-quality information system satisfies the **functionality** subgoal by performing its functions reliably, clearly, and efficiently. Table 1.1 lists some of the questions you need to ask to determine whether you have satisfied these functionality criteria. An information system satisfies the **reliability** criterion if each of its PPDSH components completely and accurately performs the system's functions and if the five components are integrated seamlessly. A reliable system uses controls to reduce the likelihood of errors, thus ensuring the completeness and accuracy of the system's inputs, stored data, and outputs. In addition, when errors are made, a reliable system recovers quickly and easily; it is "forgiving" in the sense that minor mistakes do not have disastrous consequences. For example, you can recover files deleted by mistake and "undo" actions made in error.

An information system satisfies the **clarity** criterion if its functions are consistent and predictable. This means creating a consistent user interface and providing appropriate feedback

TABLE 1.1 System quality subgoals

	Reliability	**Clarity**	**Efficiency**
People	Have the system users been adequately trained?	Are job descriptions clear?	Does the system leverage the users' skills and knowledge?
Procedures	Are procedures documented completely and accurately?	Is the user interface consistent and predictable?	Does the system avoid redundant data entry and other procedures?
		Are the user manuals written in clear, nontechnical language?	Is the data access time reasonable/acceptable to users?
Data	Is the database accurate and up to date?	Are data element names used consistently throughout the database?	Does the database make efficient use of disk space?
	Is the database complete, yet nonredundant?	Have you provided a data dictionary of the system?	Has redundant data been minimized?
			Does the software make efficient use of hardware resources?
Software	Does the software produce complete, accurate output?	Does the software provide understandable error messages and feedback?	Does the computer execute its tasks efficiently?
Hardware	Does the hardware have a long mean-time-to-failure?	Are hardware operations clearly documented?	Is printer speed acceptable?
			Is the telecommunications bandwidth appropriate for your needs?

and nontechnical error messages. For example, the graphical user interfaces for Microsoft Windows and Apple software employ standards that stipulate screen layout, menu bars, tool bars, and function key operations for all other software running in these environments. The consistency and predictability achieved by these standards greatly reduce the effort required to learn a new application and allow users to move effortlessly between applications. Another way to achieve the clarity criterion is to use consistent names for data elements and to document fully the procedures for using software and operating hardware.

An information system satisfies the **system efficiency** criterion if it executes its functions quickly and minimizes its use of people and hardware resources. An efficient system provides fast turnaround when accessing data or generating outputs; it doesn't make the user sit idly by, waiting for software or data to load or for a report to be printed. An efficient system also minimizes data entry and avoids redundant data storage.

A high-quality information system satisfies the **flexibility** subgoal by adapting to changes in the organization's needs and by being able to operate in a variety of environments. The **adaptability** criterion is satisfied if PPDSH components are loosely coupled. Earlier, we noted that the functionality subgoal requires that you develop a system whose PPDSH components are seamlessly integrated. It may seem impossible for a system's components to be both seamlessly integrated and loosely coupled, but consider this explanation. The PPDSH components are integrated if the people component can easily use the procedures component to run the software component, which seamlessly accesses and manipulates the data component and runs efficiently on the hardware component. And the PPDSH components are loosely coupled—that is, the system is adaptable—if a change in any one of these components necessitates few or no changes in the other components.

Loosely coupled components reduce the need for the system-compatibility modifications noted in the section "Systems Development Catalysts." For example, in a loosely coupled system, a change in the data component should not require major revisions of the software component (**program-data independence**). A negative example of this is the California DMV system that required 18 programmer-years of effort to update programs when the data files were changed [Bozeman 1994].

Furthermore, a loosely coupled system should be adaptable to new uses (**procedural flexibility**). For example, the procedures for maintaining data about products and generating inventory status reports should be applicable to maintaining data about customers and generating customer status reports. Such a change in purpose will require different sets of data and reports, but the procedures for entering and accessing the data and generating the reports should be very similar. In addition, both purposes should be achieved using the same hardware and software configuration.

An information system satisfies the **portability** criterion if it can operate in a variety of environments with a variety of hardware components. For example, switching to a different word-processing package should not necessitate buying a different printer (**device independence**). One of the major benefits of the UNIX operating system is that it is machine-independent; that is, it can run on a wide variety of computers, thus giving an organization the flexibility to port UNIX applications from one computer to another with little modification. Another aspect of the portability criterion is **language independence**: the ability to run programs written in a standard language under different operating systems. If the software component has been custom-written in a third-generation language such as COBOL running under IBM's VM operating system, you should be able to run these programs on a DEC VMS platform with minor revisions.

If, when revisions are mandated, the system is easy to understand, test, and modify, then the **maintainability** subgoal is satisfied. The criteria for evaluating a system's maintainability include the clarity and completeness of its documentation and its degree of modularity. Clear, complete **documentation** is needed because the people who initially develop a system are seldom the people who are responsible for maintaining or revising it. System documentation describes the five PPDSH components and serves as a road map as these components are revised. **Modularity** refers primarily to the software component; programs should be coded as loosely coupled, cohesive modules so that a change in one module does not require changes in other modules. Modularity—and reusability—are two of the most widely lauded features of OO systems. Because each object class encapsulates data and functions, each is a self-contained module that can be modified with few or no modifications to other classes.

Functionality, flexibility, maintainability—all are equally important in measuring the quality of an information system. You may be inclined to think that functionality is the most important system quality subgoal; and, clearly, when an information system is first delivered to its users, this assumption is true. However, if you consider that most business environments are highly dynamic, subject to frequent changes in personnel, objectives, and strategies, you will realize that, a bit farther down the road, flexibility and maintainability become equally if not more important. Thus, systems developers must be forward-thinking. They must develop information systems that fit today's environment but are also capable of evolving to function in tomorrow's environment to meet its as yet unspecifiable needs.

Check Your Understanding 1-4

Use the system quality criteria to evaluate the functionality, flexibility, and maintainability of Hasbro's mainframe import tracking system. If the case does not provide enough information to evaluate a subgoal, indicate "Not specified," and describe the kinds of information you would need to evaluate the subgoal.

Project Management

The second major goal of systems development, **project management**, is a process goal; it describes the criteria used to evaluate the quality of the development process. Delivering a high-quality information system is not sufficient; you must deliver the system on time, within budget, and with a high level of user commitment. Thus, how you manage the development process is just as important as the quality of the product you deliver. Yet information systems professionals have a very poor reputation on these criteria. A 1994 survey by the Institute of Management Accountants' MIS and Technology group investigated the on-budget and on-time completion rates for IS projects by polling 350 financial executives. Over one-third of the respondents said that projects exceeded the budget (by an average of 30 percent); over half noted that projects ran late (by an average of 5 months).

The **on-time criterion** measures your ability to deliver the required system within the time allotted to the project schedule. Since the purpose of the system is to help the organization meet its goals, and since a system delivered late may well frustrate that purpose, on-time delivery is obviously very important. A number of techniques have been developed to estimate the amount of time required to complete a project; in addition, a number of project management methodologies and tools are available to help you stay on schedule. Even so, a recent survey revealed that fewer than one in four companies use formal estimating techniques or adopt project management methodologies; the survey also found that companies using these techniques and methodologies were more likely to meet their delivery schedules [Hart 1994].

The **within-budget criterion** measures your ability to deliver the required system at the cost specified in the project budget. Most organizations will not fund a project until some form of cost-benefit analysis has demonstrated that the benefits of the system equal or exceed the costs of developing and maintaining the system. If the completed system ends up costing even 20 percent more than the estimate, it may not produce sufficient benefits to justify its costs. Thus, the ability to estimate the system's costs accurately is vital.

Time and budget can also be viewed as limitations that may affect the quality of the system you deliver. The triangle in Figure 1.7 illustrates the relationship between time, budget, and quality. Each leg of the triangle represents a feasible goal; for example, you can feasibly produce a high-quality information system quickly, or you can produce a system quickly and cheaply, but you cannot produce a high-quality system quickly and cheaply. Thus, project management requires that you make trade-offs. If your users need a high-quality system that supports a wide range of functions and they want it quickly, then they must be willing to provide a budget that allows you virtually unlimited people and tool resources to develop the system in a short time. In contrast, if your users need a system quickly and cheaply, they should not expect high quality or extensive functionality. They may have to be satisfied with a system that supports only the most important business functions in the initial delivery and will have to fund another project later to provide additional functions.

The third criterion of project management is **user commitment**: the degree to which the system's users and sponsors support the development project and are willing to use the system once completed. Time, budget, and commitment are interrelated in that users are less

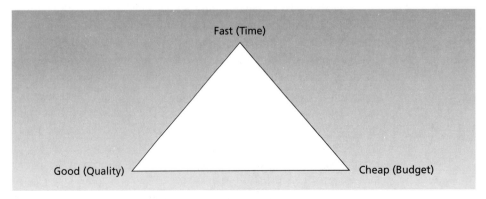

FIGURE 1.7   Trade-offs in systems development

likely to support systems that are over schedule and/or over budget. But even a high-quality system delivered on time and within budget may have low commitment if users feel that they were shut out of the development process or if they feel threatened by the system. To avoid this problem, you should practice **user-driven development**, a development approach that includes users on the development team and actively solicits their input and involves them in development activities. Chapter 3 introduces two techniques for increasing user involvement in the development process: joint application development and prototyping.

Organizational Relevance

The third goal of systems development is **organizational relevance**: the ability of an information system to contribute to organizational success. High-quality systems produced through well-managed projects are nevertheless a waste of organizational resources if they fail to help the organization meet its objectives. Generally speaking, those objectives are to increase efficiency, improve effectiveness, and/or provide a competitive advantage.

Organizational efficiency is a measure of productivity: how much time, money, or other resources are required to produce an output. Efficiency is usually the concern of operational management, which oversees the routine activities of an organization, and of transaction-processing systems (e.g., accounts payable, accounts receivable, sales processing, and payroll), which strive to maximize the number of transactions processed while minimizing the amount of resources required.

Information systems can increase efficiency by reducing the resources required to produce an output. For example, a payroll-processing system increases efficiency by reducing the labor, cost, or time required to process an organization's payroll. Similarly, the scanning systems used in grocery stores increase efficiency by increasing the number of transactions that can be processed by each checkout clerk; such a system also increases efficiency by reducing the number of data-entry errors. As a last example, consider *electronic data interchange* (EDI), the computer-to-computer transmission of electronic business documents (e.g., purchase orders, invoices, shipping documents). Organizations that have implemented EDI systems realize several efficiency benefits: faster communications, shorter turnaround cycles, lower costs, and reduced errors.

Whereas efficiency is doing things right, effectiveness is doing the right thing. **Organizational effectiveness** is a measure of how well an organization allocates its resources to achieve its goals. Effectiveness is usually the concern of tactical management, which allocates an organization's resources, and of management-support systems (e.g., information-reporting, decision-support, and executive-support systems), which strive to improve the decision-making processes of an organization. Given a limited amount of resources (time, money, personnel, supplies), the most successful organization is the one that allocates its resources most effectively.

Information systems improve organizational effectiveness by providing information for decision making and by helping managers analyze resource-allocation problems more fully. For example, the scanning systems used in grocery stores collect data that, when passed along to the product suppliers, help marketing managers evaluate the effectiveness of their advertising and promotion efforts. This information can also help an organization evaluate its shelf-management and product-pricing strategies. Information systems can also improve effectiveness by facilitating communication and data sharing. For example, teleconferencing, electronic mail, and EDI support communication across time and space; distributed databases bring information to any desktop in the organization.

Competitiveness is a measure of an organization's ability to provide more value to its customers or to provide equal value at a lower price. Although efficiency and effectiveness improve competitiveness, this objective has a broader meaning. The **competitive-forces model**, shown in Figure 1.8, describes the factors that affect an organization's ability to compete [Porter 1980]. Organizations overcome the threat of new market entrants and substitute products and the bargaining power of buyers and suppliers by employing one or more **competitive strategies**: being the low-cost producer, forming tight linkages with customers and suppliers, creating a market niche, or differentiating their products [Cash & Konsynski 1985; see also McFarlan 1984; Porter 1985]. Competitiveness is the concern of strategic management, which sets the goals for the organization and formulates strategies to achieve them.

Strategic information systems help organizations compete by using information technology to implement one or more competitive strategies. For example, Goodrich Company's Geon Vinyl Division overcame the bargaining power of customers by creating a market niche. Instead of mass producing the PVC used in a variety of consumer products, Geon Vinyl implemented a flexible manufacturing system that allowed it to produce smaller, made-to-order batches of PVC for its customers [Bartholomew 1992]. VF Corporation, the maker of Lee jeans and other apparel, implemented its Market Response System (MRS) to create tight linkages with the retailers who sell its products and to become more responsive to changes in consumer buying trends. The MRS has three components: a continuous merchandising system that collects point-of-sale data from retailers to help VF track buying trends; a flexible manufacturing system that allows VF to run smaller, more frequent production jobs; and a flow-replenishment system that creates an electronic link between VF and major retailers, giving VF the ability to monitor and automatically replenish retailer inventory [Cafasso 1993].

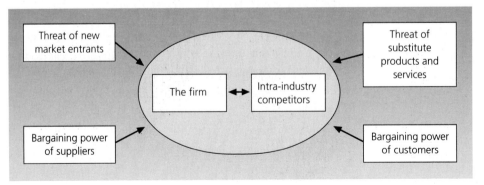

FIGURE 1.8   Competitive-forces model

Efficiency, effectiveness, competitiveness—all three are business objectives that information systems can help an organization attain.

Check Your Understanding 1-5

Evaluate the organizational relevance of Hasbro's client/server import tracking system. Does the system increase efficiency, improve effectiveness, or provide competitive advantage? If the case does not provide enough information to evaluate the system's contribution to achieving one of these objectives, indicate "Not specified," and describe the kinds of information you would need to evaluate its contribution.

◈ REVIEW OF CHAPTER LEARNING OBJECTIVES

1. *Define "system" and explain how an information system conforms to this definition.*

   A system is a set of *related components* that *work together* in a particular *environment* to perform whatever *functions* are required to achieve the system's *objective*. An information system fits this definition in that it consists of related components (people, procedures, data, software, and hardware) that work together in a particular organizational and business environment to perform functions (input, processing, output, storage, and control) that help an organization meet its objectives: to be efficient, effective, and competitive.

2. *Explain the object-oriented concepts of object class, object instance, and inheritance.*

   An object class is an abstraction or model of a real world concept; it contains attributes that describe features of interest and methods that the object performs to manipulate its data. An object instance is a specific member of an object class that is described by the values of its attributes and can perform all the methods of its object class. Inheritance is an OO concept that defines how a subclass object instance inherits all the attributes and methods of its superclass.

   An object can be the building block of almost any data or software component of an information system, including the user interface. In this text, we are most interested in business objects: the people, places, things, and transactions about which an organization must maintain data. An object-oriented information system must perform all the functions of an information system (IPOSC) and is composed of people, procedures, data, software, and hardware. However, the data and software components are packaged in a single construct, an object.

3. *Describe the phases of the system life cycle.*

   The system life cycle divides the life of an information system into two phases: development and production. During the development phase, an information system is analyzed, designed, and implemented; during the production phase, the information system is used to perform business functions. The point at which a system moves from the development phase into the production phase is called conversion.

4. *Explain the systems approach to problem solving.*

The systems approach is a problem-solving method that breaks a complex problem into pieces, designing a solution for each piece and then integrating the solutions into a complete system. As applied to information systems, the systems approach decomposes a system into subsystems and then analyzes each subsystem and the ways it interacts with other subsystems and with its environment.

5. *Define "system decomposition" and explain several ways of decomposing an information system.*

System decomposition is the process of taking apart a system to gain a full understanding of its parts. Three traditional ways of decomposing a system are by its functions (functional decomposition); by its components (people, procedures, data, software, and hardware); and by its subsystems. Today a fourth way of decomposing a system—object structure and behavior analysis—has been proposed. Here a system is analyzed in terms of the objects that comprise it.

6. *Describe the catalysts for systems development.*

The impetus for a systems development project comes from three catalysts: user demand, technology push, and strategic pull. User demand arises out of problems users have with the current system. These problems include system errors, system efficiency, system compatibility, and system enhancements. Technology push describes how new technology can be a catalyst in systems development. As new technologies make possible new, more effective and efficient ways of doing business, many organizations fund development projects to exploit these opportunities. Strategic pull describes how an organization's objectives and strategies can be an impetus for systems development. Changing strategies "pull" an organization into developing systems that support these strategies and help the organization stay competitive. Knowing which of these catalysts is the primary impetus for a development project helps you understand the problem or opportunity to be addressed and the objectives the system is supposed to help the business achieve.

7. *List and discuss the goals of systems development.*

The goals of systems development are system quality, project management, and organizational relevance. System quality is a product goal that describes the quality criteria used to evaluate the PPDSH product of systems development. A high-quality information system addresses all five components, effectively integrating people, procedures, data, software, and hardware. Subgoals of the system quality goal include functionality, flexibility, and maintainability. Project management is a process goal that describes the criteria used to evaluate the quality of the development process. Delivering a high-quality information system is not sufficient; you must deliver the system on time, within budget, and with a high level of user commitment. The third development goal, organizational relevance, evaluates the contribution that an information system makes to organizational success. An information system that satisfies this goal helps the organization become more efficient, effective, and/or competitive.

◆ KEY TERMS

adaptability
attribute
business objects
clarity
competitive strategies
competitive-forces model
competitiveness
computer-aided systems
   engineering (CASE) tool
conversion
development phase
device independence
documentation
flexibility
functional decomposition
functionality
information engineering
   (IE)
information system
information system compo-
   nents (PPDSH)
information system func-
   tions (IPOSC)
inheritance

language independence
maintainability
methodology
method
model
modularity
object class
object instance
object structure and
   behavior analysis
   (OS&BA)
object-oriented systems
   development (OOSD)
on-time criterion
organizational effectiveness
organizational efficiency
organizational relevance
portability
procedural flexibility
production phase
program-data
   independence
project management
reliability

strategic information
   systems
strategic pull
structured systems analysis
   and design (SSA&D)
system
system decomposition
system development goals
system efficiency
system environment
system life cycle
system quality
systems analysis
systems approach
systems design
techniques
technology push
tool
traditional systems development (TSD)
user commitment
user demand
user-driven development
within-budget criterion

◆ DISCUSSION QUESTIONS

1. Define the term "system" in terms of the functions a system performs.

2. Differentiate the development and production stages of the system life cycle.

3. How can adopting the systems approach help you deal with the complexity of developing an information system?

4. List an example of (a) traditional systems development methodologies and (b) object-oriented systems development methodologies. How do the two methodologies differ?

5. Discuss the kinds of problems that underlie the user-demand catalyst for systems development.

6. How do advances in technology "push" an organization to develop new systems? How do changes in business strategy "pull" an organization into systems development?

7. What characteristics describe an information system that satisfies each of the system quality subgoals of functionality, flexibility, and maintainability?

8. Why is project management an important goal of systems development?

9. Explain the difference between efficiency and effectiveness. How can information systems help an organization be more efficient and more effective?

10. How can information systems help an organization become more competitive?

◆ EXERCISES

1. Examine the world around you to identify an example of a natural or man-made system (but *not* an information system!) For example, you might select a car's combustion system, your community's transportation system, or the ecosystem of your backyard. Use the system concepts explained in Section 1.1 to describe your chosen system. What are the system's inputs and outputs? What processing must it perform to convert inputs into outputs? Describe the system's internal and external environment. In what ways is the system affected by its environment?

2. Select an information system—manual or automated—that you have used (e.g., a telephone company's directory assistance system, a library's book checkout system, your university's registration system). Use the system concepts explained in Section 1.1 to describe your chosen system. What are its inputs and outputs? What processing must it perform to convert inputs into outputs? Describe your system's internal and external system environment. In what ways is the system affected by its environment?

3. The systems approach and system decomposition are problem-solving methods used to analyze a problem and design a solution. What other problem-solving methods (e.g., the scientific method) have you learned in other courses? Compare and contrast these methods with the systems approach.

4. Read the following scenario to identify the systems development catalysts.

Business Consultants, Inc. (BCI) delivers management training seminars for businesses in the Quad-City area. To conduct the seminars, the company's trainers must transport whatever audiovisual equipment they require from BCI offices to the business sites, hotels, or convention centers where courses are held. Overhead projectors, VCRs, tape players, monitors, and other such equipment are stored in the Media Center, which is staffed by three part-time clerks and managed by Bob Seger. Tracking who has reserved which equipment for which dates is a confusing, tedious, paper-intensive task. Four times in the last week the Media Center staff has had to scramble to locate a piece of equipment for a trainer who had reserved it only to discover that his or her reservation had been misfiled. Bob Seger has requested that BCI fund development of an automated information system to deal with these problems.

5. Read the following short case to identify the systems development catalysts.[2]

In the late 1980s VF Corp. was experiencing stagnant revenues and losing market share. When the CEO, Lawrence Pugh, investigated the problem, he pinpointed VF Corp.'s Lee Jeans division as the culprit. This division had lost touch with its customers

---

[2] Adapted from R. Cafasso, "Jeans Genies." *Computerworld,* June 14, 1993, pp. 99, 102. Copyright 1995 by Computerworld, Inc., Framingham MA 01701. Reprinted from Computerworld.

and was lagging behind its competition (e.g., Levi-Strauss). Further investigation revealed that the Lee division didn't have effective tools for gathering sales data and tracking market trends; nor could it respond quickly to changes in consumer buying trends because its production cycles were too long. For example, if consumers suddenly took a fancy to bell-bottom jeans, it would be 18 months before bell-bottom jeans came rolling out of Lee factories and onto retailer shelves.

Pugh recognized that VF Corp. needed to use information systems to become more responsive and competitive. So VF Corp. launched a major development project to implement the Market Response System (MRS), which would integrate manufacturing, sales, and marketing data. The MRS would allow smaller, more frequent deliveries to—and manage the jeans inventory of—retailers; it would also gather point-of-sales data from over 300 retailers to track consumer buying trends and provide job-scheduling and factory-management capabilities so that Lee Jeans could respond quickly to these trends.

6. Read the Chapter 4 opening case, "Streamlining Order Fulfillment at CAV." Evaluate how well the new order-fulfillment system achieved the goals of system quality, project management, and organizational relevance.

◈ REFERENCES

Bartholomew, D. "Vinyl Victory." *Information Week*, May 5, 1992, pp. 32–38.

Booch, G. *Object-Oriented Analysis and Design with Applications.* Redwood City, CA: Benjamin/Cummings, 1993.

Bozeman, J. "DMV Disaster." *Computerworld*, May 9, 1994, pp. 15–16.

Cafasso, R. "Jeans Genies." *Computerworld,* June 14, 1993, pp. 99, 102.

Cash, J. I. and B. R. Konsynski. "IS Redraws Competitive Boundaries.*" Harvard Business Review*, March/April 1985, pp. 134–142.

Coad, P. and E. Yourdon. *Object-Oriented Analysis,* 2nd Ed. Englewood Cliffs, NJ: Prentice-Hall, 1990.

———. *Object-Oriented Design.* Englewood Cliffs, NJ: Yourdon Press/Prentice-Hall, 1991.

DeMarco, T. *Structured Analysis and System Specification.* Englewood Cliffs, NJ: Yourdon Press/Prentice-Hall, 1979.

Hart, J. "Pesky Projects." *Computerworld,* April 11, 1994, p. 118.

Jordan, E. W. and J. J. Machesky. *Systems Development: Requirements, Evaluation, Design, and Implementation.* Boston, MA: PWS-Kent, 1990.

Kroenke, D. *Management Information Systems,* 2nd Ed. New York: Mitchell/McGraw-Hill, 1992.

Laudon, K. C. and J. P. Laudon. "Is the Social Security Administration Ready for the 21st Century?" In *Management Information Systems*, 3rd Ed., pp. 738–748. New York: MacMillan, 1994.

Martin, J. *Information Engineering: A Trilogy.* Englewood Cliffs, NJ: Prentice-Hall, 1990.

Martin, J. and J. Odell. *Object-Oriented Analysis and Design*. Englewood Cliffs, NJ: Prentice-Hall, 1992.

McFarlan, F. W. "Information Technology Changes the Way You Compete." *Harvard Business Review*, May/June, 1984, pp. 98–103.

Porter, M. *Competitive Advantage*. New York: Free Press, 1985.

Porter, M. *Competitive Strategy*. New York: Free Press, 1980.

Rumbaugh, J., M. Blaha, W. Premerlani, and W. Lorenson. *Object-Oriented Modeling and Design*. Englewood Cliffs, NJ: Prentice-Hall, 1991.

Schlaer, S. and S. J. Mellor. *Object-Oriented Systems Analysis: Modeling the World in Data*. Englewood Cliffs, NJ: Yourdon Press Computing Series, 1988.

Yourdon, E. *Managing the Structured Techniques*. Englewood Cliffs, NJ: Prentice-Hall, 1979.

2

THE PRODUCT OF SYSTEMS DEVELOPMENT
A Closer Look

RETAIL SALES PROCESSING AND SKU REPLENISHMENT

Buyers at a major clothing retailer use its SKU Sales System to obtain up-to-date information on sales at each of its more than 70 stores nationwide. Knowing which items are "hot" and which are not helps the buyers make better stock purchasing decisions and helps the retailer manage its inventory more effectively.

When a customer makes a purchase at one of the stores, a sales clerk enters data from the item tag by scanning the *SKU—a stockkeeping unit* indicating style, color, size, and vendor—with an optical character recognition device, which relays the data to the clerk's point-of-sale (POS) terminal. The SKU is used to look up the item's price in the item file, to update the inventory file, and to post a transaction, along with a code identifying the store at which the sale was made, to the sales transaction file. The price of each item is totaled, and then the sales tax and sales total are calculated. The customer is given a receipt listing each item, its price, the sales tax, and the sales total.

Buyers monitor the sales at each store by generating reports that list the SKU, quantity purchased for resale, quantity sold, and quantity in stock. Buyers can also generate reports detailing item sales by vendor to determine how well each vendor's merchandise is selling. The more aggregate vendor sales report allows buyers to gauge which vendor's lines are most attractive to the retailer's customers. The kind of report generated is determined by the buyer, who chooses a report menu selection or enters a SKU or vendor code to select specific information to be reported.

The SKU Sales System was developed using a tiered client/server architecture, as illustrated in Figure 2.1. Each buyer has a client workstation (typically a 33-MHz 486 machine with 16 Mbytes of RAM) running Microsoft Windows for Workgroups 3.11 and Microsoft Excel spreadsheet. Each store has a local server, either a dual-processor Pentium machine or a 66-MHz PC, with 64 Mbytes of RAM. The client workstations in a store communicate

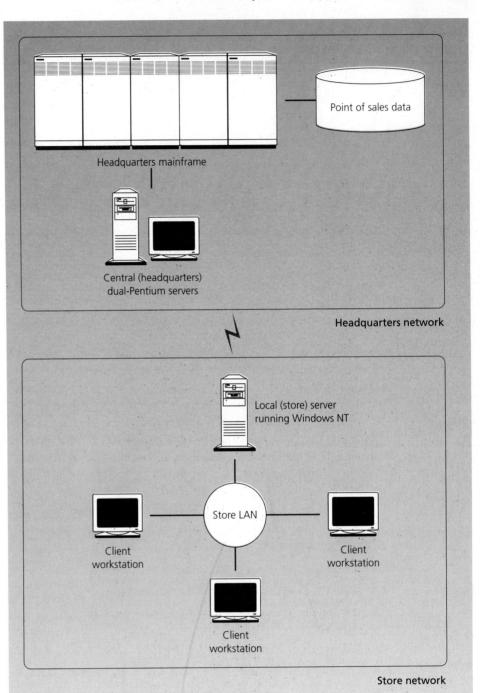

FIGURE 2.1   The SKU Sales System information architecture

with their local server through Windows NT networking software. The central servers, housed at the retailer's corporate headquarters, consist of 14 dual-processor Pentium machines, each with 256 Mbytes of RAM, running Microsoft's SQL Server for NT.

Currently, the SKU sales database contains 60 to 70 Gbytes of data, but management predicts that the database will eventually grow to 200 Gbytes. These data are maintained in an IBM IMS database housed on an IBM mainframe that collects sales transaction data from POS terminals in each store. Sales records can be sorted by store and then by SKU and/or vendor to provide a picture of how each item is selling at each store.

Buyers access SKU sales data for their store through their local server, which is used as an application, file, and print server and which performs front-end functions such as security authorization and log-in. The SKU reports are presented as Excel worksheets, thus providing a familiar, easy-to-use interface for these nontechnical buyers.

Adapted from Stuart J. Johnston, "A Good Deal for Nordstrom's Buyers," *Computerworld,* May 23, 1994, pp. 61, 65. Copyright 1995 by Computerworld, Inc., Framingham MA 01701. Reprinted from Computerworld.

The chapter opening case presents an example of an information system, describing its functions—input, processing, output, storage, and control—and its five components—people, procedures, data, software, and hardware. These functions and components represent the end-product of a major systems development effort undertaken to improve the retailer's ability to survive in the highly competitive retail industry.

Sometimes the end is a good place to start. Understanding the end product of systems development provides an anchor as we examine the highly conceptual process of analyzing and designing an information system. You should keep this end product in mind because it is the goal of all your efforts: to produce the right combination of system functions and components to serve the needs of people working in organizations.

In this chapter, you will learn the functions and components of an information system, knowledge critical for a systems analyst. After reading this chapter and completing its exercises, you should be able to

1. Distinguish between a logical function and a physical function.
2. Define the five functions of an information system.
3. Explain the sociotechnical view of information systems.
4. Define and give examples of the five components of an information system.
5. Explain how an object encapsulates the data and software components of an information system.

2.1 ◈ INFORMATION SYSTEM FUNCTIONS

An information system performs functions to help an organization meet its objectives. A **system function** is an activity or process step, which is expressed as an action verb followed by the object of the action. For example, "Enter sales data," "Calculate sales subtotal," and "Generate sales receipt" are examples of functions performed in a sales order processing system.

An information system performs five basic functions. It accepts data from its environment (*input*) and manipulates this data (*processing*) to generate a result (*output*). The inputs and outputs of an information system may be maintained for later use (*storage*). In addition, an information system employs manual and/or automated procedures to ensure the integrity of its inputs and outputs and to limit access to its processing functions and its stored data (*controls*). These functions are illustrated in Figure 2.2.

You should differentiate between the *functions* a system performs and the *technology* it uses to perform these functions; that is, you need to distinguish a logical function from a physical function. A **logical function** describes a system function independent of the technology used; a **physical function** describes a system function in terms of the technology used. For example, in the chapter opening case, one activity would be "Enter item data," a logical function. Another would be "Scan item data," a physical function in that it states how the data are entered (using an optical character recognition device). You need to distinguish logical functions from physical functions because each provides a different view of an information system and is used in different ways during systems development. This distinction and its importance will become clear when you learn about logical and physical DFDs in Technical Module A and in Chapter 10.

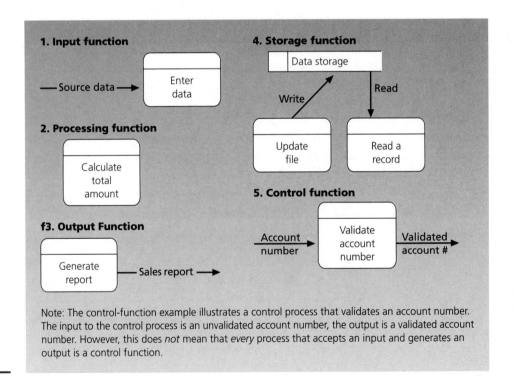

Note: The control-function example illustrates a control process that validates an account number. The input to the control process is an unvalidated account number, the output is a validated account number. However, this does *not* mean that *every* process that accepts an input and generates an output is a control function.

FIGURE 2.2   The five functions of an information system

The information system described in the chapter opening case is an *automated infor-mation system*; that is, most of its functions are performed by information technology, and its data component is maintained digitally. However, you should understand that a *manual information system* performs the same logical functions. Its processing functions are usually performed by people using motor skills and brain power, and its data are stored in paper form, for example, in a ledger book or in folders in a file cabinet, but its logical system func-tions are the same.

INPUT

Input functions describe the activities that must be performed to access data for processing. The verbs "accept," "receive," and "enter" are commonly used to state logical input func-tions. Some examples of physical input functions are reading data from keypunch cards, keying data from an invoice form, receiving purchase order data from a customer's EDI (electronic data interchange) transmission, and scanning the universal product code (UPC) from grocery items. In the chapter opening case, the logical input functions include entering item data and entering an SKU or vendor code to select sales data to be displayed in a report.

PROCESSING

Processing functions describe the ways that data are manipulated to perform business functions and to produce information of value in management decision making. Common verbs used to express logical processing functions include "calculate," "sort," "compare," and "summarize." These processes can be performed manually (by people) or automatically (by information technology). Manual processes are implemented as procedures performed by people; automated processes are implemented as instructions coded in an application pro-gram and executed by computer technology. In the chapter opening case, logical processing functions include looking up a price for each item, calculating a subtotal, calculating the sales tax, adding the subtotal and sales tax to calculate the sales total, sorting sales transac-tions by store and then by SKU, and calculating the total sales for each SKU or each vendor.

The kinds of processing performed by an information system are related to what type of information system it is. Three general classes of information systems are office automation, transaction processing, and management support systems. **Office automation systems (OAS)** perform document creation and data management processes, such as editing a docu-ment or sorting a file by a key field. They also perform scheduling and project management functions, such as identifying a time that several people can get together for a meeting and monitoring the status of a project. **Transaction processing systems (TPS)** perform routine, highly structured functions,[1] such as sales transaction processing, accounts payable and

---

[1]   A function is highly structured if its variables and operations can be predefined and programmed. For example, payroll is a highly structured function because its variables—hours worked, wage per hour, tax status, deductions—and its operations—e.g., multiply hours worked times wage per hour—are well defined, stable, and capable of being processed by a computer. A function is unstructured if its variables and operations cannot be definitively specified.

accounts receivable, and cash management. These functions require primarily mathematical and algebraic processes. **Management support systems (MSS)** perform structured functions, such as summarizing TPS data to produce the periodic reports used to control inventory and monitor sales. MSS also perform less structured functions, such as analyzing capital investments and determining the location of a new branch office. The SKU Sales System described in the chapter opening case is both a transaction processing system, which processes routine sales transactions, and a management support system, which summarizes transaction data to help buyers decide which items to reorder.

Processing functions can also be described in terms of when they are performed. In **real-time processing**, each transaction is performed as it occurs; in **batch processing**, transactions are accumulated and then processed as a batch at a later time. Each method has appropriate applications; for example, it wouldn't make sense for a retailer to batch its sales transactions (Imagine a sales clerk saying, "Oh, I'm sorry. I can't ring up your sale until there are at least five customers in line."). Real-time processing is appropriate when an immediate response is needed or when up-to-the-minute status is required, as in an airline reservation system. Batch processing is appropriate when the processing is performed on a regular schedule, such as in a payroll system.

OUTPUT

Output functions describe the activities required to generate business documents or reports. In their aggregate form, outputs are often reports—whether formal, regularly scheduled printed reports or informal, ad hoc screen reports generated in response to a database query. The outputs may also be business documents—whether paper or electronic, such as a purchase order, payment, or invoice.

Verbs such as "generate," "distribute," or "produce" are used to state logical output functions; for example, "Generate end-of-month sales report" states a logical output function without describing how the report will be generated. Some examples of physical output functions are, "Print end-of-month sales report," "Imprint check amount on a check using a magnetic ink character printer," and "Transmit an electronic payroll deposit to a bank." In the chapter opening case, the logical output functions include generating a sales receipt and generating reports summarizing sales by SKU or vendor.

STORAGE

Storage functions describe the activities required to maintain system data. In general, a storage function is an activity that accesses or transforms the database, that is, any activity that reads data from or writes data to a storage medium, whether manual or automated. The verbs "create," "update," "delete," "read," and "copy" are commonly used to state logical storage functions; the acronym **CRUD**—Create, Read, Update, Delete—is often used as a mnemonic aid for these activities. Again, notice that a logical storage function does not state the technology used (e.g., CD-ROM, magnetic tape or disk); nor does it describe how the data are organized on whatever storage medium is used.

In the chapter opening case, logical storage functions include reading the item price from the item file, updating the inventory file, and posting (i.e., writing) each transaction to the sales transaction file. Other logical storage functions relate to maintaining the item file, the inventory file, and the sales transaction file—for example, creating a new item record in the item file when a new product is received, or deleting discontinued merchandise from the item and inventory files.

CONTROL

Control functions describe the manual and automated activities performed (1) to verify the validity and accuracy of inputs and outputs and (2) to ensure the integrity of stored data. As this statement suggests, control functions are *meta-functions,* or functions on functions. That is, they are often performed on top of or simultaneously with other system functions to ensure system integrity. Control functions are classified into two groups: general controls and application controls.

General Controls

General controls are organizational policies and both manual and automated standard operating procedures designed to oversee the way systems are developed and used and to protect the system from unauthorized or malicious use. The categories of general controls include hardware, software, data security, operations, and administrative controls. *Hardware controls* limit access to system hardware, for example, by housing equipment in a restricted area. They also ensure proper hardware operation by running diagnostics tests and using parity checks to detect system malfunctions. *Software controls* monitor and restrict access to the system's software, allowing only authorized users to run certain programs or to change the program code.

Data security controls protect stored data from accidental destruction and/or unauthorized access or updating; examples include requiring redundant fail-safe procedures for erasing data and assigning read-only or read-and-update privileges to authorized users. *Operations controls* ensure that standard operating procedures are performed correctly, for example, by providing clear instructions for performing tasks; these controls also provide backup and recovery procedures to restore the system in the event of a natural disaster or system failure. *Administrative controls* protect the system through organizational policies and procedures, such as segregation of duties (for example, the person who initiates a payroll transaction is not the same person who signs the check or authorizes transmission of an electronic payment), audit trails, and supervision to ensure that control procedures are enforced.

Application Controls

Application controls are manual procedures, organizational policies, and programmed procedures built into the system's application software to validate system functions and to ensure accuracy. They apply to various specific business applications, for example, payroll and sales order processing, and are designed to ensure that the system's inputs and outputs are accurate and complete and that its processing activities are performed correctly. Thus, application controls include input, processing, and output controls.

Input controls ensure that data are entered correctly, that is, that no transcription errors occur. For example, *batch control totals* are a control technique used in batch processing. Source documents are gathered into batches, and a numeric field, such as the invoice number, on each source document in the batch is manually totaled. After the batch has been processed, the manual batch total is compared to the run control total generated by the application program. The idea is to ensure that all data are actually entered into the system. *Programmed edit checks,* another input control method, are designed to ensure that only valid data are entered. These automated procedures built into the application program validate input data by, for example, verifying that a social security number consists of nine numeric characters, that the product number entered on an Invoice data entry screen matches a product number in the Product Master file, or that the hourly wage entered on an Employee data entry screen falls within an acceptable range.

Processing controls, which verify the completeness and accuracy of data during processing, include run control totals and reasonableness tests. A *run control total* is the processing "partner" of a batch control total; as transactions are processed, the application program generates a batch total and compares it to the batch control total calculated as the transactions were entered. If the batch control total and the run control total do not match, the discrepancy is investigated.

Another example of a processing control is a *reasonableness test* (or computer matching control), which compares the current transaction to the typical transaction pattern or amount to identify possible errors or fraud. You may have seen the TV commercial in which a young woman's credit card was stolen and the thief used it to charge the expenses of a Las Vegas vacation for himself—and nine friends. The credit card company's application software had control procedures that compared current card activity to the cardholder's historical pattern of use. The thief's Las Vegas spree did not conform with the young woman's typical transaction pattern, thus triggering the system to generate an exception report. The woman did not know that her card had been stolen until a representative of the credit card company called to verify her charges!

Output controls ensure the validity of the results generated by the application program. Examples include output control totals, job logs, and report audits. *Output control totals* are compared to batch control and run control totals to verify that all transactions were processed correctly. To verify that all scheduled computer jobs were run and executed completely, computer operations personnel should review the *job log* listing all jobs and whether they ran successfully. In addition, an organization should conduct periodic *audits* of reports generated by an application to verify the completeness and accuracy of report results. The simplest output control is verifying report results by manually calculating expected results for several key output fields.

DOCUMENTING INFORMATION SYSTEMS FUNCTIONS

As a systems analyst, you will be responsible for analyzing the functions of existing information systems and specifying the functions of new information systems. When the systems you are analyzing and designing are very simple, you may be able to define these functions by stating them in text form as **functional requirements**: the IPOSC functions a system must perform to satisfy organizational needs. For example, Table 2.1 lists the functional requirements identified by analyzing the SKU Sales System described in the chapter opening case.

However, most of the time, the systems you are called upon to investigate will be so complex that you will not be able to simply list the IPOSC requirements. These systems require a more rigorous, formal analysis and design technique so that you are less likely to overlook system functions. In these cases, you will most likely create data flow diagrams to help you fully define all the inputs, processes, outputs, data stores, and controls of the system. Technical Module A defines the symbols used to create data flow diagrams and explains the rules of their construction.

Check Your Understanding 2-1

Read the case "Using Hi-Tech to Fill Government Jobs" to identify the IPOSC functions of the Clinton transition team's resume processing system. If a function is not specified in the case, indicate "Not specified." Feel free to make assumptions about unspecified functions, but be sure to indicate "Assumption" and explain why your assumption is reasonable given your knowledge of information systems.

TABLE 2.1 IPOSC functions of the SKU Sales System

Input Functions	Processing Functions	Output Functions	Storage Functions	Control Functions
The system must accept the following inputs:	The system must perform the following processes:	The system must generate the following outputs:	The system must maintain the following data:	The system must enforce the following controls:
• Item data listed on the item tag. • Vendor code or SKU to select information to be reported.	• Compare orders, sales, and current stock levels to determine SKUs to reorder. • Evaluate sales by vendor. • Calculate transaction subtotal, sales tax, and total. • Sort sales by store. • Sort sales by vendor. • Sort sales by SKU.	• Sales receipt. • SKU report. • Vendor report.	• Item data. • Inventory data. • Sales transaction data. • Vendor data. • Order data.	• Security authorization. • Log-in.

USING HIGH-TECH TO FILL GOVERNMENT JOBS

As the Clinton administration prepared to take office, one of its challenges was appointing people to the 4,000 government jobs that a new president has the discretion to fill. Given that over 100,000 people applied for these jobs, just processing the thousands of resumes that inundated the transition team offices each day was a daunting task, one that the new administration attacked with a high-tech resume-processing system.

A staff of 1,000 volunteers was aided by a Novell, Inc., local area network (LAN) that connected workers dispersed among the four floors of the transition team offices. The LAN nodes consisted of 13 Sun Microsystems workstations, 20 personal computers, and 3 optical character recognition (OCR) scanners. As resumes arrived, volunteers used the OCR scanners to convert each paper document into two computer-readable files: one file containing an exact image of the resume, and the other, an ASCII file of the resume's content.

These files were processed and stored by Resumix, a program that uses artificial intelligence techniques to search each ASCII file and build a candidate-profile file. The profile included a job classification, address and telephone number, and summary of the candidate's education, employment history and job skills. Then Resumix searched a separate database listing job requisitions and matched them with candidates from the profile database.

Once likely matches were found, they were given to a hiring manager, who then called up the resume-image files of likely candidates for closer evaluation. Hiring managers could also initiate their own searches, asking the system to perform keyword searches to identify applicants with certain skills or education. Finally, to add a personal touch, the system generated letters of acknowledgment to be sent to all applicants.

The resume-processing system was developed by and leased from Computer TaskGroup, Inc., of Buffalo, New York. Using this automated system, the Clinton transition team was able to process 2,000 resumes each day; in approximately six weeks, the system processed over 100,000 resumes, a task that would have taken at least a year if performed manually.

Adapted from Gary H. Anthes, "High-Tech Transition Helps Fill Jobs." *Computerworld,* January 18, 1993, p. 41. Copyright 1995 by Computerworld, Inc., Framingham MA 01701. Reprinted from Computerworld.

2.2 ◆ INFORMATION SYSTEM COMPONENTS

A **computer system** consists of hardware and software; in other words, a computer system is the technology used as a tool to solve a problem. To be **computer system literate**, you need to understand the operations and appropriate applications of computer hardware devices and software programs. In contrast, an information system includes not only technology but also *data* and *people* performing *procedures*. Thus, to be **information systems literate**, you need to understand both the technology and the system's data and organizational context.

This perspective on information systems is called a **sociotechnical perspective** [Bostrom and Heinen 1977] because it considers not only the technology but also the behavioral or social factors that affect how well an information system will meet the needs of the organization as a whole and of the users as individuals. The sociotechnical perspective recognizes that information systems affect the organizations in which they are used and that behavioral and organizational factors affect the design and successful use of information systems.

Thus, to develop an effective information system, you must consider not only the technological aspects of the system—the hardware and software—but also the data and organizational aspects. This means that you must analyze, design, and construct five system components: people, procedures, data, software, and hardware. We will look at the first two components, people and procedures, first.

ORGANIZATIONAL COMPONENTS OF AN INFORMATION SYSTEM: PEOPLE AND PROCEDURES

The organizational components of an information system include the people who use and develop an information system and the procedures that govern how they use the system.

People: User, Designer, Implementer

The **people** component can be subdivided into three types: users, designers, and implementers [Keen & Cummins 1994]. As shown in Figure 2.3, the mix of business knowledge and technical skills distinguishes the people in each category. Whereas users have a high degree of business knowledge and a low degree of technical skills, implementers generally have just the opposite skills mix. Designers hold the middle ground, having a good mix of business and technical skills.

The vast majority of information systems are developed for and used by people working in business functional areas, for example, manufacturing, human resources, or finance.

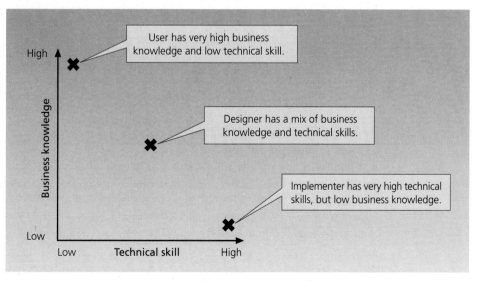

FIGURE 2.3   Level of business and technical knowledge required by each people category

These **users** are business-domain specialists who have attained a degree and/or who have developed expertise in one of the business functional areas. While you are concentrating on learning about MIS and how to develop and maintain business information systems, other business students are learning to operate and manage a business enterprise. Thus, these future users will generally lack your detailed MIS knowledge and skills. However, they will need to understand information systems well enough to use them effectively, to recognize opportunities for exploiting information technology, and to participate in systems development projects. Consequently, today most business schools require that all students complete at least one MIS course.

The user category can be subdivided into three subcategories: end-users, user-managers, and user-sponsors [Jordan and Machesky 1990]. **End-users** use the system to perform their job activities. The **user-manager** supervises the work of end-users. The **user-sponsor** authorizes project initiation and approves funding for development. Each of these subcategories has different concerns, and it is important that you know what they are. For example, end-users are most concerned about how to use the system; they want a system that makes their jobs easier. User-managers want a system that helps their subordinates work more efficiently and/or more effectively; an information system helps a user-manager "look good" if it improves the productivity of his or her department. User-sponsors are concerned with all these issues, but tend to focus on costs and benefits. They must be assured that the system is a good value; that is, the system's benefits must exceed its costs.

Designers are the people who analyze an organization, identify its processing and information requirements, and create the blueprints of a system to satisfy the users' information needs. Common job titles for designers include business analyst, systems analyst, end-user support specialist, database administrator, and network manager. Designers serve as an interface between the users who use the system and the implementers who construct it. They must be well versed in topics such as systems development techniques and tools, information architecture, systems integration, and workflow analysis. Equally important, they must have a fundamental understanding of business objectives and operations to relate their technical knowledge to the organizational context. Recognizing that *information technology* (IT) is a means to an end, not an end in itself, designers must understand how to use IT to improve organizational efficiency, effectiveness, and competitiveness. Thus, MIS majors who intend to be designers are encouraged to gain an in-depth understanding of at least one functional area (for example, by completing a minor in accounting or human resources).

Critical to a successful career as a designer are well-honed communication and interpersonal skills, an understanding of business operations, and up-to-date knowledge of development techniques and information technologies. Designers, especially business and systems analysts, must be able to interact effectively with users to determine information needs and to communicate how information technology can fill these needs. They must also understand business processes and the interdependencies and shared data flows among business functional areas. Furthermore, designers must be able to define detailed system specifications so that implementers are able to build the system.

The designer perspective on systems development is the focus of this textbook, which was written to convey the mix of technical skills and business knowledge you will need if you choose a career as a systems analyst. Thus, the majority of this textbook is devoted to analysis and design, glossing over many of the more technical issues of implementation and emphasizing only those implementation tasks that a systems analyst would be likely to perform.

Implementers, as the category name implies, implement the designers' system specifications, turning plans on paper into a functioning information system. Common job titles for implementers include network engineer, programmer, LAN specialist, and database programmer. To understand the difference between an implementer and a designer, consider these examples. Designers must understand telecommunications well enough to recommend an appropriate configuration for a local area network (LAN); they must know which topology (e.g., star, ring, bus) to recommend and be familiar with the telecommunications industry and vendors. In contrast, implementers must be more like engineers who understand how to install and maintain such a network, including the hardware, network operating system, and cabling required. Similarly, whereas a designer must be able to outline the basic program logic and to write process descriptions for the software component, an implementer must be able to interpret these specifications and to code, test, and install the programs.

No one category of the people component is more important than the others. Figure 2.4 illustrates the interdependencies among users, designers, and implementers. If an information system is to be successful, users must clearly describe their information needs and business processes, designers must understand and creatively transform these descriptions into

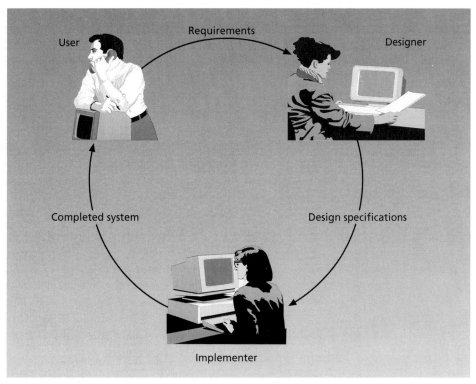

FIGURE 2.4   Interdependencies among users, designers, and implementers

an effective systems design, and implementers must build a system that conforms to the design specifications and performs its functions efficiently. The adage, "A chain is only as strong as its weakest link," comes to mind: If any of the people in the systems development chain fail to do their job conscientiously, the information system produced will not effectively meet the organization's needs.

Procedures

Simply stated, **procedures** are sets of instructions that tell people in the organization how to perform their jobs. As an organization evolves, it develops *standard operating procedures* (SOP) to guide its operations. These procedures may be formal or informal. For example, most organizations have formal, standardized procedures for processing an invoice. When invoices are received by accounts payable clerks, they follow procedures stipulated by the organization to ensure that the correct payment is made to the correct vendor on a timely basis. Invoice processing procedures include reconciling the invoice against the purchase order and shipping document to ensure that the organization pays only for goods actually ordered and received. Procedures such as these are usually documented in job descriptions and/or job manuals and are conveyed to new employees through formal on-the-job training.

An organization also develops informal procedures that are not documented in any of its manuals or job descriptions. Sometimes these informal procedures are followed instead of the organization's stipulated formal procedures. You may have experienced this discrepancy firsthand. As a new employee, you may have been trained to perform a particular task following a set of prescribed instructions, only to discover that your fellow employees never perform the task in this manner! This discrepancy is especially likely to occur if an organization's procedures are cumbersome or outdated.

Another kind of informal procedure is one that employees have evolved but that the organization has never documented. Sometimes, these undocumented procedures are inferred from the organization's policies. For example, assume that an organization has a policy that no employee may leave the work site during scheduled work hours without first gaining approval from a supervisor. Although the procedure for gaining this approval may not be formally documented, an informal, commonly accepted procedure will have evolved. Other times, these informal procedures are embedded in the **organizational culture**: the commonly shared assumptions about the organization's purpose and the practices required—and allowed—to achieve that purpose.

Your job as a systems analyst is to identify both the documented and undocumented procedures that users perform to complete job tasks in the current system and to suggest improved procedures for the new system. To achieve this purpose, you must not only study procedures documentation, such as job descriptions, policy statements, and procedures manuals, but you must also interview users and observe them as they perform their jobs to identify any informal or undocumented procedures.

Recall that procedures are instructions for people. Thus, procedures describe the manual functions required to use, operate, or maintain an information system. The procedures component of an information system can be divided into three types: application, system, and control procedures. **Control procedures**, such as backing up data, verifying input data, and restricting access to information resources, are developed to ensure the reliability and accuracy of an information system. These were discussed in Section1.1. Here we will focus on application and system procedures.

Application procedures give users instructions on how to run an application to perform a business task—that is, how and when to boot application programs, enter data, and generate reports. **System procedures** describe how to operate hardware and how to start, shut down, and maintain the system. In a mainframe system environment, system procedures are commonly performed by system administrators, data librarians, and computer operators. These procedures include loading tapes and disks, formatting disks, initiating batch processing jobs, running system diagnostics, assigning data access authorizations and network access IDs and passwords, and allocating disk space. In a desktop system environment, users perform many of these system procedures themselves. Both application and system procedures must be documented in user manuals and system manuals.

Check Your Understanding 2-2

Read the "Using High-Tech to Fill Government Jobs" case to identify the people (user, designer, implementer) and procedures (application, system, and control) component of the Clinton transition team's resume-processing system. If you are unable to identify a component because insufficient information is provided in the case, just indicate "Not specified."

THE DATA COMPONENT OF AN INFORMATION SYSTEM

Data are the core of an information system. Each organization collects, processes, and maintains a wide variety of data about employees, suppliers, products, accounts receivable, accounts payable, inventory, and so on. As a systems designer, you must be able to identify the data collected and maintained and the reports and other documents generated by the information system.

Many texts distinguish *data* from *information* by stating that data are raw, meaningless facts, whereas information is data that have been organized in a meaningful form to serve a defined purpose. In other words, data are entered into the system (input) and then manipulated (processing) to produce information (output). This distinction is usually made to an accompanying flourish of trumpets early in the text—but largely ignored in the remainder of the text, where the two terms are often used interchangeably.

As illustrated in Figure 2.5, distinguishing between data and information is useful at the aggregate level, for example, when one thinks of a sales processing system as accepting individual sales transactions as "data" and generating sales reports and invoices as "information." However, the distinction becomes blurred when one examines each discrete processing activity, as systems analysts must do to construct a model of a system's functions. At this more granular level of detail, both the input to and the output from a discrete process may be data. Furthermore, the informational output of one process may be the data input to another process. For example, in the SKU Sales System, a summary report listing sales by SKU is information (output) in the hands of a sales manager, but the same report may be data (input) in the hands of a buyer who must compare SKU sales, order quantities, and current inventory levels to decide which items to reorder.

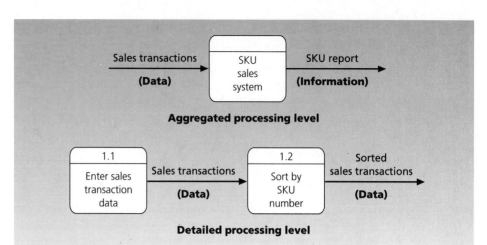

FIGURE 2.5   Data or information? The aggregate vs. the granular (detailed) perspective

Here, instead of distinguishing data from information, we distinguish three types of data: input data, stored data, and output data. **Input data** are any data entered into the system, whether by typing on a keyboard, scanning a bar code, or by any other data-entry method. **Stored data** are data maintained in a file folder or on disk or tape. **Output data** are any data generated by an information system, including documents (for example, invoices and paychecks) and reports. Let us briefly examine a supermarket transaction processing system to illustrate these three types of data. The input data is the universal product code (UPC), which is scanned by the checkout clerk. This code is used to retrieve stored data, including the product description and price. Output data include all the information listed on the grocery receipt: product description, quantity, and price; sales subtotal; sales tax; and sales total.

In the past decade, businesses have come to view their data as a valuable corporate resource to be exploited for competitive advantage. For example, Whirlpool Corporation has used its customer-service data to reduce its spare parts inventories, become more effective at monitoring the quality of the components it purchases from suppliers, and identify product defects before the company's reputation is tarnished [Verity 1994]. In addition, many companies use customer-service data as input to the design process, ensuring that a "new and improved" product or service has been improved in ways that add value to the customer.

Exploiting data as a corporate resource requires that the data be collected, organized, stored, and retrieved efficiently and effectively; in addition, the data must be accurate and current. To maximize their access and reporting flexibility, many organizations have adopted relational **database management systems (DBMS)**, which allow reports to be generated from any files that share a common attribute. The advantages and disadvantages of various data-access methods and database structures will be explained later in this text.

✓ Check Your Understanding 2-3

Identify the data component (input, stored, and output) of the Clinton transition team's resume-processing system in the "Using High-Tech to Fill Government Jobs" case.

TECHNOLOGICAL COMPONENTS OF AN INFORMATION SYSTEM: SOFTWARE AND HARDWARE

Although technology per se is not the focus of this text, this section presents a fairly detailed examination of the technological components of an information system, that is, its software and hardware. Information technology is the tool of an information system; it consists of the equipment and programs that help people to access, process, maintain, and retrieve data. Together with the data component, this technology comprises an **information architecture**: a configuration of hardware, software, telecommunications, and data designed to meet the organization's information needs. Obviously, systems analysts must be familiar with these system components. Furthermore, because information technology changes so rapidly, they must make a continued effort to stay abreast of current technology. Subscribing to one of the information systems periodicals (e.g., *Computerworld, Datamation, Infomation Week*) is one way to stay current with technical terms, products, and vendors.

Software

Software is a set of stored instructions that tell the computer what to do. Just as procedures direct the activities of people, software directs the operations of hardware. This component encompasses three basic types of software: systems software, application software, and fourth-generation tools.

System Software.   The **system software** directs the operations of the computer hardware, including not only the system unit but also all input, storage, and output devices connected to the computer. Examples of system software programs include the **operating system (OS)**, language-translation programs, and utility programs. The OS controls the operation of the computer and its disk drives, video displays, communications devices, and so on. It also acts as an interface between the hardware and any application software. Common mainframe operating systems inclue IBM's VM and VMS and Digital Equipment's VMS. Common personal computer and workstation operating systems include Microsoft's MS-DOS, IBM's PC-DOS, Apple Computer's System 7, and Sun's Solaris. UNIX is a machine-independent OS that runs on a variety of microcomputers, minicomputers, and mainframes. A special kind of OS is a **network operating system (NOS)**, which controls the activities of a telecommunications network by monitoring access and transmission activities, detecting and correcting transmission errors, and securing the network against unauthorized use (e.g., through the use of passwords and log-on procedures).

Language translation and utility programs are also classified as system software. Hardware devices understand only one language—machine language. *Language translation programs* translate programs written in higher-level languages into machine language so the computer can execute the program instructions. Programs written in human-readable, high-level languages such as COBOL, Pascal, or C must be converted to machine language before they can be executed. *Utility programs* provide the instructions for routine tasks, such as copying files, formatting a disk, and sorting data.

System software is generally the domain of system programmers who have attained computer science or engineering degrees. Thus, creating system software is not a systems designer's concern; however, choosing appropriate OS and/or NOS software is.

Application Software.   The **application software** is a program that automates a specific business function. For example, accounting application software automates the accounts receivable, accounts payable, inventory control, and payroll processes, automatically updating the general ledger as sales are made, invoices processed, inventory received, and paychecks issued. Programs that perform compensation analyses and maintain an employee job skills inventory are examples of human resources application software. Manufacturing application software includes CAD/CAM (computer-aided design and computer-aided manufacturing), MRP (material requirements planning), scheduling, numerical control, and statistical control programs.

Application software is machine-dependent or, perhaps more accurately, OS-dependent. For example, a CAD/CAM program written for an IBM mainframe running MVS as its operating system will not execute on a DEC mainframe running VMS. Similarly, an accounting package developed for PCs or PC clones running some version of DOS will not execute on an Apple Macintosh running System 7. Application software is useless without system software; in other words, application programs cannot be executed if there are no OS programs to control the hardware and to translate the application program code into machine language.

In the early days of business information systems, almost all application software had to be created "from scratch"; that is, very few software packages were available to save organizations the time and expense of custom writing their own application programs. Today, application software can be obtained from numerous sources and through various methods. These include:

◆ Custom-developed software written by the organization's information systems (IS) staff in a third-generation language such as COBOL or using a fourth-generation tool (discussed shortly)

◆ Custom-developed software written by users with a fourth-generation tool

◆ Custom-developed software written under contract by a consulting team

◆ Commercially available packaged software

Which software source an organization chooses is largely determined by factors such as complexity, availability, cost, and development time.

Fourth-Generation Tools.   The last—and most dynamic—category of software is **fourth-generation tools (4GT)**: productivity tools or fourth-generation programming languages that increase developer productivity or that allow users to develop their own applications. The primary objective of 4GTs is to allow people—possibly with limited technical skills—to develop easy-to-maintain applications with a minimum of effort [Martin 1985]. As illustrated in Figure 2.6, 4GTs maximize developer productivity, unlike previous programming

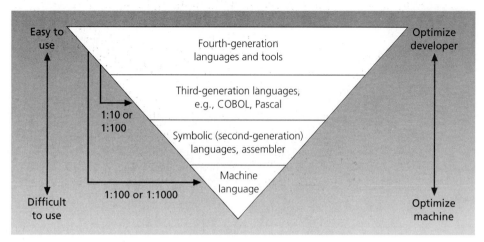

FIGURE 2.6   Fourth-generation tools maximize developer productivity

languages that attempted to maximize machine productivity. A single line of code or a single instruction in a 4GT may be equivalent to tens or hundreds, even thousands, of lines of code in a lower-level language.

The first category of 4GTs, *designer/implementer* **productivity tools**, includes fourth generation languages (for example, Information Builder's Focus and Must Software International's Nomad2) and computer-aided systems engineering (CASE) tools, such as Computer Systems Adviser's SilverRun, Texas Instruments' Information Engineering Facility (IEF), and Powersoft's PowerBuilder. Also included in this subcategory are application and report generators, such as Information Builder's FOCUS Reporter. A third subgroup of designer/implementer productivity tools consists of powerful DBMSs, such as Oracle Corporation's Oracle7, Sybase, Inc.'s SQL Server, Informix Software, Inc.'s Informix, and IBM's IMS and DB2. Such tools reduce the time and labor required to develop systems.

The second category, *user* productivity tools, facilitate application development by non-technical users. This category includes spreadsheets such as Microsoft's Excel and Lotus Development Corporation's 1-2-3; word-processing software such as Microsoft's Word and Novell's WordPerfect; PC-based DBMSs, such as Borland International's Paradox and Microsoft's Access; and presentation and desktop publishing programs, such as Software Publishing's Harvard Grahics, Microsoft's PowerPoint, and Adobe Systems, Inc.'s PageMaker. These packages are called *productivity tools* because they allow users with no programming knowledge to build their own applications. For example, using a spreadsheet package, a nonprogramming user can develop a variety of accounting and financial applications. The spreadsheet package is a 4GT; the template or worksheet, with its formatting and formulas, is an application program. Similarly, using a PC-based DBMS, a user can develop an inventory management system that not only maintains data about inventory items but also generates a daily inventory status report.

Software suites are user productivity packages that provide integrated spreadsheet, electronic mail, DBMS, presentation graphics, scheduling, and word-processing tools. Popular software suites include Microsoft's Office and Lotus Development Corporation's SmartSuite. A suite's tools work seamlessly together, allowing the user to write a report that contains a line graph generated by the spreadsheet tool, which, in turn, accessed data from the DBMS. This integration is made possible in Windows packages by a communications technology called Object Linking and Embedding (OLE), developed by Microsoft; however, a competing technology is OpenDoc, a connectivity standard developed by a consortium of vendors at Component Integration Laboratories (see, for example, [Johnston 1994]).

Workgroup and workflow tools, such as Lotus Development Corporation's Notes, are user productuvity tools that support collaborative groups and cross-functional sharing of documents and other text. Organizations use Notes to support status tracking, to-do lists, address books, and increasingly, workflow auotmation. **Workflow automation** is a growing trend in large, information-intensive industries, such as insurance, financial services, and health care; its objective is to replace today's time-consuming, sequential, paper-routing processes with electronic flows of information shared by multiple users. The advantages of using electronic forms are:

1. They are always up-to-date because any changes are replicated throughout the network automatically.

2. They can be processed by multiple users simultaneously.

3. They can be routed automatically to users.

A case in point is J&H InfoEdge, a Notes application developed by Johnsons & Higgins, a New-York-based insurance broker. InfoEdge facilitates the tracking and sharing of insurance brokerage information by creating a dynamic repository of organization-wide knowledge. Brokerage expertise and user knowledge that used to reside in the mind (or on the hard drive) of one broker are now available to all brokers in Johnson & Higgins' offices worldwide. The next step in this system's evolution is to link brokers with users, thus forming "an electronic partnership" to keep users up-to-date about the status of their accounts [Baum 1994].

As this overview demonstrates, the software component has become an increasingly important—and complex—facet of business information systems. Over the past decade, the advent of graphical user interfaces (GUI—pronounced *GOOey*), multitasking (in a microcomputer environment, the ability to have several programs active at the same time), and powerful functions has greatly increased software complexity. Constructing and maintaining this component now consumes approximately 75 percent of an information system's cost. Thus, the challenge of the next decade is to find more efficient, less costly ways to create and maintain software. The object-oriented approach introduced in Chapter 1 has been proposed as one solution to this problem.

Check Your Understanding 2-4

Identify and classify as system, application, or 4GT the software used in the Clinton transition team's resume-processing system. What processes did each category of the software perform?

Hardware

The **hardware** component consists of the physical equipment used to enter, process, output, store, and communicate data. This component includes the central processor and a host of input, output, storage, and telecommunications devices. The central processor is commonly called a *computer*; the input, output, storage, and telecommunications devices are commonly called *peripherals*. Examples of these hardware devices are provided in Table 2.2.

Computers. The data of an automated information system are manipulated by a **computer**, a processing device that performs logical and arithmetic operations on data, controls the operations of the computer and peripherals, and houses primary memory. In the early days of data processing, only one type of computer could perform these tasks: a mainframe. Today a wide variety of computers is available, ranging from the *personal digital assistant* (PDA) such as Apple's Newton, to microcomputers, workstations, minicomputers, and so on. This variety complicates your job as a systems designer in that, to design an information system, you need to understand the capabilities and appropriate applications of each computer category.

Generally speaking, computers can be classified by their speed, measured in megahertz (MHz—a million machine cycles per second) or MIPS (million instructions per second), and their primary memory capacity, i.e., random acccess memory (RAM), which is measured in megabytes (MByte = 1 million bytes) or gigabytes (GByte = 1 billion bytes). A computer's speed indicates how fast it can process software instructions; for example, a computer running at 66 MHz is twice as fast as one running at 33 MHz.

Too often students mistakenly assume that every business application requires a mainframe or, conversely, that any business application can be run on a microcomputer. To dispel this confusion, Table 2.3 indicates some of the applications typically running on each category of computer.

TABLE 2.2 Common hardware devices

Device	Examples
Input	Keyboard, mouse, magnetic ink character recognition (MICR) reader, optical character recognition (OCR) reader (e.g., a digital scanner), voice-recognition system, touch screen, pen-based input device.
Processing	Personal digital assistant (PDA), microcomputer, workstation, mini-computer, mainframe, supercomputer.
Output	VDT, printer, voice-output device, plotter, MICR inscriber.
Storage	Magnetic tape drive, magnetic disk (hard and floppy) drive, optical disk (CD-ROM and WORM) drive.
Telecommunications	*Terminal:* microcomputer or video display terminal. *Media:* twisted pair wire, coaxial cable, fiber optic cable, microwave, satellite. *Computer:* server—super PC, minicomputer, mainframe; host—minicomputer or mainframe. *Processor:* modem, multiplexer, front end processor, concentrator, controller.

Currently many large organizations are shifting from centralized mainframe-based information systems to distributed networks of smaller systems, a trend known as **downsizing**. As organizations move to smaller systems, they often develop a **client/server architecture**, in which system processes are divided between two or more computers, each performing part of the processing task. The *client* is usually a microcomputer running user-friendly software with a graphical user interface; the client provides data entry, querying, and reporting capabilities. The second computer, called a *server* or *file server*, is usually a workstation or more powerful computer (minicomputer or mainframe); the server performs the heavy-duty number crunching and database maintenance processes of the system. Notice that a client/server architecture, though discussed here under hardware, is also descriptive of how software is distributed across multiple computers.

For example, in the SKU Sales System, the client is a microcomputer running Microsoft Windows for Workgroups and Excel; the local server is a more powerful microcomputer that provides the network operating system (Windows NT) and maintains the store's database. This system is described as a tiered client/server system because the local server in each store is also networked to even more powerful dual-processor Pentium central servers in the corporate office, which are linked to an IBM mainframe. The higher-tier servers and mainframe perform the computationally intensive processes of the SKU Sales System.

Peripherals. System **peripherals** include input, output, secondary storage, and telecommunications devices. Although the term *peripheral* suggests something extra, something outside the boundary of the computer itself, peripherals are an integral part of the hardware component. Without peripherals, you could not enter, display, store, or transmit data.

Here again the variety of peripheral devices has grown over the past decade. At the advent of data processing systems, the primary means of data input were a keyboard or a punched-card reader, the primary storage device was a magnetic tape drive, and the primary

TABLE 2.3 Typical applications of each computer category

Category	Typical Applications
Microcomputer	Single-user personal productivity applications (word processing, spreadsheets, and so on), office automation, workgroup computing, LAN file server, client computer in client/server system.
Workstation	Scientific, financial, and graphics applications, such as CAD/CAM, portfolio analysis, and simulation; also used as servers on a LAN.
Minicomputer	Used by midsized organizations (universities, hospitals, and so on) with many users and applications but only a moderate online transaction processing volume; also used for departmental applications.
Mainframe	Host computer or central database server accessed by 100s of terminals and connected to dozens of tape/disk drives; high-volume, high-speed transaction processing; enterprise-wide systems.
Supercomputer	Used most commonly in scientific and military applications; now being used by a few businesses with very calculation-intensive applications.

output device was a video display terminal or line printer. Today you can choose among numerous alternatives in each peripheral category.

Input devices, hardware components that allow you to enter data into the system, include keyboard, mouse, and light pen and touch screen. Character or mark recognition devices, such as magentic ink character readers (MICR) and optical character recognition (OCR) readers, are used to input data automatically. The scanners at grocery checkout stations are an excellent example of **source data automation**: the use of input technologies that capture data in computer-readable form so that no manual data entry is required. You've experienced the benefits of this technology in the form of faster moving checkout lines and more accurate and informative grocery receipts.

Output devices include video display terminals (VDT) and printers. VDTs provide temporary display of output (sometimes called "softcopy") and are appropriate output devices for ad hoc query responses and multiple user or frequently generated reports. Printers are commonly used when a "hard copy" of the output is needed, for example, when an invoice must be mailed to a customer or a report must be used off-site. Other output devices include plotters (used to create maps or drawings), fax/modems (which are also a form of telecommunications device), and voice output, such as those used in many online registration systems and voice mail systems.

Because no computer has sufficient RAM to hold the billions of bytes of data a large organization must maintain, **secondary storage devices** are needed to provide high-capacity, nonvolatile data storage. These devices fall into two categories: **sequential-access storage devices (SASD)** and **direct-access storage devices** (**DASD**, pronounced *DAZZ dee*). A SASD, such as magnetic tape, allows only sequential access to its data; that is, if you need to read from or write to the end of the tape, the tape reader must spool through the first part of the tape to reach the correct read/write location. Because of its slow access speeds and inflexibility, magentic tape is a poor choice as a storage medium for online, real-time systems. However, it is a reasonable, low-cost choice for historical backup files and for files that usually will be processed sequentially (e.g., in a payroll application). In contrast, a DASD allows instantaneous access to data stored anywhere on the disk, because the read/write head moves to access a desired disk location. This quick access to data makes DASD the device of choice for systems requiring an immediate response.

DASD come in two forms: magnetic and optical. Magnetic direct-access storage devices include floppy disks and hard disks; optical direct-access storage devices include CD-ROM and WORM (write once, read many) optical disks. Optical DASD can store data at much higher densities than magentic DASD. Currently, the typical floppy disk has a maximum capacity of approximately 3 MBytes, whereas a 4-3/4" CD-ROM disk can store approximately 650 MBytes. However, because optical storage media are historically read-only devices, magentic disks continue to be the more popular DASD. Optical disks are used primarily for archival data storage (e.g., health records archives) or for the distribution of databases that require infrequent updates (e.g., a CD-ROM parts catalog or bibliographic database).

Yet another form of DASD commonly found today is removable-media, such as removable hard drive cartridges and magneto-optical disks. As the technology improves, the varied storage capacities and affordability of these devices will make them even more popular. Also, read/write CD-ROM drives have become affordable for the average office or small business, and will probably become more common as their prices continue to fall. If you read any comprehensive, computer hardware mail-order catalog on a regular basis, you will probably stay up-to-date on the choices and prices available.

Telecommunications Devices. A **telecommunications device** is a hardware component that allows computers to transmit data from one computer to another or from a computer to a remote peripheral device. For example, telecommunications devices are required to download data from a mainframe housed at the corporate office to another computer located in a branch office; these devices are also required to transmit a word-processing file from a computer located in your office to a central laser printer located in your department's office.

Telecommunications components include transmission media, processors, terminals, and computers. As the need to transmit data and information between various organizational units grows, such devices are becoming commonplace. They are too varied and complex to discuss in detail here.

Check Your Understanding 2-5

Identify and classify the hardware used in the Clinton transition team's resume-processing system. If a hardware device is not identified in the case, suggest the kind of device that would be appropriate. For example, no secondary storage device is indicated in the case, but, given your knowledge of these devices, you can assume what kind of device is required. Justify all your assumptions.

DOCUMENTING INFORMATION SYSTEM COMPONENTS

As a systems analyst, you will be responsible for identifying the components of an existing information system and designing the components of a new information system. The procedures component can be documented and specified using data flow diagrams, which are introduced in Technical Module A. Also commonly used are system flowcharts to document the hardware, software, and data file components of an automated information system. These are discussed in Technical Module B.

Table 2.4 presents a **function/component matrix**, a useful technique for gaining a preliminary overview of system functions and components. It helps the analyst concisely describe a system and provides a starting point for creating data flow diagrams and system flowcharts. The matrix in Table 2.4 identifies and classifies the system functions and components of the SKU Sales System. The cell contents for the People row have been defined; however, several cells' contents may be a mystery to you. You should understand that all the cells in the Procedures row refer to manual procedures performed by end-users. Similarly, all the cells in the Data row refer to data entered (Input); data accessed to perform a process (Processing); data generated (Output); data stored, whether manually or electronically (Storage); and any automated or manual activities to ensure data integrity (Control). The cells in the Software row

TABLE 2.4 SKU Sales System components and functions

People (*Users:* Sales clerks, buyers. *Designers:* Not specified. *Implementers:* Not specified)

Input	Processing	Output	Storage	Control
People who perform input procedures: Sales clerks and buyers.	*People who perform manual processing procedures:* Buyers.	*People who perform output procedures:* Sales clerks and buyers	*People who perform storage procedures:* Not specified, but assume that someone creates, updates, and deletes item and vendor records.	*People who perform control procedures:* Sales clerks and buyers.

Procedures

Input	Processing	Output	Storage	Control
Scan item tag; enter SKU or vendor code.	Manually compare orders, sales, and current stock to determine SKUs to reorder; evaluate sales by vendor.	Give sales receipt to customer and generate SKU sales report.	Not specified: assume CRUD.	Security authorization as sales clerks log on POS terminal and as buyers log on network.

Data

Input	Processing	Output	Storage	Control
SKU and vendor code	*Data accessed during processing:* Item description and item price.	Sales receipt: SKU, price, sales tax, and sales total; SKU reports: SKU, order quantity, quantity sold, quantity in stock; and vendor/SKU reports.	Item Master file, Inventory Transaction file (quantity in stock), Sales Transaction file, Vendor Master file, and Order Transaction file (quantity ordered).	Not specified.

Software

Input	Processing	Output	Storage	Control
OCR program; report menu selection screen.	Look up item price; update inventory; post transaction to Sales Transaction file; calculate sales, tax, total; sort sales records by SKU/ vendor; calculate SKU quantity sold.	Sales-processing application and Excel.	SQL Server for NT and IMS.	System: Windows for Workgroups on client workstations; and Windows NT on local servers.

Hardware

Input	Processing	Output	Storage	Control
POS terminal, OCR scanner, and mouse.	486 PCs, 66-Mhz PCs, dual-Pentium PCs, and IBM mainframe.	VDT and printer.	Not specified, but assume DASD, most likely hard drives.	Not specified.

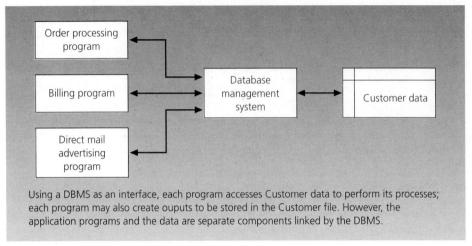

Using a DBMS as an interface, each program accesses Customer data to perform its processes; each program may also create ouputs to be stored in the Customer file. However, the application programs and the data are separate components linked by the DBMS.

FIGURE 2.7 Traditional systems view—data and software are separate components that interact to perform system funtions

refer to automated functions performed by software; thus, for example, an OCR program is needed to scan the item tag data, and a DBMS (database management system)—in this case, SQL Server for NT and IMS—is needed to store the data. Finally, the cells in the Hardware row describe the hardware devices used to perform each function; for example, we know that sales data are entered using a POS terminal and OCR scanner, and we can assume, since the Windows spreadsheet Excel is used, that a mouse is also used as an input device.

2.3 ◆ OBJECTS AS AN INFORMATION SYSTEM COMPONENT

The traditional information systems view just discussed treats data and software as two separate components. This separation reflects the traditional view's promotion of data reuse in that multiple programs are able to use the same sets of data. Today this is often done by means of a DBMS acting as an interface between the system's application programs and its data. For example, the same set of customer data may be used by an organization's order processing program, its billing program, and its direct-mail advertising program. This separation of data and software is illustrated in Figure 2.7.

In today's object-oriented (OO) view of information systems, data and software are packaged in a single construct, an *object*. Thus, system composition mirrors the composition of things in the natural world. David Taylor proposes an analogy of a system object to a living cell [1990, pp. 29–30]:

> *The basic building block out of which all living things are composed is the cell. Cells are organic "packages" that, like objects, combine related information and behavior. Most of the information is contained in protein molecules within the nucleus of the cell. The behavior, which may range from energy conversion to movement, is carried out by structures outside the nucleus.*

Cells are surrounded by a membrane that permits only certain kinds of chemical exchanges with other cells. This membrane not only protects the internal workings of the cell from outside intrusion, it also hides the complexity of the cell and presents a relatively simple interface to the rest of the organism. All interactions between cells take place through chemical messages recognized by the cell membrane and passed through to the inside of the cell.

This message-based communication greatly simplifies the way cells function. The cells don't have to read each others' protein molecules or control each others' structures to get what they need from each other—all they do is broadcast the appropriate chemical message and the receiving cell responds accordingly.[2]

Like the cell, an object is a "package" that contains data and performs behaviors by executing program code. This packaging of data and behavior into a single construct is called **encapsulation**. Each object is distinct and hides its complexity from every other object; objects interact only by sending messages, which can be recognized and acted upon only by the appropriate receiving object. The fundamental concepts of the OO approach were introduced in Chapter 1. Here we will elaborate on these concepts to illustrate how the OO systems view encapsulates data and software.

Recall that an object *class* is an abstraction or model of a real concept that defines the attributes and methods of its class members. An *attribute* is a characteristic that describes an object; a *method* is a function that the object can perform. For example, as shown in Figure 2.8, the object class ITEM specifies attributes such as StockNumber, UnitPrice, QuantityOnHand, and ReorderPoint and methods such as createItem, orderItem and giveUnitPrice. Another example of an object class is INVOICE-LINE (a set of line items on an invoice), which specifies attributes such as LineNumber and Quantity and methods such as computeExtendedPrice.

An object *instance* is a specific member of an object class. For example, one instance of the object class ITEM has "SN23-K71" as the value of its StockNumber attribute; another has "SN45-C32" as that value. Both of these instances are members of the ITEM object class; each is identified by the unique value of its StockNumber attribute. In Figure 2.8, notice that an object instance contains only the values of its attributes; however, each object instance can access and perform methods from its object class. Thus, each object has access to both its data and the program code for performing its methods.

The only means of interaction between objects is through **messages**, that is, requests from one object to another object, signaling the receiving object to perform one of its methods. For example, to carry out its computeExtendedPrice method, an INVOICE-LINE object instance must send a message to the appropriate ITEM object instance, requesting that it return the value of its UnitPrice attribute, as illustrated in Figure 2.8. Because objects interact

---

[2] Servio Corporation, *Object-Oriented Technology: A Manager's Guide,* © 1990 Servio Corporation. Reprinted by permission of Addison-Wesley Publishing Company, Inc.

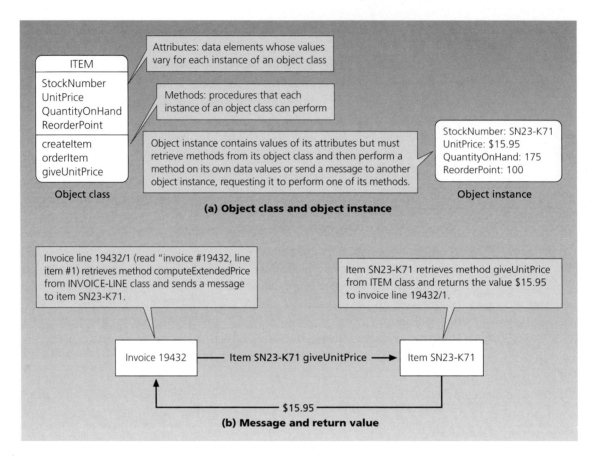

FIGURE 2.8   Fundamental object-oriented concepts

only through messages, the internal complexity of an object is hidden from other objects. Furthermore, objects facilitate the reuse of not only their data but also their program code.

We will examine these and other OO concepts more extensively in later chapters. For now, you need to understand only these concepts:

1. An OO system must perform all the functions of an information system—input, processing, output, storage, and control.

2. When you develop an OO system, you must consider all five components of an information system—people, procedures, data, software, and hardware. However, an OO system will package the data and software components as objects.

3. Each object encapsulates attributes and methods.

4. The only way for objects to interact is by sending messages.

◈ REVIEW OF CHAPTER LEARNING OBJECTIVES

1. *Distinguish between a logical function and a physical function.*

   A logical function describes an input, processing, output, storage, or control function independent of the technology used. Examples of logical functions are, "Accept data" (input); "Calculate total," and "Sort records" (processing); "Generate report" (output); "Maintain data" (storage); and "Verify user" and "Validate data" (control). In contrast, a physical function describes a system function in terms of the technology used. Examples of physical functions include, "Read data using an OCR reader" (input); "Run the sort routine to sort records alphabetically" (processing); "Print report" (output); "Update customer master tape file" (storage); and "Perform log-on procedure" (control).

2. *Define the five functions of an information system.*

   The five functions of an information system are input, processing, output, storage, and control (IPOSC). Input functions describe the activities that must be performed to access data for processing. Processing functions describe the ways that data are manipulated to perform business functions and to produce information of value in management decision making. Output functions describe the activities required to generate business documents or reports. Storage functions describe the activities required to maintain system data. In general, a storage function is an activity that accesses or transforms the database, that is, any activity that reads data from or writes data to a storage medium, whether manual or automated. Control functions describe the manual and automated activities performed (1) to verify the validity and accuracy of inputs and outputs and (2) to ensure the integrity of stored data. Control functions are often performed on top of or simultaneously with other system functions to ensure system integrity. They are classified two ways: as general controls and as application controls.

3. *Explain the sociotechnical perspective of information systems.*

   The sociotechnical perspective considers not only technology but also the behavioral or social factors that affect how well an information system will meet the needs of the organization as a whole and of the users as individuals. The sociotechnical perspective recognizes that information systems affect the organization in which they are used and that behavioral and organizational factors affect the design and successful use of information systems.

4. *Define and give examples of the five components of an information system.*

   The five components of an information system are people, procedures, data, software, and hardware (PPDSH). The people component includes three categories: users, designers, and implementers. The user category is further categorized into end-users, who use the system to perform business tasks; user-managers, who supervise end-users; and user-sponsors, who authorize and fund development projects. Designers analyze an organization, identify its processing and information requirements, and create the blueprints of a system to satisfy the users' information needs. Designers serve as an interface between the users who will use the system and the implementers who will construct it. Implementers use the design specifications to construct the system; they perform tasks such as writing programs, building databases, and installing telecommunications devices.

Procedures are sets of instructions that tell people in the organization how to perform their jobs. The procedures component is divided into three types: application, system, and control procedures. Control procedures are developed to ensure the reliability and accuracy of an information system. Application procedures instruct users on how to run an application to perform a business task. System procedures describe how to operate hardware and how to start, shut down, and maintain the system.

Data is the core of an information system. Each organization collects, processes, and maintains a wide variety of data about entities of interest to it. The data component is subdivided into three types: input data entered into the system, stored data maintained in a file, and output data generated as documents or reports.

Software is a set of stored instructions that tell the computer what to do. This component encompasses three basic types of software: system software that directs hardware operations, performs language translation, and provides utilities (e.g., a sort utility); application software that automates or supports specific business functions; and fourth-generation tools, including productivity tools and fourth-generation programming languages that increase productivity or allow users to develop their own applications.

The hardware component includes all the physical devices used to input, process, output, store, and transmit data. Hardware is classified as one of two basic types: computers and peripherals. Computer categories include supercomputer, mainframe, minicomputer, workstation, desktop computer, and portable (e.g., laptop and handheld computers). Peripheral categories include input devices, output devices, storage devices, and telecommunications devices.

5. *Explain how an object encapsulates the data and software components of an information system.*

Each object class defines the attributes that describe it and the methods that it can perform. Only the containing object can perform methods that use its data. If another object needs to use the containing object's data, it must send a message to the containing object, asking it to perform one of its methods and to return its data to the sending object. Thus, each object class is a largely independent module that is related to other object classes through messages. In this view, data and software are not separate components; instead, each object is a package containing both data and software.

◆ KEY TERMS

application controls	computer system	database management
application procedures	computer system literate	system (DBMS)
application software	control functions	designer
batch processing	control procedures	direct-access storage device
client/server architecture	CRUD	downsizing
computer	data	encapsulation

end-users
fourth-generation tool
   (4GT)
function/component matrix
functional requirements
general controls
hardware
implementer
information architecture
information systems literate
input data
input devices
input functions
logical function
management support
   systems (MSS)
message
network operating system
   (NOS)

office automation systems
   (OAS)
operating system (OS)
organizational culture
output data
output device
output functions
people
peripherals
physical function
procedures
processing function
productivity tools
real-time processing
secondary storage devices
sequential-access storage
   device
sociotechnical perspective
software

software suites
source data automation
storage functions
stored data
system function
system procedures
system software
telecommunications devices
transaction processing
   system (TPS)
user-manager
user-sponsor
users
workflow automation
workgroup and workflow
   tools

◆ DISCUSSION QUESTIONS

1. Explain the difference between a logical function and a physical function.

2. Discuss the five functions of an information system, giving examples of each.

3. Describe real-time processing and batch processing. Give an example of an application where each is appropriate.

4. Distinguish general controls from application controls. Give an example of each.

5. Discuss the three people roles in systems development.

6. "Procedures are to people what software is to hardware." Use this statement to describe the procedures component of an information system. Define three types of procedures.

7. Explain the statement, "Data is the core of an information system."

8. What is an information architecture?

9. Distinguish the purposes of the three categories of software: system, application, and fourth-generation tools. Give an example of each.

10. Describe the hardware component in terms of the IPOSC functions of an information system. What kinds of hardware are instrumental in performing each function?

11. Define encapsulation. Use this concept to explain the object-oriented view of the software and data components.

◆ EXERCISES

1. Designate each of the following functions as a logical function (LF) or physical function (PF). Rewrite all physical functions to make them logical functions.
   a. Enter item data.
   b. Calculate year-to-date earnings.
   c. Scan membership number using light pen.
   d. Back up files to floppy disk.
   e. Verify customer credit limit.
   f. Display payroll report on screen.
   g. Copy master files to magnetic tape.
   h. Generate sales receipt.

2. Designate each of the functions in Exercise 1 as an input (I), processing (P), output (O), storage (S), or control (C) function.

3. Reread the Chapter 1 opening case, "Systems Development Is Child's Play at Hasbro." Identify the logical IPOSC functions of Hasbro's import tracking system. If the case does not provide information about a particular function, indicate "Insufficient case detail" for that function.

4. Designate each of the following as system (S), application (A), designer/implementer productivity (D/IP), or user productivity (UP) software.
   a. Accounts payable program.
   b. Network operating system.
   c. CASE tool.
   d. Report generator.
   e. Disk operating system.
   f. Skills inventory program.
   g. Spreadsheet software.
   h. Computer-aided design (CAD) software.

5. Designate each of the following devices as an input (I), processing (P), output (O), storage (S), or telecommunications (T) device. If a device fits more than one category, indicate all appropriate categories and explain why each is appropriate.
   a. CD-ROM
   b. Fax/modem
   c. Laser printer
   d. Mainframe computer
   e. Video display screen
   f. Mouse
   g. OCR reader
   h. Disk drive

6. Reread the Chapter 1 opening case, "Systems Development Is Child's Play at Hasbro."
   a. Identify the PPDSH components of Hasbro's *mainframe-based* import tracking system. If the case does not provide information about a particular component, indicate "Insufficient case detail" for that component.
   b. Identify the PPDSH components of Hasbro's *LAN-based* import tracking system. If the case does not provide information about a particular component, indicate "Insufficient case detail" for that component.

7. Scan an issue of *Computerworld*, *Infomation Week*, or any other information systems journal to identify an example of each of the following not given in the chapter:
   a. Mainframe operating system
   b. Network operating system
   c. DBMS
   d. CASE tool
   e. Report generator
   f. Workgroup or workflow software package
   g. Mainframe
   h. Minicomputer
   i. Network server

◆ REFERENCES

Baum, D. "Developing Serious Apps with Notes." *Datamation,* April 15, 1994, pp. 28–32.

Bostrom, R. P., and J. S. Heinen. "MIS Problems and Failures: A Socio-technical Perspective." *MIS Quarterly*, no. 3 (1977), pp. 17–31; and no. 4 (1977), pp. 11–28.

Johnston, S. J. "Making Sense of OLE." *Computerworld,* May 23, 1994, pp. 124–125, 128.

Jordan, E. W., and J. J. Machesky. *Systems Development: Requirements, Evaluation, Design, and Implementation.* Boston, MA: PWS-Kent, 1990.

Keen, P. G. W., and J. M. Cummins. *Networks in Action: Business Choices and Telecommunications Decisions.* Belmont, CA: Wadsworth, 1994.

Martin, J. *Fourth-Generation Languages,* vol. 1 and 2. Englewood Cliffs, NJ: Prentice-Hall, 1985.

Taylor, D. *Object-Oriented Technology: A Manager's Guide.* Reading, MA: Addison-Wesley, 1990.

Verity, J. W. "The Gold Mine of Data in Customer Service." *Business Week*, March 21, 1994, pp. 113–114.

TECHNICAL MODULE A

Data Flow Diagrams

Systems analysts have traditionally used data flow diagrams to analyze and design the IPOSC requirements of a system. A **data flow diagram (DFD)** models the sources and destinations of data (external entities), the data inputs and outputs (data flows), the actions that transform inputs into outputs (processes), and the data maintained by an information system (data stores). There are two types of DFDs. A **logical DFD** models the processes that must be performed but gives no indication of how they will be performed, that is, by what person or software module. In addition, a logical DFD makes no distinction between paper data stores (e.g., folders, sheets of paper, catalogs) and digital data stores (e.g., files on magnetic tape or disk). In contrast, a **physical DFD** specifies the details of a system's physical implementation, including who performs what processes and how (e.g., manually or using information technology). Thus, a logical DFD describes logical functions whereas a physical DFD describes physical functions.

In traditional systems development, a systems analyst commonly begins analysis by creating a physical DFD of the existing system. Then the analyst transforms the physical DFD into a logical DFD and modifies it to create a new logical DFD that resolves problems in the existing system. Finally, the analyst creates a new physical DFD specifying the IPOSC functions of the new system. Today most analysts avoid the tremendous amount of labor required to draw all these diagrams and use only logical DFDs to analyze the IPOSC functions of an existing system and physical DFDs to specify the IPOSC functions of a new system. In this techinical module, we focus on logical DFDs; physical DFDs are discussed in Chapter 10.

DFD SYMBOLS

Data flow diagrams use four basic symbols, as represented in Figure A.1. Two sets of symbols are shown because both Yourdon's [1979] and Gane and Sarson's [1979] DFD symbols are widely used in traditional systems development. The two should never be mixed. For example, you should not use Yourdon's symbols for external entities and processes in combination with Gane and Sarson's symbol for data stores.

The DFD shown in Figure A.2 uses the Gane and Sarson symbols. Thus, the square labeled "Supplier" represents a source and destination of data, the arrows labeled "Notice of shipment error" and "Bill of lading" represent data flows, the rounded rectangle labeled "Verify shipment" represents a logical process that transforms the "Bill of lading" data flow into the "Verified bill of lading" data flow, and the open-ended rectangle labeled "Inventory

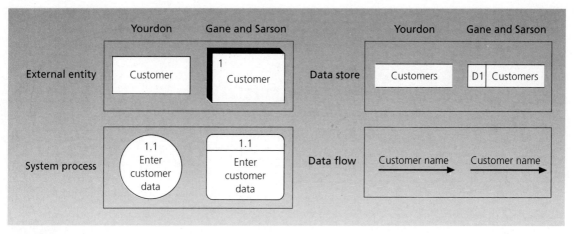

FIGURE A.1   Symbols used in data flow diagrams

Items" is a data store. In the case description provided in Figure A.2, verb phrases that indicate a process are underlined, external entities are in bold type, data flows are italicized, and data stores are shown in all capital letters.

As shown in Figure A.1, an **external entity** is represented by a labeled square or rectangle. The name of the external entity (e.g., Customer) is indicated inside the rectangle; in addition, most CASE tools used to create DFDs assign a unique number (e.g., 1 or EE1) to each external entity. In a DFD, an external entity is any person or agency outside the organization or any employee, system, or department outside the system being studied; that is, an external entity may be any entity that provides inputs to or receives outputs from the system but does not perform any system processes.

A system **process** is represented by a circle or a rounded rectangle, as shown in Figure A.1. A process is any activity—manual or automated—that transforms data. Logical DFDs model both manual and automated processes, but they make no distinction between the two. Thus, whether a process is performed by humans or by computers is not an issue in creating a logical DFD. This lack of interest in *how* a process is performed makes sense if you recall that logical DFDs document the *logical* IPOSC functions of a system. Notice that the process symbols in Figures A.1 and A.2 contain two labels: a process identification number and a process description. The **process identification number** label uniquely identifies each process and indicates its order in the sequence of processes represented. The **process description label** is always stated as an active verb phrase composed of an action verb followed by a data object; for example, "*Order* items," "*Verify* shipment," "*Update* inventory."

If you use Gane and Sarson's DFD symbols, you have the option of entering the name or location of the internal entity that performs a process in the bottom section of the process symbol, as shown in Figure A.3. However, identifying the actor or location is not required; in fact, most analysts avoid doing so because identifying the entity who performs a process violates the premise of a *logical* DFD.

A **data store** is any organized data stored for future use by the organization. For example, in a manual information system, a data store might be a telephone book, customer file folders, inventory-count sheets, or parts catalog. In an automated information system,

Carson-Plymouth Medical Devices (CPMD), an assembler of sophisticated medical products, must maintain a ready supply of high-quality components to manufacture its products. To achieve this goal, CPMD's Purchasing Department checks inventory levels each day by reviewing the INVENTORY ITEMs stock list. When the quantity on hand of a particular component reaches its economic reorder point, CPMD's Purchasing Department places a *purchase order* with its **supplier** (*supplier data* is accessed from the SUPPLIER list) for that component and files a copy in the PURCHASE ORDER file. When a **supplier** delivers a shipment along with a *bill of lading*, Shipping and Receiving (S/R) receives the shipment by performing a three-step process. First, the S/R clerk verifies the shipment by accessing a copy of the *purchase order* and comparing it to the *bill of lading*. If a received item appears on the purchase order and the bill of lading, the *verified bill of lading* and received items are passed on to Inspection. Otherwise, the S/R clerk generates a *notice of shipment error*, which is sent to the **supplier**.

Next, Inspection inspects the valid shipment items by accessing the *quality criteria* from the INSPECTION CRITERIA folder. If the item meets all the quality criteria, the inspector adds it to an *Accepted Items list*, which is forwarded to the Inventory clerk. If an item doesn't pass inspection, the inspector creates a *notice of defective shipment*, which is sent to the **supplier** along with the defective items.

Finally, the Inventory clerk updates the INVENTORY ITEMs list by adding the *current on-hand quantity* of each item to the accepted-item quantity, reflecting an *updated quantity.*

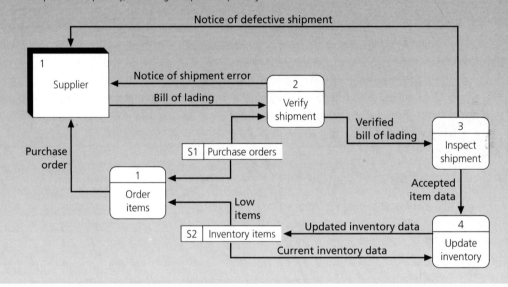

FIGURE A.2 Data flow diagram for CPMD using Gane and Sarson symbols

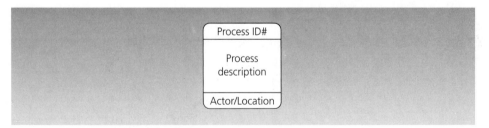

FIGURE A.3 Process symbol with actor/location section.

most data is stored in magnetic or optical form on magnetic tape, magnetic disk, or optical disk. Again, whether a data store is manual or computerized is not indicated in a logical data flow diagram. A data store is represented by a narrow rectangle, which, as shown in Figure A.1, is open in Yourdon's symbol and closed in Gane and Sarson's symbol. Notice that, when the Gane and Sarson data store symbol is used, each data store is also given an identification number, for example, S1 or D2, in addition to a name label.

You should understand that, in an automated information system, a software program is *not* a data store. A software program stored on disk contains program code that instructs hardware and manipulates data; a data store contains only data, not the instructions for processing data. Thus, software programs are not shown as data stores in DFDs.

The last symbol in Figure A.1 is an arrow representing a **data flow**. This symbol is labeled with a noun phrase describing the data flow. Data flows represent inputs to and outputs from processes; they also represent data written to or read from a data store. The arrows used to represent data flows in a DFD are usually unidirectional; that is, they point in one direction. Bidirectional data flows (a line with an arrow at both ends) are seldom used in DFDs because they represent data that is unchanged as it moves through a process. An underlying assumption in data flow diagrams is that *each data flow is unique* because each data flow into a process is transformed by the process, yielding a different data flow as an output. In fact, many CASE tools enforce unique data flows by prohibiting designers from giving two data flows the same name. Nonetheless, bidirectional data flows are sometimes used between a process and a data store to indicate data that are accessed for updating purposes only.

RULES GOVERNING DFD CONSTRUCTION

The rules governing DFD construction require that the sequence of processes move from left to right, top to bottom. To avoid a spider's web of intersecting lines, you may repeat external entities and data stores, as shown in Figure A.4. Notice that when multiple copies of these

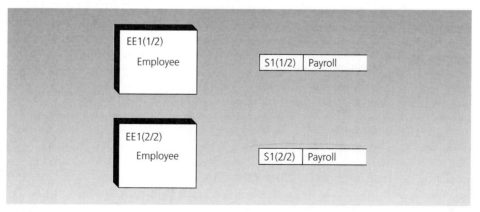

FIGURE A.4   Repeated external entity and data store symbols

entities appear in the diagram, they are labeled as 1/2 (one of two) or 2/2 (two of two), as appropriate.

If you are familiar with program flowcharts, you may wonder how to document If-Then-Else rules in a DFD. For example, the system description in Figure A.2 states, "If a received item appears on the purchase order and the bill of lading, the verified bill of lading and received items are passed on to Inspection. Otherwise, the S/R clerk generates a notice of shipment error, which is sent to the supplier." In a DFD, this If-Then-Else rule is shown by using two possible outputs of the process: the data flows for "Verified bill of lading" and "Notice of shipment error."

The four symbols described here comprise the *vocabulary* of the DFD modeling technique. As in any language, the DFD vocabulary is governed by rules of "grammar." For example, in English sentences, one uses the article "a" before singular nouns beginning with a consonant (a boy) and "an" before singular nouns beginning with a vowel (an octopus). These rules prohibit a sentence such as "An boys eats a apple."

Similarly, the rules of DFD construction prohibit a process modeler from forming certain sequences of symbols. Several such rules are illustrated in Figure A.5. The illegal constructions shown in the first four rows on the left violate the rule that *every data flow must begin or end at a process*. Thus, it is "ungrammatical" for data to flow directly (1) from one data store (DS in the figure) to another, (2) from a data store to an external entity, (3) from an external entity to a data store, or (4) from one external entity to another external entity. The reason is that we assume that data flowing from one data store to another (row 1) require some kind of process; that external entities do not have access to a system's data stores (rows 2 and 3); and that our system is not involved in data flows between external entities (row 4). In all of these situations, a process must intercede between the external entities and data stores.

Row 5 in Figure A.5 shows a **black hole**: a process or data store that receives data that are never used again. Whenever you discover a black hole in a DFD, you should more fully investigate the processes it models. It's likely a process or output has simply been overlooked. On the other hand, a black hole could indicate that the organization is indeed creating and storing data that are never used!

Row 6 shows a **magic process**: a process that spontaneously creates data from nothing, that is, from no input. A process can manipulate inputs to create new outputs—for example, by calculating a subtotal of a sales order. But it cannot create an output without first receiving some type of input. In this case, for example, the process in row 6 would have to receive customer and item data to complete a sales order. Probably, customer data were retrieved from a Customer file using the customer number, and perhaps item numbers were provided by the customer and then used to access additional item data (item description, unit, price per unit) from an Item file.

Check Your Understanding A-1

Examine the DFD shown on the top of page 69 to identify any errors in its construction. Explain why each incorrect notation is an error. Then redraw the DFD to correct each error.

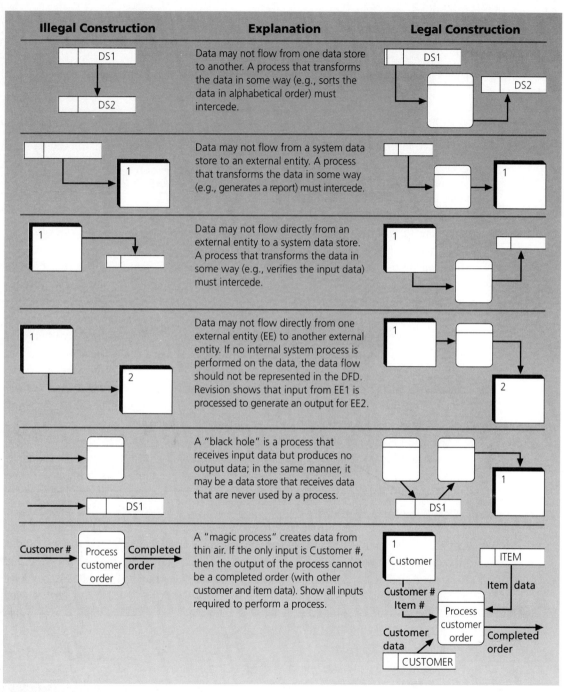

Illegal Construction	Explanation	Legal Construction
	Data may not flow from one data store to another. A process that transforms the data in some way (e.g., sorts the data in alphabetical order) must intercede.	
	Data may not flow from a system data store to an external entity. A process that transforms the data in some way (e.g., generates a report) must intercede.	
	Data may not flow directly from an external entity to a system data store. A process that transforms the data in some way (e.g., verifies the input data) must intercede.	
	Data may not flow directly from one external entity (EE) to another external entity. If no internal system process is performed on the data, the data flow should not be represented in the DFD. Revision shows that input from EE1 is processed to generate an output for EE2.	
	A "black hole" is a process that receives input data but produces no output data; in the same manner, it may be a data store that receives data that are never used by a process.	
	A "magic process" creates data from thin air. If the only input is Customer #, then the output of the process cannot be a completed order (with other customer and item data). Show all inputs required to perform a process.	

FIGURE A.5   Illegal DFD constructions

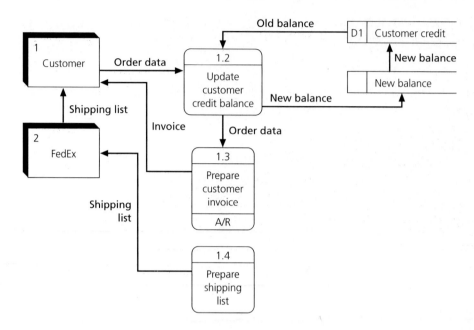

FUNCTIONAL DECOMPOSITION AND LEVELED DFDs

Data flow diagrams are the primary modeling technique of traditional systems development because they support top-down analysis and functional decomposition. Creating **leveled DFDs**—multiple DFDs in which each successive level presents a more detailed view of a process—helps manage the complexity inherent in most systems and creates a model that can be viewed at many levels of process detail. Functional decomposition, as embodied in DFDs, begins with the highest level DFD, commonly called a **context diagram**, which consolidates all processes and data stores and all internal data flows into a single process symbol representing the system. Thus, only the external entities and data flows between the system and its external entities are shown, as illustrated in Figure A.6, a context diagram of the CPMD supply management system in Figure A.2.

A **Level 0 DFD** documents the major processes of a system, as was shown in Figure A.2. Notice that the major processes are assigned process identification numbers stated as whole numbers: 1, 2, 3, and so on. In the Level 0 DFD, these process identification numbers may not always indicate a sequential ordering of processes; instead, the numbers may simply uniquely identify each process.

As illustrated in Figure A.7, a Level 0 DFD shows the **parent processes**, which may be described in more detail in a **Level 1 DFD**, which shows the **child processes** of the Level 0 DFD. Notice that Level 1 processes are assigned process identification numbers that include the parent process number plus a sequential numbering of child processes. For example, when Process 2 of the Level 0 DFD is exploded, all child processes in the Level 1-Diagram 2 DFD are numbered sequentially from 2.1 to 2.3. The first digit of this process identification number relates to the parent process; the second digit orders the child processes sequentially.

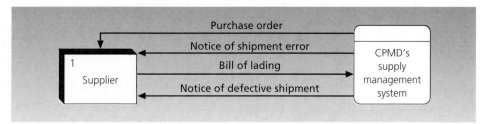

FIGURE A.6   A context diagram

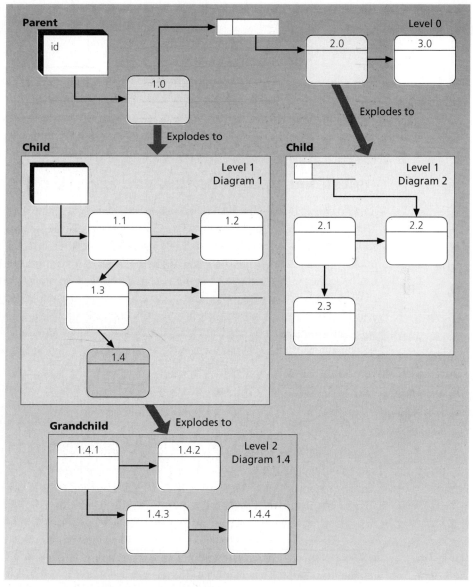

FIGURE A.7   Functional decomposition and leveled DFDs

Notice that at each level below Level 0, a separate DFD must be created for each exploded parent process. Thus, Level 1 in Figure A.7 shows two DFDs: one that explodes Process 1.0 and another that explodes Process 2.0.

Whenever a parent process is exploded to create a lower-level DFD, the parent and child diagrams must be balanced. **Balancing** requires that, at minimum, all data flows related to the parent process must also appear in the child diagram. Figure A.8 repeats the Level 0 DFD from Figure A.2, highlighting the data flows that must be balanced in the Level 1 child diagram for

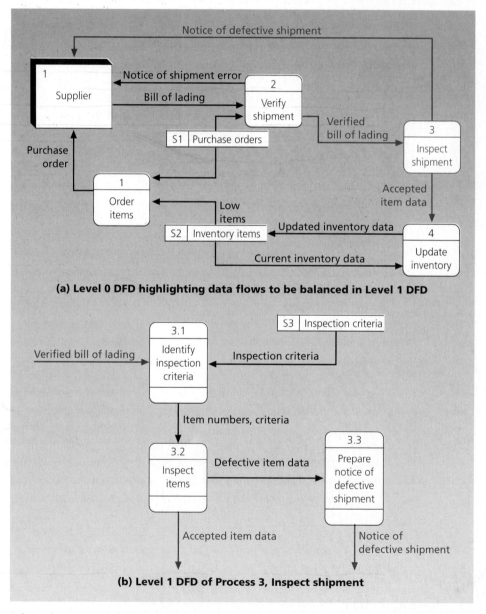

(a) Level 0 DFD highlighting data flows to be balanced in Level 1 DFD

(b) Level 1 DFD of Process 3, Inspect shipment

FIGURE A.8   Balanced parent and child diagrams

Process 3.0—"Inspect shipment." Notice that in the Level 1 child diagram, the data flows repeated from the parent diagram have no source or destination. For example, the starting point of the "Verified bill of lading" data flow is not attached to a process, data store, or external entity; similarly, the "Notice of defective shipment" data flow has no destination. These notations are legal because external entities, data stores, and parent processes from the parent diagram can, but need not, be repeated in a child diagram. Notice also that the Level 1 diagram includes additional data flows and introduces another data store, "Inspection criteria." These additions are legal because the child diagram must be balanced to the parent diagram, not the parent to the child.

Notice also that only the "Purchase orders" and "Inventory items" data stores are shown in the Level 0 DFD. Where are the "Suppliers" and "Inspection criteria" data stores that are mentioned in the case? A convention in DFD construction requires that you "push" data stores down to the lowest level. In other words, because the "Suppliers" and "Inspection Criteria" data stores are each used by only one process (Process 1 and Process 3, respectively), they are shown in the Level 1 DFDs (see e.g., Figure A.8b), but not in the Level 0 DFD. The "Purchase orders" and "Inventory items" data stores are shown in the Level 0 DFD because each is used by more than one process. The "Inventory items" data store is used by Process 1 and Process 4; the "Purchase orders" data store is used by Process 1 and Process 2.

◎   The conventions and notations used in DFD construction vary considerably. For example, you can choose to repeat or not to repeat symbols that appeared in higher-level diagrams. When an exploded process produces an output that is an input to a Level 0 process, you can choose to exclude the Level 0 process symbol in the lower-level DFD, as shown in Figure A.9a, or to include it, as shown in Figure A.9b. You may choose not to repeat the process, data store, and external entity symbols because they already were shown in the parent diagram (Level 0). You must, however, show the data flows to and from the data stores and to and from the external entity even if you do not repeat their related symbols. What is most important is that you be consistent. If you repeat data store and external entity symbols and show Level 0 process symbols in one of your exploded DFDs, do so in all of them.

Figure A.9 presents the Level 1 DFD for the parent process "Verify shipment." Here both the "Supplier" external entity and the "Purchase orders" data store symbols have been omitted because they already appeared in the Level 0 DFD. Notice that the "Verified bill of lading" data flow does not flow to any symbol. However, you should realize that some DFD notations allow you to show the Level 0 process symbol for "Inspect shipment" and to connect the "Verified bill of lading" data flow to this process symbol. In fact, the Gane and Sarson DFD notation typically adopts this convention, as shown in Figure A.9b. Notice, however, that a frame is drawn around the lower-level process to separate its processes from the higher-level process. Thus, the "Inspect shipment" process symbol is shown outside the frame. When a process frame is used, any external entities, such as the "Supplier" in Figure A.9, are also shown outside the frame.

You may wonder why the "Update inventory" process was not exploded in a Level 2 DFD. The reason is that it involves only one process that transforms data. The simple acts of reading from or writing to a data store are usually not shown as processes in a logical DFD. Thus, updating the inventory data store to reflect items received requires only one process, which reads in each item's current quantity, adds the quantity received to the current quantity, and then writes the updated quantity to the data store.

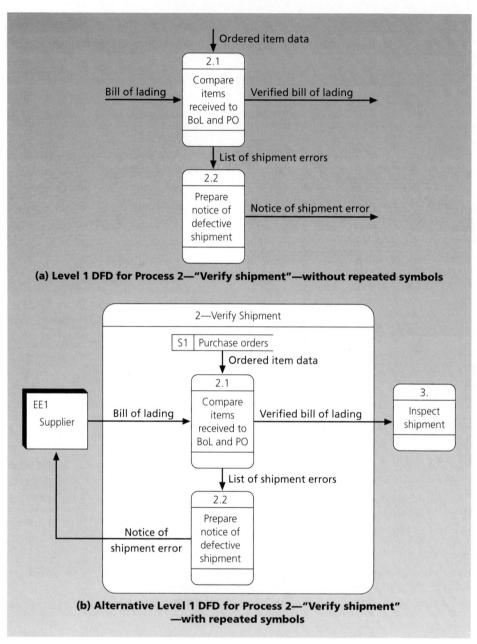

(a) Level 1 DFD for Process 2—"Verify shipment"—without repeated symbols

(b) Alternative Level 1 DFD for Process 2—"Verify shipment"
—with repeated symbols

FIGURE A.9   Level 1 DFD with and without repeated symbols from Level 0

For all intents and purposes, there is no predefined number of levels required to document a system's processes. The processes of a very complex system might be decomposed in five or six levels; those of a simple system may require only two or three levels. Generally speaking, if a diagram includes more than nine process symbols, you should consider aggregating related processes to form one or two parent processes and then decompose the parent processes in one or more lower-level diagrams. Similarly, if a process has more than four or five data flows, it is a good candidate for decomposition.

Check Your Understanding A-2

The following DFDs document a student cafeteria's process of checking out a student diner who uses a debit card to pay for a meal. First, the total cost of the meal is computed, then the student's account is debited. If the student's current debit account balance is insufficient, the student pays the remainder in cash. Examine the Level 0 and Level 1 DFDs shown here to identify any balancing errors in the child diagram. Then redraw the Level 1 DFD to eliminate these errors.

Level 0 DFD

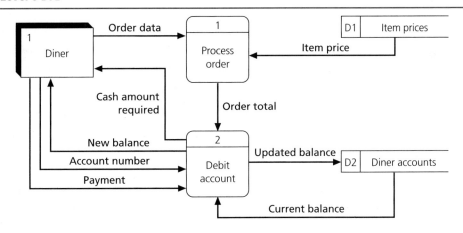

Level 1 DFD

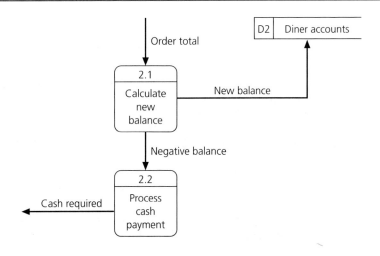

HINTS FOR CONSTRUCTING DFDs

Novice users of the DFD modeling technique may benefit from doing some preliminary analysis and planning before attempting to construct a DFD. Assume that you have been asked to construct a DFD to model the IPOSC functions in the CPMD case presented in Figure A.2. Start by creating a table that identifies the external entities, inputs, processes, outputs, and data stores as they are introduced in the case. Treat each row of the table as one major process. For example, the sentence "CPMD's Purchasing Department checks inventory levels each day by reviewing the INVENTORY ITEMs stock list." could be analyzed as shown in this table:

Process	External Entity	Input	Output	Data Store
1. Check inventory levels		Inventory levels from Inventory list	Items to reorder	Inventory items

Analyzing the next sentence, "When the quantity-on-hand of a particular component reaches its economic reorder point, CPMD's Purchasing Department places a _purchase order_ with its **supplier** (_supplier data_ is accessed from the SUPPLIER file) for that component and files a copy in the PURCHASE ORDER file," would yield a second row in the table:

Process	External Entity	Input	Output	Data Store
1. Check inventory levels		Inventory levels from Inventory list	Items to reorder	Inventory items
2. Create a purchase order	Supplier	Items to reorder; item data from Inventory; supplier data from Supplier	Purchase order to supplier and to PO file	Inventory items; supplier; purchase orders

The next sentence, "When a **supplier** delivers a shipment along with a _bill of lading,_ Shipping and Receiving (S/R) receives the shipment by performing a three-step process," describes only an external entity and an input. "Deliver shipment" is not a process within the CPMD supply management system; thus, it is not shown in the DFD. Although no processes are described in this sentence, it does alert you to the fact that receiving a shipment involves three major processes, which will probably be described in the remainder of the case.

Process	External Entity	Input	Output	Data Store
3.	Supplier	Bill of lading		

As you continue analyzing the case description, you can fill in the rest of the table:

First, the S/R clerk verifies the shipment by accessing a copy of the _purchase order_ and comparing it to the _bill of lading._ If a received item appears on the purchase order and the bill of lading, the *verified bill of lading* and received items are passed on to Inspection. Otherwise, the S/R clerk generates a *notice of shipment error*, which is sent to the **supplier**.

Process	External Entity	Input	Output	Data Store
3. Verify shipment	Supplier	Bill of lading; copy of PO (most likely from PO data store)	Verified bill of lading to next process; or notice of shipment error to supplier	Purchase orders

Next, Inspection inspects the valid shipment items by accessing the *quality criteria* from the INSPECTION CRITERIA folder. If the item meets all the quality criteria, the inspector adds it to an *Accepted Items list*, which is forwarded to the inventory clerk. If an item doesn't pass inspection, the inspector creates a *notice of defective shipment*, which is sent to the **supplier** along with the defective items.

Process	External Entity	Input	Output	Data Store
4. Inspect shipment	Supplier	Verified bill of lading; inspection criteria from Inspection Criteria folder	Accepted Items list to next process; notice of defective shipment to supplier	Inspection criteria

Finally, the inventory clerk updates the INVENTORY file by adding the *current on-hand quantity* of each item to the accepted item quantity, reflecting an *updated quantity*.

Process	External Entity	Input	Output	Data Store
5. Update inventory		Accepted Items list; current inventory levels	Updated inventory levels	Inventory items

The completed table consists of five process rows. Notice that, in the DFD shown in Figure A.2, the first two processes have been collapsed into a single process, "Order items." This is an appropriate strategy for a Level 0 DFD. However, you should also notice that, although the processes have been consolidated, all the input and output data flows, all the data stores, and the external entity shown in rows 1 and 2 have been related to this single process.

✓ Check Your Understanding A-3

1. Revise the Level 0 DFD shown in Figure A.2 to document the following component-tracking process of CPMD's supply management system. You will need to add just one

process symbol to represent this major process. Also provide the necessary Level 0 data stores, external entities, and data flows.

When certain components are used in the assembly of a medical device, CPMD needs to maintain data about the device in which the component was used. CPMD tracks this information so that if the original supplier of the component discovers a defect and must recall the component, CPMD can alert the medical supplies retailer who purchased the device in which the component was used. For example, a high rate of malfunctions was discovered in electrodes used in pacemakers that CPMD manufactured three years ago.

To comply with this requirement, as each component is used in the assembly process and then sold to a medical supplies retailer, CPMD updates its component-tracking records to indicate the model number and serial number of the medical device in which the component was used and the retailer who purchased the device. Then, if CPMD receives notice from a supplier that certain components are malfunctioning, it updates the appropriate component records to indicate that a particular component has been recalled and notifies the medical supplies retailer who purchased the affected device.

2. Create a Level 1 DFD by exploding the component-tracking process.

USING CASE TOOLS TO CONSTRUCT DFDs

Most of the DFDs shown so far were drawn using Freehand, an illustration application from Macromedia. But most illustration programs have a basic limitation—they are *only* drawing tools. In contrast, the original DFD created for Figure A.10 was made using SilverRun, a CASE tool from Computer Systems Advisors. What is the difference between a drawing tool

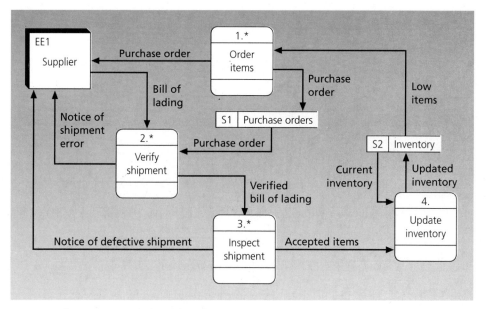

FIGURE A.10   CPMD Level 1 DFD as created in SilverRun

and a CASE tool? Both will produce attractive DFDs, and both will allow you to easily modify a DFD. But a CASE tool does much more than simply create an attractive, easy-to-modify drawing.

Notice that several of the processes shown in the Level 0 DFD in Figure A.10 have an asterisk (*) after the process identification number. The SilverRun-DFD CASE tool uses the asterisk to indicate that these processes have been exploded to a lower level. As an example of the features provided by a CASE tool, consider Figure A.11. As the Level 0 DFD shown in Figure A.10 is decomposed, SilverRun-DFD automatically carries the related processes, data stores, external entities, and data flows to the child diagram, as illustrated in Figure A.11. This CASE tool feature helps to enforce balancing between parent and child diagrams, functionality not available in a drawing tool.

In addition, a CASE tool treats your "drawings" as part of a model and can sort, modify, and analyze each aspect of the model. Figure A.12 shows SilverRun-DFD's tool palette (on the left-hand side), which allows you to create DFD shapes, draw data flows, and move between parent and child diagrams. More importantly, this figure shows SilverRun DFD's opened Model menu. Notice that this menu provides commands that allow you to view and modify textual descriptions of the various DFD components: stores, external entities, and so on. You can modify these textual descriptions to revise symbol labels, to renumber processes, and to make a number of other common revisions.

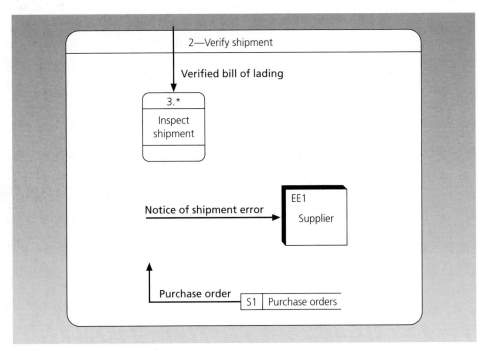

FIGURE A.11   SilverRun "head start" on balancing Level 1 DFD for Process 2

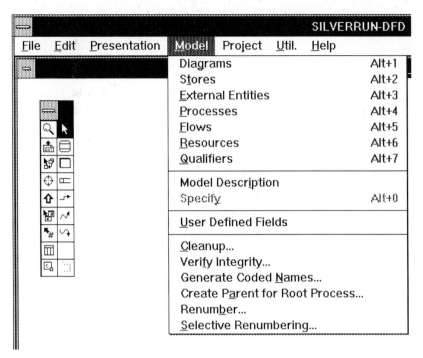

FIGURE A.12   SilverRun-DFD's Model menu

Also notice that the bottom section of this menu lists a number of commands. The most powerful command here is "Verify Integrity...." Activating this command will cause SilverRun to automatically verify the integrity of your model and to generate a report listing errors in its construction. Thus, CASE tools are *intelligent*: they provide automated procedures for applying the rules of DFD construction to your diagrams. Although SilverRun will not actually correct your model, it will give you suggestions on how to correct it.

Using a CASE tool instead of a drawing tool to create DFDs has several other benefits. For example, the project repository—sometimes called an *encyclopedia*—of a CASE tool stores not only your drawings but also valuable information about your drawings. The Project menu of SilverRun DFD in shown in Figure A.13. Granted, the purposes of the listed functions are not immediately clear. However, you should understand that a CASE tool treats your DFDs not as stand-alone drawings but as one piece of a complete systems model. Thus, for example, you can begin to specify data structures based on the data flows and data stores in your DFDs. Furthermore, if you use an integrated CASE tool, such as SilverRun, you can export model information from your DFDs into the CASE tool's data-modeling module, for example, SilverRun-ERX.

In summary, using a CASE tool to create DFDs provides several benefits. Not only can you produce attractive, easy-to-modify drawings, but you can also store valuable project in-

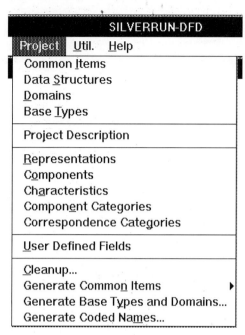

FIGURE A.13   SilverRun-DFD's Project menu

formation and integrate this information with other models to maintain a storehouse of re-usable knowledge about your organization's systems.

USES OF DATA FLOW DIAGRAMS

As a systems analyst, you will most commonly use DFDs to document the IPOSC functions of an existing information system or to specify the IPOSC functions of a new information system. The DFD is the only graphical modeling technique that represents *all* of these functions. Furthermore, leveled DFDs are the traditional modeling technique of choice for decomposing functions. And because DFDs have been used in systems analysis and design for more than a decade, many users are familiar with them. Thus, they can be an effective communication aid as you discuss system functions with users.

◆ KEY TERMS

balancing	data store	magic process
black hole	external entity	parent process
child process	Level 0 DFD	physical DFD
context diagram	Level 1 DFD	process
data flow	leveled DFDs	process description label
data flow diagram (DFD)	logical DFD	process identification number

◈ EXERCISES

1. Create a Level 0 DFD to document the IPOSC functions of Bebop Records' order processing system.

Bebop Records is a mail-order company that distributes CDs and tapes at discount prices to record-club members. When an order processing clerk receives an order form, he or she verifies that the sender is a club member by checking the Member file. If the sender is not a member, the clerk returns the order along with a membership application form. If the customer is a member, the clerk verifies the order item data by checking the Item file. Then the clerk enters the order data and saves it to the Daily Orders file. The clerk also prints an invoice and shipping list for each order, which are forwarded to Order Fulfillment.

2. Create a Level 0 DFD to document the major processes of Delta Products' order fulfillment system. Then create a balanced Level 1 DFD that more fully documents the IPOSC functions associated with the sales order processing clerk.

Delta Products Corporation is a major vendor of office supplies, furniture, and equipment. Delta's sales representatives call on customers to take orders. The sales reps write up the orders and turn them in to a sales order processing (SOP) clerk at the regional center. If the ordered items are in stock, the SOP clerk prepares a picking slip and a packing list for each order. If any of the ordered items are out of stock, the SOP clerk completes an Out of Stock Notice form, which notes the name of the customer requiring the items, and forwards it to Purchasing. A Purchasing clerk then completes a purchase order, which is mailed to a supplier. The SOP clerk notes back-ordered items on the customer's order and forwards a copy of the annotated customer order to Accounts Receivable (A/R), where an A/R clerk prepares an invoice and sends it to the customer. The SOP clerk also forwards a picking slip and packing list to the Warehouse, where stock pickers fill the order, placing ordered items into boxes along with the packing list. The boxed items and packing list are held for delivery, usually via UPS.

3. Create a context diagram of the system described in Exercise 2.

4. Create a Level 0 DFD to document the major processes of ABC Corp.'s supply requisition system; then create a balanced Level 1 DFD to document more fully the IPOSC functions associated with the buyer (given in the second paragraph).

When employees at ABC Corp. need to order supplies, they enter item data on a Purchase Requisition form. A requisition clerk assigns a requisition number and files the form in the Requisition file. Before the requisition can be filled, a supervisor must review the requisition and enter a code to approve it. The Requisition file is updated to reflect this approval.

Each day, a buyer in ABC's purchasing department accesses each approved requisition from the Requisition file and verifies the requisition approver code against the

Authorized Approver Code list. If the code is valid, the buyer then accesses a list of approved vendors. The buyer selects a vendor and calls the vendor to establish item prices. Then the buyer adds the selected vendor number, agreed upon item prices, and purchase order number to the requisition form and uses it to create a purchase order. Finally, the Requisition file is updated, a copy of the purchase order is filed in the Purchase Order file, and the purchase order is mailed to the vendor.

5. Create a context diagram of the system described in Exercise 4.

6. Create a Level 0 DFD to document the *major* processes of the payroll processing system. You may consider work-study employees to be external to the system. You may further assume (but need not document) that employees complete a payroll information form at the time of hiring; one copy of the form is maintained by the department and a second copy by Payroll.

Work-study employees in each university department provide their departmental secretary with their weekly timecards. The departmental secretary accesses the employees' hourly rate from the employee payroll file and prepares a weekly time sheet that lists each employee's name, social security number, total hours worked, and hourly rate. Then the departmental secretary files the timecards in a Timecard History folder and gives the time sheet to the department chair. If everything seems to be in order, the department chair signs the time sheet and forwards it to the university's Payroll Department. If any figures on the time sheet are unacceptable, the chair returns the sheet to the secretary, who verifies the figures and again gives the time sheet to the department chair.

In the Payroll Department, a payroll clerk calculates gross payroll earnings for each employee and then writes the earnings on the time sheet and updates the year-to-date gross earnings figure for each employee in the employee's file. (Note: Work-study students have been allocated a set figure, e.g., $1,500, that represents their total allowed gross earnings for a year.) Then the clerk accesses the employee's payroll file to determine the employee's tax status and authorized deductions. The clerk prepares the payroll checks, which are forwarded to employees. The processed time sheet is filed in a Time Sheet History folder for each pay period.

7. Create a balanced Level 1 diagram to document more fully the IPOSC functions associated with the Payroll clerk (given in paragraph 2) in Exercise 6.

8. Create a Level 0 DFD to document the IPOSC functions of All-American Bank's new accounts system.

When new customers open accounts with All-American Bank, they provide the bank with a completed new account application form. A bank clerk verifies the application data; if the form contains errors, the clerk adds the account application to an error listing, which is sent to the new accounts department. If the application data is correct, the clerk selects an account number from the available Account Numbers list and adds it to the application form. Then the clerk enters all new account data into the bank's computer and saves it to the New Accounts file. At the end of each day, the New Accounts file is accessed to (a) print a New Accounts Transaction list, which is sent to the New Accounts Department, and (b) to extract customer data, which is saved to the Customer file.

TECHNICAL MODULE B

System Flowcharts

The **system flowchart** is an analysis and design technique used to document the techno-logical components of an information system, specifically the system's hardware, software, and digital data files.

SYSTEM FLOWCHART CONSTRUCTION

The symbols used in system flowcharts are shown in Figure B.1. **Processing symbols** can represent manual as well as automated processing functions. However, only those manual processes that are required to continue an automated sequence are shown. For example, if a data entry clerk must manually sort input forms before their data are keyed into the system, this sorting process would be shown in the system flowchart by a manual processing symbol but, if a customer must complete the input form before the clerk can sort and enter the data, that form-completion process would not be shown.

The other two processing symbols represent automated processes. The *auxiliary process* symbol typically is used to represent an input/output process performed by an auxiliary device (i.e., peripheral), such as scanning a bar code, copying data from magnetic disk to tape, or printing a report. These are processes that typically execute a system software utility program or access a printer or other device driver program. In contrast, the *process* symbol represents a processing function performed by application software; for example, calculating sales order total, authorizing a credit transaction, and updating inventory status. The process symbol may be labeled with a verb phrase describing a specific process, for example, "Process payroll," or with the name of the program used to perform the process, for example, "Payroll Calculation program," or PAY1095.

As you construct a system flowchart, the processes should generally flow left to right and top to bottom. Note that this describes the general flow; in more complex flowcharts, you may not be able to adhere strictly to this rule. You should also avoid putting too much detail on a single page of the flowchart. As shown later, connector symbols are used to indicate flow across multiple pages.

Input/output symbols represent the physical devices used to enter or display data as well as the communications links, data flows, and documents that are inputs to or outputs from the system. The *keyboarding* symbol by itself represents entering data on a teletype terminal, keypad, or other "display-less" device. For example, the keyboarding symbol would be used to represent the keypad of a touchtone phone, which is used as a data entry device in an online touchtone course registration system.

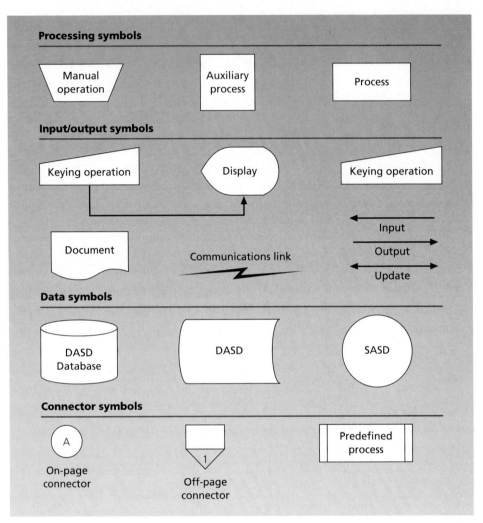

Processing symbols

Manual operation

Auxiliary process

Process

Input/output symbols

Keying operation

Display

Keying operation

Document

Communications link

Input

Output

Update

Data symbols

DASD Database

DASD

SASD

Connector symbols

A

On-page connector

1

Off-page connector

Predefined process

FIGURE B.1   System flowchart symbols

In today's information systems, most data entry is performed using a keyboard in combination with a data entry screen; this form of input operation is represented by using the keyboarding symbol in conjunction with the *display* symbol. For example, to type this sentence—that is, to enter this data into the computer—the typist used a keyboard and video display monitor, which provided feedback and presented formatting and other options in the menu and tool bar of the document window. Similarly, this combination of symbols can be used to represent entering your PIN at an automated teller machine, whose display prompts you to perform options and provides feedback on options selected, amount of cash withdrawal, and so on.

The *document* symbol represents any paper document that provides data to be entered into the system (for example, a source document such as a sales order form) or that contains information generated by the system (for example, a report, invoice, or letter). Because data on input documents must be keyed or scanned into the system (using OCR technology), an input document is always followed by a keyboarding or auxiliary process symbol. Similarly, because information on an output document is generated by a program, an output document is preceded by a process symbol. These sequences are illustrated in Figure B.2.

The other input/output symbols represent data flows. However, unlike data flows in a workflow diagram or data flow diagram, data flows in a system flowchart are unlabeled. In addition, system flowchart data flows may be bidirectional, indicating an update of a file. For example, as illustrated in Figure B.2, a Payroll program that updates a Payroll file may read the current value of a payroll record, perform a calculation to determine the new value, and write the new value back to the file. The *communications link* symbol represents an input or output transmitted over a communication line, e.g., via a network.

The **data symbols** shown in the third section of Figure B.1 represent data files. Notice that different symbols are used to indicate a direct-access storage device (DASD)—that is, magnetic or optical disk—files versus a sequential-access storage device (SASD)—that is, magnetic tape—files. Also notice that two symbols are provided for DASD files. Some texts distinguish between a DASD file and a DASD database; however, for the most part these two symbols can be used interchangeably.

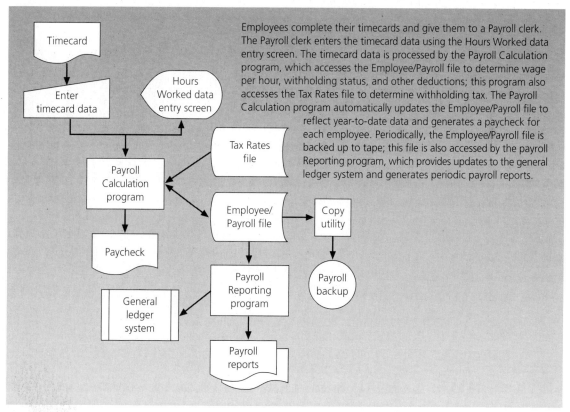

Employees complete their timecards and give them to a Payroll clerk. The Payroll clerk enters the timecard data using the Hours Worked data entry screen. The timecard data is processed by the Payroll Calculation program, which accesses the Employee/Payroll file to determine wage per hour, withholding status, and other deductions; this program also accesses the Tax Rates file to determine withholding tax. The Payroll Calculation program automatically updates the Employee/Payroll file to reflect year-to-date data and generates a paycheck for each employee. Periodically, the Employee/Payroll file is backed up to tape; this file is also accessed by the payroll Reporting program, which provides updates to the general ledger system and generates periodic payroll reports.

FIGURE B.2   Job-level system flowchart illustrating typical symbol sequences

Finally, the **connector symbols** are used (1) to indicate the flow of symbols across multiple columns or rows on a single page or across multiple pages and (2) to link the system shown in the current diagram to another system or subsystem. Notice that the *on-page connector* symbol uses letters to indicate connections; the *off-page connector* symbol uses numbers. Notice also that the *predefined process* symbol is similar to the process symbol at the top of the figure. Both are rectangular and are labeled with a verb phrase describing a process or with the name of a related system; the difference between them is the two vertical lines on both sides of the predefined process symbol. The use of the predefined process symbol is illustrated in Figure B.2, where the general ledger system is a predefined process that accepts data from the payroll system.

SYSTEM FLOWCHART LEVELS

Two levels of system flowcharts provide an overview of an information system and a detailed view of the system. As illustrated in Figure B.3, an **overview system flowchart** represents all the processes of an information system as a single process block, labeled with the name of the system. Here only the major files, inputs, and outputs are shown. In contrast, a **job-level system flowchart** (shown in Figure B.2) documents the process detail of an information system, showing each program used by an information system as a separate process block.

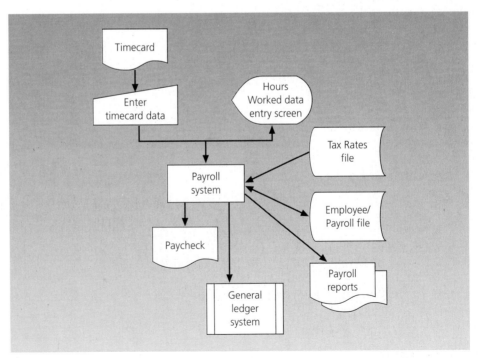

FIGURE B.3   Overview system flowchart

AVOIDING COMMON ERRORS IN SYSTEM FLOWCHARTS

One of the most common errors in system flowchart construction is omitting process blocks. You can avoid this error if you remember one simple rule: *No input, manipulation, or output of data can occur without some kind of process being performed on the data.* That is, in an automated system, software is required to perform these processes. Thus, using an OCR scanning device to input data requires an OCR program, and copying a file from one disk to another requires a copy utility program; similarly, creating a document or data and writing it to a secondary storage device requires a word-processing or database program. What

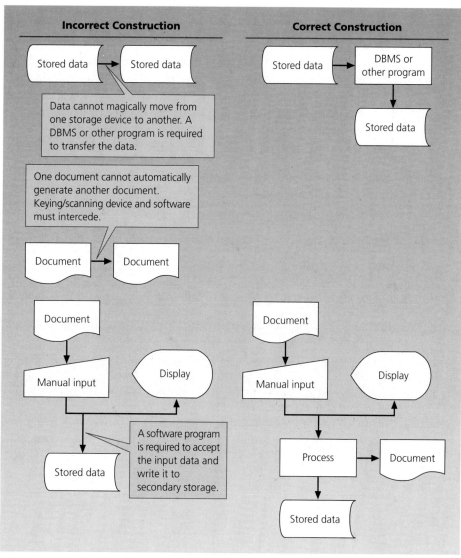

FIGURE B.4   Common errors in system flowchart construction

this means is that a process block must intercede between an input symbol and an output symbol, between an input symbol and a secondary storage symbol, and between one storage symbol and another storage symbol.

Another common error is showing paper documents as direct inputs to process blocks. Wouldn't it be wonderful if you could just lay a document next to your computer and—Presto!—the document's contents would be accessible by your software? No such luck. Again, some kind of keying or scanning device is required to input the document's contents to RAM.

These errors and their corrections are shown in Figure B.4.

USES OF SYSTEM FLOWCHARTS

System flowcharts are commonly used to document the hardware, software, and digital data of an existing information system or to represent alternative designs of a proposed information system. For example, Figure B.5 represents two alternatives for a video rental order processing system. One alternative uses OCR technology to scan the video identification number from the video tape and the customer identification number from the customer's membership card. The other requires the sales clerk to enter the video identification number and customer identification number on a Rental Order data entry screen.

◈ KEY TERMS

connector symbols	job-level system flowchart	processing symbols
data symbols	overview system flowchart	system flowchart
input/output symbols		

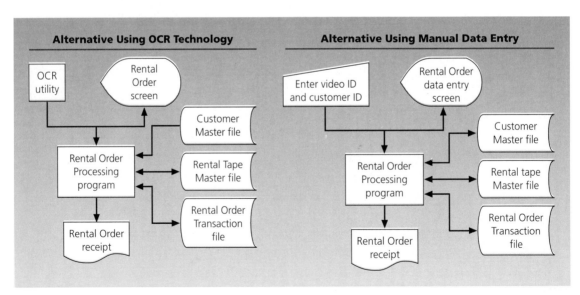

FIGURE B.5   System flowcharts documenting alternative designs

◈ EXERCISES

Note: Unless otherwise indicated, assume that all files are stored on direct access storage devices.

1. Draw a job-level system flowchart to document the following system, treating each program as a process block.

Bebop Records is a mail-order company that distributes CDs and tapes at discount prices to record club members. When an order processing clerk receives an order form he or she brings up the Enter Order data entry screen and enters the data in the Daily Orders file using Bebop's Order Entry program. At the end of each work day, Bebop's Order Processing program automatically accesses the orders from the Daily Orders file, updates the Customer file, and prints an invoice and shipping list for each order.

2. Modify the system flowchart you created in Exercise 1 to reflect the fact that, at the end of each day, the Daily Orders file is backed up to tape.

3. Draw a job-level system flowchart to document the following system, treating each program as a process block.

Cal-Neva Casualty is an auto insurance agency serving car owners in California and Nevada. When agents receive a completed policy application from a customer, they enter the policy data on the Create Policy data entry screen using program POL-361. Customer data from the policy application are saved to the Customer Master file; vehicle data, to the Vehicle Master file; and policy number, effective date, coverage, insurance rate, and other policy data, to the Policy file. Then a copy of the insurance policy is printed and sent to the customer. If the policyholder moves, the agent uses program CUST-021 to enter the customer's new address on the Update Customer data entry screen, thus updating the Customer Master file. When a customer renews his or her policy, the agent uses program POL-210 to enter the policy renewal data on the Renew Policy data entry screen, thus updating the Policy file.

As needed, the agents can use the agency's database management system (DBMS) to query the database and to generate ad hoc reports. To do this, they select a report from a menu or enter their own query on the Generate Reports screen. The DBMS displays the related report on screen or prints it on the agency's laser printer.

4. Draw an overview system flowchart of the system described in Exercise 3.

5. Draw a job-level system flowchart to document the following system, treating each system process (e.g., "Enter requisition data") as a process block.

When employees at ABC Corp. need to order supplies, they enter purchase requisition data on the Create Requisition data entry screen. The system processes this data, assigns a requisition number, and updates the Requisition file. Before the requisition can be filled, a supervisor must bring up the requisition on the Approve Requisition screen and enter a code to approve the requisition. The system updates the Requisition file to reflect this approval and also writes a record to the Requisition Audit file.

Each day, a buyer in ABC's Purchasing Department accesses each approved requisition from the Requisition file, displays it on the Finalize Requisition screen, and uses the system to verify the requisition approver code against the Authorized Approver Code file. If the code is valid, the buyer then uses the system to access and display approved vendors from the Vendor Master file on the Select Vendor data entry screen. The buyer calls the vendor to establish item prices. Then the buyer enters the selected vendor number, agreed upon item prices, and purchase order number on the Finalize Requisition data entry screen. Finally, the system updates the Requisition file, writes a record of the purchase order to the Purchase Order Master file, and prints the purchase order to be mailed to the vendor.

6. Draw an overview system flowchart to document the system described in Exercise 5. You may collapse the various requisition data entry screens described in Exercise 5 into one screen called Requisition data entry screen.

THE PROCESS OF SYSTEMS DEVELOPMENT
Two Paradigms

BANKING ON OBJECT TECHNOLOGY

What do Chase Manhattan Bank and First National Bank of Chicago have in common? Both are key players in the financial services industry, and both turned to object-oriented development to become more responsive to change. Financial services institutions operate in a highly competitive, rapidly changing world in which customer service and innovative financial offerings are the primary means of gaining a competitive advantage. Like many organizations today, Chase Manhattan and First National were crippled by the long lead times required to develop information systems to exploit these competitive opportunities. Fortunately, each bank had the "deep pockets" required to fund the change to object orientation.

As First National Bank's vice-president of technologies and development, Mark Frutig oversaw development of an object-oriented client/server system for the Securities Department. First National Bank's new securities trading system was implemented using NextStep object-oriented development environment and built on a network of Next workstations connected to Sun servers. This system processes all trade clearances and then passes the data on to a mainframe for administrative and accounting purposes.

By exploiting object inheritance in its specification of the various securities objects, First National was able to deliver the new system quickly. Perhaps even more important to the bank's continued success, the object-oriented trading system is flexible. As new securities instruments are developed, existing objects can be reused and modified, greatly reducing development time and maintenance costs. As Frutig noted, "Once we determined that all these financial securities instruments are just different ways of handling cash flows, we broke down the representation to just deal with flows. . . . The neatest thing we have been able to do is design a consistent tree of instruments, which all inherit functionality downward. This means little modification is needed when introducing a new financial security model."

Motivated by similar needs for flexibility and responsiveness, Chase Manhattan Bank also moved to object-oriented client/server systems under the direction of Jonathan Vaughan, vice-president of applications systems technology. According to Vaughan, the shift to object orientation has allowed Chase Manhattan to exploit prototyping and component-based approaches to systems development. Chase Manhattan chose Smalltalk, an object-oriented programming language, to easily integrate hardware and software components from various vendors, to build an image distribution system for customer service, and to rapidly develop a flexible query generator. The bank also used object-oriented COBOL to move mainframe applications to client/server. On the desktop, Chase Manhattan exploited OLE 2.0, Visual BASIC, and Powersoft's *PowerBuilder* to build complex applications from existing components. These development strategies have allowed Chase Manhattan to add new functions to existing applications without being stymied by the high costs and long lead times of traditional systems development.

First National's Furtig and Chase Manhattan's Vaughan both recognized that the switch to object-oriented development requires more than a change in technology or programming language. As Vaughan commented, "So how do you achieve the business benefits of object-oriented development? An effective development methodology is key . . . [as is] the discovery of objects and classification of their behavior. . . . There is an illusion that by using an object-oriented syntax (such as C++), the learning and comprehension curve can be bypassed. The essence of object orientation, however, is that it is not just another programming technique but rather a new way of approaching problems."

Adapted from J. Vaughan, "Objects' Hidden Business Benefits," and S. Cusack, "Banking on Objects," *Computerworld Client/Server Journal*, May 1994, pp. 62–63, 71. Copyright 1995 by Computerworld, Inc., Framingham MA 01701. Reprinted from Computerworld.

Chapter 2 described the *product* of systems development: an information system—comprised of people, procedures, data, software, and hardware—that performs five basic functions—input, processing, output, storage, and control—to help an organization perform its business tasks more efficiently and effectively. In this chapter, we examine the *process* of systems development. How do designers and implementers create an information system?

First, we discuss the activities and techniques of the *traditional systems development* (TSD) methodology. Recall that a methodology is a systematic description of a sequence of activities required to solve a problem. The TSD methodology is a good starting point because its concepts and variations of its techniques are still used by many organizations today; in addition, the stages and activities of the TSD methodology provide a framework for understanding the systems development life cycle. However, as the limitations and failings of the traditional approach have become evident, a number of variations on TSD have been developed, including *joint application development* (JAD) and *rapid application development* (RAD).

The chapter opening case, "Banking on Object Orientation," introduces some of the terms and technology of another development paradigm: *object-oriented systems development* (OOSD). Today organizations are adopting OOSD in an effort to reduce development time and costs. A 1995 *Computerworld* survey found that OOSD on the desktop is standard in 22 percent of the organizations surveyed and that an additional 48 percent expect it to become standard within the next two years [Heichler 1995]. Thus, it is important that you understand object-oriented concepts and techniques.

To provide you with this understanding, this text introduces a hybrid development methodology that combines aspects of OOSD and TSD. This methodology is called *Bridge* systems development because it attempts to bridge the two paradigms. After completing this chapter, you should be able to

1. Discuss the four major activities of TSD.

2. Describe some of the techniques of TSD.

3. Discuss the problems with TSD.

4. Describe several strategies to alleviate the problems with TSD.

5. Define the major activities of Bridge systems development methodology.

6. Discuss the benefits of using object technologies in systems development.

3.1 ◈ TRADITIONAL SYSTEMS DEVELOPMENT

The TSD paradigm focuses on system functions. Its primary strategy is functional decomposition in which high-level functions are successively decomposed into more detailed functions. Thus, TSD emphasizes process modeling, and systems developed under this paradigm are process-driven.

Four major TSD activities or stages are recognized: preliminary investigation, analysis, design, and implementation. These stages and their outputs are illustrated in Figure 3.1 as a waterfall, with the output of one stage cascading into the next stage. One stage must be completed before the next can begin. The dashed lines in the figure are feedback loops representing the return to an earlier stage. In a perfect world, there would be no need to return to an earlier stage; however, in real projects issues often arise during design or implementation that require more analysis or redesign. Each stage consists of a number of activities, as defined in Table 3.1 and discussed here.

PRELIMINARY INVESTIGATION

During the **preliminary investigation** stage, the objectives, constraints, and scope of the development project are identified. *Objectives* state the business benefits the system will provide. In general, an information system benefits a business by increasing efficiency, improving effectiveness, or providing a competitive advantage. For example, the SKU Sales System described in the Chapter 2 opening case was designed to help a major retailer improve its inventory control and stock purchasing processes, thus reducing stockouts and improving sales. *Constraints* state the limitations placed on the project, usually relating to time, money, and resources. For example, management may stipulate that the system must be implemented within eight months, that hardware and software costs must not exceed $100,000, and that two analysts and three programmers will be assigned to the project. The *scope* is

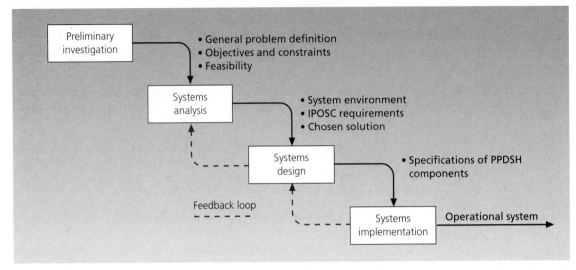

FIGURE 3.1   Traditional (waterfall) system development methodology

---

TABLE 3.1 Activities of each TSD stage

Preliminary Investigation	**Systems Design** (*continued*)

Preliminary Investigation

1. Identify objectives, constraints, and scope.
2. Estimate costs and benefits.
3. Evaluate feasibility.
4. Document objectives, constraints, and scope.
5. Get approval to begin systems analysis.

Systems Analysis

1. Analyze organizational context and requirements.
2. Analyze functional area context and requirements.
3. Analyze existing system:
   a. Physical analysis (PPDSH).
   b. Logical analysis (IPOSC).
4. Determine functionality of new system:
   a. IPOSC requirements.
   b. User characteristics.
   c. Interfaces with other systems.
5. Document requirements and get user approval to begin systems design.

Systems Design

I. General design:
   1. Specify logical design (IPOSC) and broad physical design of one or more alternative solutions.

Systems Design (*continued*)

   2. Evaluate alternatives.
   3. Choose solution or drop project.

II. Detailed design:
   1. Specify physical design (PPDSH):
      a. Design user interface.
      b. Design database.
      c. Design or acquire software.
      d. Negotiate hardware contracts.
      e. Design training and manuals.
   2. Document specifications and get user sign-off.

Systems Implementation

1. Construct components (PPDSH):
   a. Write user and systems manuals.
   b. Train users.
   c. Build the database.
   d. Code software.
   e. Prepare facility for hardware.
2. Perform unit tests.
3. Perform system tests.
4. Install components.
5. Conduct user review/acceptance test.
6. Conduct post-implementation review.

also a kind of constraint on the project, stating the system boundaries, that is, what functions are to be analyzed and redesigned by the development team.

Also during this stage, a preliminary analysis is performed to determine the feasibility, costs, and benefits of the project. The **feasibility study** addresses four major concerns: Is the system organizationally, technologically, operationally, and economically feasible? *Organizational feasibility* examines the likelihood that the proposed system will support business objectives; *operational feasibility* examines whether the proposed system is likely to be accepted by its intended users. *Technical feasibility* examines whether current technology is capable of providing the functions the proposed system is to perform. *Economic feasibility* examines whether the system's expected benefits outweigh its estimated costs. If the project is deemed feasible, then a detailed systems analysis begins.

SYSTEMS ANALYSIS

The **systems analysis** stage is devoted to understanding the system's environment, documenting the existing system's functionality, and determining the new system's requirements. The analysts investigate the current system to understand its environment, components, and functions and to identify any problems. If the current system is well documented, this task is quite easily accomplished; the analysts can simply refer to the system documentation to gain this understanding. If the current system is not well documented, just understanding the current system and its interactions with other systems can consume weeks of analysis. In fact, some organizations hire outside consultants or fund internal projects just for the purpose of describing what their current system looks like and what functions it performs! Systems analysts may need to observe the system in operation, investigate similar systems in other organizations, and interview the users who use the system.

The information compiled in this analysis is documented to describe the current system's environment and information system components (PPDSH). The system's organizational environment is commonly documented using a workflow diagram (also called a domain model), a graphical modeling technique used to represent the internal and external entities in the system's environment and the flows of data between entities. A workflow diagram of a payment reconciliation system is shown in Figure 3.2. A system flowchart in Figure 3.3 documents the hardware, software, and data components of the organization's automated information system.

After the systems analysts have a good understanding of the current system, they determine the **functional requirements**, which describe the logical IPOSC functions that the new system must perform. This activity focuses on logical IPOSC functions so that the functional requirements of the new system can be investigated without reference to a particular hardware-software-data configuration. The technique used to document system functions is the data flow diagram (DFD) discussed in Technical Module A, "Data Flow Diagrams."

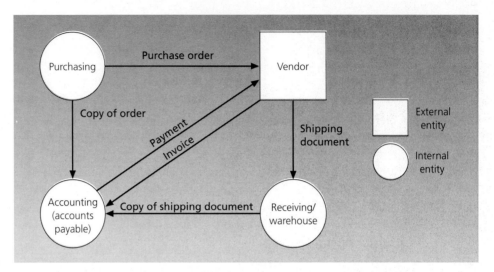

FIGURE 3.2   Workflow diagram of payment reconciliation process

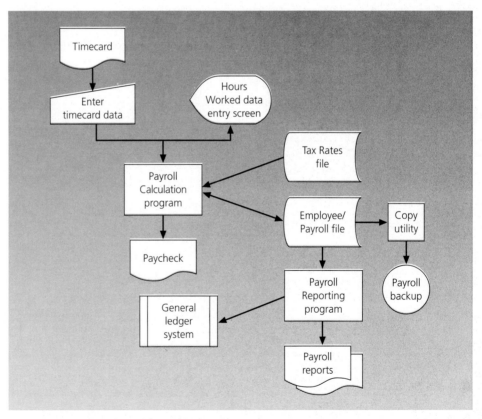

FIGURE 3.3   A system flowchart of a payroll processing system

SYSTEMS DESIGN

Systems design takes the IPOSC requirements identified during the analysis stage and synthesizes them into a new system blueprint. System design usually proceeds in two steps: general design and detailed design. For the **general design**, one or more potential designs are proposed and broadly sketched. Then these alternatives are presented to the users, who choose the design that best meets their requirements while staying within the project constraints. **Detailed design** specifies the chosen system's physical IPOSC functions in terms of the PPDSH components; the function/component matrix discussed in Chapter 2 as an analysis technique can also be used here to state the functions and component specifications of a proposed system. The outputs of the detailed design stage are specifications for the user interface, database, programs, hardware, training, and system documentation.

Several structured techniques are used during the design stage. For example, to design the software component, the designer transforms automated processes in the physical data flow diagram into a *program structure chart,* which decomposes software processes into increasingly detailed modules and shows the control paths between modules. A program structure chart illustrating some of the likely software modules of the SKU Sales System is shown in Figure 3.4. To document the detailed functions to be performed, the chart may also be supported by a *hierarchy plus input-processing-output* (HIPO) diagram, or by a program flowchart or structured text. In addition, a system flowchart of the proposed system is created to document the interrelationships among the new system's hardware, software, and data components.

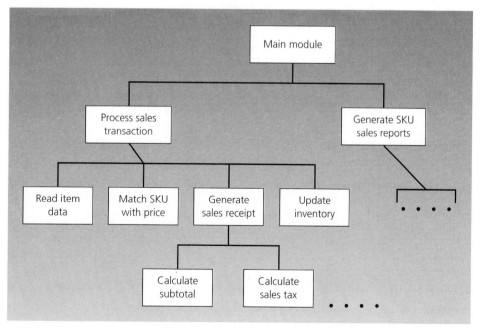

FIGURE 3.4   Program structure chart

Systems design also involves creating logical and physical models of the system's data component. An *entity-relationship diagram* (ERD) is the most popular logical data modeling technique in traditional systems development. It documents the entities about which data will be maintained (e.g., customers, parts, orders), the attributes of each entity, and the relationships between entities. This logical data model is then converted into a physical data model that specifies the structure of each file in the system's database. Physical database design also involves choosing a file organization and a data access method and defining the physical structure of each field (for example, the data type and field length).

SYSTEMS IMPLEMENTATION

Systems implementation works from the detailed design specifications to construct, test, and install the new system. During this stage, the software component is coded using structured programming techniques to reduce complexity and increase modularity. Each module of the software is tested as it is constructed. Data files are built or converted from an existing system, and the accuracy of the database is verified. Construction also involves writing user manuals and preparing the facility to house any additional hardware devices, each of which is tested individually. Manuals documenting the technical specifications and operations of the system and describing the procedures users must perform to use the system are also created at this time. Then the system as a whole is tested to ensure that all the "pieces and things" work together correctly, and users are trained to perform their new job functions. Finally, the old system is dismantled, and the new system is installed. Once the system's users have approved the system, conversion occurs and the production phase begins.

The preceding description glosses over the complexity and the many activities of systems implementation, which typically consumes more than half the time and effort of a TSD project. Systems implementation will be described more fully in Chapter 13; however, because the intended audience of this text is the designer, not the implementer, we will focus only on those implementation activities that designers are most likely to perform—for example, writing system documentation and training users.

Check Your Understanding 3-1

The numbered phrases below state activities performed during TSD. Indicate during which stage (PI—preliminary investigation, SA—systems analysis, SD—systems design, or SI—systems implementation) each activity would be most likely to occur.

_____ 1. Preparing a system flowchart of the existing system.

_____ 2. Estimating the development costs of the system.

_____ 3. Interviewing users to determine their requirements.

_____ 4. Writing programs and constructing the database.

_____ 5. Specifying the layout of screens and reports.

_____ 6. Determining the business objectives of the system.

_____ 7. Creating a program structure chart.

_____ 8. Training users and writing documentation.

_____ 9. Determining the project constraints.

_____ 10. Specifying the physical structure of the database.

3.2 ◈ PROBLEMS WITH AND ALTERNATIVES TO TRADITIONAL SYSTEMS DEVELOPMENT

Although the TSD methodology has been advocated for almost two decades, only a small minority of information systems departments in industry actually has adopted and enforced it. This section discusses the problems with TSD that have prevented its wider use and describes alternatives to it.

PROBLEMS WITH TRADITIONAL SYSTEMS DEVELOPMENT

The TSD methodology was conceived at a time when information technology consisted of "big iron"—that is, mainframes and minicomputers accessed by dumb terminals—and when almost all access to data required the intervention of a technical IS specialist. Hardware represented a major portion of the cost of systems development, and an organization's information resources were the "private property" of IS specialists. Thus, maximizing hardware efficiency and maintaining control of these resources were driving concerns. Today hardware represents a smaller portion of development costs; in addition, users are demanding access to an organization's information resources, which requires a very different system design than was common in the systems of the 1970s and early 1980s. Also, today the major development cost is incurred in paying the salaries of the designers and implementers who develop the system and in training users of the system. These and other changes in the IS arena have exposed several problems with the TSD methodology and techniques.

1. _Structured techniques are not well suited to model the requirements of today's systems._ The primary applications of information technology in the 1970s and early 1980s were large transaction processing systems (TPS) and information reporting systems that spewed out regularly scheduled reports summarizing the data collected by the TPS. Techniques of TSD—data flow diagrams, system flowcharts, program structure charts—are ideally suited for such applications because their requirements tend to be very structured and easy to specify. However, most of today's systems have a much higher level of user interaction, and many perform decision-support functions whose requirements are less structured and hence less easily defined.

Most of the modeling techniques of TSD assume that inputs are available at the time processing begins; in other words, these techniques are best applied to a batch-processing environment. However, today's systems often process transactions in real time, entering inputs as they become available and processing data on the spot. To understand the significant differences between a batch-processing system and an on-line, real-time processing system, visualize the kind of system required to process customer orders that are _mailed_ to a direct-mail retailer versus the kind of system required to process customer orders that are _taken over the phone_. In the first case, data entry clerks batch customer orders, type in the data for each order, and then save the order data on magnetic tape or disk for later processing. In the second case, a customer-service representative asks the customer for the item number, quantity, and so on for each item and is able to verify that the item is in stock and to indicate when the customer will receive the merchandise. Some retailers even train customer-service reps to suggest accessories that coordinate with a selected item or to offer alternatives if the selected item is not available.

Clearly, the second case requires a very different kind of system, with many possible processing branches, frequent interaction to gather data from the customer, and multiple accesses to the database. TSD techniques, such as data flow diagrams, are not well suited to model these requirements.

2. *The traditional systems development methodology is too costly and time consuming because of the gap between users and designers.* Recall that each of the lists of development stage activities in Table 3.1 ends with the preparation of a report and user approval of the work performed so far. In other words, developers must devote a tremendous amount of time to documenting the findings of their analysis and the specifications of their design in order to provide reports for users to review and sign off on. These reports and sign offs are necessary because the traditional approach to systems development assumes a clear division of labor between systems developers and users: systems developers analyze, design, and implement the system; users approve the requirements, design specifications, and final system implementation. The time required to prepare these reports increases the cost of development and expands the time between project inception and system delivery.

Furthermore, if the system designers are unfamiliar with the users' business functions, communication problems may arise that require more time to determine requirements. Worse yet, these communication problems may cause requirements specification to be faulty or incomplete, requiring rework of the design specifications as correct or new requirements are discovered. Both of these problems add to the cost and time to complete the system.

3. *The traditional systems development methodology is ill-suited to developing leading-edge applications.* How comfortable would you be funding a two-year, multimillion-dollar project to develop an "arostodiasist" if you had no idea what an arostodiasist is or what it looks like? How likely is it that you would be able to tell the developers what you expect the arostodiasist to do if you had no idea what it could do? Unfortunately, many users feel caught in an arostodiasist nightmare when asked to identify the functional requirements of a leading-edge—or simply, unfamiliar—application. What's more, in traditional development, users must sign off on the requirements and design specifications after seeing only a "paper model" of the system. Is it any wonder that, when the information system is finally delivered, the user takes a deep breath and says, "Oh, no. This isn't at all what I had envisioned!"

4. *The traditional systems development methodology is too inflexible for large projects.* A large project is any systems development effort requiring more than one year to complete. The danger in using the TSD methodology for such projects is the inherent delay between determining requirements and actually delivering the system. In the TSD approach, requirements are supposed to be "frozen" when the users sign off on the requirements document; under this assumption, the system that is designed and implemented will provide only the functionality detailed during requirements analysis.

However, a recent study by Capers Jones found that **creeping requirements** are a major problem in large projects. On average, user requirements grow or change about 1 percent per month. Thus, for a one-year project, if the delivered system performs only the functions determined during requirements definition, it will meet only about 90 percent of the users' requirements by the time it is delivered. For a three-year project (not uncommon, given today's complex systems), about 35 percent of the system's functionality will have to be tacked on after the requirements stage if the system is to meet the users' needs at conversion [Jones 1994].

Jones describes creeping requirements as "endemic" to large development projects, noting that they are the root cause of missed schedules and budget overruns. Even more significant are the projects that are canceled largely because of missed delivery schedules and rapidly ballooning costs. Jones found that for 1993, canceled projects represented a *waste of $14.3 billion dollars and over 285,000 effort-years* in the United States alone. If you read any of the MIS trade journals, you have probably encountered stories about such projects. Businesses that operate in a highly dynamic, even volatile environment must be able to adapt quickly to changes in their environment; the TSD methodology does not respond well to such rapid change.

ALTERNATIVE DEVELOPMENT STRATEGIES

Several variations of and additions to the TSD methodology have been suggested to alleviate the problems just outlined. Here we will describe three of these strategies: joint application development, phased development, and rapid application development.

Joint Application Development

The **joint application development (JAD)** strategy [Martin 1990] was created to overcome the communications gap between users and designers and to reduce the time and effort devoted to documenting and approving requirements and design specifications. JAD uses structured meetings that bring together users and designers to "hammer out" the requirements and general design of a system in a compressed time frame. Typically JAD sessions are conducted as a kind of mini-retreat in which users and designers are relieved of their other workday duties to focus exclusively on the development project. Depending on the complexity of the system, the JAD sessions may be scheduled for an afternoon, one or two days, or a week or more.

JAD sessions are structured in that they are conducted by a trained JAD facilitator and employ brainstorming and collaboration techniques such as the the Nominal Group Technique. Participants include the JAD facilitator; several users and designers; the user-sponsor, who acts as the champion of the project and motivates users to participate fully; a project manager, who oversees the work of the designers; and one or more scribes, who use CASE tools and prototyping tools to capture the requirements and design specifications and to generate prototypes of reports, screens, and, in some cases, program code.

An integral technique in JAD is **prototyping**: the iterative refinement of a working model. Prototyping helps to avoid the "arostodiasist" nightmare described earlier. Showing users a working model helps them better understand the features and functions of the new system; thus, they are better able to specify what they need the system to do and to know when the system is doing it correctly. During a JAD session, the users state their "first take" on requirements, and the designers and scribes formulate and generate working system models that incorporate these requirements. For example, a user might describe a report she needs the system to generate; within minutes, the designers produce a prototype report and ask her to critique it. Using her feedback, the designers generate another prototype and again show it to the user. The model-critique-refine process continues until the user approves the prototype. Once approved, the prototype may be discarded and its design specifications used to implement the working system with other tools and techniques, or the prototype may become the foundation of the production system.

JAD provides several benefits. First, it actively involves users in the analysis and design of the system, thus increasing their understanding and making them more accountable for the final system. Only through "mutual coordination" between developers and users can the learning process so vital to successful systems development be achieved [Budde & Zullighoven 1992]. Second, JAD reduces the time devoted to analysis, general design, and documentation activities. Third, JAD lessens the number of late changes in requirements, primarily because user-designer communication is improved, thus preventing the breakdowns and oversights that can plague traditional development efforts. Fourth, training and conversion are facilitated because users are more familiar with the system's features and more committed to the system's success.

Phased Development

The **phased development** strategy partitions a large system into subsystems or data capabilities and performs the TSD stages iteratively until the full system is implemented. As illustrated in Figure 3.5, a preliminary investigation is conducted to determine the objectives, constraints, and scope of the project and to identify the broad functional requirements.

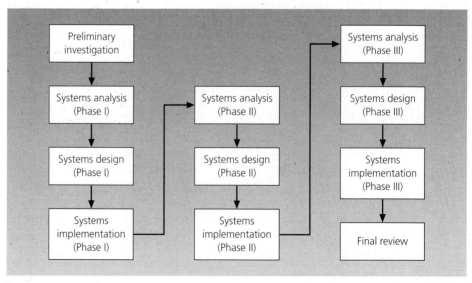

FIGURE 3.5   Phased development

These functional requirements are used to divide the system (1) into subsystems based on major processes or (2) into product deliveries based on major data capabilities (e.g., data entry, data storage, data manipulation, data retrieval, and data distribution) [Appleton 1986; Jordan & Machesky 1990].

The primary advantage of phased development is that it reduces the elapsed time between requirements analysis and system delivery, thus reducing the likelihood of creeping requirements.

Rapid Application Development

Similar to phased development and JAD, the **rapid application development (RAD)** strategy segments a system into subsystems or data capabilities and then iteratively performs the model-critique-refine process until users approve the prototype, as illustrated in Figure 3.6. What sets RAD apart from phased development and JAD is the **timebox**: a non-extendible time limit (usually 60 days) placed on the prototyping phase. Here prototyping is not performed in the JAD sessions, but as a separate process during which the designers iteratively build the prototype and submit it for user review. The output of the timebox is a working system; in other words, this strategy assumes that prototyping and CASE tools can produce efficient executable code so that the prototype becomes the production system.

Because the timebox cannot be extended, the functionality of the system may have to be limited to achieve completion within the preset time limit. This constraint forces users

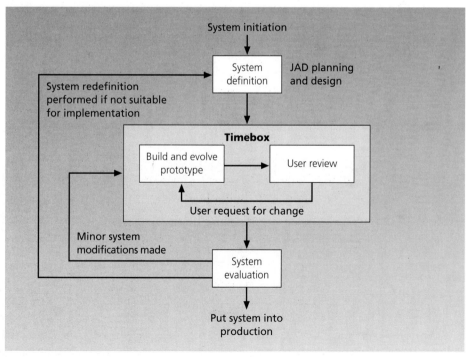

FIGURE 3.6 Rapid application development using the timebox

and designers to focus on the most important system functions, leaving the "bells and whistles" for a later iteration. The philosophy of the timebox approach is that "it is better to have a working system of limited functionality quickly than to wait two years for a more comprehensive system" [Martin 1990, pp. 22–23].

Clearly, a primary advantage of the RAD strategy is that at least some functionality is delivered quickly with incremental releases scheduled at intervals of three to six months. As with phased development, incremental delivery means that little time elapses between requirements analysis and system delivery, thus greatly reducing requirements creep. Also similar to phased development, the RAD strategy allows users to work with a limited version of a system, thereby providing greater insight into the requirements of a fuller system.

RAD provides the benefits of the JAD strategy as well: improved user-designer communication and greater user commitment to the system. Perhaps the greatest value of the RAD strategy, though, is that it avoids the financial fiasco of a canceled system. Rather than invest two years and millions of dollars to discover that a system is infeasible, the RAD strategy can be used to limit the time and expense at risk to a few months and $20,000 to $60,000.

Check Your Understanding 3-2

Indicate which strategy—phased development (PD), joint application development (JAD), prototyping (PR), and/or rapid application development (RAD)—could be used to address each of the following problems with traditional systems development.

_____ 1. The time lapse between requirements determination and delivery of the system.

_____ 2. Users' difficulty in specifying requirements.

_____ 3. The pervasive threat of creeping requirements.

_____ 4. The ineffective division of labor between users and developers.

_____ 5. The difficulty of developing leading-edge systems.

_____ 6. The problem of analyzing, designing, and implementing interactive systems.

3.3 ◈ BRIDGE SYSTEMS DEVELOPMENT METHODOLOGY: EXPLOITING OBJECT TECHNOLOGIES AND TECHNIQUES

The alternative development strategies discussed thus far address some of the problems with the traditional development methodology but not the most pressing ones: the sky-rocketing costs of software development and the exponential increase in software complexity. These problems are addressed by **object technologies**, data or software components that employ object concepts such as encapsulation and inheritance to implement an information system. Object technologies promote **reusability—** reusing existing knowledge and program code as a new system is developed or an existing system is modified—and **interoperability**—the ability to integrate applications from various sources, including custom-developed programs and commercial packages from multiple vendors, and to run these applications on a variety of hardware platforms.

To support the use of object technologies, OO analysis and design techniques define system objects that encapsulate data and methods. The idea underlying the OO approach is that, once a class has been created, it can be reused—perhaps with minor modifications—in subsequent development efforts. In the chapter opening case, both Chase Manhattan Bank and First National Bank of Chicago chose OO development because it allowed them to reuse existing classes as they built or modified systems. For example, if a CUSTOMER class was created when a customer-tracking system was developed, this same class can be reused as a home mortgage system, a 401K investment system, or *any system* related to customers is developed. To promote reusability, organizations maintain an **object class library**, a digital repository or encyclopedia containing an organization's classes.

Object technologies also promote interoperability. In the object-oriented world, almost anything can be an object—a data entry screen, a menu, even a full-blown application written in a third-generation language or running on a different hardware platform. A good illustration of interoperability is the *object linking and embedding* (OLE) technology developed by Microsoft. OLE capabilities are built into many Windows applications today, allowing users to incorporate objects from any of these applications in any other Windows OLE-compatible application.

For example, this textbook was written using Microsoft Word for Windows; many of its original figures were created using the clipart and graphics capabilities of Microsoft PowerPoint, the graphic design capabilities of Shapeware Visio, and spreadsheets and databases from Microsoft Excel and Access. The figures were not *imported* into the text document by the old-fashioned "cut-and-paste" operations; instead, they are *embedded* in the document and can be edited *within* the document. This linking and embedding of objects within Windows applications is just a hint of the potential interoperability of OO systems.

Although several OO development methodologies have been proposed, most of these methodologies focus on *software* development, not *systems* development. Thus, they largely ignore organizational analysis and any procedures performed by people. Exceptions are OO methodologies that embody aspects of TSD; for example, Martin and Odell [1992] have incorporated OO techniques in information engineering (IE), and Yourdon [1994] has made strides in bridging the traditional and OO paradigms. In addition, recent works by Jacobson [1992] and White [1995] have demonstrated a growing emphasis on using OO concepts to analyze and to mold the organization. The *Bridge systems development* methodology presented in this text is adapted from these hybrids. It melds aspects of traditional, RAD, and OO development to create a methodology that not only addresses all five system components but also incorporates object technologies and modeling techniques. Thus, it "bridges" the two major development paradigms.

Figure 3.7 illustrates the sequence of activities in the Bridge methodology. Notice that this methodology is not revolutionary; it builds on existing methodologies and requires developers to perform many of the activities of TSD. Like all full systems development life-cycle methodologies, the Bridge requires developers to conduct a preliminary investigation, to understand the existing system and its environment, to determine the requirements of the new system, and to design and implement the system. What is different about the Bridge is the iterative nature of its activities and its integration of OO and traditional analysis and design

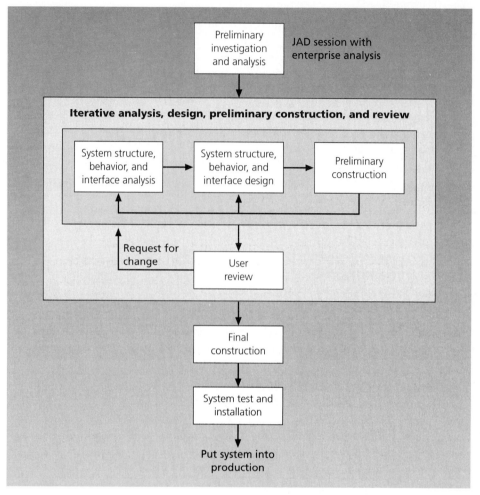

FIGURE 3.7   The Bridge systems development methodology

techniques. The activities in the Bridge systems development methodology are summarized in Table 3.2 and will now be explained in further detail.

PRELIMINARY INVESTIGATION AND ANALYSIS

The first stage in Bridge development has the same purpose as in traditional development: to understand the system's organizational context and to identify the objectives, constraints, scope, and feasibility of the development project. The difference is that here the preliminary investigation uses interactive JAD sessions to examine the organization and to discover system objects and user requirements. A key activity during this development stage is **enterprise analysis**, which provides an overview of the organization's goals, strategies, structure, data, and processes. The goal of enterprise analysis is to ensure that any information systems developed will satisfy the organizational relevance goal of systems development.

TABLE 3.2 Activities of each Bridge systems development stage

Preliminary Investigation and Analysis	**Final Construction**
1. Perform enterprise analysis (if appropriate). 2. Determine system objectives, project constraints, and scope. 3. Evaluate feasibility and get approval to proceed. 4. Conduct JAD session(s) to verify objectives, constraints, and scope; to redesign process, if necessary; and to identify requirements.	1. Construct and test production-ready database and programs (or object classes). 2. Obtain additional hardware. 3. Prepare the facility for additional hardware. 4. Test hardware components. 5. Complete user and technical documentation. 6. Train users.
Iterative Analysis, Design, Preliminary Construction, and Review	**System Test and Installation**

1. Analyze system structure and behavior.
  a. Analyze system data structures.
  b. Analyze system behaviors.
  c. Analyze system interfaces.
2. Design system structure and behavior.
  a. Design system data structures.
  b. Design system behaviors.
  c. Design system interfaces.
3. Construct preliminary system for user review.
4. Conduct user review.
5. Repeat steps 1–4, if changes are needed.
	1. Perform system test.
	2. Install components.
	3. Conduct user review/acceptance test.
	Post-Implementation
	1. Add reusable design omponents (objects) to the design/class library.
	2. Conduct post-implementation evaluation.

Techniques used in the preliminary analysis include workflow diagrams, an enterprise object model, and affinity diagrams. *Workflow diagrams* model the organization's internal and external entities and work flows and also help identify the major processes an organization must perform as it conducts its operations. Once users have verified the workflow diagrams, an enterprise object model is created to provide a very high-level view of the objects of interest to the organization. Then *affinity diagrams* relate objects in the enterprise object model to internal entities in the workflow diagrams and to the processes identified by analyzing these diagrams.

The preliminary investigation and analysis stage concludes with a JAD requirements session, in which the analyst presents initial findings and asks users to verify these findings and define the requirements of the new system. This JAD session may also include activities such as planning the project and specifying **acceptance criteria**: the system quality criteria that the system must achieve to gain user acceptance.

INTERATIVE ANALYSIS, DESIGN, PRELIMINARY CONSTRUCTION, AND REVIEW

Following the JAD requirements session, the developers iteratively analyze, design, and construct system components. During this development stage, additional JAD sessions may be needed to refine the requirements defined in the earlier JAD sessions and, as prototyping nears completion, to plan the system test, installation, and conversion.

System data structure analysis focuses on defining the object classes of the system, their attributes, and the class relationships. The primary modeling technique used in this analysis is the object relationship model (illustrated in Figure 3.8), which specifies the object classes, attributes, and relationships. As shown in the figure, one class identified during analysis may be PURCHASE-ORDER (abbreviated hereafter as PO), whose attributes include OrderDate, OrderNumber, and so on. PO is related to the CUSTOMER object class (each PO "is placed by" one CUSTOMER; each CUSTOMER "places" zero or many POs) and the ITEM class (each PO "lists" one or more ITEMs; each ITEM "is listed on" zero or many POs). **System data structure design** specifies how objects will be implemented as data structures. If the system's objects will be implemented in a relational database management system (RDBMS), the techniques and issues of system data structure design are those of traditional database design, including physical data design, access methods, and file organization.

System behavior analysis focuses on defining the processes the system must perform and the processes' actors and documents. A system *behavior* is a response to a stimulus. For example, when a user sees a screen prompt (stimulus) such as "Enter hourly wage," the expected response (behavior) is to type a currency value and press the ⟨ENTER⟩ key. Displaying this prompt is itself a behavior, perhaps in response to the user selecting a system function such as Create New Employee. "Behavior" is used instead of the more established terms "function" or "process" because it suggests a discrete event. This analysis employs data flow diagrams, use cases, and other techniques to identify behaviors. **System behavior design** specifies how behaviors will be implemented by defining the system's programs or object methods. The techniques used to analyze the behaviors of the existing system can also be used to design the behaviors of the new system. Because objects encapsulate data and behaviors, system data structure design and system behavior design are closely interrelated when the software and data components will be implemented in an OO programming language and database.

System interface analysis and design identifies the forms, screens, and reports through which human users communicate with the data, software, and hardware of the system. Activities performed here include determining what interfaces are needed and how each interface should be presented, and then designing manual forms, data entry and report screens, and

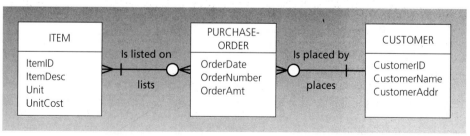

FIGURE 3.8   Object relationship model

printed reports. System interface analysis and design also defines the flow of the human-computer dialog by specifiying the screen type and menu selections for each interface screen and the flow of control between screens.

Today graphical user interfaces (GUIs) predominate in most commercial software applications. GUIs are also becoming standard in custom-developed applications as tools for constructing GUIs have become available. For example, Figure 3.9 shows the GUI of Microsoft Word. Instead of the old-fashioned character-based screens that required users to type commands, GUIs use screens with icons to represent specific functions. These icons are objects created using object technologies; in fact, GUIs are the most common applications of these techniques.

During **preliminary construction** an operational system that implements the design specifications is developed. Today most systems are implemented in an RDBMS in which *object classes* are implemented as tables, *object instances* as records, and *object attributes* as fields whose data type, length, valid values, and so on, must be defined. However, as object technology matures, more systems will be built using object database management systems (ODBMS) or hybrid DBMSs that combine the best features of ODBMS and RDBMS.

In "true" OO development, the system's programs are coded in an OO programming language, such as C++ or Smalltalk. In addition, construction makes use of the organization's class library, reusing and, where necessary, modifying existing classes. However, if the system is implemented in a non-OO programming language, it may be constructed using a variety of development tools, which are described in Chapter 8.

The purpose of the system developed during preliminary construction is to provide a functioning system for **user review**, where the system is demonstrated to the users, who may request changes in its design or identify additional requirements. Notice the feedback arrows in Figure 3.7; these feedback arrows indicate that you perform analysis, design, preliminary construction, and user review iteratively until the users accept the system, at which

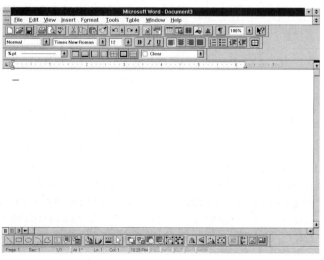

FIGURE 3.9   A graphical user interface

point the system design is frozen, and final construction begins. If the analysis-design-preliminary construction-review stage is restricted to a short time frame (e.g., 60 days), then this stage is similar to the timebox of rapid application development.

FINAL CONSTRUCTION, SYSTEM TEST AND INSTALLATION, AND POST-IMPLEMENTATION REVIEW

The activities of **final construction** in the Bridge development methodology are similar to those in traditional development. Users are trained, hardware resources are obtained, documentation is written, and the production-quality database and programs are constructed, whether in an OO or non-OO DBMS and programming language. Each component is tested to ensure its reliability and accuracy. During the **system test and installation** stage, the system as a whole is tested to ensure that all its components work well together. If the system test is successful, the system is installed and then users evaluate whether the system meets their acceptance criteria. If it does, the old system is dismantled, and the new system put into production.

The development project is brought to a close when the **post-implementation evaluation** is conducted. This evaluation is conducted a few weeks or months after conversion; its purpose is to determine how well the delivered system and the development process achieved the systems development goals. Post-implementation activities also include updating the organization's class or design library to reflect any classes or design components created during development.

Just as our description of traditional implementation activities glossed over a lot of details, our description of implementation in the Bridge methodology does the same. As noted earlier, this text focuses on analysis and design; a detailed discussion of implementation activities is not within its venue. Furthermore, if we assume that the system components are being implemented using object technologies such as an ODBMS and an OO programming language, you would need to understand the intricacies of object navigation and *object-oriented programming* (OOP) to understand the activities in this stage. But these techniques are too complex to treat adequately here; full courses—in fact, sequences of courses—are devoted to learning the concepts, syntax, and methods of ODBMS and OO programming languages. Thus, this text focuses on the implementation activities that you as a systems analyst will be most likely to perform: documenting the system, obtaining hardware and software, training users, and conducting reviews.

Check Your Understanding 3-3

The numbered phrases below state activities performed in the Bridge systems development methodology. Indicate during which stage or substage (PIA—preliminary investigation and analysis, DSA—data structure analysis, BA—behavior analysis, IAD—interface analysis and design, DSD—data structure design, BD—behavior design, PCR—preliminary construction and review, FC—final construction, STI—system test and installation, PI—post-implementation) each activity would be most likely to occur.

____ 1. Specify how objects will be implemented as data structures.

____ 2. Conduct acceptance review.

____ 3. Update the class library.

____ 4. Develop an operational system that implements the design specifications identified so far.

____ 5. Model the organization using workflow diagrams and enterprise object model.

____ 6. Identify system behaviors by creating use cases or DFDs.

____ 7. Conduct a JAD requirements workshop.

____ 8. Train users, write documentation, and construct the production database.

____ 9. Create an object relationship model.

____ 10. Specify how system behaviors will be implemented.

3.4 ◈ BENEFITS OF BRIDGE METHODOLOGY AND OBJECT TECHNOLOGIES AND MODELING TECHNIQUES

The Bridge systems development methodology achieves the benefits of JAD, prototyping, and RAD while also garnering some of the benefits of OO modeling techniques. User-developer communication is improved because the Bridge methodology uses JAD and prototyping to ensure that user input and feedback drive the development project. Increased user understanding of the proposed system design is achieved because a variety of object modeling techniques is used to analyze and to design the system. OO concepts strive to model the real world as real people view it. A CUSTOMER object is "just like" a real customer in that it has attributes that describe what it looks like and methods that describe what it can do. What's more, this same basic modeling technique is used throughout the development project; an object in the analysis stage is basically the same object in the implementation stage. Thus, OO modeling techniques provide (1) a common language that improves user-designer-implementer communication and (2) an intuitive model that improves user understanding.

In addition, the Bridge methodology adopts RAD's iterative framework to delay the point at which requirements are frozen. In fact, new requirements can be incorporated at any point while the project is in the analysis-design-preliminary construction-review stage, which extends up to the point of final construction. Thus, using this methodology to develop systems should reduce creeping requirements and improve the chances of achieving system quality and project management development goals.

When the Bridge methodology is used in combination with object technologies such as OO-CASE, ODBMS, and OO programming languages, additional benefits accrue. We've already discussed two of these benefits: reusability and interoperability. These benefits are the basis for other advantages: faster development, easier maintenance, and platform independence. Development time is reduced because implementation is facilitated; implementers spend less time "reinventing the wheel" because they are able to reuse classes developed for other systems. Maintenance is easier because each class is an independent module; modifying one class has few if any repercussions on other classes.

Platform independence is achieved if the object classes are developed in compliance with an accepted standard. The Object Management Group (OMG) has proposed and continues to develop a number of standards to ensure that objects can be used with a variety of operating systems, DBMSs, and network operating systems. The OMG's *Common Object Request Broker Architecture* (CORBA) also allows objects to communicate across heterogeneous hardware platforms.

Interoperability and platform independence make objects the implementation structure of choice for client/server systems. In fact, OO techniques greatly facilitate the division of processing tasks and data between the client system and the server system. Because each class is a self-contained module, classes can be distributed across multiple systems without creating redundancy or compatibility problems. As the information system is designed and implemented, each class can be designated as a **client object** residing on the client computer system or as a **server object** residing on the server computer system. One object communicates with another object by sending a message to request the receiving object to perform one or more of its methods.

The last benefit we will discuss here is increased flexibility. Because an information system designed and implemented using object technologies is easy to modify, requirements need not be frozen early in the development process. Even during final construction, a system implemented using object technologies is much easier to modify than a traditional system. Consequently, OO systems are less susceptible to creeping requirements.

Reusability, interoperability, improved communication, flexibility—these are just a few of the benefits of developing systems with object technologies. However, a word of caution is in order. Achieving many of the technology-related benefits is dependent on the developers complying with industry-wide standards as classes are designed and implemented. Because many of these standards are still in their infancy, attaining the promised benefits is contingent on adopting the right standards.

◆ REVIEW OF CHAPTER LEARNING OBJECTIVES

1. *Discuss the four major activities of TSD.*

During the preliminary investigation stage, the objectives, constraints, and scope of the system are identified and a preliminary analysis is performed to determine the feasibility, costs, and benefits of the project. The systems analysis stage is devoted to understanding the system's environment, documenting the existing system's functionality, and determining the new system's functional requirements. Systems design takes the IPOSC requirements identified during analysis and synthesizes them into a new system blueprint. System design usually proceeds in two steps: general design during which one or more potential designs are proposed and broadly sketched and detailed design, which specifies the chosen system's physical IPOSC functions in terms of the PPDSH components. Systems implementation works from the detailed design specifications to construct, test, and install the new system. Once the system's users have approved the system, conversion occurs and the production phase begins.

2. *Describe some of the techniques of TSD.*

A workflow diagram models the system's organizational environment, representing the internal and external entities in the system's environment and the flows of data between entities. A system flowchart documents the hardware, software, and data components of an automated information system. A data flow diagram is a process-modeling technique that documents a system's inputs, processes, outputs, data stores, and external entities. A program structure chart decomposes software processes into increasingly detailed modules and shows the control paths between modules. An entity-relationship diagram documents the entities about which data will be maintained (e.g., customers, parts, orders), the attributes of each entity, and the relationships between entities.

3. *Discuss some of the problems with TSD.*

Traditional structured techniques are not well suited to model the requirements of today's less structured, more interactive, real-time systems. In addition, the TSD methodology is too costly and time-consuming, creates a communication gap between users and designers, and relies too heavily on reports at the end of each development stage. What is more, in traditional development, users must sign off on the requirements and design specifications after seeing only a "paper model' of the system, which is inappropriate for leading-edge systems. Requirements are supposed to be "frozen" when the users sign off on the requirements document; under this assumption, the system that is designed and implemented will provide only the functionality detailed during requirements analysis. Because user requirements grow or change about 1 percent per month, creeping requirements plague a large proportion of TSD projects.

4. *Describe several strategies to alleviate the problems with TSD.*

Joint application development (JAD) overcomes the communications gap between users and designers and reduces the time and effort devoted to documenting and approving requirements and design specifications. JAD uses structured meetings that bring together users and designers to determine the requirements and general design of a system in a compressed time frame. Prototyping is the iterative refinement of a working model. Showing users a working model helps them better understand the features and functions of the new system. The phased development strategy partitions a large system into subsystems or data capabilities and performs the TSD stages iteratively until the full system is implemented. This strategy is advocated to alleviate the problem of creeping requirements. Similarly, rapid application development (RAD) also segments a system into subsystems or data capabilities. What sets RAD apart from phased development is the timebox: a non-extendible time limit (usually 60 days) placed on the prototyping phase. The output of the timebox is a working system.

5. *Describe the major activities of the Bridge systems development methodology.*

The Bridge systems development methodology combines aspects of traditional, alternative, and object-oriented methodologies and techniques. Like TSD, it begins with a preliminary investigation and analysis, but it employs JAD sessions in this and other stages to foster designer-user communication. Like RAD, the Bridge methodology's second stage iteratively performs analysis, design, preliminary construction, and review activities during which system requirements continue to evolve. The output of this stage is an operational system, which is modified for production use during final construction. Then the system is tested and subjected to a user-acceptance review. If the system meets the acceptance criteria, developers convert to the new system. A few weeks or months after conversion a post-implementation evaluation determines how well the system and the development project satisfy the goals of systems development.

6. *Discuss the benefits of using object technologies in systems development.*

The benefits of object technology include reusability, interoperability, faster development, easier maintenance, and improved user-developer communication. Reusability is achieved because developers are able to reuse existing knowledge and program code (that is, object classes) as a system is developed or modified. Thus, development time is reduced because implementers spend less time "reinventing the wheel." In addition, maintenance is easier because each class is an independent module; modifying one class has few if any repercussions on other classes. Interoperability is achieved if the system is implemented using object technologies that integrate applications from various sources, including custom-developed programs and commercial packages from multiple vendors. In addition, OO modeling techniques provide an intuitive system model that improves user-developer communication. Finally, because an information system designed and implemented using OO techniques is easy to modify, requirements need not be frozen early in the development process. Thus, OO development is less susceptible to creeping requirements.

◈ KEY TERMS

acceptance criteria
client object
creeping requirements
detailed design
enterprise analysis
feasibility study
final construction
functional requirements
general design
interoperability
joint application development (JAD)
object class library

object technology
phased development
post-implementation evaluation
preliminary investigation
preliminary construction
prototyping
rapid application development (RAD)
reusability
server object
system behavior analysis

system behavior design
system data structure analysis
system data structure design
system interface analysis
system interface design
system test and installation
systems analysis
systems design
systems implementation
timebox
user review

◈ DISCUSSION QUESTIONS

1. List and briefly describe the four major activities of traditional systems development.

2. Discuss some of the limitations of traditional systems development.

3. In your own words, explain how each of the following strategies alleviates some of the problems of traditional systems development:
   a. Joint application development.   c. Phased development.
   b. Prototyping.   d. Rapid application development.

4. List and briefly discuss the major activities of the Bridge systems development methodology. How is this methodology similar to traditional systems development? How is it different?

5. In what ways does the Bridge development methodology incorporate techniques from JAD, prototyping, and RAD?

6. Explain the difference between object structure and object behavior.

7. Define reusability in your own words.

8. Define interoperability in your own words.

9. How is user-designer-implementer communication facilitated by OO modeling techniques?

10. Compare and contrast traditional and Bridge systems development in terms of their flexibility in adapting to creeping requirements.

◈ REFERENCES

Appleton, D. "Information Asset Management." *Datamation* no 3 (February 1 1986), pp. 71–76.

Budde, R., and H. Zullighoven. "Prototyping Revisited." *Information Technology and People* 6, no 2–3 (1992), pp. 97–107.

Coad, P., and E. Yourdon. *Object-Oriented Analysis,* Englewood Cliffs, NJ: Yourdon Press/ Prentice-Hall, 1991.

————. *Object-Oriented Design*. Englewood Cliffs, NJ: Yourdon Press/Prentice-Hall, 1991.

DeMarco, T. *Structured Analysis and System Specification*. Englewood Cliffs, NJ: Prentice-Hall, 1979.

Heichler, E. "Language, Other Basics Key to Object Success." *Computerworld*, March 20, 1995, pp. 73–74.

Jacobsen, I., M. Christerson, P. Jonsson, and G. Overgaard. *Object-Oriented Software Engineering: A Use Case Driven Approach*. Reading, MA: Addison-Wesley, 1992.

Jones, C. *Assessment and Control of Software Risks*. Englewood Cliffs, NJ: Prentice-Hall, 1994.

Jordan, E. W., and J. J. Machesky. *Systems Development: Requirements, Evaluation, Design, and Implementation*. Boston, MA: PWS-Kent, 1990.

Martin, J. "Timebox Methodology." *System Builder*, April/May 1990, pp. 22–25. See also J. Martin, *Information Engineering Book III: Design and Construction*. Englewood Cliffs, NJ: Prentice-Hall, 1990.

Martin, J. *Information Engineering: A Trilogy*. Englewood Cliffs, NJ: Prentice-Hall, 1990.

Martin, J., and J. Odell. *Object-Oriented Analysis and Design*. Englewood Cliffs, NJ: Prentice-Hall, 1992.

Schlaer, S., and S. J. Mellor. *Object-Oriented Systems Analysis: Modeling the World in Data*. Englewood Cliffs, NJ: Yourdon Press/Prentice-Hall, 1988.

White, I. *Using the Booch Method: A Rational Approach*. Redwood City, CA: Benjamin-Cummings, 1995.

Yourdon, E. *Managing the Structured Techniques*. Englewood Cliffs, NJ: Prentice-Hall, 1979.

Yourdon, E. *Object-Oriented Systems Design: An Integrated Approach*. Englewood Cliffs, NJ: Yourdon Press/Prentice-Hall, 1994.

CASE ILLUSTRATION

Developing an Automated Order Processing System for ETG

The following case introduces a systems development project that will be used throughout the text to illustrate development activities and techniques. Here, an overview of the complete project is given to illustrate the activities and techniques of Bridge systems development.

CASE BACKGROUND

Entertainment to Go (ETG) is a family-run business that rents and sells movies on tape to customers in the Tri-County area. Its sales order processing procedures are quite straightforward. Customers wishing to purchase video tapes peruse the shelves of shrink-wrapped tapes and take their selected tapes to a sales clerk. The sales clerk rings up the transaction on the cash register, collects payment, and gives the customer the tapes and the yellow copy of the register receipt. However, ETG's rental order processing procedures are quite complex.

Rental customers select display boxes from the Tapes for Rent shelves and write up their own rental transactions on a two-part rental order form, listing the date of the transaction, the stock number and title of each rental tape, and the customer's name, address, and membership number (they must have a rental membership card to rent tapes). Rental customers give the order forms, selected display boxes, and their membership card to a sales clerk, who verifies the order data and then rings up the order on the cash register. The sales clerk processes payment and then staples the yellow copy of the register receipt to the yellow copy of the rental order form and the white copy of the order form to the white copy of the register receipt and gives these along with the selected display boxes and membership card to the customer.

Rental customers take their display boxes and order and receipt copies to the inventory desk, where both the customer and the inventory clerk sign both the receipt copies. The inventory clerk retains the white copies and files them alphabetically by customer name in the Filled Rental Orders file. The inventory clerk gives the yellow receipt copies and rental tapes to the customer. Rental customers give their tapes and their yellow receipt copies to the inventory clerk when they return their tapes. The inventory clerk verifies the return by retrieving the order forms from the Filled Rental Orders file, writing "Returned on <date>" on the order forms, and then filing them in the Completed Rental Orders file. The inventory clerk returns the corresponding display boxes to the Tapes for Rent shelves and reshelves the tapes in inventory.

To promote its business and enlist new members, ETG prepares a monthly newsletter that contains short descriptions of newly released rental tapes and occasional coupons. This strategy seems to have paid off in that ETG's client list swelled from a few hundred members to almost 1,000 members over the last year. Paul Cornell, patriarch of the Cornell family and president of ETG, has decided that the firm needs a better way to manage its client list, process its transactions, and maintain its inventory. Having no internal information staff and no experience in developing systems, Paul called the Small Business Administration (SBA) to learn how to hire an information systems consultant. The SBA recommended that Paul contact Victoria Hernandez, an independent business systems consultant who had conducted projects for several small businesses in the Tri-County area. Impressed with Victoria's credentials, Paul retained her to study his organization and to recommend how to redesign and automate its processes.

OVERVIEW OF ETG'S SYSTEMS DEVELOPMENT PROJECT

Preliminary Investigation and Analysis

Victoria began her investigation by conducting a JAD session one morning with Paul and a few of ETG's employees and clients. The purpose of the session was to gain an understanding of ETG's problems and the objectives and constraints of the project. As the discussion progressed, it became clear that most of ETG's problems were related to its rental order processing system. After the session, Victoria prepared a two-page report in which she described the problems and verified her understanding of the system objectives, project scope, and constraints. In a telephone conversation, Paul verified Victoria's report findings and asked her to proceed with the project.

Next, Victoria visited ETG at various times to observe its business in operation. She also requested samples of the forms, reports, and other documents used in the business operations. Then Victoria scheduled another morning JAD session with Paul, a sales clerk, and an inventory clerk to focus on defining the current order processing system. Victoria asked ETG's sales and inventory clerks to describe how they process video tape sales and rental orders; they also examined documents and files used in this process (e.g., the rental order form and membership application form) to identify order processing system objects. As the employees described the system, Victoria created first-take diagrams documenting ETG's entities, workflows, and objects (see Figure 1 on page 120 and Figure 2 on page 121).

Following the JAD session, Victoria prepared a problem definition report, in which she presented her enterprise models, summarized problems with the current system, stated the system objectives and project constraints, and evaluated the feasibility of the project. In her report, Victoria described two general design alternatives: one that employed no new information technology but redesigned current manual procedures to eliminate redundant workflows, and another that used database and bar-code technology to automate ETG's order processing procedures. Victoria presented the first alternative because it was a low-cost way of improving ETG's processes and customer service without entailing development of a computer-based information system. During another three-morning JAD workshop, Paul and the ETG employees

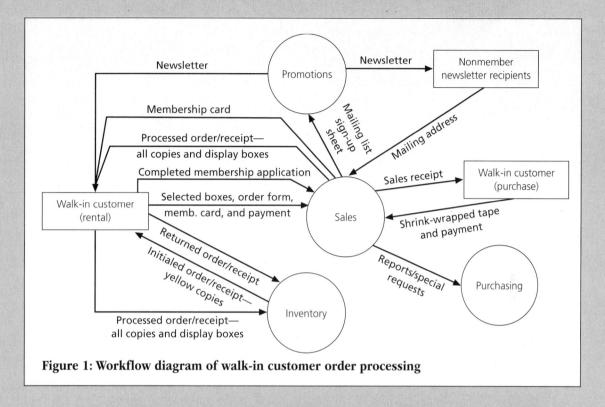

Figure 1: Workflow diagram of walk-in customer order processing

reviewed the report, verified Victoria's understanding of the project, evaluated alternatives, and analyzed the system requirements. Realizing that gaining the greatest benefits would entail automating the process, Paul authorized Victoria to begin detailed analysis and design of a computerized order processing system.

Iterative Analysis, Design, Preliminary Construction, and Review

As a part-time database instructor at the state university, Victoria knows several students who possess the skills and maturity to help her with projects. In her database class, she teaches students how to develop database applications using Microsoft Access. Victoria asked Denny Young, a particularly bright student in her class, to help her with the ETG project.

Paul opted to have systems development occur on site. He authorized Victoria to procure the necessary hardware and software and to have it installed in ETG's back office. The proposed system required installation of a microcomputer, a bar code scanner and software, a printer, and Microsoft Access, a PC-DBMS, to maintain the customer list and tape inventory data and to process transactions. Victoria consulted with a vendor to provide the hardware and software components and arranged to have the selected vendor deliver, install, and test the hardware and software.

In the meantime, Victoria and Denny studied their workflow diagrams, enterprise object model, and JAD session notes. Denny was assigned to analyze and design the system's data

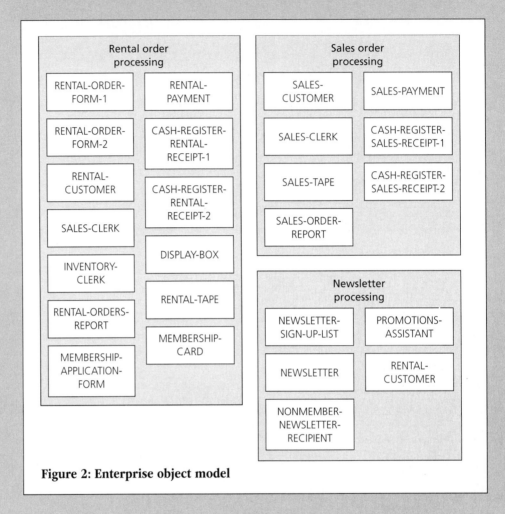

Figure 2: Enterprise object model

structures. He created an object relationship model (see Figure 3) and then used Access to prototype the database. Victoria took responsibility for the system behaviors. Working from the use cases defined during JAD, Victoria analyzed ETG's order transactions and then designed methods to automate these transactions. These methods would be implemented as Access macros.

Working together, Denny and Victoria studied their data and behavior designs to identify and to design system interfaces (e.g., Rental Order data entry screen, New Member data entry screen). Most of the interfaces were developed as Access forms and reports. Denny and Victoria also outlined test plans to verify the system's accuracy.

As pieces of the system were developed, Victoria and Denny demonstrated the system to Paul and ETG employees and incorporated their feedback into the next iteration. After two weeks of iterative construction and review, Paul approved the system design and authorized final construction.

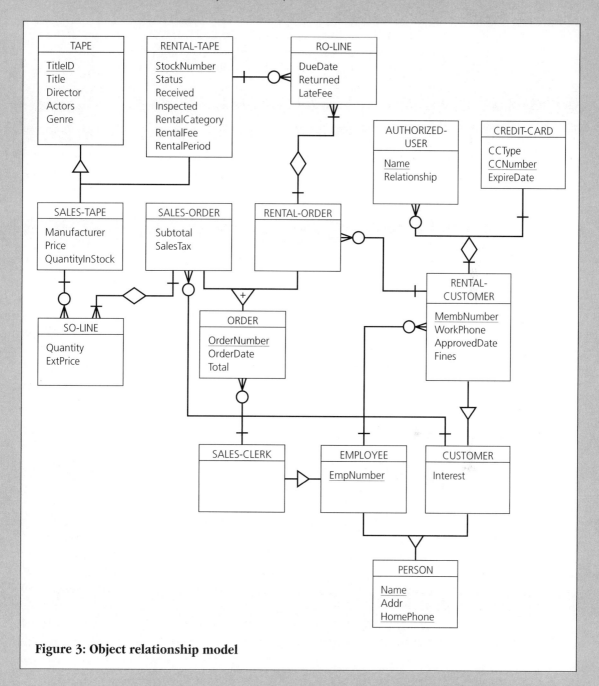

Figure 3: Object relationship model

Final Construction, Systems Test, and Installation

Victoria and Denny outlined the system documentation, user manuals, and training plans and began building the production database and fine-tuning the system interfaces and code. Again, Denny focused on the database, creating a data dictionary to document ETG's data elements and fine-tuning the physical database design to meet ETG's requirements. Constructing the physical database structures and creating data entry screens had taken just a few days. However, converting ETG's over 1,000 customer record notecards and entering the data about its 2,500 rental tapes would be far more time-consuming. In addition, a bar code label had to be affixed to each rental tape as its record was created.

Consulting with Paul, Denny decided to enlist the help of "off-duty" ETG employees. Not only would this speed up data conversion; it would also provide valuable training and experience to the clerks who were to be the system's primary users. First, Denny conducted a half-day training session for the clerks selected to help enter data; he explained hardware and software fundamentals and gave the clerks practice in entering data. Then the clerks set to work entering the customer and rental tape records; within two weeks, all the data had been entered.

In the meantime, Victoria fine-tuned the macros needed to manipulate and validate the data and to generate reports; she also wrote her sections of the system documentation and began work on the user manual. One of the sales clerks, who was working on a technical writing degree at the state university, offered to complete the user manual. Working from Victoria's outline and user-manual design specifications, the clerk prepared a user-friendly document that clearly explained all the procedures clerks would have to perform.

As final construction proceeded, ETG clerks began asking customers to complete the new membership application form. With this up-to-date data, Denny and Victoria could begin preparing the new membership cards, which had the membership number encoded as a bar code. The clerks also used this opportunity to advertise the up-and-coming system and to tell customers about the improved customer service it would provide. As part of their testing procedures, Victoria and Denny verified the scanning hardware and software using several of the newly created membership cards and bar-coded rental tapes.

When the software, hardware, and data components of the order processing system had been constructed and the user manuals written, Victoria conducted training sessions for the clerks and Paul. Then Victoria asked two of these newly initiated users to run the test conditions specified in her test plans. Testing established the validity and accuracy of the system. It was time to move the system "out front" and into production.

ETG closed for business on Wednesday so that Victoria, Denny, Paul, and three employees could conduct the system installation and conversion. They moved the hardware out of the back office and installed it at the checkout counter. They also ran a few of the most critical test conditions again to verify that all components were functioning properly. The system worked like a charm, so Victoria, Denny, Paul, and all the ETG employees had a festive dinner to celebrate the launch of the new system. At 10 A.M. Thursday, when ETG opened its doors for business, its customers were greeted by a huge banner that read "ETG Enters the Information Age!"

PART TWO

Preliminary Investigation and Analysis

In Part Two, you will begin to learn about the specific activities and techniques of the Bridge systems development methodology. Chapters 4–7 provide a detailed examination of the activities of the preliminary investigation and analysis stage. Topics and techniques addressed in these chapters include enterprise analysis (affinity diagram), enterprise modeling (organization chart, workflow diagram, and enterprise object model), and problem definition and feasibility analysis.

Chapter 4 describes the environment of an information system and discusses three trends affecting both the internal and external system environment today: business process reengineering, interorganizational information systems, and system evolution. You need to understand these trends because they represent a fundamental rethinking of the uses of information technology and highlight the importance of developing systems that can readily adapt to the changing needs of an organization.

Chapter 5 introduces enterprise analysis, the systems development activity that provides an overview of a system's internal environment and identifies the organization's information and processing needs. A modeling technique presented in this chapter is affinity diagrams, which are used to understand the internal environment of an information system and to prioritize potential systems development projects. Also discussed are three enterprise models—the organization chart, workflow diagram, and enterprise object model—that you should create prior to creating affinity diagrams. The rules for creating these models are presented in Technical Module C. The organization chart helps you document the structure of an organization. The workflow diagram is used to identify internal and external entities and the flows of data among these entities. The enterprise object model provides an overview of the organization's objects.

Chapter 6 examines how to determine system objectives, project scope, and constraints. It also discusses how to analyze the feasibility of a project, including not only economic feasibility (cost-benefit analysis) but also organizational, technical, and operational feasibility. After the systems analysts have gained a preliminary understanding of the organization and the affected information system, they document their findings in a report to the user-sponsor and end-users. This report becomes the foundation for the iterative analysis, design, and preliminary construction stage. To illustrate problem definition, Chapter 6 closes with the problem definition report Victoria Hernandez created to document the findings of her investigation of Entertainment To Go (ETG). This report also illustrates the development concepts, techniques, and issues introduced in this chapter.

Part Two ends with Chapter 7, which discusses joint application development (JAD) and describes a JAD session conducted with the ETG users.

SYSTEMS DEVELOPMENT EQUALS PLANNED ORGANIZATIONAL CHANGE

STREAMLINING ORDER FULFILLMENT AT CAV

Delivery trucks leaving the loading dock empty, customers who felt like victims, a Byzantine order fulfillment process, escalating costs, and multimillion-dollars losses—these were just a few of the problems confronting Corning Asahi Video (CAV) Products, a Corning business unit that is one of only two U.S. makers of television glass. Errors caused by CAV's outdated, inefficient order fulfillment system were costing the company more than $2 million annually in overtime, freight charges, and other associated costs. Clearly, something needed to be done—and quickly—if CAV was to stay in business.

CAV's response was to invest $570,000 in a 15-month reengineering effort that ultimately won recognition as *Computerworld*'s Reengineering Team of the Year. The benefits of the project included slashing personnel costs by $400,000 and eliminating $1.6 million in errors and cost overruns. In addition, it now takes CAV half as much time—and costs 75 percent less—to fill an order. How did CAV achieve such tremendous gains? By rethinking its order fulfillment process and deploying information technology to streamline the process.

In CAV's old order fulfillment process, customers called one of six sales representatives to place their semiannual order, which was entered on CAV's 20-year-old order processing system at corporate headquarters in New York. The system generated paper reports that were faxed to the manufacturing plant in State College, Pennsylvania. Once received, the paper orders were confirmed by telephone before production began. After confirmation, the ordered items were manufactured and shipped to customers by truck. Order processing, accounts payable, and billing functions were all performed on an old VAX; however, these systems couldn't "talk" with each other, so order data had to be reentered before an invoice could be generated. Inventory was processed manually. Altogether, the order fulfillment process involved 20 to 25 people performing 250 tasks, and each order cost an average of $2,200 and took 180 days to complete.

Given the severity of CAV's problems and its bleak financial picture, a low-cost solution had to be implemented quickly. After a preliminary investigation of its functions and of business process reengineering strategies, CAV launched its redesign project in the fall of 1991, with the stipulation that a new system be delivered by January 1993. A timeline highlighting major development milestones is shown in Table 4.1. Early on, the project team decided to use purchased software as the foundation of the new system; custom-developed programs would have cost approximately $1 million and would have taken too long to construct. The team chose DCS Logistics, a $119,000 commercial software package from Andersen Consulting. A major fear was that the software would not run on CAV's VAX platform. So Andersen conducted a seven-week on-site pilot to verify the software's compatibility and functionality. The test was successful, and the system was implemented on time and within budget.

CAV's new order fulfillment system is illustrated in Figure 4.1. CAV replaced its old disjoint systems with an integrated system, featuring a centralized database. This redesign not only eliminates redundant data entry and streamlines the order fulfillment process to about 10 tasks; it also provides easy, quick access to a variety of information about customers, products, and orders. Redesigning the order fulfillment process led CAV to reorganize its division; although no layoffs were directly caused by the process redesign, future head-count reductions in sales and other functional areas are anticipated. The success of the order fulfillment redesign effort has sparked several other process reengineering projects at CAV and a major corporate-wide project as well.

Adapted from J. Maglitta, "Glass Act," *Computerworld*, January 17, 1994, pp. 80–81, 84, 88. Copyright 1995 by Computerworld, Inc., Framingham MA 01701. Reprinted from Computerworld.

TABLE 4.1 CAV's project timeline

Mid-1991	CAV holds a 3-day "rap" session attended by 1200 employees; begins analyzing problem; gathers information about reengineering, including a one-day session with a Harvard Business School consultant and a consultation with Michael Hammer.
Fall 1991	12-member cross-functional team, consisting of 8 full-time participants—including three IS people, the customer service manager, and the quality coordinator—meets for 15 days to discuss redesign. Team devotes 3 months to interviewing customers and customer sales representatives and examining software options.
December 1991	Team decides to use purchased software as foundation for system.
January 1992	Plan presented to management; management approves and requires completion by January 1993. Redesign steering committee established.
January–April 1992	Team plans development project and begins organizational redesign.
April 1992	Andersen Consulting begins 7-week "Conference Room Pilot".
July–October 1992	Team continues organizational redesign and proves profitability of system.
August 1992	Implementation begins.
November 1992	System conversion begins.
January 1993	System goes live, completed on time and within budget.

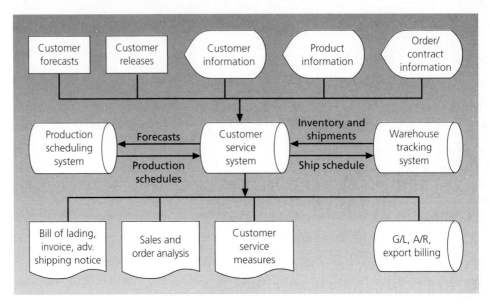

FIGURE 4.1   CAV's redesigned order fulfillment process

CSC Index, Inc., an international management consulting group based in Cambridge, Massachusetts, conducts an annual survey of IS executives in leading corporations to identify the ten most important management issues concerning organizational uses of IS. Four issues have repeatedly appeared in the top ten: reshaping business processes through information technology (IT), aligning IS and corporate goals, utilizing data, and creating an information architecture. The first issue, reshaping business processes through IT, has topped the list and defined the focus of systems development in the 1990s. The chapter opening case, "Streamlining Order Fulfillment at CAV," describes a new order fulfillment system that was the culmination of efforts to rethink a fundamental business process in light of the capabilities IT provides. This reshaping of business processes is commonly called *business process reengineering* (BPR).

The last three issues are related to redesigning old systems to exploit new technologies. Most existing systems were developed using older technologies (e.g., mainframes and dumb terminals) and traditional implementation methods (e.g., flat files and third-generation languages such as COBOL). Redesigning these systems to exploit today's telecommunications, database management, and desktop computing technologies is a costly, time-consuming, unnerving task. Yet it is a task that must be undertaken if organizations are to improve their efficiency and effectiveness and stay competitive.

In this chapter, we describe the factors in the system environment and discuss three issues, or trends, you need to understand as you begin your study of systems analysis and design—business process reengineering, interorganizational information systems, and system evolution. After completing this chapter, you should be able to

1. Describe the internal and external environment of an information system.

2. Define process thinking, and discuss the role of systems developers in redesigning business processes.

3. Explain how interorganizational information systems affect both the internal and external system environment.

4. Define system evolution and legacy systems.

5. Describe the glasshouse and client/server information architectures, and discuss some of the advantages and disadvantages of each.

6. Describe three strategies for evolving from a glasshouse architecture to a client/server architecture.

4.1 ◆ UNDERSTANDING THE ENVIRONMENT OF AN INFORMATION SYSTEM

Before an organization can begin migrating systems or redesigning processes, it first needs to understand its organizational structure, its current systems, and its information needs. The starting place for any systems development project, including business process reengineering and system evolution, is a thorough analysis of the organization, its strategies, policies, and procedures, and the interdependencies among its activities.

SYSTEM ENVIRONMENT

An information system's environment can be decomposed into its internal environment and its external environment, as shown in Figure 4.2, which illustrates the environment of CAV's order fulfillment system. The **internal environment**, or **organizational context**, includes the data maintained by the system, the people who use the system, and the organization's culture, structure, policies, and operating procedures.

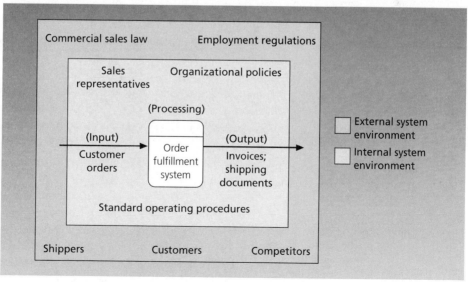

FIGURE 4.2   Environment of CAV's order fulfillment system

The typical **organizational structure** can be represented as a matrix of management levels and functional areas, as shown in Figure 4.3. The three **management levels** are *operational management,* which oversees the day-to-day business operations; *tactical management,* which allocates resources and implements the organization's strategies; and *strategic management,* which sets long-term business goals. The **business functional areas** include production, sales and marketing, finance and accounting, and human resources. Although an organization may have more than three management levels and four functional areas, the ones represented here are common to most business organizations. Knowing the management levels and functional areas served by an information system helps you understand its information and processing requirements.

The matrix shown in Figure 4.4 makes the point that a single information system, represented by one or more shaded cells, may serve the needs of a single management level within a single functional area, or it may serve the needs of multiple management levels and/or multiple business functional areas. The greater the number of functional areas and/or management levels served by an information system, the greater the complexity of the

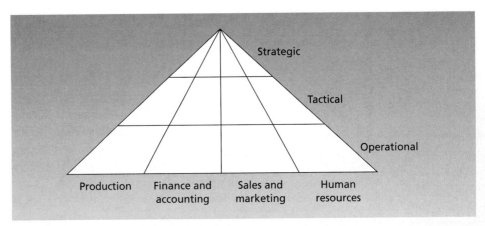

FIGURE 4.3   Organizational structure—management levels and functional areas

	Production	Finance and accounting	Sales and marketing	Human resources
Strategic				
Tactical				
Operational				

FIGURE 4.4   Business functions and management levels served by an information system

system. System complexity increases because the information and processing needs become more varied and the system is more likely to interface with many other systems. For example, CAV's order fulfillment system not only processes sales transactions—a routine activity at the operational level; it also interfaces with accounts payable, production, inventory, and shipping, and generates output used to forecast and schedule production and shipments. Thus, the CAV system is fairly complex in that it fills the information and processing needs of several business functional areas at the operational and tactical levels.

The internal environment of an information system also includes the data, people, policies, and operating procedures of the organization. These aspects of the system environment will be discussed and techniques for analyzing them will be presented in later chapters. For now, you should understand that all of these factors constitute the organizational context and must be considered fully during systems development.

An information system's **external environment** encompasses its customers, suppliers, and competitors; stakeholders in the company (e.g., stockholders); and regulations and laws that govern its operations. For example, the external environment of the CAV system includes customers and suppliers, which are examples of **external entities** that provide inputs to or receive outputs from the organization's systems. External entities are often the impetus for a system action; for examples, interactions with customers and suppliers are the impetus for sales, procurement, and shipping/receiving transactions.

An information system's external environment also includes regulations and laws that affect the organization and therefore affect the systems it develops. For example, in the United States, numerous laws govern the disposal of hazardous wastes, business employment practices, and income tax reporting; often times, organizations develop information systems to produce the reports required by these laws. These laws also affect information systems in that they may stipulate what kinds of data must be collected and how long they must be maintained. External factors affecting the CAV system include commercial sales law and fluctuations in demand for its products.

A systems development effort may fundamentally alter the internal and external environment of a system by changing how business processes are performed or how an organization interacts with external entities. Thus, systems development is properly viewed as planned organizational change. Three systems development trends currently affecting the environment of an information system are business process reengineering, interorganizational information systems, and system evolution. These trends, each of which is discussed in more detail in the remainder of this chapter, occur simultaneously but affect the system environment in different ways. *System evolution* affects the technological aspects of a system, for example, the configuration of hardware, software, data, and telecommunications resources employed by an organization to meet its information needs. In contrast, *business process reengineering* affects the internal environment—the organizational structure and processes—altering the locus of decision making and the flow of work within the organization. In addition, process reengineering often requires new technologies, thus spurring the evolution of an organization's systems. *Interorganizational information systems* profoundly affect both the internal and external system environment, spanning organizational boundaries and altering an organization's relationships with customers and suppliers.

✓ Check Your Understanding 4-1

1. Match each of the following terms with its definition.

_____ organizational context   a.   data, people, culture of the system environment

_____ operational management   b.   sets long-term goals for the organization

_____ external entity   c.   oversees day-to-day activities

_____ organizational structure   d.   people or enterprises that provide inputs to or receive outputs from an organization's systems

_____ strategic management   e.   matrix of management levels and functional areas

2. Read the following case, "Ford Has a 'Better Idea' for Accounts Payable," and answer the following questions.

   a. What management levels and functional areas does the accounts payable system support?

   b. List the system's external entities and the inputs they provide to or the outputs they receive from this system.

FORD HAS A "BETTER IDEA" FOR ACCOUNTS PAYABLE

In the midst of a severe recession in the automotive industry, Ford management set out on a cost-cutting mission. One of the areas examined was Accounts Payable (A/P), a department that employed 500 people in North America alone. Initially, Ford management set a target of cutting head count 20 percent by rethinking its accounts payable process and employing information technology to improve efficiency. However, after noting that Mazda, a somewhat smaller automotive company, employed only *five* people to handle its A/P, Ford upped its goal. Instead of cutting head count by 100, the new goal was to cut hundreds!

Ford's existing A/P process was similar to that used by most large companies. The Purchasing Department wrote a purchase order and sent a copy to A/P. When the ordered goods arrived at Receiving, a receiving clerk sent a copy of the shipping documents to A/P. After Accounts Payable received an invoice from the supplier, it matched the purchase order against the shipping documents and invoice. If all three documents agreed, an A/P clerk issued payment for the amount of the invoice. Unfortunately, the three documents often did not match. In this case, payment was delayed until an A/P clerk could trace the discrepancy. This was no small task, given that it involved matching 14 data items across the three documents.

Ford decided that eliminating the manual matching of paper documents would streamline the process, thus reducing costs. The new A/P system uses an on-line database to eliminate the flow of documents between the Accounts Payable, Purchasing, and Receiving departments. When Purchasing prepares an order, the data is entered into the on-line database. When Receiving receives a shipment, it retrieves the related purchase order record from the database and verifies the shipment against the purchase order. If the shipment corresponds to an open purchase order, the Receiving clerk enters the receiving transaction into the database; if not, the order is returned to the supplier.

The supplier's invoice has been totally eliminated. Instead, Ford's A/P system automatically issues payment after receipt of the goods has been verified. To authorize payment, the A/P application program automatically verifies just three items in the purchase order record and the receiving record—part number, unit of measure, and supplier code. If these match, the system generates a check, which is sent to the supplier.

By eliminating paper documents and manual verification, Ford was able to reduce its A/P head count by 75 percent. In addition, the organization improved the accuracy and timeliness of its financial and material control information by eliminating the discrepancies that crippled the old system.

Adaptation of "Example: Ford Motor Company" from *Reengineering the Corporation: A Manifesto for Business Revolution,* by M. Hammer and J. Champy, © 1993 by M. Hammer and J. Champy, reprinted by permission of HarperCollins Publishers, Inc.

4.2 ◆ BUSINESS PROCESS REENGINEERING

Business process reengineering is the fundamental rethinking and radical redesign of business processes to achieve dramatic improvements in critical contemporary measures of performance [Hammer & Champy 1993].

Business process reengineering (BPR)—and its various manifestations, including process innovation [Davenport & Short 1990; Davenport 1993]—has been one of the hottest topics in corporate America since Michael Hammer published his defining article, "Reengineering Work: Don't Automate, Obliterate," in 1990. As the article's title suggests, BPR is the radical rethinking of organizational structure and business processes. In philosophy, if not always in practice, BPR calls for an organizational *tabula rasa*—wiping the organization's slate clean to discover new and better ways of doing business. Starting from a clean slate is one characteristic that distinguishes BPR from *total quality management* (TQM). Other defining characteristics are summarized in Table 4.2.

As you examine Table 4.2, note that BPR is a one-time, process-oriented endeavor. Unlike TQM, which attempts to improve efficiency through continuous, incremental changes in existing tasks or functions, BPR employs a broader approach to radically transform fundamental processes. BPR is process-oriented in that it attempts to improve efficiency and effectiveness by integrating the tasks and information flows required to complete a process. Note also that information technology is the *enabler* of BPR. What this means is that organizations are able to rethink their processes because of the functionality provided by information technology. One of Hammer's most incisive analogies emphasizes this point: He compares automating current business practices to "paving cowpaths" and proposes that information technology should instead be exploited to transform business processes, thereby transforming the organization. In other words, BPR should be a strategic pull prompting organizations to develop new systems to support new ways of doing business. Table 4.3 lists some ways in which information technology can help an organization transform its processes.

TABLE 4.2 Business process reengineering versus total quality management

	Total Quality Management	**Business Process Reengineering**
Approach to Change	Incremental adjustment of an existing task or function	Radical transformation of existing process; ideally, proceeds from a "clean slate."
Frequency and Duration of Change Projects	Continuous series of relatively short, narrowly-focused initiatives; projects measured in weeks and focused on a single task or function, thereby incurring low risk.	One-time, broadly-focused initiative; projects may encompass months or years of effort and focus on all the tasks in a process, thereby incurring high risk.
Sponsorship	Sponsored by senior management but ideas for improvements come from workers.	Must be championed by a high-ranking executive with the power to make sweeping changes.
Enabling Technology	Statistical control systems that monitor the quality of an organization's output.	Information technologies, such as expert systems, imaging, and telecommunications, that support new ways of doing business.

TABLE 4.3 Examples of how information technology can change business processes

Old Rule	**Technology**	**New Rule**
Information must be processed sequentially because a document can appear in only one location at one time.	Shared databases and imaging technology	Information can be processed concurrently because electronic documents can appear simultaneously in as many places as they are needed.
Only experts can perform complex work.	Expert systems	A generalist can do the work of an expert.
Businesses must choose between a centralized or decentralized structure.	Telecommunication networks	Businesses can simultaneously reap the benefits of both structures.
Only managers have access to information, so they must make all decisions.	Decision-support tools	Information and the tools to manipulate it are provided to whoever needs them. Decision making is part of everyone's job.
Field personnel need offices where they can receive, store, retrieve, and transmit information.	Wireless data communications and portable computers	Field personnel can send and receive information wherever they are.
The best contact with a potential buyer is personal contact.	Interactive videodisc and Internet's World Wide Web	The best contact with a potential buyer is effective contact.
You have to find out where things are (e.g., a shipment en route to a customer).	Automatic identification and tracking technology	Things tell you where they are.

Adaptation of Chapter 5 from *Reengineering the Corporation: A Manifesto for Business Revolution,* by M. Hammer and J. Champy, © 1993 by M. Hammer and J. Champy, reprinted by permission of HarperCollins Publishers, Inc.

Whether BPR will radically transform organizations remains to be seen. Clearly, its effects on CAV's order fulfillment process and Ford's accounts payable system have been both positive and profound. However, both the popular and academic press are already questioning many aspects of this philosophy (see, e.g., King [1994] and Jones [1994], who attempt to tone down the hyperbole and suggest limiting the scope of BPR projects). Nonetheless, BPR is important to you as a systems developer because it represents one of the most avid campaigns to align organizational objectives and information system applications in recent years. BPR also changes your role in systems development; thus, you need to understand the tenets of BPR and your role in reengineering business processes.

PROCESS THINKING

To understand BPR, you must first understand that a **process** is a set of activities that produces an output; in business, a process creates a product or service that has value to the firm's customers. The **value chain**, illustrated in Figure 4.5, is one representation of business activities [Porter 1985]. Most business organizations are segmented into functional areas in terms of these activities. The functional areas performing the support activities are given names similar to those used in Figure 4.5: Administrative Services, Human Resource Management, Research and Development (or perhaps, Information Services), and Procurement. The primary activities are performed by Receiving and Warehousing, Production, Shipping and Distribution, Marketing and Sales, and Customer Service.

Typically, the activities in a process are performed sequentially. The sequential nature of a process is partly a constraint imposed by task dependencies—Task B cannot begin until Task A is completed—and partly a constraint imposed by paper documents. However, this second constraint has been largely eliminated; the simultaneous information access provided by shared databases, the electronic documents created by document imaging, and the communication capabilities of telecommunication networks have made it possible for many activities to be performed concurrently. For example, before the advent of these technologies, a purchase requisition had to be routed physically to each of the people whose authorization was required.

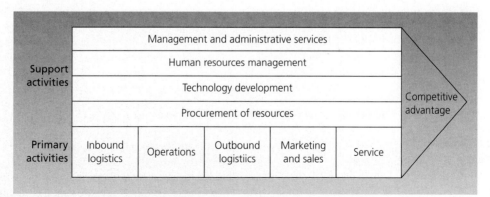

FIGURE 4.5　　Business activities and the value chain

But an electronic purchase requisition can be distributed simultaneously to all authorizers, thus reducing the time required to complete this step in the procurement process.

When organizations segment their activities into functional areas and perform activities sequentially, the interdependencies between activities tend to be ignored (see, e.g., Rockart and Short [1989] and Byrne [1993]). In addition, this segmentation fosters **"over the wall" thinking**: a functional area does its thing and then throws its output "over the wall" to the next functional area. For example, in the CAV case, focusing on activities and functional areas led the organization to develop a number of disjoint systems that could not interface with each other and thus could not share data. The people using these systems to perform their activities were a classic example of the old adage about one hand not knowing what the other hand is doing. Automating CAV's current order fulfillment activities would have been a waste of resources, a classic example of "paving cowpaths."

Fortunately for CAV, its business and IS staff recognized that order fulfillment was a disaster and used process thinking to redesign this process. **Process thinking** requires that an organization think in terms of processes, not activities or functional areas; it recognizes the cross-functional nature of business processes and seeks to integrate the flow of work required to complete a process. Another term used to describe this view is **value-chain integration**: focusing on processes integrates value-chain activities by recognizing that each activity is just one link in the process chain of creating value for customers. Process thinking and value-chain integration led CAV to launch a reengineering project to integrate the activities of order fulfillment, thus streamlining this process and eliminating redundancies, errors, and rework. By recognizing that taking orders, scheduling production, shipping goods, and billing customers were all activities in order fulfillment, CAV created a system that facilitated the flow of information through this process.

Check Your Understanding 4-2

Fill in the blank with the appropriate term.

1. _____ is a graphical representation of the primary and support activities involved in creating a service or product that provides value to customers.
2. A set of integrated activities that produces an output is called a _____.
3. _____ and _____ recognize the cross-functional nature of business processes.
4. Segmentation of business activities into functional areas encourages _____.

HOW BPR AFFECTS SYSTEMS DEVELOPMENT

What differentiates your role as a systems analyst in BPR from your role in many other systems development projects is the nature of the processes you will automate. In a typical systems development project, your task is to understand, model, and automate *existing* processes; in contrast, in a BPR project, your task is to create, model, and automate *new* processes. Thus, understanding the current process and its problems is just a first step; you must also be a creative contributor to process redesign. This will be a natural role for you as an IS professional because you will have learned process analysis and modeling techniques as you studied systems analysis and design. But it is also a challenging role because it requires a cross-functional perspective and interaction with a variety of users. Avoiding turf battles and overcoming users' inherent resistance to change are just two issues you can expect to confront in a BPR project. These issues fall into three categories: people, technology, and organization.

People Issues in BPR

One of the most common "people" issues in any systems development project is fear of change. This fear is especially prominent in the case of BPR because it may lead to not only significant changes in job tasks but also personnel reductions. Obviously, most people will not willingly participate in an effort that means they may lose their job. Fear of change also affects the IS staff, who must learn new skills to participate in BPR and to deploy the new technologies BPR often entails.

Another people issue in BPR is its emphasis on teamwork. When an organization adopts process thinking, it recognizes the need for coordination among functional areas and restructures the organization to form cross-functional teams. This team orientation requires new ways of evaluating and rewarding employees; it also means that IS professionals on the BPR team need to become more adept at interacting with users and understanding organizational concerns. The IS staff are important members of this team because they are often best qualified to provide a "big picture," enterprise-wide view of systems and processes. In contrast, most departmental users have developed a functional myopia that may lead to turf battles as processes are redesigned.

Nonetheless, IS must not appear to commandeer the BPR effort, which is fundamentally a business, not a technology, initiative. Your desire, as a systems analyst, to impose your enterprise-wide perspective and solid knowledge of what is technically feasible on the project must be tempered with the need to let users be the leaders. Thus, you must maintain a precarious balance and learn to act as a facilitator in the process redesign effort.

Technology Issues in BPR

CAV's order fulfillment system was developed using data and communications technologies that have been available for years. However, many reengineering efforts rely on leading-edge techniques and technologies, such as OO development, wireless networks, and the client/server architecture. These often unfamiliar, sometimes unproven techniques and technologies may increase the risk of project failure as they force the organization into uncharted territory. In addition, there is no clearly specified methodology to guide reengineering efforts. For these reasons, many organizations hire consultants to lead them through their initial BPR projects.

Another technology issue is that BPR requires rapid development methodologies to effect change as quickly and as inexpensively as possible. For this reason, most proponents of BPR are also proponents of the OO systems development methodology and its promised reuse of existing classes. At minimum, BPR requires a radical rethinking of systems development activities; TSD and its reliance on early freezing of requirements is inappropriate for a reengineering project [Moad 1993]. Joint application development, prototyping, and rapid application development are more flexible in adapting to the changing requirements that typify BPR projects. But many IS professionals have little or no experience with these methodologies. Thus, BPR often means that systems developers must learn new techniques as well as new technologies.

Perhaps the most important technology issue in BPR is that the organization's existing information architecture may inhibit its attempts to redesign its business processes. A 1994 survey conducted by CSC Index Inc. revealed that this was a significant concern among over half of the top executives at the firms surveyed; in fact, 11 percent stated that information technology is a major impediment to reengineering efforts [Bartholomew 1994]. Existing information systems, designed to serve departmental (i.e., functional area) needs, must be transformed to serve the cross-functional teams created by process redesign. Dealing with these *legacy systems* (discussed later, in Section 4.4) creates a major headache as organizations strive to change their structure and integrate formerly separate activities.

Organization Issues in BPR

Table 4.1 noted that one of the characteristics differentiating TQM from BPR is the people who promote and participate in each. Whereas TQM initiatives often are suggested by workers at the operational level and then gain the support of upper management, BPR initiatives usually arise at the strategic level and then are promulgated to lower levels by a high-ranking *champion,* often the CEO or a vice-president. A powerful champion is needed for BPR projects because process redesign crosses functional areas and affects the whole organization.

Understanding the strategic nature of BPR projects is important to you as a systems developer because these are among the most visible projects you will undertake in your career. High visibility places increased pressure on you to deliver tangible results as quickly as possible; changes need to be implemented before the fervor to change diminishes. In addition, you need to manage the project effectively to stay on schedule and within budget, while also helping the executive champion build user commitment to the project and to the organizational changes it will entail. Thus, it is critically important that BPR projects satisfy all the goals of systems development: a high-quality system, delivered on time and within budget, that users will support and that will help achieve organizational objectives.

You also should understand that a BPR project may fundamentally alter the structure and culture of the organization. Proponents of BPR argue that information technology is poised to reverse the negative aspects of the industrial revolution [Maglitta 1994, quoting Michael Hammer]. Table 4.4 contrasts these negative aspects of an Industrial Age organization with the positive ones of an Information Age organization. For example, streamlining processes by means of BPR often involves moving decision making to lower levels, thus changing the locus of power. Organization structure becomes less hierarchical and more of a network. Of course, this means that the information needed to make decisions must be available to more people, more specifically, to people who may not have performed these decision-making tasks before. In addition, BPR efforts that exploit *electronic data interchange* (EDI) and other interorganizational technologies dissolve organizational borders and fundamentally alter a firm's relationships with its customers and suppliers.

TABLE 4.4 Defining features of old and new organizations

	Industrial Age	**Information Age**
Organizational Structure	Rigid hierarchy with clear division of responsibility among functional areas; self-sufficent, functional "silos"	Flexible network; fewer management levels; more cross-functional teams; interdependence across and between enterprises
Leadership Focus	Autocratic command-and-control; focus on accountability	Democratic consult-and-commit; focus on empowerment and growth
Work	Managers oversee workers performing sequential, narrowly-defined tasks; emphasis on specialization yields process fragmentation	Diverse individuals and groups cooperate, performing tasks concurrently, to achieve goals; emphasis on generalists and cooperation yields process integration
Competitive Strategy	Low-cost producer; compete on the basis of cost to consumer	Product differentiation; compete on the basis of quality and responsiveness
Resource Base	Capital investments in factories; laborers	Capital investments in information technology; knowledge workers
Information Systems	Batch processing of data centralized at headquarters; emphasis on transaction processing and management reporting	Real-time processing of data distributed across a network; emphasis on communication, decision support, and collaborative work systems

So why are these organizational changes important to you as a systems developer? Because they signal an organization in a state of flux, which means that determining information and processing needs may be more difficult than it would be in a stable organization with stable procedures. Thus, the risk of project failure is increased; in fact, proponents of BPR openly acknowledge that over half of all BPR projects will fail to achieve their goals. Chapter 5 describes the factors in project risk and offers some tips for reducing that risk. For now, just realize that the massive organizational changes involved in BPR complicate your development projects.

✓ Check Your Understanding 4-3

Categorize each of the following statements as a people issue (P), a technology issue (T), or an organizational issue (O).

_____ 1. The existing information structure inhibits process redesign.

_____ 2. Employees must learn to work in teams.

_____ 3. The visibility of a BPR project makes meeting the systems development goals critical.

_____ 4. A powerful champion is required to lead the BPR effort.

_____ 5. Fear of change may raise risk of failure.

_____ 6.   BPR may fundamentally alter relationships with suppliers and customers.

_____ 7.   BPR requires rapid application development methodologies and an understanding of new information technologies.

4.3 ◆ INTERORGANIZATIONAL INFORMATION SYSTEMS

Most BPR efforts integrate only activities within the organization's value chain. However, some attempt to integrate interorganizational activities, recognizing that transactions between an organization and its external entities often directly affect the organization's efficiency and effectiveness. **Interfirm value-chain integration** recognizes the role of external entities in many organizational processes and seeks to integrate activities performed externally with the organization's internal processes.

For example, just-in-time inventory management requires coordination between a manufacturer and its suppliers to ensure that supplies are available when needed—but not before. Normally, the manufacturer monitors its own inventory and gauges materials on hand against the expected production schedule. But, when firms cooperate to integrate activities, the manufacturer gives its suppliers access to its production schedule and inventory records and requires the supplier to manage inventory levels. Thus, the manufacturer never issues a purchase order; instead, the supplier is authorized to replenish inventory automatically.

A case in point is VF Corporation (VFC), the maker of Lee jeans and other apparel, which redesigned its merchandising process to create tight linkages with the retailers who sell its products. VFC developed a continuous merchandising system to collect point-of-sale data from retailers so that VFC could track buying trends more effectively. In addition, VFC developed a flow-replenishment system that uses this electronic link to efficiently monitor and automatically replenish retailer inventory [Cafasso, June 1993].[1] Thus, VFC assumes responsibility for maintaining appropriate inventories of its products in the retailers' stores. These systems are examples of an **interorganizational information system (IIS)**: an information system that spans organizational boundaries to automate the flow of information between an organization and the external entities with which it interacts (see, e.g., Barrett and Konsynski [1982]).

Technologies such as EDI and _electronic funds transfer_ (EFT) exploit the telecommunications infrastructure to allow organizations to share data and to integrate their processes. To understand how an IIS affects an organization, consider a revised scenario of CAV's order fulfillment process. Instead of accepting orders over the telephone and sending invoices through the mail, imagine that CAV set up electronic links with its customers so that purchase order data was transmitted directly to CAV's order fulfillment system. Imagine also that CAV transmitted shipping and invoice data directly to its customers' computer systems and that CAV's customers paid for their orders through EFT, instead of by mailing a check. This hypothetical scenario is illustrated in Figure 4.6. To develop such an IIS, CAV and its customers would have to establish common data definitions, communications protocols, and procedures for transmitting data.

---

[1]   Copyright 1995 by Computerworld, Inc., Framingham MA 01701. Reprinted from Computerworld.

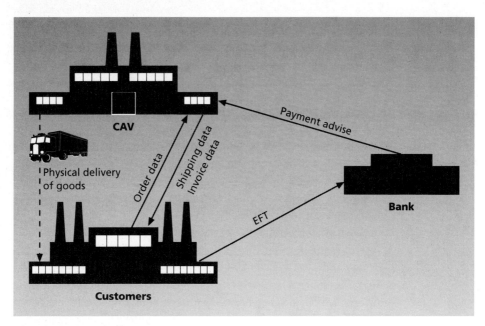

FIGURE 4.6   Interorganizational information system

The additional detail and coordination required to link an organization with its external entities make developing an IIS a complex endeavor. Nonetheless, many organizations are undertaking this difficult task in order to improve their efficiency, effectiveness, and competitiveness. From an IS perspective, what is most significant about the IIS is its impact on the scope of a development project. Normally, developers need to be concerned primarily with their own organization's structure, data, processes, and standard operating procedures. However, to develop an IIS, developers also must study the structure, data, processes, and procedures of their external entities. This broader scope increases the complexity of the system and the difficulty of determining its information and processing requirements.

Check Your Understanding 4-4

Refer to the case "Ford Has a 'Better Idea' for Accounts Payable." Explain the changes in Ford's interactions with its suppliers necessary to transform Ford's new system into an interorganizational information system. How would Ford's BPR project have been affected if one of its purposes was to create electronic links with its suppliers?

4.4 ◆ SYSTEM EVOLUTION

BPR and the development of IIS cause the organization not only to rethink its fundamental processes but also to reexamine its information architecture. Recall that an *information architecture* is a configuration of hardware, software, telecommunications, and data designed to meet an organization's information needs.

As business processes are redesigned, they often require different technologies and new ways of accessing data. For example, when decision-making authority is pushed down to lower levels in the organization, information systems must be developed to provide decision makers with the information they need. Similarly, when an organization integrates its processes with those of its external entities, information systems must be developed to link the organizations. Thus, BPR often provides the strategic pull for developing new systems employing new technologies. However, an organization cannot afford to simply discard its existing hardware and software. Instead, it must *evolve* its existing systems to a new information architecture.

The term **system evolution** is used in this text to emphasize that developers seldom create an information system from scratch; instead, most developers work to evolve an existing system from one version of itself to another and to integrate these systems as they evolve. In this section, we describe two information architectures: glasshouse and client/server. We also discuss some strategies for evolving glasshouse systems to client/server systems.

THE GLASSHOUSE INFORMATION ARCHITECTURE

A **legacy system** is an application, developed using older technologies, which is past its prime but which is so critical to the organization that it cannot be dismantled or disrupted without a severe impact on the organization. Most of today's legacy systems were developed using the earlier information architecture, sometimes referred to as the "glass house" to describe the isolation of an organization's information resources within the glass walls of the data center. In the **glasshouse information architecture**, illustrated in Figure 4.7a, dumb terminals running character-based screens are used to access data—often stored as unrelated files—from mainframes and minicomputers running software programmed in a third-generation language such as COBOL. This architecture is also called *centralized processing* or *host-based computing* because a mainframe functions as a centralized host for the organization's data and applications, giving users limited access to software and data stored and processed on the mainframe.

In the glasshouse information architecture, desktop computers are usually stand-alone devices or are equipped with terminal emulation software so that they can access data on the mainframe. In some cases, several desktop computers might be connected via a LAN, but the LAN itself is an island isolated from the organization's other information resources. This isolation of PC systems from larger platforms occurred because in the early 1980s most desktop systems were funded, developed, and maintained by individual departments, not by the organization's central data administration staff.

The primary advantages of the glasshouse information architecture are its stability, security, and manageability. Because mainframe hardware and operating systems have been fine-tuned over the past thirty years, this technology has matured and stabilized. In addition, security procedures and system management tools that handle job scheduling, data transfer, system backup/restoration, and other management operations have been developed to ensure the integrity of the system's hardware, software, and data and to manage and monitor system resources. Software and data resources are also more secure because they are housed on the mainframe host instead of being distributed on multiple systems.

The glasshouse architecture arose during an era when computers were used primarily to power transaction processing systems. Large organizations will continue to rely on this architecture and its mainframe backbone to run their transaction-intensive applications well

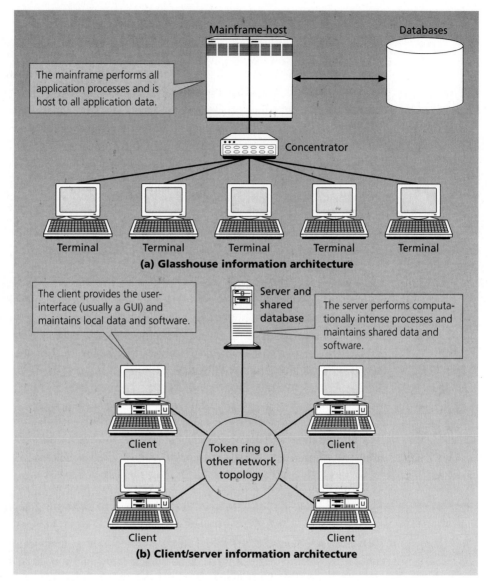

Mainframe-host

Databases

The mainframe performs all application processes and is host to all application data.

Concentrator

Terminal   Terminal   Terminal   Terminal   Terminal

(a) Glasshouse information architecture

The client provides the user-interface (usually a GUI) and maintains local data and software.

Server and shared database

The server performs computationally intense processes and maintains shared data and software.

Client   Client

Token ring or other network topology

Client   Client

(b) Client/server information architecture

FIGURE 4.7   Two information architectures

into the foreseeable future. Computing payroll for thousands of employees or processing hundreds of credit card transactions every second are just two of the high-transaction volume applications ideally suited to a mainframe-based architecture. Nonetheless, today a significant portion of an organization's information resources is devoted to information reporting and decision support processes that involve a relatively small number of users running complex, ad hoc queries against legacy databases.

A common complaint about the glasshouse information architecture is that users are virtually unable to perform these decision-support analyses. You've probably heard people talk about downloading data, a common procedure when someone wants to build a decision model on a spreadsheet using data that reside on a mainframe. Under the glasshouse information architecture, users run a terminal emulation program to log on to the mainframe and download data to a disk drive on their desktop computers. Then they launch a PC program—such as a spreadsheet or database program—and import the data to that application. Although downloading data from a mainframe is a cumbersome procedure, many nontechnical users have learned to perform this task so that they can manipulate data and view the results on a more user-friendly desktop computer. If data are stored on various host systems, users must log on System 1, download the data they need, and then log off System 1 so that they can log on System 2, download the data. . . . Needless to say, many users have difficulty just remembering all the access procedures, IDs, and passwords required to perform this process.

Another complaint about the glasshouse information architecture is its high processing costs and its demand for special technical support staff. In the early 1990s, the cost per MIP (million instructions per second) on a mainframe was approximately $100,000; in contrast, the cost per MIP was approximately $10,000 on a minicomputer and $1,000 on a desktop computer. Vigorous discounting by mainframe vendors has cut the mainframe cost per MIP in half (averaging about $40,000 per MIP in 1994); nonetheless, many organizations view migrating to a less expensive platform as a cost-cutting strategy. In addition, mainframe platforms require highly trained technical staff and a controlled environment (the "glass house" with its special electrical and air conditioning systems). To some degree, smaller systems require fewer technical personnel or a less rigidly controlled environment, so, again, organizations view smaller platforms as less labor intensive and less costly to maintain.

THE CLIENT/SERVER INFORMATION ARCHITECTURE

The information architecture being adopted by many organizations today is the highly networked **client/server architecture** illustrated in Figure 4.7b. The move to client/server is part of the **downsizing** trend: moving applications off the mainframe and onto smaller platforms. The client/server architecture is essentially a network that seamlessly integrates and—its primary differentiating characteristic—distributes data and processing among multiple computers. The **client** is usually a single-user desktop computer that provides presentation services (e.g., a graphical user interface and formatted report screens), stores data unique to the individual user's needs, and performs user-interaction intensive processes, such as querying, report writing, and sorting. The **server** is usually one or more multi-user computers that store data to be shared by multiple users and that typically perform the more computation- or database-intensive processes. Whereas most glasshouse data are stored as flat files, most client/server systems presume an SQL[2] interface to a relational DBMS.

The client/server architecture gives users greater access to data, no matter where such data reside, and allows them to view and manipulate the data more easily. Thus, end-users have

---

[2] SQL, structured query language, is a data-manipulation language used to access data from relational databases. For example, an end-user may need a report listing all customers whose accounts are more than 90 days overdue. To generate this report, the end-user writes an SQL query that extracts the relevant information from the database. The differences between the glasshouse's unrelated files (i.e., file processing environment) and a database environment are discussed in Chapter 9.

much better access to an organization's information resources than they do under the glasshouse information architecture. Additional benefits include *scalability* (the ability to increase/decrease processing and storage capacity by adding additional clients and servers) and *flexibility* (the ability to locate data and application logic wherever it seems most appropriate).

However, client/server also has its down side and may be totally inappropriate for applications that must support many users [Kennedy & Gurbaxani 1993]. A large facet of the problem is that, unlike mainframe vendors, client/server vendors have not yet developed sophisticated system management tools to help organizations manage the complex configuration of hardware, telecommunications, and database technologies required in a client/server system. Managing a system composed of so many pieces from a variety of vendors can be a nightmare for system management staff. In addition, determining how best to distribute application logic and data among multiple processors is a fine art that few developers have mastered. And although many organizations move to client/server in pursuit of lower operating costs, numerous surveys have revealed that the actual costs of operating client/server systems are not appreciably less than the costs of mainframe systems. In fact, when the additional user support and training, network, and system management costs are factored in, client/server systems may actually be more expensive [Berg 1992; Ryan 1993].

Nonetheless, many organizations are moving to client/server because of its easier data access, its faster turnaround time for ad hoc reports, the more friendly graphical user interface on the client, and—quite simply—because information technology vendors are steering them in that direction. As vendors pour more of their research and development dollars into creating and supporting client/server systems and discontinue support of older technologies, they provide a technology push prompting organizations to move in the same direction.

SYSTEM EVOLUTION STRATEGIES

Moving from the glasshouse architecture to client/server is no small task. Unless an organization is a startup company, chances are it has millions of lines of COBOL code running on legacy systems, which represent a $10 trillion investment in the U.S. alone. In addition, years of effort have been expended developing and maintaining these systems—and developing the glasshouse skills of IS designers and implementers. Organizations cannot afford to simply scrap their legacy systems; and, even if they could, their IS staffs often lack the skills to develop client/server systems. Instead, organizations must gradually evolve their legacy systems to the new information architecture.

Currently, organizations are adopting a number of strategies to facilitate system evolution. Three of these strategies "give old systems that client/server feel" without requiring developers to rewrite legacy applications [Vizard 1994]. The first strategy, **screen scraping**, is a "first-step, quick fix" strategy that uses frontware (GUI generation tools) to update the interface to a legacy application without modifying any application code. This strategy involves creating a *graphical user interface* (GUI) to the legacy system. It replaces dumb terminals with PCs, whose custom-developed GUI works like a terminal emulator but provides an easy-to-use interface for navigating legacy applications and querying legacy databases. Although this strategy does nothing to distribute processing among multiple computers, it does enable a later migration to client/server computing and maintains the data and application security that are primary benefits of glasshouse systems.

A second strategy, illustrated in Figure 4.8, uses middleware to connect a client/server LAN to existing mainframe applications and databases. **Middleware** is software that connects an end-user's client PC to a wide variety of mainframe databases. This strategy is sometimes called **upsizing** because instead of unplugging the mainframe, it "marries" the mainframe to existing PC LANs. The middleware, which is usually installed on the LAN server, handles remote procedure calls (i.e., calling for an application on a remote platform to perform a procedure) and serves as a gateway to remote databases. Middleware programs are typically able to access data stored in a variety of file formats (e.g., flat, hierarchical, network, relational). Although adopting the middleware approach is expensive—a middleware package can cost upwards of $100,000—it provides a high level of flexibility, allowing a client to access data or call procedures from any compatible legacy system. The disadvantage of this approach is that it usually increases operating costs because it requires maintaining both the legacy system and the new client/server LAN system. However, many organizations are adopting this strategy because it provides the security of a centralized host while giving end-users easy access to legacy applications and data.

Pacific Bell in San Ramon, California, adopted this strategy to upgrade its customer accounts system [Cafasso May 1993]. Before the upgrade was implemented, to solve a customer problem, a customer accounts clerk had to access several different mainframe applications,

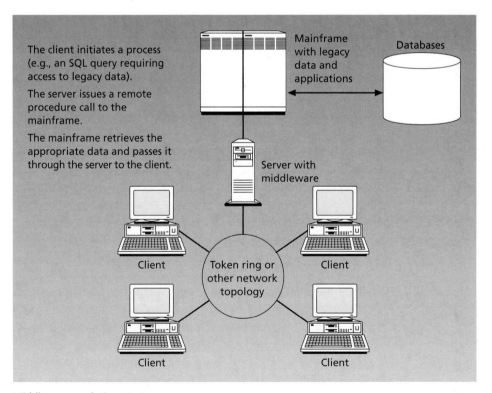

FIGURE 4.8   Middleware evolution strategy

each requiring a different log-on procedure and password. Pacific Bell implemented a client/server front end that provides a GUI and uses middleware to connect the front-end LAN system with legacy systems still housed on the mainframe. Users no longer work directly with the legacy systems; instead, they select options from the graphical front end, which are transformed into requests to be processed by two Sun Microsystems, Inc., SPARCservers. The first server creates a navigation plan describing how to access the appropriate legacy systems; the second server executes the navigation plan and retrieves data from the mainframe.

A variation of the upsizing strategy is **data staging**. This strategy uses the same technology, but, instead of allowing access to mainframe applications and data, data from the mainframe are periodically downloaded to the LAN server. Users are then able to access data on the server to perform queries and build decision models. Data staging is particularly effective when users need to perform decision-support activities that do not require real-time data.

The third strategy, **reverse engineering**, uses specialized CASE tools to analyze the code of existing applications and to reengineer the code for client/server implementation. Reverse engineering tools analyze the code, file descriptions, and database structures of existing applications, generating process and data models that capture the application's logic. Working with these models, developers can alter the design to meet new specifications, such as deploying the database using a new framework (e.g., transforming flat files into relational tables) and distributing application logic and data to the client and the server. Once the model revision is complete, the reverse engineering tool generates new code and database structures, a labor-saving process called **forward engineering**. The disadvantages of reverse engineering are its cost and long development time. Typically, IS shops have to hire consultants familiar with the tool to oversee the reverse engineering process. In addition, to verify that the reengineered system is functioning properly, many shops run the legacy system and the new client/server system in parallel, thus increasing deployment costs and delaying delivery of the new system.

The strategies described here offer ways of evolving systems that were never really designed to be radically altered. As noted in Chapter 1's discussion of systems development goals, designing for flexibility, portability, device- and language-independence is a vital concern in development projects today. After all, the leading-edge systems of today will be the legacy systems of tomorrow. To facilitate future system evolution, the shift in information architectures is being paralleled by a shift in systems development methodologies.

To ensure a smooth and efficient transformation from one system formulation to another, an information system should be viewed from a *data-driven, object-oriented perspective*. In this perspective, a system is a collection of related objects that have certain attributes and perform certain methods. These objects are implemented in self-contained software modules that are unlikely to change dramatically from one system formulation to another. Thus, object classes provide reusable building blocks as the system evolves. In addition, the object-oriented perspective produces software that can more easily be distributed over multiple processors, thus supporting the client/server architecture.

Understanding the issues, concepts, and techniques of system evolution will help you better understand a system's environment and where an organization is on the evolutionary path from glasshouse, centralized systems to more distributed client/server systems.

✓ Check Your Understanding 4-5

Indicate whether each of the following statements is true (T) or false (F).

_____ 1. Legacy systems are applications developed using microcomputers and fourth-generation languages.

_____ 2. The user-interface of a glasshouse system is usually character-based screens.

_____ 3. When personal computers are used as terminals, they must use terminal emulation software to connect to a host mainframe.

_____ 4. One advantage of the glasshouse information architecture is the low cost of its hardware.

_____ 5. The move from a glasshouse architecture to a client/server architecture is called downloading.

_____ 6. In a client/server system, the client is usually a desktop computer with a graphical user interface.

_____ 7. Flexibility and scalability are two advantages of the client/server architecture.

_____ 8. Developing and maintaining a client/server system is much less expensive than developing and maintaining a glasshouse system.

_____ 9. The screen scraping system evolution strategy basically provides a graphical user interface to a legacy system.

_____ 10. The upsizing system evolution strategy involves connecting a mainframe and a PC LAN.

◆ REVIEW OF CHAPTER LEARNING OBJECTIVES

1. *Describe the internal and external environment of an information system.*

The internal environment includes the data the system maintains, the people who use the system, and the organization's culture, structure, policies, and operating procedures. The typical organizational structure can be represented as a matrix of management levels and functional areas. The three management levels are operational management, which oversees the day-to-day business operations; tactical management, which allocates resources and implements the organization's strategies; and strategic management, which sets long-term business goals. The business functional areas include production, sales and marketing, finance and accounting, and human resources.

An information system's external environment encompasses its customers, suppliers, and competitors; stakeholders in the company (e.g., stockholders); and regulations and laws that govern its operations and therefore affect the systems it develops. These are external entities that provide inputs to or receive outputs from the organization's systems.

2. *Define process thinking and discuss the role of systems developers in redesigning business processes.*

Process thinking requires that an organization think in terms of processes, not activities functional areas; it recognizes the cross-functional nature of business processes and s to integrate the flow of work required to complete a process. Another term used to d this view is value-chain integration, which integrates value-chain activities by recognizing that each activity is just one link in the process chain of creating value for customers.

Systems developers can contribute substantially to process redesign because they understand process analysis and modeling techniques. In addition, they are better able to visualize how information technology can be used to integrate activities.

3. *Explain how interorganizational information systems affect both the internal and external system environment.*

Interorganizational information systems address the role of external entities in many organizational processes and seek to integrate activities performed externally with the organization's internal processes. From an IS perspective, what is most significant about interorganizational systems is their impact on the scope of a development project. Normally, developers need to be concerned primarily with their own organization's structure, data, processes, and standard operating procedures. However, to develop interorganizational systems, developers also must study the structure, data, processes, and procedures of their external entities and establish common data definitions, communications protocols, and procedures for transmitting data. The broader scope of such an effort increases the complexity of the system and the difficulty of determining its information and processing requirements.

4. *Define system evolution and legacy system.*

System evolution is the process of evolving an existing system from one version of itself to another. A legacy system is an application, typically developed using the glasshouse information architecture, which is past its prime but which is so critical to the organization that it cannot be dismantled or disrupted without a severe impact on the organization.

5. *Describe the glasshouse and client/server information architectures and discuss some of the advantages and disadvantages of each.*

The glasshouse information architecture uses dumb terminals running character-based screens to access data from mainframes and minicomputers running software programmed in a third-generation language such as COBOL. The primary advantages of the glasshouse information architecture are its ability to support hundreds of users and its stability, security, and manageability. Its major disadvantages include limited or difficult user data access, high processing costs, and its demand for special technical support staff.

The client/server architecture is a network that seamlessly integrates and distributes data and processing among multiple computers. The client provides presentation services (e.g., a graphical user interface and formatted report screens), stores data unique to the individual user's needs, and performs user-interaction intensive processes, such as querying, report writing, and sorting. The server stores data to be shared by multiple users and typically performs the more computation- or database-intensive processes. The advantages of the client/server architecture include greater user access to data, scalability, and flexibility. The primary disadvantages include the immaturity of client/server system management tools and the difficulty of determining how best to distribute application logic and data among multiple processors. In addition, some organizations find that the actual costs of operating downsized client/server systems are not appreciably less than—may even be greater than—the costs of mainframe systems.

6. *Describe three strategies for evolving from a glasshouse architecture to a client/server architecture.*

Organizations can adopt three strategies to facilitate evolution from a glasshouse architecture to a client/server architecture. The first strategy, screen scraping, updates the interface to a legacy application without modifying any application code. This strategy creates a GUI to the legacy system, often by replacing dumb terminals with PCs. A second strategy uses middleware to connect a client/server LAN to existing mainframe applications and databases. The third strategy, reverse engineering, uses specialized CASE tools to analyze the code of existing applications and to reengineer the code for client/server implementation.

◈ KEY TERMS

business functional areas

business process reengineering (BPR)

client

client/server information architecture

data staging

downsizing

external entities

external environment

forward engineering

glasshouse information architecture

interfirm value-chain integration

internal environment

interorganizational organizational structure

server

information systems (IIS) "over the wall" thinking

system evolution

legacy system process

upsizing

management levels process thinking

value chain

middleware reverse engineering

value-chain integration

organizational context screen scraping

◈ DISCUSSION QUESTIONS

1. List and give examples of the entities and other factors that comprise the internal environment of an information system.

2. Describe the management levels and functional areas that constitute the structure of an organization.

3. List and give examples of the entities and other factors that comprise the external environment of an information system.

4. How does a business process reengineering (BPR) initiative differ from a total quality management (TQM) initiative? How do these differences affect the level of risk in a BPR project versus that in a TQM project?

5. Give three examples of how information technology enables BPR.

6. What is a value chain? How can you use a value chain to encourage process thinki

7. For each of the following categories, discuss two issues confronted in a BPR project:
   a. People issues
   b. Technology issues
   c. Organizational issues

8. What are the defining characteristics of an interorganizational information system (IIS)? How do these characteristics affect systems development?

9. Are all legacy systems also glasshouse systems? Justify your answer.

10. Explain the division of processing and data maintenance responsibilities between a client and a server in client/server architecture.

11. Are client/server systems less expensive to operate than glasshouse systems? Why or why not?

12. Briefly explain how each of the following strategies is used to evolve from a glasshouse system to a client/server system:
    a. Screen scraping
    b. Using middleware in the upsizing strategy
    c. Data staging
    d. Reverse engineering and forward engineering

◆ EXERCISES

1. Describe the internal and external environment of your university's course registration system.

2. Reread the Chapter 1 opening case, "Systems Development Is Child's Play at Hasbro," and describe the internal and external environment of Hasbro's import tracking system.

3. Review the CYU case, "Ford Has a 'Better Idea' for Accounts Payable," and answer the following questions.
   a. What would be an appropriate name for the process addressed in Ford's BPR project? What activities are required to complete this process?
   b. How did focusing on a process instead of functional area activities help Ford to streamline its accounts payable system?

4. Review the CYU case, "Ford Has a 'Better Idea' for Accounts Payable," and answer the following questions.
   a. Discuss some of the people issues in Ford's redesign. For example, are fear of change and the need for additional training factors in Ford's redesign effort?
   b. Describe how Ford used information technology (hardware and software) to automate tasks previously performed by people following procedures.
   c. An ethical issue to think about: The Ford case euphemistically describes putting people out of work as "reducing head count." How do you feel about replacing people with technology? Is this good, bad, inevitable?

5. Compare and contrast the glasshouse information architecture and the client/server information architecture in terms of
   a. The user interface.

b. Data accessibility.
c. Processing costs.
d. Distribution of processing tasks between the desktop computer and the mainframe or server.
e. Distribution of data between the desktop computer and the mainframe or server.

◈ REFERENCES

Barrett, S., and B. Konsynski. "Inter-organizational Information Sharing Systems." *MIS Quarterly*, Special Issue 1982, pp. 93–105.

Bartholomew, D. "Technology: A Hurdle?" *Information Week*, November 7, 1994, p. 18.

Berg, L. "The Scoop on Client/Server Costs." *Computerworld,* November 16, 1992, pp. 169, 172–173, 176.

Byrne, J. A. "The Horizontal Corporation." *Business Week*, December, 20, 1993, pp. 76–81.

Cafasso, R. "From Old to New with Just a 'Click.'" *Computerworld*, May 3, 1993, p. 115.

Cafasso, R. "Jeans Genies." *Computerworld*, June 14, 1993, pp. 99, 102.

Davenport, T. E. *Process Innovation: Reengineering Work Through Information Technology*. Boston: Harvard Business School Press, 1993.

Davenport, T. E., and J. E. Short. "The New Industrial Engineering: Information Technology and Business Process Redesign." *Sloan Management Review*, Summer 1990, pp. 11–27.

Hammer, M. "Reengineering Work: Don't Automate, Obliterate." *Harvard Business Review*, July-August 1990, pp. 104–112.

Hammer, M., and J. Champy. "Explosive Thinking." *Computerworld*, May 3, 1993, pp. 123, 125.

———. *Reengineering the Corporation: A Manifesto for Business Revolution*. New York: HarperBusiness, 1993.

Jones, M. "Don't Emancipate, Exaggerate: Rhetoric, Reality and Reengineering." In R. Baskerville et al, eds. *Transforming Organizations with Information Technology*. Amsterdam: North-Holland, 1994.

Kennedy, M., and A. Gurbaxani. "When Client/Server Isn't Right." *Computerworld*, April 19, 1993, pp. 99, 101.

King, J. "Re-engineering Slammed." *Computerworld*, June 13, 1994, pp. 1, 14.

Maglitta, J. "In Depth: Michael Hammer." *Computerworld*, January 24, 1994, pp. 84–85.

Moad, J. "Does Reengineering Really Work?" *Datamation*, August 1, 1993, pp. 22–24, 28.

Ryan, H. "Sticker Shock!" *Computerworld Client/Server Journal*, November 1993, pp. 35–38.

Rockart, J. F., and J. E. Short. "IT in the 1990s: Managing Organizational Interdependence." *Sloan Management Review*, Winter 1989, pp. 7–17.

Vizard, M. "Get Your Apps Together." *Computerworld*, December 27, 1993/January 3, 1994, p. 43.

Enterprise Modeling Techniques

This technical module presents three modeling techniques useful in gaining an overview of an organization: the organization chart used to model organization structure, workflow diagrams used to model internal and external entities and the workflows between them, and the enterprise object model used to gain an overview of an organization's objects.

MODELING ORGANIZATION STRUCTURE: ORGANIZATION CHARTS

An **organization chart** is a graphical model of an organization's structure; it represents the lines of authority between the management levels and the functional areas. In this manner, an organization chart defines the framework the organization has created for performing its tasks and models the reporting structure (who reports to whom) and locus of responsibility (who is responsible for what activities) within the organization. During enterprise analysis, analysts create an organization chart to document the internal entities of the organization and to identify people to interview for a critical success factors analysis or workflow analysis.

Typically, an organization chart is represented as a hierarchy, as shown in Figure C.1. The boxes represent organizational entities responsible for strategic, tactical, or operational management of organizational units or functional areas. The lines represent the flow of information or authority between entities. The highest level of the hierarchy represents *strategic management:* the chief executive officer (CEO) and the executives who head each functional area, for example, chief financial officer (CFO), chief operating officer (COO), chief information officer (CIO). The job titles at this level may vary, depending on the size and purpose of the organization. Other examples of strategic management job titles are president, vice president of finance, vice president of operations, and so on. The middle level of the hierarchy represents *tactical management:* the managers who report to strategic management and who are responsible for implementing its strategies. The lowest level of the hierarchy represents *operational management:* the front-line supervisors who report to tactical management and who carry out its plans as they oversee the daily operations of the organization.

You should understand that the three management levels of an organization chart do not necessarily translate into a three-level hierarchy. That is, a large and complex organization may have several levels of management within the strategic, tactical, or operational management level. For example, in the organization chart shown in Figure C.1, two hierarchical levels are required to represent strategic management. The CEO oversees the activities of his or her senior executives, each of whom is responsible for planning the strategies and setting goals for one of the organization's functional areas or divisions.

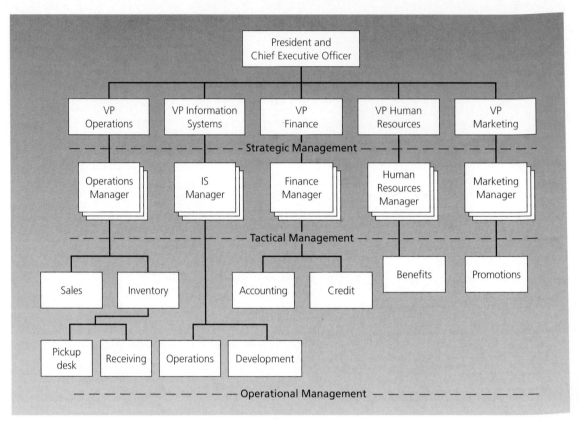

FIGURE C.1   An organization chart for Bigg's Department Stores, Inc.

You should also understand that because organizational structures vary greatly, the appearance of the organization charts modeling these structures will also vary significantly. For example, the organization chart of a large bureaucratic organization may have a dozen levels, whereas the organization chart of an entrepreneurial organization may have only two. In addition, many organizations today are moving away from a hierarchical structure with many vertical management levels to a cross-functional or horizontal structure. The organization chart of a horizontal organization typically has only two levels: the senior management level consisting of the CEO and executives responsible for finance, legal, and human resources; and the core process teams responsible for planning and performing the organization's major processes. An organization chart of a horizontal organization is illustrated in Figure C.2.

Check Your Understanding C-1

Read the following description and then draw an organization chart documenting organizational structure.

Books R Us is a wholly owned subsidiary of a major U.S. conglomerate that also operates companies in consumer products and entertainment. Books R Us is organized

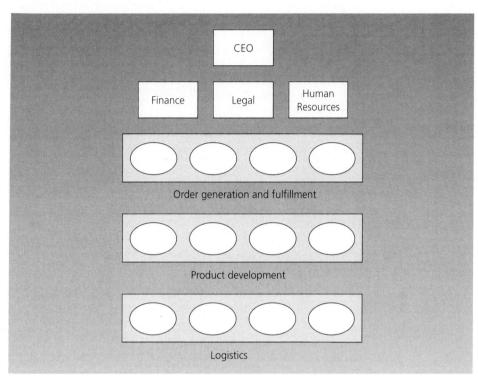

FIGURE C.2   An organization chart of a horizontal organization

a divisional bureaucracy; that is, it is divided into three divisions: College, Secondary Education, and Primary Education. These divisions are overseen by a central executive level responsible for operations (Chief Operations Officer Thomas Daniels), legal affairs (Executive Counsel Maria Chavez), and finance (Chief Financial Officer John Park). Executives at this level report to Theodore Mathers, the President and Chief Executive Officer of Books R Us.

Each division has its own divisional head as well as managers of the Human Resources, Purchasing, Marketing, Accounting, and Text Production functional areas. Monica Chandler is the divisional head who allocates resources and oversees all activities in the College Division. John Dang manages Human Resources; Polly Martin, Purchasing; Ann Young, Accounting; and William Avery, Marketing. The College Division's Text Production area, managed by Miles Standish, is further segmented by subject categories, each with its own senior editor and administrative assistant: Math and Science, Humanities, Business, and Engineering.

MODELING WORKFLOWS: WORKFLOW DIAGRAMS

Organization charts provide a static picture of an organization's structure. To understand an organization's flows of information, we need a more dynamic modeling technique. **Workflow diagrams** are a technique used to trace the flow of data—typically embodied in documents—

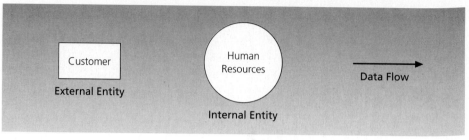

FIGURE C.3 Workflow diagram symbols

among internal and external entities[1]. Because documents are typically the inputs to and outputs of work tasks, workflow diagrams are an effective, simple technique for identifying the high-level processes an organization must perform. A **workflow**, simply stated, represents the transfer of data from one internal entity to another internal entity or between an internal and an external entity. *No workflows between external entities are shown* because such flows are outside the control of the system whose environment is being modeled.

The symbols used in workflow diagrams are shown in Figure C.3. A square represents an **external entity**: a person or business outside the boundaries of the organization, for example, a customer, vendor, or government agency. A circle represents an **internal entity**: a person or functional area within the organization, for example, a sales representative or Accounts Payable Department. The internal entities that appear in a workflow diagram should be positions or organization units shown in the organization chart. An arrow represents a workflow.

Workflow diagrams are drawn in three levels: user-level workflow diagrams, which model the entities and workflows described by a single user; combined user-level workflow diagrams, which model the entities and workflows of all users; and an organization-level workflow diagram, which models the workflows between an organization and its external entities.

User-Level Workflow Diagrams

To begin your investigation of an organization's workflows, you will need to interview users and study the organization's documented standard operating procedures. As you perform these interviews and study this documentation, your purpose is to discover the formal and informal flows of information between internal and external entities. Most organizations have formal, documented procedures stipulating how work is to be performed, who provides what information to whom, and so on. However, employees in most organizations also evolve their own informal procedures and information flows. Thus, just studying the formal documentation may not provide an accurate picture; you will need to interview users to reveal the actual flows of information.

As you conduct each interview, you create a **user-level workflow diagram** to model the entities and workflows described by a single user. To illustrate this process, let's use the

---

[1] The workflow diagramming technique presented here is an extension of the context diagram used traditional systems development. For more information about context diagrams, see, e.g., Ken Orr *Structured Requirements Definition* (Topeka, KA: Ken Orr and Associates, 1981). This technique conceptually similar to the domain analysis model used by Taylor [1995].

sales order processing (SOP) system of Bigg's Department Store as an example. The text box in Figure C.4 summarizes information gleaned from interviewing a sales clerk and a credit clerk at the store. Selected text is italicized to highlight the relevant information in the interview. In addition, entities are shown in boldface, and workflows are underlined. Notice that, at this point, you can ignore any specific descriptions of processes (for example, processing the order) and data stores (for example, the sales transaction file). These are relevant when you create process and data models, but, for now, you can ignore them because they are not represented in workflow diagrams.

Because two users were interviewed, the analyst must draw two user-level workflow diagrams: one documenting entities and workflows from the sales clerk's perspective and one from the credit clerk's perspective. The corresponding diagrams are shown in Figure C.5. Notice that the workflow diagrams do not treat the clerks as internal entities; instead the departments in which they work are given. However, if more than one entity within each department had been indicated (for example, a sales clerk and a sales manager, both working within a sales department), then the workflow diagrams would have treated each job

---

Sales Clerk Interview Summary

Two slightly different procedures are required to process a sale, depending on whether the customer pays with cash or a check or charges the sale to her account. In either case, the sales clerk writes up each order on a three-part sales form. One part of the form is the customer's copy, one is the audit copy, and one is the inventory pick-up copy. Each form lists the sales clerk's employee number; customer name, address, and phone; and item quantity, description, unit and extended price. If the customer is charging the cost of purchased items to her credit account, then the sales clerk also enters the credit account number and an approval code. If no inventory pick-up is required, the inventory pick-up copy is retained with the audit copy. The sales clerk places the audit copy of each charge receipt or sales receipt in the Sales Transaction file.

Credit customers indicate the _order item(s)_ they want to purchase and present their _charge account number_ to the **sales clerk**. The **sales clerk** processes the sale _and contacts the Credit Department, giving a_ **credit clerk** _the_ _account_

number and _sales total_. If the charge is approved, the **credit clerk** _gives the_ **sales clerk** _an_ _approval code_, which the sales clerk writes on the charge receipt. The **sales clerk** gives the **customer** a copy of the _charge receipt with the inventory pick-up copy (if appropriate)_.

Cash customers indicate the _order_ _item(s)_ they want to purchase to the **sales clerk**. The **sales clerk** processes the sale, collects _payment_ and gives the **customer** a copy of the _sales receipt along with the inventory pick-up copy (if appropriate)_.

Both types of **customer** sign the inventory pick-up receipt and give the _signed inventory pick-up copy and their sales/charge receipt_ to an **inventory pick-up clerk**. The **inventory pick-up clerk** writes his/her employee number and the serial number(s) of the item(s) on both receipts, files the inventory pick-up receipt in the Inventory Depletion file, and returns the _annotated sales/charge receipt_ to the **customer**. Then the clerk loads the item(s) in the customer's car.

Credit Clerk Interview Summary

When a credit customer wants to charge a purchase to his/her account, the **sales clerk** contacts a **credit clerk**, providing the _customer's account number and sales total_. The credit clerk accesses the customer's credit record and approves or denies the charge. If a charge is approved, _the_ **credit clerk** gives the **sales clerk** an _approval code_ and adds a record to the Approved Charges file indicating the date, customer account number, and approval code, along

with the credit clerk's employee number. At the end of each month, the credit department runs its accounts receivable program to generate updated account balances and customer account statements. The _account statements_ are mailed to **credit customers**, who submit _payment and the payment stub_ from their account statements in person or by mail to the **credit department**.

FIGURE C.4   Sales order processing system user interviews

position as an internal entity. Notice also that a user-level workflow diagram is "user-level" only in the sense that it models the viewpoint of one user. This does not mean that it contains just one internal entity, nor does it mean that it models the workflows of a single functional area. Thus, the workflow diagram in Figure C.5a shows all the entities and workflows mentioned in the sales clerk's interview. Although the interviewee was a sales clerk, the resulting workflow diagram includes the Inventory Pickup Desk and Credit Department because the sales clerk mentioned both in the interview.

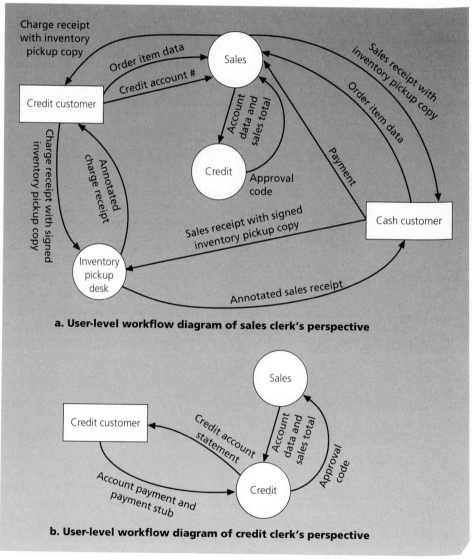

a. User-level workflow diagram of sales clerk's perspective

b. User-level workflow diagram of credit clerk's perspective

FIGURE C.5   User-level workflow diagrams of the sales order processing system

Check Your Understanding C-2

Review the following interview summary, and then draw a user-level workflow diagram to model the entities and workflows described.

> *Cal-Neva Casualty is an auto insurance company serving car owners in California and Nevada. When one of Cal-Neva's policyholders is involved in an accident, the policyholder takes his or her car to a Cal-Neva-approved body shop, fills out a claims form, and obtains an estimate of the cost to repair the car. Then the policyholder submits the estimate and the claims form to Cal-Neva's claims processing department. There a claims adjuster requests verification of coverage from a clerk in the records department and reviews the claim. If the claims adjuster approves the claim, he or she marks the claims form approved, sends the yellow copy to the policyholder and the white and green copies to the body shop, and retains the pink copy for company records. After repairing the car, the body shop has the policyholder sign its copies of the claims form, indicating that the car has been repaired to the policyholder's satisfaction. The body shop returns the signed form to the claims adjuster, who submits it to Cal-Neva's accountant. The accountant issues the body shop a check for the claim amount.*

Combined User-Level Workflow Diagram

After you have completed your interviews, you can create a **combined user-level workflow diagram** that models all the entities and workflows uncovered in your analysis. This diagram combines all of your individual user-level workflow diagrams into one diagram. For example, Figure C.6 shows the one derived from interviews with both a sales clerk and a credit clerk.

You may wonder why you need to create a combined user-level diagram. Isn't it redundant to repeat all the findings modeled in the individual diagrams? No. Your purpose in creating a combined user-level diagram is to have an integrated view of all the entities and workflows. A second purpose is to identify any inconsistencies in the user-level workflow diagrams. For example, assume that the systems analyst mentioned in the Figure C.4 text box also interviewed an inventory pickup clerk. Assume also that the inventory pickup clerk's description of the workflows was different from what the sales clerk had described. This inconsistency would become evident as you combined the sales clerk's user-level diagram with the inventory pickup clerk's user-level diagram. A third reason for creating a combined user-level workflow diagram is that an integrated view of all the entities and workflows may reveal omissions, redundancies, or inefficiencies that were not evident in the individual user-level diagrams.

In addition, the combined user-level workflow diagram can be used to identify an organization's high-level business processes, the processes that would appear on a Level 0 DFD. For example, by examining the entities and workflows in Figure C.6, we can determine that the organization performs the processes listed in Table C.1 by stating the general function of each internal entity. Although these processes are stated very generally, identifying them is important because they provide an overview of an organization's operations—useful information when conducting an enterprise analysis.

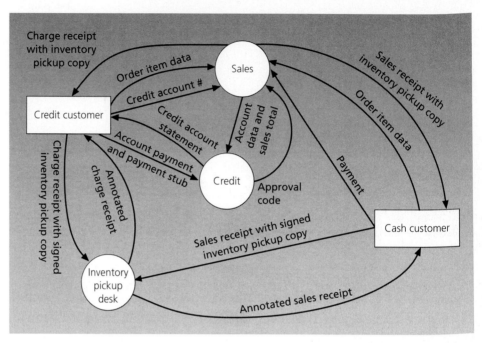

FIGURE C.6   Combined user-level workflow diagram

TABLE C.1 Major Processes of Bigg's Sales Order Processing System

1. Process sales transactions.
2. Approve credit transactions.
3. Approve removal of items from inventory.
4. Bill credit account customers.

The combined user-level diagram can also be used to define the **system boundary**, which delineates the aspects of the organization that the new system will support. In other words, you can use the combined user-level diagram to indicate—and to verify with users—which entities and workflows will be investigated further as the new information system is developed. For example, if management has stipulated that the investigation of the sales order processing system will not include the inventory pickup entity and workflows, then the system boundary would be as shown in Figure C.7.

Organization-Level Workflow Diagram

You create the **organization-level workflow diagram** after you have verified the combined user-level workflow diagram. This diagram collapses all the internal entities in the combined user-level diagram into one internal entity representing the organization or the specific pro cess you are studying. For example, the internal entities in the sales order processing co' bined user-level diagram can be collapsed into one internal entity labeled Sales C

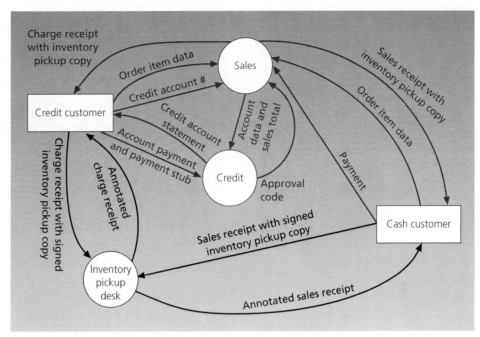

FIGURE C.7   Combined user-level workflow diagram with system boundary

Processing System. All external entities and workflows between the external entities and the sales order processing system are also modeled in this diagram. Thus, you end up with a diagram that looks like the one shown in Figure C.8.

The organization-level workflow diagram, which is equivalent to a context diagram, highlights the organization's interfaces with external entities. Like the combined user-level diagram, it also draws attention to any redundancies, omissions, and inefficiencies, especially as they relate to interactions with external entities.

Workflow diagrams provide a "quick take" on an organization's entities, workflows, and, through analysis, high-level processes. They are useful not only to document your interview findings but also to verify the accuracy of your understanding. Because workflow diagrams are a simple, easily understood modeling technique, users can review your model and point out any errors in the way you have modeled their organization's workflows, internal entities, and relationships with external entities.

MODELING ENTERPRISE OBJECTS: THE ENTERPRISE OBJECT MODEL

Creating organization charts and workflow diagrams helps you begin to identify the business objects of interest to the organization. Recall that business objects can be roles (TEACHER, STUDENT), places (CLASSROOM, LIBRARY), things (TEXTBOOK, COMPUTER), transactions (REGISTRATION, TUITION-PAYMENT), events (GRADUATION), or any tangible or intangible concept or thing. As a general rule, most internal and external entities and data flows

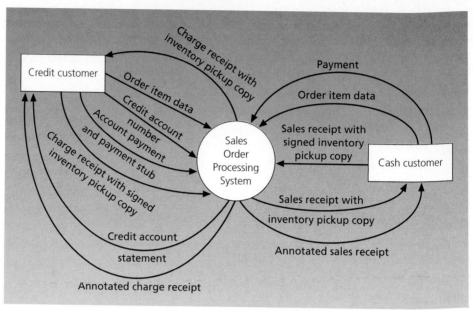

FIGURE C.8   Organization-level workflow diagram

in your workflow diagrams are potentially object classes that must be implemented in the corresponding system. However, the classes identified at this point are only **candidate classes**. As you analyze the system further, you may discover that what first appeared to be an object class is really an attribute or object instance, or simply not relevant to the system being modeled.

In this section, you will learn how to identify business objects and how to create an **enterprise object model** that groups these business objects into subjects according to the process or functional area in which they appear, or according to other relevant topics.

Identifying Candidate Classes

You can identify candidate classes by adopting one—or both—of two system perspectives: data-driven and event-driven [Yourdon 1994]. The **data-driven system perspective** focuses on the data that the system must maintain and thinks of objects in terms of what they look like. This perspective employs the following strategies:

◆ Examine source documents and reports to identify *things* about which the organization must maintain data: products, people, equipment, and so on.

◆ Examine *business events* that the organization must remember: making a sale, issuing a paycheck, buying goods and services.

◆ Examine the *roles* played by people in the system: customer, vendor, employee, manager, contractor, and so on.

◆ Examine the *physical or organizational locations and buildings* that are relevant t the system: warehouse, department, branch office, delivery dock, and so on.

For example, to start identifying the objects of interest in the sales order processing system used to illustrate workflow diagrams, you may begin by examining the source documents and reports that the system uses. Samples of a credit statement and a sales order form are shown in Figures C.9 and C.10, respectively. As you examine these documents, you should look for things, business events, roles and physical locations and buildings of interest in this system. For example, the credit statement refers to a credit customer and a credit account; thus, CREDIT-CUSTOMER and CREDIT-ACCOUNT are likely candidate classes.

The sales order form shown in Figure C.10 refers not only to customers but also to the business event of selling items. Attributes describing this event—SALES-ORDER—include OrderNumber, OrderDate, EmployeeNumber, and several others. If the customer is charging the sales total to her account, the business event is a CREDIT-ORDER and its attributes include those of a SALES-ORDER plus CreditAccountNumber and CreditApprovalCode. In addition, the sales order form refers to the items sold, whose attributes include ItemNumber, Quantity, ItemDescription, and so on. Thus, ITEM is another candidate class in this system.

These source documents and reports also identify some roles played by people in the order processing system. The sales order form indicates two roles: a customer—whether cash or

Bigg's Department Store
Credit Services Division
425 South Third Avenue
Big Town, MA 12066

Closing Date	Account Number	New Balance	Minimum Payment	Due Date
03/05/97	413-5578-3991	503.74	25.00	04/01/97

Avoid additional finance charges by paying the new balance by due date.

Man-Wa Nguyen
3639 N. Highland Ave.
Pretty Valley, MA 12068

Make check payable to **Bigg's Department Store**
Indicate amount paid $_____

- - - - - - - - - - - Detach here — Retain for your records - - - - - - - - - - -

Reference #	Posting Date	Transaction Date	Description	Amount
0294301452	02/21/97	02/19/97	Dept 57-Electronics	350.93
0294311578	02/28/97	02/28/97	Payment Received, Thank You	50.00

Previous Bal.	Finance Charge	Total Pmts	Late Charges	Total Purchases	New Bal.
199.27	3.54	50.00	0.00	350.93	503.74

FIGURE C.9   Credit account statement

Bigg's Department Store
Big Town Mall
Big Town, MA 12066

Order Number: 270054

Order Date: 2/19/97

Department Number: 53

Sales Clerk Number: 653

Sales Type: Cash ____ Credit __X__

Credit Approval Code: D93

Customer Acount Number: 413-5578-3991

Customer Name: Man-Wa Nguyen

Customer Address: 3639 N. Highland Ave, Pretty Valley, MA 12068

Customer Phone: 555-0963

Item #	Quantity	Pickup #	Item Description	Unit Price	Ext. Price
53-2371	1	92315	Stereo VHS VCR	299.99	299.99
53-10025	5		VHS tapes	4.99	24.95

Subtotal: 324.94

Sales Tax: 25.99

Total: 350.93

Cash Received: 00.00

Payment Type: n/a

Amount Charged: 350.93

I authorize Bigg's Department Store to charge the amount indicated to my account.

Credit Customer Signature: *Man-Wa Nguyen*

FIGURE C.10 Sales order form

credit—and an employee. We have already identified the CREDIT-CUSTOMER class; now we can add a CASH-CUSTOMER class and an EMPLOYEE class to our list of candidate classes.

The data-driven perspective on the sales order processing (SOP) system yields the candidate classes shown in Table C.2.

The second approach, the **event-driven system perspective**, identifies candidate classes by focusing on what an object does, not what it looks like. Adopting this perspective requires you to think about the events relevant to the system and to identify the objects that initiate, respond to, or are used in these events. Let's apply this perspective to the SOP system example. Examine the combined user-level workflow diagram in Figure C.6 and the preliminary list of processes in Table C.1 to identify the events relevant to this system. This analy

TABLE C.2 Candidate classes from the data-driven system perspective

Candidate Object	Rationale
ITEM CREDIT-ACCOUNT CREDIT-STATEMENT	ITEM, CREDIT-ACCOUNT, and CREDIT-STATEMENT are *things* about which the organization maintains data (e.g., for ITEM, stock number, description, sales price; for CREDIT-ACCOUNT, account number, credit limit, expiration date). In addition, item and credit account data are used to process a sale, and credit account data are used to issue a credit statement and process payment.
CASH-SALE CREDIT-SALE CREDIT-APPROVAL INV-PICKUP CASH-PAYMENT ACCOUNT-PAYMENT	These are all *business events* about which the organization maintains data.
CASH-CUSTOMER CREDIT-CUSTOMER SALES-CLERK CREDIT-CLERK INV-PICKUP-CLERK	These are *roles* played by people in the system. In addition, we can assume that the organization maintains data about its customers and employees; furthermore customer and employee data (e.g., sales clerk employee number; customer name, address, phone, account number, if any; inventory pickup clerk name and employee number) appear on the sales transaction form.
SALES-DEPT CREDIT-DEPT INV-PICKUP-DESK	These are all *organizational units;* however, it is not clear that the SOP system maintains data about these units.

TABLE C.3 SOP system events

◆ Cash order received.	◆ Inventory pickup receipt generated.
◆ Credit order received.	◆ Signed inventory pickup receipt received.
◆ Approval code issued.	◆ Annotated sales receipt generated.
◆ Cash payment received.	◆ Annotated charge receipt generated.
◆ Cash sales receipt generated.	◆ Credit statement generated.
◆ Charge receipt generated.	◆ Account payment received.

yields the list of events shown in Table C.3, which treats each input workflow as a "received" event and each output workflow as an "issued" or "generated" event. Your next task is to identify the roles that initiate and respond to each of the events as shown in Table C.4.

We can identify additional objects by asking, "What things are used by these events? What physical locations or organizational units are relevant to these events?" Table C.5 shows the results. This analysis yields the following candidate classes:

◆ CUSTOMER	◆ CREDIT-STATEMENT
◆ EMPLOYEE	◆ CASH-CUSTOMER
◆ DEPARTMENT	◆ CREDIT-CUSTOMER
◆ CASH-SALES-RECEIPT	◆ APPROVAL-CODE

TABLE C.4 Event-driven system perspective: roles

Event	Initiated by	Responded to by
Cash order received.	CASH-CUSTOMER	SALES-CLERK
Credit order received.	CREDIT-CUSTOMER	SALES-CLERK
Approval code issued.	SALES-CLERK	CREDIT-CLERK
Cash payment received.	CASH-CUSTOMER	SALES-CLERK
Cash sales receipt generated.	SALES-CLERK	CASH-CUSTOMER
Charge receipt generated.	SALES-CLERK	CREDIT-CUSTOMER CREDIT-CLERK
Inventory pickup receipt generated.	SALES-CLERK	CASH-CUSTOMER CREDIT-CUSTOMER
Signed inventory pickup receipt received.	CASH-CUSTOMER CREDIT-CUSTOMER	INV-PICKUP-CLERK
Annotated sales receipt generated.	INV-PICKUP-CLERK	CASH-CUSTOMER
Annotated charge receipt generated.	INV-PICKUP-CLERK	CREDIT-CUSTOMER
Credit statement generated.	CREDIT-CLERK	CREDIT-CUSTOMER
Account payment received.	CREDIT-CUSTOMER	CREDIT-CLERK

TABLE C.5 Event-driven system perspective: objects and locations or units

Event	Objects Used/Created	Location/Organizational Units
Cash order received.	ITEM	SALES-DEPARTMENT
Credit order received.	ITEM, CREDIT-ACCOUNT	SALES-DEPARTMENT
Approval code issued.	APPROVAL-CODE	CREDIT-DEPARTMENT
Cash payment received.	CASH-PAYMENT	SALES-DEPARTMENT
Cash sales receipt generated.	ITEM, SALES-RECEIPT	SALES-DEPARTMENT
Charge receipt generated.	ITEM, CHARGE-RECEIPT, CREDIT-ACCOUNT	SALES-DEPARTMENT, CREDIT-DEPARTMENT
Inventory pickup receipt generated.	ITEM, INV-PICKUP-RECEIPT	SALES-DEPARTMENT
Signed inventory pickup receipt received.	INV-PICKUP-RECEIPT	INV-PICKUP-DESK
Annotated sales receipt generated.	SALES-RECEIPT	INV-PICKUP-DESK
Annotated charge receipt generated.	CHARGE-RECEIPT	INV-PICK-UP-DESK
Credit statement generated.	CHARGE-RECEIPT, CREDIT-ACCOUNT, CREDIT-STATEMENT	CREDIT-DEPARTMENT
Account payment received.	CREDIT-STATEMENT, CREDIT-ACCOUNT, ACCOUNT-PAYMENT	CREDIT-DEPARTMENT

- CHARGE-RECEIPT
- INV-PICKUP-RECEIPT
- CASH-PAYMENT
- ACCOUNT-PAYMENT
- ITEM
- CREDIT-ACCOUNT

- SALES-CLERK
- CREDIT-CLERK
- INV-PICKUP-CLERK
- SALES-DEPARTMENT
- CREDIT-DEPARTMENT
- INV-PICKUP-DESK

Notice that most of these candidate classes are also indicated on the combined user-level workflow diagram in Figure C.6. Notice also that this list of candidate classes is almost identical to the one generated by applying the data-driven perspective shown in Table C.2. The only difference between the lists is that the data-driven list represents the business transaction of processing a cash sale as a CASH-SALE event class whereas the event-driven perspective represents this transaction in terms of the SALES-RECEIPT that embodies this transaction. The same is true for the CREDIT-SALE (CHARGE-RECEIPT) and INV-PICKUP (INV-PICKUP-RECEIPT) classes.

What this indicates is that either perspective works well to identify candidate classes. It also indicates that you may not need to go through the structured process of building the tables shown above in order to identify candidate classes. You should see that every entity and workflow on your workflow diagrams is likely to be a candidate class.

Grouping Candidate Classes in an Enterprise Object Model

Now that you have identified the organization's candidate classes, you can group them into subjects to create an enterprise object model. A **subject**[2] is a cohesive grouping of a subset of the organization's object classes; a subject is cohesive in that it groups classes that are related to each other in some way that is meaningful to the organization. Thus, your purpose in grouping classes into subjects is to provide "snapshots" of the organization's classes that are meaningful to users. These groupings are especially valuable in large organizations with hundreds of classes. By grouping related classes, you identify the subset of enterprise objects of interest to a particular set of users or to a particular system.

Object classes can be grouped in a number of ways. For example, you may want to group all the people object classes into one subject, all the document classes into another, and so on. However, if the purpose of defining subjects is to identify a cohesive subset of classes of interest in a particular system, it may be most appropriate to group them by the systems, processes, or functional areas in which they are used. Here, we form subjects by relating them to the process in which they are used. Recall that we identified four major processes in the Bigg's Department Store sales order processing system:

1. Process sales transactions.

2. Approve credit transactions.

---

[2]   *Subject* is the term applied to this concept in the Coad and Yordon OO methodology.

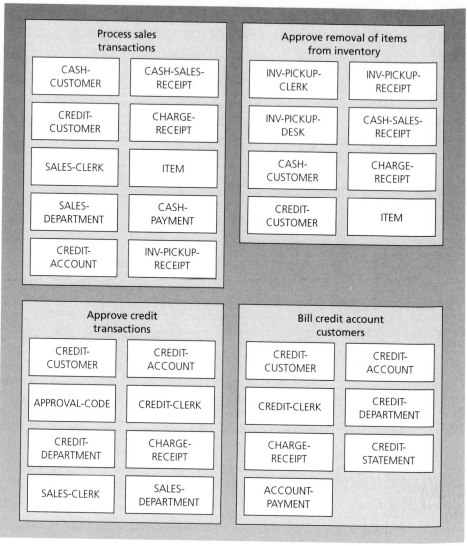

Process sales transactions

CASH-CUSTOMER	CASH-SALES-RECEIPT
CREDIT-CUSTOMER	CHARGE-RECEIPT
SALES-CLERK	ITEM
SALES-DEPARTMENT	CASH-PAYMENT
CREDIT-ACCOUNT	INV-PICKUP-RECEIPT

Approve removal of items from inventory

INV-PICKUP-CLERK	INV-PICKUP-RECEIPT
INV-PICKUP-DESK	CASH-SALES-RECEIPT
CASH-CUSTOMER	CHARGE-RECEIPT
CREDIT-CUSTOMER	ITEM

Approve credit transactions

CREDIT-CUSTOMER	CREDIT-ACCOUNT
APPROVAL-CODE	CREDIT-CLERK
CREDIT-DEPARTMENT	CHARGE-RECEIPT
SALES-CLERK	SALES-DEPARTMENT

Bill credit account customers

CREDIT-CUSTOMER	CREDIT-ACCOUNT
CREDIT-CLERK	CREDIT-DEPARTMENT
CHARGE-RECEIPT	CREDIT-STATEMENT
ACCOUNT-PAYMENT	

FIGURE C.11   Enterprise object model

3. Approve removal of items from inventory.
4. Bill credit account customers.

Assigning our candidate classes to subjects according to these processes yields the enterprise object model shown in Figure C.11. Here classes are represented as rectangles and are grouped into subjects represented as enclosed shaded boxes. However, you can create a simple enterprise object model just by listing class names under subject headings.

Notice that several classes are repeated in each subject group. These repeated classes indicate that the activities are closely related and should be integrated into one cohesive system.

◆ KEY TERMS

candidate class

combined user-level
  workflow diagram

data-driven system
  perspective

enterprise object model

event-driven system
  perspective

external entity

internal entity

organization chart

organization-level
  workflow diagram

subject

system boundary

user-level workflow diagram

workflow

workflow diagram

◆ EXERCISES

1. Create a user-level workflow diagram to document the entities and workflows of Bebop Records' order processing system.

   Bebop Records is a mail-order company that distributes CDs and tapes at discount prices to record club members. When an order processing clerk receives an order form, she or he verifies that the sender is a club member by checking the Member Master file. If the sender is not a member, the clerk returns the order along with a membership application form. If the sender is a member, the clerk verifies the order item data by checking the Item Master file. Then the clerk enters the order data and saves it to the Daily Orders file. The clerk also prints an invoice and shipping list for each order, which are forwarded to Order Fulfillment.

2. List the classes in Bebop Records' order processing system. Create an enterprise object model that groups these classes into the following subjects: things, roles, organizational units.

3. Create a user-level workflow diagram to document the entities and workflows in All-American Bank's new accounts processing system.

   When new customers open savings accounts with All-American Bank, they provide the bank with a completed new account application form. A bank clerk verifies the application data; if the form contains errors, the clerk adds the account application to an error listing, which is sent to the New Accounts Department. If the application data is correct, the clerk selects an account number from the Available Account Numbers list and adds it to the application form. Then the clerk inquires whether the customer will be making a deposit at this time. If a deposit is being made, the clerk collects the cash or check from the customer and enters the opening deposit amount on the application form. Then the clerk enters all new account data into the bank's computer and saves it to the New Accounts file. At the end of each day, the New Accounts file is accessed to print a New Accounts Transaction list, which is sent to the New Accounts Department, and to extract customer data, which is saved to the Customer Master file. In addition, the system generates a letter to the customer, indicating the customer's account number and providing information about using the account.

4. List the classes in All-American Bank's new accounts processing system. Create an enterprise object model that groups these classes into the following subjects: things, roles, and organizational units.

5. Create a user-level workflow diagram to document the entities and workflows of Delta Products' order processing system.

Delta Products Corporation is a major vendor of office supplies, furniture, and equipment. Delta's sales representatives call on customers to take orders. The sales reps write up the orders and turn them in to a sales order processing (SOP) clerk at the regional center. If the ordered items are in stock, the SOP clerk prepares a picking slip and a packing list for each order. If any of the ordered items are out of stock, the SOP clerk completes an Out of Stock Notice form, which notes the name of the customer requiring the items, and forwards it to Purchasing. A Purchasing clerk then completes a purchase order, which is mailed to a supplier. The SOP clerk notes back-ordered items on the customer's order and forwards a copy of the annotated customer order to Accounts Receivable, where an A/R clerk prepares an invoice and sends it to the customer. The SOP clerk also forwards a picking slip and packing list to the Warehouse, where stock pickers fill the order, placing ordered items into boxes along with the packing list. The boxed items and packing list are held for delivery, usually via UPS.

6. Analyze your workflow diagram from Exercise 5 to identify the major processes described in this case.

7. Create an organization-level workflow diagram to document the external entities and workflows described in Exercise 5.

8. Refer to Exercise 5 to create an enterprise object model that groups the classes in Delta Product's order processing system into subjects based on functional area (e.g., SOP, Purchasing, A/R, and so on).

9. Create two user-level workflow diagrams to document the entities and workflows in each paragraph of the payroll processing system description that follows. Then create a combined user-level workflow diagram that incorporates all the entities and workflows in the system.

Work-study employees in each university department provide their departmental secretary with their weekly timecards. The departmental secretary accesses the employees' hourly rate from the Employee Payroll file and prepares a weekly time sheet that lists each employee's name, social security number, total hours worked, and hourly rate. Then the departmental secretary files the timecards in a timecard history folder and gives the time sheet to the department chair. If everything seems to be in order, the department chair signs the time sheet and forwards it to the university's Payroll Department. If any figures on the time sheet are unacceptable, the chair returns the sheet to the secretary, who verifies the figures and again gives the time sheet to the department chair.

In the Payroll Department, a clerk calculates gross payroll earnings for each employee and then writes the earnings on the time sheet and updates the year-to-date *gross earnings figure for each employee in the employee's file. (Note: Work-study students have been allocated a set figure, e.g., $1,500, that represents their total allowed gross earnings for a year.) Then the clerk accesses the Employee Payroll file to determine the employee's tax status and authorized deductions. The clerk prepares the payroll checks, which are forwarded to employees. The processed time sheet is filed in a Time Sheet History folder for each pay period.*

10. List the classes in the payroll processing system described in Exercise 9. Create an enterprise object model that groups these objects into subjects based on (1) process timecards and (2) prepare paychecks.

◆ REFERENCES

Coad, P., and E. Yourdon. *Object-Oriented Analysis*. Englewood Cliffs, NJ: Yourdon Press/ Prentice-Hall, 1991.

———. *Object-Oriented Design*. Englewood Cliffs, NJ: Yourdon Press/Prentice-Hall, 1991.

Taylor, D. *Business Engineering with Object Technology*. New York: John Wiley & Sons, 1995.

Yourdon, E. *Object-Oriented Systems Design: An Integrated Approach*. Englewood Cliffs, NJ: Yourdon Press/Prentice-Hall, 1994.

ENTERPRISE ANALYSIS

Preliminary Investigation and Analysis

1. *Perform enterprise analysis.*
2. Determine system objectives, project constraints, and scope.
3. Evaluate feasibility and get approval to proceed.
4. Conduct JAD sessions to verify objectives, constraints, and scope; to redesign process, if necessary; and to identify requirements.

PROCESS THINKING AND WORKFLOW AUTOMATION

You don't gain the maximum impact when you . . . arbitrarily draw a boundary around a process. For us to truly redesign and become a different bank, we had to take the entire bank . . . through this exercise. [Anita Ward, senior vice-president, Texas Commerce Bank]

Want to slay the paper dragon? Start by identifying your company's workflows and then design automated processes to eliminate paper shuffling and redundant data entry. That was a lesson learned by Texas Commerce Bank and Independence One Mortgage Corp., two financial institutions that have exploited process thinking and information technology to improve productivity.

When Texas Commerce Bank (TCB) created a 401K plan called Avesta, its goals were threefold: to better manage its diversified investment funds, to closely track the impact of the plan on a customer's account, and to improve interaction between the bank and its Avesta customers. The Avesta 401K plan and its streamlined plan-management process was just one result of a massive reengineering project that yielded 15,000 suggestions for process changes.

At most banks, 401K systems are paper-intensive manual processes beleaguered by errors, delays, and redundant data entry. Typically, a plan participant must complete six complicated forms, which are submitted to the company's Human Resources Department.

There the forms are verified against personnel records and then sent to the bank that manages the plan. At the bank, a six-week paper shuffling and data entry dance begins, during which time the enrollment is not actually activated because participants may elect to make changes. Then, at the end of every payroll cycle, the client company generates a report on its 401K participants and sends it to the bank, which reconciles this report and a payroll tape to administer the plan.

To reengineer this process, TCB focused on defining and redesigning workflows independent of technology considerations. Once the workflows had been redesigned, TCB implemented workflow automation technology and an interorganizational communications link with its client companies. Now a 401K enrollee sits down at a computer at his or her employment site and completes an electronic form implemented on a PC running ViewStar Corp.'s workflow software. The enrollment data is transmitted to TCB, where a workflow system matches the enrollment data with the payroll record and then sends the data to the 401K accounting system for processing. This automated process typically requires no paper and no human intervention; in addition, it reduced operating expenses 80 percent and requires just 16—not the pre-reengineering 100—employees to administer.

Similar problems plagued Independence One Mortgage Corp. (IOMC), whose loan-origination system was so bad that the federal government threatened to revoke the bank's charter. During the mortgage-refinancing boom of the early 1990s, IOMC received an average of 100 applications, accompanied by 1,000 related documents each day. Processing an application was a largely manual process that took up to 90 days and involved 10 separate files passed between nine departments, and 30 different handoffs.

IOMC redesigned this process by replacing the 10 paper files with one electronic form, a change that saved each loan processor three hours a day! In addition, it consolidated the departments into cross-functional teams linked by an enhanced LAN, as illustrated in Figure 5.1.

Technological enhancements included adding new functionality to the Mortgage Flex software already in use and creating a LAN gateway to the existing IBM mainframe. The total cost of the project was $1.2 million; however, new hardware accounted for only $50,000 of that total. The result was that every step of the newly integrated, cross-functional loan process was supported by the Mortgage Flex system, greatly improving productivity (41 percent reduction in workforce) and reducing loan closing time from 90 days to 15 to 20 days.

Adapted from J. Maglitta, "Loan Survivors," *Computerworld,* February 27, 1995, pp. 88–91; and M. Brandel, "Texas Commerce Reinvents Itself," *Computerworld,* January 30, 1995, pp. 47, 49. Copyright 1995 by Computerworld, Inc., Framingham MA 01701. Reprinted from Computerworld.

The chapter opening case, "Process Thinking and Workflow Automation," profiles two organizations that achieved greater productivity by redesigning fundamental business processes. As the quotation opening the case suggests, both companies put their entire organizational structure "on the chopping block" and undertook massive efforts to examine every aspect of

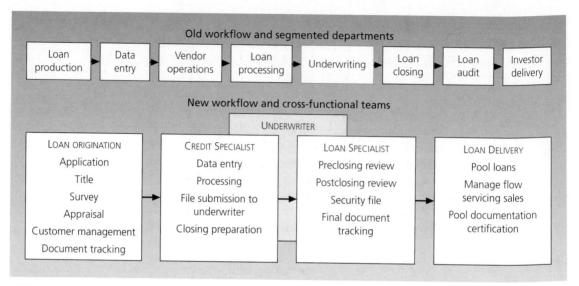

FIGURE 5.1   IOMC's redesigned work flows and organization structure

their operations to identify redundant, bottleneck activities and to determine how to streamline and integrate activities into a cohesive process.

Like the companies in this case, many businesses today are discovering that a precursor to redesigning their processes is understanding these processes and the objects, roles, activities, and business rules they involve. This chapter discusses enterprise analysis in terms of its role in helping organizations to get a "first take" on the processes and objects of interest to the enterprise. The affinity diagrams created in this analysis show where opportunities exist to create cross-functional information systems to integrate activities into a cohesive business process.

Three enterprise modeling techniques are discussed here—organization charts, workflow diagrams, and the enterprise object model. These modeling techniques are also presented in Technical Module C, "Enterprise Modeling Techniques," which you should have read before this chapter. You learned how to use these models to create affinity diagrams and how to read them to identify opportunities for integration. After completing this chapter, you should be able to

1.   Describe the top-down approach and its three levels of analysis.

2.   Discuss the purpose and techniques of enterprise analysis.

3.   Discuss the purpose and process of critical success factor (CSF) analysis.

4.   Use enterprise models to create affinity diagrams.

5.   Explain the purpose of affinity diagrams.

5.1 ◆ ENTERPRISE ANALYSIS: IDENTIFYING CROSS-FUNCTIONAL PROCESSES AND PRIORITIZING SYSTEMS DEVELOPMENT PROJECTS

The information systems department of a large organization receives more requests for services than it can possibly satisfy. Given this tremendous demand and a scarcity of resources, organizations must prioritize the requests they receive. Ideally, the method used to prioritize development projects involves analyzing the organization as a whole to determine the most pressing need for new systems and the greatest potential for organization-wide benefits from these systems. Many organizations adopt the top-down approach and conduct an enterprise analysis to do this.

ENTERPRISE ANALYSIS AND THE TOP-DOWN APPROACH

An information system does not—or at least, should not!—exist as an isolated island in the organization. Each information system affects and is affected by other organizational information systems. Thus, to avoid creating incompatible systems, or the kind of isolated systems illustrated in Chapter 4's CAV case, the analyst needs to study the organization to gain a broad perspective of its structure, processes, and information needs.

Our systems development methodology adopts the **top-down approach** to examine the environment and requirements of a system. As illustrated in Figure 5.2, this top-down approach begins by examining the organizational context, then the functional areas or management levels affected by the system under study, and finally the specific information system that is the focus of the project. This approach assumes that the environment of a system must be understood before the system itself is analyzed. It also recognizes that an information system serves an organization by performing certain business functions; thus, to ensure that the system satisfies the organizational relevance goal, the system's organizational context must be understood.

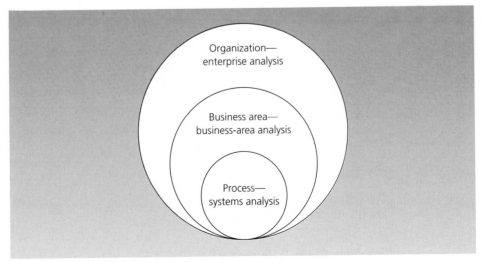

FIGURE 5.2   Top-down approach to systems development

Enterprise analysis, then, provides an overview of an organization's business objectives, structure, information needs, objects, and processes. Among the techniques used here are critical success factor (CSF) analysis, affinity diagrams, and enterprise modeling. *CSF analysis* (discussed later) involves interviewing people at various management levels to identify the factors critical to the organization's success. *Affinity diagrams* provide an organizational overview in the form of matrices relating one organizational dimension (e.g., data or object classes) to another dimension (e.g., functional areas). **Enterprise models** provide graphical representations of an organization's structure, information needs, objects, and processes. The outputs of enterprise analysis are statements of the organization's objectives or CSFs, and models of the organization's structure, objects, and workflows, including an organization chart, an enterprise object model, workflow diagrams, and affinity diagrams. The affinity diagramming technique is described later in this chapter; the other modeling techniques are presented in Technical Module C: Enterprise Modeling Techniques.

Business area analysis focuses on the functional areas and/or management levels that will use the information system and studies their information needs and processes in more detail. Systems analysts evaluate how efficiently and effectively the functional area performs its processes and to identify any interdependencies between functional areas. The techniques used here may include the ones used at the organizational level, but are usually augmented by detailed process, object, and data models. The outputs of this analysis are statements of the functional area objectives and models of its workflows, processes, and data.

Systems analysis determines the IPOSC requirements of a particular information system that will help to more efficiently and effectively perform a process, thereby meeting the organization's needs. The outputs of this analysis are detailed statements of the system objectives and functional requirements and models of the process and its objects and data.

We favor the top-down approach because it provides the emphasis on process integration and organizational relevance required to avoid developing stand-alone systems that contribute little to the organization. However, we modify this approach—as it is typically modified in practice—to focus on a subset of the enterprise. Most large organizations are so complex that analyzing and modeling the whole organization would be a never-ending task; by the time you came close to finishing the analysis, the organization probably would have changed significantly, and your enterprise models would be outdated. In practice, therefore, most organizations create an enterprise model incrementally. That is, as each systems development project is undertaken, the particular organizational subset affected by the system is analyzed and modeled. This model of an enterprise segment is maintained to reflect changes in the relevant processes and data flows. Over time, as segments are integrated with other segments, a full-scale enterprise model evolves.

CONDUCTING AN ENTERPRISE ANALYSIS

Enterprise analysis has its foundation in IBM's Business Systems Planning (BSP) technique. This technique examines an organization's existing information systems and interviews a sample of its managers to determine the kinds of information they need, the sources from which this information is collected, and the ways in which the information is used. Managers are also asked to identify their objectives and to describe the environment in which the work. The purpose of gathering this information is to provide a comprehensive overview of the organization and its functional areas, processes, information needs, and existing systems. In addition to describing the status quo, the outputs of an enterprise analysis should also define business problems and opportunities and indicate new business objectives and the automation requirements to support these objectives.

Enterprise analysis proceeds in two phases. The first phase, *identification,* focuses on defining the organization's business objectives, processes, and data. **Business objectives** state the firm's measurable goals for both the short term and the long term. For example, a manufacturing company may have business objectives such as reducing the number of defects to 1 percent within two years or reducing inventory costs by 25 percent over the next year. During the identification phase, business analysts also study current information systems to identify processes and data. A technique commonly used to perform this analysis is the affinity diagram, described in Section 5.2. The second phase, *definition,* focuses on determining which systems to build and identifying data needs shared by several functional areas or activities. Shared data is often the best indicator of the need for integrated systems. The output of the definition phase is an information systems plan that recommends new systems to develop or existing systems to integrate.

To help management identify systems that are critical to meeting the organization's objectives, you may need to conduct a critical success factors (CSF) analysis as part of your investigation. **CSF analysis** is a technique used to identify the few things an organization must do well in order to succeed in its environment (see, for example, Rockart [1979]; Bullen and Rockart [1981]; Martin [1990]). Critical success factors emanate from five sources:

1. The *industry* to which the organization belongs, for example, the auto industry or the fast-food industry.

2. The organization's *competitive strategy*, for example, creating a market niche or being the low-cost producer.

3. *Environmental factors*, such as government regulations, economic conditions, and demographics.

4. *Temporal (i.e., short-term) concerns*, such as an economic recession or trade embargo.

5. The specific *managerial focus*, for example, producing goods vs. marketing goods.

As an example of CSFs, consider an automobile manufacturer that has adopted the low-cost producer competitive strategy. Every company in the auto industry has CSFs related to the fuel economy of its products (as stipulated by the federal government) and consumers' perceptions of its image (*industry CSFs*). As a low-cost producer, our example auto company also has control of manufacturing costs and efficient dealer organization as CSFs (*competitive strategy CSFs*). Because consumers today view safety as a high priority and the government enforces auto safety standards, the company also must satisfy this CSF if it is to succeed (*environmental CSF*). A production manager in this company may identify agile manufacturing as the most critical factor in the company's ability to compete, while, for a marketing manager, effective advertising campaigns may be most important (*managerial focus CSFs*). Finally, during an economic recession, our auto manufacturer will probably add an attractive rebate program to its list of CSFs (*temporal CSF*).

To achieve these critical success factors, an organization needs to make critical decisions about how to allocate its resources, which markets to enter, and other management concerns. Such decisions require certain specific types of information. Thus, identifying CSFs ultimately helps an organization to identify its critical information needs. How well are current applications meeting these needs? What new systems should be developed to better fill these needs? Information systems that address an organization's critical information needs are most likely to help it achieve its CSFs and therefore should be given priority.

The method for conducting a CSF analysis is summarized in Figure 5.3. CSF analysis employs the top-down approach in that it begins with an understanding of management concerns and critical decisions and then defines the information needed to address these concerns and make these decisions. Furthermore, as illustrated in Figure 5.4, determining critical success factors at the organizational and process/departmental level also guides the organization's information system strategy, provides a rationale for prioritizing projects, and helps identify measurable objectives the system is to attain.

Check Your Understanding 5-1

Read the case study, "Automating Rentals at Ryder," on the next page to answer the following questions.

1. List the three levels of analysis in the top-down approach. Which business area(s) was (were) investigated in the RyderFirst project? Which information systems were analyzed and redesigned in this project?

2. Identify two factors critical to Ryder's success in the consumer truck rental industry.

3. Identify a temporal CSF that prompted development of the RyderFirst system.

4. Identify the business objectives of the RyderFirst project.

5. The case notes that inventory management was an especially important component of the RyderFirst system. Why is effective inventory management critical to this business-unit's success?

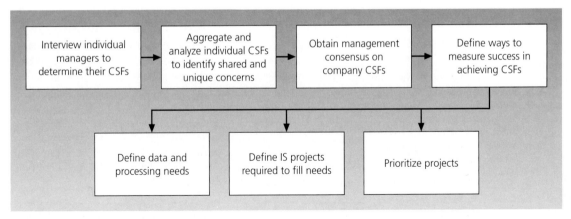

FIGURE 5.3   CSF analysis

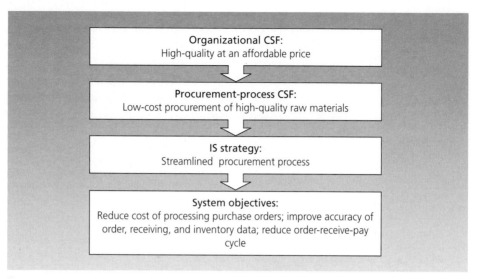

FIGURE 5.4 Relationshp of CSFs to information system (IS) strategy and system objectives

AUTOMATING RENTALS AT RYDER

Ryder System, Inc., is a diversified company of business units that include consumer truck rental, commercial truck leasing, and jet engine repair. Although the consumer truck rental unit accounts for only 25 percent of Ryder's business, it is a core business unit. Its main competitor is U-Haul Co., the number one company in this market; Ryder is number two. Excellent customer service, competitive rental rates, and maximization of unit usage (i.e., ensuring that each rental truck is in use a high percentage of the time) are keys to success in this industry. Facing an economic recession and business losses in the 1980s, Ryder undertook a five-year project to place a personal computer in each of the 4,500 offices of the independent dealers that lease Ryder trucks to consumers. The project goals were to increase revenue per unit (i.e., per rental truck) 20 percent and to decrease transfer expenses (the expense of transferring a rental truck from one dealer to another) 15 percent.

The new system, called RyderFirst, automates order entry, sales, marketing, and inventory management functions by linking local dealers to regional hosts and the headquarters mainframe. The system facilitates sales and marketing by notifying the thousands of dealers about rental rate changes and promotional campaigns. More importantly, it greatly improves inventory management by providing immediate data on the whereabouts and availability of Ryder's more than 30,000 rental trucks.

Dennis Klinger, vice president of information systems and CIO, noted that "RyderFirst is a high priority—an investment in a segment that has been under pressure. It is one of those systems that is key to the business."

Adapted from R. Cafasso, "Ryder Trucks in Automation." *Computerworld,* December 7, 1992, p. 57. Copyright 1995 by Computerworld, Inc., Framingham MA 01701. Reprinted from Computerworld.

5.2 ◆ AFFINITY DIAGRAMS

The primary technique used in enterprise analysis is an **affinity diagram**: a matrix that shows the intersection of two dimensions of the organization, for example, activities and functional areas or activities and data, as illustrated in Tables 5.1 and 5.2, respectively. Analysts create affinity diagrams during enterprise analysis for at least two reasons. First, affinity diagrams provide a broad, enterprise-wide overview of information throughout the organization; thus, they help analysts to visualize the information interdependencies among functional areas and activities and to identify opportunities to create integrated, cross-functional processes. Second, affinity diagrams help the organization to establish development priorities among potential information system applications.

Affinity diagrams are useful in obtaining a broad understanding of organizational interdependencies because they relate one aspect of the organization to another aspect. Many combinations of organizational dimensions can be modeled in affinity diagrams. For example, the diagram in Table 5.1 relates organizational activities to the functional areas that perform these

TABLE 5.1 Activity/functional-area affinity diagram

Activities	R&D	Sales	Marketing	Finance	Accounting	Personnel	Production	Procurement	Warehouse	Shipping	etc.
Design product	M		S				S				
Research market		S	M								
Determine product cost and price			M	S	S		S	S			
Enter orders		M									
Bill customers for orders					M						
Manage supplies		S					S	S	M	S	
Forecast production		S	S				M				
Schedule production		S	S				M				
Manufacture product							M				
Control inventory					M		S		M	S	
Ship orders		S					S	S		S	M
Hire employees						M	S				
Pay employees		S*			M						
etc.											

*Assumes that sales representatives are paid on commission

Key: M = Major involvement S = Some involvement

TABLE 5.2 Activity/data affinity diagram

Data

Activities	Product Description	Product Status	Materials Cost	Materials Status	Sales Order	Sales Forecast	Purchase Order	Production Schedule	Customer	Vendor	Employee	Equipment	Sales History	Promotion	Shipment	Accounts Payable	Accounts Receivable
Design product			U														
Research market	U				U				U				C				
Market product	U					U			U					C			
Determine product cost and price	C		U										U				
Enter sales orders	U	U			C				U								
Bill customers for orders	U				U				C		U*						C
Purchase and control supplies			U	U			U	C	U		C						
Pay vendors			U				U			U						C	
Forecast sales	U				U	C							U				
Schedule production				U		U		C			U	U					
Manufacture product				U													
Control product inventory	U	C			U										U		
Ship orders	U	U			CU				U						C		
Hire employees						U		U			C						
Pay employees					U*						U						
etc.																	

*Assumes that sales representatives are paid on a commission basis.

Key: C = Creates data   U = Uses data

tasks; the diagram in Table 5.2 relates organizational activities to the data created (C) or used (U) in these activities. Other combinations of affinity diagrams include functional area/ information system, activity/information system, executive/functional area, functional area/ data, information system/data, information system/business objective, and so on.

CREATING AFFINITY DIAGRAMS

If the organization you are studying is relatively simple in structure and has only a few work-flows and entities, you may be able to create an affinity diagram just by listing activities, data, functional areas, and so on. However, most of the time, you will need to create enterprise models first. Three enterprise models you can use to gain an overview of an organization are the organization chart, the workflow diagram, and the enterprise object model. Each of these modeling techniques is explained in Technical Module C, "Enterprise Modeling Techniques." Here we discuss how to use these models to create affinity diagrams.

An **organization chart** provides a graphical model of an organization's structure, representing the reporting structure (who reports to whom) and locus of responsibility (who is responsible for what activities) between the management levels and the functional areas. It defines the structure the organization has created for performing its tasks. During enterprise analysis, you create an organization chart to document the internal entities of the organization and to identify people to interview for a critical success factors analysis or workflow analysis. The internal entities shown on an organization chart become functional areas, management levels, and/or executives on your various affinity diagrams.

Workflow diagrams trace the flow of data—typically embodied in documents—among internal and external entities. The workflow diagram shown in Figure 5.5 is repeated from Technical Module C. The entities used in workflow diagrams include those shown in the organization chart (internal entities such as sales, credit, and order pickup) and any external entities with whom the organization interacts (for example, credit customer and cash customer). The internal entities of a workflow diagram typically are shown as functional areas on affinity diagrams; workflow diagram data elements (e.g., credit account #, approval code), documents (e.g., charge receipt, credit account statement), and external entities may be shown as data.

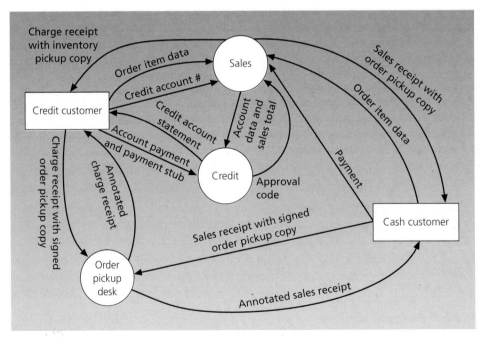

FIGURE 5.5   Combined user-level workflow diagram of Bigg's Department Store SOP system

Although workflow diagrams do not model processes, they can be used to identify the major activities an organization must perform to create and to use its workflows. The major processes identified by studying the workflow diagram in Figure 5.5 include

1. Process sales transactions (as indicated by the workflows between Sales and Customers).

2. Approve credit transactions (as indicated by the workflows between Sales and Credit).

3. Approve removal of items from inventory (as indicated by the workflow between the Customer entities and Order pickup).

4. Bill credit account customers (as indicated by the workflow between Credit and Credit customer).

These activities are shown on any affinity diagram that relates an organization's tasks to another organizational dimension.

Finally, an **enterprise object model** identifies and groups all objects of interest to the organization into subjects; each subject group represents the classes involved in a particular functional area, business process, or other classification of interest to the organization. Figure 5.6 shows the enterprise object model developed by examining the workflow diagram of Bigg's Department Store SOP System. Notice that most of the object classes in this model appeared on the workflow diagram as workflows or entities. The attributes (i.e., data) of these object classes appear as data in affinity diagrams; the business process and functional area subjects are shown as activities and functional areas in affinity diagrams.

Working from these models, we can create a variety of affinity diagrams. For example, the affinity diagram in Table 5.3 (on page 186) relates functional areas to data in Bigg's Department Store SOP system. Such data/functional-area and data/activity affinity diagrams should focus only on primary or major users and creators of data. This is especially important when looking at activities that create data. Because every activity that creates data, by default, is also a user of that data, any activity or functional area that is labeled with a "C" could also be labeled with a "U." Doing so, however, may misrepresent the significance of the relationship between that activity and data.

For example, look at the Cash Sales Receipt, Charge Receipt, and Order Pickup Receipt rows in Table 5.3. In the Sales functional-area column, the "C" in these rows represents the task of creating these receipts as sales transactions are processed; no other major use of these receipts really exists for the Sales functional area. In the Order Pickup column, on the other hand, the "C/U" in these rows indicates that there are fundamentally different activities associated with these receipts. The Order Pickup Clerk "uses" these receipts to determine which items (and how many) to give to the customer, whereas the clerk "creates" these receipts by updating them to reflect the fact that specific items (as indicated by serial numbers) have been given to the customer. Note that in Tables 5.3, 5.4 and 5.5, the shaded column indicates the functional area most widely used in the organization's activities.

The same cautions apply to activity/functional-areas affinity diagrams that indicate whether each functional area has "some" or "major" involvement in an activity. For example, in the affinity diagram shown in Table 5.4, notice that Sales has major involvement in the "Process sales transactions" activity but Credit and Order Pickup have no involvement. However, in

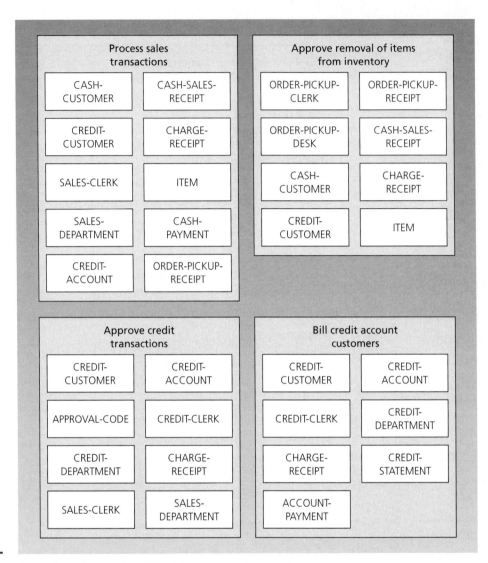

FIGURE 5.6 Enterprise object model of Bigg's Department Store SOP system

the "Approve removal of inventory items" activity, Order Pickup has major involvement, and in the "Approve credit transactions" activity, Credit has major involvement. Furthermore, Sales has some involvement in each of these activities.

These designations reflect the fact that it is possible to process a sales transaction with no involvement by Order Pickup (if the items purchased are carry out) and Credit (if the customer pays cash); however, it is not possible to approve a credit transaction or to remove items from inventory without at least some involvement by Sales. In the "Approve credit transactions" activity, Sales must request the approval; in the "Approve removal of inventory items" activity, Sales generates the order pickup receipt. Thus, Sales has at least some involvement in each of these activities.

TABLE 5.3 Data/functional-area affinity diagram

Data	Functional Area		
	Sales	Credit	Order Pickup
Account Payment		C	
Approval Code	U	C	
Cash Customer	U		
Cash Payment	C		
Cash Sales Receipt	C		C/U
Charge Receipt	C	U	C/U
Credit Account	U	C	
Credit Clerk		U	
Credit Customer	U	C	
Credit Statement		C	
Item	U		U
Order Pickup Clerk			U
Order Pickup Receipt	C		C/U
Sales Clerk	U		

TABLE 5.4 Activity/functional-area affinity diagram

Activity	Functional Area		
	Sales	Credit	Order Pickup
Process sales transactions	Major		
Approve credit transactions	Some	Major	
Approve removal of inventory items	Some		Major
Bill credit account customers		Major	

The affinity diagram in Table 5.5 relates data to activities, indicating that certain data are created by one activity and used by another. Review the user interviews in Figure C.4 and notice that certain data—for example, Sales Clerk and Order Pickup Clerk—are "used" by an activity in that their employee numbers are written on the receipt generated by processing sales and approving removal of inventory items.

Our purpose here was to use a relatively simple case description to illustrate enterprise analysis and affinity diagrams. Because the workflow diagrams and enterprise object model derived from this simple case document only a segment of the Bigg's Department Store

TABLE 5.5 Data/activity affinity diagram

	Activity			
Data	Process Sales Transactions	Approve Credit Transactions	Approve Removal of Inventory Items	Bill Credit Account Customers
Account Payment				C
Approval Code	U	C		
Cash Customer	U			
Cash Payment	C			
Cash Sales Receipt	C		C/U	
Charge Receipt	C	U	C/U	U
Credit Account	U	U		U
Credit Clerk		U		
Credit Customer	U	U		U
Credit Statement				C
Item	U		U	
Order Pickup Clerk			U	
Order Pickup Receipt	C		C/U	
Sales Clerk	U			

organization, the affinity diagrams created from these models provide insight into only a segment of the organization's functional areas, data, and activities. The incompleteness of this view is obvious in that the affinity diagrams do not indicate the creators of some of the data. For example, what functional area or activity creates the Credi Account data? In practice, your affinity diagrams should document the activities and functional areas that create each type of data. And, in practice, you would extend your enterprise analysis to ensure that the creator of each type is included in your models.

USING AFFINITY DIAGRAMS

One major use of affinity diagrams, particularly the activity/data matrix, is to identify cross-functional processes. Identifying interrelated activities and data helps an organization to assess potential information system applications that can data activities into a unified, cross-functional business process. For example, the affinity diagram in Table 5.2 indicates that Sales Order data are widely used by a number of activities. Similarly, the affinity diagram in Table 5.3 indicates that, in Bigg's SOP system, Charge Receipt data are most widely used. This widespread use suggests the possibility of integrating the activities that create and use these data into a unified process and then developing an information system that provides a common database used by all these activities.

The second major use of affinity diagrams in enterprise analysis is to evaluate which activities should be supported by information systems. Obviously, higher priority should be given to systems development projects that benefit the organization as a whole. The key, then, is to determine which information system application is likely to benefit the widest segment of the organization. The data/activity affinity diagram is especially useful in this type of analysis.

In using this matrix to identify processes to support, a systems analyst's first inclination might be to focus on those data that are used by the greatest number of activities—that is, to focus on the "U"s in the matrix. The problem with this focus is that an application that *uses* a wide variety of data may be assigned higher priority than the application that actually *creates* the data used in these activities. How beneficial is a system that requires data that do not exist? The analyst's second inclination is then to focus on the "C"s in the matrix, the activities that create the most data. But this, too, is a flawed approach because it ignores which data are used most widely. By combining the two approaches, however, we come up with a decision rule for using affinity diagrams to prioritize systems development requests:

Assign the highest priority to *applications that create the data* that are *used most widely* across the organization.

In short, this guideline says that you start by determining which data are used most widely (count the number of "U"s for each type of data), and then develop the applications that are the primary creators of that data (identify the activities with "C"s for that data). Analyzing the affinity diagram in Table 5.2 in this way shows that the Sales Order data are used by seven activities, ranging from "Research market" to "Ship orders" to "Pay employees" and that "Enter sales orders" and "Ship orders" are the two primary creators of Sales Order data. Thus, highest systems development priority should be given to applications that support "Enter sales orders" and "Ship orders," that is, the process of order fulfillment.

Check Your Understanding 5-2

Reread the case study, "Automating Rentals at Ryder," to answer the following questions.

1. We can assume that Ryder's consumer truck rental business unit performs numerous activities that were not investigated in the RyderFirst project, for example, purchasing and servicing trucks, selecting dealers, managing cash flows, etc. Which activities did the RyderFirst project address?

2. Clearly, we can assume that Rental Truck is one type of data in the RyderFirst system. Which activities are most likely to create or use this data? Why?

◈ REVIEW OF CHAPTER LEARNING OBJECTIVES

1. *Describe the top-down approach and its three levels of analysis.*

The top-down approach begins by examining the organizational context, then the functional areas or management levels affected by the system under study, and finally the specific information system that is the focus of the project. This approach assumes that the environment of a system must be understood before the system itself is analyzed. It also recognizes that an information system serves an organization by performing certain business functions; thus, to ensure that an information system satisfies the organizational relevance goal, the system's organizational context must be understood.

2. *Discuss the purpose and techniques of enterprise analysis.*

Enterprise analysis provides an overview of an organization's business objectives, structure, information needs, data, and processes. Among the techniques used here are critical success factor (CSF) analysis, affinity diagrams, and enterprise modeling. CSF analysis involves interviewing people at various management levels to identify the factors critical to the organization's success. Affinity diagrams provide an organizational overview in the form of matrices relating one organizational dimension (e.g., data) to another dimension (e.g., functional areas).

Enterprise models provide graphical representations of an organization's structure, workflows and entities. An organization chart models an organization's structure, representing the reporting structure and locus of responsibility between the management levels and the functional areas. Workflow diagrams trace the flow of data—typically embodied in documents—among internal and external entities. An enterprise object model identifies and groups all objects of interest to the organization into subjects; each subject group represents the classes involved in a particular functional area, business process, or other classification of interest to the organization.

3. *Discuss the purpose and process of critical success factor (CSF) analysis.*

CSF analysis is a technique used to identify the few things an organization must do well in order to succeed in its environment. Critical success factors emanate from five sources: industry, competitive strategy, environmental factors, temporal concerns, and managerial focus. CSF analysis employs the top-down approach in that it begins by interviewing upper management to gain an understanding of management concerns and critical decisions. Then CSF analysis defines the information—and information systems—needed to address these concerns and make these decisions. Determining critical success factors at the organizational and process/departmental level guides the organization's information system strategy, provides a rationale for prioritizing projects, and helps identify the measurable objectives an information system is to attain.

4. *Use enterprise models to create affinity diagrams.*

Enterprise models—organization charts, workflow diagrams, and enterprise object models—are used to identify the functional areas, activities, and data to be documented in affinity diagrams. All of the entities in an organization chart and the internal entities in workflow diagrams represent functional areas. The external entities and workflows in workflow diagrams and all the objects in an enterprise object model represent potential data to be used in affinity diagrams. In addition, by analyzing the workflow diagrams, you can identify major processes, which are represented as activities on affinity diagrams.

5. *Explain the purpose of affinity diagrams.*

An affinity diagram is a matrix that shows the intersection of two dimensions of the organization, for example, activities and functional areas or activities and data. Analysts create affinity diagrams during enterprise analysis (1) to gain a broad, enterprise-wide overview of information throughout the organization, thus helping analysts to visualize the information interdependencies among functional areas and activities, and (2) to help the organization to establish development priorities among potential information system applications.

◈ KEY TERMS

affinity diagram	enterprise analysis	systems analysis
business area analysis	enterprise models	top-down approach
business objective	enterprise object model	workflow diagram
CSF analysis	organization chart	

◈ DISCUSSION QUESTIONS

1. Explain how adopting the top-down approach can help you achieve the organizational relevance goal of systems development.

2. Discuss the two phases in enterprise analysis. What activities are performed in each stage? What is the purpose of these activities?

3. List and define the five sources of critical success factors.

4. Explain how conducting a CFS analysis helps you determine which information systems to develop.

5. How is each of the enterprise models—organization chart, workflow diagram, and enterprise object model—used to create affinity diagrams?

6. What are the two major uses of affinity diagrams?

◈ EXERCISES

1. Reread the short case description in Exercise 4, Chapter 1. Based on this sketch of Business Consultants, Inc., what factors are critical to the firm's success?

2. Reread the short case description in Exercise 5, Chapter 1. Based on this sketch of VF Corp.'s Lee Jeans Division, what factors are critical to the business unit's success?

3. The Chapter 2 opening case, "Retail Sales Processing and SKU Replenishment," describes some of the business operations of a major clothing retailer. Based on this sketch, what factors are critical to the retailer's success?

4. Reread the Chapter 3 opening case, "Banking on Object Technology." According to this case, what factors are critical to the success of financial institutions?

5. Create a data/activity affinity diagram by analyzing the models you created for the Delta Office Products case in Exercises 5 and 7 of Technical Module C. Analyze your affinity diagram to identify opportunities to integrate activities into a cross-functional process. Explain why these activities are candidates for integration.

6. Reread the Chapter 2 opening case, "Retail Sales Processing and SKU Replenishment." Create a functional area/activity affinity diagram to document the functional area(s) responsible for each activity.

7. Reread the Chapter 4 opening case, "Streamlining Order Fulfillment at CAV." Create an activity/data affinity diagram indicating the data created and used by each activity.

8. Analyze the affinity diagram you created in Exercise 7 to answer the following questions:
    a. Which activity creates the data used most widely by other activities?
    b. What process integration possibilities are suggested by your diagram?
    c. Explain why CAV's new order fulfillment system was so successful given your analysis of this affinity diagram.

◆ REFERENCES

Bullen, C. V., and J. F. Rockart. *A Primer on Critical Success Factors.* Center for Information Systems Research, Working Paper 69. Cambridge, MA: Sloan School of Management, MIT, June 1981.

Flaatten, P. O, et al. *Foundations of Business Systems.* Hinsdale, IL: The Dryden Press, 1989.

Martin, J. *Information Engineering: Book II, Planning and Analysis.* Englewood Cliffs, NJ: Prentice-Hall, 1990.

Rockart, J. F. "Chief Executives Define Their Own Data Needs." *Harvard Business Review,* March/April, 1979.

PROBLEM DEFINITION AND FEASIBILITY ANALYSIS

Preliminary Investigation and Analysis

1. Perform enterprise analysis.

2. *Determine system objectives, project constraints, and scope.*

3. *Evaluate feasibility and get approval to proceed.*

4. Conduct JAD sessions to verify objectives, constraints, and scope; to redesign process, if necessary; and to identify requirements.

SCOPE ON A ROPE

Beware of the friendly user who nods agreeably as you define the project you are about to undertake. Gopal Kapur, president of the Center for Project Management, notes that such users portend "scope on a rope" that will surely "hang you in the end."

The adage "Give a man enough rope and he'll surely hang himself" describes the situation for many IS projects. Project scope states the boundaries of the system to be analyzed, designed, and implemented; it states what aspects of the organization will be addressed by the project and what the project will attempt to do. When defined too loosely, scope hangs many a development team, as indicated in a recent survey by Kapur's center, which found that half of all IS projects exceed their budgets and schedules and fail to deliver the full functionality promised.

How can you avoid scope pitfalls and ensure that your project delivers on its promise? Here are some guidelines offered by the experts:

◆ Make sure that users are actively involved and understand the functionality the project will deliver. "Pin your user down—immediately," cautions Jeff Koroknay, program manager of global project management at Honeywell, Inc. You can't afford to second-guess exactly what they want the project to accomplish.

◆ State what things *will not* be attempted in the project. Joan Knutson, president of Project Management Mentors, Inc., notes that fences are built to keep things in—and out! You can clarify project scope by indicating what is "outside the fence."

◆ Understand that scope will change as the project progresses. John Tuman Jr., president of Management Technologies Group, describes scope management as "a process of discovery" in which scope must be defined iteratively. In fact, the Center for Project Management's 24-step project management methodology defines desired scope, possible scope, detailed scope, and reconfirmed scope at various points in the project.

◆ Understand that additional user demands are not the only causes of a scope change—budget or schedule slippage also affect project scope. Diana Garrett, IS program manager at Intel Corp., says, "Don't ever count on catching up later. It's not going to happen." Ray Ju, a senior project manager at Wells Fargo Bank, cautions that "if your schedule slips, then you have to either devote more people to the project, and that affects your costs, or eliminate functionality." In other words, the original project scope may have to change to stay within the project budget and schedule.

Adapted from A. LaPlante, "Scope Grope." *Computerworld,* March 20, 1995, pp. 81–82, 84. Copyright 1995 by Computerworld, Inc., Framingham MA 01701. Reprinted from Computerworld.

This chapter explains the problem definition activities of the preliminary investigation and analysis stage. After you have conducted an enterprise analysis to determine how to integrate activities and to prioritize systems to develop, your next step is to define the problem addressed by the systems development effort. You do this by (1) identifying symptoms of inefficiencies or other problems with the existing information system and (2) determining the objectives and project constraints and scope of an improved system. As the chapter opening case illustrates, poorly-defined projects are the road to ruin. Achieving the project management goal of systems development requires the analyst to define precisely what a project will do. It also requires the assessment of the feasibility of successfully designing and implementing the system. The findings from the preliminary investigation and analysis stage are documented in a problem definition report.

After completing this chapter, you should be able to

1. Define system objectives, project constraints, and project scope.

2. Name four types of feasibility, and explain how each affects an organization's decision to develop a system.

3. Define development costs, production costs, and system benefits.

4. Perform a cost-benefit analysis, and discuss its role in determining economic feasibility.

5. Use a Project Risk Evaluation form to evaluate the feasibility of a project.

6. Prepare a problem definition report to document your findings.

6.1 ◈ DEFINING THE PROBLEM: SYMPTOMS, OBJECTIVES, CONSTRAINTS, AND SCOPE

Chapter 1 noted that the catalysts for a systems development effort include user demand, technology push, and strategic pull. Whichever of these factors is the catalyst for a project, most projects are initiated in one of three ways. First, as discussed in Chapter 5, an organization may conduct an enterprise analysis to determine which systems need to be developed. Second, in organizations with their own information systems (IS) staff, a user with the authority to initiate a project submits a Request for System Services and requests a preliminary meeting with IS developers. Third, in organizations without an IS staff—or with a heavily backlogged staff—a user may request a preliminary meeting with an outsourcer or consultant. An example of a Request for System Services form is shown in Figure 6.1; similar information would be provided to an outsourcer or consultant in a request for proposal, letter, or phone conversation requesting consulting services.

Your first step is to define the problem to be addressed by the project. **Problem definition** requires you to identify symptoms that indicate a problem with the existing information system; and to determine the objectives, constraints, and scope of the development project.

IDENTIFYING SYMPTOMS

When a project is initiated by a user's Request for System Services, one of your tasks as a systems analyst is to identify symptoms indicating that the existing information system is not meeting user needs. A **symptom** is evidence that an existing information system is inefficient or ineffective. For example, in the Request for System Services shown in Figure 6.1, Ed Higgins notes inefficiencies that are symptoms that the current system is not meeting Accounting's needs. As the systems analyst, you need to determine the cause of these symptoms by (1) interviewing users and (2) observing the system in operation.

As you interview users, you should encourage them to quantify system problems. For example, how much time is too much time? How many errors are too many errors? You may need to interview supervisors and managers to determine how much time is allocated to each activity and what an acceptable error rate is. Not only will these metrics help you quantify the current problems; they will also help you to set targets for the new system to achieve and provide base figures against which to measure the new system's contributions. In this era of *total quality management* (TQM), many organizations have established targets for these measures of system efficiency. If the current information systems impede progress toward achieving these TQM targets, developing new systems may be the only way to improve efficiency.

Although interviewing end-users is an effective way to identify symptoms of system problems, you should also observe the system to gain additional information. For example, interviewing Ed Higgins may reveal that he estimates that at least 25 percent of all order pickup transactions take more than 15 minutes to complete. You need to determine the cause of this inefficiency. Observing order pickup transactions may reveal that clerks are not diligent about their jobs or that the company does not use warehouse space effectively. On the other hand, perhaps the order pickup clerks' efforts are thwarted because items listed on

Request for System Services Bigg's Department Store	Page 1 of 1

System *Sales Order Processing*	Date *August 5, 1997*

Division
  Accounting
	Supervisor
	  Ed Higgins

Extension
  2-5613
	Signature
	  Edward Higgins

Description of Problem

Current sales order processing is too cumbersome. Especially with credit transactions, customers complain about the time required to process a sale. Also, order pickup and credit statement processing are error-prone.

Requested Services

Develop sales order processing and credit account processing system that exploits new technologies to improve customer service.

(IS Use Only)

Action Taken

Scheduled preliminary meeting with Ed for 8/25 to determine objectives, constraints, and scope.

IS Signature   *Jennifer Nguyen*   Date   *August 22, 1997*

FIGURE 6.1   Request for information services form

the order pickup receipt are not in stock or perhaps data entry errors cause clerks to search in vain for nonexistent items. If items being out of stock is the root cause of the problems in order pickup, a change in the inventory control system may be needed more than a revamped sales order processing system.

DETERMINING SYSTEM OBJECTIVES

System objectives describe the business goals of the system; in other words, what benefits will the business obtain by developing the system? The benefits derived from information systems include improved efficiency, effectiveness, and competitiveness. *Efficiency* benefits include reduced labor costs, increased transactions, and improved accuracy or reliability. *Effectiveness* benefits include more complete and/or timely information for decision making. In general, the efficiency and effectiveness benefits are closely related to the characteristics of good information summarized in Table 6.1. *Competitiveness* benefits include helping the organization to implement its competitive strategy (e.g., become a low-cost producer or create tight linkages with its customers and suppliers). As further illustration of business benefits, Table 6.2 lists some of the benefits organizations can derive by using information technology to support their competitive strategies.

System objectives should be stated in *measurable terms*. For example, instead of stating a system objective as "Increase transactions per hour," you should state it as "Increase transactions per hour by 25 percent this quarter." Stating measurable objectives is facilitated if you identified measures and metrics as you interviewed users and observed the system in operation. Other examples of measurable system objectives include the following:

◆ Reduce the error rate from the current average of 5 errors per 100 transactions to less than 1 error per 100 transactions.

◆ Reduce turnaround time from the current average of 10 days to an average of 2 days.

◆ Approve credit transactions within 10 seconds by the end of the first month of processing.

TABLE 6.1 Characteristics of good information

Characteristic	Definition
Complete	Information is complete if it provides all the facts of interest to its users. For example, to satisfy the needs of sales representatives, a complete inventory status report must list each item's quantity on hand, quantity on order, and expected delivery date.
Accurate	Information is accurate if it contains no errors. For example, all calculated and retrieved values on a report must be correct, and the database must contain only valid data.
Timely	Information is timely if it is available when users need it. For example, in many organizations, a timely inventory status report is one that is up-to-the-minute, i.e., one that is updated as inventory is received or depleted.
Relevant	Information is relevant if it is useful in performing the tasks for which it is provided. For example, quantity on hand, quantity on order, and expected delivery date are all relevant information for a user trying to decide whether an order can be filled in a timely manner.
Easy to understand	Information is easy to understand if it is described and presented in a manner appropriate to its users. In other words, reports should be formatted with white space, clear headings and labels, and an appropriate report title. Field names, where feasible, should reflect the terms users employ to describe the data.
Reliable	Information is reliable if its users can depend on its accuracy, completeness, and verifiability as they use it to make decisions.
Consistent	Information is consistent if the database from which reports are generated does not contain any inconsistent data, e.g., three different records for the same customer, each listing a different address. A report is consistent if the same labels, headings, and title are always used for the same information. Two or more reports or files are consistent if the same name is used to describe shared fields.
Economical	Information is economical if the costs of gathering, manipulating, and reporting the information do not exceed the information's value to its users.

TABLE 6.2 Examples of Business Benefits

Competitive Strategy	Application/Value	
	Efficiency	Effectiveness
Be the low-cost producer.	Use source data automation and integrated manufacturing systems to increase the number of transactions performed or widgets produced from the same amount of resources.	Use information reporting and communication systems to reduce the cost of controlling the process while exploiting economies of scale.
Differentiate product or service.	Attain unparalleled quality using statistical control systems to monitor production; use sales force automation to reduce order cycle time and processing costs.	Exploit existing transaction data about customers to improve and to personalize service; use sales force automation to maintain up-to-the-minute product data.
Create a market niche.	Use database marketing to reduce the cost and effort of identifying potential markets.	Exploit existing transaction data about customers to identify and to assess the viability of new products and services.
Create tight linkages with suppliers and customers.	Use EDI, electronic mail, and the Internet to reduce costs of communicating with suppliers and customers.	Create interorganizational systems to lock in suppliers and customers, to monitor consumer trends, and to prevent stock-outs.

IDENTIFYING PROJECT SCOPE AND CONSTRAINTS

Another activity in problem definition is identifying the project scope and constraints. **Project scope** specifies what is or is not included in the study; it limits the functions and business areas addressed by the project. By stipulating the specific functions the project is to address, the user-sponsor can ensure that the project is focused. For example, the user-sponsor may stipulate that only data and processes required to control inventory are to be investigated in the project. Thus, the development team would have overstepped its boundaries if it investigated and implemented an accounts payable system. Or, as another example, the user-sponsor may stipulate that the system is to be implemented only in stores with an annual sales volume greater than $5 million.

Project scope should define the organizational, business area, and/or functional boundaries of a project. **Organizational boundaries** specify which business units, divisions, or branches of an organization are to be studied. For example, a major retailer may stipulate that a system is to be implemented for Store A; if the Store A system is a success, the system will gradually be "rolled out" to other stores. **Business-area boundaries** define which areas within the business are to be studied. For example, the retailer may stipulate that only the human resources area is to be investigated. **Process boundaries** stipulate which processes are to be investigated. For example, the retailer may stipulate that the project is to examine only the compensation analysis function within human resources. As noted in the chapter opening case, clearly specifying the system's functionality is critical to project success.

Whereas project scope stipulates what will be studied, project **constraints** limit the resources allocated to the project for analysis, design, and implementation. Resources include time, money, and personnel, all of which are limited for any organization. Examples of resource constraints include the following:

◆ Development costs must not exceed $100,000.

◆ The system must be placed in production by January 1, 1997.

◆ A team of two designers and three implementers will be assigned full-time to the project.

◆ No additional personnel may be hired to operate the system.

◆ The department's existing hardware must be integrated into the new system.

◆ No new hardware is to be purchased.

Other constraints impose user requirements that the system must satisfy. For example, the user-sponsor may stipulate that the new system must be easy to learn and use.

Sometimes the constraints imposed on a project limit your ability to achieve the system objectives. For example, the user-sponsor may expect a complex system to be operational in six months and to achieve exceptional benefits, but will devote only $15,000 and two developers to the project. In this situation, you may not be able to achieve the benefits within the constraints. You need to recognize this incompatibility of objectives and constraints as early in the project as possible. (Recall the good, fast, cheap trade-offs in Figure 1.7.) Thus, you should conduct a feasibility study as one of your first project activities. Section 6.2 presents two techniques for analyzing feasibility: the cost-benefit analysis and the project-risk evaluation.

Check Your Understanding 6-1

Identify each of the following as a statement of system objectives (O), project constraints (C), or project scope (S).

_____ 1. The proposed system will address the information needs of the sales order entry and inventory control users; accounts receivable will be automated at a later date.

_____ 2. The proposed system must incorporate existing hardware and software.

_____ 3. The proposed system will reduce transaction costs 25 percent.

_____ 4. The system must be operational by June 1.

_____ 5. Three programmer-analysts and two users will be assigned to the development team.

_____ 6. The proposed system will plan for, but will not implement, electronic links between our Purchasing Department and suppliers.

_____ 7. The proposed system will increase the accuracy, completeness, and timeliness of information.

_____ 8. The development costs must not exceed $450,000.

6.2 ◈ ECONOMIC FEASIBILITY: ESTIMATING COSTS AND BENEFITS

Early on, when an organization is just beginning to consider developing an information system, it is important to determine the system's **economic feasibility**—that is, whether it is within the appropriate realm of cost. In other words, are the anticipated benefits to be derived from the system equal to or greater than its expected costs? And can the system be developed to achieve the expected benefits within the resource constraints imposed by the user-sponsor?

To determine economic feasibility, you need to identify the expected costs and benefits of the system and perform a cost-benefit analysis.

SYSTEM COSTS

The costs of developing and operating an information system are unique to each system. **Development costs**, which are incurred during the development phase of the system life cycle, include all the costs of analyzing, designing and implementing an information system. These costs can include payroll for IS labor or hired consultants, purchasing hardware, writing or purchasing software, converting data from one file format to another, training users, preparing and duplicating documentation, preparing a special facility to house the computer system, and the costs of the myriad other activities in systems development. **Production costs**, which are incurred during the production phase of the system life cycle, are the costs of operating and maintaining the system. These can include additional labor costs for systems personnel, planned hardware and software upgrades, increased utility costs, supplies such as disks and paper, and any other costs associated with operating the production system.

All of these costs are tangible and quantifiable. But a systems development project and the operation of the delivered system may also incur intangible costs, which are more difficult to quantify. For example, how can you estimate the costs of reduced productivity and increased errors while users are adapting to the system? Similarly, how can you estimate the costs of integrating the new system with legacy systems? These potential costs are difficult to quantify, but they may make the difference between a system that is cost effective and one that is not.

SYSTEM BENEFITS

The benefits from implementing a system are as varied as the costs. **Tangible benefits** are those that can be readily quantified, that is, assigned a monetary value. These can include reduced head count, reduced cost per transaction, increased transactions per day, reduced errors and rework, new sources of income made possible by the system, and so on. **Intangible benefits** are those that are not readily quantified. For example, how do you place a dollar value on improved employee morale, improved business reputation, better customer service, and so on?

Where possible, try to quantify the intangible benefits by linking them to tangible benefits. For example, improved business reputation and better customer service may mean more customers and more repeat business, respectively. If these benefits ensue, what would be the likely increase in revenue? Similarly, improved employee morale may be linked to increased productivity or reduced absenteeism. What dollar value can be attached to these gains?

COST-BENEFIT ANALYSIS

Cost-benefit analysis is a widely used method of evaluating the cost effectiveness (economic feasibility) of a capital investment project. To conduct a cost-benefit analysis, you must identify development and production costs and expected benefits and then calculate the payback point.

You have already learned about the first two steps in a cost-benefit analysis: estimating the costs and estimating the benefits. The third step is to calculate the **payback point**: the time required to accumulate enough benefit dollars to "pay back" the cost dollars. Where a system has no production costs and its benefits are stable (that is, the dollar value of the benefits does not vary from one year to the next), you can use a simple formula to calculate the payback point:

Development costs / benefits per year = years to payback

For example, if a system costs $100,000 to develop, has no production costs, and has stable benefits of $25,000 per year, the payback point is four years.

Unfortunately, this simple formula does not fit most systems, which do incur production costs and have benefits that do vary over time. In these situations, you must use a table that accumulates costs and benefits to calculate the payback point. Table 6.3 shows a worksheet table used to perform these calculations. In this table, development costs are indicated in Year 0. Year 1 begins the day the system is put into use, and development costs for Years 1 through 5 arc zcro.

A cost-benefit analysis table indicates the development costs (in Year 0) and production costs (Years 1–5) as well as the expected benefits (Years 1–5). Total costs and total benefits are accumulated, and then benefits are subtracted from costs to determine the accumulated gain or loss. When the accumulated gain or loss figure is positive, we have achieved payback. According to Table 6.3, the XYZ Corp. Inventory System achieves payback in its third year of production, ending that year with a net savings of $8,791.

Notice that Table 6.3 includes some assumptions. Typically, a cost-benefit analysis is performed using a spreadsheet. Consequently, it is possible to take advantage of the "What If?" capabilities of a spreadsheet in performing this analysis. We have treated estimated costs and estimated benefits as assumptions that can be manipulated by our sensitivity factors for costs and benefits. For example, Table 6.3 shows that our best estimate of hardware costs is $50,000; however, we recognize that this estimate may not be accurate. Therefore, we multiply the expected hardware costs by a sensitivity factor (1.1) to evaluate the effect on costs and accumulated gain (or loss) if actual costs are 10 percent higher than our estimated hardware costs. Similarly, we use a sensitivity factor for benefits (0.9) to evaluate the effects on benefits and accumulated gain (or loss) if actual benefits are 10 percent lower than our estimated benefits.

TABLE 6.3 Cost-benefit analysis table

XYZ Corp. Inventory Management System
Cost-Benefit Analysis

Input Section

Estimated Costs			Estimated Benefits	
Hardware	$50,000.00		Inventory Savings	$1,500.00 per week
Software	$7,500.00			
Consultant	$20,000.00			
Training	$20,000.00			

Estimated Benefits

Inventory Savings $1,500.00 per week

Assumptions

Discount Rate:	10%
Sensitivity Factor (Costs):	1.1
Sensitivity Factor (Benefits):	0.9
Annual Change in Prod. Costs:	7%
Annual Change in Benefits:	5%

Estimated Costs

Hardware	$50,000.00	
Software	$7,500.00	
Consultant	$20,000.00	
Training	$20,000.00	
Supplies	$2,400.00	per year
IS Support	$18,000.00	per year
Maintenance	$2,500.00	per year

Calculations/Output Section

Costs	Year 0	Year 1	Year 2	Year 3	Year 4	Year 5
Development Costs						
Hardware	$55,000					
Software	$8,250					
Consultant	$22,000					
Training	$22,000					
Total Development Costs	**$107,250**					
Production Costs						
Supplies		$2,640	$2,825	$3,023	$3,234	$3,461
Network Support Personnel		$19,800	$21,186	$22,669	$24,256	$25,954
Maintenance/Upgrades		$2,750	$2,943	$3,148	$3,369	$3,605
Annual Production Costs		$25,190	$26,953	$28,840	$30,859	$33,019
(Present Value)		$22,900	$22,275	$21,668	$21,077	$20,502
Accumulated Costs (Development and Production Present Value)		**$130,150**	**$152,425**	**$174,093**	**$195,170**	**$215,673**

Benefits

	Year 0	Year 1	Year 2	Year 3	Year 4	Year 5
Reduced Inventory Costs		$70,200	$73,710	$77,396	$81,265	$85,329
(Present Value)		$63,818	$60,917	$58,148	$55,505	$52,982
Accumulated Benefits (Present Value)		**$63,818**	**$124,736**	**$182,884**	**$238,389**	**$291,372**
Present Value of Accumulated Gain or (Loss)		($66,332)	($27,690)	$8,791	$43,219	$75,699
Profitability Index		0.71				

Our worksheet also includes assumptions about inflation. Typically, production costs and benefits may vary from year to year. Perhaps production costs are expected to increase 7 percent and benefits are expected to increase 5 percent each year, as shown in Table 6.3. Or perhaps production costs are expected to increase 15 percent each year, while benefits are expected to decrease 10 percent each year. By including the "Assumptions" in our spreadsheet and multiplying production costs and benefits for Years 1 through 4 by the assigned annual change value, we can gain a better sense of costs and benefits over time.

The payback point can also be plotted on a line graph, as shown in Figure 6.2. Where the line for accumulated costs crosses the line for accumulated benefits, payback is achieved. This graph indicates that XYZ Corp. will recoup the costs of developing an inventory system early in the third year of production.

Why do you need to calculate the payback point? Because with today's rapidly changing information technology and business environment, an information system may become obsolete in a short time. Thus, you need to determine whether a system pays for itself before this happens. Typically, a PC-based system should pay for itself in three years; a larger system, in five to seven years.

Some organizations develop systems even though a cost-benefit analysis reveals that the system will not achieve payback within an acceptable period. Recall that cost-benefit analysis is best applied to projects whose benefits can be quantified. In some cases, the benefits of a system are more intangible and more difficult to quantify. Yet management recognizes the criticality of these systems in staying current and maintaining competitiveness. For example, scanning technology is so integral to the supermarket industry that even if developing a scanning system was not cost-effective, supermarket management would likely fund such a project in the current business environment, because not doing so would be admitting inability to compete.

A cost-benefit analysis provides a more accurate view of a firm's financial investment if it considers the time value of money. You can achieve this by projecting the present value of costs and benefits. **Present value** indicates the monetary value of certain future costs and benefits

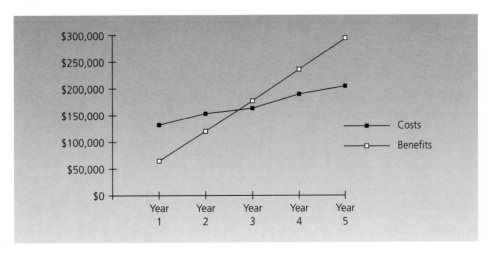

FIGURE 6.2   Line graph showing payback point

in terms of today's dollars. For example, the cost-benefit worksheet in Table 6.3 indicates the present value of production costs and benefits projected five years into the future. It is unlikely that a dollar will be worth as much five years from now as it is worth today, either because of inflation or because the firm could have invested its money in other ways. Present value is calculated using the following formula:

$$PV = \text{Payment} \times (1/(1 + c)n)$$

where c is the cost of money and n is the number of periods projected. The cost of money (also called the discount rate) represents the opportunity costs of investing in an information system rather than some other investment. If an organization could reasonably expect a 7 percent return by investing its money in mutual funds or some other "safe" investment, or if the annual inflation rate is 7 percent, then the cost of money is 7 percent (.07). The value for "Annual Production Costs (Present Value)" in Year 5 was calculated as

$$PV = \$33{,}019 \times (1/(1 + .10)^5)$$

where the cost of money is assumed to be 10 percent and production costs are projected five periods (years) into the future. The same holds true for benefits projected in the future. For example, the present value of "Reduced Inventory Costs" in Year 3 was calculated as

$$PV = \$77{,}396 \times (1/(1 + .10)^3)$$

where n is 3 because the benefits are being projected three years into the future. Indicating the present value of future costs and benefits is critical if these dollar amounts are projected a number of years into the future.

Another measure of a project's value is the **profitability index**, which compares the present value of future benefits to the value of an initial investment. The profitability index shown in Table 6.3 (.71) was calculated by dividing the present value of accumulated gain or loss ($75,699) by the development costs ($107,250). Computing a profitability index is especially helpful when a firm must decide which projects to fund. The example case is not a good investment because its profitability index is less than one. In other words, XYZ Corp. can expect to "profit" less than the development cost of its investment over the five-year projected life of the system.

✓ Check Your Understanding 6-2

1. Categorize each of the following as a development cost (DC), production cost (PC), or as a tangible benefit (TB) or intangible benefit (IB).

_____ a. Purchasing new hardware.

_____ b. Purchasing software upgrades.

_____ c. Converting data.

_____ d. Providing better customer service.

_____ e. Supplies and utilities.

_____ f. Reducing errors and rework.

    ____ g.   Increased sales.

    ____ h.   Designer and implementer labor.

    ____ i.   Improved management decision making.

    ____ j.   Salary of a system manager.

2. For each intangible benefit identified above, explain how you could quantify this intangible benefit by linking it to a tangible benefit.

6.3 ◆ EVALUATING OTHER FEASIBILITY FACTORS

Economic feasibility addresses only one of the goals of systems development: the project-management goal of developing a system within the imposed budget constraints. However, a system that is economically feasible may be infeasible for other reasons: organizational, technical, or operational. Parallel to the cost-benefit analysis for economic feasibility is the **project risk evaluation form** for organizational, technical, and operational feasibility.[1] Figure 6.3 shows a form used to address key factors that affect these feasibility concerns. **Project risk** is the likelihood that a proposed system will not satisfy the systems development goals: a high-quality system that is delivered on time, within budget, and with high user commitment and that helps the organization meet its objectives. The ratings/responses for each risk factor are −1 (no; high risk), 0 (maybe; not a factor either way), or +1 (yes; little or no risk). A +1 (little or no risk) rating for each factor would yield a total score of 14; thus, the higher the total score achieved in the evaluation, the lower is the degree of project risk associated with the project. However, each factor also needs to be considered individually because a negative rating on a few key factors can increase risk substantially. For example, negative ratings on factors 3c (developer familiarity with technology) and 4c (user commitment) and positive ratings on all other factors would yield a total score of 10, which would normally indicate relatively low risk. However, a project requiring developers to use new technologies and lacking user support is actually high-risk. Table 6.4 on page 206 summarizes some of the strategies for reducing the impact of the risk factors.

As noted in Chapter 5, one output of an enterprise analysis is a prioritized list of potential systems development projects. How does an organization decide which of these projects to pursue? To make this decision, the organization must evaluate the costs, benefits, and risks associated with each project. In general, projects tend to fall into a few categories, as illustrated in Table 6.5, shown on page 206. Generally speaking, an organization should avoid high-risk projects unless the benefits are equally high or development of the system is mandated by other factors (for example, government reporting requirements or competitive strategy). However, the adage "No pain, no gain" also applies. Few high-benefit projects are also low-risk projects. Overall, an organization should give highest priority to projects that promise significant benefits and a manageable level of risk.

---

[1] The project risk measures used in this form were adapted from Davis [1982] and Cash et al. [1988].

Project Risk Evaluation			
Project:	Completed by:		Date:
Factors affecting project risk	Rating*		Comments
1. Characteristics of the organization a. Has stable, well-defined objectives?			
b. Is guided by an information systems plan?			
c. Proposed system fits plan and addresses organizational objectives?			
2. Characteristics of the information system a. Model available/clear requirements?			
b. Automates routine, structured procedures?			
c. Affects only one business area? (No cross-functional or interorganizational links?)			
d. Can be completed in less than one year?			
e. Uses stable, proven technology?			

3. Characteristics of the developers
   a. Are experienced in chosen development
      methodology?			

b. Are skilled at determining functional requirements?			
c. Are familiar with technology and information architecture?			
4. Characteristics of the users a. Have business-area experience?			
b. Have development experience?			
c. Are committed to the project?			
Total Points			
*+1 = yes; 0 = maybe; –1 = no			

FIGURE 6.3   Project risk evaluation form. Reproduced from *Systems Development: Requirements, Evaluation, Design, and Implementation,* by E. Jordan and J. Machesky, Boston, MA: PWS-Kent, 1990. © 1990 by boyd & fraser publishing company. All rights reserved.

TABLE 6.4 Strategies to reduce project risk

Risks	Strategies to Reduce Risk
1. Objectives not defined; no information systems plan.	Conduct an enterprise analysis and/or CSF analysis before beginning detailed analysis and design.
2. Unclear requirements and/or no existing system available as model.	Use prototyping to help users identify requirements. Define requirements of new system by carefully analyzing IPOSC functions of existing system.
3. Affects more than one business area or crosses organizational boundaries.	Increase schedule and cost estimates; conduct JAD sessions with user representatives from all affected areas/organizations. Solicit the help of a high-ranking executive to champion the project.
4. Project cannot be completed in one year.	Use phased development or RAD to segment project into smaller deliverables requiring 2 to 3 months between deliveries.
5. Project requires "leading-edge" technology.	Use prototyping; hire an experienced consultant to lead the project; investigate similar systems (if available) at other organizations.
6. Developers are unfamiliar with chosen methodology.	Devote time up-front to training developers in chosen methodology; purchase and train developers in using a CASE tool that guides them through the methodology.
7. Developers are not skilled at eliciting requirements.	Use prototyping; provide additional developer training. Conduct JAD sessions led by experienced facilitator.
8. Developers are unfamiliar with technology and/or information architecture.	Hire an experienced consultant to lead the project; turn the project over to an outsourcer.
9. Users lack business expertise.	Use prototyping; interview more experienced users, perhaps at similar companies.
10. Users lack development experience.	Use JAD to guide users through analysis and design.
11. User commitment is low.	Use JAD to increase participation; assign users to development team; ask a high-ranking executive to champion the project.

TABLE 6.5 Categories of system project benefits and risks

High Priority	Project Description	Comments
↑	Quick payoff with low risk	Every organization needs at least one! Good way to demonstrate value of IS plan.
	High-risk project promising significant benefits	Nothing ventured, nothing gained. The expected benefits are worth the risks.
	Low-risk project that produces benefits over the long term	Safe bet, but no immediate payoff.
	Low-risk, low-benefit project	Why bother? Consider eliminating.
↓ Low Priority	Medium- to high-risk project with few benefits	High stakes for so-so payoff? Consider eliminating.

ORGANIZATIONAL FEASIBILITY

Even if a project is economically feasible, it may not be a wise use of organizational re sources. **Organizational feasibility** addresses concerns about how well the proposed sy tem will contribute to organizational efficiency, effectiveness, and competitiveness. In oth words, does the proposed system support the business objectives of the organization?

Important factors in determining organizational feasibility are listed in the first sectic of the project risk evaluation form, "Characteristics of the organization." First, an organiz tion must know what its objectives are to be able to identify information systems that w help it meet these objectives. An organization without well-defined objectives faces high project risk.

Second, an organization should have an **information systems (IS) plan**: a forward-looking definition of an information architecture and information systems that are aligned with the organization's strategic plan. Many organizations haphazardly develop information systems without considering how they tie into the firm's desired information architecture or how they support its strategic plan. This haphazard development yields a proliferation of in-compatible systems running on a variety of platforms and using a variety of inconsistent da-tabases, hindering efforts to integrate business processes and create cross-functional systems. Thus, organizations that relegate technology decisions to the IS staff and fail to involve se-nior management in defining an IS plan are less successful in using information technology to achieve business objectives [Fedorowitz & Konsynski 1992], thus increasing project risk.

Third, an organization must evaluate whether a proposed system fits its IS plan and ad-dresses its objectives. For example, if an organization has decided to move to a client/server architecture and to become more competitive by creating tight linkages with its customers and suppliers, it should devote its resources to building the information architecture to achieve this goal. Thus, funding an order fulfillment system project that employs a glass-house architecture without creating or at least planning for electronic links to its customers and suppliers may be a waste of organizational resources.

TECHNICAL FEASIBILITY

Technical feasibility addresses concerns about hardware and software capability, reliability, and availability and the skills of the development team. In other words, do the required hardware components exist? Are they reliable? Is the technology tried-and-true or leading-edge? Can software be purchased or custom-developed to perform the system functions? Do in-house developers have experience with these technologies? Are consultants available to guide or to implement the project?

Leading-edge technology is any hardware, software, database, or telecommunications technology that is in its infancy or is so new that few designers and implementers have de-veloped the skills to work with it. Wireless communications and, some would argue, object-oriented systems and client/server architecture are examples. Some organizations have the resources to support projects requiring leading-edge technology. For example, United States Automobile Association (USAA), an insurance company based in San Antonio, Texas, launched a project to reduce the amount of paper stored and processed in its company. At the time, imaging technology was more an idea under development than a readily available technology. But USAA had a highly skilled IS staff and the resources to work with manufacturers to develop and test this technology. So it approved the project and today saves millions of dollars annually in reduced document storage and filing costs.

Most of the questions in the second and third sections of the project risk evaluation form address technical feasibility concerns. The second section, "Characteristics of the information system," evaluates whether the technology is leading-edge and whether similar systems exist that can serve as a model. Project risk increases dramatically if no model is available *and* the technology is leading-edge. However, project risk is lower if developers can study existing systems and/or if the technology is stable and has been proven reliable. You should note that a well-conceived manual system or an automated system in another company may both serve as models for systems development.

The second section also evaluates the complexity of the proposed system. Developing an information system that affects more than one business area or that crosses organizational boundaries is a risky venture; such projects require a longer, more detailed analysis as you investigate the needs of a variety of users who may have very different perceptions of what the system should do and who should "own" what data. In addition, a project that requires more than one year to complete is vulnerable to creeping requirements, thus increasing project risk as the likelihood of delivering the right system is reduced.

The third section, "Characteristics of the developers," evaluates whether the development team has the skills required to design and implement the system. Risk factors here include skill in determining requirements and familiarity with the chosen methodology, technology, and information architecture. Project risk increases when, for example, glass-house developers skilled in the TSD methodology are assigned to develop a client/server system using an OO development methodology.

OPERATIONAL FEASIBILITY

Finally, even if a project is economically, technically, and organizationally feasible, it still may not gain management approval if it is not also operationally feasible. **Operational feasibility** addresses concerns about user acceptance, management support, and the requirements of entities and factors in the organization's external environment. If users are likely to reject the system, is management willing to deal with the employee turnover or reduced productivity that may result? If a project is a business process reengineering (BPR) effort, does it have the commitment of managers across the organization that is so vital to BPR success? Does the proposed system affect customers and suppliers in ways that require coordination with these external entities? Will the proposed system satisfy government regulations imposed on the business?

On the project risk evaluation form shown in Figure 6.3, all of the fourth section, "Characteristics of the users," and questions 2b and 2c evaluate operational feasibility. User business experience and development experience are risk factors in that users who lack this experience are less likely to be able to define their information needs and to work effectively with the development team. In addition, user acceptance is vital to a successful project and a beneficial system. Users must be committed to the project so that they will openly and completely participate in defining system requirements. Users—both end-users and managers—must also be willing to adjust to the changes in organizational structure, culture, and processes that the proposed system will entail. Otherwise, even a well-designed, high-quality system will not be accepted and will not help the organization meet its objectives.

Impact on other business areas and/or external entities must be considered for any project whose purpose is to develop a cross-functional or interorganizational system. For example, when Ford Motor Company decided to reengineer its accounts payable process, it needed to coordinate with suppliers to gain their acceptance of an invoice-free system. Going one giant step further, if an organization decides to streamline its procurement process by eliminating all paper documents and exchanging trade data via EDI, management must be assured that suppliers will implement compatible systems in support of this effort. It benefits a company not at all to develop an EDI system if none of the external entities with which it shares data do the same! And, as noted earlier, the greater complexity of systems that cross functional or organizational boundaries increases project risk.

In addition, operational feasibility entails determining how well the system will comply with legal constraints and requirements. For example, since 1970, the federal government has enacted legislation to safeguard the privacy and security of personal data. The Privacy Act of 1974 set forth guidelines that public—and to some degree, private—institutions must follow to protect individuals from an invasion of personal privacy. Other legislation governs electronic funds transfers (the Electronic Funds Transfer Act of 1979), the collection and use of data for federally funded institutions (the Education Privacy Act), and the kinds of controls a system must enforce (the Foreign Corrupt Practices Act of 1977). Furthermore, the Internal Revenue Service and the Securities and Exchange Commission stipulate what information a business must collect, maintain, and report; how and to whom the information must be reported; and for how long the information must be stored. Businesses must ensure that the systems they develop satisfy these constraints and requirements.

FEASIBILITY ANALYSIS: ONCE IS NOT ENOUGH

The findings from the feasibility analysis are documented in a **feasibility study**: a report to the user-sponsor that defines the problem; verifies the system objectives, constraints, and scope; and analyzes the likelihood of achieving the system objectives within the imposed constraints. Most organizations evaluate project feasibility only once: at the inception of the project. However, studies have shown that cost estimates made at the outset of a project may be off by as much as 80 percent, as shown in Figure 6.4 [Betts 1993]. The inaccuracy of early estimates is largely due to the lack of detailed information available early on. For example, during the preliminary investigation and analysis stage, user requirements have not been specified in detail, nor has a clear sense of the technology required to complete the project been developed. Thus, initial estimates of project cost are at best "ballpark estimates"—and that's assuming you're playing in a very large ballpark!

George J. Zawacki, president of Spectrum International, Inc., a firm that specializes in methodology and planning tools, recommends that a large project have several *funding points* scheduled to coincide with major stages in the project. At the completion of each major stage—requirements definition, preliminary design, detailed design, implementation plan—the project manager should meet with the user-sponsor to discuss progress-to-date and costs-to-date. The project manager needs to inform the user-sponsor of factors that may increase costs or delay delivery of the system and to provide a revised estimate of cost and schedule. If one adopts the iterative approach to scope definition recommended in the chapter opening case, these funding points are also an appropriate time to clarify project scope. With this information, the user-sponsor can choose a course of action: (1) cancel the project, (2) narrow the project scope to include fewer requirements, (3) provide additional time and funds, or (4) devote more resources (people, tools) to the project. Notice that options 3 and 4 are closely related; more resources will increase costs.

These options are related to the good-cheap-fast triangle introduced in Chapter 1. Given the impossibility of developing a good system cheaply and quickly, the user-sponsor has to decide whether to cancel the project, narrow the project scope (i.e., reduce functionality), or increase the schedule and budget.

Work completed	Project steps	Estimating accuracy
2%	1.1 Project proposal with **feasibility**	±80%
	1.2 User requirements	
	1.3 Systems definition	
15%	1.4 **Feasibility study**	±40%
	2.1 Preliminary design	
30%	2.2 **Feasibility study**	±20%
	3.1 Detailed design	
	3.2 Program design	
60%	3.3 **Feasibility study**	±10%
	4.1 Program and test	
	4.2 Implementation plan	
80%	4.3 **Feasibility study**	±10%
	5.1 System test	
	5.2 Installation	
	5.3 Training	
	5.4 Acceptance/changeover	

FIGURE 6.4   Estimating accuracy at five feasibility-study points. Copyright 1995 by Computerworld, Inc., Framingham MA 01701. Reprinted from Computerworld.

Check Your Understanding 6-3

Categorize each of the following as a factor in organizational (OR), technical (T), or operational (OP) feasibility.

_____ 1. Level of user commitment.

_____ 2. Developer familiarity with technology.

_____ 3. System that affects multiple business areas.

_____ 4. Information systems plan.

_____ 5. Users' business knowledge.

_____ 6. Developer familiarity with development methodology.

_____ 7. Clearly-defined objectives.

6.4 ◆ PROBLEM DEFINITION REPORT

As a business or systems analyst, you will need to prepare a number of reports throughout the life cycle of the project. Typically, the first major report is the **problem definition report** (also called a system proposal or project definition report), which presents your "first take" on the project and summarizes your findings from the preliminary investigation and analysis stage. The completed document is presented to the user-sponsor and distributed to all users and developers who will be involved in the joint application development (JAD) session(s). Thus, this report must be clear, concise, and complete; it must provide the foundation for discussing system requirements and solutions in more detail during JAD.

The purpose of the problem definition report is to document (1) your understanding of your mission, including system objectives, project constraints, and project scope; (2) your understanding of the current system, including its organizational context and the catalysts prompting the organization to develop a new system; and (3) your analysis of project risk and feasibility. The report should include an organization chart, workflow diagrams, and an enterprise object model. For small, relatively simple projects, the problem definition report may also specify general design alternatives for the new system.

REPORT ORGANIZATION

A sample outline of a problem definition report is given in Table 6.6. However, you should consult with the user-sponsor to determine the materials that he or she would like included in the report.

The problem definition report should be presented as a formal document accompanied by a *letter of transmittal*, which briefly summarizes major findings and describes your action plan for completing the next stage of development (e.g., JAD and iterative analysis and design). Other report preliminaries may include an executive summary, a table of contents, and a copy of the Information Services Request form (if applicable) or other document authorizing the project. Designed for the busy reader, an *executive summary* provides a concise (usually no more than one page) summary of the report's most important information.

TABLE 6.6 Organization of the problem definition report

I. Preliminaries
  1. Letter of transmittal.
  2. Executive summary (for short reports, include in transmittal letter).
  3. Table of contents (optional for short reports).

II. Report Body
  1. Report overview ("sets the stage" and gives reader direction and orientation).
  2. Current system environment:
      a. Organizational structure (with organization chart).
      b. Affinity diagrams (if requested by user-sponsor).
      c. System workflows (with workflow diagrams).
      d. System processes (with data flow diagrams).
      e. System data (with enterprise object model).
      f. System configuration (system flowchart, if current system is automated).
      g. Problems with current system.
  3. Project definition:
      a. System objectives.
      b. Project scope and constraints.
      c. Feasibility analysis.
  4. General Design Alternatives (optional)

III. Appendices
  1. Copies of survey instruments.
  2. Supplementary materials.

In other words, it should tell the user-sponsor what she or he needs to know to decide whether to proceed with the project. Thus, at minimum, the executive summary of the problem definition report should indicate whether the project seems feasible.

The body of the problem definition report typically contains two major sections. The first describes the current system environment, referring to the organization chart, workflow diagrams, DFDs, and enterprise object model to define the PPDSH components and IPOSC functions of the current system. The second section verifies your understanding of the system objectives, constraints, and scope; it also provides an initial analysis of the feasibility of designing and implementing a new system that will meet the system objectives while adhering to the project constraints.

For relatively simple and common applications of information technology (such as the ubiquitous TPS), it may be feasible to recommend **general design alternatives** in the problem definition report. A general design alternative describes the technology used to solve a problem. For example, a simple payroll system for a small company may employ (1) commercially-available payroll application software, (2) custom-developed COBOL application programs, or (3) custom-developed application software using a fourth-generation language, such as a spreadsheet or database tool. (Each of these options would require different resources.)

General design alternatives can also describe features of the information architecture; for example, a purchasing system might be designed to communicate orders to suppliers either by printing and mailing a purchase order or by establishing an electronic link with suppliers and transmitting purchase orders through EDI. At this stage in the project, only "general" descriptions of options should be used. Outlining general design alternatives early in the development process provides information vital to cost-benefit analysis and project risk evaluation. However, neither developers nor users should select one of the general design alternatives until requirements and system objectives and constraints are fully understood.

The report appendices include any supplementary materials that, although not vital to the report, may provide additional information of interest to readers. For example, if you surveyed customers to gain an understanding of their perceptions of the current system, you should include a copy of your survey instrument in the appendix. Other supplementary materials include articles about similar systems to help users understand possible causes of or solutions to their problems, a glossary of terms, copies of existing system documentation examined during your investigation—basically any materials of value to readers but not critical to an understanding of your findings or analysis.

GUIDELINES FOR PREPARING THE PROBLEM DEFINITION REPORT

As a formal business report, your problem definition report must exhibit effective report-writing techniques. Mastering these techniques is an important skill because ultimately your analysis is of little value if you fail to communicate it effectively. Providing a detailed discussion of report-writing techniques is beyond the scope of this textbook, but we will provide just a few general guidelines. For additional information, you should consult some of the many textbooks and popular books that describe these techniques.[2]

1. Be considerate of your audience. Remember that you are writing for busy readers. Thus, your report should be clear and concise.

   ◆ You can achieve clarity by *expressing your ideas in ordinary language*, not the jargon of MIS. For example, users do not know—and usually do not want to know—what a workflow diagram is or what cardinality is. Therefore, you need to describe these concepts in their language. *Providing logical section headings* also contributes to report clarity.

   ◆ You can achieve conciseness by *eliminating extraneous or tangential information*. As you write each sentence, ask yourself, "Do the readers need to know this to understand my findings or to decide whether to proceed with the project?" If they do not, then you need not include that sentence. *Using bullets or numbered lists* contributes to both clarity and conciseness.

---

[2] For example, a classic textbook is Lesikar, *Report Writing for Business*. However, any business communications text will provide valuable information. You also may want to consult Strunk and White, *The Elements of Style*; Fielden and Dulek, *Bottom Line Business Writing*; or Munter, *Guide to Managerial Communication*. Available in paperback form, these are inexpensive yet invaluable additions to your bookshelf.

2. Use graphics to illustrate your ideas.

◆ Technical graphics, such as workflow diagrams, enterprise object models, and other *modeling techniques should be used sparingly* in reports intended for non-MIS readers. When used, these *graphics should be clearly explained* in the text to ensure that users understand them. Relatively simple diagrams, such as workflow diagrams, are easy to understand and so should require little explanation.

◆ Nontechnical graphics should be used wherever possible to replace arcane modeling techniques. For example, you may want to *use clip-art graphics instead of formal modeling symbols* to illustrate an organization's information architecture (i.e., system flowchart).

3. Use concrete statements to express your ideas.

◆ You can achieve concreteness by *avoiding unsupported generalizations* and *providing examples to illustrate unfamiliar ideas and evidence to support your conclusions*. All major ideas should be developed fully to give readers the information they need to evaluate the project or new system design.

4. Maintain unity within each paragraph or section and coherence between paragraphs or sections.

◆ You can achieve unity by *focusing on just one major idea in each paragraph or section*. Most paragraphs should begin with a topic sentence; each section should begin with an overview of contents.

◆ You can achieve coherence by *organizing your report so that ideas flow logically* from paragraph to paragraph and from section to section. Coherence—how well your report "sticks together"—is also improved by *using transitions* (e.g., however, for example, first, second, in comparison, and so on) as you shift subpoints within a paragraph *and transitional paragraphs* as you move from section to section.

To help you better understand how to prepare a problem definition report, the case illustration that follows this chapter provides a sample report documenting Victoria Hernández's preliminary investigation and analysis of Entertainment to Go's order processing system.

◆ REVIEW OF CHAPTER LEARNING OBJECTIVES

1. *Define system objectives, project constraints, and project scope.*

System objectives, project constraints, and project scope are specified during problem definition. System objectives describe the business goals of the system—typically, improved efficiency, effectiveness, and competitiveness—stated in measurable terms. Project scope specifies what is or is not included in the study; it limits the processes and business areas addressed by the project. Project scope defines the organizational, business area, and/or process boundaries of a project. Project constraints limit the resources allocated to the project. These constraints are management limitations on resources to be used to analyze, design, and implement the system or to operate the system once delivered. Resources include time, money, and personnel. Other constraints impose user requirements that the system must satisfy.

2. *Name four types of feasibility, and explain how each affects an organization's decision to develop a system.*

The four types of feasibility are economic, organizational, technical, and operational. Economic feasibility assesses whether the costs of developing the proposed information system are justified by the benefits the organization expects to derive from the system. Economic feasibility is evaluated by performing a cost-benefit analysis.

Organizational, technical, and operational feasibility are evaluated through a project risk evaluation. Organizational feasibility assesses whether the proposed system will support the business objectives of the organization; in other words, will the new system satisfy the organizational relevance goal of systems development? Concerns here include whether the organization has clearly defined objectives and an information systems plan. Technical feasibility assesses whether the technology required by the new system is stable and readily available and whether the firm's information systems staff has the skills required to design and implement the system. Operational feasibility assesses whether the proposed system will be supported by users and management and will meet any conditions imposed by external entities (e.g., customers, suppliers, government agencies).

3. *Define development costs, production costs, and system benefits.*

Development costs are incurred during the development phase of the system life cycle and include costs such as IS labor, new hardware and software, data conversion, user training, and myriad other costs. Production costs are incurred during the production phase of the system life cycle and include costs such as additional systems personnel, utility costs, supplies, and any other costs of operating the system. System benefits are the tangible and intangible gains produced by the system. Tangible benefits include reduced labor and transaction costs, new sources of income, and any other benefit that can be readily assigned a monetary value. Intangible benefits are less readily quantified; for example, improved employee morale, enhanced business reputation, and better customer service are significant, but difficult to quantify, benefits.

4. *Perform a cost-benefit analysis, and discuss its role in determining economic feasibility.*

A cost-benefit analysis is a method of evaluating the economic feasibility of a capital investment project. To perform a cost-benefit analysis, you first identify the development and production costs and expected benefits. Then these are presented in a table and charted in a graph to determine the system's payback point—the point at which the benefit dollars exceed the cost dollars. With today's rapidly changing information technology and business environment, an information system may become obsolete in a short time. Thus, you need to determine whether a system pays for itself before then.

5. *Use a project risk evaluation form to evaluate the feasibility of a project.*

Project risk assesses the likelihood that a proposed system will satisfy the systems development goals: a high-quality system that is delivered on time, within budget, and with high user commitment and that helps the organization meet its objectives. A project risk evaluation form is a technique for evaluating and documenting the effect of key factors that affect the organizational, technical, and operational feasibility of a system.

6. *Prepare a problem definition report to document your findings.*

The problem definition report presents your "first take" on the project and summarizes your findings from the preliminary investigation and analysis stage. This report documents (1) your understanding of your mission, including system objectives, project constraints, and project scope; (2) your understanding of the current system, including its organizational context and the catalysts prompting the organization to develop a new system; and (3) your analysis of project risk and feasibility. The completed document is presented to the user-sponsor and distributed to all users and developers who will be involved in the joint application development session(s). Thus, this report must be clear, concise, and complete; it must provide the foundation for discussing system requirements and solutions in more detail during JAD.

◆ KEY TERMS

business-area boundaries	operational feasibility	profitability index
constraints	organizational boundaries	project risk
cost-benefit analysis	organizational feasibility	project risk evaluation form
development costs	payback point	project scope
economic feasibility	present value	symptom
feasibility study	problem definition	system objectives
general design alternative	problem definition report	tangible benefits
information systems (IS) plan	process boundaries	technical feasibility
intangible benefits	production costs	

◆ EXERCISES

1. Read the following short case description to identify symptoms, system objectives, and the project scope and constraints.

Business Consultants Inc. (BCI) delivers management-training seminars for businesses in the Quad-City area. To conduct the seminars, the company's trainers must transport whatever audiovisual equipment they require from BCI offices to the business sites, hotels, or convention centers where courses are held. Overhead projectors, VCRs, tape players, monitors, and other A/V equipment are stored in the Media Center, which is staffed by three part-time clerks and managed by Bob Seger. Tracking who has reserved which equipment for which dates is a confusing, tedious, paper-intensive task. Four times in the last week the Media Center staff has had to scramble to locate a piece of equipment for a trainer who had reserved it only to discover that his or her reservation had been misfiled. Bob Seger wants to develop a low-cost, easy-to-use equipment reservation and inventory system on the Media Center's personal computer using Paradox for Windows, a database management system that Bob is currently using to manage printed materials inventory.

a. What symptoms indicate that BCI's current equipment reservation and inventory system is inefficient and ineffective?

b. Given the information in the case, what objectives do you think the new reservation and inventory system is expected to achieve?

c. What is the scope of the proposed development project?

d. What constraints has Bob imposed on the development project?

2. Read the following short case description to identify symptoms and system objectives.

In the late 1980s VF Corp. was experiencing stagnant revenues and losing market share. When the CEO, Lawrence Pugh, investigated the problem, he pinpointed VF Corp.'s Lee Jeans division as the culprit. This division had lost touch with its customers and was lagging behind its competition (e.g., Levi-Strauss). Further investigation revealed that the Lee division lacked effective tools for gathering sales data and tracking market trends; nor could it respond quickly to changes in consumer buying trends because its production cycles were too long. For example, if consumers suddenly took a fancy to bell-bottom jeans, it would be 18 months before bell-bottom jeans came rolling out of Lee factories and onto retailer shelves.

Pugh recognized that VF Corp. needed to use information systems to become more responsive and competitive. So VF Corp. launched a major development project to implement the Market Response System (MRS), which would integrate manufacturing, sales, and marketing data. The MRS would allow smaller, more frequent deliveries to—and manage the jeans inventory of—retailers; it would also gather point-of-sales data from over 300 retailers to track consumer buying trends and provide job-scheduling and factory-management capabilities so that Lee Jeans could respond quickly to these trends.[3]

a. What symptoms indicate Lee Jeans' current systems were inefficient and ineffective?

b. Given the information in the case, what objectives do you think the MRS is expected to achieve?

3. Reexamine the VF Corp. case in Exercise 2 to identify the organizational, business-area, and process boundaries of the Market Response System.

---

4. Read these paragraphs to answer the questions that follow.

Tri-County Insurance is considering a project to automate its policy sales and claims-processing system. Upgrading the existing computer systems and purchasing eight additional systems and a file server will cost approximately $25,000. LAN cards, cabling, and two laser printers will cost about $5,500. In addition, the DBMS server package and other software are estimated to cost $15,000. You have estimated that consulting fees will total about $25,000 to design, implement, and install the system (includes training and documentation). Finally, paying clerks and secretaries and hiring temporary data entry clerks to enter all policy and claim data—currently stored as paper documents in four five-drawer file cabinets—will cost approximately $15,000.

Ongoing costs include the following: a combination LAN specialist/database administrator to manage and maintain the network and database ($40,000 the first year, with a 5 percent increase each subsequent year); supplies ($300 per month); and software/hardware upgrades (approximately $2,000 the first year, $3,500 the second year, and $5,000 per year in subsequent years). The quantifiable benefits to be achieved by the new system include eliminating at least one file clerk (paid $18,000 per year) and one claims adjuster (paid $28,000 per year) and increasing repeat business, generating an additional $25,000 per year in revenue.

  a. Prepare a worksheet to analyze the costs and benefits of the system.
  b. Draw a line graph to indicate the payback point.
  c. Given the results of your analysis, would you recommend that this project be funded? Justify your response.

5. Assume that the Market Response System described in Exercise 2 will be implemented using OCR and EDI technologies to collect point-of-sale data from 300 retailers who sell Lee jeans. Assume also that the system will run on an IBM ES/9000 mainframe and use DB2 as its DBMS. Complete a project risk evaluation form to evaluate the organizational, technical, and operational feasibility of the MRS project. Justify your assessment of each risk factor by referring to case specifics in the "Comments" section of the form. If you are unable to evaluate a risk factor due to insufficient information, indicate so.

6. Read this short case description and the accompanying table of costs and benefits to answer the questions that follow.

MediFact collects data about outbreaks of infectious diseases and compiles the data to produce reports of interest to local, state, and federal health agencies. The company is considering a project to replace its aging minicomputer and dumb terminals—which it leases from a major computer manufacturer—and its stand-alone desktop systems with a 25-node client/server system that would allow users to access and manipulate data more easily. The costs and benefits of the new system are summarized below:

Construction Costs

Purchase, install, and test server	$60,000
Purchase, install, and test 10 Pentium systems	$25,000

Upgrade and test fifteen 486 systems	$10,000
Purchase, install, and test network cards and cabling	$8,000
Purchase, install, and test NOS	$7,500
Purchase, install, and test DBMS	$10,000
Purchase, install, and test other software	$7,500
Convert and validate files	$3,500
Create user documentation	$10,000
Train users (includes lost productivity)	$20,000

Operating Costs

Additional user support and training	$1,000 per node/year
	5% increase/year
Hardware and software upgrades	$0 per node/Year 1
	$200 per node/Year 2
	10% increase/year
Additional utilities	First Year: $10 per node/month
	3% increase/year

Expected Benefits

Amount saved on equipment lease and maintenance	$50,000 per year
	5% increase/year
Amount saved on software licenses	$27,500 per year
	6% increase/year
Increased efficiency	$50,000 per year
	7% increase/year

a. Use a spreadsheet program to prepare a worksheet to analyze the costs and benefits of the system.

b. Generate a line chart to indicate the payback point.

c. Given the results of your analysis, would you recommend that this project be funded? Justify your response.

7. Reread Chapter 4's opening case, "Streamlining Order Fulfillment at CAV." Complete a project risk evaluation form to analyze the organizational, technical, and operational feasibility of the project. Consider the following additional information as you complete your evaluation:

a. The survival of the company depends in large part on its ability to reduce costs and improve customer service.

b. The reengineering/development team included several users and sent weekly project updates to key users.

c. Management required stable technology to implement the system, thus rejecting a general design alternative that employed a client/server.

    d.   The development team had never conducted a reeingeering project before.

    e.   The team exploited CAV's "toolbox" of development techniques as they redesigned the system.

8.   Compare the project risk factors of the CAV case to the project risk factors of the Chapter 4 Check Your Understanding case, "Ford Has a 'Better Idea' for Accounts Payable."

    a.   What factors make the Ford project *more* risky than the CAV project? Why?

    b.   What factors make the Ford project *less* risky than the CAV project? Why?

◈ REFERENCES

Betts, M. "How To Get 'Runaway Projects' on Track." *Computerworld*, March 15, 1993, p. 95.

Cash, J. I., F. W. McFarlan, J. L. McKenney, and M. R. Vitale. *Corporate Information Systems Management: Text and Cases,* 2nd ed. Homewood, IL: Irwin, 1988.

Davis, G. B. "Strategies for Information Requirements Determination." *IBM Systems Journal* 21, no 1 (1982), pp. 4–29.

Fedorowitz, J., and B. Konsynski. "Organization Support Systems: Bridging Business and Decision Processes." *Journal of Management Information Systems*, Spring 1992, pp. 5–25.

Jordan, E. W., and J. J. Machesky. *Systems Development: Requirements, Evaluation, Design, and Implementation.* Boston, MA: PWS-Kent, 1990.

Hammer, M., and G. Mangurian, "The Changing Value of Telecommunications Technology." *Sloan Management Review*, Winter 1987, p. 66.

CASE ILLUSTRATION

A Problem Definition Report for ETG

This installment of the Entertainment To Go (ETG) case illustrates the concepts and techniques of enterprise analysis and problem definition by means of a problem definition report that Victoria Hernandez prepared after her preliminary investigation of ETG.

Recall that Paul Cornell, president of ETG, asked Victoria to study all processes related to selling and renting video tapes, but to focus on walk-in customer order processing. Victoria conducted two JAD sessions, each scheduled for the morning hours before ETG opens for business. During the first JAD session, Victoria worked with Paul and a few of ETG's employees and customers to identify problems with the current system and to define the system objectives, project scope, and project constraints. During the second JAD session, Victoria, Paul, and two ETG clerks examined source documents (membership application form, rental order form, etc.) and identified the internal and external entities, workflows, processes, and objects in ETG's order processing system. In addition, Victoria visited ETG at various times during business hours to observe operations.

The following report presents Victoria's findings and briefly outlines two general design alternatives: one that requires no information technology and one that automates order processing using bar-code and database technology. As you read this report, you should keep in mind both the analysis techniques and the report-writing techniques discussed in the previous chapters. "Notes" are also provided throughout the report to call your attention to some of the report-writing techniques Victoria has employed here. In addition, occasionally notes appear in italics within brackets to emphasize particular techniques.

Hernandez & Associates
23765 North First Street
Anytown, CA 95000
(408) 555-3555

April 7, 1997

Paul Cornell, President
Entertainment To Go
3215 Main Street
Smalltown, CA 95001

Dear Mr. Cornell:

Please find enclosed the report on my preliminary investigation and analysis of ETG's order processing system. The report presents my understanding of ETG's current order processing system, providing an overview of your organization, an analysis of workflows and processes, and an initial view of ETG's objects. In addition, the report summarizes the findings from interviews of selected customers and ETG employees to identify their perceptions of problems with the existing system. Finally, the report documents system objectives and project scope and constraints. It also presents the results of a preliminary feasibility analysis and project risk evaluation.

My preliminary analysis revealed that most of the problems ETG is experiencing are related to duplication of effort and data in your rental order processing system. Because these problems should be readily alleviated by redesigning and automating your order process, I feel certain that ETG will be able to achieve its business goals within the constraints imposed on the project.

The findings in the enclosed report provide the foundation for discussion at our joint application development (JAD) session, which you have asked us to schedule for April 18–20. During the JAD session, I will ask you and your employees to verify the findings in this report and to provide more detail about ETG's requirements.

I and my student consultant Denny Young look forward to meeting with you on the 18th. In the meantime, if you have any questions or concerns, please don't hesitate to call me.

Sincerely,

Victoria Hernandez

Victoria Hernandez, CDP, MBA

Enclosure: Problem Definition Report

NOTES

Paragraph 2: Notice that Victoria's transmittal letter summarizes the major findings of her preliminary investigation, thus providing Paul with the most important information: the project is feasible. This paragraph replaces the executive summary in this short report.

Paragraph 3: Victoria also indicates the next step in the project: the JAD session scheduled for April 18–20.

Problem Definition Report
for
Entertainment To Go

Report Overview

Hernandez & Associates has been retained to develop an automated walk-in customer order processing system for Entertainment To Go (ETG). My mission is to analyze the existing system, to recommend ways to redesign the order processing activities, and then to design and implement a new system that makes this process more efficient and effective. Although I have been asked to document the workflows for all aspects of order processing, including special orders, I will focus on only the walk-in customer system in most of my analysis.

This report summarizes the findings from my preliminary investigation and analysis. The information provided in this report will serve as the foundation for the joint application development (JAD) session to be held April 18–20 at ETG.

I begin by presenting my understanding of ETG's current order processing system. This section includes an overview of the organization, an analysis of workflows and processes, and an initial view of ETG's objects. In addition, this section summarizes the findings from observation of the system in operation and interviews conducted with selected customers and ETG employees to identify their perceptions of problems with the existing system. The second section of the report documents system objectives and project scope and constraints. It also presents the results of a preliminary feasibility analysis and project risk evaluation.

NOTE

This section provides reader orientation and direction, setting the stage for the report that follows.

I. CURRENT SYSTEM ENVIRONMENT

Entertainment To Go (ETG) is a small business owned in partnership by Paul and Corita Cornell. ETG rents and sells movies on tape to a clientele of approximately 1,000 registered members. Its inventory includes approximately 2,500 rental tapes, as well as a varying stock of about 250 tapes available for purchase.

NOTE Notice that Victoria explains the organizational structure in the text of the document; she doesn't expect the organization chart to speak for itself.

Organizational Structure

ETG, like most family businesses, has a very flat organizational structure. At its head is Paul Cornell, who not only oversees daily operations but also purchases inventory and plans the firm's strategies. Paul selects stock and prepares purchase orders for vendors; he gives a copy of each purchase order to the company accountant, who handles payment. Paul's wife, Corita, prepares all the artwork and promotional literature for EGT. She also fills in for other workers on an emergency basis. The other "slots" in the organization include sales clerks who process transactions for walk-in customers, inventory clerks who maintain the tape inventory, special orders clerks who processes orders for businesses and nonprofit organizations, and a company accountant, a part-time position responsible for processing accounts receivable and accounts payable and for maintaining the company's books. All of these employees report directly to Paul, as shown in the organization chart in Figure 1.

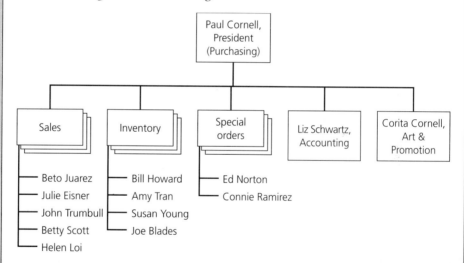

Figure 1: ETG's organization chart

Order Processing Workflows

All the people described in the organization chart are responsible in some way for performing ETG's order-processing tasks. All transactions are performed manually, assisted only by a cash register used to ring up transactions and to generate a receipt. The diagram in Figure 2 illustrates the workflows in the current walk-in customer order processing system. In this diagram, each circle represents an organizational entity, such as Sales or Purchasing; each rectangle represents an external entity, someone

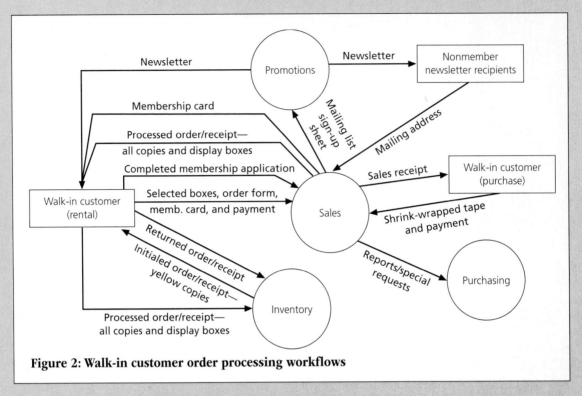

Figure 2: Walk-in customer order processing workflows

NOTE Notice that Victoria explains how to read the diagram in Figure 2. Next, she provides a textual description of the information conveyed by the diagram. Again, Victoria doesn't expect the diagram to speak for itself.

outside ETG, such as a Customer or Vendor; and each directional line indicates the flow of documents (e.g., an order form) or other data (e.g., membership number).

Rental customers select display boxes from the Tapes for Rent shelves and write up their own rental transactions on a rental order form. The rental order form lists the date of the transaction, the stock number and title of each rental tape, and the customer's name, address, and membership number (rental customers must have a rental membership card to rent tapes). The sales clerk verifies the rental order form, rings up the transaction, and processes customer payment. The sales clerk gives all copies of the register receipt and order form to the customer, who takes them to the inventory desk. The inventory clerk and customer sign all copies of the receipt; then the inventory clerk gives the customer the yellow copies and selected tapes. Rental customers give their tapes and their yellow copies to an inventory clerk when tapes are returned. The inventory clerk verifies the return by retrieving the order forms from the Filled Rental Orders file and writing "Returned on <date>" on the order forms. Then the inventory clerk returns the corresponding display boxes to the Tapes for Rent shelves and reshelves the tapes in inventory.

Figure 2 also documents the workflows required to process walk-in sales customers and to create a mailing list. *[Transitional topic sentence]* Walk-in customers who wish to purchase a tape take the shrink-wrapped tape to a sales clerk. The sales clerk rings up the sale, processes customer payment, and gives the customer the yellow copy of the register receipt and the selected tapes. The white copy of the register receipt is discarded. Sales clerks also encourage non-members to sign up to receive ETG's newsletter by providing their mailing address. The mailing list sign-up sheet is forwarded to Promotions, where newsletters are created and sent to all members and mailing list customers.

Figure 3 documents the workflows and entities in special orders processing. Special order customers call or come to the store to place their orders. The special order clerk writes up the order and checks with the inventory clerk to see if the ordered items are in stock. If they are, the special order is filled immediately by giving the tapes and a receipt to in-store customers or by mailing them to call-in customers. Special order customers can be billed later for orders. In this situation, the special order clerk forwards a copy of the order to the company accountant, who sends an invoice to the customer and processes payment when received.

Figure 4 documents the entities and workflows from the purchasing and accounts payable point of view. An additional external entity here is the vendor, who receives purchase orders and payments from ETG and who sends invoices and shipping lists to ETG. When purchasing receives an order from the vendor, the new tape data is transferred to inventory.

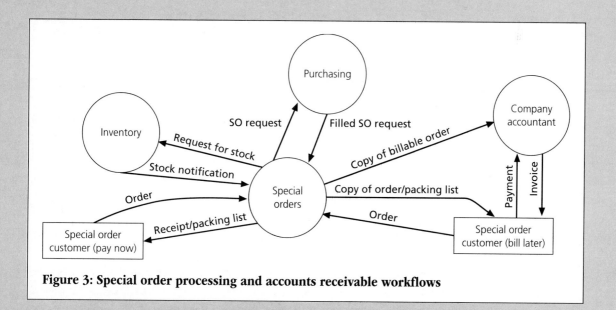

Figure 3: Special order processing and accounts receivable workflows

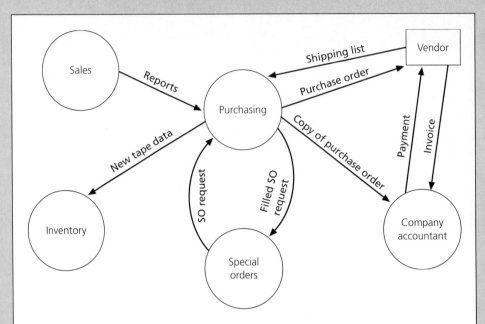

Figure 4: Purchasing and account payable workflows

Figure 5 documents the workflows for all ETG order processing activities, including special order processing. Because special order processing is not the focus of this project, additional detail about this process is not provided here. Figure 5 also highlights the workflows and entities to be investigated further in this study.

Figure 6 presents an overview of ETG's interactions with external entities. Again, workflows and entities to be investigated further are highlighted. Notice that the workflows with ETG's rental customers greatly outnumber those with its sales customers. The greater complexity of the rental order processing workflows is partly due to the fact that rental customers return their tapes whereas sales customers do not. However, the fact that the paperwork (e.g., order form) flows from the customer to the sales clerk, from the sales clerk to the customer, from the customer to the inventory clerk, from the inventory clerk to the customer, and, finally, again from the customer to the inventory clerk points to an inefficiency in this process.

NOTES

In Figure 5, Victoria uses color to indicate the system boundary, thus clearly indicating her understanding of project scope. In the paragraph after her reference to Figure 5, she makes an assertion about the inefficiency of a process and provides examples to support her assertion, thus achieving concreteness and clarity.

Notice that, on the next page, Victoria uses a numbered list for clarity and conciseness. She also uses an asterisk (*) to indicate processes outside the scope of the project. Paul can review this list quickly to verify Victoria's understanding.

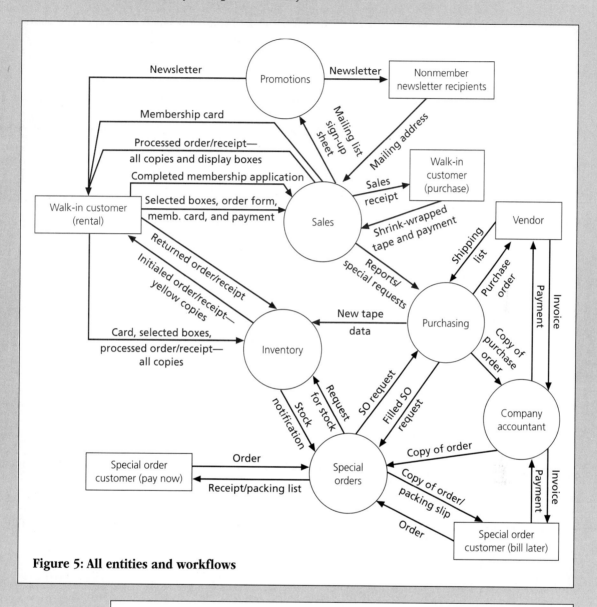

Figure 5: All entities and workflows

Figure 6 also indicates that several tasks are required to process orders. These tasks are summarized below; tasks outside the scope of the project are indicated by an asterisk.

1. Process membership applications.
2. Receive orders from customers:
   ◆ Rental orders
   ◆ Sales orders
   ◆ Special orders*

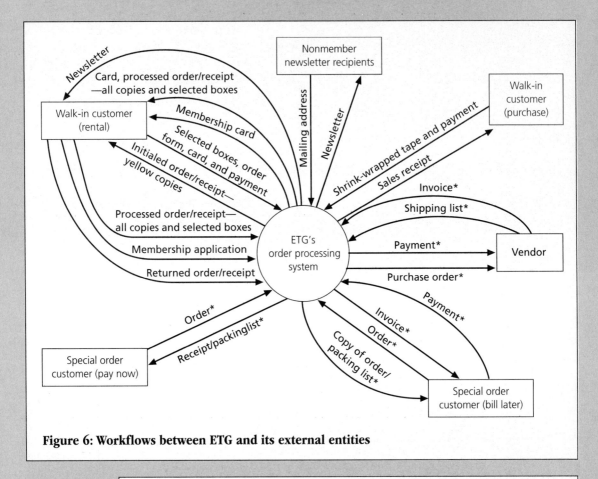

Figure 6: Workflows between ETG and its external entities

3. Generate receipts for customers:
   ◆ Rental receipt
   ◆ Sales receipt
   ◆ Special order receipt*

4. Receive selected boxes, membership card, rental order forms, and receipts from customers.

5. Receive returned rental order forms from customers.

6. Receive mailing address from non-member newsletter recipients.

7. Generate newsletter for rental customers and nonmember newsletter recipients.

8. Receive customer payments:
   ◆ Rental order payments
   ◆ Sales order payments
   ◆ Special orders paid in store*
   ◆ Special orders billed and paid later*

9. Generate invoices for bill-later special order customers.*

10. Generate purchase orders to vendors.*

11. Receive invoices from vendors.*

12. Receive shipping lists from vendors.*

13. Generate payments to vendors.*

This list includes only those processes that require interaction with ETG's vendors and customers. However, preliminary observation of the system in operation reveals that a number of internal processes must also be performed. These processes—as they relate to the walk-in customer order process—include verifying order form information, maintaining rental order form and membership files, verifying timely return of rental tapes, and restocking display boxes and tapes. These processes are analyzed more fully in the data flow diagrams shown in Figures 7 and 8.

A data flow diagram (DFD) documents the inputs to and outputs from (represented as directed arrows) each processing task (represented as a rounded box); a DFD also documents the data stores (represented by an elongated rectangle) used by a process and the external entities (represented as shaded boxes) who are sources and destinations of data flows.

NOTE

Notice that Victoria explains how to read the DFD in Figure 7. In subsequent paragraphs, she explains facets of the diagram and draws the reader's attention to problems revealed by the diagram.

A few comments about the DFDs in Figures 7 and 8 are needed. First, note that data store "D2—Tape" represents the tape data obtained from the display box or shrink-wrapped tape. I understand that you also have a file of notecards on which you describe the various titles available to rent. However, this tape notecard file is used only to answer customer inquiries about tapes available to rent. Because ETG clerks indicated that this file is seldom used in order processing, I have omitted it here. Nonetheless, we need to keep this notecard file in mind as we discuss the requirements of the new system. Second, note that data store "D5—Transaction" represents your cash register audit tape. As I understand, clerks use this audit tape to determine the total transaction volume for each day, including a breakout of the rental dollars versus the sales dollars. Third, the data flow from "Process 2.5—Process returned order" to "D2—Tape" represents the inventory clerk's returning the display boxes of completed rental orders to the display shelves.

You should also notice that the dataflow complexity uncovered in the workflow diagrams is repeated in the DFDs. Because processing the order requires two separate entities—a sales clerk and an inventory clerk—the walk-in rental customer becomes a kind of courier, transmitting documents from the sales clerk to the inventory clerk. This is especially obvious in Figure 8, where Processed Order is an output to Rental Customer in

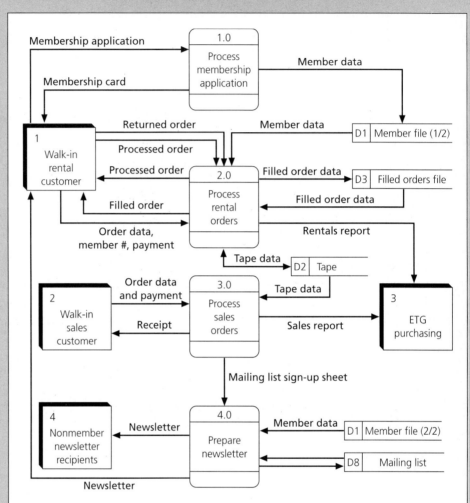

Figure 7: DFD of ETG's major processes

Process 2.3 *and* an input from Rental Customer in Process 2.4. I understand that you instituted this separation of duties to lessen the possibility of employee fraud; however, I think that you'll agree that its primary effect is to require rental customers to stand in two lines: one to ring up their rental orders, another to receive their rental tapes.

ETG Objects

The diagrams in Figures 2 through 8 also give us a preliminary view of ETG's objects. Objects represent the people, such as customers and employees; documents, such as rental order forms and reports; and things, such as membership cards and display/shrink-wrapped tapes in ETG's system. Again, my analysis focuses only on the objects in ETG's walk-in order processing system, which are documented in the enterprise object model shown in Figure 9.

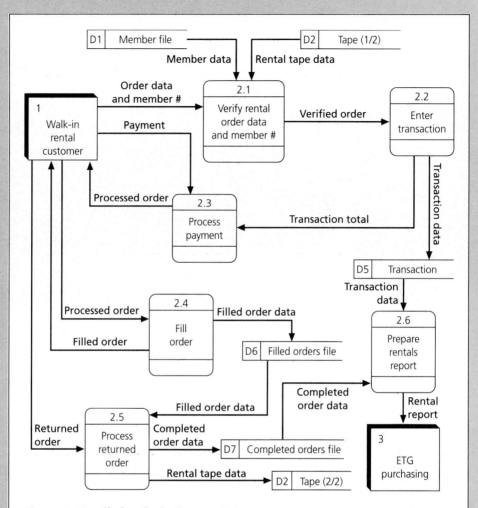

Figure 8: Detailed tasks in Process 2.0

An enterprise object model provides a preliminary list of the objects of interest to an organization. Each object is represented as a rectangle, and objects are grouped into subjects that provide a meaningful classification of objects—"meaningful" in the sense that the subject categories are of interest to the organization. In essence, the subject groupings provide views of the people, documents, and things that are relevant to the organization.

In Figure 9, ETG's objects are grouped into subjects according to the major processes performed in your order processing system: rental order processing, sales order processing, and newsletter processing. Note that the objects in membership application processing are shown in the rental order processing subject group. Where multiple copies of an object are used differently in the system—for example, the white and yellow copies of the rental order form and the cash register receipt—multiple objects are

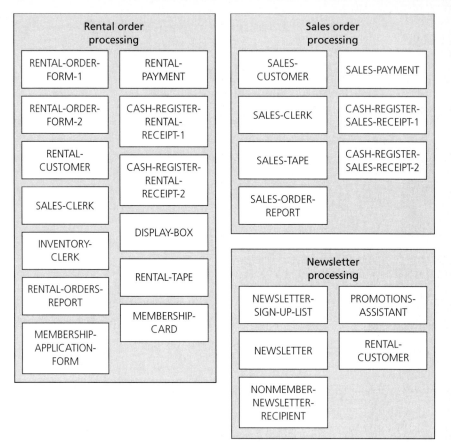

Figure 9: Enterprise object model

shown. Note also that some objects appear in multiple subjects; for example, the SALES-CLERK object appears in both the rental order processing and sales order processing subjects because sales clerks are involved in both processes. Similarly, the RENTAL-CUSTOMER object appears in both the rental order processing and newsletter processing subjects because rental customers rent tapes and receive the newsletter.

We will analyze all objects in greater detail at our next JAD session. For now, I will comment only on the DISPLAY-BOX and RENTAL-TAPE objects and the RENTAL-ORDER-FORM and CASH-REGISTER-RENTAL-RECEIPT objects. It seems that each display box is associated with exactly one rental tape, and each rental order form is associated with exactly one rental receipt. A question to be addressed at the JAD session is whether both of these objects are necessary. I understand that, to some degree, Paul may have instituted this duplication as a control to protect inventory and to create an audit trail of orders, payments, and receipts. However, it seems likely that a more efficient method could be implemented to ensure adequate accounting and inventory controls.

NOTE In the previous paragraph, Victoria supports her assertion with concrete statements describing what she believes may be a problem in the current system. She also uses ordinary language to describe the problem to ensure clarity.

Problems with the Existing System

The data and processing redundancies discussed above *[transition]* were not unduly burdensome when ETG had only a few hundred customers, but they have become too cumbersome for a growing business with a large client base. As noted in the previous discussion, the rental order process in particular seems to involve unnecessary duplication of effort and data, a duplication that, instead of safeguarding ETG's cash receipts and inventory, may be reducing ETG's efficiency and effectiveness. A JAD session with employees and customers of ETG and observation of business activities support this conclusion and revealed the following symptoms of problems with the current system:

1. Sales clerks frequently miss errors in customer-written rental orders (e.g., wrong stock number, wrong customer membership number) on busy weekend evenings when they are trying to serve so many clients in a short period of time.

2. Both rental and purchase customers often avoid ETG on weekends because the checkout line is long and typically requires a 15 to 25 minute wait.

3. Observations show that during peak weekend hours, rental tapes returned to ETG are not available for rent by other customers because inventory clerks don't have time to process returns and put display boxes back on the shelves.

4. Sales clerks complain that they waste time sifting through the piles of unprocessed display boxes and rental tapes looking for rental tapes to fill customer requests.

5. Rental customers sometimes forget to return their receipts with their tapes, requiring inventory clerks to search the Filled Rental Orders file to match returned tapes with their paperwork.

6. ETG has not instituted clear procedures for processing fines on customers who return rental tapes after their due date.

These symptoms indicate several problems with ETG's current system: redundant labor-intensive paperwork and procedures; inefficient use of resources (e.g., returned rental tapes are not being processed quickly); and imprecise procedures (e.g., for processing fines).

NOTE Again, Victoria uses a numbered list for clarity and conciseness.

II. PROJECT DEFINITION AND FEASIBILITY

System Objectives and Project Scope and Constraints

As the list of problems at the end of Section I demonstrates, most of ETG's problems are caused by its manual rental order processing system. *[Transitional sentence]* The primary objective of this project is to alleviate these problems. More specifically, any information system developed in this project is expected to

1. Reduce rental transaction errors from the current estimate of 10 percent to less than 1 percent.

2. Reduce rental transaction processing time from the current estimate of 15 minutes to less than 2 minutes.

3. Eliminate the backlog of returned rental tapes to be processed.

4. Eliminate the need for rental customers to return their receipts with their tapes.

5. Improve ETG's recordkeeping and fine-processing systems.

Although Paul has requested that all customer transactions be studied in the preliminary analysis, he has stipulated that the development project must focus primarily on the walk-in customer order processing system, as highlighted in Figure 5. ETG has allocated $30,000 to the project, which is expected to cover all costs of developing the system, including hardware, software, data conversion, training, and consulting fees. The system should be operational by September of this year.

Feasibility Analysis

In addition to defining ETG's current problems and the objectives, constraints, and scope of the project, I also analyzed project feasibility. That is, I investigated whether the project could be completed under the imposed constraints and whether the proposed system would serve ETG's business goals. My evaluation is summarized in the project risk evaluation form (see Figure 10).

NOTE In the following paragraphs, notice that Victoria provides supporting comments for each aspect of the project risk evaluation.

An initial evaluation suggests that the project is feasible on all accounts. Although no firm estimates of costs and benefits can be defined at this time, I have developed a similar system for a video rental business using bar code technology; the development costs of that system (hardware, software, and data conversion only) totaled about $20,000. So the key to coming in within budget on this project is minimizing the costs of designer and implementer labor. For this reason, I will act as project leader and will assign a student-consultant (for whom I charge a lower rate) to perform most of the design, implementation, and training activities.

Project Risk Evaluation		
Project: ETG Order Processing	**Completed by:** Victoria Hernandez	**Date:** 4/7/1997
Factors affecting project risk	Rating*	Comments
1. Characteristics of the organization a. Has stable, well defined objectives?	1	Paul has articulated plans for expansion and improved competition.
b. Is guided by an information systems plan?	0	No existing information systems, small business so less important.
c. Proposed system fits plan and addresses organizational objectives?	1	System will help ETG meet its objectives.
2. Characteristics of the information system a. Model available/clear requirements?	1	I have developed similar systems.
b. Automates routine, structured procedures?	1	Order processing is routine, clearly-defined process.
c. Affects only one business area? (No cross-functional or interorganizational links?)	0	System will encompass order processing, inventory, and, to some degree, accounting.
d. Can be completed in less than one year?	1	Estimated schedule time = 3 to 4 months.
e. Uses stable, proven technology?	1	Lots of IT options, all have been used extensively in other businesses.
3. Characteristics of the developers a. Are experienced in chosen development methodology?	1	I have used my methodology on a number of projects.
b. Are skilled at determining functional requirements?	1	Student/consultant has taken course work and participated in numerous projects.
c. Are familiar with technology and information architecture?	1	I have developed similar systems before.
4. Characteristics of the users a. Have business area experience?	1	ETG employees have an average of 2 years experience on their jobs.
b. Have development experience?	−1	None of ETG's employees have participated in an IS project before.
c. Are committed to the project?	1	Preliminary interviews suggest that all users are enthusiastice about project.
Total points	10	Low risk!

*+1 = yes; 0 = maybe; −1 = no

Figure 10: Project risk/feasibility analysis

Problems with the current system have been estimated to cost ETG at least $10,000 per year in lost business, overtime wages for the company accountant and sales clerks, and rework. In addition to eliminating these costly problems, the new system may make it feasible to increase business and to open a new store in a neighboring community—a strategic plan that has been delayed because of accounting problems related to the manual recordkeeping and order processing system. Thus, it seems likely that the costs of developing and operating the system are justified and that the system will help ETG achieve its goals. A detailed cost-benefit analysis will be provided later in the project.

Having developed a similar system, I can say with confidence that the technology is well established and should not be a barrier to development. I have experience training nontechnical sales clerks and have found that, if a sales clerk can operate a cash register, he or she can be taught to use a computer-based system. In fact, the ETG clerks I talked with expressed a great deal of interest in learning to use an automated system. Thus, I feel that the system will be readily accepted by current personnel. My only concern here is that no one at ETG has the skills to maintain a computer-based system. Therefore, we may need to factor into production costs the wages of a part-time employee or contract consultant to maintain the system.

In summary, my preliminary analysis suggests that the ETG project is very likely to contribute to organizational efficiency and competitiveness and to provide the desired benefits while meeting the imposed development constraints.

General Design Alternatives

As requested, I am providing two general design alternatives in this report. Normally, I would consider it "jumping the gun" to outline design alternatives before our JAD session; however, given my familiarity with video rental and sales transaction processing systems and ETG's desire to have the new system up and running as soon as possible, I feel comfortable offering design alternatives here.

Alternative 1 has two variations: one that requires no additional hardware and one that requires installation of an electronic security gate. In both variations, I recommend that ETG revise its current procedures in the following ways:

1. Eliminate the duplication of effort and data required in the current system by combining the sales/rentals and inventory functions into one function. The clerk who processes a rental order also retrieves the appropriate rental tapes and gives them to the customer.

2. Enlarge the sales clerk station to allow it to accommodate ETG's rental tape inventory. In other words, all rental order processing tasks occur at the sales clerk station.

3. Cross-train sales and inventory clerks so that all employees can perform both sets of tasks.

The benefits of this alternative (1A) are that it eliminates the problems of rental customers having to transfer documents between sales and inventory clerks and to stand in two lines to check out tapes.

The second variation of Alternative 1 (1B) involves the above changes plus installation of an electronic security gate near ETG's main entrance and affixing the corresponding signal label to each tape in ETG's stock. In addition, the rental tapes can be stored on the display shelves along with the display boxes because the security gate will virtually eliminate the possibility of shoplifting and employee theft.

Although Alternative 1 should reduce rental order transaction processing time to some degree, it still requires rental customers to complete the rental order form, which is in and of itself a time-consuming task. In addition, this alternative does nothing to help ETG better manage and utilize its customer, tape, and orders data, nor does it facilitate preparation of the newsletter.

Alternative 2 also has two variations, each incorporating the procedural changes of Alternative 1 and each providing a different degree of automation. Both involve creating a database of customers, tapes, and orders and automating sales and rental order processing. This alternative, like Alternative 1B, requires ETG to place the rental tapes—not just the display boxes—on its shelves and to install an electronic security gate; it also requires ETG to purchase and install a microcomputer system, printer, and database program; and to convert its data from manual to digital records.

In the first variation of Alternative 2 (2A), rental customers select tapes from the shelves and present the tapes and their membership cards to a clerk. The clerk uses an on-screen electronic form to enter the customer's membership number and the stock number of each rental tape. The software uses this data to retrieve the customer's name and address and the title of each tape. The software also computes the rental fee, saves the transaction to the rental transaction file, and prints a two-part rental form, which the customer signs. The clerk retains one copy of the form and gives the other to the customer. When customers return rental tapes, the transaction data is retrieved using the customer's membership number (if available) or the stock number(s) of the rental tapes. In addition, the software determines whether a late fee is appropriate and computes the amount of the late fee. These data are saved and called to the clerk's attention the next time the customer rents tapes; the software can also generate an overdue rental orders report.

The second variation of Alternative 2 (2B) provides a greater degree of automation by implementing bar coding technology. In this variation, membership cards and rental tapes have a computer-readable label encoding the membership number and tape stock number. To process rental transactions, the sales clerk uses a light pen to scan the card and tape labels, thus retrieving member and tape data from the database. The rest of the process is the same as variation 2A, with the exception that tapes are scanned when processing rental returns. In addition to the hardware and software described for Alternative 2A, this alternative requires ETG to purchase and install scanning hardware (primarily, a light pen) and software and to affix computer-readable labels to all membership cards and rental tapes.

Both variations of Alternative 2 have several benefits, including faster and simpler rental transaction processing and better access to and use of ETG's data. In addition, both variations simplify rental return processing, eliminating the problems that occur when customers don't return their receipt with their tapes. An added benefit is that the database of rental customers and mailing list customers can be used to create mailing labels for ETG's newsletters. Alternative 2-B has the added benefit of reducing transaction processing time even further and eliminating data entry errors.

I recommend that you delay selection of an alternative until after our JAD-Requirements session. Once we have clearly specified the functions the new system must perform, I can provide a detailed estimate of the costs and benefits of each alternative. For now, suffice it to note that Alternative 1A is the least expensive—and least beneficial—alternative and that Alternative 2B is the most expensive—and most beneficial—alternative. However, implementing any of these alternatives will alleviate, to different degrees, the problems ETG is currently experiencing.

JOINT APPLICATION DEVELOPMENT
A Technique for User-Driven Development

Preliminary Investigation and Analysis

1. Perform enterprise analysis.

2. Determine system objectives, project constraints, and scope.

3. Evaluate feasibility and get approval to proceed.

4. *Conduct JAD sessions to verify objectives, constraints, and scope; to redesign process, if necessary; and to identify requirements.*

The Chapter 3 discussion of problems with traditional systems development noted that involving users throughout the development project is critical to delivering high-quality systems that satisfy user needs. In this chapter, we examine a technique of user-driven development: joint application development (JAD). JAD ensures that the intended users of the system have a voice and an active role in systems development. It helps to sustain user involvement throughout the project stages of iterative prototyping, final construction, and system test and installation. This chapter describes how to plan and conduct JAD workshops to define and to satisfy functional requirements. After completing this chapter, you should be able to

1. Describe several types of JAD workshops.

2. Define the roles of JAD participants.

3. Discuss several tools and techniques used in JAD.

4. Explain how to prepare, conduct, and evaluate a JAD workshop.

5. List several benefits of using JAD workshops.

7.1 ◈ JAD WORKSHOPS, ROLES, AND TOOLS

Joint application development (JAD) workshops are designed to overcome the communications gap between users and designers and thus reduce the time and effort devoted to identifying, documenting, and approving requirements and design specifications. Each workshop is a structured meeting that brings together users and designers to define the requirements and general design of a system in a compressed time frame. JAD sessions are structured in that they are conducted by a trained JAD facilitator and may employ brainstorming and collaboration techniques, such as the Nominal Group Technique. Although these workshops employ a number of advanced tools, their focus is not technology per se. Instead, they focus on business needs and map these needs to system functions. This alignment of information systems with business needs helps to ensure that the organizational relevance goal of systems development is achieved.

Typically, JAD workshops are conducted as mini-retreats in which users and designers are relieved of their other workday duties to focus exclusively on the development project. Depending on the complexity of the project, each JAD workshop may consume an afternoon, one or two days, or a week. In this section, we discuss several types of JAD workshops, roles, tools, and techniques.

TYPES OF JAD WORKSHOPS

JAD workshops can be used effectively at any point in development. Here we outline some of the more common types of JAD workshops.

Joint Requirements Planning (JRP)

The **joint requirements planning (JRP) workshop** is typically held after the development team has spent a week or so gaining a basic understanding of the business area and of the current system's processes, data, and problems. The purpose of the JRP workshop is to verify the developers' understanding and to identify the requirements of the new system. This workshop also discusses project justification so that the user-sponsor can evaluate the project and make the "go/no-go" decision. Deliverables include preliminary system behavior models, system structure models, and enterprise models detailing the functional requirements; confirmation of the project scope, system objectives, and constraints; and a list of implementation issues raised during the workshop.

JAD Analysis

The purpose of the **JAD-analysis workshop** is to analyze requirements more fully and to outline the design of the new system. The intended users of the system are the most important participants in this workshop because their input is critical to assuring that the system meets user requirements. Inputs to this workshop include the basic requirements and open issues raised during JRP and the problem definition report. Deliverables include detailed models of the system's behaviors and structure.

JAD Design

The purpose of the **JAD-design workshop** is to design procedures, reports, and screens for the new system. Prototyping tools are vital to the success of this workshop. Participants also plan the construction and installation stage of the project, identifying the resources needed to implement and install the new system. Inputs include the detailed behavior and structure models from JAD analysis plus any additional design work completed in the interim. Deliverables include procedure definitions, dialog flow diagram, screen and report layouts, and plans for testing and installing the new system.

JAD Review and Confirmation

The **JAD review-and-confirmation workshop** can be scheduled at any point in the development project, whenever participants need to review the progress to date and to confirm changes made to the system. If the system is being developed using prototyping and rapid application development (RAD) techniques, a review-and-confirm session may be held after each iteration of the prototyping stage. The primary inputs are prototypes of system screens, reports, and menus. Deliverables include a list of approved changes to the prototype.

JAD ROLES

JAD workshop participants include the user-sponsor, the JAD facilitator, one or more scribes, and several users and information systems (IS) professionals. All of these participants must attend and play an active role in each workshop. Ideally, no more than 10 to 12 participants should be involved so that individual participation is maximized. The **JAD roles** and their responsibilities are as follows.

User-Sponsor

The **user-sponsor** is the high-ranking executive champion of the project who motivates users to participate fully. The user-sponsor selects users to participate in the workshop, commits resources to workshop development and delivery, and ensures that user-managers cooperate and actively participate in workshop activities. Ultimately, the user-sponsor makes the "go/no-go" decision regarding the project.

Facilitator

Typically, the **facilitator** is a business or IS professional whose knowledge of the business; diplomacy; and communication, group dynamics, and organizational skills are critical to workshop success. The facilitator is responsible for planning the workshop agenda, conducting the workshop, and summarizing the workshop results. During the workshop, the facilitator's role is that of an impartial referee and discussion leader responsible for encouraging active participation, bridging communication gaps between users and developers, negotiating between disparate factions, and ensuring coverage of the agenda and attainment of the workshop goals. If multiple JAD workshops are conducted for a single project, the same facilitator should lead each workshop.

Scribe(s)

Scribes are usually IS professionals skilled in using CASE, prototyping, and presentation tools to capture the requirements and design specifications and to generate prototypes of reports, screens, and processes (i.e., program code). Two types of scribes are commonly involved: a presentation scribe and a technical scribe. The **presentation scribe** uses word-processing, presentation, and desktop-publishing software to record the minutes of the workshop (including unresolved issues, options considered, and justifications), to generate a summary report document, and to prepare presentation graphics. The **technical scribe** uses CASE and prototyping tools to document requirements and data and process definitions, to build models, and to generate prototypes. If an integrated CASE tool containing previous business models is used, then the technical scribe may also be responsible for pointing out any inconsistencies with existing systems evident in the workshop models.

End-Users and User-Managers

The user contingent consists of the functional-area experts and managers who are best able to define business rules and processing and data requirements. In addition, these participants map critical success factors to system functions in order to ensure that the system achieves the organizational relevance goal. End-users provide valuable input on design issues and prototypes and specify training needs and acceptance criteria. User-managers are most instrumental in approving project timelines for testing, training, data conversion, and installation; they also help to define system costs and benefits and to ensure that the system addresses their critical success factors.

IS Professionals

To a large degree, IS professionals are silent observers at the JAD workshop. Their primary responsibility is to *LISTEN* to users' descriptions of business processes and data and required system functions. Thus, the most important skill you as a systems developer bring to JAD is your ability to listen effectively so that you obtain a clear, correct understanding of user needs and functional requirements. You may be called upon to comment on the technical and economic feasibility of developing certain system functions. If the JAD workshop is focusing on design, you may also be asked to develop prototypes and to present certain aspects of the design for user evaluation. However, you should understand that at a JAD workshop, the user is king; you are in attendance simply for the purpose of learning what is necessary to meet the king's needs.

JAD TOOLS AND TECHNIQUES

Tools for JAD workshops range from simple word-processing and presentation software to powerful group decision support systems and CASE and prototyping tools. In addition, JAD uses a number of group-interaction and consensus-building techniques. Here we describe several JAD tools and one consensus-building technique, the Nominal Group Technique.

Prototyping Tools

An integral technique in JAD is *prototyping:* showing users a working model to help them better understand the features and functions of the new system. Seeing a working model of the system, users are better able to specify what they need the system to do and to know when the system is doing it correctly. However, if the development team has to construct prototypes in COBOL (heaven forbid!), the effort and time required will discourage the degree of iteration desired. Thus, effective prototyping requires effective **prototyping tools**, productivity software that allows developers to illustrate and/or mimic the functions and interfaces of an information system. Chapter 8 discusses prototyping techniques and tools in detail; here we provide only a general overview of these tools.

Simple prototyping tools include word-processing and spreadsheet programs that can be used to demonstrate screen and report layouts. A more powerful prototyping tool is a PC database program, such as Microsoft Access, that employs wizards to easily derive sample forms, screens, and reports from the database definition. To capture complex processing rules, a rule-based expert system shell, such as VP-Expert, allows you to prototype these rules and test their validity. Even more powerful prototyping tools are application generators and CASE tools that can derive prototype screens and reports from process and data models stored in the tool's encyclopedia. The primary advantage of using a CASE tool to build prototypes is that all of the processing logic and design models are retained in the encyclopedia and can be used to build the final system.

Other JAD Tools and Techniques

In addition to prototyping tools, JAD workshops may also employ *spreadsheet templates* of financial models to quickly estimate the costs and return on investment of a project, *presentation packages* to build and display text and graphical aids to supplement presentations, and *project management software* to estimate project schedules, build project timelines, and monitor project progress.

Sometimes the focus of a JAD workshop is identifying critical success factors or determining strategies to exploit information technology for competitive advantage. These JAD workshops may employ a sophisticated tool such as the **group decision support system (GDSS)**, a computer-based, interactive system designed to help a group of decision makers solve unstructured problems (see, e.g., Dennis et al. [1988], DeSanctis et al. [1987], and Turoff [1991]). A GDSS embeds its hardware and software components into a structured conference facility whose layout is designed to encourage collaboration. In other words, the conference facility includes the usual configuration of tables, chairs, and audiovisual devices but, in addition, each participant has a workstation so as to anonymously enter ideas and vote for or rank alternative solutions. The workstations are connected to a file server, which collects input from each workstation, compiles the input, and displays the compilation on a common screen at the front of the room.

There are several benefits of using GDSS in a JAD workshop. First, a GDSS creates a democratic meeting atmosphere. Lower-level participants are free to express their ideas without fear of contradicting their superiors; higher-level participants are less likely to dominate the meeting and impose their ideas on other participants. Second, a GDSS encourages idea generation and divergent thinking; participants can contribute ideas without being constrained by their fear of personal criticism. Third, a GDSS helps to organize and evaluate ideas and to document the meeting activities. The GDSS software can quickly organize ideas generated during a brainstorming session or provide a group ranking of alternative solutions by compiling individual rankings.

GDSS software facilitates the use of a number of group decision-making techniques. The **Nominal Group Technique (NGT)** is a commonly supported structured technique for conducting a group interview or brainstorming session (see, e.g., Delbecq et al. [1975] or Huber [1980]). The goals of the NGT are to maximize individual participation while building group consensus. The procedure for conducting a NGT session is summarized in Table 7.1.

NGT is particularly effective when the issue being discussed is highly political, for example, the allocation of resources to projects proposed by various departments within a company. If personality or fiefdom is likely to inhibit free thinking and open expression, step 3 in Figure 7.1 may involve anonymous submission of ideas on paper or through a GDSS to minimize these factors. As stated in the ground rules, the goal is to focus on ideas, not on the people or political factions that proposed the idea.

TABLE 7.1 How to conduct a group interview using NGT

1. The facilitator explains the ground rules, announces the topic of discussion (e.g., allocation of systems development resources), and answers questions from the group to clarify the group's objective (e.g., identify selection criteria for determining which projects to fund). Ground rules include the following:

   ◆ Everyone must participate fully to ensure that the best ideas are generated.
   ◆ During group discussion, criticism must focus on ideas, not on people.
   ◆ There is no such thing as a "stupid" idea.
   ◆ Criticism should be constructive and respectful.

2. Group members work individually to "brainstorm" ideas, writing their ideas on paper or entering them on their GDSS workstation.

3. In a non-GDSS setting, the facilitator solicits an idea from each group member, listing the idea on a flipchart or chalkboard. No comments or criticisms are voiced at this point. The facilitator continues soliciting ideas, in round-robin fashion, until all ideas have been compiled. When a GDSS is used, individual ideas are compiled by the GDSS software and displayed on a common screen.

4. The facilitator opens discussion for a predefined period (e.g., 30 minutes); the group discusses the ideas and adds additional ideas as they arise.

5. When the discussion time has elapsed, each group member ranks the listed ideas on paper and submits the ranking to the facilitator; the facilitator compiles individual rankings to create a group ranking. In a GDSS setting, group members enter their rankings on their workstations, and the GDSS software compiles the rankings to produce a group ranking, which is displayed on the common screen.

6. The facilitator announces the group ranking and opens discussion. If the group decides that the group ranking is unacceptable, steps 4–5 are repeated.

✓ **Check Your Understanding 7-1**

1. Match each of the following terms with its definition.

    _____ a.   a computer-based, interactive system used to help decision makers solve unstructured problems

    _____ b.   responsible for planning the workshop agenda, conducting the workshop, and summarizing its results

    _____ c.   a structured technique used to conduct group interviews

    _____ d.   analyzes requirements and outlines the design of the new system

    _____ e.   uses CASE and prototyping tools to capture requirements and design specifications

JRP workshop

JAD-analysis workshop

JAD-design

facilitator

technical scribe

presentation scribe

prototyping tool

GDSS

NGT

2. Indicate whether each of the following statements is true (T) or false (F).

  ____ a.   JAD workshops focus on technical specifications, mapping these specifications to business needs.

  ____ b.   A JAD review-and-confirmation workshop can be scheduled after each iteration of the prototyping stage.

  ____ c.   During a JAD workshop, the primary responsibility of IS professionals is to listen to users' comments in order to understand user needs and requirements.

  ____ d.   CASE tools are not useful for prototyping system functions.

  ____ e.   NGT provides a structure for brainstorming, discussing, and ranking ideas to build group consensus.

7.2 ◆ PLANNING AND CONDUCTING A JAD WORKSHOP

Several factors are critical in successfully planning and conducting a JAD workshop [Texas Instruments 1992a]:

◆ Executive commitment to provide the required resources, time, and people.

◆ A skilled facilitator.

◆ Definition of a reasonable project scope, which may require that a large system be partitioned into smaller systems, each to be dealt with sequentially.

◆ Highly committed, well-prepared participants who are able to make decisions for their nonparticipating colleagues.

◆ A focus on business issues, not arcane technical issues.

◆ Adherence to a systems development methodology supported by a CASE tool.

◆ Use of modeling techniques that participants can comprehend.

◆ Conducive workshop facilities.

◆ Active, equal participation by all users.

PLANNING A JAD WORKSHOP

Preparing for a JAD workshop entails four activities: determining the workshop location and duration, selecting and preparing participants, planning the workshop agenda and preparing materials, and setting up the workshop room(s). The first two activities, determining location and duration and selecting participants, must be completed well in advance of the workshop. Advance planning is required to reserve facilities, hire a facilitator (if none is available in house), and ensure that selected participants will be able to attend. Although most of the preparatory activities are performed by the facilitator, scribes, and IS personnel, all aspects of the workshop plan and agenda should be reviewed and approved by the user-sponsor.

Determining Location and Duration

Ideally, a JAD workshop should be held off-site, for example in the conference rooms of a local hotel or conference center. Removing participants from the workplace decreases the likelihood that they will be interrupted by "the call of the job" and increases their ability to concentrate on workshop activities and issues. If the workshop must be held on-site, you should consider setting ground rules, such as prohibiting participants from returning to their work areas or checking voice-mail messages during workshop breaks. Attention to workshop activities and issues must be the participants' first priority if the workshop is to succeed. Participants cannot focus on defining requirements and clarifying business issues if they are worried about a mini-crisis in their business area.

Although the duration of JAD workshops varies, typically you can expect to hold two, three-to-four day workshops for a small- to medium-sized project. The more complex the application system being developed, the greater will be the amount of workshop sessions needed. Workshops work best when scheduled for a full workday (8 or 9 A.M. to 5 or 6 P.M.), rather than several half-days. The half-day spent at the work site tends to distract participants, thus requiring more time for them to "get up to speed" in the workshop.

Selecting and Preparing Participants

As noted in the previous discussion of workshop roles, you should select a facilitator who has extensive JAD experience and who has no stake in the project under consideration. If no facilitator is available in-house, you will need to hire one (perhaps from a business systems consulting group) or select a qualified employee to receive JAD facilitator training. In addition, you need to consult with affected business-area managers to select user-participants who have an excellent understanding of the business processes encompassed by the proposed system. The more indispensable a manager feels that a user is to his or her business area, the more desirable that user is as a JAD participant. You may have to work with the user-sponsor to gain the management support needed to ensure that these desirable users are released from work duties to participate in the JAD workshop. Finally, you need to appoint scribes and IS professionals to participate in the workshop.

Preparing participants involves briefing users about the workshop structure and objectives; training them, if necessary, to understand the modeling techniques to be used in the workshop; and providing them, if possible, with materials describing the project and findings from a preliminary investigation. A half-day **kick-off meeting** hosted by the user-sponsor and held a week prior to the workshop is an ideal forum for performing these activities and "gearing up" for high-level participation during the workshops.

You may want to distribute the problem definition report discussed in Chapter 6 at this time because its descriptions of objectives, constraints, scope, organizational context, work-flows, and business objects provide an excellent foundation for the workshop's more in-depth analysis and design activities. This report also provides a launching point for JAD discussions and may raise a number of issues requiring resolution during the workshop. However, if you have identified potentially contentious political issues (for example, turf battles or a high degree of fear about the system's impact on organizational culture), you should work with the user-sponsor to resolve these issues prior to the workshop.

Preparing the Agenda and Materials

Every successful meeting begins with an **agenda**, an action plan that structures the activities of the group and indicates the approximate time devoted to and person(s) responsible for leading each activity. Examples of agendas for specific workshop types are shown in Tables 7.2 and 7.3 [Texas Instruments 1992b]. A generic JAD workshop agenda contains four major activities:

1. Introduce the workshop:
    ◆ Deliver welcome (user-sponsor) and opening remarks (project manager and/or facilitator).
    ◆ Review the agenda and rules of operation (facilitator).
    ◆ Review the scope and objectives.
    ◆ Perform a team-building or ice-breaking exercise to help participants become acquainted and comfortable with each other.

2. Do the work:
    ◆ Perform the development activities appropriate to the workshop type, e.g., build data, process, or object models of the existing system or design/prototype screens and reports for the new system (facilitator).
    ◆ Document corrections, issues, models, and decisions (scribe, project manager, and IS professionals).
    ◆ Document open issues (scribe and facilitator).

3. Close the day's session (allow about 15 minutes at the end of each day):
    ◆ Review the agenda, and summarize progress; suggest any modifications that seem necessary.
    ◆ Encourage participant feedback.

4. Consolidate the workshop:
    ◆ Review objectives, goals, and agenda, and summarize results (facilitator).
    ◆ Review open issues and assign work, if any, to be completed after the workshop (facilitator, user-sponsor, and/or project manager, as appropriate).

- ◆ Describe the action plan, the "next steps" to move the project forward (project manager or facilitator).
- ◆ Evaluate workshop effectiveness (facilitator).
- ◆ Thank participants for their contributions (facilitator and/or user-sponsor).

Most of these activities are self-explanatory and descriptive of many kinds of structured meetings. We will discuss less familiar activities, such as defining the rules of operation, scribing, and handling open issues in the section on "Conducting a JAD Workshop."

TABLE 7.2 Typical agenda for two-day JRP workshop

Morning Day One

1. Getting Started:
   - ◆ Introduce participants.
   - ◆ Discuss mission and workshop objectives.
   - ◆ Define workshop deliverables.
   - ◆ Review and modify agenda.
2. Review of Organization and Current Systems:
   - ◆ Define organization's structure.
   - ◆ Describe the current workflows.
   - ◆ Describe current systems and processes performed.
   - ◆ Summarize analysis activities to date.

Afternoon Day One

3. Problem Definition:
   - ◆ Determine business objectives.
   - ◆ Define critical success factors.
   - ◆ Define system scope.
   - ◆ Determine expected system benefits.

Morning Day Two

   - ◆ Describe business activities.
   - ◆ Construct and review preliminary data models (object attribute models).
   - ◆ Construct and review preliminary process models (object behavior models).

Afternoon Day Two

4. Implementation Plan
   - ◆ Determine security and controls.
   - ◆ Identify required changes in organizational culture and/or structure.
   - ◆ Define resource limits for development and production.
   - ◆ Determine plans for converting existing data and building interfaces to current systems.
5. Open Issues

TABLE 7.3 Typical agenda for three-day JAD-design workshop

Morning Day One

1. Getting Started
   - ◆ Introduce participants.
   - ◆ Discuss mission and workshop objectives.
   - ◆ Review and modify agenda.
2. System Behaviors Design
   - ◆ Review system behavior models.
   - ◆ Map behaviors to automated and manual procedures.

Afternoon Day One

- ◆ Map behaviors to procedures (continued).
- ◆ Design manual control procedures.
- ◆ Design automated control procedures.

Morning Day Two

3. System Data Structure Design
   - ◆ Examine source documents and reports.
   - ◆ Specify entities or object classes.
   - ◆ Specify business rules governing relationships.
   - ◆ Specify attributes and identifiers.

Afternoon Day Two

4. System Interface Design
   - ◆ Design procedure steps and dialog flows.
   - ◆ Design interfaces to current systems.

Morning Day Three

5. User Interface Design
   - ◆ Design screens.
   - ◆ Design reports.

Afternoon Day Three

6. Review Installation Requirements
   - ◆ Determine how to install the new system.
   - ◆ Confirm division of responsibility among users and IS.
   - ◆ Review training and documentation needs.
7. Open Issues
   - ◆ Review issues and actions taken to date.

In addition to preparing the workshop agenda, you also need to prepare the workshop materials. These may include transparencies illustrating the most important findings and models from the problem definition report or illustrating the preliminary screen and report designs. If your audio-video resources allow, you should create and plan to display these aids using automated tools such as presentation graphics and CASE tools so that text and graphical illustrations can be modified easily as the workshop proceeds.

Setting Up the Workshop Room(s)

In addition to reserving workshop facilities, you need to ensure that the room has the appropriate equipment and supplies. A typical layout of a JAD workshop room is shown in Figure 7.1. Notice that the tables are arranged to facilitate group discussion and that several communication aids are provided: flipcharts, whiteboard, overhead projector, copier, computers for the scribes, and printer. The flipcharts, whiteboard, and overhead projector may not be needed if you have access to presentation and CASE tool software that allows you to manipulate and display images "on the fly." In any case, you will need the computers, printer, and copier to document workshop decisions and designs and to provide copies for workshop participants. Other supplies required include notepaper, additional flipchart pads, colored markers, name-card badges or placecards, and office supplies (e.g., stapler, scissors, tape).

If more than 10 participants are involved, you may need to ensure that breakout rooms are also available. The systems approach that developers apply to decompose complex systems

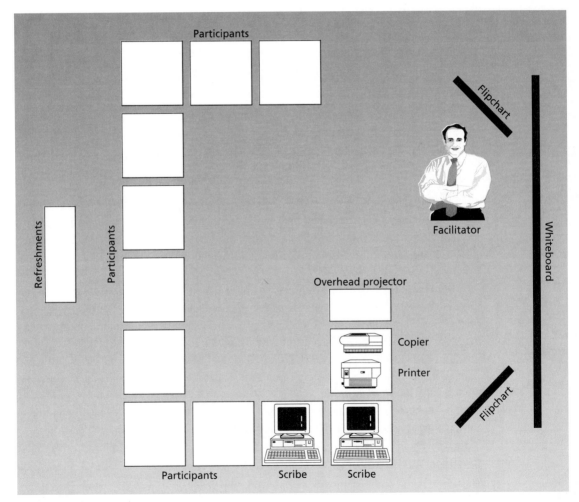

FIGURE 7.1   Layout of JAD workshop facility

problems also works well in JAD sessions when multiple tasks or issues need to be addressed simultaneously to improve productivity. At minimum, each breakout room should be equipped with a flipchart, colored markers, notepaper, and pens.

CONDUCTING A JAD WORKSHOP

The general agenda in the previous section and specific agendas in Tables 7.2 and 7.3 describe the structure and activities of a JAD workshop. Here we focus on workshop guidelines, documentation, and follow-up activities.

Rules of Operation and the Open Issues List

Every workshop needs to adhere to **rules of operation**: a set of rules specifying how participants will interact during the workshop. Examples of these rules include the following:

◆ Everyone is an equal participant; no one pulls rank.

◆ Criticize ideas, not people.

◆ Participants follow the general rules of parliamentary procedure.

◆ An issue is added to the Open Issues list if there is little hope of resolving the issue quickly.

These rules should be agreed upon by all participants; in fact, to be most effective, workshop participants should define their own set of rules. Doing so may be the focus of the ice-breaking, team-building exercise early in the workshop.

Open issues are issues raised during the workshop that cannot be resolved in a reasonable time and that seem likely to impede progress toward completing the agenda. For example, a participant may question the feasibility of implementing some aspect of the design. Users and developers may argue for and against feasibility for several minutes without agreeing on whether the design is feasible. At this point, the facilitator or one of the participants should invoke the "unresolvable issue" rule and suggest adding the feasibility issue to the Open Issues list.

The **Open Issues list** is a running record of action items to be investigated and reported on later in the same workshop or in a subsequent workshop. Beware of this list becoming a black hole into which participants discard issues they're uncomfortable addressing. Each open issue should be added to the list posted on a flipchart, whiteboard, or other medium. Participants must agree on the wording used to state the issue. At the end of each day and again at the close of the workshop, the facilitator leads the participants in reviewing the Open Issues list, prioritizing issues for resolution, and assigning a person to resolve the issue by an agreed upon date. If appropriate, the user-sponsor should be called upon to resolve political issues.

Scribing Activities

The scribe is the official transcriber of all workshop activities. Thus, JAD scribes need to be skilled in using word processing, presentation graphics, and CASE tools to ensure that all key discussion points, decisions, open issues, and models are documented accurately and completely. This responsibility is especially important—and nerve-racking—if participants draw their own models on flip charts and whiteboards. In these situations, the scribe must capture the model for later entry into the CASE tool (for example, during a break or at the end of the day). If the workshop employs a GDSS, the scribe may also be called upon to use the GDSS software to compile ideas and rankings.

At the end of each session, the scribe consolidates the materials and prepares documentation and files for the next session. In other words, part of the scribe's job is preparing session minutes, illustrations, and models to be reviewed at the next session. In some cases, the scribe or IS personnel also use agreed upon models, stored in the CASE tool's encyclopedia, to generate prototypes for review during the next session.

After completion of the workshop, the scribe produces a final set of minutes and documentation to distribute to all participants. Although the contents of this document will vary depending on the type of workshop held, examples of deliverables included in this documentation include the following:

◆ List of objectives.

◆ System/project scope.

◆ Functional requirements.

◆ Analysis of benefits and return on investment.

◆ Priority for implementing functional requirements (e.g., for several RAD projects or phased development projects.

◆ Process, data, and/or object models.

◆ Interfaces to other systems.

◆ Screen and report designs.

◆ System menus or dialog flow chart.

◆ Open Issues list and assignments.

◆ Project action plans and target dates for completion.

Workshop Evaluation

Given the emphasis on quality in organizations today, it is not at all surprising that each JAD workshop concludes with an evaluation of its effectiveness. Measures of effectiveness and comments on the JAD process are critical to refining the process and ensuring that the resources devoted to the workshop are well spent.

JAD workshops are usually evaluated in two ways: through participant feedback and through assessment by the scribe and facilitator. Workshop participants complete an assessment form similar to the one shown in Figure 7.2. The assessment form gathers feedback on how well the workshop achieved its objectives, how satisfied participants were with the time devoted to each agenda item, how effectively the facilitator and scribe filled their roles, and other measures of quality. In addition, the facilitator and scribe perform their own assessment of workshop quality. Did the right users participate? Did the participants work

Workshop Assessment Form

Your participation in this workshop is appreciated. To improve facilitator and scribe performance and the effectiveness of future workshops, we ask that you evaluate a number of factors vital to workshop success. Please return your assessment form to the user-sponsor.

JAD Workshop #1		
4/18/97 to 4/20/97, Conference Room		
Facilitator: Victoria Hernandez	Scribe: Denny Young	
Participant: Helen Loi	Organization: ETG	

Please evaluate how welll the workshop achieved its—and your—objectives:

Workshop Objectives	Excellent	Good	Below Expectation	Poor
Define ETG functional requirements				
Select a general design alternative				
Analyze workflows, processes, and data structures.				

Please assess the overall quality of the workshop:

Criterion	Excellent	Good	Below Expectation	Poor
Appropriateness of agenda items				
Time devoted to each agenda item				
Quality of user participation				
Workshop facilitator				
Workshop scribe				
Facilities				
Effectiveness of presentation materials				

Comments:

FIGURE 7.2   Sample workshop evaluation form

effectively as a team? Did each individual contribute to the results? Did the user-sponsor demonstrate commitment and motivate user participation?

✔ Check Your Understanding 7-2

Choose the best answer to complete each statement.

_____ 1. JAD critical success factors do not include
   a.   having high-level management support the JAD workshop.
   b.   having a project with reasonable scope.
   c.   resolving technical issues, not business issues.
   d.   ensuring that users are knowledgeable and participate fully.

_____ 2. The best user to select as a workshop participant is
   a.   one who has never participated in a development project.
   b.   an employee who will not be missed by his or her department.
   c.   a newly hired employee who has an open mind and is not afraid of change.
   d.   an "old hand" who knows the business inside and out.

_____ 3. Before the workshop is held,
   a.   participants must be briefed on workshop structure and the modeling techniques to be employed.
   b.   the facilitator prepares an agenda and gets the user-sponsor's approval.
   c.   the facilities for conducting the workshop must be prepared.
   d.   both a and b.
   e.   all of the above.

_____ 4. Guidelines for conducting a JAD workshop include
   a.   having participants define their own rules of operation.
   b.   creating a conducive atmosphere by avoiding personal criticisms.
   c.   preparing participants by conducting a team-building exercise at the start of each session.
   d.   both a and b.
   e.   all of the above.

_____ 5. An Open Issues list
   a.   documents issues that cannot be resolved in a reasonable time.
   b.   allows the facilitator to defer contentious issues until after the workshop.
   c.   is a "garbage can" for uncomfortable political issues.
   d.   both a and b.
   e.   all of the above.

7.3 ◆ JAD WORKSHOP BENEFITS

If planned and conducted effectively, JAD workshops provide several benefits. First, they actively involve users in the analysis and design of the system, thus increasing their understanding and making them more accountable for the final system.

Second, JAD reduces the time devoted to analysis, general design, and documentation activities. Development projects that do not use JAD rely on a series of sequential interviews of individual end-users to identify requirements. Sequential interviewing consumes a lot of time; analyzing and compiling the interviews takes yet more time. Having to reinterview some users to reconcile contradictions takes more time still. In contrast, a JAD workshop simultaneously elicits input from all participating users; if conflicts between user perspectives arise, they can be addressed during the workshop. Thus, a JAD workshop facilitates requirements determination, not only saving time but also producing an agreed upon set of requirements.

Non-JAD projects typically schedule a user review at the end of each development stage to solicit feedback and to secure permission to proceed. As preparation for the review, the development team compiles a massive report to document its findings, design specifications, and so on. Unfortunately, few users read the report, and few understand its implications for the final system. Thus, a lot of time and effort is expended for little gain. JAD reduces the number and length of written project reports by discussing issues and specifications in a face-to-face meeting.

Third, JAD lessens the number of late changes in requirements, primarily because user-designer communication is improved. Improved communication lessens the likelihood of the breakdowns and oversights that can plague traditional development efforts. And, because JAD can reduce the time elapsed between requirements specification and system implementation, requirements have less time to "creep." JAD reduces creeping requirements to less than 10 percent, especially in projects developing leading-edge applications and involving uncertainty about how to meet user needs [Jones 1994].

Fourth, training and changeover are facilitated because users are more familiar with the system's features and more committed to the system's success. Users become familiar with the system as its features evolve during the JAD workshops. As they interact with prototypes that demonstrate screens, reports, and processing logic, users develop a mental model of how the system functions. Consequently, they require less training. In fact, users who have participated in the JAD workshops can often train other users. In addition, continual, active involvement in the project increases user commitment, helping the systems analyst to maintain user interest as the system is developed and to secure their acceptance of the system when it is delivered.

◆ REVIEW OF CHAPTER LEARNING OBJECTIVES

1. *Describe several types of JAD workshops.*

The joint requirements planning (JRP) workshop verifies the developers' understanding of the project scope, objectives, and constraints and involves users to identify the functional requirements of the new system. The JAD-analysis workshop analyzes requirements more fully and outlines the design of the new system. In the JAD-design workshop, users and developers collaborate to design procedures, reports, and screens for the new system. The

JAD review-and-confirmation workshop, which can be scheduled at any point during development, reviews progress to date and confirms changes made to the system.

2. *Define the roles of JAD participants.*

The user-sponsor, usually a high-ranking executive, selects users to participate in the workshop, commits resources to workshop development and delivery, and ensures that user-managers cooperate and actively participate in workshop activities. The facilitator, an impartial referee and discussion leader, is responsible for planning the workshop agenda, conducting the workshop, and summarizing the workshop results. Scribes are usually IS professionals skilled in using CASE, prototyping, and presentation tools, who capture the requirements and design specifications and generate prototypes. End-users provide valuable input on functional requirements, design issues, and prototypes. User-managers approve project timelines for testing, training, data conversion, and installation; they also help to define system costs and benefits. The primary responsibility of IS professionals is to listen to users' descriptions of business processes and data and functional requirements; in addition, they may be called upon to build prototypes and to present aspects of the design for user evaluation.

3. *Discuss several tools and techniques used in JAD.*

JAD tools range from simple word-processing, spreadsheet, and presentation software to powerful group decision support systems, CASE, and prototyping tools. In addition, JAD uses a number of group interaction and consensus-building techniques. A group decision support system (GDSS) is an interactive information system that employs idea collection and organization software to help a group of decision makers solve unstructured problems. Using a GDSS in a JAD workshop helps to create a democratic meeting atmosphere in which participants feel comfortable contributing ideas. A group decision-making technique supported by a GDSS and used in JAD workshops is the Nominal Group Technique (NGT), a structured technique for conducting a group interview or brainstorming session that maximizes individual participation while building a group consensus.

4. *Explain how to prepare, conduct, and evaluate a JAD workshop.*

Preparing for a JAD workshop entails four activities: determining the workshop location and duration, selecting and preparing participants, planning the workshop agenda and preparing materials, and setting up the workshop room(s).

Typically, a JAD workshop proceeds in three major stages: introduction, work activities, consolidation. The introduction stage reviews the workshop agenda, scope, and objectives; defines the rules of operation; and gives participants a chance to get acquainted and to become a team. During the work activities stage, participants perform the development activities appropriate to the workshop type; the scribe captures ideas and models to document the decisions reached during these activities. During the consolidation stage, the workshop is brought to a close by reviewing objectives and progress towards achieving the objectives, planning the next steps in the project, and evaluating the workshop's effectiveness. As the facilitator conducts the workshop, he or she compiles a list of open issues and works with the group to assign resolution of these issues to various participants.

JAD workshops are usually evaluated by having workshop participants complete an assessment form; in addition, the facilitator and scribe(s) meet to assess workshop quality and to identify ways to improve their performance.

5. *List several benefits of using JAD workshops.*

JAD workshops actively involve users in the analysis and design of the system, thus increasing their understanding and making them more accountable for the final system. They also reduce the time devoted to analysis, general design, and documentation activities. Moreover, JAD lessens the number of late changes in requirements, primarily because user-designer communication is improved and because JAD reduces the time elapsed between requirements specification and system implementation. Still another benefit of JAD is the way it facilitates training and changeover because users are more familiar with the system's features and more committed to the system's success.

◆ KEY TERMS

agenda	JAD-design workshop	Open Issues list
facilitator	joint application develop-	open issue
group decision support	ment (JAD)	presentation scribe
system (GDSS)	joint requirements planning	prototyping tools
JAD review-and-confirma-	(JRP) workshop	rules of operation
tion workshop	kick-off meeting	scribes
JAD roles	Nominal Group Technique	technical scribe
JAD-analysis workshop	(NGT)	user-sponsor

◆ DISCUSSION QUESTIONS

1. Review the model of the Bridge systems development methodology provided in Figure 3.7 and Table 3.2. What types of JAD workshops are likely to be conducted during each stage of a Bridge project?

2. What are the responsibilities of systems analysts before, during, and after a JAD workshop?

3. Discuss the responsibilities and skills of a presentation scribe and a technical scribe. What kinds of tools does each scribe need to perform his or her job effectively?

4. How do JAD workshops support user-driven development?

5. Define the Nominal Group Technique and explain how it is used in a JAD workshop.

6. What is a group decision support system (GDSS)? How can it be used in a JAD workshop? What are the benefits of using a GDSS during a JAD workshop?

7. Discuss JAD's critical success factors. How can you ensure that they are achieved?

8. Explain how end-users, user-managers, and other participants are selected and prepared to participate in a JAD workshop.

9. Explain how the rules of operation and Open Issues list facilitate conducting a JAD workshop.

10. How does JAD help (a) to alleviate the problem of creeping requirements? (b) to improve user-developer communication?

◆ REFERENCES

Delbecq, A. L., A. H. Van de Ven, and D. H. Gustafson. *Group Techniques for Program Planning*. Glenview, IL: Scott, Foresman and Company, 1975.

Denrus, A. R., J. F. George, L. M. Jessup, J. F. Nunamaker, and D. R. Vogel. "Information Technology to Support Electronic Meetings." *MIS Quarterly* 12, no. 4 (December 1988).

DeSanctis, G., and R. B. Gallupe. "A Foundation for the Study of Group Support Systems." *Management Science* 33, no. 5 (May 1987).

Huber, G. "Chapter 11: Special Group Techniques: Procedures and Examples." *Managerial Decision Making*. Glenview, IL: Scott, Foresman and Company, 1980.

Jones, C. *Assessment and Control of Software Risks*. Englewood Cliffs, NJ: Prentice-Hall (Yourdon Press), 1994.

Martin, J. *Information Engineering: Book I, Introduction*. Englewood Cliffs, NJ: Prentice-Hall, 1990.

———. *Information Engineering: Book III, Design and Construction*. Englewood Cliffs, NJ: Prentice-Hall, 1990.

Turoff, M. "Computer-Mediated Communication Requirements for Group Support." *Journal of Organization Computing* 1, no. 1 (January–March 1991).

Texas Instruments Incorporated [1992a]. *Rapid Application Development Guide*. TI Part Number 2579082. April 1992.

Texas Instruments Incorporated [1992b]. *Scribing in JAD*. TI Part Number 2579084. April 1992.

CASE ILLUSTRATION

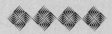

Conducting a JAD Workshop for ETG

This case installment describes a JAD workshop that Victoria and her student-consultant, Denny Young, conducted for ETG. The workshop presented here—and continued as chapter opening cases in Chapters 9, 10, and 11—combines elements of joint requirements planning (JRP), JAD analysis, and JAD design. Working from the problem definition report, the participants perform analysis activities, such as verifying the findings of the report, creating models of the system's behaviors and structure, defining ETG's business rules, and elaborating the requirements of the new walk-in customer order processing system. They also perform design activities, such as selecting a general design alternative and specifying the procedures, database, and interfaces of the new system.

The case illustration is presented as a narrative including references to figures from the problem definition report and providing a few additional figures. Some of the additional figures are ones that Victoria and Denny prepared for the JAD workshop; others are ones that were created during the workshop. Figure 1 gives the agenda for the workshop, but you should note that this case installment describes only selected agenda activities. Blank lines indicate breaks in time or in the flow of the narrative. In addition, some portions of the case are italicized to highlight statements about functional requirements.

The participants in the JAD workshop—Victoria, Denny, Paul, Corita, Linda Schwartz (company accountant) and several of the most experienced ETG clerks (Beto Juarez and Helen Loi from Sales and Susan Young and Bill Howard from Inventory)—met in the conference room of Victoria's office suite on three mornings before ETG business hours. They brought along their copies of the problem definition report to use as a reference throughout the workshop. In addition, Victoria prepared the workshop agenda in Figure 1 that was distributed at the beginning of the first session.

WORKSHOP INTRODUCTION

Victoria and Paul opened the workshop by welcoming the participants and encouraging everyone to participate fully in workshop activities. Then Victoria reviewed the agenda, focusing on Session One activities, and Denny defined the objectives of the workshop and explained how the workshop would be conducted.

"Victoria and I will be wearing multiple hats during these sessions. In addition to our role as analysts, we will also act as facilitators and scribes. What this means is that we will

AGENDA
JAD Workshop for
ETG's Walk-in Order Processing System
April 18–20, 1997

Session One, Tuesday, April 18, 8:00 a.m. - 12:30 p.m.

I. Introduction
   - Welcome participants (Victoria & Paul)
   - Review the agenda (Victoria)
   - Define workshop procedures and objective (Denny)

II. Review of Problem Definition Report
   - Verify scope, objectives, and constraints (All)

   Session Break & Snack (10:00 – 10:30)

   - Verify workflows, processes, and objects (All)
   - State problems new system will address (All)
   - Define functional requirements (All)

III. Session Close
   - Resolve open issues and make work assignments (Denny)

Session Two, Wednesday, April 19, 8:00 a.m. – 12:30 p.m.

I. Introduction
   - Review Session Two agenda (Victoria)
   - Review decisions/progress made in Session One (Denny & Paul)
   - Discuss open issues (Paul)

II. Discussion and Selection of Design Alternatives
   - Review general design alternatives (All)
   - Analyze costs and benefits (Victoria)
   - Select alternative (Paul and Linda)

   Session Break & Snack (10:00 – 10:30)

III. Definition of Selected Design Alternative (lead by Victoria)
   - Specify use cases describing the new system's major functions (Victoria)
   - Discuss user requirements of selected alternative (All)

IV. Session Close
   - Resolve open issues and make work assignments (Denny)

Session Three, Thursday, April 20, 8:00 a.m. – 12:30 p.m.

I. Introduction
   - Review Session Three agenda (Victoria)
   - Review decisions/progress made in Session Two (Denny & Paul)
   - Discuss open issues (Paul)

II. Definition of Business Objects and Rules (led by Denny)
   - Verify objects in order processing system (All)
   - Analyze use cases (All)
   - Define business rules governing the new system (All)

   Session Break & Snack (10:00 – 10:30)

III. Preliminary Design of User Interface (led by Denny)
   - Design forms (All)
   - Design input screens (All)
   - Design reports (All)

IV. Session Close
   - Summarize decisions and review progress (Victoria & Paul)
   - Plan resolution of open issues (Victoria & Paul)
   - Define the action plan (Victoria & Denny)
   - Evaluate effectiveness (All)
   - Thank participants (Victoria & Paul)

Figure 1: Agenda for ETG's two-day JAD workshop

lead the session discussions and take notes to document our findings and any decisions you make. What this doesn't mean is that we "rule the roost"—so to speak. What I mean is that you—the users—are the star players here. YOU make the decisions. We're here to listen to you, to learn what you expect the system to do, how you want it to work. So you should never hesitate to speak up, raise issues, disagree with what Victoria or I say.

"A general procedure or policy used in most JAD sessions regards the Open Issues list. Any time an issue is raised that can't be resolved after a short discussion, it is added to the Open Issues list. At the end of each session, we will revisit these Open Issues, perhaps assigning someone to investigate the issue and report back to all of us. You should understand that the open issues list isn't some kind of big rug that we sweep things under. In fact, if you feel that an issue has been given the short end of the stick, say so. One goal of a JAD workshop is to raise and to resolve these issues.

"Throughout the sessions, I or Victoria will be using a number of computerized tools to display diagrams and tables and, later on, to prototype the design of the user interface. Selected screens produced by these tools will be displayed on the whiteboard so that everyone can see them, suggest revisions, and then see the revised diagrams. These tools will help us capture your knowledge of ETG and the requirements and design specifications of the new system." Denny took a few minutes to demonstrate the computer screen projection system and to explain some of the diagrams the participants would be examining.

"Okay. Let's get to work!"

CONFIRMATION OF SYSTEM OBJECTIVES AND PROJECT SCOPE AND CONSTRAINTS

Victoria began the problem definition report confirmation by asking the workshop participants to verify the project scope and constraints and the system objectives.

"If you will please turn to the 'Project Definition and Feasibility' section of your report, you'll see a subheading 'System Objectives and Project Scope and Constraints.' We'll begin here to verify that we all have the same ideas about the nature of the project and about the ways in which the new order processing system will benefit ETG. First, let's look at the system objectives. As we verify these objectives, we'll also need to relate them to the problems listed in the report. We want to be sure that the system addresses these problems, or we need to decide that certain problems won't be addressed by the new system. Notice that Denny has also projected these objectives on the whiteboard. As you suggest revisions, he'll modify the list displayed. Does anyone have any suggestions, additions, or deletions?"

The participants reviewed the objectives silently for a few minutes. Susan Young, one of the inventory clerks, timidly raised her hand. "Susan, do you have a suggestion?" Victoria said, a note of encouragement in her voice.

"Yes," Susan said and then paused. "I don't understand how you plan to achieve the objectives about reducing the returned-tape backlog and reducing checkout time. I guess, to be honest, I'm really concerned about losing my job. As I read the report, I felt that you were saying that I was redundant."

"I got the same impression," Bill Howard added. "I don't see what role inventory clerks will play in the new system."

"OK, Susan, Bill," Victoria responded. "I believe that you've raised an important issue, but it's one that I can't address. Let's just take a moment to let Paul comment on your statement and then return to our discussion of objectives. Paul?"

Paul paused to clear his throat and then addressed his response to all the ETG employees present. "I can't guarantee that some clerks won't lose their jobs. Part of being more efficient is requiring less manpower to perform a job. However, my hope is that, by providing better customer service, we will increase the number of transactions that need to be processed. That means that the amount of work will increase and that we'll need everyone's help. No promises, but you should know that I didn't undertake this effort in an attempt to reduce payroll."

"Does that address your concern, Susan and Bill?" Victoria asked.

"Good enough, for now. Several of us clerks have wondered if this wasn't just another 'downsizing' disguised as 'reengineering,' " Susan responded.

"Paul's a good guy. I'll take his word for his real intention," Bill agreed.

"Good," Victoria said, signaling the resolution of the issue. "As I listened to Paul's response, though, I think I heard him state some system objectives not in our original list. Paul said something about improved customer service and increased sales and rentals. Paul, should we add these to the list of objectives?"

"Definitely. Those are really the most important objectives. But I guess that they were so implicit in everything else that I never thought to make them explicit. Yes, let's make them explicit in our project definition." Denny revised the objectives and projected the Revised Objectives list on the whiteboard.

"If I may, I'd like to interject another issue, more related to scope, I guess, than to objectives. The newsletter—and more generally, promotions—isn't mentioned in the objectives but is included in the project scope," Corita added. "It seems to me that we need to decide whether or how the new system will address promotions and newsletter processing."

"That's a very good point, Corita," Victoria responded, "and an issue that we need to discuss. If newsletter production is to be addressed fully, you need to think about purchasing additional hardware and desktop-publishing software."

"In an effort to address the most pressing concerns," Paul interjected, "I suggest that we focus on order processing for the time being. Corita, I know that you'd like to use desktop publishing to produce the newsletter. And I realize that we haven't leveraged the newsletter as well as we might to increase business. But—"

"But! Before you reject the idea, I think we should at least consider the costs and benefits," Corita countered. "Let's at least consider the feasibility of using desktop publishing."

"Corita has raised an issue that requires more information before we can address it fully," Victoria interjected. "Unless you decide to eliminate newsletter production from the project scope, we probably should do as Corita suggests. Shall we tentatively add increased promotions to our system objectives?"

"Yes," Paul answered, "I have no qualms about including promotions in general within the project scope. I'm just not ready to adopt desktop publishing at this time."

"For now, let's add a statement about newsletter production to our Open Issues list," Victoria continued. "Corita, since you raised the issue, you have first-cut at stating precisely what the issue is." Victoria stood in front of the Open Issues flipchart, ready to record Corita's statement.

"Okay, let me think a minute. Okay, 'Should newsletter production be automated in the new—' No, that's not quite it. 'Would automating newsletter production as part of the new system be cost effective?' Does that state your concern, Paul?"

"Yes, it does. If it makes sense—and saves or makes dollars—to automate now instead of undertaking another project later, then we should include newsletter production in this project. Otherwise, we should just plan the new system to allow . . . connection to the promotions . . . stuff. I don't know how to say what I mean."

"I think I understand your point," Victoria responded. "The new system should, at minimum, be designed to support Promotions' current data needs. In other words, even if desktop publishing isn't included in this project, *the new system must capture and give Promotions access to member and mailing list data and must support any promotional activities that Corita defines.* Is that right, Paul?"

"Sounds right."

"Does this statement reflect your concerns, Corita?"

"At least as they relate to promotions in general."

"Good. Then let's add the issue to the Open Issues list." As Victoria wrote Corita's revised statement on the flipchart, she added, "By the way, we'll plan how to investigate this issue at the end of today's session. Are there any more revisions to the objectives? . . . No? Then, Denny, would you please display the revised objectives?" (see Figure 2).

REVIEW OF WORKFLOW DIAGRAMS

The workshop was progressing well, with the participants verifying the workflow diagrams as Denny projected them. Then Corita raised a question.

"Here I go again," Corita sighed. "Either I've missed the boat or you're missing an important workflow between Promotions and Sales. You show member and newsletter sign-up data coming to me from Sales, but you don't show my giving Sales definitions of new promotional campaigns. Not that the omission is your fault, Victoria. I may have forgotten to mention this when we talked before."

---

1. Improve customer service by
   - Reducing rental transaction errors from the current estimate of 10 percent to less than 1 percent.
   - Reducing rental transaction processing time from the current estimate of 15 minutes to less than 2 minutes.
   - Eliminating the need for rental customers to return their receipts with their tapes.
2. Increase sales and rentals by
   - Eliminating the backlog of returned rental tapes to be processed.
   - More effectively managing promotions to generate new and repeat business.
3. Improve ETG's recordkeeping and fine-processing systems.

Figure 2: Revised system objectives for ETG's order processing system

"Whatever the cause of the omission, I'm just pleased that it's come to light now. That's the value of these workshops—correcting omissions, errors, misperceptions, et cetera. So none of you should hesitate to point out errors. I won't be offended!"

"Good," Beto said. "Then you won't be offended when I say that the diagrams totally ignore processing of overdue fines. I don't see any lines showing fines and fine payments. Yet *determining fines and processing fine payments will be necessary in any system we devise.*"

Linda Schwartz spoke up for the first time. "I don't see any mention of the audit tape and copies of the sales and rentals reports that I receive. At the end of each day, the sales clerks remove the cash register audit tape and count the money in the register. Both the audit tape and the cash are locked in the safe. I retrieve these each morning in order to prepare general ledger entries. You've noted that I receive copies of special orders, but omitted the cash register audit tape and the daily sales/rentals data that I receive."

"Excellent!" Victoria said. "You're doing an exceptional job critiquing these diagrams."

As the ETG users continued to point out errors and omissions, Denny revised the appropriate diagrams, adding the workflows and labels (see Figure 3). "Is this right?" Denny asked, as he displayed each revised diagram to the users.

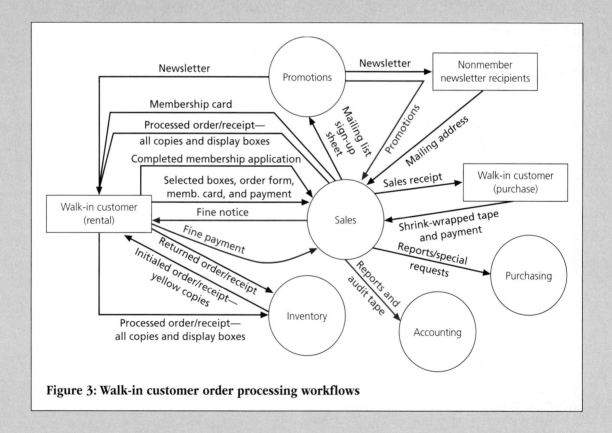

Figure 3: Walk-in customer order processing workflows

DEFINITION OF INTERFACES TO OTHER SYSTEMS

"Denny has displayed a diagram that highlights the workflows between other ETG departments and the order processing system (see Figure 4). The new system combines Sales and Inventory. The other organizational units shown here either create data for or use data from Order Processing," Victoria noted, as she used a pointer to trace the shared work flows on the projected diagram.

"As Corita pointed out earlier today, *Promotions needs both member data and the mailing list sign-up sheet from Order Processing.* Notice also that *Purchasing needs reports from and provides new tape data to Order Processing.* These workflows suggest the need for interfaces between these departments. In addition, *Accounting needs summary data about sales and rentals receipts.*"

"There's also a connection between Special Orders and Inventory," Paul noted. "The special order clerks often contact an inventory clerk to *verify tape availability for our commercial and bulk-order customers.*"

"Okay, let's summarize the new system's interfaces to other systems," Victoria said. "We've got to give Purchasing access to sales/rentals report data, Accounting access to audit and sales/rentals receipts data, Special Orders access to inventory data—by the way, is that just sales tape inventory or both sales and rental tapes?"

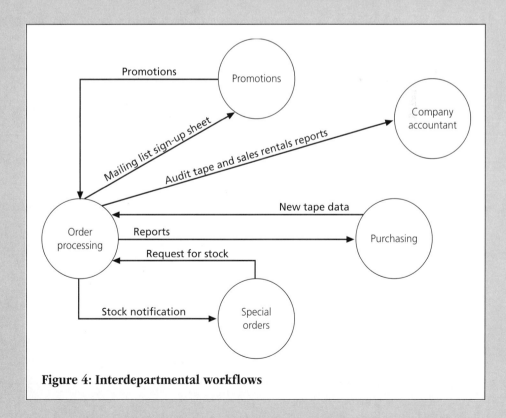

Figure 4: Interdepartmental workflows

"Mostly sales tapes, Victoria, but occasionally special-order customers rent tapes as well," Paul answered.

"Thanks, Paul. So both sales and rental tape inventory for Special Orders and, last but not least, member and mailing list sign-up data to Promotions. Good. We'll address how these other departments will access order processing data when we design the new system."

DEFINITION OF REQUIREMENTS

"Okay, I think we're ready to specify the requirements of the new system. In a few minutes, we'll examine a list of requirements that Denny and I compiled based on our preliminary analysis, DFDs, and comments that you've made today. One skill every good analyst learns is to listen for requirements. Denny is especially proficient in this skill and has been adding requirements to the list as he takes notes on our discussion. Let's review the requirements list to see if we've captured your needs accurately." (See Figure 5.)

"As you can see, we've categorized requirements into system functions: input, processing, output, storage, and control—the IPOSC functions, if you will," Victoria said. "Our Requirements list must state explicitly all the major functions the system will need to perform. Please review the list and suggest additions, deletions, or modifications."

The ETG users examined the list and concluded that it looked complete. Victoria continued, "I think we've defined *most* of the requirements, but you should understand that it's entirely natural for new requirements to arise as we more fully define the system's procedures, database, and interfaces. You'll also probably come up with additional needs and wants as you examine the prototypes Denny and I create. However, these should not require significant modification of the project scope."

Victoria looked at her wristwatch. "Well, it's 12:30 and we've just barely made it through our agenda. I think you'll agree that we've had a very productive morning. I'm a little concerned about being squeezed for time in the remaining sessions. Paul, will it be possible to run an hour longer to make sure that we get through everything on the agenda?"

"Sure. In fact, I'll have pizza delivered at noon—if you don't mind the mess! That way we can work through lunch and still open the store at two."

"Thanks, Paul. I won't mind 'the mess' at all, as long as one of the pizzas has anchovies! Tomorrow, we'll begin by discussing and selecting a general design alternative. I have several handouts that more fully describe these options. Please review these by tomorrow morning so that we'll have a bit of a head start on the agenda," Victoria said as she distributed handouts describing each alternative and its costs and benefits. "Okay, as our last order of business today, let's take just a few minutes to make work assignments and then you all can be on your way. The only unresolved open issue seems to be Corita's question about including desktop publishing as part of the new system. As we discussed requirements, we seemed to agree that Promotions is within the scope of the project and that the new system must support Promotions' data needs. The only unresolved issue is whether desktop-publishing capability would be a cost-effective addition to the project scope. Would anyone like to volunteer to investigate this issue?"

Input Functions: The system must accept the following inputs:

- new sales and rental tape data from Purchasing
- new-member data from Membership Application forms
- sales order and rental order transaction data, including employee number, member number, and tape stock number
- new customer mailing list data from the newsletter sign-up sheet
- definitions of promotional campaigns from Promotions

Processing Functions: The system must perform the following processes:

- assign membership number to new members
- assign order number and date to each order
- assign rental fee and due date to each rental order line item
- calculate transaction subtotal, sales tax, and total
- process cash and check payments
- determine the availability of rental and sales tapes for Special Orders
- sort transactions by type (rental vs. sale)
- identify overdue rental tapes/orders
- calculate overdue tape fines
- process payment of overdue tape fines

Output Functions: The system must generate the following outputs:

- sales order form
- rental order form
- membership cards
- sales and rentals summary report for Accounting and Purchasing
- overdue-tapes report
- newsletter mailing labels for Promotions
- cash receipts report for Accounting

Storage Functions: The system must maintain the following data:

- sales and rental tape data
- rental customers (members)
- sales and rental order transaction data
- cash receipts data
- employee data
- nonmember newsletter recipients' names and addresses

Control Functions: The system must enforce the following controls:

- verify rental tape data at checkout and return
- verify rental order payment before allowing rental tapes to be removed from the premises
- verify membership status before allowing customer to rent tapes
- verify on-time return of rental tapes
- limit system access to authorized users

Figure 5: The new system's IPOSC requirements

Denny, Corita, and Susan Young raised their hands. Denny said, "I know someone who can give us some price quotes on hardware and software. So if Susan and Corita can estimate the potential benefits from automating newsletter processing, we could meet later tonight and put together a cost-benefit analysis."

"Great idea, Denny," Corita replied. "I've given the issue a lot of thought and should have no trouble coming up with a list of benefits. And Susan? Didn't you say that you investigated desktop publishing for one of your courses?"

"Sure did. And I even saved the articles just in case an opportunity such as this arose," Susan responded. "I get off work at six. Should we meet at about seven tonight?"

The next morning, the JAD workshop continued with the report on desktop publishing. Paul and Corita, the user-sponsors, decided that, although automating newsletter production was desirable, it was a system function that was only indirectly related to order processing. In addition, broadening the scope to include desktop publishing would require a significant investment in additional hardware and software, making it almost impossible to satisfy the $30,000 project budget constraint. Paul convinced Corita to delay implementation of desktop-publishing capability until after the order processing system was up and running.

The next topic on the agenda was selection of a general design alternative. Victoria presented each alternative and its costs and benefits (see the "General Design Alternatives" section of the problem definition report for a description of the alternatives; see Figure 6 on page 270 for Victoria's comparative cost-benefit analysis worksheet). Then she encouraged the ETG participants to ask questions and to evaluate the alternatives. "A prime consideration as you evaluate these alternatives should be how well and how completely each solves the problems and satisfies the requirements that you identified yesterday. Last night I printed and made copies of the Requirements list that we discussed yesterday [Figure 5]," Victoria said, as she distributed the handouts.

Paul reviewed the problems and requirements and then said, "It seems that any of the alternatives you described will satisfy our requirements, Victoria. The main difference is the degree to which each really solves our problems. I mean, we could 'calculate transaction subtotal' and all that with a cash register like we do now; and we could track rental transactions and all that manually. But doing so would not 'improve recordkeeping' or reduce transaction time and errors, et cetera. I tend to favor the fullest solution that you proposed, what you called Alternative 2B in your report. Part of the reason I don't want to address desktop publishing at this time is that I really want to solve our order processing problems as completely as we can afford to do. Your cost-benefit analysis of option 2B comes in under budget, but there's a chance that, when all is said and done, the actual cost will be a bit higher. How do the rest of you feel?"

The ETG users agreed that the alternatives should be evaluated in terms of how well each helps ETG achieve its objectives. Denny quickly put together an evaluation worksheet. He decided to use the Nominal Group Technique to have individuals prepare their individual ratings and then compile a group rating. The design alternative evaluation worksheet and group ratings are shown in Figure 7 on page 271. The bar-code alternative was the clear winner. Although this alternative's total costs over three years would be approximately $10,000 greater than the keyboard-entry alternative, its greater benefits and contribution to ETG objectives justified the additional cost.

Entertainment to Go Walk-in Customer Order Processing System	Costs and Benefits of the Four General Design Alternatives			
Development Costs	**1A**	**1B**	**2A**	**2B**
Computer Hardware				
1 Pentium clone system*	$0	$0	$3,000	$3,000
1 tape back-up drive			$500	$500
1 impact printer	$0	$0	$450	$450
1 bar code reader	$0	$0	$0	$500
1 bar code labeler	$0	$0	$0	$500
Software				
Microsoft Office Professional	$0	$0	$600	$600
Bar coding software	$0	$0	$0	$400
Other				
Electronic security gate	$0	$1,000	$1,000	$1,000
Security labels for tapes	$0	$250	$250	$250
Bar code labels for tapes and membership cards				$250
Consulting	$3,000	$3,500	$8,500	$10,000
Data conversion	$0	$0	$3,500	$4,000
Training	$500	$500	$2,500	$2,500
Facility remodeling	$4,000	$4,000	$2,500	$2,500
Total Development Costs	**$7,500**	**$9,250**	**$22,800**	**$26,540**
Production Costs (Years 1–3)				
Computer supplies	$0	$0	$500	$750
Hardware/software upgrades	$0	$0	$500	$1,000
Parttime Systems Manager	$0	$0	$14,400	$21,600
Total Production Costs Years 1–3	**$0**	**$0**	**$15,400**	**$23,350**
Production Costs Present Value			$12,225	$18,536
Total Costs	**$7,500**	**$9,250**	**$35,025**	**$44,986**
Benefits (Years 1–3)				
Improved customer service	$6,000	$6,000	$30,000	$45,000
Increased productivity	$4,500	$4,500	$15,000	$20,000
Reduced shrinkage	$0	$2,000	$2,000	$2,000
Reduced rework due to errors	$1,500	$1,500	$3,000	$6,000
Improved fine processing	$0	$0	$2,500	$2,500
Improved management information	$0	$0	$5,000	$5,000
Total Benefits for Production Years 1–3	**$12,000**	**$14,000**	**$52,500**	**$75,500**
Present Value of Benefits	**$9,526**	**$11,114**	**$41,676**	**$59,934**
Net Gain or (Loss)	**$2,026**	**$1,864**	**$6,651**	**$14,948**
Profitability Index	**1.27**	**1.20**	**1.83**	**2.27**
Assumptions				
Discount rate used to compute present value	0.08			
Systems manager fee per hour	$40			
Assumed hours/month for Alternative 2A	10			
Assumed hours/month for Alternative 2B	15			

*16 MB RAM, 1Gbyte HD, DOS and Windows

Figure 6: Cost-benefit analysis of the four general design alternatives

| Alternative | | 1A | | 1B | | 2A | | 2B | |
Objective	Weight	Raw Score	Weighted Score	Raw Score	Weighted Score	Raw Score	Weighted Score	Raw Score	Weighted Score
Reduced errors	4	7	28	7	28	9	36	10	40
Improved productivity	5	5	25	5	25	8	40	10	50
Better service	5	5	25	5	25	9	45	10	50
Increased tape turnover	4	5	20	5	20	8	32	9	36
More effective promotions	4	0	0	0	0	8	32	8	32
Improved recordkeeping	4	0	0	0	0	10	40	10	40
Total Weighted Score			98		98		225		248

Note: Weight ranges from 1 (not important) to 5 (very important).
Raw score for each criterion ranges from 0 (no contribution to objective) to 10 (major contribution to objective).
The weighted score is the product of the criterion weight times the criterion raw score.

Figure 7: Design alternative evaluation worksheet

PART THREE

Iterative Analysis, Design, Preliminary Construction, and Review

Iterative Analysis, Design, Preliminary Construction, and Review

1. Analyze system structure and behavior.
   a. Analyze system data structures.
   b. Analyze system behavior.
   c. Analyze system interfaces.
2. Design system structure and behavior.
   a. Design system data structures.
   b. Design system behavior.
   c. Design system interfaces.
3. Construct prototype for user review.
4. Conduct user review.
5. Repeat steps 1–4, if changes are needed.

Part Three covers the iterative analysis, design, preliminary construction, and review stage of systems development. Now that you have completed the enterprise analysis and problem definition, you are ready to perform the activities that students usually find the most interesting and exciting: designing and prototyping the new system!

The activities in this stage require you to define more fully the requirements of the new system and to design and to construct a prototype (i.e., a preliminary system) that fulfills these requirements. The activities you will perform include the following:

◆ Studying source documents and existing data stores to define the system's data structures.

◆ Specifying system behaviors that will be implemented as manual procedures and programs or object methods.

◆ Specifying and designing user interfaces, including data entry screens, menus, and reports.

◆ Constructing a preliminary database and programs to implement your design specification.

- Demonstrating your prototype to users.
- Refining your prototype based on user feedback.

Additional modeling techniques used during this stage include

- The object relationship model, which specifies the system's data objects and their relationships.
- Physical DFDs, which specify the IPOSC functions of the new system.
- Dialog flow diagrams, which specify the system's menus and screens (i.e., interfaces).
- Behavior specification techniques, which use diagrams and structured text to specify system behaviors.

Part Three begins with Chapter 8, which discusses prototyping and rapid application development (RAD). One objective of this chapter is to help you understand a concept central to RAD and other iterative development methodologies: *Although the discussion of analysis, design, preliminary construction, and review activities is presented in a sequential, linear fashion in Part Three, you should realize that these activities are not sequential; in fact, they tend to overlap and iterate through this development stage.* Chapter 8 also discusses the techniques and tools required for successful RAD and prototyping projects.

Technical Module D presents the object relationship model, which is used to analyze the data structures of a system. Chapter 9 continues the discussion of system data structure analysis and design. In this chapter, you will learn about the concepts and issues in physical database design, focusing on relational and object database management systems. Chapter 9 also explains how to convert an object relationship model into a relational database design.

Chapter 10 takes a closer look at the activities and techniques of system behavior analysis and design. In this chapter, you will learn how to specify the behaviors of the new system. Here you will focus on the system's object methods and messages. You will learn to determine how system functions should be performed (e.g., batch vs. real-time); you will also learn how to construct and to partition a physical DFD, to design programs, and to specify system behaviors using structured text.

Chapter 11 focuses on the system interface: the menus, screens, and reports that bridge the human-computer boundary. You will learn about the concepts and issues in user interface design and construct a dialog flow diagram to specify the interfaces and the flow of control between them.

Chapter 12 explains how to conduct a user review and how to prepare a report defining the design specifications of the new system. The design specification report is the foundation for the final construction, system test, and installation stage of systems development. In this report, you document the design of the new system and detail the activities required to construct, test, and install the production system.

The Part Three ETG case illustration is about the activities of this development stage, describing how Victoria and Denny design and prototype a new order processing system for ETG.

RAPID APPLICATION DEVELOPMENT AND PROTOTYPING

In Chapter 3, you learned about creeping requirements, a problem that plagues projects using the traditional development methodology, which performs activities in a linear, waterfall sequence and requires that requirements be frozen before design begins. Creeping requirements are endemic, averaging 35 percent in a recent study of 60 projects [Jones 1994]. However, given the rapidly changing business environment, we must expect some requirements creep. The real problem is the lack of—or failure to use—effective methods and strategies to minimize the impact of requirements creep on the project management and system quality development goals. In essence, we must learn to develop more adaptable systems using more flexible development methodologies.

The JAD technique discussed in Chapter 7 offers a valuable means of controlling requirements creep. As noted in that chapter, JAD reduces requirements creep to less than 10 percent, especially in leading-edge application projects with uncertainty about how to meet user needs. Other strategies effective in reducing requirements creep are prototyping and iterative development, such as rapid application development (RAD).

These strategies are presented as an introduction to the iterative analysis, design, preliminary construction, and review stage. You should understand that the sequential, linear nature of a textbook is not amenable to representing iterative processes. Thus, although the remainder of Part Three will discuss these activities linearly, you should bear in mind that *these activities are not performed linearly;* that is, they are not sequential. In real projects, you may move from analysis to design, back to analysis, on to design, then to preliminary construction and back to design, then conduct a user review, and so on, as the structure and behavior of the information system unfold.

After completing this chapter, you should be able to

1. Define prototyping and describe several prototyping tools.

2. Compare and contrast requirements prototyping and evolutionary prototyping, giving examples of how each is used.

3. Discuss the advantages and disadvantages of prototyping.

4. Define rapid application development (RAD), distinguishing it from traditional systems development, phased development, and prototyping.

5. Discuss the objectives of RAD.

6. List and explain the four ingredients required for RAD success.

7. Describe the benefits of RAD.

8.1   ◆   PROTOTYPING

In the 1970s many IS academics and professionals held a negative view of **prototyping**—the iterative refinement of a working model of an information system. The term "quick and dirty" was often applied to the prototyping strategy, indicating the low regard in which it was held: "quick" in the sense of plunging into design and construction without adequately defining requirements; "dirty" in the sense of delivering an undocumented system that was difficult to maintain. In essence, prototyping was regarded as an unstructured method that, though possibly suitable for defining the human-computer interface, was unacceptable in regular practice.

However, in the early 1980s, several studies demonstrated that prototyping produced highly desirable benefits: shortened development time, greater usability, improved developer-user communication, and reduced deadline effect, among others (see e.g., Alavi [1984], Boehm et al. [1984], and Mason & Carey [1983]). Over the past decade, the prototyping strategy has been amended to overcome its perceived disadvantages: the seemingly unplanned, uncontrollable, unmanageable nature of its process; the difficulty in integrating the prototyped system with other systems; and the less coherent system design it yielded as compared to other methods. Today, prototyping is widely recognized as an effective systems development strategy that developers are encouraged to exploit in almost every project.

TWO PROTOTYPING STRATEGIES: REQUIREMENTS AND EVOLUTIONARY

Two prototyping strategies are commonly employed today. The first, **requirements prototyping**, uses a prototype to determine the requirements of a proposed information system. Showing users a working model of the system helps them to understand its features and functions, to specify what they need the system to do (its requirements) and to see where the system is performing correctly. Then, using user feedback, the designers generate another prototype and again show it to the users. The model-critique-refine process continues until the prototype is approved. Once approved, the prototype is discarded, and its design specifications are used to implement the production system with other tools and techniques. For example, the prototype might be constructed using a fourth-generation language (4GL) or prototyping tool, but the production system might be implemented in COBOL.

Requirements prototyping is commonly used as a requirements determination strategy [Davis 1982] that can be employed during the systems analysis stage of any development methodology, as illustrated in Figure 8.1. It is particularly effective in defining the requirements of leading-edge systems and in designing the human-computer interface. However, requirements prototyping is essentially an "add-on" technique for improving user-developer communication; it is not, in and of itself, a systems development methodology because it does not address all development activities. The conditions under which requirements prototyping is likely to be effective are summarized in Table 8.1.

In contrast, the second prototyping strategy, **evolutionary prototyping**, is a fully realized systems development methodology. Evolutionary prototyping may use the same techniques

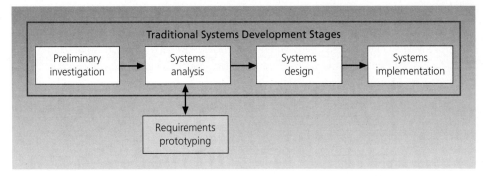

FIGURE 8.1   Requirements prototyping as "add-on" technique in traditional systems development

TABLE 8.1 When to use requirements prototyping

Conditions Supporting Requirements Prototyping	Conditions Not Supporting Requirements Prototyping
The proposed system is leading-edge; thus, users do not understand its requirements, and no model (e.g., existing system) is readily available.	Users clearly understand the requirements of the proposed system, or you can model the new system from existing systems in your own or another organization.
The proposed system automates a real-time, highly interactive application (e.g., a decision support or executive information system), with many complex user interfaces.	The proposed system is processing-intensive and/or batch-oriented (e.g., transaction processing systems for payroll, accounts payable, sales order processing, etc.) with few user interfaces.
You need to strengthen user commitment to the project and system. Prototyping improves user-developer communication and involves users more fully in the development project.	Users are too busy or unwilling to invest the time to critique your prototype as it evolves.

and tools as requirements prototyping with one important difference: instead of being discarded, the prototype becomes the production system. Thus, evolutionary prototyping constructs a preliminary system release, a process that requires more time and effort than requirements prototyping and is feasible only if advanced tools capable of generating efficient, bug-free programs and database structures are available. Other conditions conducive to evolutionary prototyping are summarized in Table 8.2.

The activities in evolutionary prototyping are illustrated in Figure 8.2. Notice that you first define the proposed system's functional requirements at a high level of generality. This "first take" on requirements provides the starting point for iteratively analyzing, designing, constructing a prototype, and reviewing the prototype with users. You pay more attention to design, construction, and review here than in requirements prototyping because the end-product of this process will become a production system. Thus, while requirements prototyping may involve one or two developers working a week or less, or may be performed during a single JAD session, evolutionary prototyping involves the whole development team and consumes the majority of the project schedule.

In its fullest incarnation, evolutionary prototyping is indistinguishable from an iterative systems development methodology such as rapid application development. Thus, we will explore its techniques, tools, and benefits more fully in Section 8.2, "Rapid Application Development."

TABLE 8.2 When to use evolutionary prototyping

Conditions Supporting Evolutionary Prototyping	Conditions Not Supporting Evolutionary Prototyping
The proposed system is leading-edge; thus, you cannot safely freeze requirements before beginning design and implementation.	The requirements of the proposed system are clearly understood and unlikely to change.
The proposed system is being developed for a dynamic environment in which business needs are constantly changing.	The proposed system is being developed for a stable business environment.
The proposed system automates a real-time, highly interactive application (e.g., a decision support or executive information system), with many complex user interfaces.	The proposed system is processing-intensive and/or batch-oriented (e.g., transaction processing systems for payroll, accounts payable, sales order processing, etc.). This is the kind of project in which traditional systems development works well!
The proposed system is small- to medium-sized and has few critical interfaces with other systems.	The proposed system is large, with numerous interfaces with other systems.
Your development team has at least a small cadre of developers trained in the use of advanced tools.	No one on your development team has previous experience with advanced tools. Develop this expertise first.

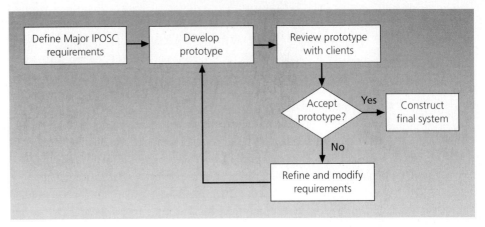

FIGURE 8.2   Activities in evolutionary prototyping

PROTOTYPING TOOLS

Prototyping is feasible and cost effective only if developers have the ability to use advanced tools. **Prototyping tools** range from the simple to the powerful. Simple prototyping tools include word-processing and spreadsheet programs that can be used to illustrate screen and report layouts. A more powerful prototyping tool is a PC database program that employs wizards to easily derive sample forms, screens, and reports from the database definition. For example, Microsoft Access provides a number of wizards that let you simulate user interfaces in a matter of minutes. Access also provides "button wizards" that make it easy to simulate the flow of control between screens. Other prototyping tools include fourth-generation languages, such as FOCUS, Natural, and NOMAD2, and the rapid development tools discussed later in this chapter.

When one objective of a prototype is to capture complex processing rules, a rule-based expert system shell, such as VP-Expert, may be needed. For example, assume that your task is to build a system to automate benefits determination for welfare applicants. The rules governing who qualifies for what benefits are complex, with numerous logic branches depending on the values of certain attributes (e.g., number of dependents, monthly income, etc.). An easy-to-use tool such as VP-Expert allows you to prototype these rules and test their validity; given a set of attributes, if the prototype identifies the correct benefits, you know that you have expressed the rules correctly.

The most powerful prototyping tools are application generators and CASE tools that can derive screens and reports from process and data models stored in the tool's encyclopedia. The primary advantage of using a CASE tool to build prototypes is that all of the processing logic and design models are retained in the encyclopedia and can be used to build the final system. An integrated CASE (sometimes called i-CASE) tool provides toolsets addressing all development activities, from planning and analysis to design and construction. The models created by these toolsets can be integrated and stored in the tool's encyclopedia so that the output of one toolset is the input to another toolset. In addition, many CASE tools provide a code generator that can convert design models into executable code and database structures.

ADVANTAGES AND DISADVANTAGES OF PROTOTYPING

The greatest advantage of prototyping is its ability to control requirements creep, thus improving system quality. Prototyping alone can reduce requirements creep to less than 10 percent; in conjunction with JAD, prototyping reduces requirements creep to less than 5 percent [Jones 1994]. This advantage justifies your including some prototyping in almost any development project. In addition, prototyping increases user involvement and commitment. Users feel that they are an integral part of the development effort because their insights and feedback are incorporated into the system design. And because users become familiar with system features and functions as they work with the prototype, training them to use the new system is facilitated.

The disadvantages of prototyping vary depending on the prototyping strategy used. In requirements prototyping, a frequent problem is that users develop false expectations about how quickly the system will be delivered. Having seen a prototype developed in days or weeks, they expect the production system to be delivered with equivalent speed. Another problem is that users may be disappointed if discrepancies exist between the prototype and the production system. For example, the prototype, which used a small test database, may have responded to a query in one to two seconds; in contrast, the full production system, which must access the full database and perhaps compete with other users' database accesses, may require five to ten seconds to return a response.

Disadvantages commonly arising in the evolutionary prototyping strategy relate primarily to project-management issues. How can you plan a project schedule if you cannot specify exactly what tasks are required and how much time each task will consume? At what point should you begin to develop user and system documentation? Should the documentation evolve in concert with the prototype? How do you gauge whether your project is on schedule when there are no clearly defined criteria for deciding that the prototype is "done"? This is the most troublesome issue in evolutionary prototyping: deciding when enough is enough. At what point has the prototype evolved sufficiently to undergo final construction and testing and to be placed in production?

Consider an analogy. Before the advent of word-processing software on microcomputers, you manually typed your manuscripts. If you made a typographical error, you had to use correction fluid, or—for highly critical papers—you had to retype the page. If you decided to change a sentence after it had been typed, you had to discard the page and start again. Your formatting options were limited to variable margins, underlining, and—well, that was about it! You were seldom tempted to refine your prose after it had been typed because doing so required too much effort. Good enough would just have to be good enough.

Contrast this scenario with how you prepare manuscripts using a word-processing program. Do you find yourself endlessly editing and revising your sentences? Do you waste time fiddling with various formatting options? Probably so, because experimentation is so easy that you lose sight of the time and effort expended until you suddenly realize that it is almost midnight, and you've devoted two hours to writing the first paragraph of a report due at 9:00 tomorrow morning!

The same kind of endless tinkering is fatal to a systems development project. Some developers become so obsessed with getting a particular data entry screen just right that they expend undue time and effort on what may be an insignificant piece of the whole system. In the meantime, the project clock is winding down, and the database and programs are only half-completed. Thus, discipline and the ability to focus on the whole system, not just one piece, are critical to evolutionary prototyping success.

Check Your Understanding 8-1

Categorize each of the following statements as descriptive of requirements prototyping (R), evolutionary prototyping (E), or both (B).

_____ 1. The iterative refinement of a working model of an information system.

_____ 2. The prototype becomes the production system.

_____ 3. Improves developer-user communication.

_____ 4. An "add-in" technique used to determine requirements.

_____ 5. The prototype is discarded.

_____ 6. Feasible only if tools are available that can generate code and database structures.

_____ 7. A full systems development methodology.

_____ 8. Effective when requirements cannot be frozen before design begins.

_____ 9. A strategy for strengthening user commitment.

_____ 10. May be difficult to control project schedule if this strategy is used.

8.2 ◈ RAPID APPLICATION DEVELOPMENT

Rapid application development (RAD) is a systems development methodology that employs evolutionary prototyping and phased development techniques to deliver limited functionality in a short timeframe. If additional functionality is needed, the initial project's schedule is not extended; instead, another project is funded to enhance the first project's delivered system to provide added functions. Over repeated small projects, the system evolves to produce greater and greater functionality. Similar to phased development, RAD requires that you be able to identify a small set of requirements that can be delivered within a few months. And, as in phased development, this small set of requirements may be derived by segmenting a system into subsystems or data capabilities or by clustering and prioritizing functional requirements into subsets that can be delivered iteratively over a series of small projects.

Although often discussed in the same category as JAD and prototyping, RAD is a full-fledged systems development methodology, as shown in Figure 8.3. It is not just an add-on technique. One feature that distinguishes RAD from requirements prototyping is that the output of the timebox is a production system. RAD differs from evolutionary prototyping and

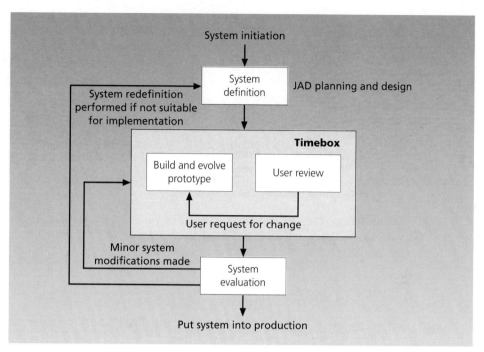

FIGURE 8.3 Activities in rapid application development

phased development because of the **timebox**: a nonextendible time limit (usually 60 days) placed on the evolutionary prototyping stage. Once the requirements set for a project has been identified, you iteratively perform the analysis, design, prototype construction and review process until the time limit expires or you have satisfied the requirements—whichever comes first.

Because the timebox cannot be extended, the functionality of the system may have to be limited. This constraint forces users and designers to focus on the most important system functions, leaving the "bells and whistles" for a later iteration. The philosophy of the timebox approach is that "it is better to have a working system of limited functionality quickly than to wait two years for a more comprehensive system" [Martin 1990, pp. 22–23]. Furthermore, the short span of elapsed time from project inception to system delivery guards against the dreaded requirements creep.

OBJECTIVES AND INGREDIENTS OF RAD PROJECTS

The objectives of the RAD methodology are to deliver a high-quality system inexpensively and quickly. RAD attempts to overcome—perhaps disprove—the limitations illustrated by the cheap-fast-good triangle discussed in Chapter 1. Proponents of RAD insist that all three goals are attainable simultaneously, representing the development goals as overlapping circles, as shown in Figure 8.4. Achieving all three goals requires that a RAD project exploit four ingredients: tools, methodology, people, and management [Texas Instruments 1992a].

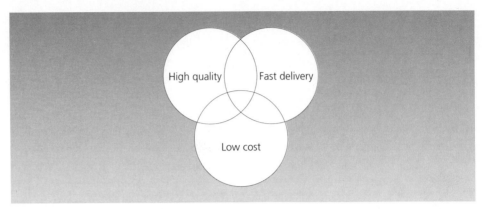

FIGURE 8.4   RAD objective: to quickly and inexpensively produce a high-quality system

Tools

The secret to RAD is reducing the time and effort devoted to creating the software component. Accordingly, RAD success is dependent on the availability of tools that allow developers to quickly and easily create applications. Several categories of tools are required: graphical user interface (GUI) generators and cross-platform development tools, frontware, fourth-generation languages (4GLs) and relational database management (RDBMS) tools, and CASE tools.

The first category, **graphical user interface (GUI) generators**, allow developers to quickly create visual representations of user interfaces and then generate the underlying source code. Examples of these tools include AppMaker (Macintosh), Instant Windows, XFaceMaker, and WindowsMaker. **Cross-platform development tools**, such as Galaxy and Open Interface, perform the same functions, but differ from GUI generators in that, from a single graphical representation, they can generate the code for user interfaces running on multiple platforms (e.g., in Windows and UNIX).

Another major category of tools is **frontware**, also called *screen scrapers*, which allows developers to create GUI front ends that emulate dumb terminal connections to existing mainframe applications. Easel (Easel Corp.) and EDA/SQL (Information Builders) are two examples of frontware tools. These tools support data access from a variety of databases (flat files; network, hierarchical, and relational databases) running on a variety of hardware platforms.

The third category of tools, more mature and robust than GUI generators and frontware, include **fourth-generation languages (4GLs)**, which are full-featured programming languages that in some cases also provide a database management system (DBMS). Examples of 4GLs are FOCUS (Information Builders), Natural (Software AG), and Powerhouse (Cognos, Inc.). These 4GLs greatly reduce programming labor by creating programs with far fewer lines of code than would be required using a 3GL. Because coding effort is reduced, development time is also shortened. In addition, most 4GLs support multiple database types and run on multiple platforms from desktops to mainframes; some are also fully supported by CASE tools that automatically generate 4GL code.

Also within the third category that facilitate database development are **relational database management system (RDBMS) tools**, such as SQL Forms (Oracle) and Informix-4GL (Informix). Increasingly, RDBMS vendors are offering their own CASE product or providing interfaces to existing CASE tools. Developers specify the database design using the tool, which then generates the database structures, thus reducing development time and effort.

A variation of 4GLs are **graphical 4GLs**, programming languages that support rapid development by combining many of the features of GUI generators, frontware, and RDBMS tools with object-oriented constructs. Graphical 4GLs include SQLWindows (Gupta), VisualAge (IBM), ObjectView (Knowledgeware), Visual Basic (Microsoft), Visual Works (ParcPlace), and Powerbuilder (Powersoft). Some graphical 4GL tools provide prebuilt modules, allowing developers to "piece together" the software component and greatly reducing the amount of programming effort required. For example, Visual Basic modules (VBX) are available from a variety of third-party vendors who provide components ranging from GUI buttons to modules that perform complex numerical analyses. The trend in software development is **component-based application development:** constructing applications by "snapping in" and customizing prebuilt modules. Many graphical 4GL tools support this trend. In addition, many graphical 4GLs also provide data-modeling capabilities, support multiple platforms and databases, and can coordinate the movement of data between server and client.

The fourth category of tools includes traditional CASE tools, which are the most mature and robust of all tool categories, making them more suitable for large, stable, mission-critical applications. Many CASE tools support all stages and activities of systems development; in addition, they usually enforce a development methodology. Unfortunately, adherence to the tool's methodology may have the effect of lengthening development time. However, some CASE tool vendors—for example, IEF by Texas Instruments—recommend strategies for using their tools in RAD projects [Texas Instruments 1992a]. A benefit of using CASE tools in RAD is that all analysis and design models are retained in the tool's encyclopedia and can be reused in later projects.

Object-oriented technolgoies are also integral to RAD. OO's promise of reusable classes can reduce the time and effort devoted to software construction, consequently reducing development time.

Methodology

RAD success requires that developers adhere to the RAD methodology, which integrates advanced development techniques, such as JAD and prototyping, and clearly defines development tasks throughout the project. The Texas Instruments' (TI) *Rapid Application Development Guide* provides a clear, concise, detailed description of this methodology and recommends how to schedule and manage a RAD project. Although TI's model of the RAD methodology is structured somewhat differently and sometimes uses different names to describe development activities and stages, the fundamentals are the same as the methodology shown in Figure 8.3.

People

As important as tool availability and adherence to the RAD methodology are, involving the right people in the project is critical. Without the involvement and commitment of users, RAD will fail. RAD requires a user-sponsor who can make things happen by motivating user participation and removing any political or bureaucratic barriers that might impede the project. Because RAD uses JAD sessions throughout the development project, key users and managers must be committed to attending and enthusiastically participating in these sessions. This requirement means that many valuable employees will not be attending to their "real" jobs for several days during the project.

In addition, RAD requires a highly skilled development team. The term **SWAT Team** is sometimes used to describe these developers: Skilled With Advanced Tools. A SWAT Team is a small group—typically no more than five people—of experienced, well-trained developers who can work together efficiently and effectively. Ideally, this team should include individuals who have worked together on many projects, thus developing an understanding of each other's work styles and skills. Through their project experience, the SWAT team may have developed its own library of reusable designs, which can be used to speed development even further.

Management

In addition to a committed user-sponsor, RAD success also requires that management demonstrate support by helping to manage the change in organizational culture that RAD requires. RAD breaks down the traditional barriers between IS and business functional areas, demanding that each attend to the concerns and needs of the other. Users must learn about IS, and developers must learn about business processes and issues. Management must agree that decisions made in the JAD sessions are equivalent to the formal sign-off employed in traditional systems development. In other words, the development team is not required to produce lengthy specification documents, nor does it need to conduct a time-consuming (read "project delaying") review and approval process.

In addition, management must ensure that effective project-management tools and techniques are employed so that the value of RAD is clearly demonstrated by measures of performance and system quality. Demonstrated benefits are key to motivating the required change in organizational culture.

BENEFITS OF RAPID APPLICATION DEVELOPMENT

The primary advantage of RAD is that at least some functionality is delivered quickly, with incremental releases scheduled at three to six month intervals. As with phased development, incremental delivery means that little time elapses between requirements analysis and system delivery, thus greatly reducing requirements creep. Also similar to phased development, the RAD strategy allows users to work with a limited version of a system, thereby providing greater insight into the requirements of the fuller system.

RAD improves user-designer communication as well, and it increases user commitment to the system as users are continuously called upon to define their needs and to critique the evolving system. Finally, the RAD strategy avoids the financial fiasco of a canceled system. Rather than invest two years and millions of dollars to discover that a system is infeasible, an organization can use RAD to limit the time and expense at risk to a few months and perhaps only tens of thousands of dollars.

✔ Check Your Understanding 8-2

1. Use the terms "requirements prototyping," "evolutionary prototyping," "phased development," and "JAD" to fill the blanks.

    a. RAD is similar to _____ in that both are full systems development methodologies.

    b. RAD differs from _____ and _____ in that RAD imposes a timebox, whereas the others do not.

    c. RAD is similar to _____ in that both segment a system into subsystems, or small sets of requirements to be implemented over several short projects.

    d. RAD is similar to _____ in that it requires committed users and managers who are willing to participate actively in the development project.

2. Fill in the blanks with the appropriate term.

    a. Reducing the time and effort required to develop the _____ component of an information system is the secret to RAD.

    b. A _____ is a full-featured programming language that may also provide database management functions.

    c. A _____ is a small group of very experienced developers who are skilled in the use of advanced tools.

    d. _____ is a trend in software development in which application programs are constructed from prebuilt modules.

◆ REVIEW OF CHAPTER LEARNING OBJECTIVES

1. *Define prototyping and describe several prototyping tools.*

Prototyping is the iterative refinement of a working model of an information system. It typically requires a variety of tools, ranging from simple word-processing, graphics, and spreadsheet software to fourth-generation languages, application generators, and CASE tools.

2. *Compare and contrast requirements prototyping and evolutionary prototyping, giving examples of how each is used.*

Requirements prototyping is a requirements determination strategy in which developers construct a prototype to help users define system requirements. Showing users a working model of the system helps them to understand its features and functions. Once approved, the prototype is discarded, and its design specifications are used to implement the working system with other tools and techniques. In contrast, evolutionary prototyping is a full systems development methodology in which the prototype becomes the production system. Evolutionary prototyping, RAD, and other iterative methodologies are similar in that each advocates iterative analysis, design, and prototyping as an effective strategy for developing an information system.

3. *Discuss the advantages and disadvantages of prototyping.*

One of the greatest benefits of prototyping is its reduction of requirements creep. Because requirements are frozen later in a prototyping project than in a traditional systems development project, creeping requirements are less likely to damage system quality. Prototyping also improves user-developer communication and user commitment. Disadvantages of requirements prototyping include (a) unrealistic user expectations about how quickly the production system will be delivered and (b) user disappointment regarding discrepancies between the prototype and the production system. Disadvantages of evolutionary prototyping are primarily related to project-management issues: When is the prototype "done"?

4. *Define rapid application development (RAD), distinguishing it from traditional systems development, phased development, and prototyping.*

RAD is a systems development methodology that employs evolutionary prototyping and phased development techniques to deliver limited functionality in a short timeframe. A feature that distinguishes RAD from traditional systems development is its iterative analysis, design, prototyping, and user review stage. A feature that distinguishes it from evolutionary prototyping and phased development is the **timebox:** a nonextendible time limit (usually 60 days) placed on the evolutionary prototyping stage. A feature that distinguishes RAD from requirements prototyping is that the output of the timebox is a working system. Thus, the RAD strategy assumes the availability of prototyping, CASE, and other advanced tools that can produce efficient, executable code and database structures.

5. *Discuss the objectives of RAD.*

RAD's objectives are to deliver a high-quality system inexpensively and quickly. RAD attempts to overcome the long-held proposition that a *good* system cannot be delivered both *quickly* and *cheaply*. Proponents of RAD insist that all three goals are attainable.

6. *List and explain the four ingredients required for successful RAD.*

Achieving RAD goals requires that a RAD project exploit four ingredients: tools, methodology, people, and management. Tools must be available to allow developers to quickly and easily create applications, namely, graphical user interface (GUI) generators and cross-platform development tools, frontware, 4GLs and RDBMS tools, and CASE tools. The RAD methodology must integrate advanced development techniques, such as JAD and prototyping, and clearly define development tasks throughout the project. People must include a committed user-sponsor; knowledgeable, enthusiastic users; a highly skilled development team; and supportive management to facilitate the necessary change in organizational culture and ensures the use of effective project-management tools.

7. *Describe the benefits of RAD.*

RAD provides all the benefits of prototyping: reduced requirements creep, improved user-developer communication, and increased user commitment. In addition, RAD avoids the financial fiasco of a canceled system by forcing users and developers to limit project scope and system requirements so that a working system can be delivered with a few months.

◈ KEY TERMS

component-based application development

cross-platform development tools

evolutionary prototyping

fourth-generation language (4GL)

frontware

graphical 4GL

graphical user interface (GUI) generators

prototyping

prototyping tools

rapid application development (RAD)

relational database management (RDBMS) tools

requirements prototyping

SWAT Team

timebox

◈ DISCUSSION QUESTIONS

1. Under what conditions is requirements prototyping an effective "add-on" technique in a traditional systems development project?

2. Would evolutionary prototyping be an effective systems development strategy for a large-scale, long-term (i.e., two or more years) project? Why or why not?

3. How does RAD eliminate the problem of endless tinkering that can plague an evolutionary prototyping project?

4. RAD is best employed for small- to medium-sized system projects. If an organization needs to develop a large system and wants to use RAD, how should it do so?

5. Evolutionary prototyping and RAD are considered full systems development methodologies. Why?

6. List the three objectives of RAD. Do you believe that RAD can achieve all three of its objectives simultaneously? Why or why not?

7. Define and give examples of each of the categories of RAD tools.

8. What is component-based application development? In what ways does this software development trend support RAD's objectives?

9. What is a SWAT team? How does a SWAT team help to meet the three RAD objectives?

◈ REFERENCES

Alavi, M. "An Assessment of the Prototyping Approach to Information Systems Development." *Communications of the ACM* 27, no. 6 (June 1984), pp. 556–563.

Boehm, B., T. E. Gray, and T. Seewaldt. "Prototyping Versus Specifying: A Multiproject Experiment." *IEEE Transactions on Software Engineering* SE-10, no. 3 (1984), pp. 298–311.

Budde, R., and H. Zullighoven. "Prototyping Revisited." In *Information Technology and People* 6, no. 2–3 (1992), pp. 97–107.

Davis, G. B. "Strategies for Information Requirements Determination." *IBM Systems Journal* 21, no. 1 (1982), pp. 4–29.

Jones, C. *Assessment and Control of Software Risks*. Englewood Cliffs, NJ: Prentice Hall (Yourdon Press), 1994.

Martin, J. "Timebox Methodology." *System Builder,* April/May 1990, pp. 22–25.

———. *Information Engineering Book III: Design and Construction*. Englewood Cliffs, NJ: Prentice-Hall, 1990.

Mason, R. E. A., and T. T. Carey. "Prototyping Interactive Information Systems." *Communications of the ACM* 26, no. 5 (May 1983), pp. 347–354.

Texas Instruments Incorporated [1992a]. *Rapid Application Development Guide*. TI Part Number 2579082. April 1992.

Texas Instruments Incorporated [1992b]. *Scribing in JAD*. TI Part Number 2579084. April 1992.

Modeling Object Classes, Attributes, and Relationships

In previous chapters, you have learned that the most important feature that distinguishes traditional systems development (TSD) from object-oriented systems development (OOSD) is their treatment of the data and software components. TSD treats these as separate components and uses different techniques to analyze and design a system's data from those used to analyze and design its functions or processes (i.e., software). In contrast, OOSD encapsulates data (attributes) and functions (methods) into objects. However you envision implementing data and processes in the system, a crucial analysis and design activity is defining the data requirements of the system. Both TSD and OOSD use similar techniques to perform this activity.

In TSD, this activity is called **data modeling**, whose fundamental construct is an **entity:** a person, place, thing, event, or concept about which data is collected and maintained. In OOSD, this activity is called **object structure analysis and design**, whose fundamental construct is an object class that has both attributes (data) and methods. Whatever its name, the basic purpose of this activity is the same: to define the data that a system must maintain. Here we discuss the basic concepts of and present a technique for modeling the system's data component.

You may wonder, why create a model of the data? Why not just create the database and be done with it? Indeed, for a very simple application, it may be practical to "Just do it!" But most business applications are complex and include many people, things, places, and transactions about which data must be maintained. To create a database that is both efficient (provides fast access to data and minimizes storage requirements) and effective (provides all the necessary data and allows users to access and manipulate the data in a variety of ways), you need to understand fully what the pieces of data are and how they relate to one another.

Identifying the data needed in an application often involves reviewing dozens of reports and forms and interviewing numerous users. For example, if you were analyzing the Bigg's Department Store sales order processing system, you would need to examine, at minimum, documents such as the sales receipt and account statement; any reports generated from the sales processing activity, such as sales by department; and the customer, account, product, and other files maintained to process sales. You would also need to consult with users and managers to learn about additional data and reports they would like to have.

Furthermore, you would need to analyze your enterprise models and DFDs to identify likely entities and classes. As a general rule, many internal and external entities and workflows in your workflow diagrams are potentially entities or classes that must be implemented in the corresponding system. The same is true of the data flows and data stores modeled in DFDs.

System data structure analysis and design is usually performed in two steps. In the first step, **logical data design** (the focus of this technical module), you define the things about which the organization must maintain data and indicate how these things are related to each other. In traditional systems development, the modeling technique most commonly used to perform this step is the entity-relationship diagram, which will be described briefly. Because of our interest in integrating traditional and object-oriented modeling techniques, the object relationship model will be described in greater detail. In the second step of data modeling, **physical database design**, the logical model is used to define the physical database, including the file organization, access methods, database architecture, and so on. Physical database design is addressed in Chapter 9.

LOGICAL DATA MODELING CONCEPTS

The concepts of logical data design are very similar to object-oriented concepts introduced earlier in this text. The basic concept in traditional data modeling is an **entity**: a person, place, thing, or event about which data is collected and maintained. An entity is very similar to an object class. However, entities represent only data; they do not encapsulate data and methods as object classes do. Examples of entities/object classes in a sales order processing system are CUSTOMER, PRODUCT, SALES-TRANSACTION, and SALES-CLERK.

Each class or entity is described by one or more **attributes**: the properties or characteristics that the user needs to know about it. For example, CUSTOMER might be described by the attributes of CustomerName, Street, City, State, ZipCode, and PhoneNumber. A SALES-TRANSACTION might be described by attributes such as OrderDate, OrderNumber, TransactionType, Subtotal, SalesTax, and Total. Notice that attribute names are indicated in mixed case with no spaces.

An **instance** of an object class (or simply, object) consists of the values for the attributes that describe a particular person, place, or thing. For example, "Dan Harding, 123 Elm Street, San Jose, CA, 95192, 937-4219" describes one CUSTOMER object. An example of an instance of a SALES-TRANSACTION is "02/11/95, 17654, Cash, 399.99, 33.99, 433.98." Many organizations require that each object have at least one attribute value that uniquely identifies it. For example, a SALES-TRANSACTION object is most likely uniquely identified by the attribute OrderNumber. The attribute that uniquely identifies an instance is called an **identifier**. As illustrated in Table D.1, the value assigned to the attribute OrderNumber is used to uniquely identify each sales transaction. Thus, we can distinguish the SALES-TRANSACTION instance identified by the OrderNumber 17655 from the SALES-TRANSACTION instance identified by OrderNumber 17656 even though all of their other attributes are the same.

Object classes/entities are related to each other in various ways. For example, in the Bigg's Department Store sales order processing system introduced in Technical Module C, "Enterprise Modeling Techniques," a CUSTOMER is related to a SALES-TRANSACTION in that a CUSTOMER

TABLE D.1 Instances with unique identifiers

OrderDate	OrderNumber (identifier)	Transaction Type	Subtotal	SalesTax	Total
02/11/97	17654	Cash	399.99	34.00	433.99
02/11/97	17655	Credit	199.99	17.00	216.99
02/11/97	17656	Credit	199.99	17.00	216.99

initiates a SALES-TRANSACTION. A **relationship** models business policies stipulating how one instance is related to another instance. In our example, the relationship between a CUSTOMER instance and a SALES-TRANSACTION instance is named "initiates": an instance of CUSTOMER "initiates" an instance of SALES-TRANSACTION. Relationship names can also be assigned to the reverse relationship: an instance of SALES-TRANSACTION "is initiated by" an instance of CUSTOMER. Because relationship names are sometimes trivial, they may often be omitted without diminishing the descriptiveness of the model.

Relationships are described in terms of their **cardinality**: the number of instances of A that can or must be related to one instance of B. To fully describe a relationship, you need to state both its minimum cardinality and its maximum cardinality. **Minimum cardinality** states how many instances of A *must* be associated with one instance of B; in other words, each instance of B must be related to x instances of A. The minimum cardinality of a relationship is usually zero or 1. **Maximum cardinality** states how many instances of A *may* be associated with one instance of B; in other words, each instance of B may be related to x instances of A. The maximum cardinality of a relationship is usually 1 or many. A graphical illustration of cardinality is provided in Figure D.1.

For example, an organizational policy may state that data are maintained about all customers (those who have made at least one purchase) and all prospective customers (those who have been identified as prospects but who have not yet made a purchase). According to

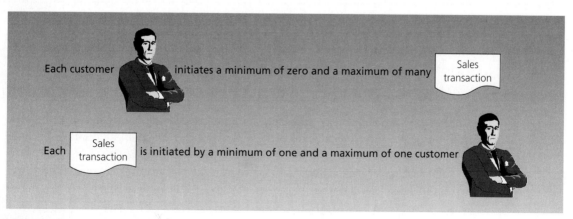

FIGURE D.1 Illustration of the cardinalities of object relationships

this policy, the minimum cardinality of CUSTOMER to SALES-TRANSACTION is zero, and the maximum cardinality is many. Looking at the reverse relationship, an organization may stipulate that each sales transaction is initiated by exactly one customer. Given this business rule, the minimum cardinality of SALES-TRANSACTION to CUSTOMER is 1; the maximum cardinality is also 1.

When the minimum cardinality of a relationship is 1, an **existence dependency** is created. That is, an instance of SALES-TRANSACTION cannot exist if no instance of the related CUSTOMER exists. In other words, an instance of a SALES-TRANSACTION cannot be created unless or until the related instance of CUSTOMER exists. In practical terms, the existence dependency between SALES-TRANSACTION and CUSTOMER means that a sales clerk cannot create a sales transaction for Dan Harding if Dan Harding does not exist in the organization's customer file. Another example of an existence dependency is evident in the relationship between a SALES-TRANSACTION and a SALES-TRANSACTION-LINE (abbreviated as ST-LINE). An instance of an ST-LINE cannot exist if the SALES-TRANSACTION instance of which it is a part does not also exist.

The cardinality of a relationship is determined by business rules. **Business rules** define, among other things, the relationships between things of interest to an organization. For example, the management of Shady Oaks Apartments stipulates that two reserved parking spaces are assigned to each apartment. Although many organizations may have the same entities or object classes and the same names for the relationships, the cardinality of these relationships may differ from one organization to the next because of their business rules.

Consider the cardinality of the relationship of COURSE to STUDENT. Small State University policy stipulates that no more than 35 students may be enrolled in any one course; thus, the maximum cardinality of COURSE to STUDENT is 35. In contrast, Big State University policy stipulates that the maximum number of students enrolled in a course is 200; thus, the maximum cardinality of COURSE to STUDENT at Big State University is 200. To discover the maximum cardinality of COURSE to STUDENT, you would have to study the university rules or interview an administrator.

TRADITIONAL DATA MODELING TECHNIQUE: ENTITY-RELATIONSHIP DIAGRAM

The logical data design technique most commonly used in traditional systems development is the **entity-relationship (E-R) diagram**. This diagram uses a number of notational conventions to model the concepts just defined. Object classes (called entities in this technique) are represented as rectangles, and relationships are represented as diamonds. For example, Figure D.2 shows how CUSTOMER and SALES-TRANSACTION and their relationship are modeled in an E-R diagram.

Notice that the name of the relationship—"initiates"—is provided inside the relationship diamond. Also provided in the relationship diamond is the relationship type, "1:N." The three **relationship types** are 1:1 (read "one-to-one," indicating that each instance of the first entity can be related to at most one instance of the second entity), 1:N (read "one-to-many,"

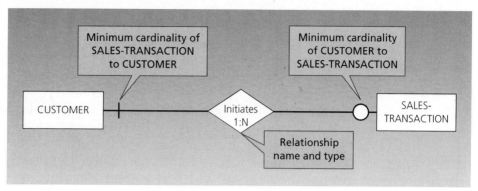

FIGURE D.2   Entity-relationship diagram example

indicating that each instance of the first entity can be related to many instances of the second entity), and N:M, (read "many-to-many," indicating that many instances of the first entity can be related to many instances of the second entity). These numbers indicate the maximum cardinality of each entity in the relationship. For example, the 1 in the "1:N" notation in Figure D.2 is closest to CUSTOMER, indicating that at most one customer may be related to each sales transaction. The N in the "1:N" notation is closest to SALES-TRANSACTION, indicating that many sales transactions may be related to each customer.

However, the relationship type does not indicate the minimum cardinality of the relationship. We must add a bar at the CUSTOMER end of the relationship line to indicate that each sales transaction is initiated by a minimum of one customer; furthermore, we must add a circle at the SALES-TRANSACTION end of the relationship line to indicate that a customer can initiate a minimum of zero sales transactions.

The E-R diagram employs additional notational conventions to model attributes, identifiers, and various kinds of relationships and entities, which are not discussed here. Many students, especially introductory-level students, are overwhelmed by the notational complexity of the E-R diagram. For this reason, we prefer the simpler object relationship model.

OBJECT-ORIENTED MODELING TECHNIQUE: OBJECT RELATIONSHIP MODEL

An **object relationship model** [Martin & Odell 1992; Yourdon 1994] is an expressive technique for documenting object classes and their attributes and relationships. The symbols used in an object relationship model, shown in Figure D.3, are similar to those of the traditional E-R diagram, but omit the relationship diamond and combine the representation of minimum/maximum cardinality into one notation. Like the E-R diagram, the object relationship model represents an object class as a rectangle labeled with the name in all capital letters.

An object relationship is indicated by a line connecting one object class to another. A relationship line can be labeled with the name of the relationship. Unlike the E-R diagram's diamond relationship notation, which notes only the name of the relationship between the first class and the second class, the object relationship line here can be labeled to indicate two-way relationships. The label above (to the left of) the relationship line indicates the name of the relationship of the class on the left (top) to the class on the right (bottom); the label beneath (to the right of) the relationship line indicates the name of the relationship of the class on the right (bottom) to the class on the left (top). In a complex object relationship model, with many classes and many relationships, you may choose to omit relationship labels—or at least to eliminate the reverse (right-to-left, bottom-to-top) relationship labels—so as to reduce clutter. Relationship names are required only if two classes have two or more relationships.

In the object relationship model, both the minimum and maximum cardinalities of a relationship are represented by the type of relationship line connection used. The examples in Figure D.3 show several connections representing the possible minimum-maximum cardinality combinations. You should understand that, although cardinalities are shown in Figure D.3 as being one-way (from left-hand to right-hand), they are actually two-way, just as relationships are two-way. In an object relationship model, both ends of the relationship line must have connection symbols indicating cardinality. So, for example, one instance of

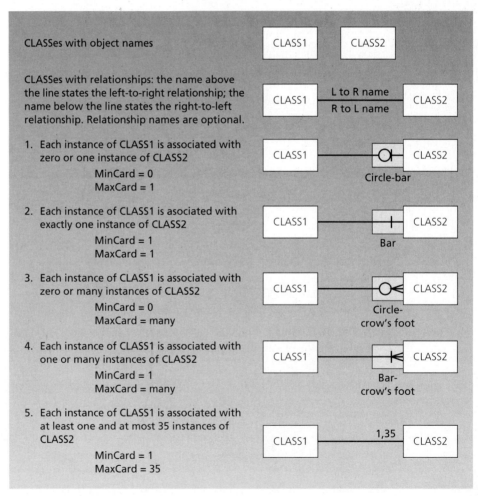

FIGURE D.3 Symbols used in an object relationship model

CLASS1 may be related to one or many instances of CLASS2, and one instance of CLASS2 may be related to exactly one instance of CLASS1.

Examples 2 and 4 in Figure D.3 model an existence dependency between CLASS1 and CLASS2. No instance of CLASS1 can exist unless at least one instance of CLASS2 also exists. Example 2 illustrates how you would model the existence dependency between SALES-TRANSACTION and CUSTOMER that was discussed in the example above: an instance of a SALES-TRANSACTION can exist only if an instance of the related CUSTOMER object exists. In example 2, the bar on the right-hand side of the relationship line indicates that both the minimum cardinality and the maximum cardinality of the relationship are 1. Example 4 illustrates an existence dependency in which the minimum cardinality of the relationship is 1 (indicated by the bar), but the maximum cardinality is many (indicated by the crow's foot).

Example 5 in Figure D.3 shows an alternative method used to indicate cardinality. Instead of using bars, circles, and crow's feet on relationship lines, you may state the cardinality as n_1, n_2, where n_1 indicates the minimum cardinality, and n_2 indicates the maximum cardinality: for example, 1,N (minimum cardinality = 1, maximum cardinality = many); 0,1 (minimum cardinality = 0, maximum cardinality = 1); or, as shown in the example, 1,35 (minimum cardinality = 1, maximum cardinality = 35). This notation eliminates symbols that are unfamiliar to users and allows you to indicate an exact number for both minimum and maximum cardinality.

For example, consider the cardinality of the relationship between FOOTBALL-TEAM and FOOTBALL-PLAYER. Each team must have a minimum of 11 players and may have a maximum of 45 players (assuming NFL rules). Furthermore, each player may play for exactly one team. This relationship and its cardinalities are illustrated in Figure D.4. Notice that the cardinality between the left-hand class (FOOTBALL-TEAM) and the right-hand class (FOOTBALL-PLAYER) is shown at the top right-hand end of the line (11,45); each football team must have at least 11 players and may have at most 45 players. The cardinality between the right-hand class (FOOTBALL-PLAYER) and the left-hand class (FOOTBALL-TEAM) is shown at the bottom, left-hand end of the line (1,1); each football player must play for at least one team and may play for at most one team. Again, you may choose to omit the relationship names.

So far, we have discussed and modeled only one way in which object classes may be related to each other. An instance of CLASS1 may "collaborate" with an instance of CLASS2. In a **collaboration relationship**, object instances are related because one instance needs data contained in another instance. For example, an instance of SALES-TRANSACTION and an instance

Each instance of FOOTBALL-TEAM is associated with at least 11 and at most 45 instances of FOOTBALL-PLAYER. Each instance of FOOTBALL-PLAYER is associated with exactly one instance of FOOTBALL-TEAM.

| FOOTBALL-TEAM | has | 11,45 | FOOTBALL-PLAYER |
| | 1,1 | plays for | |

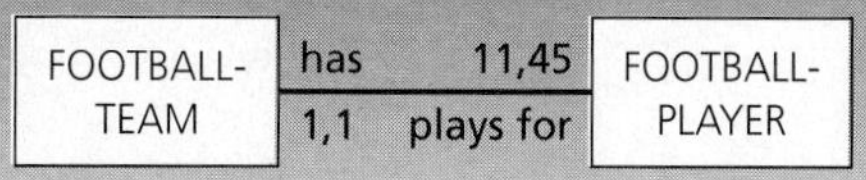

FIGURE D.4   Alternative method of indicating cardinalities

of CUSTOMER are related because the SALES-TRANSACTION instance needs to use data contained in the CUSTOMER instance: name, address, and so on. These related objects collaborate in that SALES-TRANSACTION must send a message to the appropriate CUSTOMER instance requesting that it perform a method to return a data value to the SALES-TRANSACTION instance. Two other relationships—specialization and composition—are discussed next.

SPECIALIZATION: THE IS-A RELATIONSHIP

Figure D.5 demonstrates how to model a **specialization**, or **IS-A**, **relationship**, which describes an object relationship in which an instance of CLASS2 is a specialized case of an instance of CLASS1. A **subclass** (sometimes called a **child**) inherits the attributes and methods of its **superclass** (sometimes called the **parent**). The IS-A relationship creates an identity between an instance of the subclass and an instance of the superclass.

The identity between a subclass and a superclass is one-way in that an instance of SUBCLASS2 IS-A instance of SUPERCLASS1, but an instance of SUPERCLASS1 is not necessarily an instance of SUBCLASS2. For example, an instance of the subclass TEACHER is also an instance of the superclass PERSON. However, an instance of PERSON is not necessarily an instance of TEACHER. Otherwise, every person, to be a person, would also have to be a teacher!

The one-way identity of the IS-A relationship is indicated by the triangle on the relationship line. The triangle points from the subclasses to the superclass, indicating that the IS-A relationship flows from CLASS2 and CLASS3 to CLASS1.

Thinking in terms of set theory and Venn diagrams may help you understand the specialization relationship. In a *Venn diagram,* each object class is a set modeled as a circle, and each object instance is modeled as a dot. A subclass is modeled as a circle within another circle. The Venn diagram in Figure D.6a models the relationship between the superclass PERSON and the subclass TEACHER. Notice that the object instance of Sandy Dewitz is a *single* object instance that is a member of both the PERSON superclass and the TEACHER subclass.

Each instance of a superclass—for example, Sandy Dewitz the PERSON—can be related to multiple subclasses. In a Venn diagram, nonexclusive subclasses are modeled as overlapping circles. Thus, as shown in Figure D.6b, an instance of the PERSON superclass can be an instance of the TEACHER subclass, of the PHD subclass, of the FEMALE subclass,

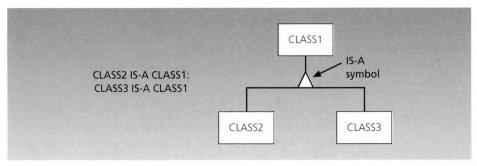

FIGURE D.5   Notation for the IS-A relationship

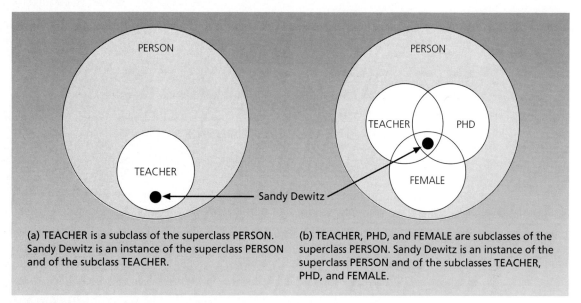

(a) TEACHER is a subclass of the superclass PERSON. Sandy Dewitz is an instance of the superclass PERSON and of the subclass TEACHER.

(b) TEACHER, PHD, and FEMALE are subclasses of the superclass PERSON. Sandy Dewitz is an instance of the superclass PERSON and of the subclasses TEACHER, PHD, and FEMALE.

FIGURE D.6   Venn diagrams illustrating superclass-subclass (IS-A) relationships

and so on. As another example, recall the object-oriented fable about Cathy the VET and Fred the DOG-OWNER in Chapter 1. Recall that Cathy was an instance of the superclass PERSON and of both the subclasses VET and DOG-OWNER. See Figure 1.3 in Chapter 1 for the Venn diagram illustration of this concept.

Some object-oriented methodologies (see, for example, [Embly et al. 1992]) provide several notations to indicate whether the subclasses of a superclass are mutually exclusive, complete, and so on. For our purposes, we will adopt just one additional notation: a plus sign (+). Placing a plus sign inside the IS-A triangle indicates that the subclasses are mutually exclusive (for example, MALE and FEMALE). No plus sign inside the IS-A triangle indicates that the subclasses are not mutually exclusive; in other words, a single instance of the superclass can be an instance of more than one subclass.

COMPOSITION: THE HAS-A RELATIONSHIP

Another object relationship that has been standardized and formally modeled in all OOA&D methodologies is the **composition**, or **HAS-A**, **relationship**, which describes the case when one object instance is composed of one or more instances of another object class. For example, a person has two arms, two legs, a torso, and a head. A car is composed of a body, an engine, seats, and so forth. Note that the HAS-A relationship is reserved for object classes that are components of other object classes. The HAS-A relationship *may not be used* to relate an attribute to the object class that it describes. For example, it would be incorrect to say that CAR (object class) HAS-A VehicleIdentificationNumber (attribute).

An example of a business object that illustrates the composition relationship is a SALES-TRANSACTION. Each SALES-TRANSACTION HAS-A ST-LINE, which lists detailed data about each item—including the stock number, description, and unit price—and indicates the quantity and extended price. Thus, we can say that each instance of a SALES-TRANSACTION is composed of one or more instances of an ST-LINE. Looking at the relationship in the opposite direction, we can say that each instance of an ST-LINE is part of exactly one SALES-TRANSACTION. Figure D.7 illustrates the notation used to represent this relationship. Notice that the composition relationship uses a diamond to connect the component object classes to the composite object class.

The composition relationship differs from the specialization relationship in that there is no identity between the classes in the composition relationship. An instance of ST-LINE is not an instance of SALES-TRANSACTION; it is simply one component that comprises an instance of a SALES-TRANSACTION. Whereas no cardinality need be indicated for the specialization relationship, minimum and maximum cardinalities must be expressed for the composition relationship to indicate how many of each component object comprise each composite object.

The composition relationship also differs from the specialization relationship in that inheritance does not apply to classes related by the composition relationship. If class A is a part of class B, and class B is a part of class C, then class A is a part of class C. However, classes A, B, and C cannot be described using the same attributes, nor do they perform the same methods. For example, a bolt is a part of an engine, and an engine is a part of a car, but a bolt does not inherit any of its attributes or methods from the engine or the car.

To illustrate the object relationship model in use, Figure D.8 gives the object relationship model segments for the Bigg's Department Store sales order processing system. A text description of each relationship is presented and then the corresponding object relationship model segment. Figure D.9 provides a unified object relationship model of the sales order processing system.

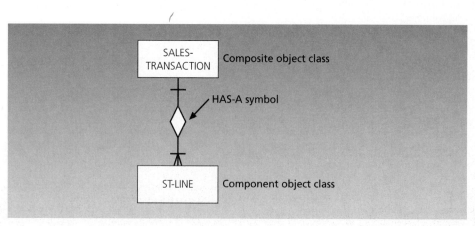

FIGURE D.7   Notation for the HAS-A relationship

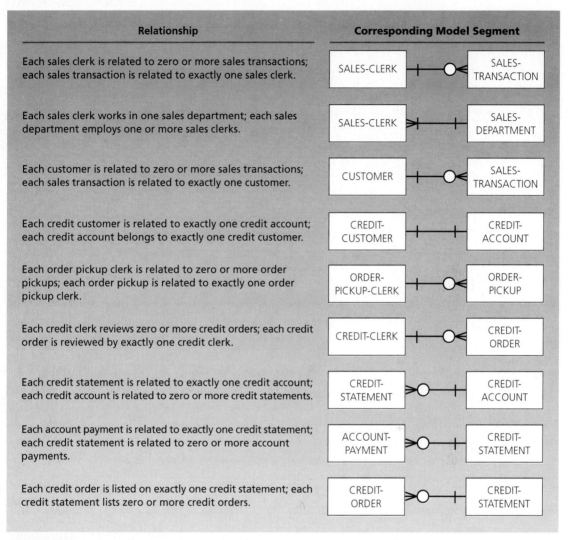

Relationship	Corresponding Model Segment
Each sales clerk is related to zero or more sales transactions; each sales transaction is related to exactly one sales clerk.	SALES-CLERK ├──O< SALES-TRANSACTION
Each sales clerk works in one sales department; each sales department employs one or more sales clerks.	SALES-CLERK >──┤ SALES-DEPARTMENT
Each customer is related to zero or more sales transactions; each sales transaction is related to exactly one customer.	CUSTOMER ├──O< SALES-TRANSACTION
Each credit customer is related to exactly one credit account; each credit account belongs to exactly one credit customer.	CREDIT-CUSTOMER ├──┤ CREDIT-ACCOUNT
Each order pickup clerk is related to zero or more order pickups; each order pickup is related to exactly one order pickup clerk.	ORDER-PICKUP-CLERK ├──O< ORDER-PICKUP
Each credit clerk reviews zero or more credit orders; each credit order is reviewed by exactly one credit clerk.	CREDIT-CLERK ├──O< CREDIT-ORDER
Each credit statement is related to exactly one credit account; each credit account is related to zero or more credit statements.	CREDIT-STATEMENT >O──┤ CREDIT-ACCOUNT
Each account payment is related to exactly one credit statement; each credit statement is related to zero or more account payments.	ACCOUNT-PAYMENT >O──┤ CREDIT-STATEMENT
Each credit order is listed on exactly one credit statement; each credit statement lists zero or more credit orders.	CREDIT-ORDER >O──┤ CREDIT-STATEMENT

FIGURE D.8a Relationships and corresponding object relationship model segments

 Check Your Understanding D-1

1. Create an object relationship model segment similar to those shown in Figure D.8 for each of the following business rules governing the Bigg's Department Store special order division.

   a. Each special order clerk can process zero to many special orders; each special order is processed by exactly one special order clerk.

   b. Each special order customer places zero or more special orders; each special order is placed by exactly one special order customer.

   c. Each special order has one or more line items; each line item belongs to exactly one special order.

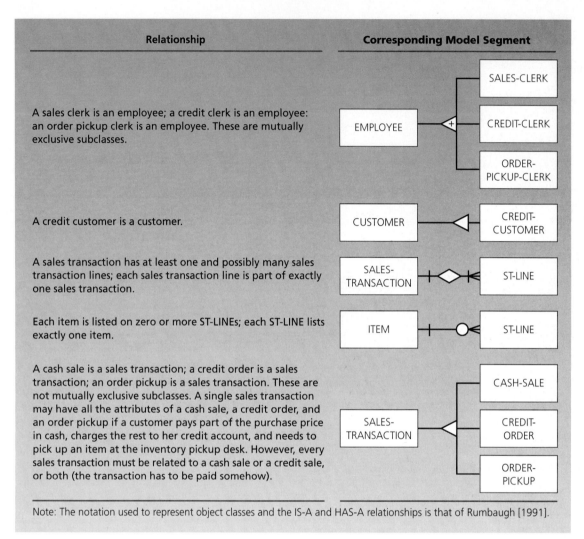

Relationship	Corresponding Model Segment
A sales clerk is an employee; a credit clerk is an employee; an order pickup clerk is an employee. These are mutually exclusive subclasses.	EMPLOYEE — SALES-CLERK, CREDIT-CLERK, ORDER-PICKUP-CLERK
A credit customer is a customer.	CUSTOMER — CREDIT-CUSTOMER
A sales transaction has at least one and possibly many sales transaction lines; each sales transaction line is part of exactly one sales transaction.	SALES-TRANSACTION — ST-LINE
Each item is listed on zero or more ST-LINEs; each ST-LINE lists exactly one item.	ITEM — ST-LINE
A cash sale is a sales transaction; a credit order is a sales transaction; an order pickup is a sales transaction. These are not mutually exclusive subclasses. A single sales transaction may have all the attributes of a cash sale, a credit order, and an order pickup if a customer pays part of the purchase price in cash, charges the rest to her credit account, and needs to pick up an item at the inventory pickup desk. However, every sales transaction must be related to a cash sale or a credit sale, or both (the transaction has to be paid somehow).	SALES-TRANSACTION — CASH-SALE, CREDIT-ORDER, ORDER-PICKUP

Note: The notation used to represent object classes and the IS-A and HAS-A relationships is that of Rumbaugh [1991].

FIGURE D.8b   Relationships and corresponding object relationship model segments

      d.   Each line item lists exactly one item; each item is listed on zero or more line items.

      e.   Each special order is paid by zero or one payment; each payment pays exactly one special order.

      f.   Each special order may be billed by zero or one invoice; each invoice bills exactly one special order.

      g.   Each special order customer may receive zero or many invoices; each invoice is received by exactly one special order customer.

      h.   Each invoice is paid by zero or one payment; each payment pays exactly one invoice.

2.   Integrate your object model segments to create an object relationship model (see Figure D.9) of the special order division.

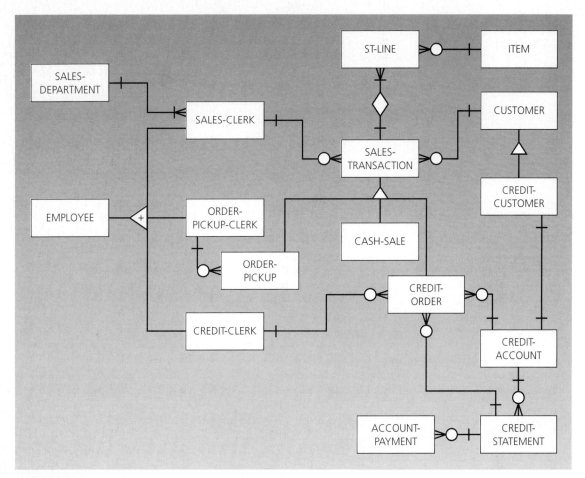

FIGURE D.9   Completed object relationship model

IDENTIFYING OBJECT CLASSES, RELATIONSHIPS, AND ATTRIBUTES

Creating an object relationship model is fairly simple when you are given explicit statements of object classes and business rules. To help you learn to determine object classes, relationships, and attributes through your own analysis, this section analyzes the objects in the Bigg's Department Store sales order processing system. You may want to review the identification of candidate classes for Bigg's Department Store in Technical Module C before reading the rest of this section.

Identifying Classes

The object classes presented in the enterprise object model in Figure D.10 (repeated here from Figure C.11) are only candidate classes. In other words, the object classes listed here *may or may not* indeed be object classes.

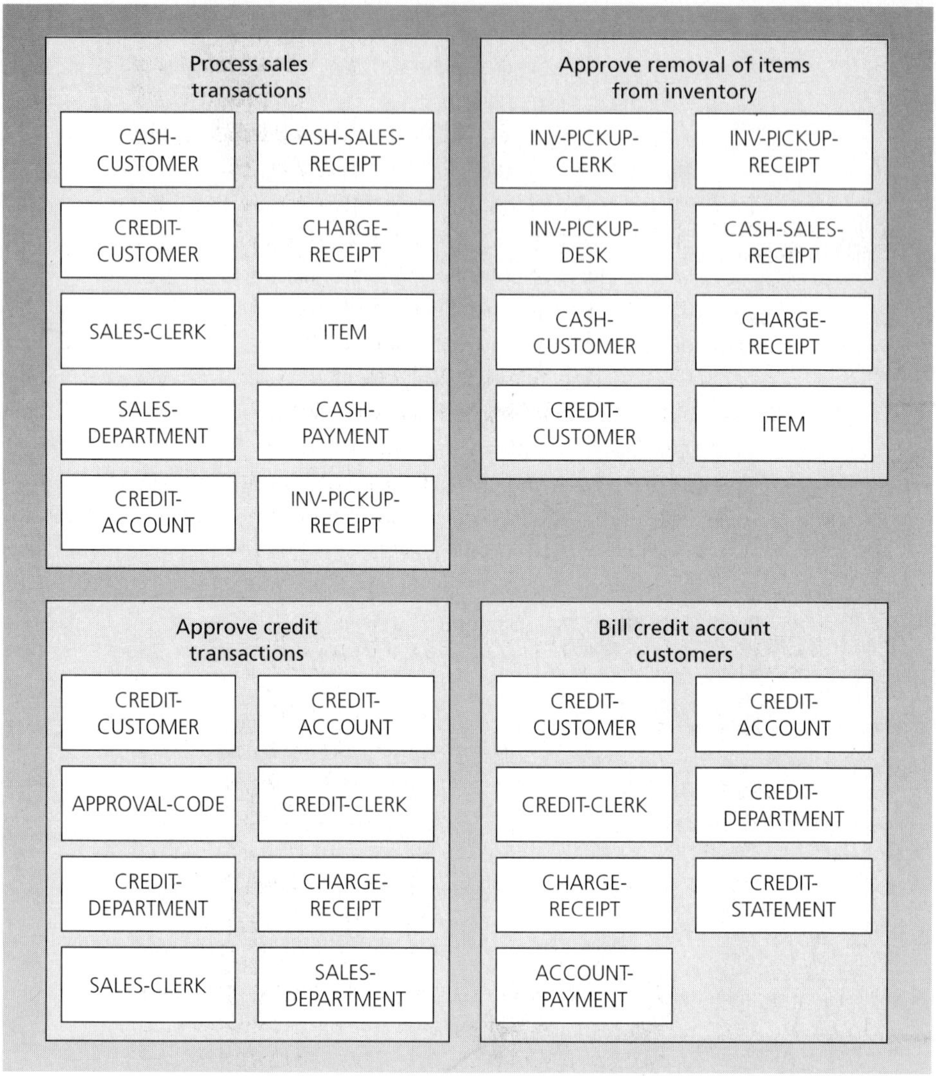

Process sales transactions	
CASH-CUSTOMER	CASH-SALES-RECEIPT
CREDIT-CUSTOMER	CHARGE-RECEIPT
SALES-CLERK	ITEM
SALES-DEPARTMENT	CASH-PAYMENT
CREDIT-ACCOUNT	INV-PICKUP-RECEIPT

Approve removal of items from inventory	
INV-PICKUP-CLERK	INV-PICKUP-RECEIPT
INV-PICKUP-DESK	CASH-SALES-RECEIPT
CASH-CUSTOMER	CHARGE-RECEIPT
CREDIT-CUSTOMER	ITEM

Approve credit transactions	
CREDIT-CUSTOMER	CREDIT-ACCOUNT
APPROVAL-CODE	CREDIT-CLERK
CREDIT-DEPARTMENT	CHARGE-RECEIPT
SALES-CLERK	SALES-DEPARTMENT

Bill credit account customers	
CREDIT-CUSTOMER	CREDIT-ACCOUNT
CREDIT-CLERK	CREDIT-DEPARTMENT
CHARGE-RECEIPT	CREDIT-STATEMENT
ACCOUNT-PAYMENT	

FIGURE D.10   Enterprise object model (repeated from Figure C.11)

In your first attempt to generate object classes, you are likely to identify more than are actually needed in the system. Contrary to many things in life, more is not better when it comes to object classes. Identifying too many object classes complicates development and yields a system that requires far more object-messaging than necessary. How do you evaluate candidate object classes to weed out the unnecessary ones? A few rules of thumb can guide your determination [Coad & Yourdon 1991]:

1. *Each class has data (i.e., attributes) that it must remember.* You should be able to name at least one attribute for each object class.

2. *Each class has more than one attribute.* In some cases, a class may have only one attribute; in very rare cases, it may have no attributes. But, generally speaking, each object class will be described by several attributes. Usually, if an object class seems to have only one

attribute, it is really an attribute of another object class. An exception to this rule is a subclass, which may have only one attribute or no attributes different from its superclass but does have different methods.

3. *All instances of the object class share the same attributes and methods.* You need to determine that all instances of the object class have the same attributes and perform the same methods. If you find yourself thinking that some attributes do not describe some instances of an object class or that some methods do not apply to certain instances, you may need to distinguish a superclass from its subclass.

As discussed in Technical Module C, we can identify multiple attributes for most of the candidate classes listed in the enterprise object model. Two exceptions are the CREDIT-DEPARTMENT and INV-PICKUP-DESK. If you review the process description provided in Figure C.4 and the sample credit statement and sales transaction forms shown in Figures D.11 and D.12, respectively, it seems that no data are tracked about these departments. At this point, it seems that the CREDIT-DEPARTMENT and the INV-PICKUP-DESK are not *critical* object classes in the sales order processing system; they may be classes in the enterprise as a whole, or they may be instances of the general class, DEPARTMENT.

In contrast, we know that the attributes of SALES-DEPARTMENT include DeptNumber and DeptName (i.e., "57" and "Electronics," as shown in the credit-statement line item in

Bigg's Department Store
Credit Services Division
425 South Third Avenue
Big Town, MA 12066

Closing Date	Account Number	New Balance	Minimum Payment	Due Date
03/05/97	413-5578-3991	503.74	25.00	04/01/97

Avoid additional finance charges by paying the new balance by due date.

Man-Wa Nguyen   Make check payable to **Bigg's Department Store**
3639 N. Highland Ave.   Indicate amount paid $_____
Pretty Valley, MA 12068

Detach here — Retain for your records

Reference #	Posting Date	Transaction Date	Description	Amount
0294301452	02/21/97	02/19/97	Dept 57-Electronics	350.93
0294311578	02/28/97	02/28/97	Payment Received, Thank You	50.00

Previous Bal.	Finance Charge	Total Pmts	Late Charges	Total Purchases	New Bal.
199.27	3.54	50.00	0.00	350.93	503.74

FIGURE D.11   Credit statement

Bigg's Department Store
Big Town Mall
Big Town, MA 12066

Order Number: 270054   Order Date: 2/19/97
Department Number: 20   Sales Clerk Number: 653
Sales Type: Cash X Credit ____   Credit Approval Code:_____

Customer Acount Number: _____
Customer Name: Herman Osterich _____
Customer Address: Route 1, Small Town, MA 12068 _____
Customer Phone: 555-7367 _____

Item #	Quantity	Pickup #	Item Description	Unit Price	Ext. Price
20-925100	1		Microwave Oven (recond.)	199.99	199.99

Subtotal:	199.99
Sales Tax:	17.00
Total:	216.99
Cash Received:	216.99
Payment Type:	Check
Amount Charged:	00.00

I authorize Bigg's Department Store to charge the amount indicated to my account.
Credit Customer Signature: _____

FIGURE D.12   Sales transaction form

Figure D.11 and in the sales order header in Figure D.12). Because a sales department is described by more than one attribute, SALES-DEPARTMENT is a class in the Bigg's Department Store sales order processing system. This suggests that we may need to define DEPARTMENT as a superclass and treat SALES-DEPARTMENT, CREDIT-DEPARTMENT, and INV-PICKUP-DESK as subclasses. However, in an effort to reduce the complexity of our model, for the time being we will include only the SALES-DEPARTMENT object class.

At first glance, it seems that the only data tracked about employees are their employee numbers. However, we can assume that Bigg's Department Store maintains more data about its employees than just their employee numbers. At minimum, the attributes EmpNumber and EmpName are needed to describe each employee. Thus, EMPLOYEE is probably a class in this system. Furthermore, the description of sales processing activities indicates that sales clerks, credit clerks, and inventory clerks perform different functions, so it seems reasonable to treat SALES-CLERK, CREDIT-CLERK, and INV-PICKUP-CLERK as subclasses of EMPLOYEE because each subclass may perform different methods.

What about CASH-PAYMENT? If you examine the sales transaction form, you will see that two pieces of data are collected about cash payments: cash received and payment type (e.g., cash or check). However, these data describe a CASH-SALE (whose attributes are AmountReceived and PaymentType), so it may be redundant to treat CASH-PAYMENT separately. The same is true of APPROVAL-CODE, which should be represented as an attribute of CREDIT-ORDER, not as an object class in and of itself.

The enterprise object model shows two types of customer objects: CASH-CUSTOMER and CREDIT-CUSTOMER. When represented in the object relationship model in Figure D.9, the CASH-CUSTOMER candidate class is collapsed into the CUSTOMER superclass because it seems likely that a CASH-CUSTOMER has all the attributes and methods of a CUSTOMER. The only significantly different type of customer is a credit customer, who is related to a credit account and can perform methods such as making an account payment. Thus, the only subclass of CUSTOMER represented in our model is CREDIT-CUSTOMER.

The enterprise object model also lists three types of receipt object classes: CASH-SALES-RECEIPT, CHARGE-RECEIPT, and INV-PICKUP-RECEIPT. In the object relationship model for the Bigg's Department Store sales order processing system, these candidate classes have been renamed to reflect the kind of sales transaction each receipt is used to perform. In addition, the three transaction types—CASH-SALE, CREDIT-ORDER, and ORDER-PICKUP—are treated as subclasses of the superclass SALES-TRANSACTION. The reason for creating this specialization relationship will become clear when we discuss attributes.

In summary, it seems that our initial list of candidate classes was too long. We identified more classes than may be necessary in the sales order processing system. Note the word "may" in the previous sentence. As we prototype the system and integrate it with other systems, it may be necessary to add or to delete object classes or to rethink our definition of some classes to conform with existing classes in other systems.

Check Your Understanding D-2

Examine the Pet License Application form in Figure D.A to identify its object classes.

Identifying Object Relationships

As you examine source documents and interview users, you also need to analyze the relationships between classes. For example, each CREDIT-STATEMENT instance reports data about exactly one CREDIT-CUSTOMER instance and one CREDIT-ACCOUNT instance. How do we know this? Because the credit statement form provides space for one account number and one credit customer. In addition, each CREDIT-STATEMENT reports possibly many instances of CREDIT-ORDER and ACCOUNT-PAYMENT, as indicated by the multiple lines provided in this section of the credit statement form.

Looking at the sales transaction form, we know that each instance of an ST-LINE is related to exactly one instance of an ITEM because each item line of the sales order form allows space for only one item number, description, and unit price. Furthermore, we assume

---

Applicant — Please complete the following information:

Owner name: _____

Owner address: _____ Phone: _____

Pet type (check one):   Dog ___ Cat ___ Pet name: _____

Color: _____ Age: _____ Breed: _____

Date of last rabies vaccination: _____

Check one in each row: Male ___ Female ___

Neutered ___ Fertile ___

Cats only — date of last feline leukemia vaccination: _____

Shaded Area for Office Use Only

License number: _____ County: _____ Issue Date: _____ Expiration date: _____

Fee paid: _____ Discount: Senior ___ Guide dog ___

FIGURE D.A   Pet License Application form

that each instance of an ITEM can appear on zero or many instances of an ST-LINE because Bigg's Department Store probably sells many instances of each item (for example, many VCRs model 2371 can be sold). We know that each instance of a SALES-TRANSACTION can have one or many instances of an ST-LINE because it would not make sense to fill out a sales order form if the customer was not purchasing at least one item and because several item lines are provided on the form.

Although this discussion has not explicated all the object relationships represented by these documents, it should make clear the process you need to follow to do so yourself. You already know a lot about the world around you. The key to being a good data modeler is to exploit your knowledge and experience of the real world and your common sense—and to verify your model with users!

Check Your Understanding D-3

Reexamine the Pet License Application form in Figure D.A to create relationships between the object classes and to indicate the minimum and maximum cardinalities of each relationship. Your finished model should look similar to the object relationship model shown in Figure D.9.

Identifying Object Attributes

Assigning attributes to object classes is one of the more difficult tasks for novice data modelers. Clearly, most of the labels (e.g., Order Number, Customer Name, Sales Type) and column headers (e.g., Item Number, Quantity, Reference Number) in the two sample forms can be modeled as attributes. But how do you determine to which object class each attribute belongs?

Distributing attributes among the object classes related to the credit statement and sales transaction forms is a significant challenge. Although you have determined that the credit statement reports data about instances of several object classes—CREDIT-STATEMENT, CREDIT-CUSTOMER, CREDIT-ACCOUNT, CREDIT-ORDER, and ACCOUNT-PAYMENT—and that a sales transaction collects data about instances of several object classes—CASH-SALE, CREDIT-ORDER, INVENTORY-PICKUP, CUSTOMER, ITEM, CREDIT-ACCOUNT—how do you decide which attributes belong to which object class? A few guidelines will help you:

1. Each object class appears only once in the object relationship model.

2. Each attribute appears only once in the object relationship model.

3. An attribute should be assigned to the object class that it most logically describes.

Rules 1 and 2 are pretty clear-cut: your object relationship model must not repeat object class names or attribute names. A word of caution: Don't try to sidestep these rules by using synonyms for class and attribute names! For example, you would be "cheating" if you called the credit account number an AccountNumber attribute in CREDIT-ACCOUNT and CustomerNumber in CUSTOMER. If AccountNumber in an instance of CREDIT-ACCOUNT has the same value as CustomerNumber in an instance of the related CUSTOMER, then they are the same attribute, and one of the synonymous attributes must be deleted.

Rule 3 is more ambiguous. Given that each attribute is assigned to only one object class, you must determine to which class each attribute is most directly related. For example, the CustomerName attribute appears on a sales transaction form and on a credit statement. Is CustomerName an attribute of SALES-TRANSACTION, CREDIT-STATEMENT, or both? None of the above; it is an attribute of CUSTOMER because CustomerName logically describes a customer, not a sales form or credit statement. However, CUSTOMER collaborates with SALES-TRANSACTION and CREDIT-STATEMENT. Thus, when a SALES-TRANSACTION instance needs to know the value of CustomerName in a CUSTOMER instance, it must have a method that sends a message to the CUSTOMER instance requesting this data.

Similarly, the AccountNumber attribute appears on a sales form and a credit statement and, on first glance, may seem to be an attribute of CREDIT-ORDER, CREDIT-STATEMENT, or CUSTOMER. However, AccountNumber is an attribute of CREDIT-ACCOUNT because it is most descriptive of this object class. Again, if instances of the other object classes need to know an account number, they must send a message to the CREDIT-ACCOUNT instance requesting this data.

Are you getting the idea? Because each attribute name can appear only once in the object relationship model, you assign each attribute to the object class that it best describes and use collaboration relationships to show that this object must provide data to other objects. Another helpful guideline is to start with those object classes whose existence is not dependent on another object class. For example, a CUSTOMER instance can exist without a related SALES-TRANSACTION instance (minimum cardinality = 0), but a SALES-TRANSACTION instance cannot exist without a related instance of a CUSTOMER. In this case, you would begin by assigning attributes to CUSTOMER.

Another challenge in assigning attributes involves superclass versus subclass objects. Here, you should begin by defining the attributes of the superclass and then continue defining the attributes that make each subclass a specialization of the superclass. For example, the sales transaction form, shown in Figure D.12, collects data about several kinds of sales transactions. Recall that the sales order processing system description provided in Technical Module C stated that

> *the sales clerk writes up each order on a three-part sales form. One part of the form is the customer's copy, one is the audit copy, and one is the inventory pickup copy. Each form lists the sales clerk's employee number; customer name, address, and phone; item quantity, description, unit and extended price; and the transaction subtotal, sales tax, and total. If the customer is paying cash, the sales clerk checks the cash sales type and enters the amount and type of payment received (cash or check). If the customer is charging the cost of purchased items to her credit account, then the sales clerk also enters the credit account number and an approval code. If inventory pickup is required, the sales order also lists an inventory pickup number, and the sales clerk gives the inventory pickup copy to the customer. If no inventory pickup is required, the inventory pickup copy is retained with the audit copy. The sales clerk places the audit copy of each transaction in the Sales Transaction file.*

Examining the sales transaction form, we can see that attributes describing every SALES-TRANSACTION include OrderNumber, OrderDate, TransactionType, and summary attributes, such as Subtotal, SalesTax, and Total. If the customer is paying cash, the sales transaction is a CASH-SALE, and its additional attributes include AmountReceived and PaymentType. If the customer is charging the purchase to his or her account, the transaction is a CREDIT-ORDER, and its attributes include those of a SALES-TRANSACTION plus AmountCharged and ApprovalCode. In addition, the customer must be a CREDIT-CUSTOMER, who has all the attributes of a CUSTOMER, including Name, Address, and PhoneNumber, but also has a relationship to CREDIT-ACCOUNT. If the customer is picking up items from inventory, the SALES-TRANSACTION is also an ORDER-PICKUP, which has the attribute PickupNumber.

Because all these transactions have attributes in common and each has attributes unique to its type of transaction, we should model CASH-SALE, CREDIT-ORDER, and ORDER-PICKUP as subclasses of the superclass SALES-TRANSACTION. The distribution of attributes among these data objects is shown in Figure D.13. Notice that the IS-A triangle does not contain a plus sign, indicating that these subclasses are not mutually exclusive. Therefore, a single instance of a SALES-TRANSACTION can be an instance of a CASH-SALE, a CREDIT-ORDER, *and* an ORDER-PICKUP. The only restriction is that an instance of a SALES-TRANSACTION must always be an instance of a CASH-SALE or a CREDIT-ORDER, or both.

Determining Identifiers

The final task in our analysis is to determine the identifier of each object class. Figure D.14 shows a complete object relationship model that also indicates the attributes and identifiers of the object classes. Identifiers are underscored. Notice that in most cases an object class is

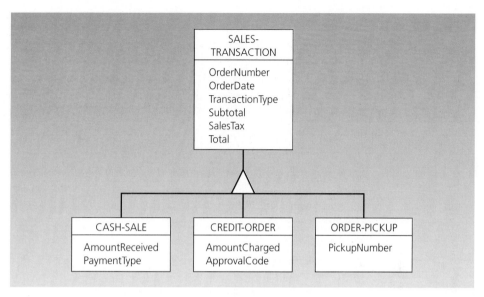

FIGURE D.13 Distribution of attributes among a superclass and subclasses

identified by a numeric attribute: DeptNumber, ItemNumber, and so on. Notice also that some object classes do not have an identifier, for example, SALES-CLERK, and CASH-SALE. As you will learn when we discuss physical database design in Chapter 9, subclass objects usually assume the identifier of their superclass. Thus, SALES-CLERK assumes the identifier EmpNumber from EMPLOYEE, and CASH-SALE assumes the identifier OrderNumber from SALES-TRANSACTION. In other cases, an object class assumes the identifier(s) of the other object class(es) to which it is related. For example, each instance of ST-LINE will be identified by the identifiers of its related SALES-TRANSACTION and ITEM instances.

 ## Check Your Understanding D-4

Revise the object relationship model you created for Check Your Understanding D-3, assigning attributes to and indicating the identifier of each object class based on your reexamination of the Pet License Application form. Your finished model should look similar to the one shown in Figure D.14.

USES OF OBJECT RELATIONSHIP MODELS

Creating an object relationship model helps you to understand two facets of an information system: (1) the data structures required by the system and (2) some of the messages required to allow objects to communicate with one another. The object relationship model documents the findings of your logical data structure analysis and design and is the foundation upon which the physical design of the system's database is built. It also indicates which classes will need to use the data of other classes. If two classes are related, they will need to communicate with each other. Thus, the object relationship model can be used to identify some of the messages that are required to allow objects to access each other's data and methods.

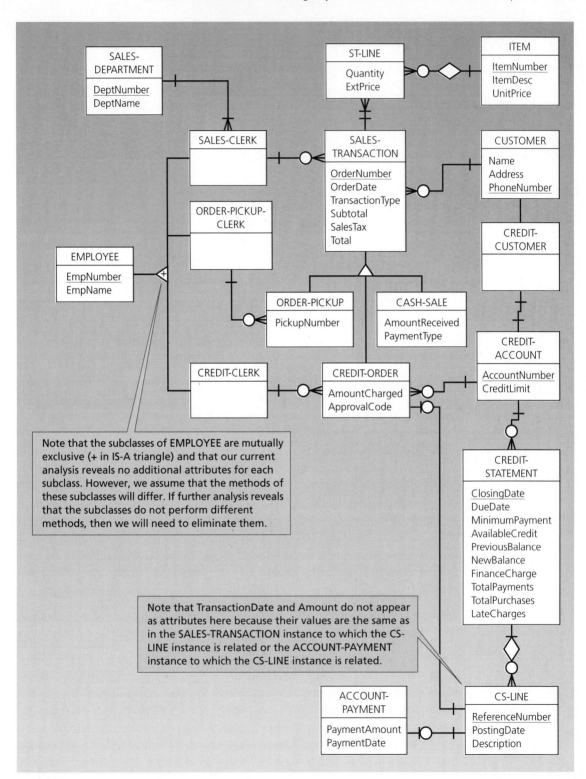

FIGURE D.14 Object relationship model with attributes and identifiers

◈ KEY TERMS

attributes	existence dependency	relationship
business rules	identifier	relationship types (1:1, 1:N,
cardinality	instance	N:M)
collaboration relationship	logical data design	specialization (IS-A)
composition (or HAS-A)	maximum cardinality	relationship
relationship	minimum cardinality	subclass (child)
data modeling	object relationship model	superclass (parent)
entity	object structure analysis and	
entity-relationship (E-R)	design	
diagram	physical database design	

◈ EXERCISES

1. Read the following short case description to create an object relationship model of Property Management Associates' property management system. Show attributes and identifiers in your model.

    Property Management Associates (PMA) is a property-management company that oversees commercial rental properties. As part of its rent-collection operation, PMA maintains data about the properties (or units) it manages. For each unit, PMA tracks the unit address, owner name, size (in square feet), number of rooms, and special facilities (e.g., private restrooms, private entrance, reception area, etc.). These units are leased by businesses (i.e., the tenants), who sign a lease agreement stating the beginning occupancy date, ending occupancy date, lease terms (e.g., no smoking in facility), deposit paid, monthly rent, and rent-due date (e.g., the 10th of each month). PMA also maintains data about each tenant, including tenant name, tenant business phone, nature of business (e.g., ice cream shop, legal services), credit rating, and at least two references. Each lease agreement represents only one tenant and one unit; however, each tenant may sign many leases (e.g., renew the current lease or lease another unit), and each unit may, over time, be covered by many lease agreements.

2. Read the following short case to create an object relationship model of Bankrupt Airlines Ticketing System. Show attributes and identifiers in your model.

    Bankrupt Airlines offers numerous flights between destinations in the western United States every day. Information maintained about flights includes flight number, departure time, departure city, arrival time, arrival city, and seats available. To reserve a seat on one of Bankrupt's flights, a customer calls a toll-free number and gives the ticketing agent his or her name, address, and credit card number. The ticketing agent issues a ticket stating the ticket number, departure date, ticket class (e.g., first, coach), ticket conditions (e.g., no refund), and fare. Although each flight can be booked by many customers and each customer can book many flights, Bankrupt's ticketing policies require that each customer must have a ticket to board each flight and that each ticket must be issued to only one passenger.

3. Review the case description and sample registration card shown here. Then draw an object relationship model to represent the classes in the DMV's vehicle-registration system. Given the abbreviations in the form, you may find it difficult to assign attributes and an identifier to each object class. Give it your best effort!

Type	Registration Valid From		Type	License Number	
Auto	11/08/93 to 11/08/94		91	2ZZN281	

Vehicle Identification Number				Make	
2YVHW31A9M5143404				Mazda	

Body Type	Cyls.	Date First Sold	Class	Yr	Yr. Model	Type Veh.	MP
CP		00/00/00	DJ	91	91	170	G

Date Issued	Ax.	Wc.	Unladen Weight		VALID	Total Fees Paid	
11/18/93						$328	

* * * * * * * For California Title Information * * * * * * * * * * * * * *
* * * * * * * Contact Any DMV Office * * * * * * * * * * * * * * * * * *

Registered Owner
Jones Andrew T.
4321 West San Carlos Street
San Jose, CA 95192

Lienholder
None

The State of California requires that every vehicle operated on its roads be registered with the Department of Motor Vehicles (DMV). Each year, the owner of the vehicle must return a vehicle-registration form and pay a fee to register his or her vehicle. On alternate years, the owner must also submit a smog-inspection certificate showing that the vehicle to be registered meets California emission standards. Upon receiving the fee (and smog inspection certificate), the DMV issues a registration card (shown here) and a sticker to affix to the vehicle's license plates. Each registration contains data about one vehicle and one owner and is related to zero or one smog-inspection certificate. Each owner can be related to many registrations, but each vehicle can be listed on only one registration. Each smog-inspection certificate is related to one registration.

4. The McMahon Agency is run by Allie McMahon, a musician's agent who forms contracts between bands and local clubs, taking a percentage of the booking rate in payment. Allie gathers and maintains information about clubs and bands on 3 x 5 cards that she files in two recipe boxes, one marked "Bands" and the other marked "Clubs." She maintains copies of her booking contracts in a folder labeled "Contracts." Examples of these data stores are provided on the next page. Create an object relationship model with attributes and identifiers to model the object classes and relationships in Allie's contract-management system.

Sample Contract

Band:	NWO	Club:	SJL
Booking Date:	May 30, 1994	Play Hours:	9 pm to 1 am
Restraints:	volume ordinance no smoking/drinking on stage		
Booking Rate:	$400	Cancellation:	72 hours notice
Payment Terms:	Check for the full amount made to the order of The McMahon Agency; payment due within 10 days after booking date.		

Sample Band Card

Band Name:	New World Order	Band Code:	NWO
Band Members:	*Jay Partridge(Drums) Paul Murdock(Bass), Al Dryer(Sax), Bo Diddle(Rhythm)	Phone:	(408) 456-3901
Music:	R&B	Features:	Lots of Robert Cray and own tunes; great vocals
Black-out:	Most Su-Tues	Minimum Rate:	$250 per nite
Agent's Fee:	15%, last negotiated 10/1/95		

* Denotes Band Leader

Note: Address and phone number for each band member are maintained on Allie's rolodex.

Sample Club Card

Club Name:	San Jose Lives	Club Code:	SJL
Address:	1403 First Street San Jose, CA 95193	Club Phone:	(408) 444-3321
Manager:	Jim Jones	Manager Phone:	(408) 333-4432
Music:	R&B	Restraints:	15 min break, volume control, dress code
Play Hours:	9-12 S-W; 9-1 Th-Sa	Play Rate:	$300-500 per nite
Cancellation Policy:	72 hours notice, no fine; less, $100 fine		

5. Create an object relationship model to model the relationships, attributes and identifiers of the object classes in Your Good Health Clinic's patient-records and appointment-scheduling system shown below and on the next page.

Patient Information Form
Your Good Health Clinic

Please supply the following information for our records.

Full Name: *Alicia Navarone*   Date of birth: *10-9-58*

Current address: *1253 North Pine Ridge Blvd, San Jose, CA 95190*

Home Phone: *(408) 299-7765*   Work phone: *(415) 912-4376*

Sex (check one): M ___ F *X*   Occupation: *Environmental Health Specialist*

For office use only

Patient-ID: 189-0321-88   Primary Physician: Schwartz

Your Good Health Clinic List of Physicians				
Physician Name	**Specialty**	**Hospital Affiliation**	**Phone**	**Pager**
Martina Andresen	Sprts Med.	St. Mary's	3416	555-4447
Aaron Yamamoto	Cardiology	Stanford Medical Center	3417	555-6668
William Schwartz	Internal Med.	Santa Clara County General	3418	555-7779

Appointment Schedule for 12/15/97				
Physician	**Appt. Time**	**Patient**	**Phone**	**Complaint**
Yamamoto	8:00 a.m.	Sam Goldwin	555-7849	Chest pain
Yamamoto	8:30 a.m.	Betty Rambler	237-0096	Cardiovascular exam
	etc.			
Schwartz	8:00 a.m.	Alicia Navarone	299-7765	Sore throat and fever
Schwartz	8:15 a.m.	Ben Casey	991-8080	Annual physical
	etc.			
Andresen	8:00 a.m.	Steve Young	664-8712	Annual physical
Andresen	9:00 a.m.	Bobby Bonds	771-6190	Pulled muscle in leg
	etc.			

6. Data about work-study employees is maintained on the three source documents shown below and on the next page. Create an object relationship model to model the relationships, attributes, and identifiers of the object classes represented in these documents. You may assume that each employee punches in and out only once each workday.

Work-Study Employee Payroll Information
Applicant: Please provide the following information for payroll purposes.

Full name: _Susan Marie Stevens_   SSN: _555-33-4444_

Tax status: _Single_   Authorized Deductions:

Exemptions: _1_   Type   Amount

                                    1. ___Tuition___   25.00/wk

                                    2. ___Parking:___   4.50/wk

---

Office use only

Department employed in: _Marketing_

Hourly rate: _7.85_

Work-Study allocation: _2000.00_

YTD gross pay: _1351.97_   Last updated: _11/1/97_

```
                       Timecard for:  Susan Stevens
                               SSN:  555-33-4444
                 Pay Period Ending:  10/29/97

        Date              Time-In           Time-Out

        10/24             1000              1159
        10/25             1000              1203
        10/26             1300              1700
        10/27             1300              1700
        etc.
```

Time Sheet for <u>Marketing</u> **Department**
Pay Period Ending <u>10/29/97</u>

SSN	Employee Name	Hrly Rate	Hrs Worked	Gross
123-45-6789	Tran Pham	8.50	22	187.00
555-33-4444	Susan Stevens	7.85	20	157.00
etc.				

◈ REFERENCES

Embly, D. W., B. D. Kurtz, and S. N. Woodfield. *Object-Oriented Systems Analysis: A Model-Driven Approach.* Englewood Cliffs, NJ: Yourdon Press/Prentice-Hall, 1992.

Kroenke, D. *Database Processing,* 5th ed. Englewood Cliffs, NJ: Prentice-Hall, 1995.

Martin, J., and J. Odell. *Object-Oriented Analysis and Design.* Englewood Cliffs, NJ: Prentice-Hall, 1992.

Rumbaugh, J., et al. *Object-Oriented Modeling and Design.* Englewood Cliffs, NJ: Prentice-Hall, 1991.

Taylor, D. *Business Engineering with Object Technology.* New York: John Wiley & Sons, 1995.

Yourdon, E. *Object-Oriented Systems Design: An Integrated Approach.* Englewood Cliffs, NJ: Yourdon Press/Prentice-Hall, 1994.

ANALYZING AND DESIGNING SYSTEM DATA STRUCTURES

Iterative Analysis, Design, Preliminary Construction, and Review

1. Analyze system structure and behavior.
   a. *Analyze system data structures.*
   b. Analyze system behavior.
   c. Analyze system interfaces.

2. Design system structure and behavior.
   a. *Design system data structures.*
   b. Design system behavior.
   c. Design system interfaces.

3. Construct prototype for user review.

4. Conduct user review.

5. Repeat steps 1–4 if changes are needed.

JAD WORKSHOP EXCERPT: DEFINING USE CASES, CLASSES, ATTRIBUTES, AND RELATIONSHIPS

Victoria continued the ETG JAD workshop by initiating a discussion of the kinds of business transactions that ETG's new order processing system would have to support. "Our next task is to define use cases. Use cases specify sequences of behaviors that must be performed in the order processing system, for example, adding a new rental customer or renting a tape. If you look through your problem definition report, you'll find a list of high-level processing tasks identified during my enterprise analysis of ETG. Based on this, Denny and I have compiled a preliminary list of use cases, which Denny will now project on the whiteboard." (See Figure 9.1 for a mapping of use cases to high-level processes.)

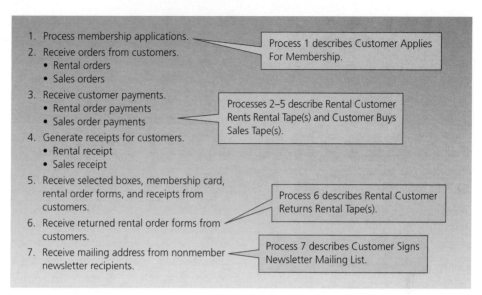

1. Process membership applications.

   Process 1 describes Customer Applies For Membership.

2. Receive orders from customers.
   * Rental orders
   * Sales orders

3. Receive customer payments.
   * Rental order payments
   * Sales order payments

   Processes 2–5 describe Rental Customer Rents Rental Tape(s) and Customer Buys Sales Tape(s).

4. Generate receipts for customers.
   * Rental receipt
   * Sales receipt

5. Receive selected boxes, membership card, rental order forms, and receipts from customers.

   Process 6 describes Rental Customer Returns Rental Tape(s).

6. Receive returned rental order forms from customers.

7. Receive mailing address from nonmember newsletter recipients.

   Process 7 describes Customer Signs Newsletter Mailing List.

FIGURE 9.1   Identifying use cases in ETG's order processing system

Denny displayed the list of use cases:

◆   Customer Applies For Membership

◆   Rental Customer Rents Rental Tape(s)

◆   Customer Buys Sales Tape(s)

◆   Rental Customer Returns Rental Tape(s)

◆   Customer Signs Newsletter Mailing List

◆   Special Orders Requests Tape Availability

◆   Management Requests Reports

◆   Promotions Requests Mailing Labels

"Let's take a moment to review this list and to determine if it is complete. Can you think of any additional business transactions that should be listed here?" Victoria asked.

"It seems that these are all related to customers or other departments. What about the processes of maintaining the database?" Paul asked.

"You're right in thinking that the system will have to maintain data, Paul. Denny will focus on defining aspects of the database in just a few moments. Implicit in his discussion is that the system will support all the create, read, update, and delete functions required to maintain ETG's data."

Corita asked, "Should we also have some way of dealing with a rental customer using a coupon or 'bonus points' to pay for a rental order? Or is that part of renting a tape?"

Victoria answered, "You should consider two factors to decide that: One, is a payment a discrete transaction? In other words, do customers ever just make payments separate from the transaction of purchasing or renting tapes? Two, does the payment method used distinctly define a rental transaction? For example, in a department store, a customer making a credit account payment is a distinct transaction; in addition, cash orders are processed differently than credit orders in that they require different inputs, access different files, and generate different outputs. Does the method of payment significantly differentiate a transaction in your order processing system?"

"What would be the implications for the system?" Paul asked. "I mean, are we talking about having a separate screen for cash rental orders versus coupon rental orders versus cash sales orders, and so on? If so, that seems unnecessary."

"You're right, Paul. It would be," Victoria said. "However, different ways of handling payments would not require different screens. Only the logic behind the screen would be different. Let's not delve too far into interfaces at this point. We need to define the activities the system will support before we decide what interfaces are needed. Corita, you raised the question in the first place. What do you think?"

"Making a payment is part of a rental transaction and a sales transaction and a fine processing transaction. So payment processing should be defined as something we can use in all three," Corita said.

"Fine processing transaction?" Victoria interrupted. "Clearly we need to add Customer Makes Payment to our use-case list. But I think Corita has mentioned another use case missing in our preliminary list. Is fine processing part of renting a tape, or is it a transaction in and of itself?"

"Both," Beto replied. "Customers often pay fines when they return overdue tapes, but they can also pay fines separately or as part of a rental order transaction."

"That's true," Paul added. "In fact, we have a business policy requiring rental customers to pay fines before they can rent tapes."

"But that's a policy that's not always enforced," Corita noted. "For example, if a kid comes in to rent a tape using his dad's membership card, I'll just ask him to tell his dad about the fines—assuming I know about them! Our fine records have been pretty sloppy and almost impossible to use effectively. Anyway, I'll just tell the kid about the fine and then go ahead and rent the tape."

"Okay, let's plan to address fine payment policy later on when we define system behaviors in more detail. For now, let's add 'Rental Customer Pays Fines' as a use case. Is that okay with everyone?"

Helen responded, "Sounds great. Given that, it seems to me that we've defined all the major transactions in the order processing system. Well, not *defined*—but at least *identified*. I'd like to *define* these transactions further."

"Okay, Helen," Victoria laughed. "I can see that you're anxious to forge ahead. But first we all need to agree that the use cases listed represent all the major order processing transactions you perform. Any other comments? ... Okay, then let's take Helen's suggestion and begin to define a scenario for each use case. We need to determine the tasks, objects—and, later on, the interfaces—involved in each transaction. Our purpose at this point is just to state what has to be done, not who at ETG will do it or how. Thus, for the most part, the only people mentioned in the use case should be external entities such as customers. Let's begin with the Rental Customer Rents Rental Tape(s) transaction. Denny will capture your description and project it on the whiteboard as it is built. How should this transaction be performed in the new system?"

Susan said, "What's this *Rental* Customer *Rents Rental* Tapes() business. Why not just call it Customer Rents Tape(s)?"

Victoria laughed. "It does sound kind of redundant, doesn't it? My reason for being so precise is that you've stated that only *rental* customers can rent tapes and that the only tapes that can be rented are *rental* tapes. In other words, a nonmember customer—or, for that matter, a rental customer—cannot rent a *sales* tape. I've tried to incorporate these business rules in the name of this transaction."

"All right," Susan responded, "as long as I know that there's a method to your madness."

"There usually is, Susan," Victoria said. "But you're right to question me anyway. It's important that my view of the system accurately reflects your view. So, fire away!"

"By this point, you know that I will do just that," Susan teased. "Someone has to keep you honest."

"Good, I'll depend on it. Can you start us off, Susan? How should a rental transaction begin in the new system?"

As the ETG participants described the steps in a rental transaction, Denny used word-processing software to capture their description and display it on the whiteboard. They described rental customers' presenting their membership cards and selected tapes to the order desk and so on. Then Paul interrupted, "Victoria, I'd like to add a control on the new rental orders process. Since the authorized users of each membership will be easily accessible on the system, I think it makes sense to verify that someone is an authorized user before we let him or her use a member's card."

"But how will you enforce that rule in practice?" Beto asked. "If little Jimmy Smith presents his mother's membership card, how do I know that he's who he says he is?"

"Well, at minimum, he knows his name and that he's Betty Smith's son," Paul explained, "and, if his mom listed him as an authorized user on her membership application form, then his name and the fact that he's her son will appear in the authorized users list. Is that right, Victoria?"

"Yes, Paul. We can easily display a list of authorized users on demand, but you should realize that it's not a foolproof control."

"No, but it gives me a modicum of protection. If Jimmy is an authorized user and Jimmy rents videos without his mother's permission, his mother is still responsible for returning the tapes on time and in good condition."

The ETG participants continued to define the tasks involved in processing rental orders. Just as it seemed that they were satisfied with their description, Corita asked, "What about 3/3 rental orders? We haven't addressed how they are processed?"

"Is a 3/3 order handled in a different way, Corita?"

"Well, only in the sense that the sales clerk needs to treat it as a 3 standard tapes for $3.00 transaction instead of a 3 standard tapes for $10.50 transaction."

"Okay," Victoria replied, "then would it be appropriate to treat a 3/3 rental order transaction as a special case of a rental order transaction?"

Linda, the company accountant, responded. "The main thing is that I don't think we should have collected $10.50 when we've really only collected $3.00. However you can avoid that kind of error is fine with me."

"In a later session, you'll have a chance to verify that the new system avoids that error. For now, Denny, please add the 3/3 rental order transaction as a special case of Rental Customer Rents Rental Tapes." Victoria asked Denny to project the completed use-case specification on the whiteboard (see Figure 9.2).

Use Case Name: Rental Customer Rents Rental Tape(s)
Use Case Purpose: Describes the process of renting rental tapes to rental customers
Uses: Rental Customer Pays Fines; Customer Makes Payment
Extended by: Rental Customer Rents 3/3 Rental Tapes

Typical Course of Events:

1. Use case is initiated when a <u>rental customer</u> selects <u>rental tapes</u> from the display shelves and presents a <u>membership card</u> and the selected rental tapes for check out.
2. The <u>rental order</u> is completed, indicating a valid *employee number,* a valid *member number, order number,* and *order date.*
3. For each rental tape being rented, a <u>rental-order line</u> is created, giving the *stock number, title, rental category,* and *rental fee* of each rental tape; in addition, the *due date* calculated for each rental tape is shown on the rental-order line.
4. The <u>rental order</u> is completed by calculating and entering a *total cost* for the order.
5. Customer makes <u>payment</u>.
6. The rental order form is printed and the customer signs it. The customer is given one copy of the form; the other copy is retained for the audit file.

Alternative Courses of Events:

a. At step 1, if a rental customer does not have his membership card with him, his *telephone number* can be used to determine the appropriate member number.
b. At step 2, if the customer claims to be an <u>authorized user</u>, the rental customer's authorized user list is displayed. If the customer is not listed, the transaction is cancelled, and the membership card is confiscated.
c. At step 2, if an invalid employee number is provided, the transaction is cancelled.
d. At step 2, if the rental customer provides an invalid member number, the transaction is cancelled, and the membership card is confiscated. If the member number is valid but the rental customer has unpaid *fines,* fines are processed before the transaction proceeds. If customer is unable to pay the fines, the transaction is cancelled. (see Rental Customer Pays Fines use case.)
e. At step 5, if the customer cannot make payment, the transaction is cancelled.

(a) Rental Customer Rents Rental Tape(s)

Use Case Name: Rental Customer Returns Rental Tape(s)
Use Case Purpose: Describes the processing of returned rental tapes
Uses: Rental Customer Pays Fines

Typical Course of Events:

1. Use case is initiated when a <u>rental customer</u> returns <u>rental tapes</u>.
2. For each rental tape being returned, the *stock number* is used to access the <u>rental-order</u> record.
3. The *return date and time* for each tape is determined, and the status of the tape is updated (i.e., status = on shelf).
4. If the tape was returned on time, no further processing is required.
5. If the tape was returned late, the amount of the *overdue fine* is calculated, the appropriate rental customer record is accessed, and *fines* is updated.
6. If the rental customer wants to pay the fine when the tape is returned, fines are processed (see Rental Customer Pays Fines).

(b) Rental Customer Returns Rental Tape(s)

FIGURE 9.2 Use-case specifications (*continued on next page*)

Use Case Name: Customer Buys Sales Tape(s)
Use Case Purpose: Describes the process of selling sales tapes to customers
Uses: Customer Makes Payment

Typical Course of Events:

1. Use case is initiated when a customer selects sales tapes from shelves and presents selected tapes for check out.
2. The sales order form header is completed, indicating a valid *employee number*, an optional *member number, order number*, and *order date*.
3. For each sales tape title being rented, a sales-order line is created, giving the *quantity, title ID, title, selling price*, and *extended price*.
4. The sales order form is completed by calculating the *subtotal, sales tax*, and *total* for the order.
5. Customer makes payment.
6. The sales order form is printed. The customer is given one copy of the form; the other copy is retained for the audit file.

Alternative Courses of Events:

a. At step 2, if an invalid employee number is provided, the transaction is cancelled.
b. At step 5, if the customer cannot make payment, the transaction is cancelled.

(c) Customer Buys Sales Tape(s)

Use Case Name: Customer Applies For Membership
Use Case Purpose: Describes the process of processing a membership application and creating a new rental customer record

Typical Course of Events:

1. Use case is initiated when a customer completes a membership application form.
2. As the membership form data are entered into the system, the *address* is verified against the customer's checkbook, driver's license, or other ID; the *credit card type, number*, and *expiration date* are verified by examining the customer's credit card.
3. A membership card indicating the customer's *membership number* is created and given to the customer.

Alternative Courses of Events:

a. At step 1, if incomplete information is provided, the application form is returned to the customer and complete information is requested.
b. At step 2, if the customer leaves the membership form for later processing, the address, etc. are verified before the customer leaves.

(d) Customer Applies For Membership

FIGURE 9.2 Use-case specifications (*continued*)

The ETG participants continued to work with Victoria to define use cases, preparing a use-case specification like the ones shown in Figure 9.2 for each use case.

After a short break, Denny took over. His objective was to analyze the use cases to verify the list of candidate classes and to clarify the rules governing ETG's order processing system. Denny and Victoria need to understand ETG's business rules in order to design the system behaviors, database, data entry screens, and reports.

Denny began by reviewing the list of candidate classes identified during preliminary analysis (see Figure 9.3). "Okay, let's see if we can eliminate some of these now that you've outlined how the new system will behave. This list represents all the business people and things in your current order processing system. As I examined this list, it seemed that you might be calling the same things by different names or be using redundant documents or things in your system. For example, you use multiple receipts: one copy of the rental order form is a receipt and all copies of the cash register receipt are receipts. Are all these forms necessary in the new system?"

"Not really," Beto replied. "In the new system, as we described it in the use cases, the order form and the receipt are the same document—the receipt is simply a copy of the order form (see Figure 9.4). Assuming that the new system generates the order form only after payment has been made, we don't need the cash register receipt. What's more, in the new system, we could allow a single transaction to include both rentals and sales."

"Is that something you'd like to consider, Paul?" Denny asked.

"I like the idea of having just one order document instead of two, but I prefer that sales and rentals be written up on separate forms," Paul replied.

"Okay," Denny commented. "Then every transaction will have certain data—date, order number, employee number, and total. According to the use cases, each rental order

---

RENTAL-ORDER-FORM-1   (treat as interface)
RENTAL-ORDER-FORM-2   (treat as interface; add RENTAL-ORDER and SALES-ORDER as
                                    subclasses of ORDER; separate forms for each)

RENTAL-CUSTOMER
SALES-CLERK
~~INVENTORY-CLERK~~ (position no longer exists)
RENTAL-ORDERS-REPORT (treat as interface)
MEMBERSHIP-APPLICATION-FORM (treat as interface)
~~RENTAL-PAYMENT~~ (see below)
~~CASH-REGISTER-RENTAL-RECEIPT-1~~
~~CASH-REGISTER-RENTAL-RECEIPT-2~~
~~DISPLAY-BOX~~
RENTAL-TAPE   (a subclass of TAPE, but many RENTAL-TAPE instances—each with its own
                StockNumber—can be related to one instance of TAPE)
~~MEMBERSHIP-CARD~~ (same as RENTAL-CUSTOMER; may treat as interface)
~~SALES-~~CUSTOMER (RENTAL-CUSTOMER is-a CUSTOMER)
SALES-TAPE (subclass of TAPE)
SALES-ORDER-REPORT (treat as interface)
~~SALES-~~PAYMENT (superclass with ORDER-PAYMENT and FINE-PAYMENT subclasses)
~~CASH-REGISTER-SALES-RECEIPT-1~~ (treat as SALES-ORDER-FORM interface)
~~CASH-REGISTER-SALES-RECEIPT-2~~
NEWSLETTER-SIGN-UP-LIST (treat as interface)
~~NEWSLETTER~~ (removed from project scope)
~~NONMEMBER-NEWSLETTER-RECIPIENT~~ (same as CUSTOMER)
~~PROMOTIONS-ASSISTANT~~ (not relevant given project scope)

FIGURE 9.3   Annotated candidate classes identified during preliminary analysis

Entertainment To Go
153 North Victory Street
Scotts Valley, CA 95066
(408) 555-9000

Order Number: 10054   Order Date: 3/22//97

Sales Clerk: Julie   Checked out by: Joe
Due Date: 3/23/97   Date Returned: *3/23/97*
Checked in by: *Amy*   Late Fee:

Rental Customer: Please complete the shaded portion below.

Customer Membership Number: *C152*
Customer Name: *Paula Cassidy*
Customer Address: *3039 N. Highland Ave., Scotts Valley, CA 95066*
Customer Phone: *555-3491*

Videos Rented:

Video Stock #	Video Title	Category	Rental Fee
W115-92	*When Harry Met Sally*	*S*	*$3.50*
S421-90	*Shark!*	*E*	*$2.50*

Total: *$6.00*

Rented videos must be returned by 6:00 p.m. on the due date shown to avoid a late fee.

Customer Signature: *Paula Cassidy*

FIGURE 9.4   ETG's current rental order form

must also be related to a rental customer and one or more rental tapes and will have additional attributes, such as due date and rental fee. Sales order transactions may not be related to any specific customer but must be related to at least one sales tape." Denny drew a line through the RENTAL-ORDER-FORM and CASH-REGISTER-RECEIPT candidate classes and wrote "Order form—2 copies; separate forms for sales and rentals" in their place. He also added an ORDER superclass and noted that a SALES-ORDER is an ORDER and a RENTAL-ORDER is an ORDER. "Good. That will eliminate a lot of redundancy in the new system. Next, let's look at the EMPLOYEE objects. Paul, would I be right in assuming that you maintain the same data about each employee—name, address, phone, employee number?"

"Yes, that's right."

"Currently, you differentiate a sales clerk from an inventory clerk from a promotions assistant. However, under the general design alternative you've chosen, sales clerks and inventory clerks will have the same responsibilities. Can we eliminate the INVENTORY-CLERK?

"Yes," Susan agreed, "as long as you eliminate the object but not the people who fill that role! Remember Paul's promise to try to keep all 'used-to-be inventory clerks' on staff."

Denny crossed out the INVENTORY-CLERK object class. "Okay, next let's look at some of the customer classes, such as RENTAL-CUSTOMER, SALES-CUSTOMER, NONMEMBER-NEWSLETTER-RECIPIENT. Do you maintain some data about every customer but different data about rental versus sales customers? In other words, how many different kinds of customers do you really have?"

Helen shook her head. "We don't really maintain data about all customers. I mean, we maintain data about all rental customers—membership number, a credit card number, things like that—but we don't maintain any data about most of our sales customers. What I'm trying to say is that we have a master customer list in which we list the name and address of every customer—sales or rental—who has a membership or who has signed up for our mailing list. Those who sign the mailing list provide their name, address, and phone number and indicate their favorite movie genre, etc. But we don't have any data for customers who just buy tapes from us. Also, a rental customer can buy tapes as well as rent tapes, so I guess that sometimes a rental customer is a sales customer."

Denny paused to consider this information. "Then what you're saying is that, for your purposes, anyone can buy a sales tape, every customer for whom you know the name and address receives a newsletter, but only rental customers can rent tapes. Is that right?"

"Sounds right. Is there a problem with that?" Paul asked.

"No problem," Denny assured Paul. "All it means is that I need to rethink the way I've described customers so far." Denny crossed out the SALES-CUSTOMER and NON-MEMBER-NEWSLETTER-RECIPIENT classes, added a CUSTOMER superclass, and noted that a RENTAL-CUSTOMER is a CUSTOMER. "I think we're doing a great job of eliminating some of the redundancy in your system. Let's examine the RENTAL-CUSTOMER, MEMBERSHIP-APPLICATION-FORM, and MEMBERSHIP-CARD objects next. Clearly these are three distinct things in your current system and in the proposed system as you've described it in your use cases. But would it be accurate to say that all three are different names for data about a rental customer?"

Beto responded, "That's true. I guess you could say that we use the membership application to collect information about rental customers and then use the membership card to verify that someone is a member."

"Okay, but does all the data on the membership application and the membership card describe a rental customer? What I'm trying to get at is whether these three things need to be treated as different classes with different attributes. Perhaps we can answer this question by defining the attributes of each."

"If you look at our membership application form," Helen said, "you can see we collect the usual information about name, address, phone numbers (see Figure 9.5). We also require that customers give us information about a major credit card so that if they keep a tape or incur excessive fines, we have some recourse."

Entertainment To Go
Membership Application Form

Name: _____
          (first)   (initial)   (last)

Address: _____
                    (street)

_____
          (city)   (state)   (zip code)

Home phone: _____ Work phone: _____

Major credit card: Visa ____ MC ____ _____
                                              No.   Exp. date:

Authorized users of membership card:

Name   Relationship

_____

_____

_____

_____

_____

By signing this form, I agree to abide by the membership rule as explained on the back of each sales transaction form.

_____
          (signature)   (date)

For ETG Use Only

Membership #: _____ Approved by: _____ Date approved: _____

FIGURE 9.5   ETG's current membership application form

     Denny examined the form. "This form and the membership card are really interfaces, so we'll leave them for Victoria to address later. I see that you also ask for the names of authorized users. I recall that authorized users were mentioned in the Rental Customer use case. Are these people considered members too?"

     "Not directly," Helen responded. "Only the primary applicant is a member. But, if the member wants to, he can let someone else rent tapes under his or her membership—you know, like kids or roommates."

     "Then an authorized user can't exist without the member's authorization, right?"

     "I guess that's right, if you mean "exist" in the sense of existing in our records," Beto replied. "Each member has only one membership card that lists his membership number. Authorized users don't have their own membership cards."

"Okay, then the data on the membership application describes one rental customer, but each rental customer may have zero or more authorized users. Is that right, Beto?"

"That's right, Denny. One membership application, one member, one membership card, but potentially many authorized users."

Denny added an AUTHORIZED-USER and a CREDIT-CARD class to his list and noted that a RENTAL-CUSTOMER has one CREDIT-CARD and zero or more AUTHORIZED-USERs. "Next, let's look at the RENTAL-TAPE and SALES-TAPE. Would it be accurate to say that both of these objects belong to a more general class, TAPE? In other words, is some of the data the same whether a tape is a rental tape or a sales tape?"

"That's true," Paul answered, referring Denny to sample tape records maintained on 3 x 5 notecards and a breakdown of rental fees and rental periods for each category of rental tape (see Figure 9.6). "For example, we maintain data about the tape title, director, actors, and genre whether the tape is for rent or for sale. But we also maintain different data for each tape type. For example, we assign a rental category and a unique stock number to each rental tape, but not to sales tapes. By the way, although it's not indicated here, I would like to track the quantity of each sales tape title in stock. And Special Orders needs to know if rental tapes are available. At least in the new system, we won't have to track display boxes too."

"That's right. I bet you're glad that you won't need to maintain a display box for every rental tape." Denny crossed display box off his list. "But something you just said makes me wonder if RENTAL-TAPE should be treated as a subclass of TAPE. You said that there can be multiple 'When Harry Met Sally' rental tapes, with each tracked individually by a unique stock number. In contrast, all 'When Harry Met Sally' sales tapes are indistinguishable and are lumped in quantity in stock. That's going to require not only different attributes

Rental Tape Stock Number: W115-92
Rental Category: New Rel.___ Standard _X_ Educ ___
Title: When Harry Met Sally
Director: Rob Reiner
Actors: Billy Crystal, Meg Ryan
Genre: Romantic comedy
Received: 10/26/93
Last Inspected: 9/15/96

Tape Title Number: J274-94
Sales Tape Mfr. #: 74643-01304
Title: Jurassic Park
Director: Steven Spielberg
Actors: Sam Neil, Laura Dern
Genre: Sci-Fi
Price: $21.99

Rental Categories

Cat	Fee	Days
N	4.50	1
S	3.50	1
E	2.50	2

FIGURE 9.6   Samples of ETG's current tape records and category details

but also different methods for dealing with each type of tape. Fortunately for me, it's Victoria's job to sort out the methods." Denny created an object relationship model segment to represent his initial understanding of the tape classes (see Figure 9.7).

Denny continued asking questions about ETG's use cases and business rules. As each rule was clarified, he created another object relationship model segment (see selected examples in Figure 9.8). "Okay, I think I've got enough information to begin designing and constructing a model of your new system's classes and attributes (see Figure 9.9 on page 330). It's Victoria's turn now. She's going to help you examine the system behaviors and interfaces more fully."

(continued in Chapter 10 opening case)

The chapter opening case presents an excerpt of the JAD workshop that Victoria and Denny conducted to help ETG define its new order processing system. By analyzing use cases, source documents, and business rules, Denny was able to identify classes, attributes, and relationships and to create an object relationship model. Working from this model, Denny can design and construct the system's database. The process Denny follows to perform these development tasks will be used to illustrate logical and physical database design in this chapter.

Database design and construction addresses the data—and, to some extent, the procedures and software—components of the PPDSH information system model. This activity also designs many of the input, output, storage, and control functions of the IPOSC information

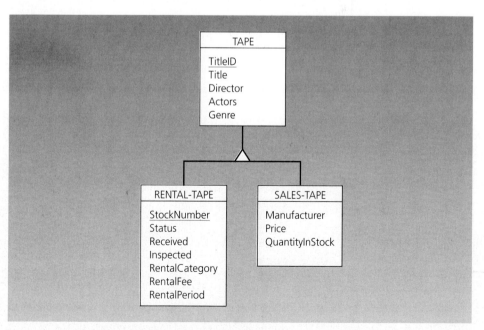

FIGURE 9.7 Denny's model of TAPE, RENTAL-TAPE, and SALES-TAPE

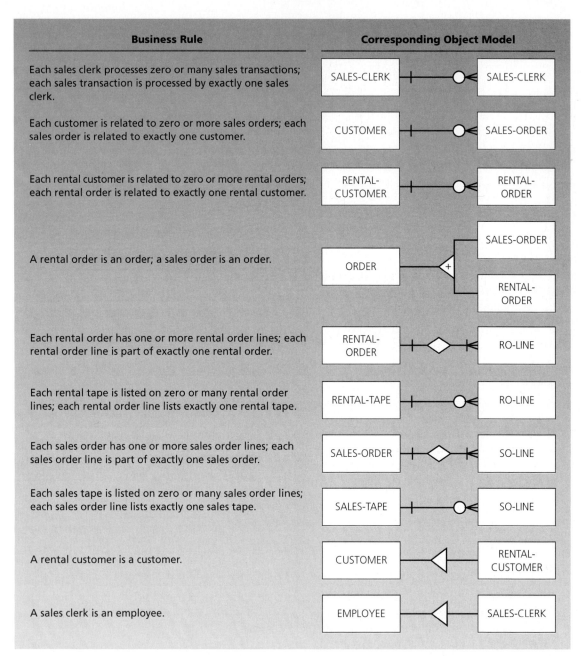

Business Rule	Corresponding Object Model
Each sales clerk processes zero or many sales transactions; each sales transaction is processed by exactly one sales clerk.	SALES-CLERK ── SALES-CLERK
Each customer is related to zero or more sales orders; each sales order is related to exactly one customer.	CUSTOMER ── SALES-ORDER
Each rental customer is related to zero or more rental orders; each rental order is related to exactly one rental customer.	RENTAL-CUSTOMER ── RENTAL-ORDER
A rental order is an order; a sales order is an order.	ORDER ──+── SALES-ORDER / RENTAL-ORDER
Each rental order has one or more rental order lines; each rental order line is part of exactly one rental order.	RENTAL-ORDER ──◇── RO-LINE
Each rental tape is listed on zero or many rental order lines; each rental order line lists exactly one rental tape.	RENTAL-TAPE ── RO-LINE
Each sales order has one or more sales order lines; each sales order line is part of exactly one sales order.	SALES-ORDER ──◇── SO-LINE
Each sales tape is listed on zero or many sales order lines; each sales order line lists exactly one sales tape.	SALES-TAPE ── SO-LINE
A rental customer is a customer.	CUSTOMER ──◁── RENTAL-CUSTOMER
A sales clerk is an employee.	EMPLOYEE ──◁── SALES-CLERK

FIGURE 9.8 Additional ETG business rules mapped to object relationship model segments

system model. Designing a database requires you to understand the data the system must collect (input data), the reports it must generate (output data), and the records it must maintain (stored data). In addition, as you design a database, you must consider the procedures users will follow to enter, access, and manipulate data and the control functions required to protect the database from intentional or unintentional corruption.

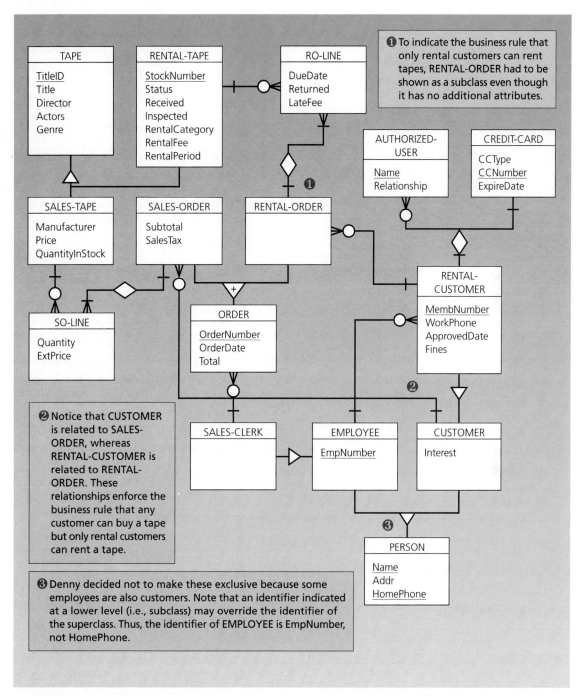

FIGURE 9.9   Object relationship model of ETG's proposed walk-in customer order processing system

This chapter explains how to specify the logical and physical design of a database. **Logical database design** specifies data elements, logical records, keys, and relationships; **physical database design** specifies the file organization, physical records, and indexes for each file. After completing this chapter, you should be able to

1. Define what a use case is and explain its purpose in systems analysis and design.

2. Define several database concepts.

3. Discuss the problems with conventional file processing that are alleviated by implementing a database management system (DBMS).

4. Define four database structures and discuss the advantages and disadvantages of each.

5. Explain the criteria for evaluating database quality, including strategies for attaining these criteria.

6. Convert an object relationship model into a logical database design (relational DBMS).

7. Specify a physical database design using a data dictionary.

9.1 ◈ A USE-CASE APPROACH TO SYSTEMS ANALYSIS AND DESIGN

Many object-oriented analysis and design methodologies (e.g., [Booch 1994], [Jacobson et al. 1992], [Taylor 1995], and [White 1994]) have adopted the concept of a use case to analyze system data structures and behaviors. A **use case** is "a sequence of transactions in a system whose task is to yield a result of measurable value to an individual actor of the system" [Jacobson et al. 1995, p. 105]. More simply, you can think of a use case as an atomic sequence of activities that produces something of value to an external entity or a user.[1] For example, selling a product to a customer yields something of value to a customer, and generating management reports (we hope) yields something of value to a manager.

In essence, use cases describe transactions that the system performs, thus describing the things a system contains and the behaviors a system must support. Use cases provide an external view of the system, treating the system as a black box whose internal operations cannot be viewed. Thus, use cases present a nontechnical system view that users can more fully comprehend. For this reason, Jacobson [1995] recommends that users and designers collaborate to define use cases as a method of specifying the system's functional requirements. Use cases can also be used to identify and to define the system's classes, methods, and messages; to serve as test cases to verify that the system meets its requirements; to provide the basis for creating user documentation; and to specify the functionality of "minisystem" prototypes [White 1994].

Figure 9.2 gave the Rental Customer Rents Rental Tape(s) use-case specification for ETG's new order processing system. Notice that a use case can be written in ordinary English. Later, when we have fully defined the classes, methods, and messages in this use case,

---

[1] Although Jacobson limits use cases to descriptions of system processes that yield value to external entities, other methodologists have extended use cases to include system processes that yield value to *both external entities and users of the system* (see, e.g., [White 1994]). We adopt the latter approach here.

we will express its classes and sequence of behaviors more formally. However, for the time being, your main concern is expressing use cases in clear, easily-understood language so that users can verify them.

General guidelines for writing use cases include

1. Segment the use case into discrete activities by numbering each step.
2. Show alternative courses of events separately.
3. Use specialization and composition relationships to model a use case that is a special case of another use case or that is part of another use case.

Let's examine each of these guidelines further.

Guidelines 1 and 2 are closely related. Segmenting the use case into discrete activities is helpful because it allows you to specify alternative courses of events at each activity. For example, in the Rental Customer Rents Rental Tape(s) use case shown in Figure 9.2, alternative courses of events can occur at activities 1, 2, and 5. Showing these as alternatives instead of as "branches" within the use case simplifies the use case and emphasizes the typical course of events. Nonetheless, showing alternative courses of events is critical to a complete specification of the use case.

Guideline 3 also is designed to simplify use-case specifications. Just as an object class can be a specialization or a part of another object class, a use case can be a specialization or a part of another use case. For example, the use-case specification in Figure 9.2 indicates that the Rental Customer Rents Rental Tape(s) use case uses the Customer Makes Payment use case; in other words, the use case Customer Makes Payment *is part of* the use case Rental Customer Rents Rental Tape(s). The use-case specification also indicates that it is extended by the use case Rental Customer Rents 3/3 Rental Tapes, which is a specialized case. Figure 9.10 defines the "extends," "extended by," "uses," and "used by" relationships [Jacobson 1995].

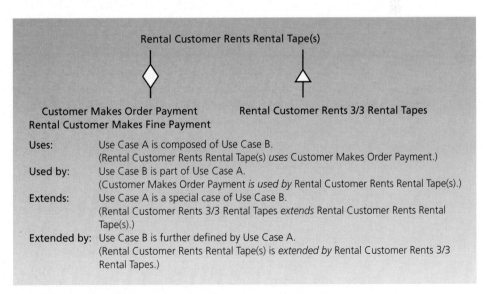

Uses:	Use Case A is composed of Use Case B.
	(Rental Customer Rents Rental Tape(s) *uses* Customer Makes Order Payment.)
Used by:	Use Case B is part of Use Case A.
	(Customer Makes Order Payment *is used by* Rental Customer Rents Rental Tape(s).)
Extends:	Use Case A is a special case of Use Case B.
	(Rental Customer Rents 3/3 Rental Tapes *extends* Rental Customer Rents Rental Tape(s).)
Extended by:	Use Case B is further defined by Use Case A.
	(Rental Customer Rents Rental Tape(s) is *extended by* Rental Customer Rents 3/3 Rental Tapes.)

FIGURE 9.10   Definition of specialization and composition use-case relationships

By exploiting the specialization and composition use case relationships, you achieve the modularity, reusability, and simplicity that are hallmarks of object-oriented analysis and design.

In the chapter opening case, use cases were analyzed to identify the object classes of ETG's order processing system. To identify object classes in a use case, begin by searching for nouns that describe roles, things, places, and so on. Following the guidelines recommended in the section "Identifying Candidate Classes" of Technical Module C will also be helpful here. In the use cases shown in Figure 9.2, things that are likely to be object classes, such as rental customer, rental tape, rental order, and RO-line, have been underlined, and things that are likely to be attributes have been italicized.

Figure 9.11 isolates the object relationship model segment containing the classes of the Rental Customer Rents Rental Tape(s) use case. A real-world object relationship model can contain dozens, even hundreds, of object classes. Segmenting an object relationship model

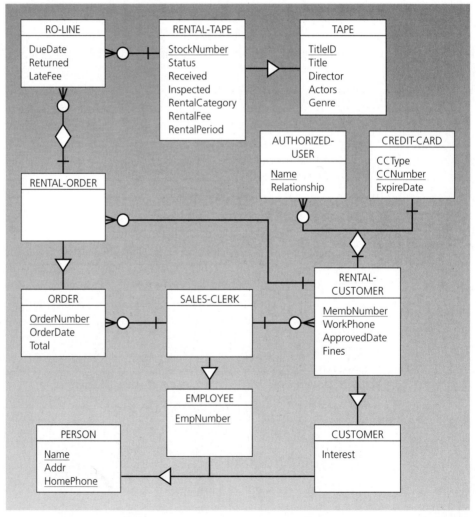

FIGURE 9.11   Object relationship model segment with classes in Rental Customer Rents Rental Tape(s) use case

into use-case views is a helpful technique for reducing complexity, allowing you to focus on one view at a time. Each use-case view is equivalent to a subject in the enterprise object model and should be examined to verify (1) that all necessary classes have been identified and (2) that each class's attributes describe the characteristics of interest in the use case. For example, clearly one class required in the Rental Customer Rents Rental Tape(s) use case is RENTAL-CUSTOMER. Do the attributes of RENTAL-CUSTOMER provide all the data necessary to use this class in this use case? In other words, does the RENTAL-CUSTOMER class "know" everything it needs to know to participate in this use case? It would seem so, given that the only RENTAL-CUSTOMER attributes specifically mentioned in the use case are membership number and fines.

By successively analyzing each use case and physically examining any source documents used in the case (for example, ETG's membership application form), you can begin to define a system's data structures, or more generally, its classes and attributes. Keep in mind that the classes uncovered in system data structure analysis and design may change as you undertake system behavior analysis and design. This evolution of classes is a natural and desirable effect as you iterate through analysis and design activities.

9.2 ◆ INTRODUCTION TO DATABASE CONCEPTS

As you learned to construct an object relationship model in Technical Module D, you learned several logical data modeling terms. Here you will learn the physical database design equivalents of these terms. To help you relate these two sets of terms, Table 9.1 lists the logical data modeling terms and "translates" them into physical database design terms. A **field** or **data element**, which is equivalent to an attribute in logical data modeling, is the smallest unit of data consisting of a combination of characters that describe one feature of an object class; for example, CustomerName, ZipCode, HourlyWage.

A **logical record** is a collection of related fields that describe one instance of an object class; for example, a Customer record containing the fields CustomerName, CustomerAddress, etc. A **physical record** is a unit of data stored at a disk address and transferred to main memory as a single "chunk." Thus, a physical record may correspond to one or more instances of a logical record. Records are uniquely identified by a **primary key**, which is usually the

TABLE 9.1 Relating concepts of logical data modeling and physical database design

Logical Data Modeling	Physical Database Design
Attribute	Data element; field
Object instance	Logical record
Object class	File; table; relation
Identifier	Primary key
Relationship	Foreign key; pointer
Object relationship model	Database

identifier assigned during logical data modeling. Records are related to one another through the use of a **foreign key**—the primary key of a related record included as a field of another record—or through the use of a **pointer**, which gives the address of the related record.

A **file**, which is loosely equivalent to an object class, is a collection of related records; for example, all Customer records are stored in a Customer file. The term "loosely equivalent" is used here because, as you will see later, a single object class may be implemented as one or more files. What is more, multiple object classes may be implemented as a single file.

An **index** is a file that relates the value of one or more fields to the physical storage address where the related record is located. You may find this concept easier to understand if you think of a book index, which maps key words to the text page(s) where they occur. Files can be indexed in several ways. Usually, though, a file is indexed on the values of the primary key. However, other nonkey fields can also be used, in which case the index is a **secondary index**.

A **database** is a collection of related files. David Kroenke, who has written several textbooks on database processing, defines a database as "a self-describing collection of integrated records" [1995, pp. 13–16]. A database is indeed more than the data it contains. It also contains a description of its logical and physical structure, called a **schema**, which is written in a *data definition language* (DDL) and which describes the logical and physical data structures as well as the validation rules, access authorizations, and other aspects of the database. The structure of the database may also be documented in a **data dictionary**, which defines all the data structures (for example, data elements and records) of the database. You will learn how to construct a data dictionary in Section 9.5.

Databases are managed by software called a **database management system (DBMS)**, which provides an interface between an organization's data and the programs that must use this data. When an organization uses a DBMS to manage its data, all access to data is governed by and processed through the DBMS. The significance of this fact is made clear when one compares a conventional file-processing environment to a DBMS environment.

CONVENTIONAL FILE PROCESSING VERSUS DATABASE MANAGEMENT

In the **conventional file-processing environment** that prevailed until the 1970s but is less common today, data are organized in unrelated files by functional area. Each functional area's files are independent; thus, if the Marketing Department needs information from the Accounting Department, IS professionals have to write programs to extract the accounting data that marketing needs. In addition, all reports that users need must be programmed by IS personnel; thus, no ad hoc reports are available.

Several problems exist in the conventional file-processing environment. One of the most pernicious is **program-data dependence**: any time the format of the data changes, all the programs that use that data also must be modified. You may recall that the California Department of Motor Vehicles (DMV) experienced this problem. When the DMV needed to add a social security number field to its vehicle-registration and driver-license files, the task of modifying all the programs that accessed these files consumed 18 programmer-years of effort. Program-data dependence means that each program must describe the structure of each file it accesses. If you have done any programming in COBOL, you are no doubt familiar with the PIC statements required to describe the input picture of each file used by a COBOL program, for example,

Total-finance-charges	PIC 999.99
Amount-financed	PIC 9999.99
Number-of-payments	PIC 99
Annual-interest-rate	PIC 99.999

If the structure of this file changes, then a programmer must go into each program and modify the PIC statements to reflect the changes in file structure. Thus, file and program maintenance are very costly and time-consuming in a conventional file-processing environment.

Other problems with conventional file processing include data redundancy, inconsistency, and confusion. **Data redundancy** occurs when the same data are stored in multiple files. For example, when files are independent, data common to several files must be repeated in each file. This redundancy is illustrated in Table 9.2, which shows how student data would be stored in conventional file processing. Notice that StudentName, StudentSSN, and StudentAddress must appear in all three files.

Data inconsistency occurs when data are modified in one file but not in others. For example, if a student moves, all three files—Student Billing, Student Advising, and Student Transcript—must be modified to reflect this address change. However, if the new address is

Table 9.2 Data redundancy in conventional file-processing environment

Files	Data	Applications
Student Billing file	StudentName StudentSSN StudentAddress CreditLoad Tuition	Student Billing program
Student Advising file	StudentName StudentSSN StudentAddress Major Minor Advisor	Student Advising program
Student Transcript file	StudentName StudentSSN StudentAddress {Semester CourseNumber CourseTitle CourseCredits CourseGrade}	Student Transcript program

Note: Data enclosed in braces {} indicates a repeating group.

entered into only one of these files, the data about this student will be inconsistent: The Student Billing file may list the student's new address "425 Elm Street" whereas the Student Advising and Student Transcript files list the old address, "3571 Poplar Avenue." **Data confusion** occurs when different users use different terms to describe data. For example, users of the Student Billing program may use the name "StudentID" instead of "StudentSSN" to describe a student's social security number.

Furthermore, because files are independent from each other, the conventional file-processing environment lacks flexibility and does not support data sharing. These problems yield a complex web of paperwork that must be exchanged among functional area users. Because users in one functional area are unable to access other areas' data on the computer, they must rely on printed reports and often must retype data from another area's report into their own application.

In contrast to the conventional file-processing environment, the DBMS environment consolidates an organization's data into an integrated database that can be used by a variety of functional areas to support a variety of applications. Thus, an interface is provided between data and the programs that must use the data. Figure 9.12 illustrates how the data in Table 9.2 would be organized in a relational database management system (RDBMS). Notice that the repeated student data—StudentName, StudentSSN, StudentAddress—are organized as a separate file, the Student Master file. Notice also that the other files are related to the Student Master file through StudentSSN, which is a primary key in the Student Master file and both a foreign key and a primary key in the other student files.

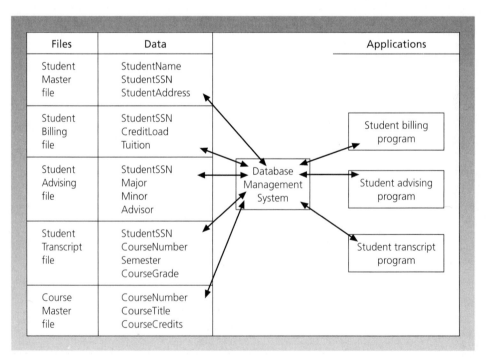

FIGURE 9.12   Reduction of data redundancy in a DBMS environment

The DBMS interface between data and programs provides several advantages. First, it reduces program-data dependence because data are organized by the DBMS independent of the programs that use the data. Programs are not affected if new data are added to a file or if the structure of data in an existing file changes. Second, the DBMS environment reduces data redundancy because all common data that must be known by several files—for example, the StudentName, StudentAddress, and StudentSSN fields in our example—do not need to be repeated in each file. Instead, any file that contains the StudentSSN can access StudentName and StudentAddress from the Student Master file. Third, the DBMS environment increases data integrity by reducing the likelihood of data inconsistency and data confusion. For example, in a DBMS environment, if a student moves, his or her address must be modified in only the Student Master file, not in every file that contains student data. Fourth, flexibility and data sharing are improved because the organization has an integrated database instead of stand-alone files. Thus, if a Marketing Department user needs to access Accounting Department data, the DBMS facilitates this data sharing by providing more user-friendly, standardized access procedures.

Nonetheless, the DBMS environment does have some disadvantages. Some of its disadvantages are related to high one-time, start-up costs, including the cost of the DBMS software (a mainframe DBMS can cost hundreds of thousands of dollars!), the conversion from file processing to a database, and the potential need for more sophisticated hardware and software. In addition, a DBMS environment typically incurs higher operating costs because it requires highly skilled personnel to create and to administer the database. Another disadvantage is the greater complexity of the DBMS environment where potentially hundreds or thousands of files may be integrated. Finally, a DBMS environment is more vulnerable than a conventional file-processing environment, and it is more difficult to repair the damage if failure does occur because multiple applications may be affected. Furthermore, although data in a DBMS are typically more secure, if security is breached, the interloper may have access to more data than would be the case in a conventional file-processing environment.

Check Your Understanding 9-1

1. Match each of the following terms with its definition.

____ field	a. a field or data element that uniquely identifies each record.
____ physical record	b. a collection of related records.
____ file	c. a primary key used as a data element in another relation.
____ database	d. a self-describing set of integrated records.
____ primary key	e. a collection of characters equivalent to an attribute of a class.
____ foreign key	f. a unit of data stored and accessed as one chunk.

2. Fill in the blanks with the appropriate term.

   a. _____ means that each time the data structure changes, the programs that use the data must also be modified.

b. The conventional file-processing environment is plagued by_____
    because data are not always updated in every file where they occur.

c. A DBMS reduces _____ by minimizing the repetition of data elements
    throughout the database.

d. Because a DBMS acts as an _____ between data and programs,
    program-data dependence is alleviated.

e. Three disadvantages of the DBMS environment are _____,
    _____, and _____.

DATABASE STRUCTURES

Database structures are categorized by the type of data model they support. Three data models have commonly been implemented in DBMS: hierarchical, network, and relational. A fourth DBMS type, object-oriented, has arisen in recent years.

A **hierarchical DBMS** organizes data in a hierarchy in which each "parent" can have many "children" but each "child" can have only one "parent." In Figure 9.13 the MIS Department record is a parent and the Professor Andrews record is a child of the MIS Department record. A hierarchical DBMS, then, supports one-to-many relationships in that each parent record can have many child records, but each child record can have only one parent record. For example, each instructor in Figure 9.13 is related to many courses, but each course can be related to only one instructor. An advantage of a hierarchical DBMS is that it is very efficient and can quickly process a large number of records because it uses pointers to link two related records. These pointers have to be defined when the database is built; in other words, the database designer must know in advance the kinds of access paths through

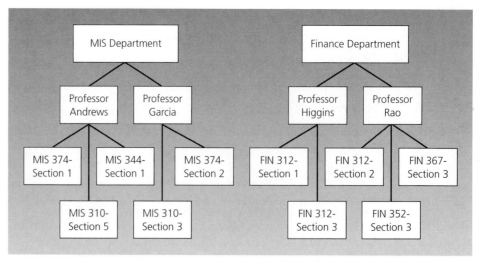

FIGURE 9.13 Hierarchical database model

the database an application will require. Thus, a hierarchical DBMS is a good choice for applications that involve very few types of prespecified queries but lots of data.

A **network DBMS** is somewhat more flexible in that it supports many-to-many relationships in which each child record can have many parent records (see Figure 9.14). However, because it, too, uses pointers to implement relationships, a network DBMS also requires that all the relationships be specified when the database is created. In addition, it is not as efficient as a hierarchical DBMS, making it better suited for applications with limited links among records or a lower volume of data. Databases created with either a hierarchical or network DBMS are difficult to modify and provide low flexibility in terms of supporting ad hoc or changing report needs. However, both are commonly used in high transaction-volume applications that require quick access to data.

A **relational DBMS** (or **RDBMS**), which represents each object class or entity as a **table** (formally called a **relation**), produces the most flexible database because it uses foreign keys to relate two records. In an RDBMS, if two records share a field, they can be linked. For example, in Table 9.3, the Professor Andrews Faculty record is related to the MIS Department record because it contains DeptName as a foreign key. What this means is that all of the information about the MIS department—that its DeptChair is Professor Wright and its DeptOffice is in BT 351, for example—can be accessed from the Department table; thus, these data need not be repeated in the Faculty table. This method of relating records in an RDBMS is the same as that illustrated in Figure 9.12, where StudentSSN, the key of the Student Master file, is repeated in the Student Billing, Student Advising, and Student Transcript files. The flexibility of an RDBMS makes it desirable for decision-support applications in which users directly access the database. However, it may not support efficient

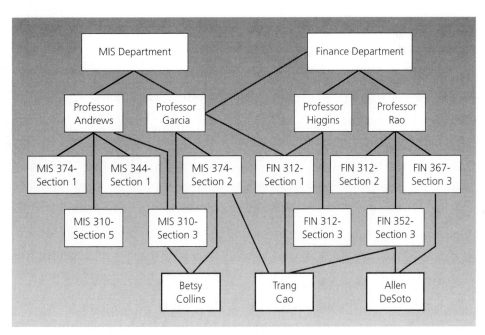

FIGURE 9.14   Network data model

TABLE 9.3 Relational data model

Department

DeptName	DeptChair	DeptOffice	DeptPhone
MIS	Wright	BT 351	5-6714
Finance	Dean	BT 751	5-2394

Faculty

FacName	FacRank	FacOffice	FacPhone	DeptName
Andrews	Professor	BT 347	5-1294	MIS
Garcia	Assoc. Prof.	BT 359	5-3495	MIS
Higgins	Asst. Prof.	BT 735	5-3491	Finance
Rao	Professor	BT 572	5-2317	Finance

Course

CrsNumb	CrsTitle	CrsCredit	CrsTime	CrsRoom	FacName
MIS 374-1	Systems Analysis and Design	3	930–1045 TTh	BC 301	Andrews
MIS 374-3	Systems Analysis and Design	3	1330–1445 MW	BC 305	Garcia
MIS 374-5	Systems Analysis and Design	3	1100–1215 TTh	BC 301	Andrews
. . .					
FIN 312-2	Principles of Finance	3	1800–2045	BC 208	Rao
. . .					

Note: The ellipses in the Course table indicate that additional course records will appear in this table.

data access, making it less desirable for transaction-processing applications with high transaction volumes.

Object-oriented DBMS (or **OODBMS**) is the latest development in database structures. OODBMS were developed to manage the *persistent objects,* those that continue to exist between program executions, used in object-oriented programming. Until recently, poor management of persistent objects has been a weakness of many object-oriented applications. Smalltalk, one of the most mature object-oriented programming languages, maintains persistent objects by storing the final state of the system at the end of a program run. This technique works well for single-user systems but is inappropriate for the kinds of concurrent multi-user systems found in most organizations. Other ways of stepping around the issue of storing persistent objects include (1) removing methods from objects and (2) breaking objects into segments, and then creating an object data interface to object-oriented application programs so that object data can be stored in a network, hierarchical, or relational database.

A true OODBMS is able to store objects without disassembling them into data files. An OODBMS combines the network model's ability to handle complex data structures with the relational model's flexibility. Two types of OODBMS are available today: passive and active. A *passive OODBMS* separates object attributes from object methods, essentially managing object data as a static system component; it must be used in conjunction with an application written in an object-oriented programming language. In contrast, an *active OODBMS* stores object attributes and methods together and can be used with applications written in both object-oriented (OO) and non-OO programming languages. Thus it is "active" in the sense that object methods can be executed from within the DBMS. As a result, an active OODBMS can be self-monitoring; for example, triggers can be implemented in the OODBMS so that when the QuantityOnHand attribute of an instance of the INVENTORY-ITEM class is less than 100, the INVENTORY-ITEM object's placeOrder method is executed automatically.

An advantage of using an OODBMS is the ability to store and to rapidly retrieve a wide variety of complex information, including images, voice recordings, and other multimedia data. Nonetheless, at the time that this text is being written, OODBMS are not widely used in business applications, largely because most organizations have hundreds or thousands of megabytes of legacy data organized in network, hierarchical, or relational databases. Although it seems likely that OODBMS will evolve—perhaps as a hybrid relational-OO data structure—and become more widely used in future applications, the three models described here account for the vast majority of DBMS in use today. If you want to learn more about this topic, you should consult the references listed at the end of this chapter.

✓ Check Your Understanding 9-2

Choose the best answer to complete each statement.

1. Low flexibility and difficult modification are disadvantages of
   a. a network DBMS
   b. a hierarchical DBMS
   c. a relational DBMS (RDBMS)
   d. both a and b
   e. all of the above

2. A _____ allows each child record to be related to only one parent record.
   a. network DBMS
   b. hierarchical DBMS
   c. relational DBMS (RDBMS)
   d. both a and b
   e. all of the above

3. A _____ uses foreign keys to relate records.
   a. network DBMS
   b. hierarchical DBMS
   c. relational DBMS (RDBMS)
   d. OODBMS
   e. all of the above

4. A _____ is best suited for use in applications that process a large volume of data in clearly specified ways (e.g., a transaction-processing system).
   a. network DBMS
   b. hierarchical DBMS
   c. relational DBMS
   d. both a and b
   e. all of the above

5. A(n) _____ stores both attributes and methods and can execute its methods within the database.
   a. network DBMS
   b. passive OODBMS
   c. relational DBMS (RDBMS)
   d. active OODBMS
   e. none of the above

9.3 ◈ DATABASE DESIGN QUALITY CRITERIA

Before we examine how to design a relational database, you need to understand some of the criteria for evaluating the quality of a database design. As with all things in life, database design requires you to weigh the advantages and disadvantages of various options and to make compromises. Ideally, a database should be efficient, flexible, and accurate. Notice that these criteria are those of the system-quality goal of systems development. Just as you want the system as a whole to be reliable, clear, efficient, flexible, and easy to maintain, you want to design a database that achieves these same characteristics. Nonetheless, sometimes you must trade a measure of efficiency for greater flexibility or a measure of flexibility for greater efficiency. In no case, however, should you compromise the reliability—accuracy, timeliness, and completeness—of your database. Each of these database quality criteria is defined here, along with some strategies for attaining them.

EFFICIENCY

Three questions help you to evaluate the efficiency of your database design:

1. Does the database make efficient use of physical storage?
2. Is the time required to process a query or to update the database acceptable to users?
3. Has redundant data been minimized?

The first two questions require you to consider alternative ways of organizing data in, and accessing data from, physical storage. **File-access methods** describe how records are accessed from physical storage. There are two methods: direct and sequential. **Physical file organization** describes the way that records are organized on disk or tape: sequential, direct, or indexed sequential.

In the **sequential file organization**, the records of a file are stored and accessed in sequence, either by the value of their key field or by the order in which they were created. This file organization is most efficient (1) when the records of a file are usually processed sequentially and (2) when the most important applications using the file typically access many of the records. Files used in payroll processing, customer account processing, and other batch-processing applications are candidates for sequential file organization. In the **direct file organization**, records are assigned a disk address derived from the value of their key fields. This file organization is most efficient when the records of a file must be accessed one at a time, in real time, and in no predictable order, for example, in an airline reservation system.

In the **indexed sequential file organization**, the records of a file can be stored in any order and accessed sequentially or directly because an index is used to locate each record. An index matches the value of a field of interest—for example, a phone number—to the physical location where the corresponding record is located. This file organization is a compromise between sequential and direct file organization and is most appropriate when a file is used by a variety of applications that need to access records on a variety of fields, thus requiring several indexes. For example, a credit clerk may need to bring up a customer's name and address by entering the customer's account number, thus requiring that the customer file be indexed by account number, which is probably the primary key. In contrast, a sales clerk may need to bring up this same data by entering the customer's phone number, thus requiring that the customer file be indexed on phone number.

The third question—has data redundancy been minimized?—concerns the problem addressed earlier in Table 9.2 and Figure 9.12. In a relational database, data redundancy is reduced through a process called **normalization**. Although a full discussion of normalization is beyond the scope of this text, you need to have a basic understanding of this concept to design an efficient, flexible database. The goal of normalization is to devise logical records whose fields are defined wholly by the record's primary key. We can illustrate normalization using ETG's video rental order form, shown in Figure 9.4.

The unnormalized view of the data in this form is shown in Table 9.4. In the unnormalized view, all data on the form about the order, customer, and tape are represented as a single logical record, and data about tapes rented are listed as repeating groups. In contrast, the normalized view of video rental form data, shown in Table 9.5, segments the data into object classes and represents each object class as a table. Related records on all of the tables are linked through shared fields. For example, the RENTAL-CUSTOMER instance identified by Memb# C152 is related to the ORDER instance 10054 because Memb# is a field in both tables and has the value C152 in both records. In addition, the RENTAL-TAPE instances S421-90 and W115-92 are related to the ORDER-LINE instances because the Stock# is a field in both the RENTAL-TAPE and ORDER-LINE tables and has the same values in both sets of records. Finally, the ORDER-LINE instances are related to ORDER instance 10054 because the Order# is a field in both the ORDER-LINE and ORDER tables and has the same value in each record.

In all of the normalized records defined in Table 9.5, the field values of each record are wholly defined by the primary key of the record. For example, all the field values of the RENTAL-CUSTOMER record whose primary key is C152 describe one instance of a rental customer whose name is Paula Cassidy; whose address is 3639 N. Highland Ave., Scotts Valley, CA 95066; and whose home phone is 555-3491. Similarly, all field values of the RENTAL-TAPE record whose primary key is S421-90 describe one instance of a rental tape, in this case, an educational tape whose title is *Shark!* In addition, each ORDER-LINE record is related to one ORDER and one RENTAL-TAPE. All the relevant data about each ORDER-LINE record—who checked out the tape, when the tape is due, when the tape was returned, who checked in the tape, and what the late fee is—are given in the ORDER-LINE table. These data cannot be stored in the ORDER table because a customer could check out multiple tapes on a single order and return one tape on time and the others late.

TABLE 9.4 Unnormalized view of video rental order form data

Order#	SClerk	Rdate	Ddate	ChOut	Return	ChIn	Lfee		
10054	Julie	4/22/97	4/23/97	Joe	4/23/97	Amy	0		
Memb#	**Name**	**Addr**	**Phone**	**Stock#**	**Title**		**Cat**	**Rfee**	**Total**
C152	Paula	3639 . . .	555 . . .	W115-92	When Harry . . .		S	$3.50	$6.00
				S421-90	Shark!		E	$2.50	

TABLE 9.5 Normalized view of video rental order form data*

ORDER

Order#	Sclerk	Odate	Memb#	Total
10054	Julie	4/22/97	C152	6.00

RENTAL-CUSTOMER

Memb#	Name	Addr	HPhone
C152	Paula Cassidy	3639 N. Highland Ave., Scotts Valley, CA 95066	555-3491

ORDER-LINE

Order#	Stock#	CheckOut	DueDate	Returned	CheckIn	Lfee
10054	S421-90	Joe	4/23/97	4/23/97	Amy	0
10054	W115-92	Joe	4/23/97	4/23/97	Amy	0

RENTAL-TAPE   **RENTAL-CATEGORY**

Stock#	Title	Cat	Cat	Rfee
S421-90	Shark!	E	N	4.50
W115-92	When Harry Met Sally	S	S	3.50
			E	2.50

*Note that the relations here are not the same as those that Denny defines in Table 9.6. Denny's relations are different because he is modeling the data requirements of the new order processing system, not the old one. Thus, his model in Figure 9.9 and relations in Table 9.6 incorporate requirements identified during the JAD workshop.

FLEXIBILITY

Flexibility is concerned with the adaptability and maintainability of the database. Two questions help you to evaluate the flexibility of your database design:

1. Are the data structured in such a way that they can be used by a variety of applications?

2. Can the database be easily adapted to changes in current applications or to the requirements of future applications?

In a relational database, both of these questions are addressed through normalization. A normalized database is flexible because it treats each object class as a distinct table and uses foreign keys to link related tables.

Another reason that a normalized database is flexible in that it reduces data redundancy, therefore facilitating database updates. An example of this ease of updating is seen in the RENTAL-TAPE and RENTAL-CATEGORY tables shown in Table 9.5. If rental fee were treated as a field in the RENTAL-TAPE table (as Denny originally designed this object class in Figure 9.9), each time ETG wanted to change its rental fees, a clerk would have to update each RENTAL-TAPE record individually. By treating rental category as a separate table, ETG can change all of its rental fees by modifying just the three RENTAL-CATEGORY records.

INTEGRITY

Database integrity is concerned with the *reliability* and *clarity* criteria of the system quality development goal and with the *control* function of the information system functions model. Three questions help you to evaluate the integrity of your database design:

1. Are the data accurate, up-to-date, consistent, and complete?
2. Are data element names used consistently throughout the database?
3. Are the data secured from system failures and unauthorized access?

Maintaining database integrity is more related to the procedures you design for users to create, read, update, and delete records than to the design of the database itself. However, you can improve data consistency by creating a normalized database, thus limiting the number of files that require updating when a field value changes. Using consistent field names throughout the database will also improve the consistency of the database and reduce data confusion. Ensuring database completeness requires you to investigate the users' data needs thoroughly and to design a database to satisfy these needs.

To ensure accuracy, you will need to define controls to prevent invalid data from being stored in the database. For example, validation rules prohibit users from entering invalid data. A **validation rule** defines the valid values of an object instance's attributes. For example, the object class EMPLOYEE may be described by the attribute Wage. A business rule may state that the valid values of the Wage attribute range from $4.25 to $25.00. In other words, no hourly employee in the organization is paid less than $4.25 per hour and none is paid more than $25.00 per hour. When the EMPLOYEE object class is implemented in a computerized human resources/payroll application, its validation rules will prohibit users from entering invalid data. For example, consider the case of a human resources data entry clerk attempting to create a new instance of EMPLOYEE to maintain data about a newly hired employee. If the clerk enters $3.50 as the value of the new hire's Wage attribute, the system will display an error message: "Invalid wage—valid range is $4.25 – $25.00."

Securing the database from system failures and unauthorized access involves designing error recovery, backup, and system access procedures to safeguard data. Error recovery procedures address how to recover from an abnormal program termination or hardware failure that could corrupt the database. Backup procedures prescribe how and when to backup the database; for example, files may be copied to magnetic tape at the end of each day. Unauthorized access is prevented by defining access authorizations in the database schema and by designing system log-on procedures.

9.4 ◆ TRANSFORMING AN OBJECT RELATIONSHIP MODEL INTO A LOGICAL DATABASE DESIGN

Working from your object relationship model, you can quite easily create a logical database design. Here, we focus on relational database design because RDBMS is most commonly used in today's organizations. The design of a relational database is typically represented as a set of relations expressed in the following format:

RELATION-NAME (<u>PrimaryKey</u>, Field1, Field2, ... FieldN, *ForeignKey*)

where the name of the relation (or table) is given in capital letters, the primary key of each relation is underlined, and foreign keys are italicized. For example, the relations designed from the TAPE, SALES-TAPE, RENTAL-TAPE, and RENTAL-CATEGORY data object classes can be represented as

TAPE (<u>TitleID</u>, Title, Director, Actors, Genre)
SALES-TAPE (*<u>TitleID</u>*, Manufacturer, Price, QuantityInStock)
RENTAL-TAPE (<u>StockNumber</u>, *Category*, Status, Received, Inspected, *TitleID*)
RENTAL-CATEGORY (<u>Category</u>, RentalFee, RentalPeriod)

Notice that TitleID is a primary key in TAPE and a foreign key in RENTAL-TAPE; it is both a primary key and a foreign key in SALES-TAPE. Similarly Category is a primary key in RENTAL-CATEGORY and a foreign key in RENTAL-TAPE.

Table 9.6 shows the relations that Denny defined as he designed the database for ETG's order processing system.

STEPS IN TRANSFORMING AN OBJECT CLASS INTO A RELATION

You transform an object class into one or more relations by performing the following process:

1. Each object class becomes one relation. See the following sections on "Aggregating Records" and "Segmenting Records" for exceptions to this rule.

TABLE 9.6 Relations (tables) in ETG's order processing database

CUSTOMER (<u>CustID</u>, FirstName, MidInitial, LastName, TermOfAddress, Street, City, State, ZipCode, HomePhone, Interest)

RENTAL-CUSTOMER (<u>MembNumber</u>, WorkPhone, CCType, CCNumber, CCExpDate, *EmpNumber*, ApprovedDate, Fines, *CustID*)

AUTHORIZED-USER (*<u>MembNumber</u>*, <u>Name</u>, Relationship)

EMPLOYEE (<u>EmpNumber</u>, FirstName, MidInitial, LastName, Street, City, State, ZipCode)

RENTAL-ORDER (<u>OrderNumber</u>, OrderDate, *EmpNumber*, *MembNumber*, Total)

RO-LINE (*<u>OrderNumber</u>*, *<u>StockNumber</u>*, DueDate, Returned, LateFee)

SALES-ORDER (<u>OrderNumber</u>, OrderDate, *EmpNumber*, *CustID*, Subtotal, SalesTax, Total)

SO-LINE (*<u>OrderNumber</u>*, *<u>TitleID</u>*, Quantity, ExtPrice)

TAPE (<u>TitleID</u>, Title, Director, Actors, Genre)

RENTAL-TAPE (<u>StockNumber</u>, *Category*, Received, Inspected, Status, *TitleID*)

RENTAL-CATEGORY (<u>Category</u>, RentalFee, RentalPeriod)

SALES-TAPE (*<u>TitleID</u>*, Manufacturer, Price, QuantityInStock)

2. Each attribute becomes a field in the relation. See the following section on "Segmenting Attributes" for exceptions to this rule.

3. The identifier of each class becomes the primary key of the relation. Note that the primary key of an object subclass is the primary key of its object superclass. If no identifier was defined for an object class in the object relationship model, its primary key may be composed from the identifier(s) of its related class(es). For example, in Figure 9.9, no identifier was indicated for the SO-LINE and RO-LINE classes. When these classes are transformed into relations, the primary key of SO-LINE is OrderNumber and TitleID (the identifiers of ORDER and SALES-TAPE); the primary key of RO-LINE is OrderNumber and StockNumber (the identifiers of RENTAL-ORDER and RENTAL-TAPE).

4. Each relationship is represented as a foreign key. For 1:N relationships, the foreign key is placed in the "many" relation. For example, each RENTAL-CUSTOMER instance can be related to many RENTAL-ORDER instances; thus, the primary key of RENTAL-CUSTOMER (MembNumber) becomes a foreign key in RENTAL-ORDER. For N:M relationships, a new relation is created whose only attributes are the identifiers of the related classes, which are both foreign keys and primary keys in the new relation.

ADDITIONAL GUIDELINES

Defining relations would be extremely simple if you could just follow the four steps outlined in the preceding section. Unfortunately, these steps are only general heuristics. To maximize database efficiency and flexibility, you need to understand some of the more specific guidelines governing logical database design.

Aggregating Records

One way to improve database efficiency is to aggregate records that will be used together. Record aggregation is allowed only when the records' relationship is 1:1 or 0:1. For example, although Denny's object relationship model shows CREDIT-CARD as a separate class, with each CREDIT-CARD instance related to exactly one RENTAL-CUSTOMER instance, he combined these classes into a single relation in his database design. That is, the attributes of the CREDIT-CARD object class are included in the RENTAL-CUSTOMER relation. Similarly, although SALES-CLERK is shown as a subclass of EMPLOYEE, which is a subclass of PERSON, Denny uses just one relation, EMPLOYEE, to contain all the data describing employees. Why? Because accessing and reading two or three records to describe an employee requires more access time than reading one record. The same design decision was made in collapsing the ORDER superclass into its subclasses SALES-ORDER and RENTAL-ORDER.

Segmenting Records

Sometimes what was represented as a single object class in the object relationship model becomes two or more relations in a logical database design. For example, in his object relationship model, Denny represented RENTAL-TAPE as a single object class. Yet, in his relations, Denny segmented the attributes of RENTAL-TAPE into two relations, RENTAL-TAPE and

RENTAL-CATEGORY. RENTAL-TAPE contains the primary key of RENTAL-CATEGORY (Category) as a foreign key. As just explained, this segmentation facilitates the task of updating the rental fee charged for each tape.

Segmenting Attributes

To support flexible use of fields in the database, you may need to decompose some of the attributes in your object relationship model. For example, in his object relationship model, Denny used the attributes of EmpName and CustomerName. However, in his EMPLOYEE and CUSTOMER relations, he segmented these attributes to represent the first, middle, and last names as separate data elements and added a TermOfAddress data element so that each person can be addressed as "Mr.," "Ms.," and so on. Denny also decomposed the address attributes in the same manner. Segmenting these attributes will allow ETG to use name or address data elements individually or in combination, for example, in a personalized letter addressed to each employee or customer.

Linking Records

The object relationship model indicates which object classes are related to which other classes. It also indicates the cardinality of these relationships. As you transform your object relationship model into a logical database design, you can represent these relationships in a number of ways: pointers, foreign keys, and so on. In a relational database, records are linked through the use of foreign keys. Using the primary key of one record as a foreign key in another record creates a relationship between the records in the tables. For example, in Table 9.6, each AUTHO-RIZED-USER record is linked to a RENTAL-CUSTOMER record by placing the value of the primary key of RENTAL-CUSTOMER (MembNumber) in the related AUTHORIZED-USER record. Notice that MembNumber is a foreign key (indicated by italics) in AUTHORIZED-USER because each RENTAL-CUSTOMER instance can have many AUTHORIZED-USER instances, but each AUTHORIZED-USER instance has only one RENTAL-CUSTOMER instance.

This example illustrates one rule for linking records: *The record that has a maximum cardinality of 1 always provides the foreign key for the related record that has a maximum cardinality of many.* Why? Because a fundamental rule of the relational data model and relational databases forbids the use of repeating groups of fields. If the primary key of the "many" record were used as a foreign key in the "1" record, repeating fields would result, as illustrated in Figure 9.15. Thus, because each RENTAL-CATEGORY record can be related to many RENTAL-TAPE records, but each RENTAL-TAPE record is related to at most one RENTAL-CATEGORY record, Category is a foreign key in RENTAL-TAPE. Other examples of this rule include SALES-ORDER/SO-LINE, RENTAL-ORDER/RO-LINE, SALES-TAPE/SO-LINE, EMPLOYEE/RENTAL-ORDER, EMPLOYEE/SALES-ORDER, TAPE/SALES-TAPE, TAPE/RENTAL-TAPE, EMPLOYEE/RENTAL-MEMBER, RENTAL-CUSTOMER/RENTAL-ORDER, and CUSTOMER/SALES-ORDER.

For many-to-many relationships, you need to define three relations: one for each of the object classes and one for their relationship, which contains *only* the primary keys of the other two relations, as illustrated in Table 9.7.

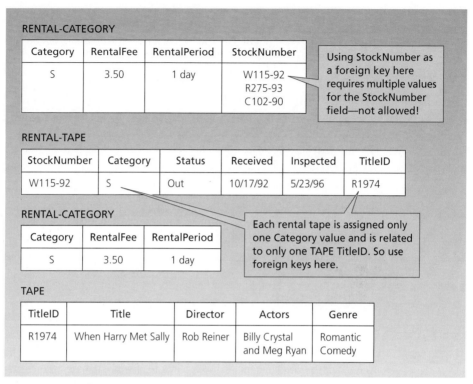

FIGURE 9.15   Correct use of foreign keys

TABLE 9.7 Linking two many-to-many relations by creating a third relation

RELATION1 (<u>PrimaryKey1</u>, . . .)
RELATION2 (<u>PrimaryKey2</u>, . . .)
RELATION3 (<u>*PrimaryKey1*</u>, <u>*PrimaryKey2*</u>)

 Check Your Understanding 9-3

Transform the object relationship model in Figure 9.A into relations.

9.5 ◆ USING A DATA DICTIONARY TO SPECIFY PHYSICAL DATABASE DESIGN

After you have specified the logical structure of your database using relations, your next task is to define its physical structure. Physical database design involves the following tasks:

1. Determine the physical file organization and physical record size.

2. Determine the indexes (primary and secondary) required to support efficient, flexible data access.

3. Specify the properties of each field and record.

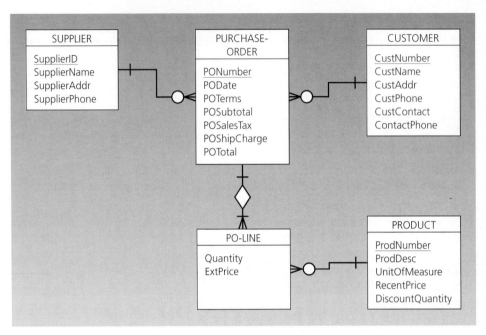

FIGURE 9-A   Object relationship model for Check Your Understanding 9-3

These database characteristics are defined in the database schema and in the system's data dictionary. Schemas and the data-definition languages used to create them are beyond the scope of this text. You will learn more about these database concepts in a course devoted entirely to database design and implementation. Here, we explain how to use a data dictionary to specify several aspects of your physical database design.

A data dictionary defines each data structure in a database. In essence, it records data about data (called *metadata*). Ideally, an organization should have one data dictionary that defines all the data used in all its applications. One integrated data dictionary helps to avoid the proliferation of synonymous field names and the data confusion it creates.

You can create a data dictionary in a number of ways. Your data dictionary may be a word-processed document that devotes a page to each table and data element definition. If you are creating a data dictionary manually, you should use the symbols shown in Table 9.8. If you use a CASE tool to analyze and design information systems, it is likely that the CASE tool provides a data-dictionary feature. In addition, most DBMS products on the market today will automatically generate a data dictionary derived from user input during database design. For example, Microsoft Access, a personal computer RDBMS, allows users to define not only the structure, relationships, and indexes of each table but also several properties of each field. Figure 9.16 shows the Access interface used to define tables and fields.

Notice that for each field of a table, you must specify a field name; you may also indicate the primary key (note the key icon in front of the MembNumber field). Many DBMS products will automatically assign a surrogate key to a table if you do not specify a primary key. (A surrogate key is a system-controlled counter field that uniquely identifies each record.) In addition, for each field, you can specify a data type (text, numeric, date/time, etc.) and a

TABLE 9.8 Data-definition symbols

Data Structure Symbols: Used to specify the data elements in a table or file		Data Type Symbols: Used to specify the format or input/output picture of a data element	
=	Is composed of	X	Any character
+	And	9	Numeric character
[ ]	Selection	A	Alphabetic character
( )	Optional	Z	Leading zeros as spaces
{ }	Repeating element or group	.	Period, e.g., 99.99
		,	Comma, e.g., 99,999
Example:		-	Hyphen, e.g., 999-9999 for local telephone number
RENTAL-CUSTOMER =			
MembNumber +	CCExpDate +	/	Slash, e.g., 99/99/99 for date
(WorkPhone) +	EmpNumber +		
CCType +	ApprovedDate +		
CCNumber +	Fines		
WorkPhone =	CCType =		
AreaCode +	[MasterCard, Visa, Discover]		
LocalNumber			

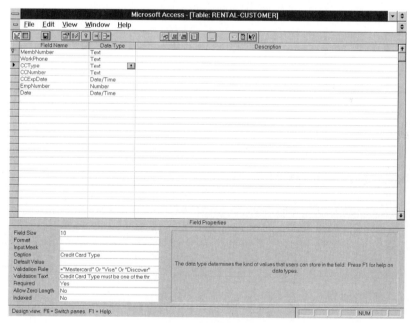

FIGURE 9.16   Microsoft Access user interface for specifying tables and field properties

number of field properties, such as field size, format, input picture (or mask), default value, validation rule, and so on. Access then uses these table and field definitions to create a data dictionary. Figure 9.17 shows an excerpt from Access's data dictionary entry for the RENTAL-CUSTOMER table that Denny defined.

TABLE:	**RENTAL-CUSTOMER**	**Page 1**

Properties

Date Created:	7/22/96 7:55:31 AM	Def/ Updatable:	Yes
Last Updated:	7/31/96 2:49:23 PM	Record Count:	0

Columns

Name	Type	Size
MembNumber	Text	6

 Definition: A number that uniquely identifies each rental membership customer
 Caption: Membership Number
 Format: "a99999"
 Input Mask: "a99999"
 Required: Yes

WorkPhone	Text	10

 Definition: The phone number at which a member can be reached during the day
 Caption: Work Phone
 Input Mask: !\(999") "000\-0000;;-
 Required: No

CCType	Text	10

 Definition: The type of credit card (e.g., MasterCard)
 Caption: Credit Card Type
 Required: Yes
 Validation Rule: ="MasterCard" Or "Visa" Or "Discover"
 Validation Text: Credit Card Type must be MasterCard, Visa, or Discover.

EmpNumber	Number(Integer)	2

 Definition: A number that uniquely identifies each employee
 Caption: Approved by
 Decimal Places: 0
 Required: Yes
 Validation Rule: *Requires EMPLOYEE table lookup to verify that the number entered is a valid employee number*
 Validation Text: Value entered must be a valid employee number.

Relationships

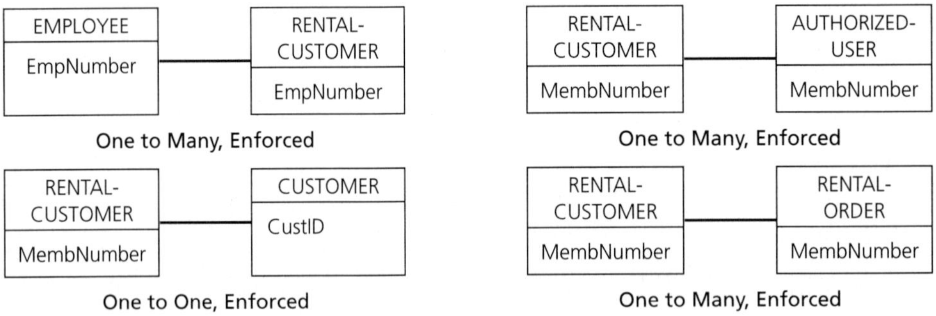

EMPLOYEE	RENTAL-CUSTOMER
EmpNumber	EmpNumber

One to Many, Enforced

RENTAL-CUSTOMER	AUTHORIZED-USER
MembNumber	MembNumber

One to Many, Enforced

RENTAL-CUSTOMER	CUSTOMER
MembNumber	CustID

One to One, Enforced

RENTAL-CUSTOMER	RENTAL-ORDER
MembNumber	MembNumber

One to Many, Enforced

Table Indexes

Name	Number of Fields
Primary Key	1

 Required: Yes
 Unique: Yes
 Fields: MembNumber, Ascending

FIGURE 9.17   Excerpted data-dictionary entry for RENTAL-CUSTOMER

In addition to the field and table descriptions shown in Figure 9.17, a data dictionary may also specify physical file organization, physical record length, aliases for each field, table locations, the names of programs that use each table, data responsibilities (the business unit responsible for creating and maintaining the data) and authorizations (the users who are authorized to create, read, update, or delete a record), and any other information deemed important by the organization. For each field, a data-dictionary entry may also indicate whether the value is base (a field value keyed into the system and stored in a file) or derived (the output of a system process, for example, a subtotal calculated by the system) and what the source of the field value is (input by user, provided by system, and so on).

◈ REVIEW OF CHAPTER LEARNING OBJECTIVES

1. *Define what a use case is and explain its purpose in systems analysis and design.*

A use case is a sequence of transactions in a system that produces something of value to an external entity or user. For example, selling a product to a customer yields something of value to the customer. Use cases describe the behaviors a system must support; they are used to identify and to define the system's classes, methods, and messages; to serve as test cases to verify that the system meets its requirements; and to specify the functionality of "minisystem" prototypes.

2. *Define several database concepts.*

A field or data element, which is equivalent to an attribute in logical data modeling, is the smallest unit of data consisting of a combination of characters. A record is a collection of related fields that describe one instance of an object class. A physical record is a unit of data stored at a disk address and transferred to main memory as a single "chunk." A primary key is a data element that uniquely identifies each record. Records are related to one another through the use of a foreign key—the primary key of a related record included as a field of another record—or through the use of a pointer, which gives the address of the related record. A file, which is loosely equivalent to an object class, is a collection of related records; for example, all CUSTOMER records are stored in a Customer file. A database is a collection of related files.

3. *Discuss the problems with conventional file processing that are alleviated by implementing a database management system (DBMS).*

Problems common in a conventional file-processing environment but alleviated in a DBMS environment include program-data dependence, data redundancy, data inconsistency, and data confusion. Because programs in a conventional file-processing environment contain descriptions of the files they use, any time the format of the data changes, all the programs that use that data also must be modified (program-data dependence). Program-data dependence is not a problem in a DBMS environment because the DBMS acts as an interface between programs and data.

Data redundancy occurs in a conventional file-processing environment because the same data are stored in multiple files. For example, when files are independent, data common to several files must be repeated in each file. Data redundancy is reduced in a DBMS environment because files can be related to each other using foreign keys and pointers.

In conventional file processing, data redundancy has two pernicious side effects: data inconsistency and data confusion. When data are repeated in several files, several files must be updated if the data change. Data inconsistency occurs when data are modified in one file but not in others. Data confusion occurs when different users use different terms to describe the same data. Because a DBMS reduces data redundancy, it also reduces data inconsistency and data confusion. In addition, the data dictionary or schema defines all the data elements in the database, thus reducing the incidence of data confusion.

4. *Define four types of DBMS architecture, and discuss the advantages and disadvantages of each.*

A hierarchical DBMS organizes data in a hierarchy in which each "parent" can have many "children" but each "child" can have only one "parent." An advantage of a hierarchical DBMS is that it is very efficient and can quickly process a large number of records because it uses pointers to link related records. Disadvantages include its inflexibility and the difficulty of modification. A network DBMS is somewhat more flexible in that it supports many-to-many relationships. However, it is just as difficult to modify and is not as efficient as a hierarchical DBMS. A relational DBMS (RDBMS) represents each object class as a table (or relation) and uses foreign keys to relate records. The database created with an RDBMS is the most flexible and easiest to modify; however, it generally is not as efficient as one created with a hierarchical or network DBMS. An object-oriented DBMS (OODBMS) stores object attributes and methods together, can handle complex data structures easily, and is very flexible.

5. *Explain the criteria for evaluating database quality, including strategies for attaining these criteria.*

A database is efficient if it minimizes the use of physical storage, processes queries and updates quickly, and contains little redundant data. Achieving storage and processing efficiency requires that a designer select an appropriate physical file organization and file access method. In an RDBMS environment, minimizing redundant data requires that a designer normalize tables so that the values of each record are completely defined by the table's primary key.

A database is flexible if it can be used by a variety of applications and easily adapts to changing data needs. The key to flexibility in an RDBMS environment is normalization.

The integrity of a database relates to its reliability and clarity. A database is reliable if its data is accurate, up to date, consistent, and complete. Reliability is achieved by securing the database against unauthorized access and system failure and by designing procedures to prevent data entry errors and unauthorized access and to recover data in the event of a system error. A database is clear if its data elements are used consistently. You can improve clarity by creating a normalized database and defining each data element in the data dictionary or schema.

6. *Convert an object relationship model into a relational database design.*

An object relationship model can be converted into a relational database design by performing the following steps: (a) transforming each data object class into a relation, (b) transforming each attribute into a data element or field in the relation, (c) transforming each identifier into the primary key of the relation, and (d) linking relations by using foreign keys (1:N relationships) or by creating a new relation (N:M relationships).

7. *Specify a physical database design using a data dictionary.*

A data dictionary is used to define each data element (field) and table (file) in the database. The data dictionary specifies the physical file organization; physical record length; data type, format, and aliases for each field; table locations; the names of programs that use each table; data responsibilities and authorizations; and any other information deemed important by the organization. Many CASE tools and DBMS products provide facilities for creating a data dictionary. If you create a data dictionary manually, you should follow the data-definition conventions of your organization.

◈ KEY TERMS

conventional file-processing
  environment
data confusion
data dictionary
data inconsistency
data redundancy
database
database management
  system (DBMS)
database structure
direct file organization
field (or data) element
file

file-access method
foreign key
hierarchical DBMS
index
indexed sequential file
  organization
logical database design
logical record
network DBMS
normalization
object-oriented DBMS
  (OODBMS)
physical database design

physical file organization
physical record
pointer
primary key
program-data dependence
relational DBMS (or
  RDBMS)
schema
secondary index
sequential file organization
table or relation
use case
validation rule

◈ DISCUSSION QUESTIONS

1. What is a use case? How are use cases used in system data structure analysis and design?

2. Differentiate each of the following database concept pairs:
   a. Record versus file
   b. File versus database
   c. Data element or field versus primary key
   d. Primary key versus foreign key

3. Explain how the problems of conventional file processing are alleviated by a DBMS.

4. Define and give one advantage and one disadvantage of each of the three traditional database structures:
   a. Hierarchical
   b. Network
   c. Relational

5. What features distinguish an OODBMS from the traditional database structures?

6. Explain the difference between a passive OODBMS and an active OODBMS.

7. Discuss the three criteria used to evaluate database quality.

8. List and define the three physical file organizations, giving an example of an application where each is appropriate. Which criteria of database quality does selecting an appropriate physical file-organization and file-access method help you achieve?

9. In your own words, explain the statement, "A table is normalized if every data element of the table is completely determined by the table's primary key." Give an example of a normalized table, other than those presented in the chapter.

10. Which criteria of database quality does normalization help you achieve?

11. List three examples of procedures that can protect database integrity.

12. Discuss the four steps in transforming an object relationship model into a relational database design.

13. Under what conditions should two or more object classes be transformed into a single relation?

14. Under what conditions should a single object class be transformed into two or more relations?

15. Explain how foreign keys are used to link relations.

16. What is a data dictionary? How can creating one data dictionary for all the organization's applications reduce data confusion?

◆ EXERCISES

1. Transform the following object relationship model into relations. State any assumptions made as you transformed the model into relations.

2. Transform the following object relationship model into relations. State any assumptions made as you transformed the model into relations.

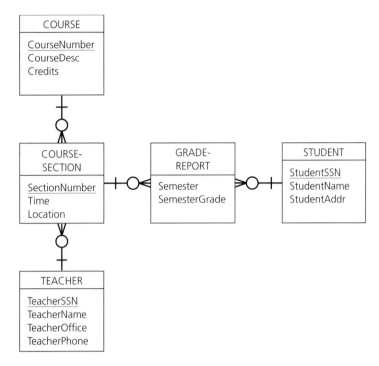

3. Transform the object relationship model for Bigg's Department Store (see Figure D.14) into relations. State any assumptions made as you transformed the model into relations.

Note: Exercises 4–8 assume that you have completed the related exercises in Technical Module D and have learned the correct object relationship model representation for each exercise.

4. Specify the relations for the property-management system object relationship model you created in Exercise 1 of Technical Module D, page 312. Indicate any assumptions you made as you transformed the model into a relational database design.

5. Specify the relations for the Bankrupt Airlines ticketing system object relationship model you created in Exercise 2 of Technical Module D, page 312. Indicate any assumptions you made as you transformed the model into a relational database design.

6. Specify the relations for the contract-management system object relationship model you created in Exercise 4 of Technical Module D, page 313. Indicate any assumptions you made as you transformed the model into a relational database design.

7. Specify the relations for the patient-records and appointment-scheduling system object relationship model you created in Exercise 5 of Technical Module D, page 314. Indicate any assumptions you made as you transformed the model into a relational database design.

8. Specify the relations for the payroll-processing system object relationship model you created in Exercise 6 of Technical Module D, page 315. Indicate any assumptions you made as you transformed the model into a relational database design.

9. Examine the sample tape records shown in Figure 9.6 and the relations shown in Table 9.6. Design data-dictionary entries for the TAPE, SALES-TAPE, and RENTAL-TAPE tables, specifying each data element's data type and input/output picture using the symbols presented in Table 9.8.

◆ REFERENCES

Booch, G. *Object-Oriented Analysis and Design with Applications*. Redwood City, CA: Benjamin/Cummings, 1994.

Jacobson, I. "Basic Use-Case Modeling." *Report on Object Analysis and Design* 1, no. 2, (1995), pp. 15–19.

Jacobson, I., M. Christerson, P. Jonsson, and G. Overgaard. *Object-Oriented Software Engineering: A Use Case Driven Approach*. Reading, MA: Addison-Wesley, 1992.

Jacobson, I., M. Ericsson, and A. Jacobson. *The Object Advantage: Business Process Reengineering with Object Technology*. Reading, MA: Addison-Wesley, 1995.

Kroenke, D. *Database Processing, 5th ed*. Englewood Cliffs, NJ: Prentice-Hall, 1995.

Martin, J., and J. Odell. *Object-Oriented Analysis and Design*. Englewood Cliffs, NJ: Prentice-Hall, 1992. See especially Chapter 13.

Rumbaugh, J., M. Blaha, W. Premerlani, F. Eddy, and W. Lorensen. *Object-Oriented Modeling and Design*. Englewood Cliffs, NJ: Prentice-Hall, 1991. These authors discuss how to map an object model to a relational database structure.

Tasker, D., and B. Von Halle. "Database Design: An Object for Everyone." *Database Programming and Design*, June 1995, pp. 11–16.

Taylor, D. *Object-Oriented Technology: A Manager's Guide*. Reading, MA: Addison-Wesley, 1990. Chapter 6 provides an excellent, easy-to-understand explanation of OODBMS.

Taylor, D. *Business Engineering with Object Technology*. New York: John Wiley and Sons, 1995.

Yourdon, E. *Object-Oriented Systems Design: An Integrated Approach*. Englewood Cliffs, NJ: Yourdon Press/Prentice-Hall, 1994. See especially Chapter 19.

White, I. *Using the Booch Method: A Rational Approach*. Redwood City, CA: Benjamin/Cummings, 1994.

10

ANALYZING AND DESIGNING SYSTEM BEHAVIORS

Iterative Analysis, Design, Preliminary Construction, and Review

1. Analyze system structure and behavior.
   a. Analyze system data structures.
   b. *Analyze system behavior.*
   c. Analyze system interfaces.

2. Design system structure and behavior.
   a. Design system data structures.
   b. *Design system behavior.*
   c. Design system interfaces.

3. Construct prototype for user review.

4. Conduct user review.

5. Repeat steps 1–4 if changes are needed.

JAD WORKSHOP EXCERPT: ANALYZING AND DESIGNING ETG'S SYSTEM BEHAVIORS

Victoria continued the ETG JAD workshop by analyzing ETG's use cases to understand more fully the behaviors that ETG's new order processing system would have to support.

"We defined several use cases earlier in this workshop. Working with Denny, you analyzed these use cases to define the classes or things of interest in your new order processing system. Now we need to discuss more fully the behaviors of the new system. Denny, please display the list of use cases again." Denny projected the list of use cases on the whiteboard:

1. Customer Applies For Membership
2. Rental Customer Rents Rental Tape(s)
3. Customer Buys Sales Tape(s)
4. Rental Customer Returns Rental Tape(s)
5. Customer Signs Newsletter Mailing List
6. Rental Customer Pays Fines (may be used in 2 and 4)
7. Customer Makes Payment (used in 2, 3, and 6)
8. Rental Customer Rents 3/3 Rental Tapes (a special case of 2)
9. Special Orders Requests Tape Availability
10. Management Requests Reports
11. Promotions Requests Mailing Labels

"Again, let's start with the Rental Customer Rents Rental Tape(s) use case. Denny has highlighted the verb phrases in that use case and will project it on the whiteboard for you now (see Figure 10.1). What seems like ages ago now, we developed a preliminary list of requirements for the new system, delineating the input, processing, output, storage, and control functions that the system would need to perform. I think you'll see that many of those requirements appear in this use case as system behaviors: calculate total cost of order, verify membership status, verify authorized user status, determine date due, and so on.

"What we need to do next is to understand any business rules governing how these behaviors are performed. We need to define these business rules so that—whether automated or manual—the behaviors we design will reflect your way of doing business. For example, from our earlier discussions, I've surmised that ETG has defined certain policies and procedures for handling payments. For one thing, you accept check payments only for orders more than $10, is that right?"

"That's right," Paul said, "although we sometimes make an exception for our longtime members or frequent customers. It doesn't make sense to go by the book if it means losing a valued customer. In addition, we require two forms of identification—you know, like a driver's license, membership card, or credit card—with each check payment."

"Okay, what other policies or procedures govern payment processing?" Victoria asked.

"This seems like a good time to bring up coupons," Corita volunteered. "Our newsletter often contains coupons, for example, a dollar off the rental fee of a new rental tape. We also run promotions in which existing customers receive a coupon good for a free rental of a new tape if they get a friend to complete a membership application. We treat coupons as cash payments, except that if the value of the coupon is more than the amount due, we don't give the customer any change. However, if the value of the coupon is less than the amount due, we collect the remainder in cash."

"So, if a customer chooses a 3/3 rental—valued at $3.00—instead of a new tape rental, valued at $4.50, it's okay?" Victoria asked, encouraging Corita to clarify coupon-payment rules.

"Yes, as long as the order amount is less than or equal to the value of the coupon," Corita explained.

"The main thing," Linda added, "is that the clerk writes the actual dollar value of the order on the coupon if the order's value is less than the preprinted coupon value. In other words, in the case you just described, the clerk should cross out '$4.50' and write '$3.00' in its place."

Use Case Name: Rental Customer Rents Rental Tape(s)
Use Case Purpose: Describes the process of renting rental tapes to rental customers
Uses: Rental Customer Pays Fines; Customer Makes Payment
Extended by: Rental Customer Rents 3/3 Rental Tapes

Typical Course of Events:

1. Use case is initiated when a <u>customer selects rental tapes</u> from shelves and <u>presents membership card and selected rental tapes</u> for check out.
2. The <u>rental order form header is completed</u>, indicating a <u>valid employee number</u>, a <u>valid member number</u>, order number, and order date.
3. For each rental tape being rented, a <u>rental order line is created</u>, giving the stock number, title, rental category, and rental fee of each rental tape; in addition, the <u>due date calculated for each rental tape</u> is shown on the rental order line.
4. The <u>rental order form footer</u> is completed by <u>calculating</u> and entering <u>a total cost for the order</u>.
5. <u>Customer makes payment.</u> (See Customer Makes Payment use case.)
6. The <u>rental order form is printed</u> and the <u>customer signs it</u>. The <u>customer is given one copy</u> of the form; the <u>other copy is retained</u> for the audit file.

Alternative Courses of Events:

Alternative A: At step 1, if a rental customer does not have his membership card with him, his telephone number can be used to <u>determine the appropriate member number</u>.

Alternative B: At step 2, if the <u>customer claims to be an authorized user</u>, the rental customer's <u>authorized user list is displayed</u>. If the customer is not listed, the <u>transaction is canceled</u>, and the <u>membership card is confiscated</u>.

Alternative C: At step 2, if an invalid employee number is provided, the transaction is canceled.

Alternative D: At step 2, if the rental customer provides an invalid member number, the transaction is canceled, and the membership card is confiscated. If the member number is valid but the <u>rental customer has unpaid fines</u>, <u>fines are processed</u> before the transaction proceeds. If customer is unable to pay the fines, the transaction is canceled.

Alternative E: At steps 3 and 4, if the order is a 3/3 tape rental, see Rental Customer Rents 3/3 Rental Tapes use case.

Alternative F: At step 5, if the customer cannot make payment, the transaction is canceled.

FIGURE 10.1a Identifying behaviors in the Rental Customer Rents Rental Tape(s) use case

"OK, I think that's *pretty* clear," Victoria said as she moved to the flipchart. "Let's use something we analysts call structured text to define payment-processing alternatives and the rules governing each." Soliciting input from the ETG participants, Victoria created a structured text description of payment processing (see Table 10.1 on page 364).

As the workshop continued, Victoria and the ETG users defined business rules governing a number of system behaviors. For example, Victoria verified that sales tax is added to sales orders but not to rental orders. She also learned that to replace the cash register audit tape used in the old system, all payments in the new system would have to be recorded in a Cash Receipts Audit file giving the employee number, order number, payment method, and payment amount for order payments and the employee number, membership number, payment method, and payment amount for fine payments.

Use Case Name: Rental Customer Rents 3/3 Rental Tapes
Use Case Purpose: Describes the process of renting 3/3 rental tapes to rental customers
Extends: Rental Customer Rents Rental Tape(s)

Typical Course of Events:

Steps 2, and 4–6 are the same as shown in Rental Customer Rents Rental Tape(s).

1. Use case is initiated when a customer presents membership card and selected rental tapes for checkout; selection includes 3 rental tapes (must be category S or E).
3. For each 3/3 tape, <u>a 3/3 rental order line is created</u>, giving the stock number, title, rental category of each tape and indicating a rental fee of 0.00. In addition, the <u>due date calculated for each rental tape</u> is shown on the rental order line. Then, <u>another 3/3 rental order line is created</u> indicating "3/3 order" as the title, "P" as the rental category, and $3.00 as the rental fee; no stock number is given.

Use Case Name: Customer Makes Payment
Use Case Purpose: Describes the processing of payments for rental and sales orders
Used by: Rental Customer Rents Rental Tape(s), Customer Buys Sales Tape(s)

Typical Course of Events:

1. Use case is initiated when a <u>customer is informed of total amount due</u> and presents cash or a personal check to <u>make payment</u>.
2. a. If customer presents cash payment, the <u>cash is placed in the cash drawer</u>.
   b. The <u>amount of change due (if any) is calculated and given to the customer</u>.
3. a. If customer presents a personal check for exactly the amount due, <u>two forms of identification are requested</u>. The <u>identifying numbers</u> of these identification forms (e.g., driver's license number, credit card number) <u>are written in the top right-hand corner of the check</u>.
   b. The <u>check is placed in the cash drawer</u>.
4. The <u>payment method (cash or check), amount, date, order number, and employee number of the clerk receiving the payment are recorded</u>.

Use Case Name: Rental Customer Pays Fines
Use Case Purpose: Describes the processing of fine payments for rental orders
Used by: Rental Customer Rents Rental Tape(s)
Uses: Customer Makes Payment

Typical Course of Events:

1. Use case is initiated when a <u>rental customer is informed that he has unpaid fines or inquires if he has unpaid fines</u>.
2. <u>Rental customer is informed of the total amount due and asked how much of the total he wants to pay</u>.
3. Customer makes payment (see Customer Makes Payment use case steps 2 and 3 only).
4. The <u>fine payment amount is subtracted from the current fines</u>, giving an updated fine total.
5. The <u>payment method (cash or check), amount, date, member number, and employee number of the clerk receiving the payment are recorded</u>.

FIGURE 10.1b Identifying use case behaviors in Rental Customer Rents 3/3 Rental Tapes, Customer Makes Payment, and Rental Customer Pays Fines

TABLE 10.1 Structured-text description of manual payment-processing procedures

---

if Customer is paying cash then
      ring as cash payment;
      calculate change due (if any) and give to customer;
      place cash in cash drawer;
else if   Customer is paying by check and OrderTotal > $10.00 or
      (OrderTotal $10.00 and manager appr oves payment method) then
      verify two forms of ID (membership card, credit card, driver's license);
      ring as cash payment;
      place check in cash drawer;
else if   Customer is paying by coupon and coupon value Or derTotal then
      ring as cash payment;
      place coupon in cash drawer;
// Note that no cash is refunded for coupon payments //
else if   Customer is paying by coupon and coupon value < OrderTotal then
      ring as cash payment;
      place coupon in cash drawer;
      calculate amount due;
      continue as cash/check payment;
end;

This discussion of systems behaviors revealed that an object class not adequately defined in the earlier discussion was PAYMENT, which seemed to be an integral part of several use cases: Customer Makes Payment, Rental Customer Rents Rental Tape(s), Customer Buys Sales Tape(s), and Rental Customer Pays Fines. In fact, as the ETG users made clear during the JAD workshop, payments are so fundamental to ETG's order processing system that order payments and fine payments required different behaviors. Thus, Victoria and Denny needed to add PAYMENT and its subclasses, FINE-PAYMENT and ORDER-PAYMENT, to the object relationship model.

As the group discussed policies governing rental orders and fine payments, Victoria discovered that without management approval, a rental customer who has more than $10 in unpaid fines cannot rent tapes. However, she also learned that this policy is seldom enforced in practice. Consulting with the ETG users and Denny, Victoria got Paul's approval to provide flexible support of this business rule by (1) adding FINE as a subclass of RO-LINE and creating a composition relationship between FINE and RENTAL-CUSTOMER; (2) including a FineComments attribute in the RENTAL-CUSTOMER class; (3) whenever a rental order was processed, displaying the unpaid fines and comments on attempts made to collect them (e.g., "letter sent 4/28, called 5/3, reminded in store 5/9"); and (4) empowering sales clerks to decide whether to enforce the policy or to simply remind the customer that fines were unpaid. The object relationship model segment shown in Figure 10.2 includes the PAYMENT and FINE classes identified during the discussion of use cases.

As the participants discussed the Rental Customer Rents 3/3 Tapes use case, Victoria concluded that processsing rental orders and processing 3/3 rental orders required many of the same behaviors. So she decided to treat 3/3-ORDER as a subclass of RENTAL-ORDER. Victoria also realized that designing the behaviors in this use case would give her a chance to exploit another feature of the object-oriented approach: polymorphism!

continued in Chapter 11 opening case

The chapter opening case illustrates some of the system behavior analysis and design activities that Victoria and Denny performed to define the behaviors of ETG's new order processing system. A **system behavior** (or, simply, *behavior*) is a response to a stimulus. For example, when a user sees a screen prompt "Enter Hourly Wage," the expected response to this stimulus is the behavior of typing a currency value and pressing the ENTER key. The system's displaying this prompt is itself also a behavior, perhaps in response to the user's selecting a system function such as Create New Employee. The stimulus for a behavior also

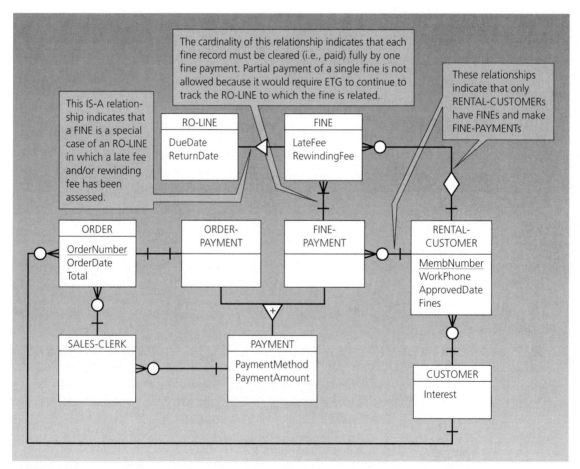

FIGURE 10.2   Augmented object relationship model segment showing PAYMENT and FINE classes

can be satisfaction of a condition; for example, when the value of QuantityInStock for a particular inventory item is less than 100, the expected response is the behavior of reordering the item. We use the term *behavior* instead of the more established terms *function* or *process* because behavior suggests a discrete event and applies to acts performed by either a human or a machine in response to either another behavior or a condition.

In this chapter, you will learn two approaches to system behavior analysis and design: the traditional approach and the object-oriented approach. In the traditional approach, you will use physical data flow diagrams (DFDs) to design the manual and automated behaviors of a proposed system. Then you will partition these DFDs to identify programs and determine whether each program should be implemented as a batch process or a real-time process. Finally, you will specify each program's functions using program structure charts and structured-text process descriptions. In the object-oriented approach, you will extend your analysis of use cases to identify system behaviors. Then you will use structured-text and object behavior modeling techniques to design the methods and messages required to perform these behaviors. Whether your intent is to implement a traditional system or an object-oriented system, the purpose of **system behavior analysis and design** is the same: to determine what behaviors the system needs to support and to design manual and automated procedures to perform these behaviors. After completing this chapter, you should be able to

1. Compare and contrast the traditional and object-oriented approaches to system behavior analysis and design.

2. Explain the purpose of physical DFDs in system behavior analysis and design.

3. Discuss the characteristics that differentiate a physical DFD from a logical DFD.

4. Partition a physical DFD to group manual procedures and to define discrete programs.

5. Convert a physical DFD into a program structure chart and/or structured-text process descriptions.

6. Explain encapsulation and its impact on object-oriented system behavior design.

7. Specify system behaviors in use cases and object relationship models.

8. Create class specifications.

9. Discuss several criteria for evaluating system behavior design quality.

10.1 ◈ SYSTEM BEHAVIOR ANALYSIS AND DESIGN: TWO APPROACHES

Figure 10.3 illustrates the activities of system behavior analysis and design as they typically occur in traditional systems development and in object-oriented systems development. In this section, we highlight the activities of each approach, comment on how each treats the data and software components, and weigh the relative advantages and disadvantages of each.

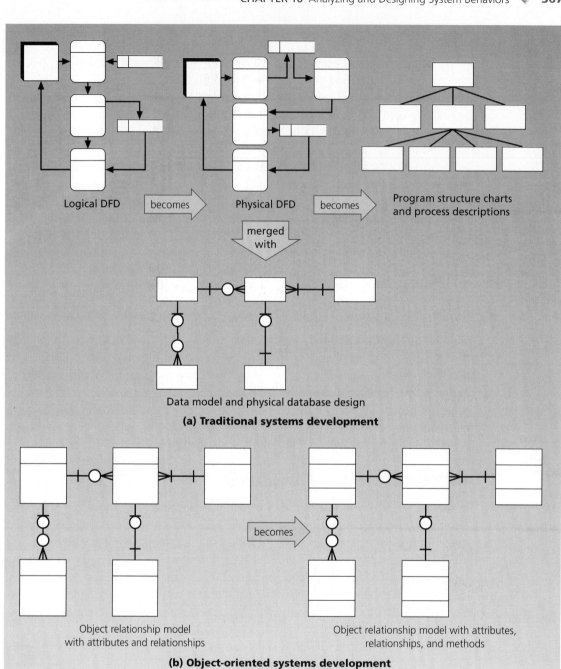

Logical DFD → becomes → Physical DFD → becomes → Program structure charts and process descriptions

merged with

Data model and physical database design

(a) Traditional systems development

Object relationship model with attributes and relationships → becomes → Object relationship model with attributes, relationships, and methods

(b) Object-oriented systems development

FIGURE 10.3   Activities of system behavior analysis and design

THE TRADITIONAL APPROACH

In traditional systems development, you first identify a new system's IPOSC requirements and then create logical and physical DFDs, program structure charts, and structured text to design the manual and automated behaviors of the new system. The automated behaviors are implemented as a collection of application programs that manipulate data stored in a database. Because data and software are treated as separate information system components, you need to create different models to specify the software component (DFDs and their related structure charts and/or process descriptions) from those that you created to specify the data component (the logical data model and its related physical database design).

Ivar Jacobson, the author of the use-case method described in Chapter 9, considers this disconnection between data and behaviors a major weakness of the traditional approach because it requires people to "think like computers." He believes a more desirable technique would model business processes and data the way that business people think of them, thus yielding models that people can more easily understand [Jacobson et al. 1995].

Nonetheless, the traditional approach offers several advantages: its maturity, its well-defined quality criteria, and its CASE tool support. Traditional analysis and design techniques have been refined over the two decades since their inception. What began as structured programming in the late 1960s evolved into structured analysis and design techniques in the mid- and late 1970s. Numerous textbooks and reference manuals have been written documenting these techniques, and thousands of MIS practitioners have put them to the test constructing a wide variety of information systems for a wide variety of applications. Based on these experiences, quality criteria for evaluating the design of an information system have been defined and now serve as guidelines to ensure system quality. In addition, most CASE tools currently on the market support traditional systems development methodologies.

THE OBJECT-ORIENTED APPROACH

In contrast to traditional systems development, object-oriented (OO) systems development requires you to analyze use cases to specify the behaviors a system must support and then extend your object relationship model to include methods to perform these behaviors. For example, the Rental Customer Rents Rental Tape(s) use case specified in Figure 10.1 requires methods such as verifyMembNumber, determineDueDate, calculateTotal, and displayUsers; it also requires messages to allow objects to collaborate. Because data and the behaviors that manipulate data are encapsulated in objects, you use a single construct—an object class—to design both the data structures and the behaviors of the new system.

Thus, system behavior design is simply an extension of system data structure design. Consequently, model consistency is maintained as development proceeds from analysis through design to implementation. This consistency is a great benefit of the OO approach, since it reduces complexity, improves understanding, and yields models that more closely map to real-world concepts. However, the OO approach is far less mature than the traditional approach—a mere infant compared to its middle-aged traditional counterpart. Although currently OO programming languages and techniques are well defined, building on SIMULA, an OO programming language developed in the 1960s, OO analysis and design techniques are only beginning to evolve. The first OO texts appeared in the late 1980s, and CASE tool support emerged only in the early 1990s.[1]

OO techniques for analyzing and modeling the data content of and relationships between classes are well defined, building on the traditional logical data model and refining the specialization (is-a) and composition (has-a) relationships. But OO system behavior analysis and design techniques are generally less mature—critics would say less formal, less rigorous, and less testable, and "goodness" criteria for evaluating the quality of OO designs are still emerging. Nonetheless, some OO methodologies such as those of Booch [1993] and Rumbaugh [1991], are maturing rapidly and are supported by "industrial strength" CASE tools (Rational Software Corporation's Rational Rose and Martin Marietta Corporation's OMTool,[2] respectively).

Although the future seems to be object-oriented, at the time this text is being written, most organizations are still using traditional techniques to analyze and to design system behaviors. To prepare you for this dichotomous reality, this chapter discusses the activities and techniques of both the traditional and the object-oriented approaches.

10.2 ◈ TRADITIONAL SYSTEM BEHAVIOR ANALYSIS AND DESIGN

Because traditional systems development separates system data structure analysis and design from system behavior analysis and design, a fundamental question arises: Which should be done first? Should data structures be designed and then the behaviors that manipulate the data? Or should behaviors be designed first? The way that system data structure analysis and design was presented in the Chapter 9 opening case indicates that we recommend the latter case.

Recall that Victoria first led the ETG users to specify use cases and then Denny stepped in to analyze and design the data structures of the new order processing system. Use cases, which can replace the logical DFDs created in traditional analysis and design, give a logical view of major system behaviors, providing a foundation for data structure analysis and design and the more detailed system behavior analysis and design discussed in this chapter. Thus, at least a general understanding of the new system's behaviors is a precursor to detailed data structure analysis and design.

This section explains the steps of traditional system behavior design:

1. Create leveled physical DFDs to design system behaviors.

2. Partition your physical DFDs to identify programs.

3. Determine how each program should be implemented: batch processing or real-time processing.

4. Create a program structure chart for each program.

5. Use structured text to write process descriptions and to model business rules.

---

[1] See Yourdon [1994]. Chapter 24 provides a listing of OO CASE tool vendors.

[2] More specifically, OMTool supports a convergence of the Booch method and Rumbaugh's Object Modeling Technique and is the product of an alliance between Martin Marietta Advanced Concepts Center and Rational Software Corporation.

CREATING PHYSICAL DATA FLOW DIAGRAMS

A **physical data flow diagram (DFD)** is a traditional process-modeling technique used to specify *how* the IPOSC functions will be implemented in a new information system. Notice the emphasis on "how" in the preceding sentence. During the preliminary investigation and analysis stage, you create logical DFDs of the existing information system to document *what* this system does (i.e., its logical IPOSC functions). Now you need to create physical DFDs to design *how* these functions—and any additional functions identified during analysis—will be performed in the new system. Figure 10.4 shows a Level 0 physical DFD of ETG's new order processing

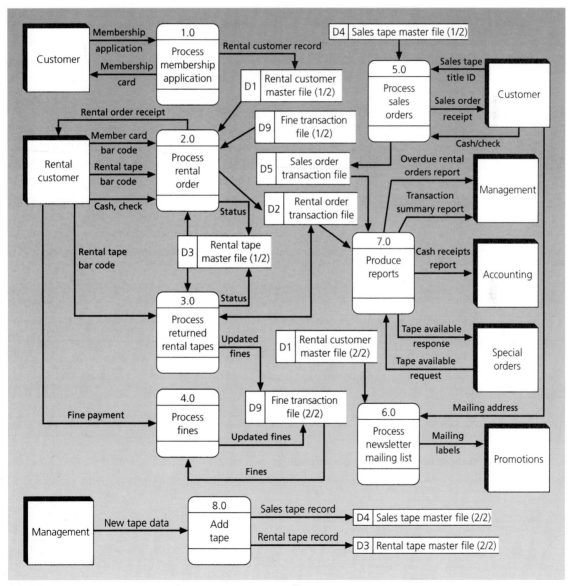

FIGURE 10.4 Level 0 physical DFD of ETG's new order processing system

system; Figure 10.5 shows a Level 1 physical DFD of ETG's rental orders process; and Figure 10.6 (on page 372) shows a Level 2 physical DFD of Process 2.2—Complete rental order line(s). As these diagrams show, physical DFDs are similar to logical DFDs in that both can be leveled and balanced to detail system functions more fully. In addition, all the rules that govern logical DFD construction (see Technical Module A) also govern physical DFD construction.

However, a physical DFD differs from a logical DFD in several ways. Whereas a logical DFD describes a process independent of the information technology used to implement the process, a physical DFD is created with the chosen technology in mind. For example, in the logical DFD of ETG's rental orders process (see Figure 8 in Victoria's problem definition report), Process 2.2 is labeled "Enter transaction," which gives no indication of how transaction data are entered or who/what performs this process. In contrast, in the physical DFD shown in Figure 10.6, the corresponding physical process is labeled "Scan member number bar code." This process label indicates that a scanning device is used to read the member number, which is represented as a bar code. In addition, the agent/location section of the process bubble indicates that this process is performed by a sales clerk. Thus, a physical DFD describes a system's *physical* IPOSC functions; it also distinguishes between manual and automated processes.

A physical DFD also differs from a logical DFD in that its data stores are labeled with the actual file names and indicate whether each is a *master file* (a relatively stable file containing records of customers, suppliers, products, and similar entities) or a transaction file (a file that maintains records of business transactions, such as sales order records, purchase order records, or payroll records). For example, the physical DFD in Figure 10.4 labels the file

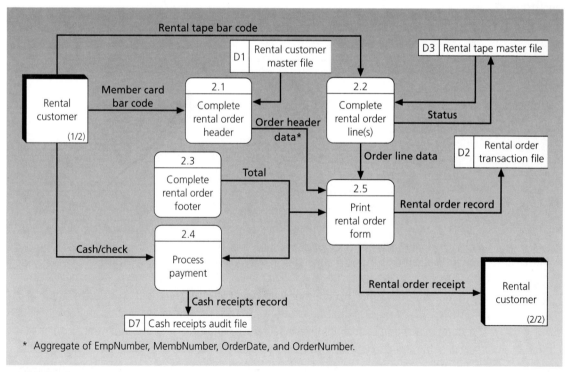

* Aggregate of EmpNumber, MembNumber, OrderDate, and OrderNumber.

FIGURE 10.5   Level 1 physical DFD of Process 2.0—Process rental orders

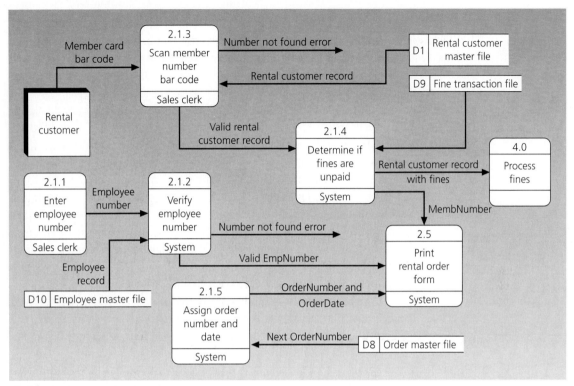

FIGURE 10.6   Level 2 physical DFD of Process 2.1—Complete rental order header

containing member data as "Rental customer master file." Physical DFDs can also show temporary files used to hold intermediate data created during processing.

The data flows of a physical DFD are often labeled differently from those in logical DFDs as well. For example, instead of using a logical data flow labeled "Payment," a physical DFD may label the same data flow "Cash, check, or credit card." Similarly, as shown in Figure 10.4, a physical data flow may specify the actual field name (MembNumber, DueDate, Fines), give a record name (Rental customer record), or describe the data "carrier" (Membership application form, Rental tape bar code, Rental order receipt, Cash receipts report).

Physical DFDs also more clearly indicate the sequence in which processes are to be performed. Indicating sequence is important because physical DFDs are used to document manual procedures and to prepare program structure charts. Just as a recipe indicates that the cook must mix the cake ingredients before baking the cake, a physical DFD indicates that line item data must be entered before a total is computed or that records must be sorted before a file is updated.

Another difference between logical and physical DFDs is that physical DFDs are more specific. Physical DFDs indicate control processes, such as verifying user authorization (for example, requiring an employee to enter an employee number and verifying the entry against the Employee Master file) and validating input fields (for example, verifying that an item price input field is of the appropriate data type and is within a specified range of values, or validating a membership number input field by determining that it exists in the Rental Customer Master file). Physical DFDs also may show transaction audit files, such as the Cash Receipts Audit file that ETG's company accountant uses to audit cash transactions.

Check Your Understanding 10-1

Indicate whether each of the following characteristics describes a logical DFD (L), a physical DFD (P), or both (B).

_____ 1.   Documents external entities, processes, data stores, and data flows.

_____ 2.   Specifies how the physical IPOSC requirements will be implemented.

_____ 3.   Makes no distinction between manual and automated processes.

_____ 4.   Shows temporary files created during processing.

_____ 5.   Forbids data flows between external entities and data stores.

_____ 6.   Includes control processes such as user authorization and data validation.

_____ 7.   Supports functional decomposition through leveling and balancing.

_____ 8.   Uses actual file names and distinguishes between master and transaction files.

PARTITIONING A PHYSICAL DFD INTO PROGRAMS

After you have created leveled physical DFDs, you examine your diagrams to categorize DFD processes into those that will be implemented as application programs and those that will be documented as manual procedures. Recall that Chapter 4 defined a *process* as a set of activities that produces an output. More specifically, a **process** is a unit of work that is performed within a defined time frame and that follows a specified sequence. A **partition** segments a physical DFD into discrete programs; that is, each partition represents a program that will be executed to support a business process. If two processes are performed at different times or by different users, they will usually require separate programs so they should be segmented into different partitions.

Oftentimes each of the major system processes documented on a Level 0 DFD can be partitioned into a discrete program. For example, each major process in the Level 0 physical DFD of ETG's new order processing system shown in Figure 10.4 will become a separate partition. Other times you may need to examine lower-level DFDs to define partitions and to distinguish manual and automated processes. For example, Figure 10.7 presents a partitioned Level 1 physical DFD for Process 7.0—Produce reports. (Notice that partitions are indicated by drawing a box around one or more process bubbles.) Here the benefits of partitioning lower-level DFDs are quite evident. Because the reports generated in this process are produced at different times (for example, the Cash Receipts report is produced every business day, but the Transactions Summary report is produced weekly), most of them will require different programs.

For each manual process, you write a *procedures description* that explains how the user performs the process. For example, in the ETG system, sales clerks will manually scan bar codes to capture the rental tape stock number and the rental customer membership number;

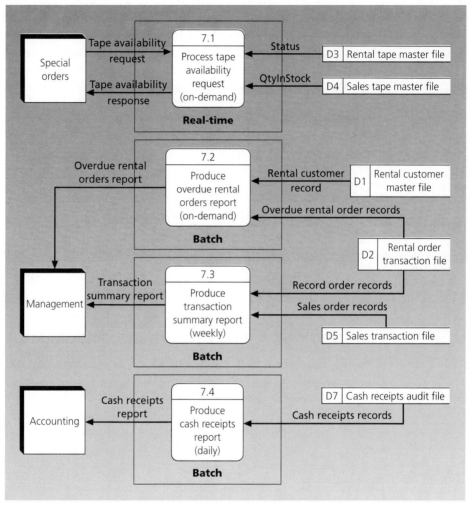

FIGURE 10.7   Partitioned Level 1 physical DFD of Process 7.0—Produce reports

they will also verify authorized users and process customer payments. A procedures description should state the business policies governing a manual process (for example, allowing only authorized users to rent tapes using a member's card and requiring two forms of identification to process a check payment). It should also explain how to perform each task in the process (for example, how to scan a bar code, how to verify an authorized user, and how to process a check or coupon payment). Table 10.2 shows an example of a manual procedure description.

DECIDING ON BATCH VERSUS REAL-TIME PROCESSING

For each automated process, you determine if batch processing or real-time processing is more appropriate. Typically, a transaction that interacts with an external entity and that requires an immediate response (processing a customer phone sales order) or that must be processed as it

TABLE 10.2 Sample of a manual procedure description

Procedure:	**Processing a Rental Order**

Stimulus:	Customer presents rental tapes and membership card for checkout.
Frequency:	Performed repeatedly throughout each business day.
Inputs:	Employee number (keyed)
	Membership number (scanned from membership card)
	Rental tape stock number (scanned from tape)
Outputs:	Rental order form

Structured-Text Process Description:

```
enter employee number;
scan membership card bar code;
verify user's status and eligibility to rent tapes (i.e., authorized user, unpaid fines);
if user status can't be verified or if user has excessive fines then
      cancel order and confiscate membership card; [state ETG User and Fine Policies]
      abort procedure;
end if;
if user wants to pay fines then
      process fine payment; [refer to Processing Fine Payments]
      continue procedure;
end if;
while there are tapes to process do
      scan tape bar code;
end while;
collect payment; [refer to Processing Order Payments]
print rental order form;
get customer's signature;
distribute copies;
end procedure;
```

occurs (processing a department store sales transaction) should be implemented as a real-time process. For example, the Tape Availability report shown in Figure 10.7 requires an immediate response so that Special Orders can complete a special order; similarly, processing rental and sales orders, rental tape returns, and fines must be performed on demand repeatedly throughout the day. Thus, these processes should be implemented as real-time processes. In contrast, a transaction that does not require human intervention (updating a master file by merging it with a transaction file), that generates its outputs from only stored data (generating monthly customer billing statements), or that does not require an immediate response (processing direct-mail sales orders) can be implemented as a batch process. The programs to generate mailing labels and most of the reports in ETG's order processing system are examples of programs suitable for batch processing.

After this analysis, you should have a good sense of the basic processing logic required to support the application being designed. Based on this understanding, you can decide how the software component of the information system should be implemented: by purchasing prepackaged software or by custom-developing the application programs. In many cases, you may be able to avoid software development altogether if a commercial software package fills your needs. If you will be considering a commercial package, your next task is to specify the criteria that a commercial package would have to satisfy. These criteria are derived from your functional requirements and from your physical DFDs. Evaluating and acquiring commercial software packages are discussed in Chapter 13.

If you decide to custom-develop the programs, your next behavior analysis and design activity is to design the application program required for each partition. Techniques used to specify conventional programs include program structure charts, pseudocode, structured text, decision tables, and decision trees. Here we discuss two of these techniques: program structure charts and structured text.

Check Your Understanding 10-2

Partition the physical DFDs shown below and on the facing page to identify programs. Determine how each program should be implemented: as a batch process or as a real-time process. Justify your choice.

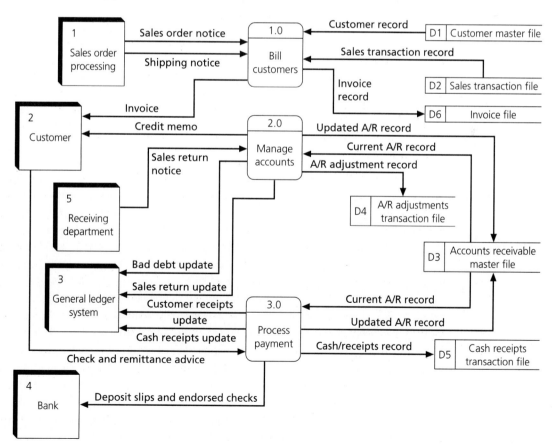

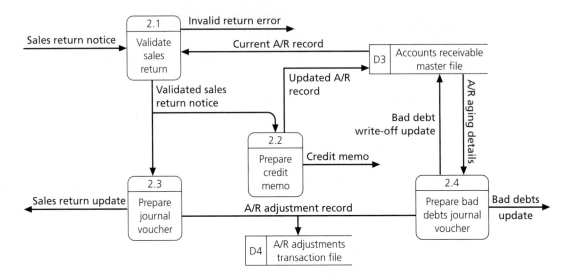

TRANSFORMING A PHYSICAL DFD INTO A PROGRAM STRUCTURE CHART

A **program structure chart** (also called a *hierarchy chart* or, simply, a *structure chart*) is a traditional design technique that employs functional decomposition to specify the structure and functions of an application program. Because we assume that you have learned—or will learn—about program structure charts in a programming course, we provide only an overview of chart construction here. The symbols used to create a program structure chart are shown in Figure 10.8, along with defintions of a **module**, **data flow**, **control flow**, loop, selection, and module connection.

The functions that a program must perform are represented as a hierarchy of modules, with modules at a lower level specifying more detail of a function shown in a module at a higher level. For example, in Figure 10.9 (on page 379), the nine modules at Level 3 indicate that the major functions of the Level 1 module ETG order processing system are Add Member, Process Rental Order, Process Sales Order, Process Rental Returns, Process Fines, Check Stock Availability, Generate Reports, Generate Mailing Labels, and Add Tape. This structure chart provides an overview of ETG's order processing system; each of the modules at Level 3 will be defined as a program and will become the Level 1 module in the structure chart of each program; in addition, each of the Level 5 modules will become a program. For example, the structure chart in Figure 10.10 (on page 380) presents the design of the Process Rental Orders program.

A structure chart differs from a physical DFD not only in the way it looks but also in the kinds of information it conveys. Although DFDs provide a system view that is comprehensible by users, a programmer needs more specific information to turn a design on paper into program code. For example, structure charts indicate what data are read from or written to a file, what control conditions must be enforced, and other details required to construct a program. You transform a physical DFD into a structure chart by performing two forms of analysis:

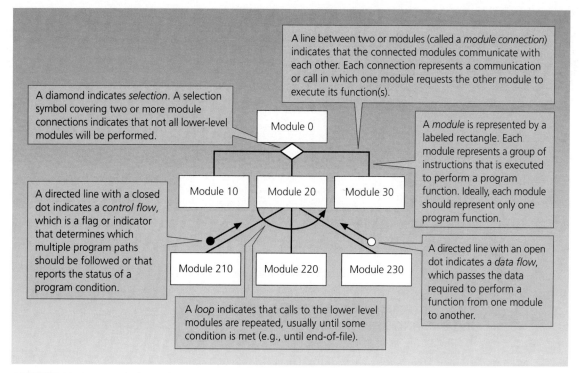

FIGURE 10.8   Symbols used in program structure charts

1. **Transform analysis**—used to segment sequential DFD processes into input, process-ing, and output functions. For example, the six second-level modules of Process Rental Order, shown in Figure 10.10, are performed sequentially to accept inputs about tapes and customers, to process the transaction, and to generate the Rental order record and Rental order form.

2. **Transaction analysis**—used to segment DFD processes into alternate flows of control depending on a condition or user selection (e.g., a menu selection). For example, in Figure 10.9, the Produce Report module will call one of the lower-level modules—Gen-erate Cash Receipts Report, Generate Transaction Summary Report, and Generate Over-due Rental Orders Report—based on the user's selection.

Generally speaking, each DFD process will appear as a structure chart module. You can see this relationship if you compare the physical DFDs in Figures 10.5 and 10.6 to the structure chart in Figure 10.10; notice that the processes in Figure 10.5 become Level 2 modules and those in Figure 10.6 become Level 3 and 4 modules. This mapping of DFD processes to structure chart modules is further illustrated in Figure 10.11 (on page 381). In addition, each data flow that reads data from or writes data to a data store or accepts user input is treated as a separate module in a program structure chart.

A few guidelines will help you use structure charts effectively:

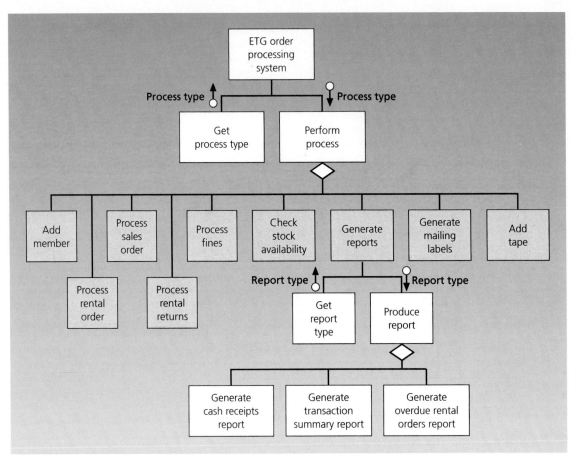

FIGURE 10.9 Overview program structure chart of ETG's order processing system

1. Level 1 of a structure chart may have only one module (sometimes called the *boss module, executive module,* or *main module*); this highest-level module is the command center of the program in that it invokes or calls modules at Level 2, which in turn call modules at Level 3, and so on. Ultimately, control always returns to the Level 1 module.

2. *Each module should perform only one function.* Note that "one function" does not mean one behavior or one program statement. Modules at higher levels of the structure chart may specify a "single" function that can be further decomposed.

3. Modules at each level should be arranged in sequential order; that is, the left-hand modules should specify functions that must be performed before the functions of the right-hand modules. An exception to this general rule is modules that represent alternative functions selected by a higher-level module.

4. The selection symbol should be used to indicate that not all modules at the next lower level will be performed. For example, in Figure 10.9, the diamond attached to the Produce Report module indicates that only one of the lower-level modules—Generate Cash Receipts Report, for example—will be called to execute its functions.

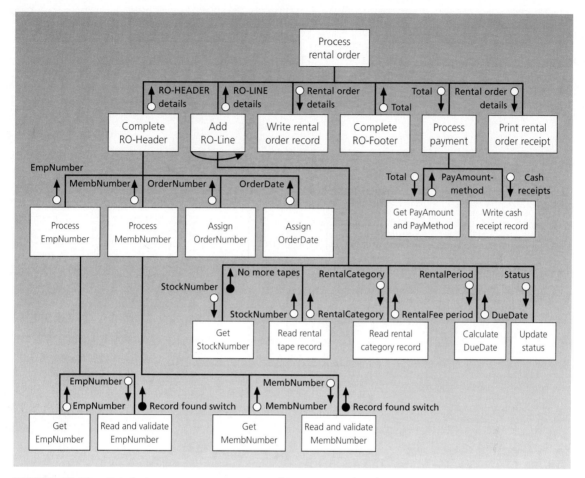

FIGURE 10.10   Detailed program structure chart of Process Rental Orders program

5. The loop symbol should be used to indicate that some or all of the modules at the next lower level will be performed repeatedly until a specified condition is met. For example, in Figure 10.10, the loop attached to the Add RO-Line module indicates that the lower-level modules—Get StockNumber and so on—will be performed until the control flow No More Tapes is true.

6. The data elements passed between modules should be specified by labeling each data flow symbol with the name assigned to each element in the physical database design. Where several fields of a record must be passed, you can create a data structure that aggregates fields and assume that the aggregate data structure will be defined in the program. For example, in Figure 10.10, the data flow labeled RO-Header Details is a data structure aggregating EmpNumber, MembNumber, OrderNumber, and OrderDate. *Only the data required to perform the receiving module's task should be passed between modules.*

7. Control flows should be used to indicate a control flag or other value that is used to direct the flow of control or to report the status of a condition. Generally speaking, *control flows*

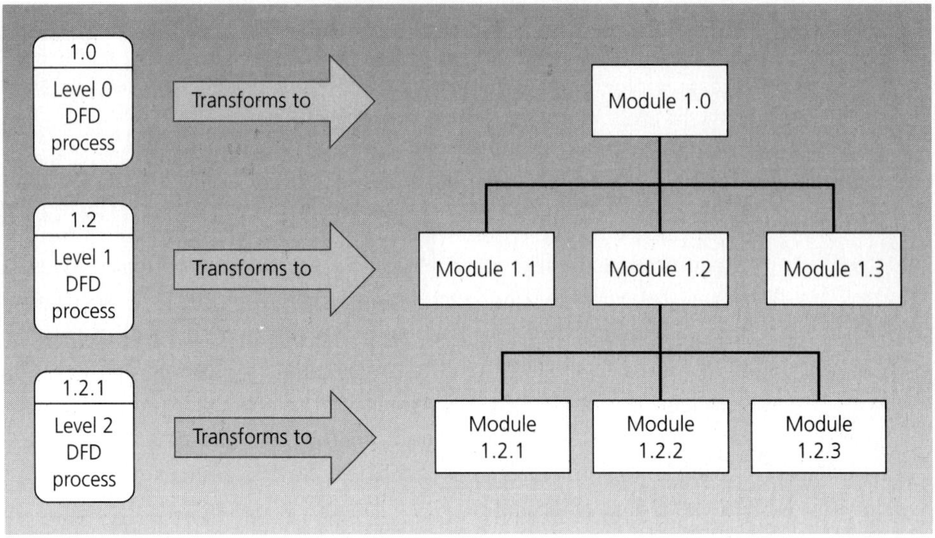

FIGURE 10.11 Mapping DFD bubbles to structure chart modules

should move from a lower-level module to a higher-level module. In addition, *at most one control flow should exist between any two modules.*

8. Each program structure chart should be reviewed and evaluated to ensure that the design works before coding begins. This verification process, called a **structured walkthrough**, requires someone other than the chart's creator to simulate program execution by "walking through" the structure chart's processes and flows of data and control.

Program structure charts employ the top-down approach and functional decomposition to increase software modularity, understandability, maintainability, and reusability. As you create the chart, your goal is to maximize **cohesiveness** and to minimize **coupling** [Jordan & Machesky 1990]. The italicized sentences in guidelines 2, 6, and 7 indicate how to achieve these goals. A cohesive design specifies only one function per module, and the function of each module can be clearly expressed as verb plus object. For example, a module called "Complete RO-Footer and Print Rental Order" is almost certainly not cohesive because it performs two functions. It would be better to create two separate, cohesive modules—"Complete RO-Footer" and "Print Rental Order"—to perform these two functions.

To reduce coupling, you should minimize the number of data and control flows passed between modules. Although data coupling is a natural result of module communication, passing only the data needed to perform a module's function reduces data coupling. To minimize control coupling, you should avoid control flows that allow one module to determine the processing of another module. For example, in Figure 10.9, a control flow should not determine which report is generated; instead, ReportType should be a variable (data flow) assigned a value in the Get Report Type module. Then, based on the value of this variable, the Produce Report module will select which report to generate.

Check Your Understanding 10-3

Create a program structure chart to design a program to process rental tape returns. The physical DFDs of this process are shown in Figure 10.12.

SPECIFYING SYSTEM BEHAVIORS IN STRUCTURED TEXT

Structured text (also called *structured English*) uses a quasi-formal language to specify system behaviors and business rules [Yourdon Inc. 1993]. It is a quasi-formal language in that it combines formal expressions and indentation rules with everyday language. The standard constructs in structured text are **sequence**, **selection**, and **iteration**. These constructs are defined as containing conditions and statements, which can be expressed in everyday language. Thus, the meaning and syntax of only a small set of basic expressions is constrained—or "structured"—in structured text. Definitions of the basic constructs and examples of expressions follow (see also Table 10.3).

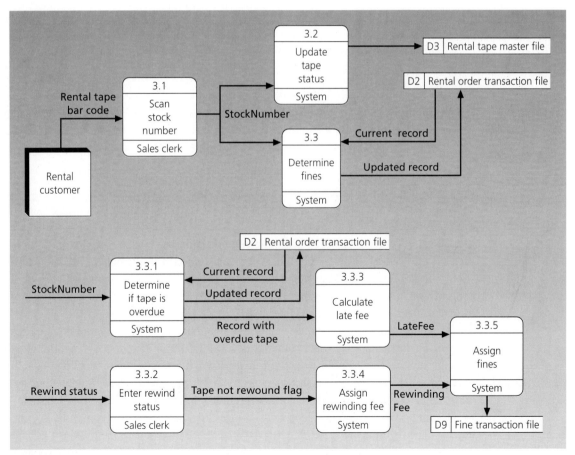

FIGURE 10.12   Physical DFDs of Process 3.0—Process returned rental tapes

TABLE 10.3 Standard constructs and expressions in structured text

Standard Construct	Example

in sequence do
   <statement>;
end;
	in sequence do
	    print Rental-Customer.Name;
	    print Rental-Customer.WorkPhone;
	    end;

Selection Expressions	

if <condition> **then**
   <statement>;
else
   <statement>;
end;
	if EmpNumber is valid then
	    move EmpNumber to RO-Header;
	   else
	    display error message "Access denied Invalid
	       Employee Number";
	    return to main menu;
	    end;

if <condition> **then**
   <statement>;
elseif <condition> **then**
   <statement>;
end;
	accept ReportType;
	if ReportType = "TS" then
	    perform Generate Transaction Summary Report;
	elseif ReportType = "CR" then
	    perform Generate Cash Receipts Report;
	elseif ReportType = "OR" then
	    perform Generate Overdue Rental Orders Report;
	    end;

Iteration Expressions	

for each <entity or data flow>
   <statement>;
end ;
	for each Rental-Customer
	    print mailing label;
	    end;

while <condition> **do**
   <statement>;
end ;
	accept first Rental-Tape.StockNumber
	while there are tapes to process do
	    read Rental-Tape record;
	    read Tape record;
	    move Rental-Tape.StockNumber to RO-Line;
	    move Tape.Title to RO-Line;
	    read Rental-Category record;
	    move Rental-Category.RentalFee to RO-Line;
	    DueDate = Date$ + RentalPeriod;
	    move DueDate to RO-Line;
	    write RO-Line;
	    Rental-Tape.Status = "Rented";
	    accept another Rental-Tape.StockNumber;
	    end;

repeat
   <statement>;
until <condition> **;**
end;
	repeat
	    accept Rental-Tape.StockNumber;
	    read Rental-Tape record;
	    read Tape record;
	    move Rental-Tape.StockNumber to RO-Line;
	    move Tape.Title to RO-Line;
	    read Rental-Category record;
	    move Rental-Category.RentalFee to RO-Line;
	    DueDate = Date$ + RentalPeriod;
	    move DueDate to RO-Line;
	    write RO-Line;
	    Rental-Tape.Status = "Rented";
	    display prompt "More tapes? (Y/N)";
	until response = "N";
	    end;

◆ **Sequence:** perform <statement$_1$>, then perform <statement$_2$>, . . . perform <statement$_n$>. A statement can be a simple action (e.g., read a record) or one of the constructs in Table 10.3 (e.g., repeat . . . until)

◆ **Selection:** test for one or more conditions; depending on which condition is true, perform a statement or set of statements. The simplest form of selection is the if <condition> then <statement> construct. A condition is a boolean expression, one that can be evaluated as true or false (e.g., x   10).

◆ **Iteration:** perform the same behavior(s) repeatedly; the number of iterations may be fixed or may be determined by a test condition.

By using these expressions in combination, you can define a variety of manual and automated behaviors. The benefit of using structured text is that it helps to clarify system behaviors and the business rules that govern them; it also uncovers any ambiguities or misunderstandings as behaviors and rules are made explicit. Furthermore, structured-text descriptions of automated behaviors give programmers the detailed specifications they need to write program code. Thus, the system behaviors of every structure chart module should be specified in structured text.

This section has presented only a cursory view of traditional system behavior design. Some traditional systems development methodologies would have you also create process specifications, data-flow specifications, and a host of other documents and models, but even this cursory view reveals the tremendous effort expended up front before system construction can begin. It also reveals why traditional techniques are not highly amenable to rapid application development and prototyping. If one accepts the traditional approach's assumption that design must be completed before program coding and other implementation activities can begin, then it is easy to understand why late changes in requirements are so disruptive. If you have spent several days (weeks?) creating physical DFDs, program structure charts, and structured-text descriptions of system behaviors, you would be less than thrilled with having to revise these specifications to meet new requirements. Thus, the "structure" of traditional structured techniques tends to promote rigidity rather than the adaptability to changing needs that today's organizations need. However, an advantage of this detailed behavior specification is that if you create these specifications with an integrated CASE tool, the CASE tool's code generator can often generate program code from your data and behavior models and structured-text descriptions.

10.3 ◈ OBJECT-ORIENTED SYSTEM BEHAVIOR ANALYSIS AND DESIGN

The object-oriented (OO) approach to system behavior analysis and design presented in this section follows no particular OO methodology. Instead, it discusses fundamental concepts of OO behavior analysis and design and provides simple techniques for designing system behaviors using these concepts. The goal of this section is to help you make the transition from the traditional programs-versus-data way of thinking to the OO objects-have-data-and-perform-methods way of thinking. The transition requires a clear understanding of the key

OO concepts of encapsulation, method, service interface, message, and—the big one—polymorphism. Although several of these concepts were introduced briefly earlier in this text, each is explicated more fully here. Then a five-step process for analyzing and designing system behaviors is presented.

KEY CONCEPTS OF OBJECT-ORIENTED SYSTEM BEHAVIOR

The concept of **encapsulation** is fundamental to the OO approach. You already know that a single construct, an object class, encapsulates data (attributes) and behaviors (methods), but you may not understand how encapsulation affects system behavior analysis and design. In the traditional approach, programs "know" about the data they use because they read data from various files, manipulate the data, and write the processed data to the same or other files. In essence, programs "throw open the door" to files and then pick and choose the data they need from each file or record. In contrast, in the OO approach, data is the sacred reserve of the object in which it is contained. Encapsulation means that no other object can directly read or change another object's data; only the containing object can manipulate its own data. Because data is hidden from other objects, the term *information hiding* is sometimes used as a synonym for encapsulation.

What this means is that each object class controls its own data and can define methods (1) to manipulate its data for its own purposes and (2) to report data to or to perform manipulations of its data for another object. Every class must perform the CRUD functions of creating, reading, updating, or deleting an instance of an object class. Methods that perform these CRUD functions are sometimes called *implicit methods* because systems analysts assume that every class will have these methods and thus do not explicitly design them as part of the system. In fact, the CRUD methods are sometimes assigned to an abstract superclass—for example, DATA-OBJECT, and every class that needs to use these methods is treated as a subclass of DATA-OBJECT.

Private methods are performed for the object's own benefit and are not known to any other object. An example of a private method is one in which an object manipulates the value of one or more attributes to determine the value of another of its attributes. For example, the SALES-ORDER class may define attributes such as Subtotal, SalesTax, and Total. Using the method calculateTotal, a SALES-ORDER object can add the value of its Subtotal attribute to the value of its SalesTax attribute to determine the value of its Total attribute.

In practice, classes have very few private methods. In fact, private methods are most often used to relate the class or its attributes to abstract classes such as NAME, STRING, DATE, TIME, or the abstract DATA-OBJECT class mentioned earlier. These are abstract classes in that they are not intended to have *instances*—to hold data; instead, they define the format, data type, and validation rules of commonly used data types. Thus, the RO-LINE class in ETG's system might have private methods to relate its date attributes DueDate and ReturnDate to the abstract class DATE. Because these concepts are more appropriate to a database or advanced OO analysis and design course, we mention them just as a point of interest. If you want to investigate abstract classes on your own, see the references listed at the end of Chapters 9 and 10.

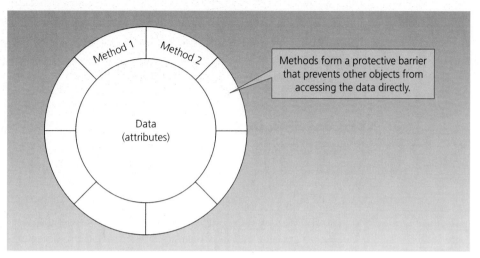

FIGURE 10.13   An object's service interface

A **service** (or **public**) **method** "services" the needs of other objects, and it is "public" in the sense that other objects know about its existence. Public methods form the **service interface** of an object[3]: that is, the "face" that an object presents to other objects. You may find these concepts easier to understand if you visualize an object as shown in Figure 10.13. An object's data and private methods are hidden; only its public methods—its service interface—are exposed. And this exposure is limited to the other objects' knowing that the method exists; they do not know, nor do they need to know, how the method is performed.

Encapsulation provides two benefits. One, it protects each object's data by allowing only the object itself to manipulate its data, thus preventing the data corruption that can occur in traditional systems in which multiple programs access and manipulate data stored in a single file. Two, encapsulation reduces the rippling effect so often seen in conventional systems in which a change in a data structure necessitates a change in the programs that use it and a change in one part of a program necessitates changes in other parts of the program. In an OO system, the "what" (data) and "how" (methods) of an object class are known only to the object class. Thus, a single class can be changed without requiring changes to other classes.

The effect of encapsulation is that objects must have some way to communicate so that they can request services. Enter, messages! Recall that a **message** is a request from one object to another object—or even to itself—signaling the receiving object to perform one of the methods in its service interface. Messages are a key component of system behavior analysis and design because they are the stimulus that triggers performance of a method. Messages can be expressed as

<receiving object instance> <method>: <parameters>

where <receiving object instance> gives the value of the identifier of the receiving object instance, <method> indicates the name of a method in the receiving object's service interface,

---

[3]   Technically, we should say "service interface of an object *class*" because object instances contain only data; methods are "retrieved" from the instance's class.

and <parameters> indicates any information the receiving object needs to know to do its job. For example, the message

　　　rental-categoryN reportRentalFee

requests the RENTAL-CATEGORY object instance whose identifier is N to return a value for the attribute RentalFee.

Just as the execution of program statements must be properly sequenced in a conventional system, the sending of messages and the performance of methods must be properly sequenced in an OO system. The actual composition and relaying of messages is an implementation issue that depends on the programming language used. Our goal during design is simply to specify more formal use cases—or system scenarios—that define appropriate sequences of behavior. The activities required to achieve this goal are discussed in the next section, "Designing Object-Oriented System Behaviors."

No discussion of OO concepts would be complete without a nod to *polymorphism*—a big word that can clear a room almost as effectively as yelling "Fire!" To ease your way into this concept, let us begin with an example. As Victoria examined the Rental Customer Rents 3/3 Rental Tape(s) use case, she realized that it extends—or is a special case of—Rental Customer Rents Rental Tape(s). A regular rental order adds rental order lines by using the tape's stock number to look up the tape's rental category and then getting the rental period and rental fee from the appropriate RENTAL-CATEGORY instance. However, a 3/3 rental order does not apply the normal rental fee, nor does it apply the normal rental period. Instead, it verifies that the selected tape is eligible—that is, is a standard (S) or educational (E) category tape—and then overrides the normal rental fee (3.50) and rental period (one day), creating an additional line item indicating "3/3 order" as the title, "3.00" as the rental fee, and today's date plus three days as the due date. Everything else about a 3/3 rental order is the same as a regular rental order. Victoria has uncovered an excellent opportunity to put polymorphism to work.

If she defines 3/3-ORDER as a subclass of RENTAL-ORDER, she can exploit inheritance and use all the attributes and methods of RENTAL-ORDER in 3/3-ORDER. What is more, she can override the RENTAL-ORDER addLineItem method by defining it as a method in 3/3-ORDER. *When an attribute or method appears both in a superclass and one of its subclasses, the attribute or method defined in the subclass overrides—or substitutes for—the attribute or method in the superclass.* Thus, although it can be called by the same message, a singularly named method—addLineItem—performs different functions depending on whether it is invoked as part of a RENTAL-ORDER or a 3/3-ORDER. That is the power of polymorphism.

So what does polymorphism mean? *Poly* means "many"; *morph* means "shapes." Thus, **polymorphism** is the ability of an attribute or method to take many shapes, to have many implementations. Another example of polymorphism arises in the subclasses of TAPE. SALES-TAPE instances are "lumped" by TitleID; thus, SALES-TAPE has the attribute QtyInStock, which indicates the number of any one sales tape title in ETG's inventory. In contrast, RENTAL-TAPE instances are individuated by StockNumber; each is treated as a separate entity. To know how many of a particular title of rental tape ETG has, the number of instances of that rental tape title must be counted. Thus, the message "J274-94 (the tape TitleID) reportQuantity" will trigger different behaviors depending on whether it is reporting on SALES-TAPE instances or RENTAL-TAPE instances.

Because polymorphism is an effect of how classes are implemented, it is really more related to implementation than to analysis and design. Nonetheless, you should understand the power of polymorphism so that you can design system behaviors to exploit it.

Check Your Understanding 10-4

Indicate which OO concept each of the following statements describe: encapsulation (E), method (M), private method (PRM), public method (PUM), message (MS), or polymorphism (P).

_____ 1. A function performed by an object for its own benefit.

_____ 2. A stimulus causing an object to perform a method.

_____ 3. The hiding of data within an object.

_____ 4. A function performed by an object for the benefit of another object.

_____ 5. An automated behavior performed by a class.

_____ 6. The hiding of different implementations behind a common interface.

_____ 7. A method contained in a class's service interface.

_____ 8. Requires that objects communicate to request each other's services.

DESIGNING OBJECT-ORIENTED SYSTEM BEHAVIORS

The OO approach to system behavior analysis and design extends the object relationship model by adding methods to perform the automated behaviors revealed in use cases. Use cases provide a logical view of the behaviors an information system must support. Traditional behavior design transforms use cases into physical DFDs and program structure charts that specify program functions and the sequence of module execution. Similarly, your goal in OO system behavior design is to transform use cases into object class methods and the messages that trigger these methods. A five-step process for this follows.

1. Analyze use cases to identify classes and behaviors.

2. Define methods and assign to object classes.

3. Extend the object relationship model to include methods, and create a class specification for each class in the model.

4. Reflect classes, methods, and messages in formal use cases.

5. "Walk through" formal use cases to verify design.

Step 1: Analyze Use Cases to Identify Classes and Behaviors

During system data structure analysis and design, you identified the classes used in each use case. Behavior analysis may bring to light additional classes. For example, in the chapter opening case, Victoria realized that the classes FINE and PAYMENT and the subclasses FINE-PAYMENT and ORDER-PAYMENT were necessary to support ETG's system behaviors. Figure 10.14 shows the modified object relationship model segment for the Rental Customer Rents Rental Tape(s) use case, which will be used to illustrate OO behavior analysis and design.

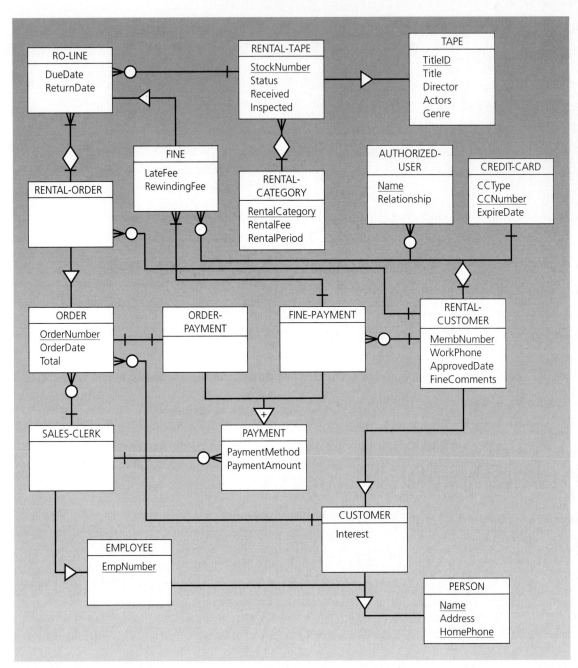

FIGURE 10.14 Object relationship model segment of classes in Rental Customer Rents Rental Tape(s) use case

Your next task is to identify use-case behaviors by highlighting verb phrases in the use case, as Victoria did during the JAD workshop (see Figure 10.1). A preliminary examination of this use case yields the list of behaviors shown in Table 10.4. This list includes both manual and automated behaviors. Manual behaviors to be performed by humans will require a manual

TABLE 10.4 Behaviors in Rental Customer Rents Rental Tape(s) use case

◆ Select tapes (manual).	◆ Report rental fee.
◆ Present tapes and membership card (manual).	◆ Report rental period.
◆ Report member number.	◆ Determine due date.
◆ Determine membership number from phone number.	◆ Change rental tape status.
	◆ Complete rental order form footer.
◆ Claim authorized user status (manual).	◆ Calculate order total.
◆ Verify authorized user status (manual/automated).	◆ Tell customer the order total (manual).
◆ Report fines.	◆ Present payment (manual).
◆ Update fines.	◆ Calculate change due (manual).
◆ Pay fine.	◆ Give change to customer (manual).
◆ Complete rental order form header.	◆ Obtain two forms of ID (manual).
◆ Verify employee number.	◆ Write ID numbers on check (manual).
◆ Verify member number.	◆ Print order form.
◆ Give order number and date.	◆ Get customer signature (manual).
◆ Add rental order line(s).	◆ Distribute copies of order form (manual).
◆ Verify stock number.	◆ Confiscate membership card (manual).
◆ Report title.	◆ Cancel transaction.
◆ Report rental category.	◆ Record cash receipt.

procedures description just as in the traditional approach. Automated behaviors will become methods and will be assigned to object classes.

Strategies for identifying behaviors include the following:

1. Examine the object relationship model segment for the use case. As you examine the classes, ask, "What roles does each class play? What are the responsibilities of each class?" For example, a RENTAL-CUSTOMER instance can initiate a rental order transaction and pay for the order; a SALES-CLERK instance can create an instance of a RENTAL-ORDER (i.e., by selecting the Process Rental Orders system function). A RENTAL-TAPE instance can change its Status. An RO-LINE instance can accept the StockNumber of a RENTAL-TAPE instance. Get the idea? Object thinking requires you to treat objects as dynamic entities capable of action. What actions are each object class responsible for performing?

2. As you examine the object relationship model, ask, "How are relationships between objects created and broken? What methods are required to create/break these relationships?" [Yourdon 1994]. For example, each instance of an AUTHORIZED-USER is related to an instance of a RENTAL-CUSTOMER. By including the methods addUser and deleteUser in RENTAL-CUSTOMER we design RENTAL-CUSTOMER to create/break this relationship.

3. As you examine the attributes of each class, ask, "Do any other objects need to use this attribute? What method allows these other objects to use the attribute?" For example, each instance of an RO-LINE needs to use an instance of a TAPE Title attribute. Including the method reportTitle in TAPE allows an instance of a TAPE to communicate its Title to an instance of an RO-LINE.

4. Act out the use case to gain a better understanding of how objects will collaborate. Assign each design team member to play the role of an object class—someone should play the role of an RO-LINE, someone else the role of a RENTAL-ORDER, a third person the role

of a RENTAL-TAPE, and so on. Then walk through the Rental Customer Rents Rental Tape(s) use case. Doing so will help you to understand the behaviors (methods) that must be performed and to determine which class is logically responsible for each method.

A word of caution as you apply strategies 2 and 3: do not confuse the relations defined in Chapter 9 with object attributes. The classes there evolved as Victoria and Denny continued working with ETG users to design the system. Also, object classes, as implemented in an OO programming language or database management system do not use foreign keys; they use pointers to relate one object instance to another object instance. Therefore, although the *relation* RENTAL-CUSTOMER was defined as including the EmpNumber as a foreign key, EmpNumber is not an attribute of the *object class* RENTAL-CUSTOMER.

Instead, as indicated in strategy 2, you need to define a method for relating an EMPLOYEE instance to a RENTAL-CUSTOMER instance. For example, the method approveApplicant contained in EMPLOYEE could be used to create this relationship. Similarly, in Chapter 9, the relation RENTAL-TAPE was defined as including RentalCategory as a foreign key. Again, you would not include RentalCategory as an attribute of RENTAL-TAPE, but you would define a method—for example, assignCategory—for creating this relationship. Figure 10.15 illustrates how relationships are created and broken via methods.

Step 2: Define Methods and Assign to Object Classes

List the classes and assign each automated behavior to a class. For example, Table 10.5 lists the rental order processing behaviors for which each of the classes used in ETG's rental order processing system is responsible; it also gives the name of the method that performs this behavior. A few guidelines will help you assign methods to classes:

1. Each class specifies the kinds of things its instances can know (attributes) and do (methods). Keep in mind that an object instance is an abstraction; it is not a human

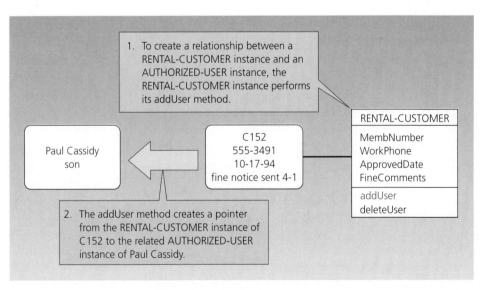

FIGURE 10.15 Illustration of object method creating a relationship

TABLE 10.5 Behaviors and methods of each class in the Rental Customer Rents Rental Tape(s) use case

Entity Class	Behaviors	Methods
EMPLOYEE	◆ Verify employee number	isEmployee
RENTAL-CUSTOMER	◆ Verify membership number	isMember
	◆ Determine membership number from phone number	getMembNumber(WorkPhone)
	◆ Determine if fines are unpaid	hasFines
	◆ Report fines	reportFineComments
	◆ Relate to fines incurred	incurFine(FINE)
	◆ Pay fine	payFines(FINE, FINE-PAYMENT)
	◆ Pay for order	makePayment(ORDER-PAYMENT)
	◆ Authorize membership user	addUser(USER)
ORDER	◆ Set order number	setOrderNumber(OrderNumber)
	◆ Set order date	setOrderDate(OrderDate)
	◆ Relate to Employee	assignEmployee(EMPLOYEE)
	◆ Cancel order	cancelOrder
RENTAL-ORDER	◆ Relate to RENTAL-CUSTOMER instance	AssignCustomer(RENTAL-CUSTOMER)
	◆ Add an RO-LINE instance (i.e., relate to RO-LINE instance)	addLineItem
	◆ Calculate order total	calculateTotal
	◆ Print rental-order form	printForm
RO-LINE	◆ Accept stock number (i.e., relate to RENTAL-TAPE instance)	assignRentalTape(RENTAL-TAPE)
RENTAL-TAPE	◆ Verify stock number	isTape
	◆ Change status	setStatus(Status)
	◆ Relate to TAPE instance	assignTape(TAPE)
	◆ Relate to RENTAL-CATEGORY instance	assignCategory(RENTAL-CATEGORY)
TAPE	◆ Report title	reportTitle
RENTAL-CATEGORY	◆ Report rental fee	reportFee
	◆ Calculate due date	determineDueDate
FINE	◆ Report fines	reportFines(RENTAL-CUSTOMER)
	◆ Determine late fee	calculateLateFee
	◆ Assign rewinding fee	setRewindingFee(RewindingFee)
	◆ Remove paid fines	removeFine
AUTHORIZED-USER	◆ Verify authorized user status	displayUsers(RENTAL-CUSTOMER)
PAYMENT	◆ Accept payment method and amount	setPayMethod(PayMethod)
		setPayAmount(PayAmount)
	◆ Relate to EMPLOYEE instance	assignEmployee(EMPLOYEE)
ORDER-PAYMENT	◆ Pay for order (i.e., relate to ORDER instance)	pay(ORDER)
FINE-PAYMENT	◆ Pay for fine (i.e., relate to FINE instance)	pay(FINE)

being or any kind of physical, tangible entity. Instead, it is the computer system's representation of the data about and the automated functions perfomed by this abstraction.

2. Methods, the automated behaviors performed by object instances, should be distributed fairly evenly among classes so that you avoid having a few "control" objects and many "data" objects [Taylor 1995].

3. When possible, a method should be assigned to the class that knows the attributes needed to perform the method; when no single class knows all the attributes used in the method, you should assign the method to the class that would logically be expected to perform the method. Then you create additional methods to give this class access to the other classes' attributes. For example, one of the classes used in the Rental Customer Rents Rental Tape(s) use case must be responsible for determining the due date of each rental tape. The RO-LINE class lists DueDate as an attribute and, on first glance, seems the logical choice for housing the determineDueDate method. However, it would be better to assign this method to RENTAL-CATEGORY and have RO-LINE send a message to the appropriate RENTAL-CATEGORY instance asking it to perform the method and to return a value for DueDate in response. Why? Because the value of DueDate is dependent on the value of RentalPeriod within a particular RENTAL-CATEGORY instance. The RENTAL-CATEGORY instance knows the value of RentalPeriod; thus, it is the better choice.[4]

4. Methods used to create and break relationships should be assigned to the class that controls the relationship. If you recall the discussion of existence dependency in Technical Module D, the concept of a "controlling class" makes sense. Assume that an instance of CLASS-1 can exist without being related to an instance of CLASS-2, but an instance of CLASS-2 cannot exist without being related to an instance of CLASS-1. In this case, CLASS-1 is the controlling class. For example, a RENTAL-CUSTOMER instance can exist without being related to an AUTHORIZED-USER instance, but the reverse is not true. Thus, RENTAL-CUSTOMER is the controlling class in this relationship and should contain methods for making and breaking the relationship to AUTHORIZED-USER instances..

5. A method that changes the state of an object should be assigned to that object's class. For example, the method setStatus changes the status of a RENTAL-TAPE instance; thus setStatus should be assigned to the RENTAL-TAPE class.

The process of defining methods and assigning them to classes often will lead you to rethink your definition of classes. You may end up adding classes, deleting classes, or merging two or more classes into a single class. Figuring out which methods should be performed by

---

4   You may wonder why not just write an IF-THEN-ELSE method in RO-LINE that determines DueDate? If Category = N then DueDate = Today +1 else if Category = S then . . . . Yourdon explains why this is not a good choice: "If the method involves a lot of code, look at it closely; if it contains IF-THEN-ELSE statements . . . it's a *strong* indication that the method's class has been poorly factored—that is, procedural code is being used to make decisions that should have been made in the inheritance hierarchy (i.e., by creating subclasses)" [1994, pp. 308–309].

each class is more an art than a science. You may do well to follow Peter Coad's advice: "When in doubt, act it out!"[5]

Check Your Understanding 10-5

Based on the following short statements describing the function of a method, determine to which class it should be assigned.

1. The method reportStatus returns the value "overdue" or "paid" to indicate that an instance of ACCOUNT has missed or made a payment. Should this method be assigned to ACCOUNT or to PAYMENT? Why?

2. The method addAccount creates a relationship between a CUSTOMER instance and an ACCOUNT instance. Each CUSTOMER object can be related to zero or many ACCOUNT objects, but each ACCOUNT object must be related to exactly one CUSTOMER object. Should this method be assigned to ACCOUNT or to CUSTOMER? Why?

3. The method calculateExtPrice multiplies the quantity of a line item by the price of the line item. Quantity is an attribute of LINE-ITEM; Price is an attribute of PRODUCT. Should this method be assigned to LINE-ITEM or to PRODUCT? Why?

Step 3: Extend Object Relationship Model to Include Methods and Create Class Specifications

The next step is to extend the object relationship model to include methods. First, any additional or modified classes defined during use-case analysis are added to the object relationship model. Then methods are assigned to the classes chosen during step 2. The extended object relationship model segment for Rental Customer Rents Rental Tape(s) is shown in Figure 10.16. Notice that methods are shown in the bottom segment of the object class and begin with a lower-case verb followed by an upper-case noun. This is the syntax convention adopted in this textbook; other conventions include using all lowercase letters and separating the words of a method name with hyphens (e.g., report-status [Yourdon 1994]), or with an underscore (e.g., report_status [Booch 1993]), or with spaces (e.g., report status [Rumbaugh 1991]). The syntax itself is not important for our purposes; it is just a way of distinguishing methods (doSomething) from attributes (ClassTrait).

After you have extended your object relationship model, you specify each class and its relationships, attributes, and methods in a **class specification**, which is essentially the OO equivalent of a data dictionary. For each class, you specify the following:

◆ Object class name.

◆ Business definition of the object class—what it means to the user.

---

[5] In addition to coauthoring an OO methodology with Edward Yourdon, Peter Coad is also the creator of *The Object Game*, a videotape and game pieces designed to illustrate object thinking. At several points in the videotape, Coad encourages his designers to play the role of objects and to act out the behaviors each must perform.

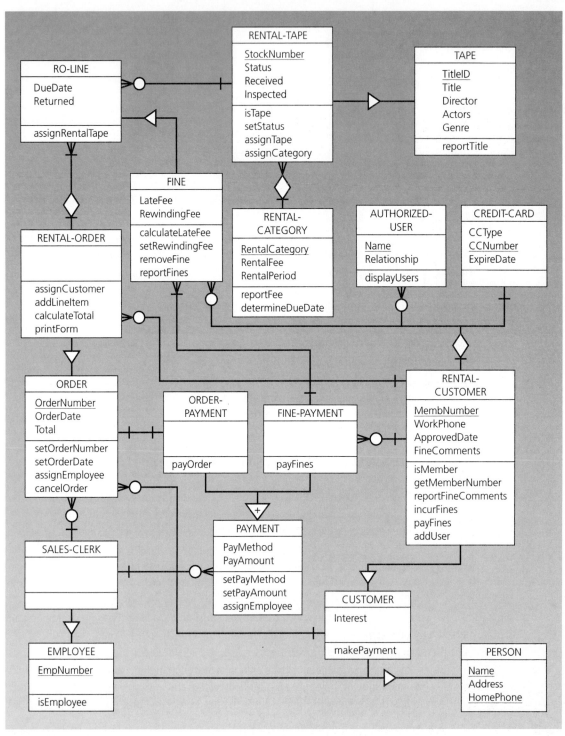

FIGURE 10.16 Extended object relationship model (with methods) for Rental Customer Rents Rental Tape(s)

◆ Relationships, noting the classes that this class collaborates with and any specialization or composition relationships.

◆ Attribute definitions, similar to those provided in a data dictionary; at minimum, the data type (e.g., currency, text, yes/no, and so on) should be indicated.

◆ Service interface, listing the class's public methods.

◆ Method definitions, including how the method is performed and what data it needs; structured text is useful here.

An example of a class specification is given in Table 10.6.

Step 4: Reflect Classes, Methods, and Messages in Formal Use Cases

Now that you know the classes, attributes, and methods required for each use case, you can revise your use cases to reflect them. For example, the Rental Customer Rents Rental Tape(s) use case can be revised as shown in Table 10.7 on page 398.[6] In this notation, a behavior requiring object communication is indicated as <receiving class>, <method>. When you walk through a specific instance of the formal use case, you would use the message notation described earlier, substituting the object instance for the <receiving class>.

Step 5: Walk Through Formal Use Cases to Verify Design

Your final task is to walk through each formal use-case description to verify that the appropriate classes, attributes, and methods have been designed to perform the use case. Assign class roles, and act out the use case. You may find it helpful to pass a token between class-role actors to simulate the flow of control from object to object.

10.4 ◆ CRITERIA FOR EVALUATING SYSTEM BEHAVIOR DESIGN

Just as we needed criteria by which to evaluate the quality of a data structure design, we also need criteria by which to evaluate the quality of a behavior design. There are numerous ways to design an information system to solve a problem, but some designs are better than others. As noted earlier, the traditional approach, because of its longevity, has provided fairly rigorous and reliable "goodness" criteria. In contrast, the OO approach, because of its relative youth, has so far established what some refer to as a "tribal folklore" [Yourdon 1994]. Nonetheless, this "tribal folklore" provides some insights into what good OO designs look like.

As with all things, you must weigh quality against cost. Your goal as you design system behaviors is to maximize goodness while minimizing cost. In other words, you want to design the best system you can, given your budget and schedule constraints. Another goal as you design an information system is to weigh present functionality against future adaptability and maintainability. If a system must be delivered in three months, present functionality will win, hands down. However, if you have the luxury of time and resources, you should

---

[6] The notation shown here for expressing formal use cases is that of Taylor [1995].

TABLE 10.6 Class specification

Class Name:	Rental-Customer
Definition:	A customer who has completed a membership application at ETG and has been approved to rent tapes.
Relationships:	is-a Customer
	has-a Credit-Card (1,1)
	has-a Authorized-User (0,N)
	has-a Fine (0,N)
	collaborates with Rental-Order, Fine-Payment

Attributes:	MembNumber	{text}
	a number that uniquely identifies each rental customer	
	WorkPhone	{text}
	the phone number at which the member can be reached during the day	
	ApprovedDate	{date}
	the date on which the member's application was approved	
	FineComments	{memo}
	comments describing attempts to collect unpaid fines	

Public Methods (Service Interface):

isMember
- Purpose: Verifies membership
- Arguments: None
- Return Value: Boolean (yes/no)

getMembNumber
- Purpose: Retrieves a membership number based on the member's work phone
- Arguments: WorkPhone
- Return Value: MembNumber

reportFineComments
- Purpose: Displays comments about attempts to collect fines
- Arguments: None
- Return Value: FineComments

incurFine
- Purpose: Creates a relationship between a FINE instance and the RENTAL-CUSTOMER instance
- Arguments: FINE
- Return Value: none

payFine
- Purpose: Creates a relationship between a FINE-PAYMENT instance and the RENTAL-CUSTOMER instance
- Arguments: FINE-PAYMENT, FINE
- Return Value: none

addUser
- Purpose: Creates a relationship between an AUTHORIZED-USER instance and the RENTAL-CUSTOMER instance
- Arguments: AUTHORIZED-USER
- Return Value: none

Structured Text:

Repeat
  read RENTAL-CUSTOMER record;
  if membNumber = scannedNumber then
    membership-is-valid;
until membership-is-valid or end-of-file;
end;

TABLE 10.7 Formal specification of the Rental Customer Rents Rental Tape(s) use case

(A sales clerk calls up the Rental Order screen and enters his or her employee number.)
    EMPLOYEE, isEmployee
    RENTAL-ORDER, assignEmployee(EMPLOYEE)
    RENTAL-ORDER, setOrderNumber   [method inherited from ORDER]
    RENTAL-ORDER, setOrderDate   [method inherited from ORDER]

(The sales clerk scans the membership card bar code.)
    RENTAL-CUSTOMER, isMember
    RENTAL-ORDER, assignCustomer(RENTAL-CUSTOMER)
    RENTAL-CUSTOMER, hasFines

(If the rental customer has fines, the system displays fines and comments.)
    FINE, reportFines(RENTAL-CUSTOMER)
    RENTAL-CUSTOMER, reportFineComments

(If the customer wants to pay fines, the sales clerk selects the Process Fines option.)
    RENTAL-CUSTOMER, payFines(FINE, FINE-PAYMENT)
    FINE-PAYMENT, assignEmployee(EMPLOYEE)   [method inherited from PAYMENT]
    FINE-PAYMENT, setPayMethod(PayMethod)   [method inherited from PAYMENT]
    FINE-PAYMENT, setPayAmount(PayAmount)   [method inherited from PAYMENT]
    FINE-PAYMENT, payFine(FINE)
    FINE, removeFine

(If the customer claims to be an authorized user, the sales clerk selects an option to display authorized users.)
    AUTHORIZED-USER, displayUsers(RENTAL-CUSTOMER)

(The sales clerk scans the rental tape bar code.)
    RENTAL-TAPE, isTape
    RENTAL-ORDER, addLineItem
    RO-LINE, addTape(RENTAL-TAPE)
    RENTAL-TAPE, reportTitle   [method inherited from TAPE]
    RENTAL-CATEGORY, reportFee
    RENTAL-CATEGORY, determineDueDate
    RENTAL-TAPE, setStatus('Rented')

(The sales clerk indicates that there are no more tapes to process.)
    RENTAL-ORDER, calculateTotal

(The sales clerk informs the customer of the amount due and processes the payment.)
    RENTAL-CUSTOMER, makePayment(ORDER-PAYMENT)   [method inherited from
                                                                       CUSTOMER]
    ORDER-PAYMENT, assignEmployee(EMPLOYEE)   [method inherited from PAYMENT]
    ORDER-PAYMENT, setPayMethod(PayMethod)   [method inherited from PAYMENT]
    ORDER-PAYMENT, setPayAmount(PayAmount)   [method inherited from PAYMENT]
    ORDER-PAYMENT, payOrder(ORDER)

(The sales clerk prints the order form.)
    RENTAL-ORDER, printForm

always strive to design a system that will be adaptable and easy to maintain. Indeed, future adaptability and maintainability—more specifically, reusability—are especially important in OO analysis and design. The time and energy invested in designing reusable classes will pay huge dividends in future projects.

Here we discuss several criteria used to evaluate system behavior design [Yourdon 1994]. The first two, coupling and cohesiveness, have already been discussed in terms of traditional system behavior design—that is, program structure charts.

COUPLING

A high-quality system behavior design minimizes coupling—whether between modules in a program structure chart or between object classes in an object relationship model. The more loosely coupled the modules or objects are, the greater their reusability. You have already learned some guidelines to reduce coupling in program structure charts. Guidelines for reducing coupling in OO behavior designs include the following:

◆ No message should require more than three parameters. In other words, you should not have to pass a lot of data between objects.

◆ No messages should be sent from a subclass to access data defined in a superclass. Inheritance takes care of this data-sharing automatically.

◆ Coupling is a natural side effect of specialization and composition relationships. However, collaboration relationships should not be so strong that CLASS-1 is useless without CLASS-2.

COHESIVENESS

A high-quality system behavior design maximizes cohesiveness. A cohesive design specifies only one function per module or one function per method. The function of each module or method should be clearly expressed as verb plus object. For example, instead of a method called completeRO-Footer that also prints the rental order, two separate methods should be created for these two functions if cohesiveness is to be maximized. In addition, in the OO approach, overriding of attributes and methods defined in a superclass should be a relatively rare phenomenon. If you design many subclasses that override their superclasses, you may be misunderstanding the use of inheritance and the specialization relationship.

CLARITY

A high-quality design speaks for itself. Can someone other than the designer read the program structure chart or formal use-case specification? The design should not rely on hidden assumptions or tacit knowledge. A clear design also uses consistent syntax and vocabulary. A powerful advantage of the OO approach is its model consistency; the same basic model is used throughout analysis and design and carried into implementation, thus improving clarity.

COMPLEXITY VERSUS REUSABILITY

In Shakespeare's *Romeo and Juliet*, Mercutio, having been stabbed in a sword fight, comments (rather sardonically!) that his wound is "not so deep as a well nor so wide as a church-door, but 'tis enough, t'will serve." Generally speaking, an OO design should embody the same characteristics: neither too deep (too many layers of specialization) nor too wide (too little specialization). A general guideline is that the design should have no more than 7 ±2 levels of specialization. You have to weigh the reusability achieved by "deep" designs against the complexity that these designs create.

SIMPLICITY

An object class that contains 20 attributes and 30 methods is not simple. Too many methods suggest an application-specific definition of object classes, which yields classes that are difficult to reuse. A general guideline is that each class should have at most five to six methods; and whatever the number of methods, the number of attributes should be at most twice the number of methods. Each method (in the traditional approach, each module) should perform a function describable in less than one page of C++ code (or ten lines of Smalltalk!). Another guideline cautions you to avoid procedure-focused IF-THEN-ELSE statements in the definition of methods. If such selection constructs seem to be needed, you probably need to create subclasses and let inheritance do its job.

COMPACTNESS

As you have seen in the ETG case, even a fairly simple system can require many classes. If such a simple system requires so many classes, imagine designing the behaviors of an information system to control the space shuttle! This criterion is related to the complexity versus reusability trade-off, in that it acknowledges that the more classes a system has, the more complex the system is. Thus, you should avoid inventing unnecessary classes.

"ACT-ABILITY"

The play's the thing! A high-quality OO design can be acted out by humans role-playing objects. A high-quality traditional design can be verified in a structured walkthrough. If you have effectively modeled the system's business domain, the mappings between real-world objects and system objects should be transparent.

◆ REVIEW OF CHAPTER LEARNING OBJECTIVES

1. *Compare and contrast the traditional and object-oriented approaches to system behavior analysis and design.*

   The traditional approach to system behavior analysis and design uses physical data flow diagrams (DFDs) to design the manual and automated behaviors of a proposed system.

Then these DFDs are partitioned to identify programs and determine whether each program should be implemented as a batch process or a real-time process. Finally, each program's functions are specified using program structure charts and structured-text process descriptions. In the object-oriented approach, use cases are analyzed to identify manual and automated system behaviors. Automated behaviors are transformed into class methods and messages, which are specified using structured text.

The traditional approach offers several advantages: mature techniques, well-defined quality criteria, and CASE tool support. However, its disconnection between data and behaviors requires that a systems analyst prepare different models to specify the data and software components. In contrast, the OO approach simply adds methods to the model of classes, attributes, and relationships created during system data-structure analysis and design. Because data (attributes) and behaviors (methods) are encapsulated in objects, a single construct—an object class—is used to specify both the data structures and the behaviors of the new system. Thus, model consistency is maintained as development proceeds from analysis through design to implementation.

2. *Explain the purpose of physical DFDs in system behavior analysis and design.*

Physical DFDs are used to specify how the IPOSC functions will be implemented in a new information system. They specify system behaviors in terms of the technology used to perform the behaviors. Leveled physical DFDs are analyzed to identify manual and automated behaviors and to partition automated behaviors into programs.

3. *Discuss the characteristics that differentiate a physical DFD from a logical DFD.*

A physical DFD differs from a logical DFD in several ways. First, logical DFDs describe system functions independent of the technology used to implement these functions; in contrast, physical DFDs are created with the implementation technology in mind. Second, physical DFDs distinguish manual processes from automated processes. Third, the data flows and data stores of a physical DFD are labeled using the field and file names selected during database design. Fourth, physical DFDs more clearly indicate behavior sequence and specify control processes, temporary data stores, and transaction audit files.

4. *Partition a physical DFD to group manual procedures and to define discrete programs.*

A partition segments a physical DFD into discrete application programs that will be executed to support a business process. If two processes are performed at different times or by different users, they will usually require separate programs; thus, they should be segmented into different partitions. Typically, each process bubble on the Level 0 physical DFD can be treated as a separate partition. However, lower-level DFDs must also be studied to determine if some of their processes will require different programs and to group manual processes into procedures. Each partition of an automated process is further analyzed to determine whether real-time or batch processing is appropriate. Each partition of a manual process is documented in a manual procedure description.

5. *Convert a physical DFD into a program structure chart or structured text process descriptions.*

A program structure chart specifies the structure and functions of an application program. Similar to a DFD, a structure chart uses the top-down approach and functional decomposition to define a hierarchy of program modules. A physical DFD is transformed into a program structure chart through transform analysis (segmenting sequential DFD processes into input, processing, and output modules) and transaction analysis (segmenting DFD processes into alternate flows of control). Generally, each DFD process bubble will appear as a module in the corresponding program structure chart.

Structured text uses standard constructs (sequence, selection, and iteration) to specify system behaviors and business rules in more detail. Both manual and automated behaviors can be defined using structured text. In particular, the processing internal to every program structure chart module should be defined using structured-text process descriptions.

6. *Explain encapsulation and its impact on object-oriented system behavior design.*

Encapsulation means that no other object can directly read or change another object's data; only the containing object can manipulate its own data. Because data is "hidden" from other objects, each object class must define methods (a) to manipulate its own data for its own purposes (private methods) and (b) to report data to or perform manipulations of its data for another object (public methods).

The effect of encapsulation is that objects must have some way to communicate so that they can request services. Messages between objects are usually the stimulus that triggers a method to execute. Thus, a vital activity in OO system behavior design is specifying formal use cases that define sequences of behavior—that is, the messages to be sent and the methods to be performed.

7. *Specify system behaviors in use cases and object relationship models.*

Use cases provide a logical view of the behaviors an information system must support. A major activity in OO system behavior design is transforming these use cases into a design that specifies object class methods and the sequencing of messages and methods. This transformation begins by analyzing use cases to identify system behaviors; the object relationship model is also examined to identify behaviors required to manipulate attributes and to make/break relationships. Once identified, manual behaviors are grouped into procedures and then documented in manual procedures descriptions; automated behaviors become methods that are assigned to classes. Some guidelines for assigning methods to classes include the following: (1) assign private methods to the class that knows the attributes needed to perform the method, (2) assign a method that changes the state of an object to the class whose object instance is affected by the method, and (3) assign methods that make/break relationships to the class that controls the relationship. The final step is to revise the object relationship model to include methods.

8. *Create class specifications.*

   The relationships, attributes, and methods of each class are documented in a class specification. For each class, the following specifications should be given: class name and business definition; collaboration, specialization, and composition relationships; attribute definitions; service interface; and structured text descriptions of method functions.

9. *Discuss several criteria for evaluating system behavior design quality.*

   The criteria for evaluating system behavior design quality include coupling, cohesiveness, clarity, complexity versus reusability, simplicity, compactness, and "act-ability." A good design is loosely coupled, meaning that data flows between structure chart modules and messages between classes are minimized. A good design is also cohesive, meaning that each module or method specifies just one function that can be clearly expressed as verb plus object. A good design is also clear; it contains no hidden assumptions and uses consistent syntax and vocabulary. In addition, it balances complexity and reusability; a structure chart or a class hierarchy with 20 levels is probably too complex. A good design is simple; the function of each module or method can be expressed in a page of code or less. And a good design is compact; this criterion reminds you that small is beautiful and that a design with more modules or objects is not necessarily better than one with fewer modules or objects. Finally, a good design can be acted out; you should be able to "walk through" the flow of control in a program structure chart and mimic the flow of messages and the execution of methods in a formal use case.

◆ KEY TERMS

class specification	partition	service (or public) method
cohesiveness	physical data flow diagram	service interface
control flow	(DFD)	structured text
coupling	polymorphism	structured walkthrough
data flow	private method	system behavior
encapsulation	process	system behavior analysis
iteration	program structure chart	and design
message	selection	transaction analysis
module	sequence	transform analysis

◆ DISCUSSION QUESTIONS

1. Compare and contrast the modeling of data and behaviors in the traditional versus the OO approach.

2. List and discuss three advantages of the traditional approach to system behavior design.

3. Explain the benefits of the consistent models that characterize the OO approach to system behavior design.

4. How does a physical DFD differ from a logical DFD? Why are these differences important in system behavior design?

5. How are physical DFDs used to identify the application programs required by a system?

6. In what circumstances is real-time processing required? In what circumstances is batch processing a viable alternative?

7. Explain each of the following program structure chart constructs:
   a. Module
   b. Data flow
   c. Control flow
   d. Looping
   e. Selection

8. Discuss some guidelines for minimizing coupling and maximizing cohesiveness in program design.

9. Explain each of the following structured-text constructs, and give an example of a structured-text expression using each:
   a. Sequence
   b. Selection
   c. Iteration

10. What is encapsulation? How does it affect OO system behavior design? Discuss two benefits of encapsulation.

11. Distinguish between a private method and a public method. Which type of method is part of a class's service interface?

12. What is polymorphism? How does it contribute to design simplicity and reusability?

13. Explain the five-step process of identifying and specifying object behaviors.

14. Discuss two strategies for identifying behaviors.

15. Discuss three guidelines for assigning methods to classes.

16. Describe the kinds of information provided in a class specification.

17. Explain each of the following criteria for evaluating behavior design, and provide a guideline for satisfying each criterion:
   a. Coupling
   b. Cohesiveness
   c. Clarity
   d. Complexity versus reusability
   e. Simplicity
   f. Compactness
   g. "Act-ability"

◆ EXERCISES

1. Create a Level 0 physical DFD to design the IPOSC functions of Bebop Records' order processing system.

Bebop Records is a mail-order company that distributes CDs and tapes at discount prices to record club members. Order processing clerks man a bank of telephones to receive phone orders from customers 24 hours a day. When a caller places an order, the order processing clerk verifies that the caller is a club member by checking the Member Master file. If the caller is not a member, the clerk calls up the Create New Member screen and solicits appropriate data from the caller. The system assigns a membership number to the new member record and saves it to the Member Master file. To process the order, the clerk calls up the Enter Order screen, enters the order data (including item number, which is verified by the Item Master file), and saves it to the Daily Orders Transaction file. At regular intervals throughout the day, the system accesses the Daily Orders Transaction file to generate an invoice and shipping list for each order, which are printed and forwarded to Order Fulfillment.

2. Create a Level 0 physical DFD to design the IPOSC processes of All-American Bank's new-accounts system.

When a new customer opens an account with All-American Bank, he or she provides the bank with a completed new-account application form. A clerk processes the application by calling up the Create New Account screen and entering the data from the application form. The system assigns an account number and saves the account record to the Accounts Master file. At the end of each day, the Accounts Master file is accessed to print a New Accounts Transaction list, which is sent to the New Accounts Department, and to extract customer data, which is saved to the Customer Master file.

3. Create a Level 0 physical DFD to document the major processes of Delta Products' order fulfillment system. Then create a balanced Level 1 physical DFD that more fully documents the IPOSC functions of creating a sales order record.

Delta Products Corporation is a major vendor of office supplies, furniture, and equipment. Delta's sales representatives call on customers to take orders. The sales reps write up the orders on sales order forms and turn them in to a sales order processing (SOP) clerk at the regional center. The SOP clerk calls up the Order Entry screen and enters the order details. To create the order header, the clerk enters a customer account number, which the system uses to verify that the customer exists (by consulting the Customer Master file) and to retrieve the appropriate billing and shipping addresses for the order header. In addition, the system assigns an order number and order date to each order.

To create order line items, the clerk enters the quantity and product number. The system uses the product number to access the appropriate record in the Product Master file, filling in the description, unit of measure (e.g., each, case, etc.), and unit price of each item. The system also determines if the item is in stock. If the item is in stock, the system automatically calculates the extended price of each line item; if the item is not in stock, the system notes "back-ordered" on the item line and generates an Out Of Stock notice record, which notes the customer account number, product number, and quantity desired; this record is saved to the Stock-Out Transaction file.

To create the order footer, the system calculates the order subtotal and applies appropriate customer discounts by accessing the discount rate from the Customer Master file. The system also calculates sales tax on the discounted price by consulting the Sales Tax Master file to determine the appropriate tax rate for the customer's state. Finally, the system calculates the order total by adding the discounted subtotal and sales tax. The system saves a record of the order to the Sales Order Transaction file.

At the end of each day, the system accesses the Sales Order Transaction file to extract data to print a picking slip and a packing list for each order, which are forwarded to the warehouse. Stock pickers use the picking slip to select items from warehouse shelves, placing ordered items into boxes along with the packing list. The boxed items and packing list are held for shipment the next morning, usually via UPS.

4. Create a Level 0 physical DFD to design the *major* processes of ABC's supply requisition system; then create a balanced Level 1 physical DFD to specify more fully the IPOSC functions associated with the buyer (given in the second paragraph).

When employees at ABC Corp. need to order supplies, they complete a purchase requisition form by calling up the Create Requisition screen and filling in requisition details, including product number (verified against the Product Master file). The system assigns a requisition number, and the data are saved to the Requisition Transaction file. Before the requisition can be filled, a supervisor must review the requisition by calling up the Approve Requisition screen and then must enter a code to approve it. The system updates the Requisition Transaction file to reflect this approval and also writes a record to the Requisition Audit file.

Each day, a buyer in ABC's Purchasing Department accesses each approved requisition from the Requisition file by calling up the Fill Requisition screen and using the system to verify the requisition's approver code against the Authorized Approver Code Master file. If the code is invalid, the requisition record is flagged to signal an error. At the end of each day, the system runs a program to print an exception report listing invalid requisitions for manual investigation. If the code is valid, the buyer then accesses a list of approved vendors from the Vendor Master file. The buyer selects a vendor and calls that vendor to establish item prices. Then the buyer adds the selected vendor number, agreed item prices, and purchase order number to the requisition. Finally, the system updates the Requisition Transaction file, writes a record of the purchase order to the Purchase Order Master file, and prints the purchase order, which is mailed to the vendor.

5. Partition the Level 0 DFD you created in Exercise 1. Determine whether each program should be implemented using batch or real-time processing. Justify your choice.

6. Partition the Level 0 DFD you created in Exercise 2. Determine whether each program should be implemented using batch or real-time processing. Justify your choice.

7. Partition the Level 0 DFD you created in Exercise 3. Determine whether each program should be implemented using batch or real-time processing. Justify your choice.

8. Partition the Level 0 DFD you created in Exercise 4. Determine whether each program should be implemented using batch or real-time processing. Justify your choice.

9. Create a program structure chart to design a program to support the Create Order process of the Level 1 physical DFD you created in Exercise 3.

10. Create a program structure chart to design a program to support the Fill Requisition process of the Level 1 physical DFD you created in Exercise 4.

11. Select three modules in the program structure chart you created for Exercise 9 and write structured-text process descriptions to define the internal processing of each module.

12. Select three modules in the program structure chart you created for Exercise 10 and write structured-text process descriptions to define the internal processing of each module.

13. Examine the process description provided in Exercise 3 and create a Customer Places Order use case similar to the one shown in Figure 10.1. Your use case should be a logical view of the system, so you can ignore screens, files, and so forth.
   a. Identify the classes involved in the use case.
   b. Identify the system behaviors in the use case and determine whether each behavior is manual or automated.
   c. For each automated behavior, specify a method and assign it to one of the classes. Justify your assignment.
   d. Select two of your classes and write a class specification for each.

14. Examine the process description provided in Exercise 4 and create a Buyer Fills Requisition use case similar to the one shown in Figure 10.1. Your use case should be a logical view of the system, so you can ignore screens, files, and so forth.
   a. Identify the classes involved in the use case.
   b. Identify the system behaviors in the use case and determine whether each behavior is manual or automated.
   c. For each automated behavior, specify a method and assign it to one of the classes. Justify your assignment.
   d. Select two of your classes and write a class specification for each.

◆ REFERENCES

Booch, G. *Object-Oriented Analysis and Design with Applications.* Redwood City, CA: Benjamin/Cummings, 1993.

Coad, P. *The Object Game.* Austin, TX: Object International, Inc. This is a video plus game pieces that Coad designed to promote object thinking. Copies of the game can be purchased at specialty bookstores or by contacting Object International at 1-800-OOA-2-OOP.

Jacobson, I., M. Christerson, P. Jonsson, and G. Overgaard. *Object-Oriented Software Engineering: A Use Case Driven Approach.* Reading, MA: Addison-Wesley, 1992.

Jacobson, I., M. Ericsson, and A. Jacobson. *The Object Advantage: Business Process Reengineering with Object Technology.* Workingham, England: Addison-Wesley, 1995.

Jordan, E. W., and J. J. Machesky. *Systems Development: Requirements, Evaluation, Design, and Implementation*. Boston, MA: PWS-Kent, 1990.

Martin, J., and J. Odell. *Object-Oriented Analysis and Design*. Englewood Cliffs, NJ: Prentice-Hall, 1992.

Rumbaugh, J., M. Blaha, W. Premerlani, F. Eddy, and W. Lorensen. *Object-Oriented Modeling and Design*. Englewood Cliffs, NJ: Prentice-Hall, 1991.

Taylor, D. *Object-Oriented Technology: A Manager's Guide*. Reading, MA: Addison-Wesley, 1990.

Taylor, D. *Business Engineering with Object Technology*. New York: John Wiley and Sons, 1995.

Yourdon, E. *Object-Oriented Systems Design: An Integrated Approach*. Englewood Cliffs, NJ: Yourdon Press/Prentice-Hall, 1994.

Yourdon Inc. *Yourdon Systems Method: Model-Driven Systems Development*. Englewood Cliffs, NJ: PTR Prentice-Hall, 1993.

White, I. *Using the Booch Method: A Rational Approach*. Redwood City, CA: Benjamin/Cummings, 1994.

ANALYZING AND DESIGNING SYSTEM INTERFACES

Iterative Analysis, Design, Preliminary Construction, and Review

1. Analyze system structure and behavior.
   a. Analyze system data structures.
   b. Analyze system behavior.
   c. *Analyze system interfaces.*

2. Design system structure and behavior.
   a. Design system data structures.
   b. Design system behavior.
   c. *Design system interfaces.*

3. Construct prototype for user review.

4. Conduct user review.

5. Repeat steps 1–4, if changes are needed.

JAD WORKSHOP EXCERPT:
ANALYZING AND DESIGNING ETG'S USER INTERFACES

"Well, we've reached the last task of this JAD workshop—preliminary design of the user interfaces," Victoria said. "Contrary to what the agenda says, Denny's going to man the computer and wear his scribe hat, and I'm going to lead us through this task. Denny will be capturing your comments and working in the background so that we can prototype one or two screens for you this morning."

"You mean you're going to start actually building the system already?" Paul marveled, turning his attention to Denny.

"In only a very rudimentary way," Denny responded. "During the break, I used Access to do a preliminary design of a few of the tables. I want to use these tables to give you a sneak preview of the system's interfaces before we bring down the curtain on this workshop. We'll be showing you all the interfaces during the coming weeks as we evolve the system."

"Speaking of 'all the interfaces,'" Victoria interrupted. "Creating a list of these interfaces is our first activity. User interfaces include any documents and reports used or created by the system; data entry screens and menus are also user interfaces. Once again, we'll analyze the order processing use cases to determine the system's interfaces. Denny has displayed the Rental Customer Rents Rental Tape(s) use case that we defined earlier (see Figure 11.1). Note that several aspects of the use case are highlighted to indicate where interfaces are needed."

Use Case Name: Rental Customer Rents Rental Tape(s)
Use Case Purpose: Describes the process of renting rental tapes to rental customers
Uses: Rental Customer Pays Fines; Customer Makes Payment
Extended by: Rental Customer Rents 3/3 Rental Tapes

Typical Course of Events:

1. Use case is initiated when a customer selects rental tapes from shelves and presents membership card and selected rental tapes for checkout.
2. The rental order form header is completed, indicating a valid employee number, a valid member number, order number, and order date.
3. For each rental tape being rented, a rental order line is created, giving the stock number, title, rental category, and rental fee of each rental tape; in addition, the due date calculated for each rental tape is shown on the rental order line.
4. The rental order form footer is completed by calculating and entering a total cost for the order.
5. Customer makes payment. (See Customer Makes Payment use case.)
6. The rental order form is printed, and the customer signs it. The customer is given one copy of the form; the other copy is retained for the audit file.

Alternative Courses of Events:

Alternative A: At step 1, if a rental customer does not have the membership card, the member's telephone number can be used to determine the appropriate member number.

Alternative B: At step 2, if the customer claims to be an authorized user, the rental customer's authorized user list is displayed. If the customer is not listed, the transaction is canceled, and the membership card is confiscated.

Alternative C: At step 2, if an invalid employee number is provided, the transaction is canceled.

Alternative D: At step 2, if the rental customer provides an invalid member number, the transaction is canceled, and the membership card is confiscated. If the member number is valid but the rental customer has unpaid fines, fines are processed before the transaction proceeds. If customer is unable to pay the fines, the transaction is canceled.

Alternative E: At steps 3 and 4, if the order is a 3/3 tape rental, see Rental Customer Rents 3/3 Rental Tapes use case.

Alternative F: At step 5, if the customer cannot make payment, the transaction is canceled.

FIGURE 11.1   Rental Customer Rents Rental Tape(s) use case with Victoria's annotations

Working with the ETG users, Victoria analyzed each use case, creating a list of the interfaces in the order processing system (see Table 11.1). As each interface was identified, Victoria asked the ETG users to make preliminary design decisions, such as whether a report should be printed or displayed on screen. While they were discussing the overdue rental orders report, Linda, the company accountant, raised an issue.

"It seems to me that we haven't adequately addressed the problem of unpaid fines. I know that Paul hesitates to charge $4.50 a day for each day that a new rental tape is overdue, so waiting until customers appear in the store again to notify them that they have fines or haven't returned a tape isn't sufficient. It seems we really need several ways of processing fines. First, we need to generate a daily report that lists new tapes due back the previous day but not returned. The clerks could use this report to call customers to remind them to return their tapes. Second, we need to generate a monthly report listing unpaid fines. We can use this report to send notices to the appropriate customers."

"I think you're right, Linda. And you've described what sound like effective ways of dealing with the fines problem. But what about our 'contract' with Victoria and Denny?" Paul asked. "Aren't you adding functions that weren't defined in our list of requirements?"

"May I comment on that?" Victoria interrupted. "Recall that I said our requirements list is subject to minor changes as the system evolves. The additional requirement of creating a daily report listing overdue tapes is one of those minor changes. It doesn't require us to collect additional data or to reformulate the system significantly, and implementing such a report won't add even a half-day's work to our schedule. Linda has put forth a good idea. Don't let your concern about our 'contract' dissuade you from it."

"Then let's do it," Paul decided. "I love getting more 'oomph' for my money. If you can provide this added function at no additional cost, I'm all for it."

When the participants had finished their analysis of required interfaces, Victoria moved on to the final workshop task. "Our job now is to determine how the interfaces you've just identified should be presented; in other words, how you envision working with the system."

TABLE 11.1 User interfaces in ETG's order processing system

External Documents	Data Entry Screens	Reports*	Human-Computer Dialog
◆ Membership application form	◆ Add member	◆ Transaction summary report-P	Menu screens:
◆ Membership card	◆ Process order	◆ Overdue rentals report-P	◆ System
◆ Rental order receipt	• Sales order	◆ Cash receipts report-P	◆ Print reports
◆ Sales order receipt	• Rental order	◆ Mailing labels-P	◆ Check tape stock
◆ Fine receipt	• Find member	◆ Stock availability-S	
◆ New tape description	◆ Process return	◆ Authorized users list-S	
	◆ Process fines	◆ Fine details-S	
	◆ Update mailing list		
	◆ CRUD master files		
	◆ Add tape		

*P = printed; S = screen

Corita interrupted, "I'm not sure that's feasible. How can *we* tell *you* how to design the interfaces when we don't really know what an interface is or how to implement one?"

"I appreciate your concern, Corita," Victoria responded. "But I think you know more than you think you know. From our earlier discussions, I know that each of you has, at minimum, used a word-processing package that employed a graphical user interface. So you're familiar with menus, buttons, icons, pop-up windows, and so on. You're also familiar with the documents used or created by the order processing system; for example, the membership application and the order receipt. And you know best how you want information presented in a report and whether the report should be printed or displayed on screen.

"Your task today isn't to *create* these interfaces; that's our job. But you do know enough about what's possible—and what you want—in an interface to comment on how you'd like certain interface features and functions to look, how a document or report should be organized, and so on. You can tell us, for example, that you want certain data displayed on a screen or that you want the data displayed only if a certain function is activated and whether you want that function activated by clicking a button or selecting a command from a submenu. That's what I mean when I say 'envisioning the system interfaces.' You don't have to create them; just imagine aloud how you'd like them to look—how you envision working with the system. Okay?"

"Thanks for the reassurance, Victoria," Corita answered.

"Sounds like fun," Susan added. "Let's do it!"

"I love your 'can-do' spirit, Susan," Victoria said with a laugh. "Would you like to get us started?"

"Sure. What do you need to know?"

"Let's begin with rental order processing. A customer has just approached the sales counter with his membership card and selected tapes. What's the first thing you imagine doing?"

"I usually start with a smile and a wisecrack about his selection of tapes. You know, some of the 'personal-touch/treat-each-customer-as-special' stuff that is the heart of good customer relations."

"Okay. So you've smiled and added your personal touch. What's next?"

"Ummm . . . I do something that brings the rental order form up on the screen."

"What 'something' do you do?"

"There's a screen with a bunch of options listed. I select the one for processing a rental order, and—Presto!—the rental order form appears."

"What's on the form when it first appears?"

"Well, there has to be some way for me to enter my employee number and the customer's membership number. Do I also have to enter the order number and date?"

"You could. But it's easier to have the system assign them automatically. Do you want to see the order number and date even if the system assigns them?"

"Yeah, I guess I would. I'm used to seeing them on the paper order form. Seeing them on the screen would reassure me that the system is doing its thing."

"Okay, then we'll be sure to include them. We've agreed that the membership number will be entered by scanning a bar code on the membership card. How will you know when it's time to scan the bar code?"

"Because the rental order form doesn't appear until I've entered the employee number. If I enter a valid number, the screen appears with the cursor on the Membership Number entry field. That's my cue to scan the bar code."

"You've scanned the bar code on the customer's membership card. What happens next?"

Susan looked around the table at her fellow ETG employees. "Hey, guys, feel free to break in anytime. I'm surely not the only one here who has 'vision.'"

"I'll bite," Beto jumped in. "Maybe I haven't scanned the bar code because the customer forgot to bring his card. So . . . there's the cursor, sitting on Membership Number, but I can't enter one. The computer, being the smart guy it is, provides an alternative. Over on the right-hand side of the screen, there's a 'Get membership number' button that's active whenever the cursor is on Membership Number. So I just click the button, and a window pops up asking me to enter the customer's phone number. I do as I'm asked, and the system figures out the membership number and plunks it into the entry field for me."

As Beto talked, Helen's amazement grew. "That's great, Beto. I really like your vision of how we do that. May I add to your vision?"

"The crystal ball is all yours, Helen."

"Okay. I scan the bar code, but the computer can't match it to any membership number—maybe because there's a scratch or something on the bar code. So it displays an error message and asks me if I want to enter the membership number manually. I do, and the system uses that to bring up a match."

Paul chimed in, "Good point, Helen. That's a good backup strategy in case there's something wrong with the card. Of course, you offer to prepare a new card for the customer so that won't happen again."

"Of course. And once I've validated the membership number, the system fills in a box on the screen called 'Unpaid fines.' I inform the customer that he or she has fines, and, if the fine amount is high or if the customer wants information about the fines, I click another button called Display Fines and—to use Susan's expression—Presto! A window pops open showing details about each fine—the order number, date, tape title, type of fine, and amount. I can do the same thing if I want to see a list of authorized users. Just click a button, and a window appears with the Authorized Users list."

Victoria said, laughing, "I can see you're really getting into this!"

As the ETG users continued envisioning the new system, Victoria and Denny noted their design decisions on printed copies of each use case. They will use these notes to guide them as they prototype the interfaces.

The final session of the three-day workshop was drawing to a close. Denny wanted to be sure that the ETG users maintained their current high level of enthusiasm about the design process and the proposed system. So he decided to build a quick prototype of the Rental Order data entry screen based on the users' design decisions.

"Here's my first take on the header of the Rental Order Form data entry screen," Denny announced (see Figure 11.2). "What do you think?"

An almost unanimous "Great!" arose from the ETG users. But Linda's sharp eyes saw something that raised a question. "Why are some of the fields white and others gray?"

"Just a convention for distinguishing between data values that must be entered and those that are retrieved from the database or assigned by the system. The only data value the user enters in this header is Membership Number."

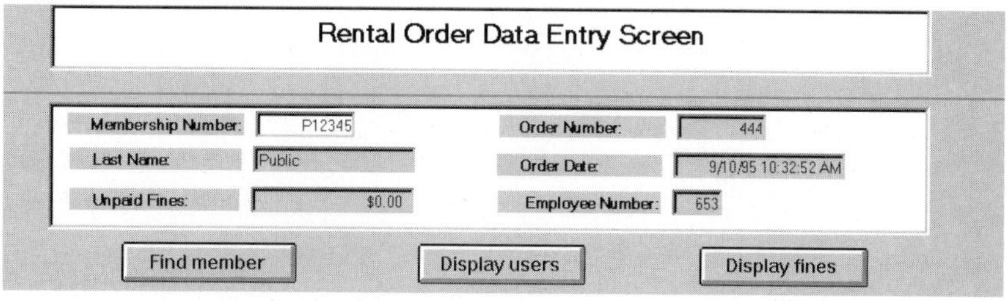

FIGURE 11.2 Denny's prototype of the rental order header

"I like your displaying the customer's name," Susan commented. "With that information, my 'personal touch' can be even more personal!"

"I'm impressed," Paul mused. "If the speed with which you implemented this screen is any indication, I bet you and Victoria will have the system up and running by this time tomorrow!"

"Whoa!," Victoria cautioned. "What you're seeing here is the equivalent of a stage prop. Until we build the database and write macros to perform system functions, that screen is just a pretty facade. It doesn't do anything except look good."

"Darn," Susan teased. "You've destroyed my 'vision' of you and Denny as superhuman beings who, with the aid of your trusty computer, create rental orders out of chaos."

A **user interface** includes the system aspects that are "visible" to users and that allow users to interact with the system's data, software, and hardware. When the first computers were developed, the user interface was decidedly unfriendly. Users stood at large panels of switches, which were connected and disconnected in complicated combinations to issue commands and input data to the computer. If you have ever seen an old-fashioned telephone switchboard, you can visualize how tedious this interaction was! And you can also understand that users had to be highly trained technicians. Soon, character-based screens were developed that listed menus of options, but required knowledge of the system's command language, or used arcane keystroke combinations to support human-computer interaction. With the advent of more sophisticated bit-mapped screens in the 1980s, the user interface became more friendly, using menus, icons, and tool bars and supporting "point-and-click" interaction.

As information systems have shifted from being primarily batch processing systems to supporting real-time processing, the importance of the user interface has increased. Batch processing systems require almost no human intervention; once a process is initiated by a human user, information technology does the rest. For example, a batch customer billing system reads input data from the Customer Account file, determines the amount to be billed, and generates a billing statement for each of the possibly thousands of customers. However, real-time processing systems usually perform one transaction at a time and require human users to select the process to be performed and to enter critical data elements. Thus, real-time processing systems are event driven, requiring many more interfaces to allow users to provide the command and data inputs that signal which event (i.e., process) will occur next.

ETG's order processing system is, for the most part, a real-time system. All order transactions are processed one at a time while the customer is in the store. Thus, this system requires several user interfaces to allow users to select what kind of process to perform (e.g., processing a rental order or processing a rental return) and to enter the data needed to perform these processes (e.g., membership number, rental tape stock number).

The chapter opening case illustrates some of the activities that must be performed to analyze and design user interfaces for a system. First, the tasks to be supported by the system are analyzed. Based on the physical data flow diagrams or use cases of the proposed system, the user interfaces required for the system are identified. Then, based on an understanding of the system's tasks and intended users, the design of each user interface is specified and aligned with the users' skill level and the logical flow of their tasks. Finally, prototypes of the interfaces are constructed and demonstrated to the users to gain their feedback.

This chapter discusses four user interface categories, the process of creating these interfaces, and several guidelines for effective interface design. After completing this chapter, you should be able to

1. Define "user interface" and describe four types, giving guidelines for designing each.

2. Define "direct manipulation" and discuss its advantages and disadvantages.

3. Describe a five-step process for analyzing and designing user interfaces.

4. Explain how to identify user interfaces from physical DFDs and use cases.

5. Create a dialog flow diagram to document the system's major interfaces and the flow of control between them.

6. Discuss four user documentation issues.

7. List some guidelines for good design and explain how to apply each guideline to user interface design.

11.1 ◈ TYPES OF USER INTERFACES

Hearing the term "user interface," you probably envision a Windows or Macintosh screen with icons, tool bars, buttons, pop-up windows, and so on. Although these screen environments are good examples of user interfaces, the term has a broader meaning when applied to business applications. A user interface is any portion of the application that allows users to input data or commands into or receive outputs from the system. Thus, user interfaces include documents, data entry screens, printed and screen reports, and the human-computer dialog, as illustrated in Figure 11.3. These user interfaces and a few guidelines for designing them are explained here. User documentation, which is also a type of user interface vital to effective human-system interaction, is discussed in Section 11.3.

EXTERNAL DOCUMENTS

External documents include all the tangible "pieces of paper" that are used to gather inputs to or that are generated as outputs from the system. Examples include application forms,

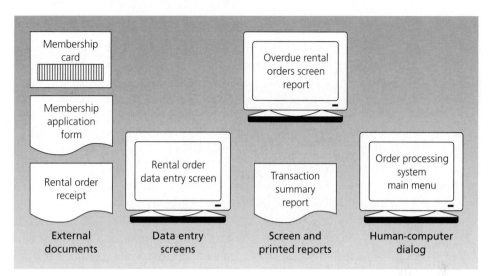

FIGURE 11.3   The four types of user interfaces

purchase orders, invoices, checks, bills of lading—the myriad documents used or generated by a system. A well-designed external document presents a positive image of the organization; it is attractive, easy to read and easy to understand. If the document requires action by its receiver (e.g., an invoice, monthly utility bill, or credit card statement that requires the receiver to make payment), it clearly indicates the action required and the process for completing the action.

DATA ENTRY SCREENS

Data entry screens are used to enter data into the system. Generally speaking, a data entry screen is needed (1) for each of the system's master files or object classes so that records or object instances can be created, edited, and deleted and (2) for each transaction the system automates so that data about the transaction can be captured by the system.

A well-designed data entry screen facilitates data entry, reduces errors, and increases productivity. One way to facilitate data entry is to have the screen mirror the layout of the source document from which data are to be entered. For example, if a medical clinic uses a Patient Information form to collect information about new patients, the layout of data elements on the Patient Information data entry screen should be similar to the layout of the form. User productivity can be increased and data entry errors reduced by minimizing the amount of data entered by the user. Figure 11.4 shows the Rental Order data entry screen Denny designed for ETG. Notice that a sales clerk need enter only three data elements to complete a rental order transaction: employee number (actually entered on an earlier screen and passed to this screen), membership number, and rental tape stock number. The other data elements are assigned by the system (e.g., order date and number, rental fee, and due date), retrieved from the system's database using record keys (e.g., rental customer name, tape title), or calculated by the system (e.g., order total).

Other guidelines for data entry screen design include the following:

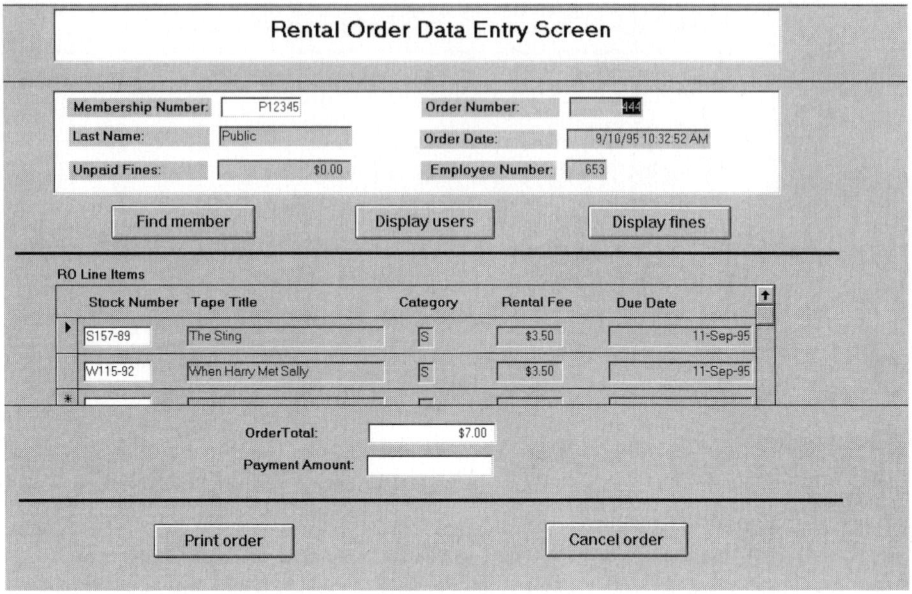

FIGURE 11.4 Rental order data entry screen for the ETG order processing system

1. Assign a title and screen number to each data entry screen. Center the title at the top of the screen; indicate the screen number, page number (if the screen runs more than one "page"), and system date in a consistent location.

2. Avoid cluttered screens. Use *white space* generously and group logically related items (e.g., all the components of an address) to increase readability. Use a top-down, left-to-right flow of user-entered items.

3. If function keys are used, provide a mapping of function keys to functions performed at the bottom of the screen.

4. Use color appropriately, generally no more than five colors per screen.

REPORTS

Reports summarize and organize data in a format meaningful to their intended users. They differ from external documents in that reports are generally intended for internal use and are produced by sorting, calculating, and compiling data stored in the system's database. Reports can be printed ("**hard copy**") or displayed on screen ("**soft copy**"). Factors in determining which output method to use include the number of users, the length and complexity of the report, and the duration of the report's usefulness, as shown in Table 11.2. In general, short reports that have only a few users and that are used for a short period of time can be generated as screen reports; longer reports that have many users and that are used over a longer time frame should be printed for distribution.

A well-designed report is easy to scan, highlights important facts, and uses a consistent, symmetrical layout; the last two characteristics help achieve the first one. "Scan-ability" is increased by avoiding clutter (e.g., using wide margins and liberal white space between items),

TABLE 11.2 Criteria for selecting screen or printed reports

	Screen Report	**Printed Report**
Number of users	Few	Many
Length and complexity	Fits on 1 or 2 screens	Requires 3 or more screens
	Has ten or fewer data elements	Has more than 10 data elements
Duration of usefulness	Short duration—less than one week	Long duration—more than one week

providing labels and column headers to identify symmetrically aligned information, and using formatting options such as boldface type, shading, or boxes to highlight important facts. A word of caution about formatting options: Do not overuse them; overuse *reduces* clarity and "scan-ability."

Sometimes, no matter how effectively you design a report, it will contain too much data for the user to comprehend easily. In these situations, you should create graphs to encapsulate the most important information in the report. The three basic types of graphs are line graphs, bar graphs, and pie charts. A **line graph** represents data as points in time, where the *x*-axis is a time line and the *y*-axis gives the quantity of the item being measured (e.g., dollar sales or units sold). Thus, each point represents the value of the item being measured at a particular point in time; the points are connected to show the trend over time (e.g., increasing sales over the past year). In a **bar graph**, each bar represents one data component, for example, the number of widgets sold in a particular month. Bar graphs are especially effective for comparing figures for various time frames (e.g., sales by each computer manufacturer for several quarters) or for various scenarios (e.g., expected profits before and after a merger). A **pie chart** consists of a "pie" sliced into various pieces, the size of the piece representing the percentage that each data component contributes to the whole (e.g., the percentage of sales that each department contributed to total store sales). Using color in graphs will improve the user's ability to extract information [Headley 1990].

HUMAN-COMPUTER DIALOG

A **human-computer dialog** is the style of interaction between the system and its users. Types of dialogs include command, menu, form-filling, direct manipulation, or a combination of these. The primary considerations in selecting a dialog type are the level of user expertise and the frequency of use.

A **command dialog** triggers the execution of system functions by employing a command language that defines the valid terms and syntax for interaction. For example, to interact with early versions of dBASE, a popular file management tool, users typed "dot commands," so called because each command began with a period. Thus, they typed the command *.create report <reportname>* to generate a report. DOS is another example of a command dialog, wherein, for example, a user enters the command *copy a:letter.doc b:* to copy a file named "letter.doc" from one diskette to another. Although command dialogs are appropriate for computer-literate frequent users, they are inappropriate for most typical business users. Learning, using, and remembering a command language is simply too demanding for many users. A **menu dialog**, which lists several possible actions and requires the user to select an option, is preferable. You are probably familiar with the pull-down menus of Macintosh and Windows applications, which use a mouse to select ("point") and to activate ("click") a menu option. These are examples of today's menu dialog. However, before the advent of bit-mapped screens, a menu dialog consisted of a character-based screen listing various options and a prompt requesting the user to enter an option. However implemented, menu dialogs are especially appropriate for infrequent (or inexpert) users because no command language must be learned and remembered.

On the other hand, expert or frequent users may be frustrated by having to cascade through a hierarchy of menus to find a desired command. Thus, most menu dialogs today also provide shortcut key combinations that allow the user to execute a command directly. For example, the Microsoft Word Edit menu shown in Figure 11.5 provides two types of shortcut keys: single-stroke key commands, such as R (Repeat New Default) and F (Find), which are typed after the Edit menu has been opened; and combination keystroke commands, such as CTRL-Y and CTRL-F, which can be activated without opening the Edit menu.

A third type of human-computer dialog is a **form-filling dialog**, which typically replicates a source document and, as its name suggests, requires the user to "fill in the form." One advantage of this dialog type is that it exploits the user's familiarity with the source document to increase ease of use. Another is that it limits the range of possible actions to a few constrained choices, such as moving the cursor and entering and editing text. Thus, form-filling dialog is appropriate for novice and infrequent users.

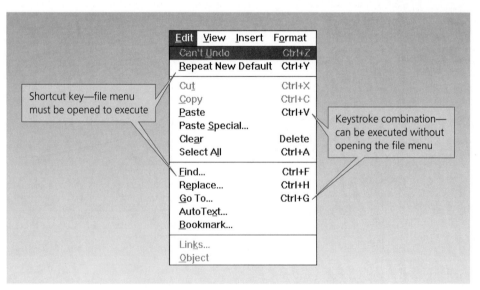

FIGURE 11.5   Menu dialog with shortcut keys

A **direct manipulation dialog** is one in which a pointing device such as a mouse is used to manipulate screen objects that perform system functions [Schneiderman 1983]. The "point-and-click" menu selection process described earlier is an example of direct manipulation. Other examples include "double-clicking" an icon to launch an application or to open a file, using "drag-and-drop" to copy a file from one directory to another, and single-clicking a button or tool icon to perform functions such as "Print" and "Cancel."

Direct-manipulation interfaces are best understood by examining a graphical user interface (GUI). Figure 11.6 shows a screen captured from Microsoft Word; the elements of the screen are labeled to indicate common GUI components. To interact with Word—that is, to directly manipulate objects on a Word screen—a user employs a mouse to pull down menus, click buttons, highlight text, move the cursor, select tools, and so on. Note the term "objects" in the previous sentence. Direct-manipulation interfaces are a prime example of the successful application of object-oriented technology. Each window, menu, icon, and so on is an object that remembers data (i.e., the contents of a window or the state of a toggle button) and performs functions. The ability to define window, menu, and icon superclasses and then to create specialized subclasses of each is the key to efficient GUI design and implementation.

Direct manipulation interfaces provide several benefits. Ease of learning is increased because users are not required to remember commands. For example, instead of remembering a print command, a user prints the current document by clicking the printer icon in the tool bar. Ease of use and productivity are increased because users are not required to spiral through several menus to perform common operations such as setting the font or formatting

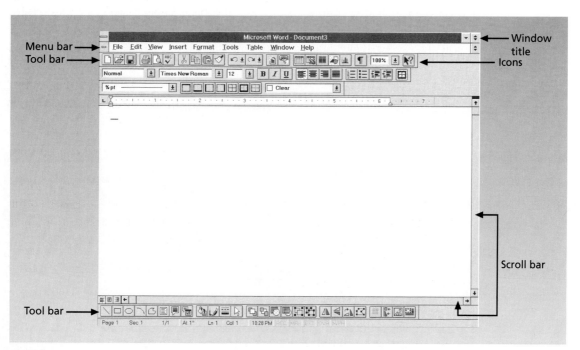

FIGURE 11.6   The graphical user interface of Microsoft Word

bulleted lists. Instead, these functions are clearly visible and easily performed on the document screen. Some other benefits of direct manipulation interfaces include the following [Schneiderman 1982]:

◆ Novice users quickly learn the system's basic functions.

◆ Expert users are more productive.

◆ Intermittent users are reminded of commonly used functions.

◆ Few error messages are needed.

◆ Users get immediate feedback on the effects of their actions.

◆ Anxiety is reduced because the system is more easily understood and allows actions to be reversed.

Designing and implementing such interfaces is no small task. To understand the relative complexity of a command dialog versus a direct-manipulation dialog, consider this fact: Most pre-GUI word-processing packages were sold as a single 360 Kbytes diskette and ran on computers with 64 to 128 Kbytes of RAM; today's GUI word-processing packages are sold as eight to ten 1.4 Mbytes diskettes and require 10 to 20 Mbytes of hard disk space and 4 to 8 Mbytes of RAM to operate efficiently. What is more, the "simple" task of opening a window may require five or six pages of C++ code! Fortunately, a number of tools are available to help reduce the time and effort required to custom-develop a GUI, including the GUI generators discussed in the Chapter 8 overview of RAD tools. In addition, component-based software development is supported by vendors who create and sell *Visual Basic modules* (commonly called VBXs) containing the code for manipulating windows, creating buttons, and so on.

The greater complexity of a direct-manipulation GUI makes interface design a task for experts. An understanding of human cognition and graphic design is necessary to avoid many of the undesirable consequences of poor design, such as applications that are difficult to learn and use. Both Apple Computer Corp. and Microsoft Corp. employ cognitive psychologists, GUI experts, and graphic designers to create their GUIs; in fact, to design its groupware software, Microsoft Corp. enlisted the help of anthropologists, who understand how groups interact.

Clearly then, giving you all the knowledge to design effective GUIs is beyond the scope of this textbook. (See Rettig [1992] for suggestions on designing a user interface "when you don't know how.") However, many of the guidelines for creating effective GUIs have been codified. To help you avoid the pitfalls of GUI design, we present several guidelines later in this chapter. Furthermore, because you are likely to be involved in analyzing and creating a variety of user interfaces, we present a five-step process to guide you in this endeavor.

✓ Check Your Understanding 11-1

1. Classify each of the following interfaces as an external document (ED), data entry screen (DES), report (R), or human-computer dialog (HCD).

____ a. A semester grade report sent to a student's home address.

____ b. A pop-up window displaying an error message.

_____ c. A document that summarizes sales by salesperson (500 total) by region (10 total) for the month of June.

_____ d. A window that prompts the user to input item number and quantity.

_____ e. A window listing the name, phone number, amount due, and days past due for each delinquent account.

_____ f. A tool bar.

_____ g. A monthly checking account statement.

_____ h. A window that lists a menu of options.

2. Examine the interfaces you classified as reports in Exercise 1. Determine whether each should be printed or displayed on screen. Justify your choice.

11.2 ◆ THE PROCESS OF INTERFACE ANALYSIS AND DESIGN

Because a good interface combines aesthetics, usability, and functionality, designing user interfaces is as much an art as it is a science. Following is a five-step process for analyzing and designing user interfaces:

1. Analyze the users and their tasks.

2. Identify the system's user interfaces.

3. Select a dialog type for each interface.

4. Develop a prototype.

5. Review and revise as needed.

ANALYZE THE USERS AND THEIR TASKS

The first step in interface analysis and design is to analyze the users and their tasks. A new system is easier to learn and to use if it is aligned with the user's method of completing a task, and if its flow of activity parallels the user's task flow. Hence **task analysis** is used to identify, categorize, and define the procedures users employ to perform work tasks. Then the new system is designed to support those methods where possible. Of course, inefficient or ineffective ones must be changed.

Questions to answer as you analyze users and their tasks include the following:

1. *Who are the intended users?* This question investigates characteristics of the intended users: their level of expertise at performing the task, their experience using automated systems, and any other relevant factors. The answers will influence your choice of a human-computer dialog and the amount and type of documentation, help screens, and other support your interface provides the users.

2. *What are the users' goals in performing the task?* Users' goals may be more complex than is apparent from simple observation of their performing a task. For example, observing a grocery store clerk check out a customer may lead you to conclude that the clerk's goals

are simply to efficiently process each item and to generate a receipt. However, the clerk's goals may also include providing friendly, helpful customer service and maintaining a clean, orderly work area. Determining users' goals helps you to identify criteria for evaluating interface design. A good design helps users to achieve their goals.

3. *What information do users need to perform the task?* This question investigates the inputs to the task: what the user must know and what data the user must access to perform the task. For example, a grocery checkout clerk must know the produce code assigned to each variety of fresh fruit and vegetable. How can these codes be made available to the clerk in a way that reduces the need to memorize them but that does not interfere with task performance?

4. *What information do users generate as they perform the task?* This question examines the outputs of the task: what outputs must be generated and how each should be generated. Should these outputs be displayed in real time, or can they be compiled (batched) and generated as a single output? For example, as a grocery checkout clerk processes each item, its description and price and a running subtotal can be displayed immediately. This real-time feedback facilitates error detection ("Oops! The shelf label indicated that those potato chips were on sale for 99 cents, not $1.59.") However, achieving this benefit requires a more sophisticated interface, one that serves the needs of both the clerk *and* the customer (in this case, a secondary user).

5. *What methods do users employ to perform the task?* This question investigates the shortcuts, rules of thumb, and other methods that users have developed to facilitate task completion. For example, a grocery checkout clerk often needs to ring up multiple purchases of the same item (e.g., four cans of the same cat food). How can you design an interface that facilitates this task? Methods used to perform a task can be identified by interviewing expert users, observing users as they perform the task, and examining physical DFDs or use cases describing system behaviors.

IDENTIFY REQUIRED USER INTERFACES

After you have gained an understanding of the users and their tasks, your next step is to examine physical DFDs or use cases of the proposed system to identify the documents, data entry screens, printed and screen reports, and other interfaces it requires. Figure 11.7 shows the Level 0 physical DFD of ETG's proposed order processing system, with highlighted data flows that require a user interface. Notice that a user interface is required whenever a manual process interacts with an automated process or an external entity provides input to or receives output from a process. For example, the "Membership application" data flow from Customer to Process 1.0 requires an external document—the membership application form—and a data entry screen to input the data from the form. The "Member card bar code" and "Rental tape bar code" data flows from Rental-Customer to Process 2.0 require an external document—the membership card—and a Rental Order data entry screen to accept the membership number and rental tape stock number. You should understand that each interface data flow will not necessarily require a different interface. For example, the member number and rental tape stock number can both be captured by a single Rental Order data entry screen.

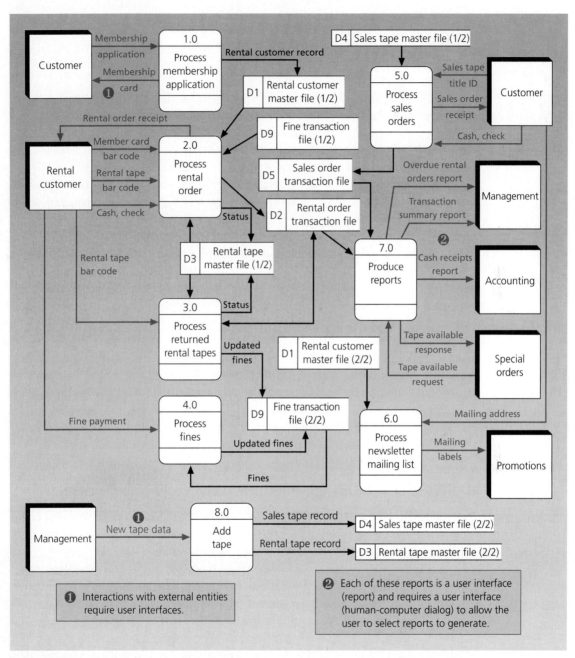

FIGURE 11.7   Physical Level 0 DFD of ETG's new order processing system with highlighted interface data flows

The physical DFD in Figure 11.8 examines the process of completing the rental order header more fully. Notice that the data flow from Process 2.1.6—Display fines—an automated process performed by the system—to Process 2.1.7—Determine if fines must be paid—a manual process performed by the sales clerk—requires an interface, most likely a

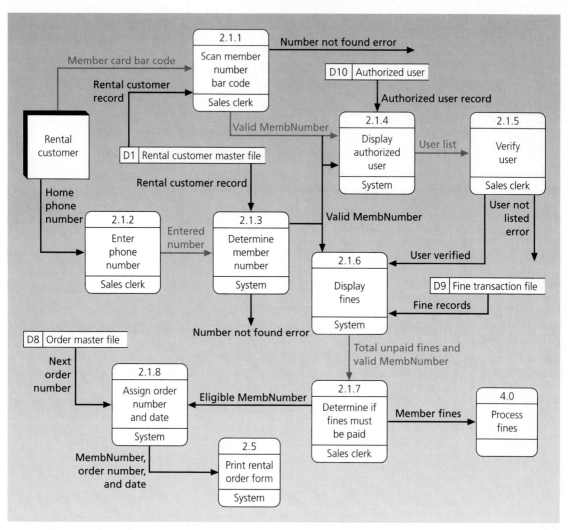

FIGURE 11.8   Lower-level physical DFD with highlighted interface data flows

screen that displays fine data and prompts the user to respond to the question "Pay fines now?" The same is true of the data flow between Process 2.1.4—Display authorized users and Process 2.1.5—Verify user.

Similar strategies are used to analyze use cases. Refer again to ETG's Rental Customer Rents Rental Tape(s) use case in Figure 11.1. Phrases that indicate aspects of the user interface are highlighted. Notice that any time the sales clerk must interact with the system—e.g., by entering an employee number, selecting a command button, or responding to a prompt—a user interface is needed. The same is true of the system's communications with the user; displaying prompts, report screens, and error messages are user interface functions. Again, each interaction or communication does not necessarily require a *different* interface; instead, several interactions or communications may be performed by a single interface.

SELECT A DIALOG TYPE AND DEVELOP A PROTOTYPE

Now that you understand the system's users and their tasks and have identified the required interfaces, you can begin to design and to prototype these interfaces. Following a three-step process will help you to complete this task [Yourdon 1994]:

1. Design the command hierarchy.
2. Design detailed interactions between user and system.
3. Design the interface objects required to manage the interactions.

Designing Command Hierarchy

During the first step of designing the command hierarchy, you identify the major screens (in today's parlance, "windows") that users will employ to access and to perform system functions. Basically, what you are doing is providing

1. A view of the system's functions or object methods in the form of menus or command buttons.
2. A way for the system to accept inputs from the user in the form of data entry screens.
3. A way for the system to display information to the user in the form of screen reports and error messages.

A technique used to model the command hierarchy is the **dialog flow diagram**, which shows the major screens or windows of the system as labeled rectangles and indicates the flow of control between screens as directional arrows. The symbols used in a dialog flow diagram are explained in Figure 11.9.

Figure 11.10 gives the dialog flow diagram for ETG's order processing system. Notice that this dialog flow is presented as a four-level hierarchy of functions, beginning with the topmost system menu. Each screen at the next lower level must be accessible from the preceding

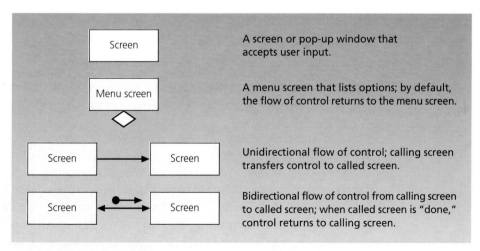

FIGURE 11.9   Dialog flow diagram symbols

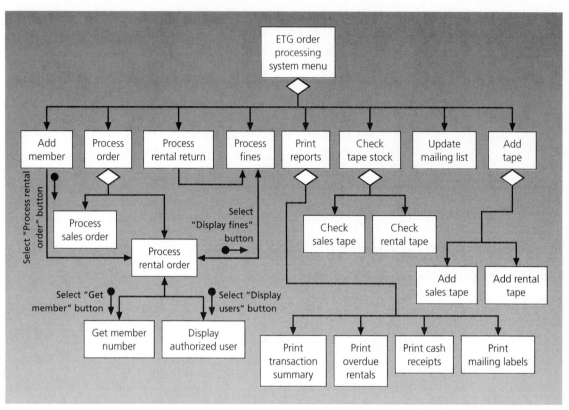

FIGURE 11.10 Dialog flow diagram for ETG's order processing system

screen. Thus, each of the screens—Add Member, Process Order, and so on to Add Tape—must be options on the system's main menu screen. Similarly, "Process sales order" and "Process rental order" must be options on the Process Order screen. Figure 11.11 shows the system menu for ETG's order processing system. Notice that all eight second-level screens are accessible from this menu. Figure 11.12 gives the second-level Print reports menu screen, using radio buttons to constrain the user to one selection and giving the user the option to preview the report before printing it.

Figure 11.4, ETG's Rental Order data entry screen (a third-level screen), provides command buttons so that the user can access the Find Member and Display Users screens (fourth-level screens) or the Process Fines screen (a second-level screen). Notice that, in the diagram in Figure 11.10, the flow of control between these screens is determined by a command button selection and that control returns to the calling screen ("Process rental order"). You may wonder why the notation in this situation is different from the notation for a menu screen. The primary difference is that, on a menu screen, the flow of control will *always* be transferred to *one* of the menu options; however, on a "regular" screen used to enter data (e.g., rental order transaction data) or to specify parameters (e.g., the begin and end dates for a report), the flow of control may be transferred to *none* of the screens called by the command buttons or to *one or all* of them sequentially.

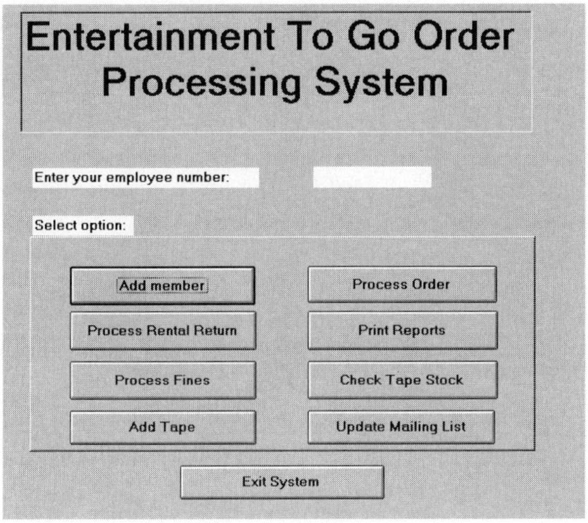

FIGURE 11.11 ETG's system (main) menu screen

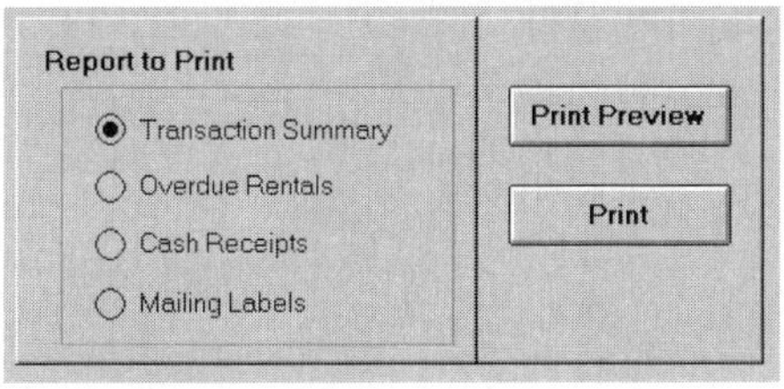

FIGURE 11.12 ETG's Print Reports menu screen

Notice that, for the most part, control in the Figure 11.10 dialog flow diagram flows from a calling menu screen (e.g., "Process order") to a called screen (e.g., "Process rental order") and then returns to the calling menu screen after the called screen has performed its function. Thus, the only permissible "moves" are between these screens. Two exceptions are (1) the "Process rental order" screen, which can be called by the "Process order" screen or the "Add member" screen, and (2) the "Process fines" screen, which can be called by the system menu screen, the "Process rental return" screen, or the "Process rental order" screen. Notice that, in the first case, the flow of control does not return to "Add member" after a rental order has been processed. This is indicated by the unidirectional dialog flow arrow, which points from "Add member" to "Process rental order." Notice that in the second case, after "Process fines" has completed its function, the flow of control returns to the "Process rental order" screen, as indicated by the bidirectional arrow connecting these screens.

You may have noticed that a dialog flow diagram looks a lot like a program structure chart. This resemblance is more than coincidental. A dialog flow diagram presents the structure of the system's user interfaces; these interfaces allow users to interact with system processes, whose structure is documented in a program structure chart. Thus, the structures of both diagrams are similar. The flow of control between system interfaces also tends to mimic the flow of control between program modules, which suggests that examining your program structure chart can help you design the flow of control between interfaces. Furthermore, you should compare these two diagrams to ensure that the interface structure design supports the program structure design.

Designing Detailed Interactions Between User and System

During the second step of designing detailed interactions, you make the design decisions that determine the look and functionality of the system's user interfaces. For example, you may decide to use command buttons instead of a menu bar within a data entry screen to allow users to open related screens (see, for example, Figure 11.4). You also determine which data elements will be entered by users versus those that will be retrieved, calculated, or assigned by the system's software. Other design decisions include whether a report should be printed or displayed on screen and how external documents and reports should be formatted.

The discussion of user interfaces in Section 11.1 provided several guidelines to help you make these decisions. Some specific guidelines for making GUI design decisions are presented in Table 11.3, which indicates appropriate window objects for triggering a process based on the frequency of access, and Table 11.4, which indicates the type of text entry field to use in various situations. Additional guidelines are provided in Section 11.4.

Whenever feasible, you should involve users in making design decisions. Conducting an "envisioning" session as Victoria did during the JAD workshop is an effective way of involving users. Not only does this envisioning help you design user-friendly interfaces, it also ensures that your interfaces support the users' task flow. The output of an envisioning session is a detailed use case, such as the one shown in Figure 11.13, which describes how a task is performed given the structure of the related interfaces.

This detailed use case indicates the state the system must be in (e.g., "Waiting for stock number" and "Waiting to print receipt") before certain functions can be performed. For

TABLE 11.3 Guidelines for selecting window objects to trigger a process

Frequency of Access	Number of Selections	Appropriate GUI Object
Infrequent	Many	Pull-down menu, pop-up window
Infrequent	Few	Button or tool pallet
Frequent	Few	Button with hot-key or function key
Most frequent	—	Default button

TABLE 11.4 Guidelines for selecting window objects to enter text

Text Characteristics	Appropriate GUI Object
Single line	Text entry field
Fixed number of lines	Multiple text entry fields
Indefinite number of lines	Scrollable multiline text entry field
Tabular	Matrix window object

Use Case Name: Rental Customer Rents Rental Tape(s)
Use Case Purpose: Describes the process of renting rental tapes to rental customers
Uses: Rental Customer Pays Fines; Customer Makes Payment
Extended by: Rental Customer Rents 3/3 Rental Tapes

Typical Course of Events:

The <u>main menu</u> is displayed on the screen; waiting for employee number and menu selection:
- When a customer presents membership card and selected rental tapes for check out, this use case is initiated by the sales clerk's <u>entering a valid employee number and selecting "Process order" from the main menu. The Process Orders menu is displayed.</u>

Waiting for menu selection:
- The sales clerk selects "Process rental orders."

The <u>rental order screen</u> is displayed; waiting for member number:
- The <u>sales clerk scans the member number from the membership card</u>, and the system verifies that the member number is valid and that the rental customer has no unpaid fines.
- If the member number is valid, the <u>system completes the rental order header</u>, indicating a valid employee number, a valid member number, order number, and order date.
- The <u>system prompts the sales clerk to enter a rental tape stock number.</u>

Waiting for stock number:
- The <u>sales clerk scans the stock number from the rental tape</u>.
- For each rental tape being rented, the <u>system creates a rental order line</u>, giving the stock number, title, rental category, and rental fee of each rental tape; in addition, the due date calculated for each rental tape is shown on the rental order line.
- The <u>system prompts the sales clerk to enter another rental tape stock number or to signal the end of the order</u>.
- If another stock number is entered, the system creates another rental order line.

Waiting for end of order indicator:
- When the sales clerk signals the end of the order, the <u>system creates a rental order footer</u> by calculating and displaying the total cost for the order.
- Customer makes payment. (See Customer Makes Payment use case.)

Waiting to print receipt:
- The <u>sales clerk requests that the receipt be printed</u>.
- The <u>system prints the rental order receipt</u>.
- The customer signs the rental order receipt.
- The customer is given one copy of the receipt; the other copy is retained for the audit file.

FIGURE 11.13 Detailed use case for Rental Customer Rents Rental Tape(s) (*continued on next page*)

example, the rental order screen must be displayed before the system can accept the membership number that the sales clerk scans from the membership card; similarly, the order header must be completed before the system can accept a tape stock number. The system would display an error message if the sales clerk scanned the tape stock number instead of the membership number when the rental order screen first appeared. A detailed use case also indicates the user interface features employed to perform system functions—for example, selecting a particular command button to open a screen or to print a receipt—and the types of controls and corresponding error messages required to ensure system integrity (e.g., validating employee number, membership number, and rental tape stock number).

Alternative Courses of Events:

An invalid employee number is entered:
- The system displays an error message and prompts the sales clerk to try again.

An invalid menu selection is entered:
- The system displays an error message and prompts the sales clerk to try again.

The customer does not have his or her membership card:
- At "Waiting for member number," the sales clerk selects a command button, and the system displays a pop-up screen and prompts the sales clerk to enter the customer's home phone number.

    Waiting for home phone number:
    - The sales clerk enters the rental customer's home phone number.
    - The system matches the home phone number with the appropriate member number and creates the rental order header.
    - If no match is found, the system displays an error message.

Member number is invalid:
- The system prompts the sales clerk to enter the member number manually.
- If three successive attempts to validate the member number fail, the system cancels the transaction and prompts the sales clerk to confiscate the membership card.

The rental customer has fines:
- The sales clerk can select a command button to cause the system to display fines and prompt the sales clerk to determine whether fines must be paid before the transaction proceeds.
- If the sales clerk decides that fines must be paid, fines are processed before the transaction proceeds. (See Rental Customer Pays Fines use case.)
- If the sales clerk decides that fines need not be paid at this time, the system creates a rental order header.

The customer claims to be an authorized user:
- The sales clerk clicks a command button to display the rental customer's Authorized User list.
- The system displays the list and prompts the sales clerk to validate the customer.

    Waiting for validation:
    - The sales clerk asks the customer for his or her name and relationship to the member.
    - If the customer is listed, the sales clerk types "Y" to validate the user.
    - If the customer is not listed, the sales clerk types "N"; the system cancels the transaction and prompts the sales clerk to confiscate the membership card.

The rental tape stock number is invalid:
- The system prompts the sales clerk to enter the stock number manually.
- If three successive attempts to validate the stock number fail, the system prompts the sales clerk to mark the rental tape for manual verification.

FIGURE 11.13   Detailed use case for Rental Customer Rents Rental Tape(s) (*continued*)

Designing Interface Objects Required to Manage Interactions

The last step in prototype development, designing the interface objects required to manage the interactions, transforms your design decisions into tangible interfaces. Depending on the resources and tools available, you can prototype user interfaces by drawing report and screen layouts on graph paper or using a word-processing, spreadsheet, or graphics program. Ideally, you will have access to a GUI generator or the interface design capabilities of a DBMS. For example, Microsoft Access can be used to design and construct all the typical components of a GUI—menu bars, tool bars, buttons, pop-up windows, and so on—and a variety of user interfaces, including data entry and menu screens and printed and screen reports. All of the user interfaces shown as illustrations in this chapter were constructed using Access.

You may not realize it, but if you choose to construct user interfaces employing a GUI generator or a DBMS such as Microsoft Access, you are practicing object-oriented design. Each window, button, icon, and so on created using these tools is an object, which remembers its attributes and performs methods. "What attributes and methods?" you may ask. The attributes of a data entry user interface (called a *form* in Access) include properties such as its size, the location of various text and data entry fields in the window, whether its contents can be edited, and so on. Its methods include displaying itself (i.e., opening its window), accepting inputs, requesting data from business objects, calculating the value of certain fields, and so on.

To distinguish these window, button, and icon objects from the business objects designed earlier, we call them **interface objects**[1]: objects that provide a bridge between users in the real world and business objects in an automated system. Interface objects capture and display the system's data; for example, in ETG's order processing system, the "Process rental order" interface object (a data entry screen) collects data about a rental order transaction. Interface objects also initiate system processes. For example, the "Process rental order" interface object has a "Print order" interface object (a command button) that causes the system to print the rental order receipt.

However, you should note that, in most cases, the interface objects created by a GUI generator are not "true" objects. Although each interface object encapsulates attributes and methods, only a few GUI generators support inheritance and polymorphism among interface objects. Thus, these tools are more appropriately called "object-based" rather than "object-oriented." Nonetheless, creating an object relationship model of an application's interface objects is useful. Documenting the specialization and composition relationships between interface objects, as illustrated in Figure 11.14, highlights their commonality, facilitating reuse of many design components. For example, we can stipulate the dimensions, font characteristics, background color, and so on of a Title Bar interface object and reuse this design specification for each window in the application.

An important activity in interface object design is *mapping* business objects to the interface objects that use them. This mapping indicates constraints and collaborations that must be captured as the interface is designed; it also determines which attributes must appear as data elements in each user interface. Figure 11.15 maps ETG's Rental Order Form interface object and its components to ETG's business objects. The business objects mapped to the Rental Order Form (in essence, the order header and footer) indicate that each form must contain data about exactly one RENTAL-CUSTOMER and must be paid by exactly one ORDER-PAYMENT (constraints). This mapping also indicates that, because a rental customer can have many fines, the total fine amount will have to be calculated before it can be displayed in the rental order header (collaboration between RENTAL-CUSTOMER and FINE). The mapping between the RO-Line subform and its business object model segment indicates that the Rental Order data entry screen must allow the user to enter at least one and possibly many line items and

---

[1]   See Tasker and Von Halle [1995] for a fuller treatment of interface objects and the interrelationships between interface objects and business objects.

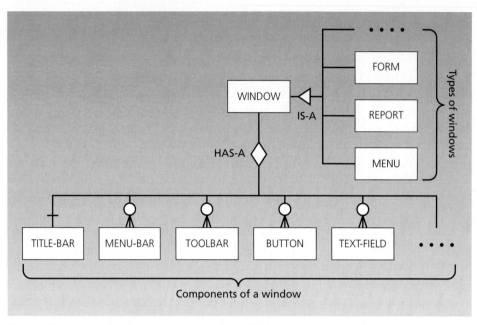

FIGURE 11.14 IS-A and HAS-A relationships between interface objects

that building each line item requires collaboration between RENTAL-CATEGORY, RENTAL-TAPE, and TAPE object instances.

As important as it is to map interface objects to business objects, the two sets of objects should be kept separate so that changes in an interface object will not require changes in the related business objects.

REVIEW THE PROTOTYPE WITH USERS AND REVISE AS NEEDED

The last activity in prototyping the user interfaces is to review the prototype with users to gain their feedback. This critical activity not only validates the design but also builds user commitment because users feel that their needs and opinions were considered [Appleton 1993]. In software development companies and large organizations, user interfaces may be subjected to a **usability test**, whose purpose is to ensure that system interfaces are easy to learn and use and that they support the desired level of user productivity. Such tests are typically conducted by human-computer interface specialists who videotape users working with the system in order to identify where users are most prone to make errors and to evaluate user reactions and assess productivity.

For example, Nynex Corp., a telecommunications company that provides telephone service to the New York area, needed to select workstations for a new system. One of the workstation vendors submitted a proposal claiming that its workstation interfaces would make operators 10 to 20 percent more efficient. Given that reducing the time to process a call just one second saves the company $3 million a year, Nynex was understandably excited by the proposal. However, usability tests revealed that operators using the workstations were actually 3 percent less efficient than those using the existing system [Dix 1993].

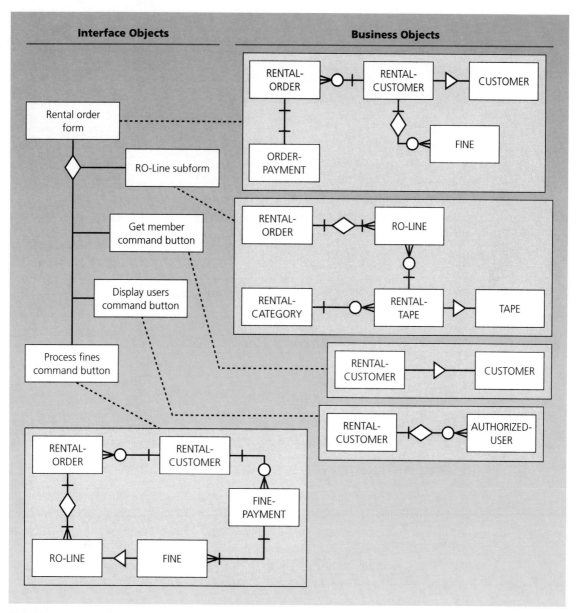

FIGURE 11.15 The mapping of interface objects to business objects

The usability of a GUI is especially critical. On average, providing the training, help desk, and other services required to support GUIs costs an organization $1,200 to $1,500 per user per year. A small improvement in the usability of the interface can yield substantial savings.

Although you may not be able to conduct a formal usability test, you should conduct user reviews repeatedly during the iterative analysis, design, and prototyping stage. As you construct interface facades like the one Denny demonstrated during the JAD session, you can show them to users to gain feedback about how they look. Do users find them attractive and easy to read? Does each data entry or report interface provide the desired data elements? After the functionality of an interface has been programmed (e.g., a data entry screen interface actually accepts and processes data), users can work with the interface to evaluate its "feel"—that is, how smoothly and efficiently users can move from field to field on a data entry screen, select menu options, and so on. Finally, when all the system's interfaces are operational, users can evaluate the functionality of the system's full human-computer dialog. Can they move easily between screens? Have you provided all the links between screens that they need? Does the user get lost, or is he or she always certain how to return to a previous screen or move to another screen? The ETG case installment that concludes Part Three illustrates this iterative review of system interfaces.

✓ Check Your Understanding 11-2

Choose the best answer to complete each statement.

_____ 1. Understanding a system's users
    a. determines your choice of an appropriate human-computer dialog.
    b. is critical to designing a system that is easy to learn and use.
    c. involves investigating their goals in completing a task.
    d. all of the above.
    e. only b and c.

_____ 2. Task analysis involves
    a. determining the inputs and outputs of a task.
    b. identifying the methods users have developed to complete a task.
    c. examining program structure charts.
    d. all of the above.
    e. only a and b.

_____ 3. Generally speaking, a user interface is required
    a. to accept an input from an external entity.
    b. to provide an output for an external entity.
    c. so that a manual process can interact with an automated process.
    d. all of the above.
    e. only a and c.

_____ 4. Dialog flow diagrams
    a. document all interfaces, including external documents.
    b. are similar in structure to the system's program structure chart.
    c. show the flow of control between interfaces.
    d. all of the above.
    e. only b and c.

_____ 5. All of the following statements are true except
    a. Interface objects perform functions but do not remember data.
    b. Business objects should be loosely coupled with their related interface objects.

    c.   An interface object can be composed of other interface objects.

    d.   All of the above statements are true.

_____ 6.   Mapping interface objects to the business objects they use

    a.   identifies constraints on interface design.

    b.   helps the designer determine the data elements that must appear on a data entry screen.

    c.   indicates collaborations that must be captured as the interface is designed.

    d.   all of the above.

    e.   only a and c.

_____ 7.   A user review of interface prototypes should be conducted

    a.   only after interfaces are fully operational.

    b.   repeatedly throughout the iterative analysis and design stage.

    c.   to gain user feedback and to increase user commitment.

    d.   both a and c.

    e.   both b and c.

11.3 ◆ USER DOCUMENTATION

User documentation is the part of the user interface that describes how to use the system. User documentation may include the following components:

◆ A **user guide** that describes the system and explains its use.

◆ A reference card that summarizes basic functions and commands.

◆ Specialized guides that describe how to install the application or explain system error messages.

◆ **Tutorials** that instruct users in the system's basic functionality.

◆ An **on-line help system** that basically replicates the user guide and assists users in understanding and using system features and functions.

Because good documentation is no substitute for good design, system designers should work with system documenters to integrate documentation into the product. In fact, designers and documenters should work concurrently so that documentation evolves as the system evolves. Working in tandem also provides valuable feedback about the system's design. Generally speaking, a poorly designed system is difficult to document; thus, documenters can serve as front-line testers of the system's usability.

    This section discusses some of the issues in user documentation and suggests guidelines to ensure that this aspect of the user interface is as well conceived as the system itself.

ISSUES IN USER DOCUMENTATION

A number of issues need to be addressed as user documentation is designed and written. The title of an insightful article on user documentation raises the single most critical issue: "Nobody Reads Documentation" [Rettig 1991]. It is a sad but true fact that most people adopt the "If all else fails, read the documentation" strategy to learn how to use an information system. This is especially true of users, who want to complete a job task, not study a 300-page manual to learn the procedures for using application software.

Thus, one issue in creating user documentation is determining *how material should be presented*. Should you provide both a user guide and an online help system? Do you need to develop tutorials and create an installation guide explaining how to install the software and configure it for different platforms? How you answer these questions depends to some degree on who your intended users are and how much training they will receive. In organizations where information systems professionals are responsible for software installation and system configuration, these procedures would be part of the technical documentation, not the user documentation. The amount of upfront training also affects how the material is presented. If an organization provides little formal training, then the benefits of including tutorials will almost certainly justify the costs of creating them.

Today the trend is to create self-documenting systems instead of making documentation a separate, add-on product. For example, many commercially available software packages provide on-line help systems and/or cue cards that explain how to perform a task. In addition, most GUIs use the status bar to display a brief explanation of what a menu option or tool bar icon does.

Another issue is determining *how the material should be organized* to make it most useful to and accessible by users. There are three approaches to organizing content [Rettig 1991]:

1. **Software-oriented documentation** focuses on commands used to work with the software. The user guide is organized alphabetically by command name, providing a definition of each command's purpose and syntax (e.g., format <disk drive name> :). A problem with this approach is that the user must know the software—or, at minimum, be a wizard at intuiting the likely name of a command—to know how to use the documentation.

2. **Menu-oriented documentation** organizes user guide content by describing the commands available in each menu. Again, an understanding of the software is required in that the user must understand what kinds of commands are likely to be grouped in each menu. An additional problem is that finding descriptions of commands in submenus may be difficult; for example, where should the user look to find out how to print a file to disk? Under "Print" or "Save"?

3. **Task-oriented documentation** organizes content by task, describing system commands in terms of the tasks the user will perform to use the application. For example, user guide chapters for the ETG order processing system may be titled "How to Add a New Member," "How to Process a Rental Order," "How to Add a New Tape," and so on. This approach puts the burden of knowledge on the documenter, not on the user. Instead of the user having to understand the system, the documenter must understand the tasks the user will perform. Instead of treating each system command or function as an independent entity, this approach describes system functions in the context of a task that the user needs to perform.

A third issue is determining *how much material should be presented*. There must be enough to guide users but not so much as to overwhelm them. Users are more likely to consult a 50-page user guide than a 500-page one. When the task-oriented approach is adopted, the question, "What material should be included in the documentation?" is answered by determining what tasks the typical user will most commonly perform. Focusing on what most users must know to perform their job tasks reduces the amount of material in the user guide. Less frequently performed tasks can be relegated to an "advanced" or supplemental user guide. Supplemental materials, such as overviews, summaries, command indexes, and so on can be minimized or cut altogether.

A fourth issue is *how to test the documentation*. Yes, *test* the documentation! Errors in the user documentation are unpardonable sins because they devastate the users' confidence in the system's accuracy and reliability. Thus, just as all other aspects of the system must be tested, so must the user documentation—but not by designers and documenters, because they have too much tacit knowledge about the system. Documentation that is clear to them may be obscure and incomplete to users. Having a few representative users try to perform use-case tasks by using the documentation is the best test of its clarity and completeness.

CREATING USER DOCUMENTATION

As noted earlier, user documentation should be created concurrently with system design and construction. If you employ use cases throughout your analysis and design and select the task-oriented approach, the user guide—the most common form of user documentation—will evolve as the system evolves. A task-oriented user guide describes all the manual procedures performed by users and relates each user interface to the procedure that uses it. Each major task is treated as a chapter. Additional chapters may provide supplemental material, such as explanations of error messages or a glossary defining important terms.

A detailed use case, such as the one given in Figure 11.13, is the foundation for a task-oriented user guide. Each use case explains how to perform a task. All you need to do is to revise the use case to reference specific interface components and to map each use case to pictures of the interface(s) it uses. Thus, instead of referring to "a window," "a command button," "a menu option," "a prompt," "an error message," and so on, you include a screen shot of the interface in the user guide and specify the name or content of each window, button, option, prompt, or error message in the use case.

To illustrate the transformation of use cases into a user guide, Figure 11.13 provides an excerpt of the "How to Process a Rental Order" chapter of ETG's user guide. Note that the Figure 11.16 use case indicates that "The system prompts the sales clerk to enter a rental tape stock number." The user guide in Figure 11.16 provides a picture of the interface in this state, describes the "prompt," and explains how the user should respond to it. Similarly, the use-case sentence, "The sales clerk selects a command button . . ." becomes, "Click on the 'Find Member' button" in the user guide; "The system displays an error message . . ." becomes, "If no record of this member is found, the system displays the error message "User not found."'

The user guide sample chapter shown in Figure 11.16 begins with a summary of the task it describes, including a description of the inputs the user will enter and the outputs the system will generate. Note also that task procedures are framed in terms of user actions and system responses. This mapping of user actions to system responses helps users to predict what the system will do. To improve clarity and completeness, exceptions to the typical

CHAPTER 3: HOW TO PROCESS A RENTAL ORDER

Stimulus: Customer presents rental tapes and membership card for checkout.
Frequency: Performed repeatedly throughout each business day.
Inputs: Employee number (keyed)
Membership number (scanned from membership card)
Rental tape stock number (scanned from tape)
Payment amount (keyed)
Outputs: Printed rental order form
Rental order transaction record
Cash receipts transaction record

SECTION 1: TYPICAL COURSE OF EVENTS

1. At the main menu, enter your employee number.

   The system verifies your employee number, displaying the error message, "Invalid employee number" if your entry is invalid.

2. Select "Process rental order" from the main menu.

   The Rental Order data entry screen appears. Your employee number appears in the Employee Number text entry box. A blinking cursor is located in the Membership Number text entry box.

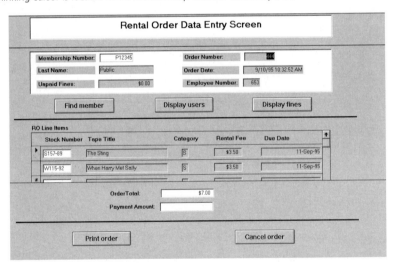

NOTE: At any point in this process, you may click the
"Cancel order" button to back out of the order.

3. Scan membership card bar code and press enter.

   (For more information about scanning bar codes, see "Using the Scanning Device" in this manual.)

   If the membership number is valid, the system fills in the Last Name and Unpaid Fines text boxes and assigns values to the Order Number and Order Date text boxes. The system also displays a blank item line and locates a blinking cursor in the Stock Number text entry box. Continue at step 4.

FIGURE 11.16   Excerpt from ETG's user guide, page 1

If the membership number is invalid, the system displays the error message "Invalid membership number." Scan the bar code again. If the system is again unable to verify the membership number, manually enter the membership number printed beneath the bar code. If these measures fail, see Section 3, Troubleshooting, later in this chapter.

If the member does not have his or her membership card, see "Finding a Member Number" under Section 2, Alternative Courses of Events, later in this chapter.

If the member claims to be an authorized user, see "Verifying Users" under Section 2, Alternative Courses of Events, later in this chapter.

If the member has unpaid fines, see "Processing Fines" in Chapter 5.

For each rental tape being checked out, perform steps 4 and 5:

4. **Scan the stock number bar code from the rental tape.**

   The system fills in the Tape Title, Category, Rental Fee, and Due Date text boxes.

   If this data is correct, continue at step 5.

   If the stock number is invalid, the system displays the error message, "Invalid stock number." Scan the bar code again. If the system is again unable to verify the stock number, manually enter the stock number printed beneath the bar code. If these measures fail, see Section 3, Troubleshooting, later in this chapter.

5. **Press the Enter key to accept the line item.**

   The system displays another blank item line with a blinking cursor located in the Stock Number text entry box.

   To process additional rental tapes, repeat steps 4 and 5.

   To signal that there are no more rental tapes to process, press the Enter key.

   The system calculates the order total and displays it in the Order Total text box. Continue at Step 6.

---

6. **Collect payment and enter the amount collected in the "Payment amount" text entry box.**

   . . . .

7. **Click the "Print order" button to print the rental order receipt.**

   . . . .

SECTION 2: ALTERNATIVE COURSES OF EVENTS

Finding a Member Number

1. **Click the "Find member" button.**

   The system opens a pop-up window, as shown below:

   [A screen shot of the pop-up window would be provided here.]

   A blinking cursor is located in the Home Phone text entry box.

2. **Type the member's home phone number and press Enter.**

   The system retrieves the membership number, closes the pop-up window, and displays the membership number in the Membership Number text entry box of the Rental Order data entry screen. The system also fills in the other text boxes in the header.

   Continue at step 4, "Scan the stock number bar code from the rental tape," in Section 1.

Note: Ellipses in this figure indicate that text has been omitted.

FIGURE 11.16 Excerpt from ETG's user guide, page 2

course of events are noted in the task procedure description, but the methods for dealing with these exceptions are given in different sections of the user guide.

✓ Check Your Understanding 11-3

Indicate whether each of the following statements is true (T) or false (F).

_____ 1. A poorly designed system is easy to learn and use if its user documentation is clear and complete.

_____ 2. Documenters and designers should work together to create user documentation.

_____ 3. Designers should serve as test subjects to verify the clarity and completeness of user documentation.

_____ 4. The user documentation for some systems will not describe how to install software.

_____ 5. One factor in determining how user documentation material should be presented is the amount of training an organization provides.

_____ 6. A self-documenting system provides an on-line help system and uses pop-up windows or balloons to explain menu options and the function of tool bar icons.

_____ 7. Software-oriented documentation is most appropriate for expert users who already understand the system.

_____ 8. Creating task-oriented documentation requires the writer to understand users' tasks.

_____ 9. A 200-page user guide is almost certainly more complete and more usable than a 50-page user guide.

_____ 10. An effective user guide maps user interfaces to the tasks performed.

11.4 ◈ CRITERIA FOR EVALUATING USER INTERFACE DESIGNS

Just as we needed criteria to evaluate system data structure and behavior designs, we need criteria to evaluate user interface designs. Donald Norman, a cognitive psychologist who has studied interface design, offers several principles that we can use as our criteria [1988]. These guidelines are phrased as questions. If you have created a good design, you should be able to answer each question with a confident "Yes!"

1. *Does the design help the user develop an accurate mental model of the system?* The **user's mental model** of the system consists of the concepts he or she uses to explain the behavior of the system. This mental model causes users to develop expectations about the outcome of their actions: "If I do X, the system will do Y." A well-designed interface helps users map what they want to do to what they can do, what they did to how the system responded. If the mappings are right, the user will develop the correct mental model of the system, enabling them to understand and, therefore, to use the system correctly.

To foster a correct mental model, today's GUIs exploit **metaphors** that associate one concept or thing with another concept or thing: for example, "window" and "desktop." "Opening" and "closing" a window, clicking on a printer icon to print a document or a diskette icon to save a file, clicking a blank page icon to open a new file—all are functions users grasp easily because the metaphors work. However, if the interface design uses inappropriate metaphors, it causes users to misinterpret the system's features or functions, thus fostering an incorrect mental model and impeding system understanding and use. For example, a popular electronic mail package provides a paper clip icon in its tool bar. Most people associate a paper clip with *attaching* one document to another; but this package uses this icon to *copy* selected items to the clipboard [Gavron 1994]. You can imagine the number of users who misinterpreted this icon!

Guidelines for achieving this criterion include the following:

◆ Make clear what actions are currently possible. For example, the File menu in Figure 11.5 shows available options in dark type and "grays out" other options. Going a step further, the interface can be designed to reveal only those functions that a user is authorized to execute. Similarly, if a user is not supposed to change the value of certain data elements on a data entry screen—for example, the unit price of an item—those values can be retrieved from the database and displayed as locked (i.e., unalterable) fields.

◆ Provide timely feedback about the effect of user actions. For example, when the user saves a file, a message might indicate that the file is being saved. In addition, it might show, for example, an hourglass indicating that the system is busy performing the requested function. This reminds the user that the system cannot accept any inputs until the current process is completed.

◆ Anticipate errors and design the system to help users avoid them. If an error could have disastrous consequences, the system should require the user to verify the command (e.g., formatting a hard drive, deleting a file, or replacing a large block of text with another block of text) before it is executed. A good design also provides reliable, clear mechanisms for recovering from errors. For example, the Undo command in Word's Edit menu (and the corresponding icon in the tool bar) is an effective way to allow users to reverse previous actions.

2. *Does the design simplify the users' tasks?* A treatise on user interfaces in relation to human cognition is beyond the scope of this textbook. Suffice it to say, an understanding of humans as information processors is a prerequisite to effective interface design. For example, one of the most important findings from studies of human cognition is that we "human information processors" have a limited capacity to process and store information. In fact, processing more than 7±2 pieces or "chunks" of information at a time is virtually impossible for most of us [Miller 1956]. Furthermore, we need help to recall facts that we have learned but have not used recently.

Relating these findings to user interface design suggests that if an automated information system increases the amount of information that we must store and process, its effect will be to impede—rather than to support—task performance. Some guidelines for ensuring that a design does not complicate the user's task follow:

◆ Minimize user memory load by employing menus, function key mappings, pop-up windows, tool bars, and so on to remind users of frequently used features and functions. Limit the number of menu options, open windows, and so on to adhere to the 7±2 rule.

◆ When designing data entry and report screens, follow the *Rule of 1.7* [Sarna & Febish 1994]: At the normal viewing distance from a monitor, the human eye can focus on an area only 1.7 inches in diameter. Thus, each circle with a diameter of 1.7 inches is a natural "chunk" for the human information processor. Arranging data elements on the screen into logical chunks of data, each chunk related to one task or one concept, will focus the user's attention and simplify task completion.

◆ Create a simple, natural dialogue. This goal is becoming more difficult to achieve, especially in commercial software where more and more—and more!—features and functions are added to each product release. Few users will or can avail themselves of all these features. To improve usability, simplicity, and clarity, move seldom used features, functions, or information from the main application screens to submenus and screens.

◆ Provide shortcuts to exploit the experience of expert users. Shortcut keys and keystroke combinations make an interface more flexible and thus more usable by a broader range of users.

3. *Does the design make visible the system's features and functions?* A well-designed user interface makes clear what can and should be done. For example, an external document such as a credit card statement clearly indicates the minimum payment amount and due date and the address to which payment should be sent. Likewise, a human-computer dialog should not open with a blank screen, leaving the user to ponder what she or he is supposed to do. Instead, it should open with a menu, buttons, tool bar, or a combination of the three so that the user knows what functions are available. Other guidelines for achieving visibility include the following:

◆ Provide clear, understandable, relevant feedback. An hourglass, a clock, a gauge moving from 0 percent to 100 percent are all standard—and valuable—feedback mechanisms used to indicate that the system is busy.

◆ Clearly indicate how to exit the system, cancel a command, or close a window. Users need to know "the way out."

◆ Avoid technical jargon and cryptic system language in designing error messages. Where possible, suggest an action to recover from the error.

◆ Use color, boxes, and font changes sparingly and logically to improve visibility and to focus the user's attention. For example, in a human-computer dialog, you might display error messages in red and highlight the screen title in larger letters on a blue background. In a printed report or external document, you might box in the most important information. Note, however, that too many colors, too many boxed in chunks of information, or too many changes in font and type size distract the user, making it difficult to focus on what is important.

4. *Is the design consistent? Does it conform to user interface standards?* If users are to develop an appropriate mental model of the system, the interface must be consistent and its behaviors predictable. Many organizations develop **user interface standards** (also known

TABLE 11.5 Benefits derived from user interface standards

Developers	Users
◆ Fewer design alternatives, i.e., less design complexity	◆ Consistency within and between business functions and applications
◆ Greater portability of interface to other applications and platforms	◆ Reduced learning curve
◆ Easier maintenance	◆ Fewer errors
◆ Less need for user support	◆ Greater satisfaction
◆ Reusable templates for menus, help screens, training manuals, and user manuals	◆ Increased productivity

as *application standards*) that specify design decisions, such as those suggested in Tables 11.3 and 11.4 and stipulate templates for window components, such as the title bar, type and location of options on a menu bar, and so on. Developing and enforcing user interface standards yields several benefits, both for designers and users, as summarized in Table 11.5.

Although standardization is usually a plus, replacing standard, generic menu options with ones specific to the application and tailored to the user's language can make system functions more obvious. For example, if the only relevant file in an application is the Vendor Master file and the only relevant tasks are creating, updating, and deleting vendor records, why not replace the generic File menu with a Vendor menu and the generic Edit menu with a Tasks menu [Comaford 1994]?

◆ REVIEW OF CHAPTER LEARNING OBJECTIVES

1. *Define "user interface" and describe four types of user interfaces, giving guidelines for designing each.*

    A user interface includes those aspects of the system that allow users to interact with its data, software, and hardware. Types of user interfaces include

    a. *External documents*—all the tangible documents that are used to gather inputs to or that are generated as outputs from the system. External documents should create a positive image of the organization, be easy to read, and clearly indicate the expected response, if any.

    b. *Data entry screens*—the application windows used to enter, edit, and delete data. Data entry screens should be designed to reduce errors and increase user productivity (e.g., by mirroring any source documents from which data are entered and limiting the amount of data to be entered).

    c. *Reports*—system outputs that sort, calculate, or compile information in a form meaningful to their intended users. Reports can be printed or displayed on screen. However, only short reports that have few users and a short duration of usefulness should be displayed on screen. A report should be aesthetically pleasing (e.g., be symmetrical and make liberal use of white space) and call attention to important facts (e.g., by selectively using formatting options such as boldface type, underlining, and shading or by using graphs to illustrate salient points).

d. *Human-computer dialog*—the style of interaction between the system and its users. Types of human-computer dialogs include command, menu, form-filling, and direct-manipulation. The predominant dialog should be appropriate for the users' level of expertise and frequency of use. Novice or infrequent users benefit from menu, form-filling, and direct-manipulation dialogs because these do not require learning a command language.

2. *Define "direct manipulation" and discuss its advantages and disadvantages.*

Direct manipulation employs a pointing device such as a mouse to manipulate screen objects that perform system functions. The advantages of a direct-manipulation user interface include its ease of learning and use and its adaptability to various skill levels. However, designing and implementing such complex interfaces is a task for experts.

3. *Describe a five-step process for analyzing and designing user interfaces.*

A process for analyzing and designing interfaces follows:

a. *Analyze the users and their tasks.* Perform a task analysis to determine user characteristics and goals and to identify the inputs and outputs of each task and users' methods for completing the task.

b. *Identify the system's user interfaces.* Examine physical DFDs and use cases to identify the required interfaces.

c. *Select a dialog type for each interface.* The predominant dialog employed in a system must be appropriate given the characteristics of the system's users. The dialog itself can be designed by asking users to envision working with the system and by creating a dialog flow diagram that documents the major interfaces and the flow of control between them.

d. *Develop a prototype.* Map interface objects to the business objects they use to determine the constraints and collaborations that must be captured as the interface is constructed. Whenever feasible, use a GUI generator to build the prototype interfaces.

e. *Review and revise as needed.* Conduct frequent user reviews to gain user feedback and to increase user commitment. Reviews can be conducted to evaluate the "look" of nonoperational interfaces, the "feel" of each interface, and the flow between interfaces.

4. *Explain how to identify user interfaces from physical DFDs and use cases.*

Physical DFDs indicate system behaviors and interactions between external entities and the system and between users and the system. A user interface is needed any time an external entity provides inputs to or receives outputs from the system or a manual process (i.e., behavior performed by a user) provides input to or receives output from an automated process (i.e., behavior performed by software). User interfaces can also be identified by examining use cases for these same kinds of interactions. Any time a user must interact with the system—e.g., by entering data, selecting a command button, or responding to a prompt, a user interface is needed. The same is true of the system's communications with the user; displaying prompts, report screens, and error messages are user interface functions.

5. *Create a dialog flow diagram to document the system's major interfaces and the flow of control between them.*

A dialog flow diagram shows the major screens or windows of the system as a hierarchy of labeled rectangles and indicates the flow of control between screens as directional arrows. For the most part, control in a dialog flow diagram flows from a calling screen to a called screen and then returns to the calling screen after the called screen has performed its function. The structure and flow of control in a dialog flow diagram are usually similar to the structure and flow of control in the related program structure chart.

6. *Discuss four user documentation issues.*

One user documentation issue is *how material should be presented.* Today the user documentation of commercially available software packages provides on-line help systems and/or cue cards, thus integrating documentation with the application. Another issue is *how the material should be organized.* Three ways of organizing content are software-oriented, menu-oriented, and task-oriented; generally speaking, the most effective is task-orientation, which describes system commands in terms of the tasks the user will perform using the application. A third issue is determining *how much material should be presented.* A user guide can be made less intimidating by focusing on what users must know to perform their job tasks and minimizing supplemental materials such as overviews and command indexes. A fourth issue is *how to test the documentation;* having users perform use-case tasks using the documentation is the best test of its clarity and completeness.

7. *List some guidelines for good design and explain how to apply each guideline to user interface design.*

   a. Help the user create an accurate mental model of the system by exploiting effective metaphors, employing the user's language, making clear what actions are possible, providing timely feedback about the effect of user actions, and designing the system to avoid errors or to make recovery easy.

   b. Simplify the task structure by minimizing user memory load (e.g., use menus, tool bars, and so on instead of an obscure command language) and focusing on the features and functions that users are most likely to use.

   c. Make the system's functions visible by clearly indicating the system's current state, providing clear feedback, and reducing clutter.

   d. Be consistent; employ user interface standards whenever feasible to maintain a consistent "look" and "feel" across interfaces and across applications.

◈ KEY TERMS

bar graph	menu dialog	task analysis
command dialog	menu-oriented documenta-	task-oriented documentation
data entry screen	tion	tutorial
dialog flow diagram	metaphor	usability test
direct-manipulation dialog	online help system	user documentation
external document	pie chart	user guide
form-filling dialog	report	user interface
hard copy	soft copy	user interface standards
human-computer dialog	software-oriented	user's mental model
interface object	documentation	
line graph		

◈ DISCUSSION QUESTIONS

1. Define and give an example of each of the following user interfaces:
   a. External document
   b. Data entry screen
   c. Report
   d. Human-computer dialog

2. Discuss two guidelines for designing each type of user interface.

3. How do user characteristics influence the choice of a human-computer dialog? Which dialog types are appropriate for novice users? For expert users? How can a dialog be made flexible to support both kinds of users?

4. In your own words, explain "direct manipulation." How have direct manipulation interfaces benefited users? In what ways do they place additional burdens on designers and implementers?

5. List and briefly explain the five steps in interface analysis and design.

6. What must a designer know about users to design effective interfaces?

7. What must a designer know about the users' tasks to design effective interfaces?

8. How can physical DFDs and use cases be used to identify user interfaces?

9. Explain how a dialog flow diagram is used to design the command hierarchy.

10. Why is the structure of a system's dialog flow diagram similar to the structure of its program structure chart?

11. Explain how to use "envisioning" to design the detailed interactions between users and the system.

12. What is an interface object? How does it differ from a business object?

13. What can an analyst learn by mapping business objects to the interface objects that use them?

14. Describe three points at which users should review interfaces.

15. Define "self-documenting system" in terms of how user documentation is presented.

16. Briefly explain three ways to organize user documentation. Which is most effective? Why?

17. Why should user documentation be tested? How should it be tested?

18. List four general design principles. For each principle, explain two user interface design guidelines.

◈ EXERCISES

1. Examine ETG's current video rental order form, shown in Figure 9.1.
   a. What type of user interface is this?
   b. Use the interface design guidelines and criteria discussed in Sections 11.1 and 11.4 to evaluate this user interface.
   c. How can this interface be improved?

2. Examine the Microsoft Access user interface shown in Figure 9.16.
   a. What type of human-computer dialog is used in this interface?
   b. Use the interface design guidelines and criteria discussed in Sections 11.1 and 11.4 to evaluate this user interface.
   c. How can this interface be improved?

3. Examine ETG's current membership application form shown in Figure 9.5.
   a. What type of user interface is this?
   b. Use the interface design guidelines and criteria discussed in Sections 11.1 and 11.4 to evaluate this user interface.
   c. How can this interface be improved?

4. Examine the user interface shown in Figure 11.4.
   a. What type of user interface is this?
   b. Use the interface design guidelines and criteria discussed in Sections 11.1 and 11.4 to evaluate this user interface.
   c. How can this interface be improved?

5. Examine Bigg's Department Store's credit statement, shown as Figure D.11 in Technical Module D.
   a. What type of user interface is this?
   b. Use the interface design guidelines and criteria discussed in Sections 11.1 and 11.4 to evaluate this user interface.
   c. How can this interface be improved?

6. Figure 10.7 gives the physical DFD of ETG's reports generation process. Identify the user interfaces required to perform this process, and explain why each is needed.

7. Examine the physical DFDs of ETG's rental returns process shown in Figure 10.12. Identify the user interfaces required, and explain why each is needed.

8. Figure 10.1b gives the Customer Makes Payment use case. Identify the user interfaces required to perform this use case, and explain why each is needed.

9. Examine the Customer Buys Sales Tape(s) use case given in Figure 9.2c. Identify the user interfaces required, and explain why each is needed.

10. Perform a task analysis to describe ETG users and the task of processing sales orders. You may need to review ETG case installments and the chapter opening cases in Chapters 9 through 11 to complete this exercise.

   a. Who are the intended users? What is their level of expertise at performing this task? At using automated systems?
   b. What are the users' goals in performing this task?
   c. What information do users need to perform this task?
   d. What information do users generate as they perform this task?
   e. What methods do users employ to perform this task?

11. Using whatever resources you have available—graph paper, word-processing or graphics program, or GUI generator, design a data entry screen so that ETG users can enter and save data from the membership application form shown in Figure 9.5.

12. Using whatever resources you have available—graph paper, word-processing or graphics program, or GUI generator, design a Sales Order data entry screen for ETG's order processing system.

◈ REFERENCES

Appleton, E. L. "Put Usability to the Test." *Datamation*, July 15, 1993, pp. 61–62.

Comaford, C. "Meaningful Menu Makes the GUI." *Windows Sources*, May 1994, pp. 228–229.

Dix, L. Z. "Users' Champion." *Computerworld*, July 5, 1993, pp. 71–72.

Hoadley, E. D. "Investigating the Effects of Color." *Communications of the ACM,* February 1990.

Miller, G. A. "The Magical Number Seven, Plus or Minus Two: Some Limits on Our Capacity to Process Information." *Psychological Review* 63 (1956), pp. 63, 81–97.

Molich, R., and J. Nielsen. "Improving a Human-Computer Dialogue." *Communications of the ACM*, March 1990, pp. 338–348.

Nielsen, J. "Traditional Dialogue Design Applied to Modern User Interfaces." *Communications of the ACM*, October 1990, pp. 109–117.

Norman, D. A. *The Design of Everyday Things*. New York: Doubleday, 1988.

Norman, D. A., and S. W. Draper. *User Centered System Design: New Perspectives on Human-Computer Interaction*. Hillsdale, NJ: Lawrence Erlbaum Associates, 1986.

Rettig, M. "Interface Design When You Don't Know How." *Communications of the ACM* 35, no. 1 (January 1992), pp. 29–34.

Sarna, D. E. Y., and G. J. Febish. "What Makes a GUI Work?" *Datamation*, July 15, 1994, pp. 29, 82.

Schneiderman, B. "The Future of Interactive Systems and the Emergence of Direct Manipulation." *Behavior and Information Technology* 1 (1982), pp. 237–256.

———. "Direct Manipulation: A Step Beyond Programming Languages." IEEE Computer 16, no. 8 (1983), pp. 57–69.

Tasker, D., and B. Von Halle. "Database Design: An Object for Everyone." *Database Programming and Design*, June 1995, pp. 11–16.

Tasker, D., and B. Von Halle. "Database Design: Where the Wild Things Are." *Database Programming and Design*, May 1995, pp. 13–16.

Yourdon, E. *Object-Oriented Systems Design: An Integrated Approach*. Englewood Cliffs, NJ: Yourdon Press/Prentice-Hall, 1994. See especially Chapter 19.

DOCUMENTING DESIGN SPECIFICATIONS

Iterative Analysis, Design, Preliminary Construction, and Review

1. Analyze system structure and behavior.
   a. Analyze system data structures.
   b. Analyze system behavior.
   c. Analyze system interfaces.

2. Design system structure and behavior.
   a. Design system data structures.
   b. Design system behavior.
   c. Design system interfaces.

3. Construct prototype for user review.

4. *Conduct user review.*

5. Repeat steps 1–4, if changes are needed.

Throughout the iterative analysis, design, and preliminary construction stage of systems development, developers work with users to evolve the new system. When the time allotted for this stage has elapsed, the developers must finalize the design specifications and plan the project's final construction, testing, and installation activities. The design specifications are documented in a report, which is presented to the users at a JAD-review-and-confirmation workshop. At the workshop, the users review the preliminary system, indicate modifications or enhancements required in the production system, and approve the developers' plans for constructing, testing, and installing the production system.

   This chapter discusses the purposes, audience, and contents of the design specification report and explains the activities of the JAD-review-and-confirmation workshop. It also describes the planning that must occur before the last development stage begins. After completing this chapter, you should be able to

1. Explain the purposes and identify the intended readers of the design specification report.

2. List and discuss the contents of each section of the design specification report.

3. Describe the activities performed and the issues addressed in a JAD-review-and-confirmation workshop.

4. Use a Gantt chart to document a plan.

5. Describe the purpose and contents of three plans: the construction plan, the test plan, and the installation plan.

12.1 ◈ PREPARING AND VERIFYING THE DESIGN SPECIFICATION REPORT

The two major activities remaining in the iterative analysis, design, and preliminary construction stage are to prepare the design specification report and to conduct a JAD-confirmation session to gain user approval of the design.

The **design specification report** documents the system data structure, behavior, and user interface designs that have evolved, and it outlines a plan to complete the project. Thus, it serves two purposes: (1) it documents the system's design so that when future modifications are required, the new development team will have a clear, complete description of the system; and (2) it communicates the design specifications and the developers' plan for implementing the production system to the users, who must approve both the design and plan before final construction can begin. Consequently, the design specification report has two audiences, each with very different needs. Its technical documentation of design specifications is prepared for future developers, who may be called upon to modify or enhance the system or to integrate it with another newly developed system. Its nontechnical presentation of these specifications is prepared for users, who need to understand the design so that they can approve it and signal the beginning of the final construction, system test, and installation activities. Specifically, users need to understand how the PPDSH components have been integrated to produce a system that performs the IPOSC requirements identified during analysis.

PREPARING THE DESIGN SPECIFICATION REPORT

The report-writing guidelines presented in Chapter 6 are equally applicable to the design specification report. Although some of the content of this report differs from the problem definition report, its presentation style is quite similar. You can use the sample problem definition report at the end of Chapter 6 as a model as you prepare several sections of the design specification report.

The contents of the design specification report vary somewhat depending on the nature of the particular project and the system it documents. A sample report outline is given in Table 12.1. Generally speaking, the report will contain the following material:

◆ A system overview providing a nontechnical description of system components and functions as they relate to the functional requirements.

TABLE 12.1 Contents of design specification report

A. Preliminaries
   Letter of transmittal
   Executive summary (for short reports, include in transmittal letter)
   Table of contents (optional for short reports)

B. Report Body
   Report overview
   System overview
   Technical specifications (may be placed in appendices and referenced in System overview)
   Construction plan
   Test plan
   Installation and training plans

C. Appendices

◆ The finalized versions of various system models, e.g., physical DFDs, data models and physical database design, class specifications, program structure chart, and so on.

◆ Estimates of performance requirements to be used in acquiring hardware and/or software and in testing the system.

◆ Construction plan.

◆ Test plan.

◆ Installation and training plans.

The first section of the design specification report, the **system overview**, describes the system components and functions in a manner and language appropriate for the system's non-technical users. Its purpose is to provide easy-to-understand explanations of the final system design and to relate aspects of this design to the functional requirements identified earlier in the project. Because the final prototype serves as "living" illustration of the system's design, this section of the report should focus on explaining how the production system will satisfy the most important functional requirements.

The contents of the system overview include the following:

◆ Restatement of system objectives and project constraints.

◆ Restatement of detailed IPOSC requirements.

◆ Description of the new system's components and functions.

◆ Discussion of how the system design meets the system objectives and satisfies the IPOSC requirements while conforming to the project constraints.

◆ Summary of changes in organizational structure, job descriptions, procedures, and/or workflows required to support the new system.

Note that this section opens with restatements of the system objectives, project constraints, and IPOSC requirements. These were initially stated in the problem definition report, but they may have changed during JAD workshops and iterative analysis and design. For example,

ETG modified its system objectives and added or clarified some IPOSC requirements during the JAD workshops. Objectives and requirements must be clearly stated here because they will be verified during the JAD-review-and-confirmation workshop and will become inputs to the acceptance and post-implementation reviews conducted at the end of the project.

After presentation of restated objectives and requirements, the system overview continues with a description of the new system's components and functions. Here you explain how the PPDSH components have been integrated into a cohesive system. You also explain how this system configuration will perform the IPOSC functions. Although much of this section may consist of textual discussions, wherever possible, you should include graphical illustrations. For example, Figure 12.1 gives an excerpt of the design specification report that Victoria and Denny prepared for ETG. Notice that portions of the text descriptions have been italicized to highlight the IPOSC requirements embodied in the design.

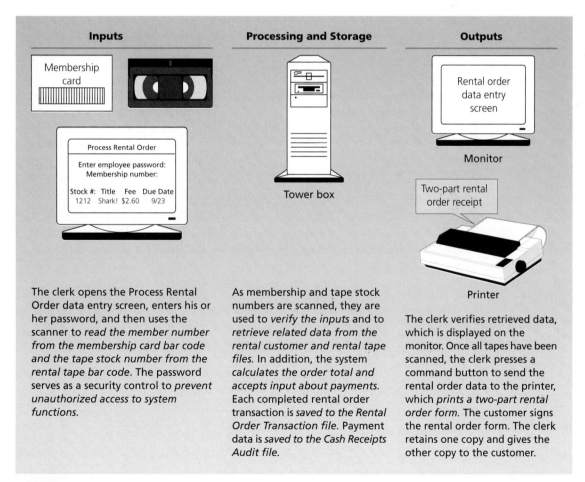

Inputs	Processing and Storage	Outputs

The clerk opens the Process Rental Order data entry screen, enters his or her password, and then uses the scanner to *read the member number from the membership card bar code and the tape stock number from the rental tape bar code*. The password serves as a security control to *prevent unauthorized access to system functions*.

As membership and tape stock numbers are scanned, they are used to *verify the inputs* and to *retrieve related data from the rental customer and rental tape files*. In addition, the system *calculates the order total and accepts input about payments*. Each completed rental order transaction is *saved to the Rental Order Transaction file*. Payment data is *saved to the Cash Receipts Audit file*.

The clerk verifies retrieved data, which is displayed on the monitor. Once all tapes have been scanned, the clerk presses a command button to send the rental order data to the printer, which *prints a two-part rental order form*. The customer signs the rental order form. The clerk retains one copy and gives the other copy to the customer.

FIGURE 12.1 Graphical illustation of system components and functions

Another major section of the design specification report, the **technical specifications**, provides final models of the system, including the physical DFDs, object relationship or other data model, class specifications or physical database design, use cases, dialog flow diagram, program structure charts, system flowchart, structured-text procedure descriptions, and so on. The content of this section depends on the modeling techniques used to analyze and design the system's data structures and behaviors. If an integrated CASE tool was used to analyze and design the system, many of these models can be generated from the tool's project encyclopedia. The technical specifications may also include detailed **performance requirements**—factors such as response time, transaction volume, data volume, and so on—for use in acquiring software, hardware devices, and telecommunications capabilities.

The technical documentation presented in this section should be complete and accurate so that future developers can use it to gain an understanding of the system when revisions or enhancements are needed. Preparing this documentation now will spare you having to do it during final construction. However, this section of the design specification report can be created at a later date without significantly affecting the users' ability to approve the system design—assuming that the system overview provides a complete view of system functions and components. In fact, it may be feasible to provide these technical models and specifications in an appendix and simply refer your reader to them at appropriate points in the system overview.

Next the **construction plan** indicates the tasks that must be performed to finalize the system, including who will perform these activities, when they will be performed, and what additional resources, if any, will be required. If the iterative analysis and design stage yields a complete, production-ready system, very little work will remain for final construction. However, in larger, more complex projects, considerable time and effort may be needed to gear up the preliminary system for production. For example, a prototype database and programs may have been constructed on a stand-alone desktop computer, but the production system must be upgraded to operate in a networked environment. The design specification report should also provide a test plan and an installation plan. The **test plan** indicates the testing strategy to be employed, defines test scenarios, and assigns responsibility for testing activities to users and developers. The **installation plan** indicates the chosen installation strategy, schedules and assigns responsibility for all installation activities, and identifies any additional resources needed.

At this point, you may find it difficult to visualize these plans because many of the activities included in them have not been discussed yet. You will learn more about final construction, testing, and installation in Chapter 13.

✓ Check Your Understanding 12-1

Indicate in which section of the design specification report (SO—system overview or TS—technical specifications) each of the following would be found.

_____ 1. Restatement of system objectives.

_____ 2. Dialog flow diagram and system flowchart.

_____ 3. Summary of changes in organizational structure, policies, and workflows.

_____ 4. Discussion of how the system meets the IPOSC requirements.

_____ 5. IPOSC requirements and project scope.

_____ 6. Program structure chart or class specifications.

_____ 7. DFDs and/or use cases.

_____ 8. Object relationship model.

_____ 9. Description of system components.

_____ 10. Performance requirements.

VERIFYING THE DESIGN SPECIFICATION REPORT: JAD-REVIEW-AND-CONFIRMATION WORKSHOP

The design specification report documents the system design, telling users how it fulfills their functional requirements. However, "telling" is seldom as effective as "showing." Thus, you also need to conduct a JAD-review-and-confirmation workshop to demonstrate the preliminary system. As this evolved, it was demonstrated informally to selected users, but the workshop presents a formal review in which users approve not only the system design but also the development team's construction, testing, and installation plans. The inputs to this workshop are the design specification report and the preliminary system.

Reviewing and Confirming the System Design

The first major activity of the review-and-confirmation workshop is to approve the system design. The development team demonstrates the system's functions, noting how each function satisfies the IPOSC requirements identified earlier in the project. This demonstration is particularly effective if one or more users are called upon to execute these functions using the preliminary system. If the demonstration environment does not simulate the production environment, the development team should alert users to this fact and explain how system performance may differ during production. For example, perhaps the prototype was developed as a stand-alone system but the production system will operate in a networked environment. If response time will be longer or certain system features will be modified when the system is scaled up for network operation, developers should explain these differences.

During the demonstration, users pose questions, ask for clarification of design features, and generally evaluate how well the system design meets their needs. Developers and/or the scribe document any desired changes or enhancements. Ideally, the users will approve the design "as is" and request no changes or only minor changes. If modifications or enhancements are proposed, the workshop facilitator leads the participants in a discussion to

1. Decide whether to approve the design "as is" or with modifications.

2. Determine which modifications and enhancements must be made for the design to be accepted.

3. Prioritize these design changes.

The project manager and developers may be called upon to evaluate the feasibility of implementing the proposed changes and to estimate the additional resources—time, labor, budget—required to do so. If significant changes are proposed, the JAD participants, in essence, conduct an informal, on-the-spot feasibility study. If the changes are infeasible or if implementing them requires substantial additional resources, exceeding the budget and schedule, the user-sponsor may opt to cancel the project.

Thus, the review-and-confirmation workshop must yield a formal "sign-off" if the project is to move to the final systems development stage. If the user-sponsor approves the preliminary system with no or minor changes, the development team moves forward to perform final construction, system test, and installation activities. If significant changes are required, one or more additional iterations of the analysis-design-preliminary construction stage and another review-and-confirmation workshop may be needed. The worst-case scenario is that the user-sponsor finds the system completely unacceptable and cancels the project—an unlikely outcome if the system was subjected to frequent informal reviews and the user-sponsor was kept abreast of the outcome of these reviews.

Reviewing and Confirming the Construction, Test, and Installation Plans

Assuming that the user-sponsor approves the move to final construction, the second major activity of the JAD workshop is to review and confirm the plans for constructing and testing the system and converting from the old system to the new. Section 12.2 describes the contents of and issues addressed in these plans. Here the activities of reviewing and confirming the plans are described. Chapter 13 explains the activities performed and the issues addressed during the last stage of systems development.

The JAD facilitator presents each plan, soliciting comments and questions from the user-participants, which are answered by the project manager or other IS participants. Two important considerations during this discussion are (1) agreeing on the division of responsibilities between users and developers and (2) approving the schedule. For example, the construction plan may indicate that a select group of users is responsible for writing the user documentation or revising job descriptions; similarly, the test plan may make users responsible for creating test data and performing usability tests, or the installation plan may require users to perform the tedious task of converting manual records to digital records. Approving the installation schedule is a critical concern for the user-sponsor because some of the activities performed during this development stage can disrupt the organization's daily operations and/or take users away from their normal duties. Such disruptive activities must be scheduled to avoid peak business periods and to minimize the negative effects on the organization.

If the construction plan includes acquiring additional hardware or software, the JAD workshop is an appropriate forum for verifying performance requirements and defining selection criteria so that the acquisition process (discussed more fully in Chapter 13) can commence as soon as possible—so that these desired resources are available in a timely manner.

As the test plan is discussed, users are asked to provide the criteria that will be used to evaluate the final system during the acceptance review. These **acceptance criteria** state the system quality criteria necessary for user acceptance. These may have been defined during an earlier JAD workshop but should nevertheless be revisited and verified as part of the test plan. Acceptance criteria may address *system efficiency* (e.g., response time, transaction volume, non-redundant data and procedures), *system clarity* (e.g., usability, quality of reports and user interfaces, amount and quality of documentation), and *system reliability* (e.g., appropriate integrity and security controls, mean-time-to-failure, backup and recovery procedures). Looking to the future, the acceptance criteria may also address *system maintainability* (e.g., amount and quality of technical documentation, modularity of software, ease of maintenance) and *system flexibility* (e.g., portability to different platforms, adaptability to changes in procedures or other components).

Generally speaking, users should identify about ten such criteria. Too few criteria provide an inadequate verification of system quality; too many yield an acceptance review that essentially replicates a full-scale system test.

✓ Check Your Understanding 12-2

Indicate whether each of the following statements is true (T) or false (F).

_____ 1. During the JAD-review-and-confirmation workshop, only developers should be allowed to demonstrate the prototype because only they understand how it functions.

_____ 2. No design changes may be proposed during the design review-and-confirmation workshop; the system must be accepted "as is" or rejected.

_____ 3. Both users and developers may be assigned responsibility for final construction, testing, and conversion activities.

_____ 4. Even if the system design is unacceptable, the project's user-sponsor has no choice but to continue funding the project through final construction, testing, and installation.

_____ 5. The installation schedule must be approved by the user-sponsor to ensure that its activities are scheduled to minimize disruption of business operations.

_____ 6. Acceptance criteria state the system quality criteria the system must satisfy to be accepted by users.

_____ 7. Users should identify at least 25 acceptance criteria to ensure adequate verification of system quality.

12.2 ◆ PLANNING FINAL CONSTRUCTION, SYSTEM TEST, AND INSTALLATION ACTIVITIES

As the iterative analysis and design stage is brought to a close, planning begins for the last development stage: final construction, system test, and installation. To ensure that the system meets its system quality goals and that the project meets its project management goals, the project manager must carefully plan the activities of this final stage. An approved preliminary system must be transformed into a production system that satisfies the system objectives. Moreover, the process of converting from the old system to the new must be a smooth one, minimizing any disruptions of the organization's daily operations.

Planning involves the following tasks:

1. Identifying activities to be performed.
2. Determining dependencies between these activities.
3. Assigning personnel and resources to each activity.
4. Scheduling the begin date and end date of each activity.

The second task, determining **task dependencies**, requires that the project manager understand the inputs and outputs of each task so that activities are scheduled in the correct sequence. If Activity 1 provides outputs that are inputs to Activity 2, then Activity 1 must be completed before Activity 2 can begin. For example, user documentation cannot be written until the features and functions of the system are stable; that is, the system's data structures, behaviors, and user interfaces must be fully defined before a manual documenting these features and functions can be completed. Thus, a task dependency for the "create user documentation" activity is the definition of system data structures, behaviors, and user interfaces.

A **Gantt chart**, shown in Figure 12.2, is a tool used to perform the four project-planning tasks just outlined. It combines textual and graphical elements to document *what task* will be performed *by whom* using *what resources* over *what time frame*. Critical points in the schedule can also be indicated on the Gantt chart. As shown in the figure, a diamond symbolizes a **milestone**—the completion of a task that produces a measurable output of critical importance to meeting the project schedule. For example, Task 1 is an activity that produces a milestone; if Task 1 is not completed on schedule, Task 2 will begin later than planned, thus delaying project completion. Milestones aid in monitoring a project schedule by calling the project manager's attention to critical tasks that must be completed on time.

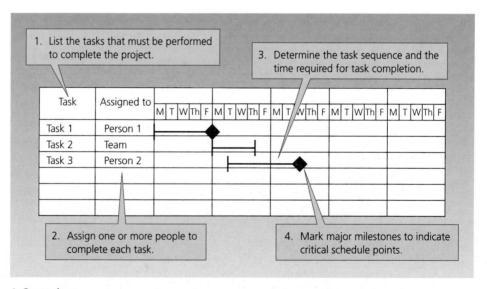

FIGURE 12.2   A Gantt chart

CONSTRUCTION PLAN

The construction plan identifies the activities required to transform the preliminary system into a production-grade system. These activities include

1. Creating the production database and software.
2. Writing user and technical documentation.
3. Preparing training materials.
4. Acquiring hardware and telecommunication devices.
5. Preparing the facility to house these devices.

The construction plan also identifies and suggests strategies for obtaining any additional resources that will be needed, such as CASE tools, GUI generators, a DBMS—any of the tools discussed in Chapter 8 as critical to the success of a rapid application development (RAD) project.

Two **final construction strategies** are the single-team versus the multiple-team approach and the single-phase versus the multiple-phase approach. Which approach is employed depends on how much time and effort is required to transform the preliminary system into a production-grade system. In the typical RAD project, final construction is performed in one phase by one small team of four or five developers and consumes at most two or three months of a six-month project schedule. A smaller, simpler system may require a smaller team and less than a month. In contrast, for a larger, more complex system, construction activities may be completed by a single team but spread over multiple phases, each phase delivering a portion of the total system functionality. Another approach to large projects is to perform the activities in one phase but to assign them to multiple teams working concurrently on different aspects of the system. For example, one team may be responsible for acquiring hardware and software, another for creating the production database, yet another for writing user documentation, and so on.

Thus, the complexity of the construction plan also depends on how complex the system is and how much functionality has already been implemented in the preliminary system. If multiple teams and/or multiple phases are required for final construction, the construction plan must indicate the activities, personnel, resources, and schedule for each team and/or phase.

Figure 12.3 gives the construction plan that Victoria created for the ETG project. Notice that this small, relatively simple project requires only two developers and a handful of users to be involved in final construction. Notice also that because the preliminary system implemented so much of the system's functionality, most construction activities require only a few days to finalize the various system components. Furthermore, because hardware and software were acquired earlier in the project, no effort need be devoted to this activity now. Finally, notice that ETG users play a significant role in completing the construction tasks; this involvement will facilitate training and increase user commitment.

TEST PLAN

Testing examines the PPDSH components and the IPOSC functions to verify that they satisfy the functionality criteria of the quality goal of system development. That is, the system must be

Construction Schedule for ETG's Order Processing System								
Construction Activity	Assigned To	Resources	6/5 to 6/7	6/8 to 6/9	6/12 to 6/14	6/15 to 6/16	6/19 to 6/21	6/22 to 6/23
Finalize data structures	Denny	Access, ORM, physical DB design						
Complete data dictionary and system documentation	Denny	Access, ORM, physical DB design						
Finalize and unit test user interfaces	Victoria	Access, detailed use cases						
Finalize and unit test macros	Victoria	Access, detailed use cases, structured-text procedures						
Plan training	Victoria	Detailed use cases, user manual outline						
Create user manual and new job descriptions	Paul, Susan, Denny	WP, use cases, structured-text procedures						
Prepare and test membership cards	Beto, Denny	Cards, bar code labeler, scanning HW/SW						
Prepare and test tape labels	Helen, Denny	Tape security labels, bar code labeler, scanning HW/SW						

FIGURE 12.3   Example of a construction plan

tested to ensure that it is accurate, reliable, clear, efficient, flexible, and maintainable. The test plan indicates the extent of testing to be performed and the chosen testing strategy; it also outlines the testing procedure and determines who will test what and when. The extent of testing required depends on several factors [Texas Instruments 1992]:

◆ System complexity, including procedural complexity and the stability of the chosen information architecture.

◆ The degree to which reusable code and design elements have been used to construct the system.

◆ The impact of system failure on the organization.

The greater the system complexity and impact of failure, and the smaller the extent to which reusable components were employed, the more fully the system must be tested. These factors and their effect on the choice of a testing strategy are discussed and illustrated in Chapter 13.

Two fundamental **testing strategies** are the black-box strategy and the glass-box strategy [Rettig 1991]. The *black-box strategy,* as its name implies, treats the system as a black box; if, given certain inputs, the system generates the correct outputs, the system is assumed to be correct. In contrast, the *glass-box strategy* looks "inside the box" and verifies system components and functions by, for example, examining each line of code. The test plan indicates which of these strategies will be employed and justifies this choice. It also outlines the kinds of tests to be performed and the testing procedure to be followed. The **testing procedure** stipulates how test data will be created, what test cases will be run, who will perform each test, and how the results will be documented. A Gantt chart is an effective tool for documenting the test schedule and responsibilities. A test specification form, which is discussed in Chapter 13, can be used to document each test and its results.

Figure 12.4 gives the test plan that Victoria developed for ETG's order processing system. Again, notice the high level of user participation in the testing activities. Notice also that, by detailing each type of test to be performed, Victoria's test schedule also documents the test cases to be developed.

Test Plan for ETG's Order Processing System

Testing Strategy

Unit Tests. Each hardware component, each Access Basic macro, and each interface was thoroughly tested as the preliminary system was developed. These will be tested individually again as the final system components are implemented. Because the software component has been implemented as a number of single-purpose macros, we feel confident in using the black-box testing strategy to test these macros. The compatibility of the hardware devices has already been demonstrated to some degree as we used these devices to build the system. In addition, these devices will be subjected to stress and volume tests to evaluate their capacity and performance limits.

System Test. A system test will be conducted to verify the efficiency and effectiveness of the system and to ensure that all components work together as an integrated whole. The clarity and accuracy of the user documentation will be verified by having users follow user manual instructions to execute test cases. These tests will also verify the accuracy and completeness of the software and data components. We will use the black-box testing strategy for our system test. In addition, Denny and I will subject the system to stress and volume tests to determine its maximum capacity and performance limits.

Testing Procedure

The detailed use cases defined during our earlier JAD workshops will serve as test cases. Working with test data, we will ask users, following directions in the user guide, to execute each use case. If the system performs as described in the use case and generates the correct outputs, we can assume that it is functioning correctly. To support this assumption, we will also design test cases to force errors, thus ensuring that the system recognizes, reponds correctly to, and recovers smoothly from errors. Test specification forms will be used to document the test cases and results.

Test Data

Test data will be derived from historical records of actual membership application, rental order, sales order, newsletter sign-up and fine-processing transactions. In addition, a subset of the Master file records (e.g., Rental Tape, Sales Tape, Customer, Rental Customer) will be ported to the test environment to be used as test data.

Test Schedule

The schedule for performing the various system tests is documented in the Test Plan Gantt chart.

FIGURE 12.4   Example of a test plan, page 1

Testing Schedule for ETG's Order Processing System									
Test Activity	Assigned To	6/26	6/27	6/28 AM	6/28 PM	6/29 AM	6/29 PM	6/30	7/5 AM
Create test data	Denny, Beto	░	◆						
Test system									
• Verify tape label scanning process	Denny, Helen, Bill		░						
• Verify card label scanning process	Denny, Helen, Bill		░						
• Verify membership application use case	Denny, John, Susan			░					
• Verify rental order processing use case	Denny, John, Susan			░					
• Verify sales order processing use case	Denny, John, Susan			░					
• Verify fine processing use case	Denny, John, Susan			░					
• Verify rental return processing use case	Denny, Helen, Beto				░				
• Verify newsletter sign-up processing use case	Denny, Helen, Beto, Corita				░				
• Verify tape availability request use case	Denny, Helen, Beto, Connie				░				
• Verify management reporting use case	Denny, Helen, Beto, Paul, Linda				░				
• Verify mailing labels processing use case	Denny, Helen, Beto, Corita				░				
Test backup, security, and recovery procedures									
• Verify system startup/ shut-down procedures	Denny, Beto, Susan, Paul					░			
• Verify daily data backup procedures	Denny, Beto, Susan, Paul					░			
• Verify weekly historical backup procedures	Denny, Beto, Susan, Paul					░			
• Verify tape and customer record maintenance	Denny, Beto, Susan, Paul						░		
• Verify system failure recovery procedures	Denny, Beto, Susan, Paul						░		
• Verify security controls	Denny, Linda, Paul						░		
Conduct volume test	Victoria, Denny							░	
Conduct stress test	Victoria, Denny							░	
Review test results with ETG	All								░

FIGURE 12.4   Example of a test plan, page 2

INSTALLATION PLAN

After the system components and functions have been verified, it is time to convert from the old system to the new system. The installation plan

◆ Identifies, schedules, and assigns responsibility for installation activities.

◆ Specifies user training requirements and outlines a training plan.

◆ Specifies an installation strategy and describes a fall-back plan in the event of system failure.

◆ Indicates how changes in organizational culture—e.g., organizational structure, job descriptions, procedures, and/or workflows—will be implemented.

Figure 12.5 gives the installation plan that Victoria created for the ETG project.

Installation activities include training users, converting data, dismantling the old system and installing new hardware and software, acquiring supplies, creating a user and system documentation library, and so on. Factors of concern here are dividing responsibilities between users and developers, setting an installation date, planning the training schedule and materials, and minimizing the time required to switch from the old system to the new system. The project manager should create a Gantt chart that schedules these activities in a logical sequence, taking into consideration task dependencies. Also, as noted earlier, the project's user-sponsor should be consulted to ensure that installation activities do not disrupt the organization's daily operations.

The **training plan** defines the user training requirements, including required materials and equipment and the training schedule. Because a detailed training plan is developed during final construction, only an overview of training requirements is needed in the installation plan.

An **installation strategy** defines how the old system will be dismantled and replaced by the new system. The four installation strategies are

◆ *Direct cutover*—the old system is entirely dismantled and immediately replaced by the new system.

◆ *Phased installation*—conversion to the new system occurs in phases, e.g., by subsystem or geographic location.

◆ *Pilot installation*—one location, division, or branch office performs a direct cutover; the system is installed at other locations if the pilot is successful.

◆ *Parallel operation*—both the old and the new system are operated concurrently until the user-sponsor has been assured of the new system's accuracy and reliability.

These strategies and the rationale for selecting each one are presented in Chapter 13. In addition, the installation plan must recommend a **fall-back plan** that specifies how daily operations will be continued in the event of system failure.

The installation plan should also address any changes in organizational structure, policies, procedures, or workflows engendered by the new system. As noted in Chapter 4, systems development is planned organizational change. Consequently, an additional purpose of the installation plan is to identify the required changes and to suggest strategies for implementing these changes.

Installation Plan for ETG's Order Processing System

Installation Strategy

We will use the direct cutover strategy to convert from the old manual system to the new automated system. Manual order processing will cease at the close of business on Tuesday, July 18. ETG will be closed for business Wednesday, July 19, so that we can complete the conversion. When ETG opens for business Thursday morning, July 20, the new automated system will be in place. As a fall-back in the unlikely event of system failure, we will maintain ETG's manual sales and rental order forms so that processing of these transactions can continue. The installation schedule is documented in the Installation Plan Gantt chart.

Training Requirements

All ETG clerks will need training in the normal operation of the new order processing system, including all transaction processing procedures and tape availability processing procedures. In addition, two clerks, Paul, and Linda will be trained to generate periodic management reports and to perform database maintenance, file backup, and system recovery procedures. We estimate that training in normal processing procedures will require one four-hour session. Training in backup and recovery procedures will require another four-hour session. Both of these sessions are scheduled in the Gantt chart.

Because ETG has no facilities appropriate for use as a classroom, we recommend that the training sessions be conducted in the office suite conference room where we held the JAD workshop. To provide an acceptable level of hands-on training, we will set up at least five computer systems—comparable in "look" and "feel" to ETG's computer system—running the fully tested order processing software. The cost of renting this hardware was factored into the training costs estimated in our cost-benefit analysis. The conference room is equipped with all the audiovisual equipment we will need. Instructional materials include the following:

- A guide to Windows and an explanation of fundamental computer concepts. These are Hernandez & Associates copyrighted materials.
- ETG Order Processing System user guide.
- Transparencies and other instructional materials developed specifically for ETG. These materials will become the property of ETG and can be used to train new hires in the future.

Implementing Changes in Organizational Culture

Changes in organizational structure, policies, and procedures entailed by the new system include the following:

- Elimination of four inventory clerk positions.
- Reassignment of three inventory clerks to sales clerk positions; Susan Young will be reassigned to work with Corita in Promotions.
- Creation of a "system go-fer" position (to be defined further during construction; basically, the person filling this position—Beto has volunteered!—is responsible for maintaining ETG's database, generating periodic and on-demand reports, and other duties).
- Creation of a part-time systems manager position (to be filled by contracting with an independent consultant; contract should be filled by July 14).
- Stipulation and enforcement of a "tighter" fine-payment policy; clerks will be oriented to this policy during training.

We anticipate no adverse effects from the changes in procedures, policies, job descriptions, and so on, that the new system will entail. The ETG "family" has proven to be an enthusiastic, flexible group of people. After their job-loss concerns were assuaged, the ETG clerks embraced the planned changes as an opportunity to improve their job skills by becoming "information systems literate."

FIGURE 12.5   Example of an installation plan (page 1)

Installation Schedule for ETG's Order Processing System											
Installation Activity	**Assigned To**	7/6 to 7/9	7/10 AM	7/11 AM	7/12	7/13	7/14	7/17	7/18	7/19 AM	7/19 4PM
Complete contract for system manager position	Paul, Linda, Victoria						◆				
Train users											
• Data entry	Denny	7/6AM									
• Normal processing	Victoria										
• Backup, recovery	Denny										
Convert data	Denny and off-duty clerks										
Create user and system documentation library	Victoria, Susan										
Obtain and store supplies	Beto, Helen										
Prepare facility	Construction crew, Denny								◆		
Install hardware	Victoria, Denny, Paul, Beto, Bill, Susan										
Install software	Victoria, Denny, Paul, Beto, Bill, Susan										
Verify installed system	Victoria, Denny, Paul, Beto, Bill, Susan										
Conduct user acceptance review	All										

FIGURE 12.5   Example of an installation plan (page 2)

Check Your Understanding 12-3

Indicate the plan that addresses each of the following activities or issues: final construction plan (FC), test plan (T), or installation plan (I). A single activity or issue may be relevant to one or more plans.

_____ 1.   Changes in organizational structure, culture, workflows, and procedures.

_____ 2.   Activities required to transform the preliminary system into a production-grade system.

_____ 3.   System accuracy, reliability, and clarity.

_____ 4.   Transforming manual records into digital records.

_____ 5.   Minimizing disruption of business operations.

_____ 6.   Assigning multiple teams or scheduling multiple phases to complete activities.

_____ 7.   Determining who will perform what activity, using what resources, in what time frame.

_____ 8. Identifying training requirements and planning training activities.

_____ 9. Selecting a black-box or a glass-box strategy.

_____ 10. Selecting a strategy by evaluating system complexity and the impact of system failure.

◆ REVIEW OF CHAPTER LEARNING OBJECTIVES

1. _Explain the purposes and identify the intended readers of the design specification report._

   The design specification report serves two purposes: (1) it documents the system's design, providing a clear, complete description of the system to guide future development; and (2) it communicates the design specifications and the developers' plans for implementing the production system to the users. Thus, the design specification report has two audiences, each with very different needs: (1) future developers, who may be called upon to modify or enhance the system or to integrate it with another newly developed system; and (2) users, who need to understand the PPDSH components and the IPOSC functions to evaluate how well the system will serve the organization's information-processing needs.

2. _List and discuss the contents of each section of the design specification report._

   The _system overview_ describes the system components and functions, providing easy-to-understand explanations of the final system design and relating aspects of this design to the functional requirements identified earlier in the project. The _technical specifications_ section provides final models of the system, including the physical DFDs, object relationship or other data model, class specifications or physical database design, use cases, dialog flow diagram, program structure charts, system flowchart, structured-text procedure descriptions, and so on. The content of this section depends on the modeling techniques used to analyze and design the system's data structures and behaviors. The _construction plan_ indicates the tasks that must be performed to finalize the system, including who will perform these activities, when they will be performed, and any additional resources required to construct the production system. The _test plan_ indicates the testing strategy to be employed, defines test scenarios, and assigns responsibility for testing activities to users and developers. The _installation plan_ indicates the chosen installation strategy, schedules and assigns responsibility for all installation activities, and identifies any additional resources needed.

3. _Describe the activities performed and the issues addressed in a JAD-review-and-confirmation workshop._

   The JAD-review-and-confirmation workshop is a formal review in which user participants (1) review the system design and the development team's construction, testing, and conversion plans; (2) verify performance requirements and identify selection criteria for hardware and software acquisition; and (3) define acceptance criteria to be used to evaluate the final system. Issues addressed in the system design review include (1) whether to approve the design as is or with modifications, (2) which modifications and enhancements must be made for the design to be accepted, and (3) prioritization of design changes. The project manager and developers may be called upon to evaluate the feasibility of implementing the proposed changes and to estimate the additional resources—time, labor, budget—required to do so. Issues addressed during the planning review include agreeing on the division of responsibilities between users and developers and approving the schedule.

4. *Use a Gantt chart to document a plan.*

    A Gantt chart is a planning tool that combines textual and graphical elements to document *what task* will be performed *by whom* using *what resources* over *what time frame*. It is also used to monitor the status of a project. Critical points in the schedule are indicated on the Gantt chart as *milestones,* tasks that produce a measurable output of critical importance to meeting the project schedule. Milestones aid in monitoring a project schedule by calling the project manager's attention to critical tasks that must be completed on time.

5. *Describe the purpose and contents of three plans: the construction plan, the test plan, and the installation plan.*

    The *construction plan* identifies, assigns responsibility for, and schedules the activities required to transform the preliminary system into a production system. Activities addressed in the construction plan include creating the production database and software, writing user and technical documentation, preparing training materials, acquiring hardware and telecommunication devices, and preparing the facility to house these devices. The construction plan also identifies and suggests strategies for obtaining any additional resources required to construct the production system.

    The *test plan* indicates the extent of testing to be performed and the chosen testing strategy, outlines the testing procedure, and determines who will test what and when.

    The *installation plan* identifies, schedules, and assigns responsibility for installation activities; determines the user training requirements and outlines a training plan; selects an installation strategy and describes a fall-back plan in the event of system failure.

◆ KEY TERMS

acceptance criteria	installation plan	technical specifications
construction plan	installation strategy	test plan
design specification report	milestone	testing procedure
fall-back plan	performance requirements	testing strategies
final construction strategies	system overview	training plan
Gantt chart	task dependency	

◆ DISCUSSION QUESTIONS

1. Identify the two purposes and audiences of a design specification report. Which sections of the report serve each purpose and are directed at each audience?

2. In what ways is a design specification report similar to a problem definition report? How is it different?

3. Describe the contents of the *system overview* section of a design specification report.

4. Describe the contents of the *technical specifications* section of a design specification report.

5. Explain the statement "The JAD-review-and-confirmation workshop serves as a formal 'sign-off.'"

6. Discuss the three possible outcomes of a JAD-review-and-confirmation workshop.

7. Explain the steps that ensue if users require modifications before accepting the system design.

8. List the four major planning activities. How is a Gantt chart used to perform these activities and to monitor the project schedule?

9. Describe the purpose, contents, and issues of a construction plan.

10. Explain two construction strategies.

11. Describe the purpose, contents, and issues of a test plan.

12. Describe the purpose, contents, and issues of an installation plan.

◆ EXERCISES

1. Examine the physical DFDs of ETG's rental return process shown in Figure 10.12 and the list of IPOSC requirements given in Figure 5 of the ETG JAD case. Then create a graphic (similar to the one in Figure 12.1) that transforms the technical design specifications of the DFDs into a graphical illustration that documents these specifications but also is easy for users to understand and relates system design features to the IPOSC requirements.

2. Reread the Delta Products case problem given in Exercise 10.3 of Chapter 10. Assume that Delta has designed the order fulfillment system to run on a local area network (LAN) comprised of desktop computers linked to a centralized file server. The Order Entry screen runs on the SOP clerk's desktop computer; all files are stored in the centralized file server. Create a graphic (similar to the one in Figure 12.1) that illustrates the order fulfillment system's components and functions and relates these design elements to the following IPOSC requirements:

◆ Receive written sales orders from sales representatives.
◆ Verify customer before processing order.
◆ Retrieve customer billing and shipping address from customer record.

◆ Accept product number and quantity as real-time inputs.

◆ Determine product availability.

◆ Calculate extended price, subtotal, discount, discounted subtotal, sales tax, and total for each order.

◆ Create a sales order transaction record.

Note: Illustrate *only* those aspects of the design that embody these requirements.

3. Reread the ABC Corp. case problem given in Exercise 10.4 of Chapter 10. Assume that ABC has designed the supply requisition system to run on a LAN comprised of desktop computers linked to a centralized minicomputer that functions as a file server. The user interfaces run on the desktop computers; all files are stored on the centralized file server. Create a graphic (similar to the one in Figure 12.1) that illustrates the supply requisition system's components and functions and relates these design elements to the following IPOSC requirements:

◆ Complete purchase requisition forms.

◆ Approve purchase requisitions.

◆ Verify requisition approver codes.

◆ Select vendors.

◆ Generate purchase orders.

◆ Maintain a Requisition Transaction file, a Vendor Master file, and a Purchase Order Master file.

4. Construct a Gantt chart to document the construction plan described in the following case problem.

Pat Collins, the project manager of Delta's order fulfillment systems development project, assigned a team of four developers and two users to finish system construction. Martin Valasquez, a database programmer, and Vivian Wong, a senior SOP administrative assistant, were assigned the task of finalizing database structure; Pat estimated that this task would require two weeks to complete because Vivian would be available only five to eight hours per week. In addition, Martin would need access to Delta's DBMS. Bobbie Devine, a GUI designer, and Matt LeBarr, an SOP clerk, were assigned the task of finalizing user interfaces, which Pat estimated would take three weeks and could be done concurrently with final database construction. A resource required to complete this task was a GUI generator and access to the database definitions. John Reynolds and Patti Stevens, two programmer/analysts, were assigned the task of finalizing the programs, which would take three weeks and could not begin until the database and user interfaces were completed.

After Martin and Vivian completed database construction, they were to begin work on the user guide, a task that would require access to desktop publishing software, would take three weeks, and could not begin until the database and user interfaces were completed. After Bobbie and Matt completed interface construction, they were to create the system documentation, which would require access to Delta's CASE tool and would consume two weeks. When the two users, Vivian and Matt, completed their other tasks, they were to plan the training sessions and revise job descriptions, tasks that would require the resources of the user manual and presentation software and would consume two weeks. When all the developers completed their other tasks, they were to plan the system test, which would require approximately one week.

5. Construct a Gantt chart to plan the testing activities described in the following table. The test team consists of three developers (D1, D2, and D3) and two users (U1 and U2).

Testing Activity	People Assigned	Time Required	Task Dependencies
Create test data	D1, U1, U2	3 days	
Test hardware using vendor tests	D2, D3	2 days	
Test network using vendor tests	D2, D3	2 days	Completion of hardware test
Conduct system test	D1, D2, D3, U1, U2	8 days	Creation of test data; completion of hardware and network tests
Test operations procedures	D1, U1	3 days	Completion of system test
Conduct volume test	D2, U2	2 days	Completion of system test
Conduct stress test	D3	2 days	Completion of system test
Review results with users	All	1 day	Completion of all tests

6. Construct a Gantt chart to plan the installation activities listed in the following table. The installation team consists of a facilities crew (to prepare the facility), four developers (D1 through D4), and three users (U1 through U3).

Installation Activity	Person Assigned	Time Required	Task Dependencies
Create system library	D1, U1	2 days	
Prepare facility	Facilities crew, U2	10 days	
Install hardware	D2, D3, D4, U3	4 days	Completion of facility
Install system software and DBMS	D2, D4, U3	2 days	Installation of hardware
Install application software	D2, D4, U3	2 days	Installation of system software
Convert database	D2, D3, U2	3 days	Installation of system software and DBMS
Train users	D1, D3, U1	5 days	
Conduct user acceptance review	All	1 day	Completion of all other tasks

◈ REFERENCES

Rettig, M. "Testing Made Palatable." *Communications of the ACM* 34, no. 5 (May 1991), pp. 25–29.

Texas Instruments, Incorporated. *Rapid Application Development Guide.* TI Part Number 2579082, 1992.

CASE ILLUSTRATION

Iterative Analysis, Design, Preliminary Construction, and Review

This installment of the ETG case is quite brief, largely because many activities of the iterative analysis, design, and preliminary construction development stage have been illustrated in Chapters 9 through 12. These chapters also presented many of the system data structure, behavior, and user interface models and the final construction, test, and installation plans, along with other outputs generated during this stage. Thus, this case installment just summarizes those activities and outputs.

After the JAD workshop, Victoria and Denny set to work designing and prototyping ETG's order processing system data structures, behaviors, and user interfaces. Paul opted to have this phase of the development project occur on site so that Victoria and Denny would have easy access to ETG employees for informal prototype reviews.

Paul authorized Victoria to procure the necessary hardware and software and to have it installed in ETG's back office. The proposed system required installation of a microcomputer, a bar code scanner and its software, a printer, and, finally, Microsoft Access, a PC-DBMS, to maintain the customer list and tape inventory data and to process transactions. Access was chosen both for its ease of use and its powerful features and capabilities—and because both Victoria and Denny were fairly accomplished Access developers. Victoria consulted with a vendor to provide the hardware and software components and arranged to have the vendor deliver, install, and test the hardware and software.

In the meantime, Victoria and Denny studied the models and notes generated during the JAD workshop. Denny was assigned to continue the analysis and design of the system's data structures. He revised the object relationship model to take into account data requirements identified during the discussion of system behaviors and user interfaces. He also met with Linda Schwartz to clarify the cash receipts and transaction data she needed to perform her accounting functions and to produce the reports she wanted. Then he used Access to prototype the database. Denny consulted informally with Paul and any available clerks to review each table as he designed it and to verify that the database contained all the data elements ETG needed.

Victoria took responsibility for the system behaviors. Working from the use cases defined during the JAD workshop, she analyzed ETG's transactions and then designed behaviors to perform these transactions. Victoria wrote structured text to design the system's automated behaviors, which would be implemented as Access macros embedded in the system's user interfaces. She described manual behaviors in use cases and/or structured text; these would serve as the foundation of the system's user documentation.

Working together, Denny and Victoria studied their data structure and behavior designs to design the system's user interfaces (e.g., Rental Order data entry screen, New Member data entry screen). Because Victoria was busy with three other projects, Denny was assigned the task of constructing the user interfaces. First, Denny designed the layouts of all system menus, data entry screens, and printed and screen reports using the form and report design capabilities of Access. As each user interface layout was designed, he asked ETG users to assess the "look" of each interface, focusing not only on the layout but also on the data captured or displayed by each interface. Usually, the ETG users were very pleased; on occasion, they requested that Denny revise the layout or add/remove a data element or command button.

Next, working from Victoria's structured-text process descriptions, Denny created the Access macros that would "activate" the user interfaces. Each command button, each calculated or retrieved data element on a screen or report, each validation routine used to verify inputs (e.g., employee number, membership number, tape stock number, and so on) required a macro written in Access Basic. As Denny finished programming the behaviors of each user interface, he asked two or three ETG users to test the interface's "feel." Finally, when all the code for all the user interfaces had been completed, Denny asked several ETG users to verify their functionality and to assess the flow of control between interfaces.

After a few weeks of iterative prototyping and review, the design was stable and the preliminary system complete. Victoria prepared a design specification report, incorporating the final design models and illustrating the design specifications in "user-friendly" graphics. She also planned the activities of the last development stage: final construction, system test, and installation. Working with Denny, Victoria outlined the final construction activities, test plans to verify the system's accuracy, and an installation schedule that Paul recommended to minimize disruption. The system installation was scheduled for a midweek morning, a period of low activity at ETG.

As they planned the activities of the final stage, Victoria and Denny assigned ETG users to tasks based on their interests, aptitudes, and ETG work schedules. Having interacted with the staff so frequently during the past few weeks, Victoria felt as confident about assessing their skills as she did about assessing the skills of her students. She assigned Susan to construct the user manual because of her technical writing expertise; she assigned Beto and Helen to help Denny prepare and test the bar-code labels because of their attention to detail. Beto and Susan were also assigned extensive testing responsibilities because Victoria knew that she could depend on them to speak up if they found something wrong or unacceptable.

Victoria was especially pleased with the degree of support and assistance Beto had provided during the JAD workshops and prototype reviews. He seemed to have an affinity for working with information systems, and, in fact, had volunteered for the database maintenance, report generation, and other routine system duties that would need to be performed during production. To prepare him for these duties, Victoria made sure that Beto had an active role in creating test data, converting data into digital records, and installing the hardware and software.

Victoria scheduled a JAD-review-and-confirmation workshop to be conducted one morning at her office suite. Denny opened the workshop session by explaining its purpose and describing the system's hardware, software, and data components. Then Victoria called upon Beto and Susan to demonstrate the major system functions and procedures embodied in the prototype system. Victoria displayed the IPOSC requirements defined during the earlier JAD session and checked off each requirement as the ETG participants reviewed the preliminary system and agreed that a requirement had been satisfied. The ETG users concurred that the system design satisfied all the requirements, but requested a few minor changes in the user interfaces. As the project's user-sponsor, Paul approved the system design on the condition that the suggested changes be made during final construction.

Next, Victoria presented her plans for final construction, testing, and installation. Because she had consulted with Paul as she devised her plans, they were accepted without revision. Paul approved the plans and authorized final construction.

PART FOUR

Final Construction, Testing, Installation, and Review

Part Four examines the final construction, system test and installation, and post-implementation review stages of the Bridge systems development methodology. The activities in these stages require you to implement the construction, testing, and installation plans you outlined in your design specification report. The activities you will perform include the following:

◆ Finalize the people, procedures, data, software, and hardware components of the system.

  ◆ Revise job descriptions and train users.
  ◆ Create user and technical documentation.
  ◆ Build the production database.
  ◆ Acquire or refine the programs or object classes that perform system behaviors.
  ◆ Acquire additional hardware devices.
  ◆ Prepare the facility.

◆ Test each component separately (unit test) and the system as a whole (system test).

  ◆ Create test data.
  ◆ Prepare test specifications.
  ◆ Run and document tests.

◆ Install the system and conduct a user acceptance review.

◆ Conduct a post-implementation evaluation to evaluate the development product (the new system) and process (the development project).

Although implementing an information system requires highly technical tasks such as installing and testing a new operating system and installing telecommunications devices and cabling, these are not discussed here. Instead, Part Four adopts the perspective of a system *designer*, not a system implementer. Training users, writing documentation, acquiring hardware and software, performing system tests, and conducting an acceptance review and a post-implementation evaluation are the implementation tasks that system designers are most likely to perform. Consequently, these activities are the focus of Chapter 13 and of the ETG case illustration that concludes Part Four.

FINAL CONSTRUCTION, TESTING, INSTALLATION, AND REVIEW

Final Construction

1. Construct and test production-ready database and programs (or object classes).
2. Obtain additional hardware.
3. Prepare the facility for additional hardware.
4. Test hardware components.
5. Complete user and technical documentation.
6. Train users.

System Test and Installation

1. Perform system test.
2. Install components.
3. Conduct user review/acceptance test.

Post-Implementation

1. Add reusable design components (object classes) to the design-class library.
2. Conduct post-implementation evaluation.

The activities of the last development stage in the Bridge methodology are similar to those in traditional development. Users are trained, hardware resources are obtained, documentation is written, and the production-quality data and software components are constructed, whether in an OO or non-OO DBMS and programming language. As each information system component is constructed, it is tested to ensure its reliability and accuracy. Then the system as a whole is tested to ensure that all the components work together correctly and that the new system is effectively integrated with other systems. If the system test is successful, a user acceptance review is conducted in which users evaluate whether the system meets their acceptance criteria. If it does, the old system is dismantled, and the new system is put into production.

Just as users participated actively in analyzing and designing the new system, they should also be actively involved in constructing, testing, installing, and reviewing the system. Users can write their own user guide, prepare test data and stipulate test conditions, perform testing procedures, and so on. Maintaining user involvement during these critical activities not only builds user commitment, it also facilitates training and system installation because involved users have a better understanding of the system and of the development process. Moreover, they have some insight into what a complex, difficult undertaking system development is, thus improving user-developer communication. An added bonus is that users who have executed system tests successfully have greater confidence in the system's accuracy and reliability.

In this chapter, you will learn about the final construction, testing, installation, and review activities that system designers are most likely to perform. After completing this chapter, you should be able to

1. Explain the activities of final construction.
2. Discuss the software and hardware acquisition process.
3. Plan user training activities.
4. Define "integrated performance support system" and discuss its advantages over traditional user training.
5. Distinguish the development/test environment from the production environment.
6. Differentiate between black-box testing and glass-box testing.
7. Create test specifications to plan and to document system-testing procedures.
8. List four installation strategies and discuss the advantages and disadvantages of each.
9. Define and explain the purpose of a post-implementation evaluation.

13.1 ◈ FINAL CONSTRUCTION OF THE PPDSH COMPONENTS

Final construction is the process of making "production-ready" the preliminary system that evolved during iterative analysis and design. Activities required to finalize the PPDSH components of the system include the following:

1. Construct and verify the data component.
2. Construct (acquire) and verify the software component.
3. Acquire and verify the hardware component.
4. Prepare the facility.
5. Construct and verify documentation.
6. Train users and assign production responsibilities.

In the typical rapid application development (RAD) project, these activities consume two weeks to two months of a six-month project schedule. However, creating extensive documentation and/or training hundreds of users can easily double or triple this estimate. Thus, the time and effort devoted to final construction depends on several factors:

1. Has most of the system's IPOSC functionality been embodied in the prototype?
2. Does the new system require additional hardware, especially communications devices?
3. Does the new system require a new operating system, network operating system, and/or DBMS?
4. Are extensive user and technical documentation required?
5. Do a large number of users (i.e., more than 50) require extensive training (i.e., more than one or two days)?

If the answer to question 1 is "No" and the answers to questions 2 through 5 are "Yes," you can expect to devote more time and effort to construction activities.

CONSTRUCTING AND VERIFYING THE DATA COMPONENT

During the iterative analysis, design, and preliminary construction stage, the system data structures were defined and the physical database was designed and prototyped. If the physical database design was created using a CASE tool, the system's database structures may have been constructed by the CASE tool's database-generation facility. If not, you may have created these structures using your selected DBMS. (Refer to Figure 9.16 to examine the Microsoft Access user interface for defining tables and fields.) At this point, the database consists of empty tables; in other words, the structure of the database is complete, but it is an empty shell ready to be filled with data.

One of the most crucial construction activities is **file conversion** (also called *data conversion*): the process of converting from manual to digital files or from digital files in one format or structure to digital files in another format or structure. In general, the following activities are performed to convert data from one form to another:

1. Set a date for *freezing* the database. From the freeze date to the completion of file conversion, no updates are made to the existing database. Instead, they are tracked separately (e.g., in an automated system, required updates may be saved to a different file) and performed after file conversion.
2. Back up existing system data.
3. Convert the data.
4. Verify the converted data.
5. Perform accumulated updates.

During final construction, if the existing system maintained data manually, these data must be entered into the tables by keying each record, a very labor-intensive, time-consuming task that requires the use of controls to verify the validity, completeness, and accuracy of the entered records. To ensure **validity**, you verify that only authorized, genuine data are entered. This means all records must be reviewed prior to being entered into the new system. To ensure **completeness**, you verify that *all* valid data are entered by using batch controls or hash totals to manage the number of records entered. To ensure **accuracy**, you verify that only *correct* data are entered. This goal can be achieved by employing input validation routines to verify the format and range of each data element and to generate exception reports listing any records that fail the validation criteria. Inaccurate records are then reviewed, corrected, and reentered [Gelinas et al. 1990].

If the existing system maintained data in digital form but the new system requires a different database structure, the digital records must be converted from the old structure to the new. This conversion is usually performed using data-conversion software. For example, Microsoft Access provides a conversion facility that converts data to and from the Access database structure. These conversion programs usually also provide error-checking routines to verify that the conversion was performed successfully, that is, that the converted data are an accurate and complete "copy" of the original data. However, conversion software cannot ensure that the *original* data were valid, complete, and accurate.

CONSTRUCTING (ACQUIRING) AND VERIFYING THE SOFTWARE

The software component includes both system and application software. In some development projects, the new system uses the organization's existing operating system, database management system, and/or network operating system. In this case, your only task is to verify that the new application software is compatible with the existing system software. In other development projects, the new system software must be acquired from a software vendor. Then your job is more complicated, requiring you to define the system software's technical requirements, evaluate various alternatives, and select the best product for your organization. The acquisition and verification processes are discussed here.

Application software can be obtained from numerous sources and through various methods, including

◆ Custom-developed software written by the organization's IS staff in a third- or fourth-generation language or an object-oriented language.

◆ Custom-developed software generated by the code generator of a CASE tool.

◆ Custom-developed software written by users using a fourth-generation tool.

◆ Custom-developed software written under contract by a consulting team (*outsourcing*).

◆ Commercially available packaged software.

If the software component is being written in a third-generation language and if a CASE tool was used to design system behaviors, programs may be generated using the CASE tool's code-generation facility. Otherwise, programmers—guided by the program structure charts and structured text created during design—code the programs using structured programming techniques to reduce complexity and increase modularity. As each module of the software is constructed, it is subjected to a **unit test** to verify its correctness. Each tested module is integrated with the other tested modules, and an **integration test** is conducted to verify the flow of control and data between modules. These tests are best performed by the module programmer and his or her peers. In some organizations, the tested software is then turned over to "code busters" whose job is to subject the programs to extreme conditions, which usually can reveal coding errors or omissions that the programming team overlooked.

If the software is being constructed using an object-oriented programming language, each object class must be verified as it is constructed. Each set of code used to implement an object class is equivalent to a program module in traditional programming; each must be subjected to a unit test and, when integrated with other classes, an integration test. Rettig [1991] describes a Smalltalk class, called the Test Manager, that his programming team created to automatically verify each object class. The Test Manager tested all the paths through the code written to implement each class and also verified class interactions when classes were integrated.

If the software component will be constructed from one or more commercially available packages, an evaluation and acquisition process ensues. With developer support, users are good candidates to perform many of the tasks in this process. Depending on the cost and complexity of the software, you may be able to simply visit an approved vendor and select a package directly, or you may need to create a **request for proposal (RFP)** or a **request for quotation (RFQ)** to be submitted to several vendors. A RFQ is used when you have already selected a product and need price quotations from several vendors; a RFP is used when you know the functional requirements and features of the software but have no specific product in mind. Vendor responses are then evaluated using **selection criteria**, which establish the features and functions necessary to satisfy the functional requirements and other organizational needs according to the development team and the users. Examples of selection criteria are given in Table 13.1. The selected package(s) must be tested to verify vendor claims about data and transaction volume, response time, and *throughput* (the quantity of work completed in a set time period) and to ensure that the software performs the required functions and is compatible with existing software and hardware.

ACQUIRING AND VERIFYING HARDWARE

The hardware acquisition process is similar to the software acquisition process just described. Before RFPs or RFQs can be sent to vendors, the development team and users must determine the technical and performance specifications for each hardware component. For computers, these specifications include processor memory size and expandability; *cycle time,* or *millions of instructions per second* (MIPS); number of communication ports supported; *mean time between failure* (MTBF), and so on. For secondary storage devices, these specifications include type (tape, floppy, fixed, CD-ROM, etc.), capacity, and access time. Hardware selection criteria are derived from an examination of the data and transaction volumes, response time, and other performance factors that the system requires. They include cost, maintenance, delivery schedule, documentation, vendor reputation and service, compatibility with existing devices, flexibility, expandability, and reliability.

Before contracts for purchasing or leasing hardware components are completed, the development team may need to verify vendor claims about data and transaction volumes, response time, throughput, and other performance factors. These performance factors are usually presented as **benchmarks**: comparative throughput measures given a *typical* user

TABLE 13.1 Selection criteria used to evaluate software for acquisition

Technical Criteria	Vendor Criteria
◆ Functional requirements • Does the software perform all the IPOSC functions required in the system?	◆ Reputation and stability
	◆ Quality of service
◆ Capacity • What data and transaction volumes does it support?	◆ Licensing agreement
	◆ Training program • Does the vendor provide low-cost user and/or operator training?
◆ Response time	

◆ Standardization and portability
  • Is the software written in a standard language?
  • Can it be ported to different operating system or hardware platforms?
	◆ Technical support
	  • Does the vendor provide a toll-free 24-hour hotline to answer user questions?

◆ Customization (flexibility)
  • Can the software be modified to meet organization-specific requirements?
	◆ Maintenance agreement
	  • Does the vendor notify you about upgrades?
	  • Are the cost and installation of upgrades covered in the maintenance agreement?

◆ Controls • Does the software provide security, data validation, and other control functions?	
◆ User documentation	
◆ Ease of use and learning	

workload processed on each vendor's hardware. Although many benchmarks have been somewhat standardized in recent years, they do not always provide a valid comparison of vendor equipment. Thus, especially for large systems requiring mainframe computers and numerous tape and disk drive devices, you may need to perform your own benchmark tests using your data, software, and typical data and transaction volumes.

PREPARING THE FACILITY

Construction also involves preparing the facility to house any additional hardware devices. Processors, secondary storage devices, printers, network and communications devices—all require a reliable, uninterrupted power source, and some may require special air conditioning and ventilation as well as security and disaster-protection features. Thus, well in advance of the expected installation date you need to identify the facility requirements and plan how to satisfy them. Questions to be addressed in the process include the following:

◆ Has a reliable, secure, uninterrupted electrical supply been provided?

◆ Does the facility have adequate, conveniently located power outlets?

◆ Is a raised floor required to conceal electrical, ventilation, and other equipment and cables?

- ◆ Is the computer room large enough to house all the equipment while providing adequate ventilation and work space?

- ◆ Is the computer room secure from unauthorized access?

- ◆ Has a fire detection system been installed?

- ◆ Has space been allotted and have shelves been provided for a tape/disk library; operations, system, and user documentation; computer supplies, and so on?

- ◆ In the users' area, does the lighting level and direction reduce glare on computer screens?

- ◆ Have plans been made for running communication lines, e.g., for a local area network or for a client/server system?

CONSTRUCTING AND VERIFYING DOCUMENTATION

Chapter 11 discussed user documentation as part of the user interface, explaining several user documentation issues and giving an example of a user guide. Created along with the user documentation is the **technical documentation** (also called *system documentation*) of the system's design, prepared for the benefit of future developers who will maintain and evolve the system. This technical documentation, a first draft of which was developed as part of the design specification report, provides the final physical DFDs, object relationship or other data model, class specifications or physical database design, use cases, dialog flow diagram, program structure charts, system flowchart, structured text-procedure descriptions, and so on.

The **operations manual** (also called the *technical operations manual*) is created at the same time to describe the procedures for starting and shutting down the system, performing routine data backup, recovering from system failure, and employing security and access controls. The content and complexity of the operations manual depend on the system platform. Operations for mainframe and networked environments are more complex than those for a system running on a stand-alone desktop computer. Procedures for loading and unloading tapes and disks, performing daily file backups, administering security and access controls, allocating disk space, running batch jobs, and so on, are included in the operations manual.

One technique used to verify user and operations documentation is to conduct user walk-throughs of the normal, operating, and recovery procedures described. Your goal as a systems analyst is to verify the completeness, clarity, and accuracy of those procedures. Have all procedures—and all the steps in each procedure—been adequately described? Further verification of the user and operations guides is achieved during the system test if users and operators consult these guides as they perform test procedures.

TRAINING USERS AND ASSIGNING PRODUCTION RESPONSIBILITIES

Training the users is a critical and potentially costly activity. The user documentation must be completed and tested in advance of the training sessions. In addition, the type of training, schedule, participants, and curriculum must be determined and the required materials and equipment identified. An effective tool for performing these planning activities is the **training**

plan, which outlines the training schedule, objectives, materials, and so on and which is approved by the user-sponsor before training begins. Figure 13.1 gives the training plan that Victoria prepared for ETG.

Training incurs both direct and indirect costs. Direct costs for instructors, equipment, and materials average $150 to $350 per person per day; indirect costs include (1) the lost

---

TRAINING PLAN FOR ETG USERS

Type of Training	Schedule	Location	Participants
Data entry procedures	July 6, 8:00 to 10:00 AM	Victoria's conference room	Beto, Julie, John, Betty, Bill, Amy, Susan
Normal procedures	July 10, 8:00 to noon	Victoria's conference room	Julie, John, Betty, Bill, Amy, Susan, Corita, Helen, Beto, Paul
Backup/operating procedures	July 10, 1:00 to 5:00 PM	Victoria's conference room	Beto, Helen, Linda, Paul

OBJECTIVES

Data Entry Training	Normal User Training	Backup/Operations Training
Participants will learn • fundamental computer concepts • Windows user interface concepts • data entry procedures	Participants will be able to • perform all transaction processing procedures • perform all tape availability processing procedures	Participants will be able to • generate periodic management reports • create, update, and delete master file records • perform file backup and system recovery procedures

MATERIALS AND EQUIPMENT

Type/Title	Quantity	Cost
Computer system running the fully tested order processing software (systems will be available 7/6–7/10 for data entry by off-duty clerks)	5	$50/day/system = $750 no cost for weekends
A Guide to Windows *Fundamental Computer Concepts* (Hernandez & Associates copyrighted materials)	10 each	$5.00 each × 20 = $100
ETG Order Processing System User Guide	10	Developed for ETG
Overhead transparency projector	1	Provided by office suite
Transparencies	misc.	Developed for ETG

APPROVAL

_____   _____
       (user-sponsor)   (date)

FIGURE 13.1   Training plan for ETG's order processing system

productivity of employees taken away from their normal duties and (2) the opportunity costs incurred because system benefits are delayed while users wait to be trained. Together, these costs can add up to millions of dollars for a large company—an investment some feel is wasted, given that users forget as much as 90 percent of what they learned in training.

In an effort to lower costs and to improve user performance, the **integrated performance support system (IPSS)** has been developed as an alternative to traditional instructor-led training. This well-conceived blend of computer-based training (CBT) programs, interactive tutorials, videotaped instruction, printed and on-line user documentation, and help-desk support is designed to guide the user on a "just in time" basis. Instead of overloading users with information during a two-week training session, IPSS provides one or two days of instructor-led training and then turns the users loose. As they require information about how to perform specific tasks, the IPSS guides them to the appropriate training material. In some cases the expert-system component of the IPSS can offer the user advice; in other cases, the user may be directed to work through a CBT program or interactive tutorial, watch a videotape, consult the user documentation, or call the help desk. Although an IPSS can be costly to develop (typically between $100,000 and $1 million), many organizations view it as a good investment because it can reduce training costs 50 percent or more for large systems with many users [Dublin 1993].

In addition to training the users, final construction also involves assigning responsibility for production roles. For example, who will order and maintain system supplies? Who will perform system startup and shut-down? Who will run reports? Who will perform master file updates? These responsibilities must be determined (1) so that each user's job tasks are clearly defined and (2) so that appropriate access authorizations can be assigned. Significant changes in job responsibilities may require that the job descriptions and/or titles of certain users be modified. Furthermore, knowing which tasks will be performed by which users determines the system functions each user is authorized to perform. For example, if only selected users can run reports or perform master file updates, only these users should be allowed to execute the system functions to perform these tasks. Because these access authorizations are usually set as the software and data are constructed, they should be determined early in the final construction process.

✓ Check Your Understanding 13-1

Match each of the following terms with its definition.

_____ unit test

_____ user documentation

_____ file conversion

_____ integrated performance support system

_____ operations manual

_____ training plan

_____ selection criteria

_____ benchmarks

_____ request for quotation

_____ integration test

_____ technical documentation

a. describes how to perform startup, shut-down, and recovery procedures.

b. combines computer-based training, printed manuals, videotapes, and face-to-face sessions to teach users system functions.

c. involves verifying data accuracy, completeness, and validity.

d. serves as a reference for system maintenance and modification.

e. specifies the features and functions required to satisfy the system's functional requirements.

f. measurements used to compare vendor products.

g. verifies the flow of control between program modules.

h. specifies training materials and objectives.

13.2 ◈ SYSTEM TEST AND INSTALLATION

During the **system test and installation**, the system as a whole is tested to ensure that all its components work well together. If the system test is successful, a JAD-review-and-confirmation workshop follows in which users evaluate the system against their acceptance criteria. If the system satisfies these criteria, the old system is dismantled, and the new system is put into production. System testing and installation involves a five-step process:

1. Choose a testing strategy.

2. Prepare test specifications and create test data.

3. Perform system tests.

4. Install the system.

5. Conduct the user acceptance review.

The choice of a testing strategy and an installation strategy should have been made and documented in the design specification report. Here we explain these strategies and appropriate applications of each in more detail. Our discussion requires that we revisit the *system life cycle.* Recall that this life cycle recognizes two phases: development and production. Each phase represents a fundamentally different system environment: the **development/test environment** in which a system is designed, constructed, and tested; and the **production environment** in which a system is used to perform the organization's daily operations. A system under development should never be used to perform production functions; similarly, no aspect of the production system should be "contaminated" by the development environment. In simple words, *the two environments should never overlap!* The clear separation of these two environments is especially critical during testing. Because the new system has not been proven accurate or reliable, it must be isolated from the production system.

Two critical precautions should be derived from this discussion. One, if the new system uses components of the production system (e.g., the same hardware, software, and/or data), steps must be taken to safeguard these components. For example, the software or data must be copied to the development/test environment so that the production programs and data are not affected by errors or crashes during construction or testing. Two, "live" production data should never be used as test data.

CHOOSING A TESTING STRATEGY

Two fundamental testing strategies are the black-box strategy and the glass-box strategy (also called *white-box* or *program-based testing*) [Rettig 1991]. As its name implies, the **black-box testing strategy** treats the system as a box whose contents cannot be discerned. This strategy assumes that if, given certain inputs, the "box" (i.e., the system) generates the correct outputs, then the contents of the box (i.e., the system's programs, data structures, interfaces and so on) must be correct. In contrast, the **glass-box testing strategy** looks "inside the box" to verify system components and functions by examining each line of code and each data structure. The black-box strategy is more appropriate when the purpose of a test is to verify system functions or user specifications; thus, it is best used to verify the system as a whole or to test purchased software. Because the glass-box strategy verifies program code and data structures, it is best used to verify individual program modules or system components and to test custom-developed software. For example, both the unit test and the integration test should use the glass-box testing strategy to verify software at the code level.

PREPARING TEST SPECIFICATIONS AND CREATING TEST DATA

A **test specification** outlines the procedures for testing the system; it serves both to plan and to document the results of unit and system tests. If you developed use cases during analysis and design, each use case must be scrutinized to identify system functions to be tested. A test specification is complete only if it forces the system to execute all of its functions, including error-recognition routines. Figure 13.2 gives an excerpt of the test specification that Denny and Beto prepared to verify the Rental Customer Rents Rental Tape(s) use case (the related data entry screen can be viewed in Figure 11.4). Notice that both valid and invalid input data conditions are tested. When valid input data are entered (e.g., "c152"), correct output should be produced (e.g., Paula Cassidy's name appears in the Member Name screen field); when invalid data are entered (e.g., "a111" or "c-152"), the system should recognize it as invalid and display the appropriate error message. Notice also that both the absence and the presence of a condition are tested; for example, Denny and Beto created test conditions for customers with and without unpaid fines.

The test specifications in Figure 13.2 verify that a particular kind of transaction is performed properly. In addition to testing every transaction, other functions that must be tested include report generation, query response, and end-of-period functions. The latter are easily overlooked but must be verified so that the system does not "explode" at a critical point in the business cycle (e.g., end-of-month or end-of-quarter processing). In addition, the functionality of user interface features, such as command buttons, function keys, tool icons, and so on, must be verified.

Users are prime candidates to help prepare test specifications because they are familiar with procedures and the kinds of errors that a user is likely to make. Developers are also appropriate preparers because they are familiar with the error-trapping procedures built into the system. Thus, the ideal test specification team consists of at least one user and one developer.

To determine whether the system is performing its input data verification, data retrieval, and report generation functions correctly, appropriate test conditions must be run against a set

	Test Specification for ___ETG's Order Processing System___ (system)				Page: 1 of 3

Designed by:
  Denny and Beto

Module or Screen:
  Rental Customer Rents Rental Tape use case

Test Data Source:
  Data sets #1–4

Objectives:
  To verify accuracy of RO interface and macros

Test Condition #	Description of Condition	Test Steps	Expected Results	Executed by/ Results
Rental-1	Incorrect format for membership number	Enter "c-152" at the membership number prompt.	System recognizes format error and displays error message.	
Rental-2	Invalid membership number	Enter "a111" at the membership number prompt.	System recognizes error and displays "Member not found" error message.	
Rental-3	Valid membership number	Enter "c152" at the membership number prompt.	System retrieves Paula Cassidy's record; displays last name.	
Rental-4	Member has fines	Enter "a359" at the membership number prompt.	System displays "14.50" in the Unpaid Fines field.	
Rental-5	Member has no fines	Enter "c152" at the membership number prompt.	System displays "0.00" in the Unpaid Fines field.	

FIGURE 13.2   Test specification for ETG's Rental Order use case. Reproduced from *Systems Development: Requirements, Evaluation, Design, and Implementation,* by E. Jordan and J. Machesky. Boston, MA: PWS-Kent, 1990. Copyright 1990 by boyd & fraser publishing company. All rights reserved.

of valid stored data called **test data**. Sources of test data include data sets created by users or selected subsets of historical production data copied to the test environment. Generally speaking, several small test data sets tailored for a specific purpose are more effective than one large, general-purpose set. For example, Table 13.2 gives four test data sets that Denny and Beto created to test the Rental Customer Rents Rental Tape(s) use case. Notice that these sets contain *only valid data*. In other words, no specious data (e.g., the invalid membership number "a111" or an incorrectly formatted membership number such as "c-152") may appear in these data sets. To ensure that all test data elements are correctly formatted, you must refer to the data dictionary to determine each data element's correct format.

    Both the test data sets and the test specifications should be saved for reuse as the system is maintained or modified.

PERFORMING SYSTEM TESTS

The **system test** simulates the production environment as closely as possible to verify that all components are integrated effectively and that the system performs its functions accurately,

TABLE 13.2 Test data sets to verify the Rental Customer Rents Rental Tape(s) use case

Test Data Set #1				Test Data Set #2				
RENTAL-CUSTOMER				RENTAL-ORDER				
Memb#	First Name	Last Name		Order#	Memb#			
a359	Bob	Andresen		10054	c152			
c152	Paula	Cassidy		10153	a359			
				10184	c152			
				12051	a359			
Test Data Set #3				**Test Data Set #4**				
RO-LINE				FINE				
Order#	Stock#	DueDate	ReturnDate	Order#	Stock#	LateFee	RewindFee	
10054	W115-92	4/23/95	4/23/95	10153	P345-95	13.50	0	
10153	P345-95	4/30/95	5/3/95	12051	D104-94	0	1.00	
10184	S421-90	5/24/95	5/24/95					
12051	D104-94	5/28/95	5/28/95					

reliably, and efficiently. First, the test procedures outlined in the *test specification* are run using small test data sets. The results of each test are documented in the "Executed by/Results" column of the test specification form. If the system fails a test, the failure is noted on the form, indicating how the actual result differed from the expected result. After completion of the system test, developers review each discrepancy, tracing its cause and prescribing a solution. Then users and developers meet to prioritize errors for correction. Critical errors must be repaired and the system test repeated; correcting less critical errors may be delayed until prior to the acceptance review or after implementation.

After these tests verify the system functions, *stress and volume tests* should be conducted in a simulated production environment. Simulating the production environment requires that the data volume, transaction volume, number of simultaneous users, and so on during the system test approximate those of the production system environment. A system that performs well at a very low data or transaction volume may perform poorly (e.g., unacceptable response time) at a higher data or transaction volume. Your goal in performing a **stress test** is to simulate hardware malfunctions, extreme data and transaction volumes, and other conditions in order to ensure that the system degrades gracefully under extreme conditions. The **volume test** (also called a *capacity test*) is conducted to verify that the system meets the required response time, throughput, and demand levels set by users.

Because testing can be an expensive, time-consuming endeavor, its cost should not exceed its benefits. How thoroughly the system should be tested depends on its complexity and the consequences of its failure. A system whose errors or failure would significantly affect the organization should be more thoroughly tested than one whose impact would be minimal. If reusable components or commercially available software have been incorporated into the new system, less testing—at least of these components—may be required.

Check Your Understanding 13-2

1. Indicate whether each of the following statements describes black-box testing (BB) or glass-box testing (GB).

    _____ a. Focuses on system functions and user specifications.

    _____ b. Commonly used by programmers performing unit tests.

    _____ c. Verifies system functions at the code level.

    _____ d. Verifies system functions on the basis of their producing correct outputs.

    _____ e. Commonly used to verify purchased software.

2. Indicate whether each of the following statements is true (T) or false (F).

    _____ a. The system should be tested in the production environment.

    _____ b. One source of test data is historical production data copied to the test environment.

    _____ c. Only developers should prepare test specifications and test data because they are the only ones familiar with the system.

    _____ d. Several small test data sets tailored for a specific purpose are more effective than one large, general-purpose test data set.

    _____ e. Test data sets contain both valid and invalid data.

INSTALLING THE SYSTEM

After the system has been verified to operate correctly, you are ready to install the system components in the production environment. Installation activities include

1. Installing the production database.

2. Loading the new software into the production program library.

3. Installing additional hardware.

4. Updating the documentation library.

An installation date and an installation strategy were determined as part of the installation plan you prepared for the Design Specification report. Choosing an installation date is especially critical for an automated transaction processing system. Just as a retailer must suspend business to perform a physical inventory count, at some point, an organization installing a new information system must suspend its operations to perform the installation. The old production IPOSC functions must be suspended and the old PPDSH components removed so that the new processes can be initiated and the new components installed.

Because this suspension leaves the organization "in the lurch" until installation is completed, the installation date must be scheduled to minimize the time that production activities will be disrupted. For most organizations, weekends or holidays are appropriate times to suspend production and to install the new system because these are times of low production activity. For ETG, just the opposite is true. Weekends are the busiest periods for a video rental store, so installation was scheduled for midweek.

Installation Strategies

An *installation strategy* defines a process for converting from the old production system to the new. Four installation strategies—direct cutover, pilot installation, phased installation, and parallel operation—were outlined in Chapter 12. Here these strategies are discussed in detail and weighed in terms of their relative advantages and disadvantages.

The **direct cutover** strategy immediately replaces the old production system with the newly developed system. For example, at the close of business on Friday, the old system is dismantled, and when workers return Monday morning, the new system is up and running. The primary advantages of the direct cutover strategy are its low cost and its immediate accumulation of benefits. Its primary disadvantages are that it allows users no time to adjust gradually to the new system and that it provides no "fall-back" should the system not perform as expected. Thus, the direct cutover strategy is appropriate for small, relatively simple systems whose failure would not seriously impact the organization. Thorough unit and system testing are critical if this strategy is to be employed safely.

The **pilot installation** strategy uses the direct cutover strategy to install the new system at one location, division, or branch office; if the pilot is successful, the system is installed at other locations. For the pilot location, the advantages and disadvantages of this strategy are similar to those of the direct cutover strategy. However, the old system in operation at other locations can serve as a fall-back, and the impact of failure on the organization is limited to the pilot location. Thus, this strategy is somewhat less risky than direct cutover. In addition, lessons learned at the pilot installation location can be applied as the system is installed at other locations. The main drawback of this strategy is that the other locations cannot begin accruing the system's benefits immediately. For example, if the system is piloted at Location A for six months before it is installed at other locations, and if the pilot system is a smashing success, the other locations incur opportunity costs: the loss of the six months' benefits they would have received if the system had been installed immediately at their locations.

In **phased installation**, conversion from the old production system to the new occurs in phases, for example, by subsystem or geographic location. *Phasing installation by location* is similar to the pilot installation strategy except that, in this strategy, installation at the other locations is a given. In contrast, in the pilot installation strategy, the system is installed at the other locations only if it proves successful at the pilot location. The advantages and disadvantages of phasing installation by location are similar to those of the pilot installation strategy. *Phasing installation by subsystem* is the natural choice when full system functionality is delivered through a phased development project or multiple RAD projects. The advantages of the phased installation strategy are that it simplifies installation and allows users time to adjust gradually to the new system. Installation is simplified because, instead of converting all components and functions in one massive, complex effort, the conversion occurs in stages, thus reducing the complexity and effort of the undertaking.

The **parallel operation** installation strategy is the most complex and resource-intensive. In this strategy, both the old production system and the new are operated concurrently until the user-sponsor has been assured of the new system's accuracy and reliability. What this means is that all the PPDSH components and IPOSC functions of the two systems are "live" at the same time. Consider this example: Assume that Victoria chose the parallel operation strategy to install ETG's order processing system. Customers would complete the rental order form and give it to a sales clerk. The clerk would manually verify the information on the form and add additional data. Then the clerk would also process the transaction using the computer-based system, scanning the membership card and tape stock number bar codes, printing the rental order receipt, and so on. During this period of parallel operation, ETG would gain none of the increased productivity promised by the new system; instead, productivity would decline—as would customer service—because the workload and paperwork would be doubled.

This example illustrates the primary disadvantages of the parallel operation strategy: increased workload, duplicated paperwork, reduced productivity, and stressed users. Furthermore, if both the new and old systems use the same computer resources, the strain of running both systems concurrently may increase turnaround time, even causing system crashes. Nonetheless, the parallel operation installation strategy is a good choice—perhaps the only choice—for systems whose failure would cripple the organization. The primary advantages of this strategy are (1) the safety net it provides—if the new system fails, the old system is a ready fall-back—and (2) the opportunity it provides to verify the new system by validating its outputs against those of the old system.

CONDUCTING THE USER ACCEPTANCE REVIEW

Finally, you are ready to conduct what should be the last JAD workshop of the project: the **user acceptance review**, which is essentially a final test to ensure that the system satisfies the users' acceptance criteria. Typically, users focus on system quality, usability, reliability, security, and performance; your job is to assure them that the system meets these criteria. If users were involved in the system test, they already have some assurance that the system is usable and reliable, and they have seen how well the system performs in a simulated production environment. Now you must assure them that it performs equally well in the real production environment. In many organizations, a form such as the one shown in Figure 13.3, is used to document the acceptance criteria and the user-sponsor's approval. Your goal is to have the user-sponsor approve each acceptance criterion.

This goal may be achieved by repeating some of the test procedures performed during the system test. Following a *test script* (e.g., a detailed use case or test specification), the users subject the system to various tests, the results of which you note in a test log. Users may also evaluate the user documentation; interfaces such as human-computer dialog, reports, and data entry screens; normal, security, backup and recovery procedures; and system performance criteria such as response time. Throughout this evaluation, users identify omitted or unacceptable functions and features and desired changes or enhancements. Then they prioritize the modifications to be completed, noting whether each must be completed before or after system conversion. Only after the user-sponsor has signed off on all the acceptance criteria is the development team "home free." In other words, the project is not finished until the user-sponsor says so.

Acceptance Review Approval Form for ETG's Order Processing System		
Prepared by: Victoria Hernandez	**Acceptance Review Date:** July 19, 1997	**Page:** 1 of 1
Acceptance Criterion	Results/Comments	Approved by/ Date
Accurately and reliably performs all use-case functions.		
Processes a rental order transaction (2 tapes, no fines) in less than two minutes.		
Determines tape availability in less than ten seconds.		
Prints rental/sales receipt in thirty seconds or less.		
Is easy to learn and use.		
Generates easy-to-read, complete, and accurate management reports.		
Maintains complete, accurate record of all cash receipts.		
Prints correctly formatted mailing labels in approximatley thirty minutes.		
Provides clear, accurate, complete user documentation.		
Provides clear, accurate, complete technical and operations documentation.		

FIGURE 13.3   Acceptance review approval form

Once the system's users have approved the system, conversion occurs, and the production phase begins. **Conversion** is the point at which responsibility for the system shifts from the development team to the production users. Achieving conversion may require multiple acceptance reviews; if the pilot or phased installation strategy is chosen, an acceptance review must be conducted at the conclusion of each installation.

Check Your Understanding 13-3

Read the short scenarios below and select an appropriate installation strategy given the details provided. Justify your choice.

1. A hospital has developed a real-time system that monitors an intensive-care patient's vital signs and alerts the nurse if critical conditions are detected.

2. A regional bank with branch offices in several communities is planning to install a new automated teller machine (ATM) system at each branch office. Bank officials are concerned about minimizing risk and installation cost and complexity.

3. A family-owned hardware store is planning to install an inventory control system whose software component consists of an award-winning inventory package.

4. A family-owned hardware store is planning to install an integrated accounting system whose software component consists of award-winning sales order processing, inventory control, accounts payable, payroll, and general ledger packages.

13.3 ◈ POST-IMPLEMENTATION ACTIVITIES

Although conversion marks the point at which the system moves out of development and into production, the development project is not formally brought to a close until the organization's class/design library has been updated and a post-implementation evaluation has been conducted. Then the cycle of system maintenance and system evolution begins.

UPDATING A CLASS/DESIGN LIBRARY

One post-implementation activity is to update the organization's class or design library. In a traditional development environment reusable design elements, such as enterprise models, data models, subroutine code, and specifications of commonly used procedures—as well as test data and test specifications—can be maintained in a CASE tool's *encyclopedia*. This is the design repository that future development projects can leverage to reduce the time and effort devoted to analysis, design, and construction. In an object-oriented development environment, reusable classes are maintained in the organization's class library.

Earlier in this text, you learned that the key to delivering systems more quickly is *reuse* of the software component and that reusability is one of the advantages of object technology. But software reuse does not just happen on its own: Organizations that adopt object-oriented development techniques and programming languages do not automatically gain the benefits of reuse. In fact, as noted earlier, reusability can also be achieved using traditional techniques and programming languages. Thus, the key to reuse is less a technical issue than an organizational issue [Griss 1995]: Has the organization implemented reward systems, processes, tools, and repositories to promote reuse?

To pay more than lip service to reuse, an organization must institute compensation systems that reward developers for reusing the design elements or classes created by others. The organization must also facilitate reuse by providing easy access to reusable components. No class or design model will be reused if finding it takes longer than reinventing it! Furthermore, developers must know that a particular "wheel" has already been invented if they are to avoid reinventing it yet again. Thus, the organization must implement design/object catalogs, browsers, and other tools that facilitate location and reuse of classes and design models. Procedures that encourage and support reuse must also be instituted. For example, Jacobson et al. [1995] recommend that the organization appoint a *reuse coordinator:* a person or group responsible for identifying opportunities for and promoting reuse. At minimum, the organization should adopt methodologies and guidelines that support reuse and school its developers in designing for reuse. Only by planning for and promoting design and software reuse can an organization leverage these valuable assets.

CONDUCTING POST-IMPLEMENTATION EVALUATION

The **post-implementation evaluation** is performed a few weeks or months after conversion to determine how well the delivered system and the development process itself achieved the systems development goals: system quality, project management, and organizational relevance. Too often, organizations fail to assess their development projects and the information systems they deliver. Thus, no one in the organization knows whether the system actually achieved its promised benefits; furthermore, the organization misses an excellent opportunity to improve its development processes.

The post-implementation evaluation seeks to answer several questions [Gulliver 1987]:

◆ Did the delivered system achieve its objectives?

◆ Are users satisfied with the system's quality?

◆ Was the project managed effectively?

◆ What did the project actually cost?

◆ How much time and effort did the project actually require?

◆ What factors contributed to the success or failure of the project?

The answers to these questions are derived by gathering user and developer perceptions of the development process and product and by evaluating several critical measures of system performance (system reliability, response time, accuracy of system outputs, and so on). An evaluation team of several users and developors employs a variety of techniques to collect this information: conducting surveys, one-on-one interviews, or a JAD-review workshop; observing the system in use; studying project documents; and collecting data about system performance.

The evaluation team's findings are presented in the post-implementation evaluation report; Table 13.3 outlines the typical sections and contents of this report. The *project overview* describes any factors necessary for the reader's understanding of the project: its users, developers, purpose, risk factors, and any other information related to understanding the technical, organizational, and social issues the project faced. The *method of evaluation* section describes how the development process and product were assessed; copies of survey instruments, interview questions, system performance measurement tests, and so on, should be placed in the *appendices*.

The *results* section addresses each of the development goals individually, summarizing both user and developer perceptions and objective measures of goal achievement. See Table 1.1 in the Chapter 1 discussion of system development goals for questions used to assess system functionality. User and developer responses to these questions provide subjective measurements of system quality. Objective measures of *system quality* include the performance measures noted earlier (system reliability, response time, accuracy of system outputs, etc.). Objective measures of *project management* include estimated versus actual cost and estimated

TABLE 13.3 Contents of the post-implementation evaluation report

I. Preliminaries
   A. Letter of transmittal
   B. Executive summary (for short reports, include in the transmittal letter)
      Summarize evaluation method and results, highlighting lessons learned.
   C. Table of contents (optional for short reports)

II. Report Body
   A. Project overview
      1. Description of the system's users
      2. Description of the system's developers
      3. Description of the project
         a. Project risk factors (size, complexity, etc.)
         b. System objectives
         c. Other objectives
         d. Project constraints and scope
         e. Tools and methodology used
         f. Critical project events
   B. Method of evaluation
   C. Results—system quality
      1. User perceptions
      2. Developer perceptions
      3. Objective measures
   D. Results—project management
      1. User perceptions
      2. Developer perceptions
      3. Objective measures
   E. Results—organizational relevance
      1. User perceptions
      2. Developer perceptions
      3. Objective measures
   F. Conclusions and recommendations*

III. Appendices
   A. Copies of survey instruments
   B. Organization chart
   C. Selected project documentation

*Conclusions and recommendations may be placed at the beginning of the report body for emphasis.

versus actual schedule. Objective measures of *organizational relevance* include data about improvements in the organization's

1. Efficiency (e.g., reduced error rate, cycle time, and so on).

2. Effectiveness (e.g., more timely, complete, and accurate information for management decision making).

3. Competitiveness (e.g., reduced cost, improved quality, increased repeat business or market share).

The *conclusions and recommendations* section summarizes the lessons learned, including mistakes and successes. This is the most valuable section of the report because it suggests how the organization can learn from its past mistakes and repeat its successes. Only by performing this critical project assessment can an organization continuously improve the quality of its development process and its information systems.

MAINTAINING AND EVOLVING THE SYSTEM

Although this textbook has focused on the initial development of an automated information system, you should understand that what happens *after* initial development represents the majority of the system's lifetime costs. An information system operates in a dynamic environment where change is the norm. Thus, you should expect that a newly developed system will require maintenance and modification almost from the day it is installed. Consider that the accounting information systems in many large organizations were "born" in the 1960s and still "draw breath" today, albeit in an altered form. They may now run on more powerful hardware, their software may have been modified (patched!) numerous times, and their data may have changed structure or been moved to magnetic disk. But the fundamental IPOSC functions are largely the same.

Recall that one of the subgoals of the system quality development goal is *maintainability*: creating information systems that are clearly documented and amenable to modification. Any changes in the existing system require that the system be thoroughly understood and thoroughly tested after the modifications have been made. Thus, providing clear, complete, accurate technical documentation and saving test data and specifications for reuse are just two ways that you contribute to achieving this goal. Another subgoal is *flexibility:* creating information systems that are adaptable to changes in their components. A change in one component should not necessitate a change in the other components. By selecting "open" data, software, and hardware components, you contribute to the achievement of the flexibility subgoal.

In the remainder of this section, we discuss system maintenance and system evolution. **System maintenance**, the modification of one or more system components, is largely a technology-driven undertaking that does not involve users. In contrast, **system evolution**, the modification of system functions, is a business-driven undertaking that requires significant user involvement and commitment.

System Maintenance

System maintenance addresses technical issues, such as making program code more efficient or modifying certain hardware or software components. For example, design errors or omissions may be discovered while the system is in production. Correcting these does not require a full-scale development project, largely because the intended design is already documented in the system's design specification report. Instead, the system must be modified to satisfy the performance or functional specifications already defined.

Another example of system maintenance is upgrading selected hardware or software components. If the latest version of a particular software package provides desirable functionality, the maintenance staff may be called upon to install the upgrade on the affected users' computer system(s). If this version also requires greater primary memory or faster processing speeds, the hardware may need to be upgraded (e.g., a personal computer might be upgraded from 8 Mbytes to 16 Mbytes or a math coprocessor or a Pentium microprocessor might be installed). System maintenance may also include modifications to the telecommunications media and software (e.g., replacing coaxial cable with fiber optic cable, installing an additional communications hub, or upgrading to a newer version of the network operating system).

System maintenance does not require approval to launch a project, nor does it require the formation of a development team. Instead, in most organizations, requests for maintenance are submitted to the IS maintenance staff, where they are prioritized and completed as time and resources allow. Only those requests that require significant investments of time, labor, or money (e.g., upgrading 100 386-PCs with Pentium processors or a new software release) are subjected to a formal approval process.

System Evolution

System evolution, which involves both users and developers, addresses system performance issues that affect organizational efficiency, effectiveness, and competitiveness. Systems evolve to fulfill new functional requirements, to provide desired enhancements, and to employ new technologies. Evolving the system requires that another development project be launched. Thus, the system life cycle is indeed a cycle; a system is developed, put into production, returned to development, returned to production, and so on. The augmented view of the system life cycle in Figure 13.4 emphasizes that the system must be evolved—that is, returned to development—because the business is constantly evolving while the system is in production.

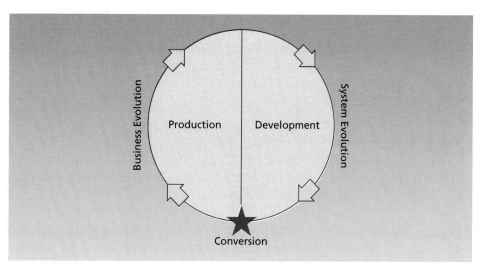

FIGURE 13.4   Augmented view of system life cycle

To better manage system evolution, some organizations institute a **change management** process, which includes the following elements:

1. A change review board is appointed to assess and approve requested changes.

2. The user group requesting system changes submits a formal change request to the change review board.

3. The change review board evaluates the request and passes it to the IS department, which analyzes its implications on the current production system.

4. IS prepares a change analysis report for the review board.

5. Based on the merit of the request (e.g., need, expected benefits) and the change analysis report, the review board approves or rejects the request.

6. If approved, a new project is launched, followed by a change acceptance review to evaluate the success and effects of the development effort and the system evolution.

✦ REVIEW OF CHAPTER LEARNING OBJECTIVES

1. *Explain the activities of final construction.*

   The activities of final construction include the following:

   a. *Construct and verify the data component.* One of the most crucial construction activities is *file conversion*: the process of converting from manual to digital files or from digital files in one format or structure to digital files in another format or structure. After the database has been constructed, its validity, completeness, and accuracy must be verified.

   b. *Construct (acquire) and verify the software component.* The software component includes both system and application software. If software is to be purchased from a vendor, a formal acquisition, evaluation, and verification process ensues. If software is being custom-developed, programmers code and unit test each module/object class and then integrate the modules/object classes and perform integration tests.

   c. *Acquire and verify the hardware component.* Requests for proposals/quotations detailing the technical and performance specifications of each hardware component are submitted to vendors. The responses are evaluated and vendor claims are verified. Then a contract for purchase or lease of the hardware is prepared.

   d. *Prepare the facility.* The work area and/or computer room may need to be modified to house additional hardware. Factors to consider in preparing the facility include a reliable, uninterrupted power source; air conditioning and ventilation; security and disaster protection; lighting and work-area comfort; and allocation of space for tape/disk libraries, documentation, and supplies.

   e. *Construct and verify documentation.* The user, technical, and operations manuals must be written and their clarity, accuracy, and completeness verified.

f. *Train users and assign production responsibilities.* One or more developers and users should create a training plan that specifies the training schedule, objectives, materials, and so on and that is approved by the user-sponsor. Traditional training is conducted by instructors who explain the system and give users practice in performing its functions in face-to-face training sessions. Final construction also involves assigning responsibility for production roles so that each user's job tasks are clearly defined and appropriate access authorizations can be assigned.

2. *Discuss the software and hardware acquisition process.*

To acquire software and/or hardware, you may need to create a request for proposal (RFP) or a request for quotation (RFQ) to be submitted to several vendors. Vendor responses are evaluated using selection criteria established by the development team and users as to the features and functions necessary to satisfy the system's functional requirements and other organizational needs. The selected products must be tested to verify vendor claims and to ensure that they perform the required functions and are compatible with the organization's existing software and hardware.

3. *Plan user training activities.*

The type of training, schedule, participants, and curriculum must be determined and the required materials and equipment identified. An effective tool for performing these planning activities is the training plan, which outlines the training schedule, objectives, materials, and so on, and which is approved by the user-sponsor before training begins. The user documentation must be completed and tested in advance of the training sessions.

4. *Define "integrated performance support system" and discuss its advantages over traditional user training.*

Integrated performance support systems augment face-to-face training with computer-based training programs, interactive tutorials, videotaped instruction, printed and online user documentation, and help-desk support designed to guide the user on a "just in time" basis. Compared to traditional training methods, an IPSS can reduce training costs 50 percent or more for large systems with many users. In addition, an IPSS may be more effective because it supports user learning needs on an "on demand" basis.

5. *Distinguish the development/test environment from the production environment.*

Each phase of the system life cycle—development and production—requires a fundamentally different system environment. A system under development should never be used to perform production functions; similarly, no aspect of the production system should be "contaminated" by the development environment. The clear separation of these two environments is especially critical during testing. For example, "live" production data should never be used as test data.

6. *Differentiate between black-box testing and glass-box testing.*

The black-box testing strategy treats the system as a box whose contents cannot be discerned. This strategy assumes that if, given certain inputs, the system generates the correct outputs, then the system's programs, data structures, interfaces, and so on, must be correct. In contrast, the glass-box strategy looks "inside the box" to verify system components and functions by examining each line of code and each data structure.

7. *Create test specifications to plan and to document system testing procedures.*

Test specifications outline the procedures for testing the system, serving both to plan and to document the results of unit and system tests. A test specification is complete only if it forces the system to execute all of its functions, including error-recognition routines. Both test data and test specifications should be saved for reuse when the system is modified or enhanced.

8. *List four installation strategies and discuss the advantages and disadvantages of each.*

The four installation strategies are direct cutover, pilot installation, phased installation, and parallel operation. The primary advantages of the *direct cutover* strategy are its low cost and its immediate accumulation of benefits. Its primary disadvantages are that it allows no gradual adjustment to the new system and provides no fall-back should the system not perform as expected. The *pilot installation* strategy is somewhat less risky than direct cutover and allows lessons learned from the pilot installation to be applied as the system is installed at other locations. Its main drawback is that the other locations cannot begin accruing the system's benefits immediately. The advantages and disadvantages of *phased installation* by location are similar to those of the pilot installation strategy. Phasing installation by subsystem simplifies installation and allows users time to adjust gradually to the new system. The *parallel operation* installation strategy is the most complex and resource-intensive, often resulting in increased workload, duplicated paperwork, reduced productivity, and stressed users. The primary advantages of this strategy are the safety net and the opportunity to verify the new system by validating its outputs against those of the old system.

9. *Define and explain the purpose of a post-implementation evaluation.*

A post-implementation evaluation is conducted to determine how well the delivered system and the development process itself have achieved the systems development goals of system quality, project management, and organizational relevance. An evaluation team of several users and developers gathers user and developer perceptions of the development process and product, then evaluates several critical measures of system performance. The evaluation team's findings are presented in a Post-Implementation Evaluation report.

◆ KEY TERMS

accuracy	conversion	final construction
benchmark	development/test	glass-box testing strategy
black-box testing strategy	environment	integrated performance
change management	direct cutover	support system (IPSS)
completeness	file conversion	integration test

operations manual	request for quotation (RFQ)	test data
parallel operation	selection criteria	test specification
phased installation	stress test	training plan
pilot installation	system evolution	unit test
post-implementation evaluation	system maintenance	user acceptance review
	system test	validity
production environment	system test and installation	volume test
request for proposal (RFP)	technical documentation	

◆ DISCUSSION QUESTIONS

1. What factors influence the time and effort devoted to final construction?

2. What is file conversion? Explain the activities it entails.

3. How can you verify the validity, completeness, and accuracy of the new system's data component?

4. List five sources from which the software component can be obtained.

5. How can you verify the new system's software component?

6. Explain how to acquire software and hardware from a vendor.

7. How can you verify the new system's hardware component?

8. List several factors that must be considered as the system facility is prepared.

9. Differentiate between the system's technical documentation and its operations manual by describing the users and contents of each.

10. How can you verify the accuracy, completeness, and clarity of documentation?

11. What is an integrated performance support system (IPSS)? What are the benefits of an IPSS compared with traditional instructor-led training sessions?

12. Why is it critical that you never allow the development/test environment and the production environment to overlap?

13. Give an appropriate use of each of the testing strategies: black-box and glass-box.

14. Explain the statement, "A test specification serves both to plan and to document the results of unit and system tests."

15. Discuss the advantages and disadvantages of each installation strategy.

16. What steps must an organization take to promote and to support design and software reuse?

17. How can conducting a post-implementation evaluation help an organization improve its development processes?

18. Distinguish between system maintenance and system evolution.

◆ EXERCISES

1. Examine the Appointment data entry screen shown in Figure 13.5. Create test data and write five test conditions to verify this data entry screen. You may assume that field type tests (e.g., for alphabetic versus numeric data) are automatically performed by the DBMS; your task is to test functionality, not field types. (See Exercise 5 in Technical Module D for more case detail.)

   Description of Screen Functionality: *The user enters an appointment date and physician's name, causing the system to retrieve a table showing appointments for that physician on that date. To add an entry, the user tabs to an open timeslot and enters the patient ID; the system retrieves the patient name and phone number and moves the cursor to the complaint column. The user enters the patient's complaint. To cancel an entry, the user tabs to the selected row and presses the* (DELETE) *key. To modify an entry, the user tabs to the selected cell, presses* (F6), *and enters a new value.*

2. Examine the Enter Booking Contract data entry screen shown in Figure 13.6. Create test data and write five test conditions to verify this data entry screen. You may assume that

---

Appointment Data Entry Screen

Enter Appointment Date: *MM/DD/YY*
Enter Physician: *AAAAAAAAAAAAAAAAA*

Appointment for \<Physician\> on \<Date\>

Appointment Time	Patient ID	Patient Name	Patient Phone	Complaint
8:00				
8:15	336-1194-38	Ben Carey	337-7773	Annual exam
8:30	336-1194-38	Ben Carey	337-7773	Annual exam
8:45	336-1194-38	Ben Carey	337-7773	Annual exam
9:00	336-1194-38	Ben Carey	337-7773	Annual exam
9:15	109-3344-12	Mark Warren	773-3337	headaches
etc....				
4:45				

To **ADD** entry: Tab to open timeslot; enter patient ID and complaint.
To **CANCEL** entry: Tab to row and press [Delete] key.
To **MODIFY** entry: Tab to cell and press [F6]; enter new value.
To **SAVE** and **EXIT**: Press [F2]
To **EXIT** without saving: Press [F9]

FIGURE 13.5   Data entry screen for Exercise 1

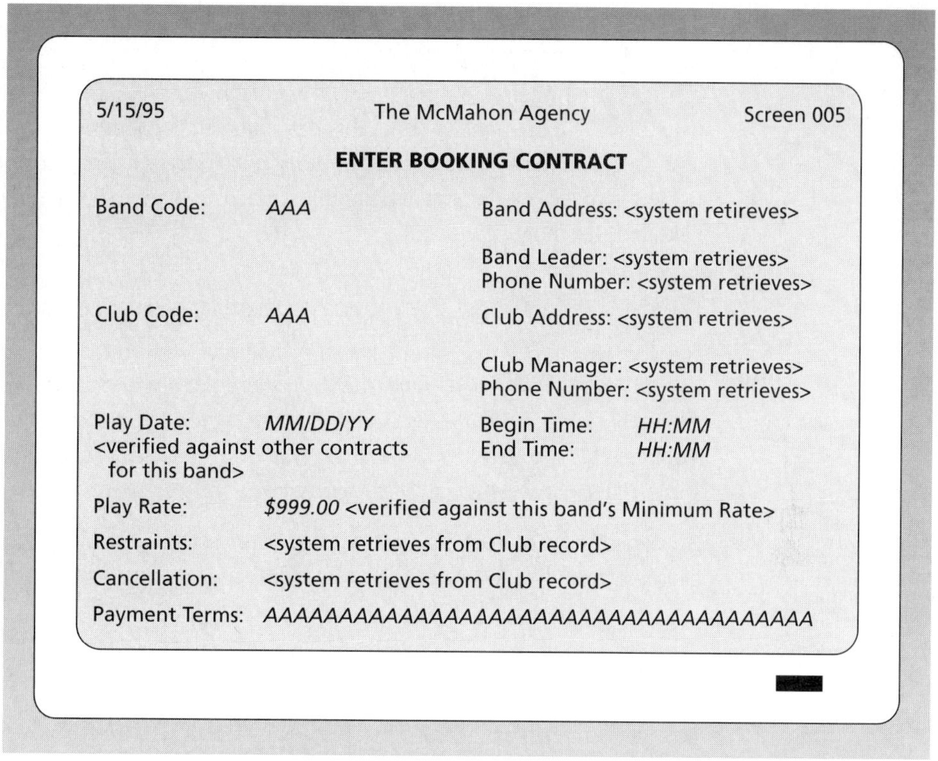

┌───┐
│ 5/15/95   The McMahon Agency   Screen 005 │
│   │
│   **ENTER BOOKING CONTRACT**   │
│   │
│ Band Code: *AAA*   Band Address: <system retreves> │
│   │
│   Band Leader: <system retrieves> │
│   Phone Number: <system retrieves> │
│   │
│ Club Code: *AAA*   Club Address: <system retrieves> │
│   │
│   Club Manager: <system retrieves> │
│   Phone Number: <system retrieves> │
│   │
│ Play Date: *MM/DD/YY*   Begin Time: *HH:MM*   │
│ <verified against other contracts   End Time: *HH:MM*   │
│   for this band>   │
│   │
│ Play Rate: *$999.00* <verified against this band's Minimum Rate> │
│   │
│ Restraints: <system retrieves from Club record>   │
│   │
│ Cancellation: <system retrieves from Club record>   │
│   │
│ Payment Terms: *AAAAAAAAAAAAAAAAAAAAAAAAAAAAAAAAAAAAAAAAAAAA* │
└───┘

FIGURE 13.6   Data entry screen for Exercise 2

field type tests (e.g., for alphabetic versus numeric data) are automatically performed by the DBMS; your task is to test functionality, not field types. (See Exercise 4 of Technical Module D for more case detail.)

Description of Screen Functionality: *Fields shown in italics are entered by the user. All other data is retrieved from the database. The Play Date and Play Rate are verified against data in the database. If a Play Date for which the band has already been scheduled is entered, the system displays the error message, "Band already scheduled. Please enter a different date." If a Play Rate less than the band's minimum play rate is entered, the system displays the error message, "Play Rate is less than band's minimum. Please enter a different rate."*

3. Examine the data entry screen you created for Exercise 11 in Chapter 11. Create test data and write five test conditions to verify this data entry screen. You may assume that field type tests (e.g., for alphabetic versus numeric data) are automatically performed by the DBMS; your task is to test functionality, not field types.

4. Examine the data entry screen you created for Exercise 12 in Chapter 11. Create test data and write five test conditions to verify this data entry screen. You may assume that field type tests (e.g., for alphabetic versus numeric data) are automatically performed by the DBMS; your task is to test functionality, not field types.

5. Reread the Chapter 4 opening case, "Streamlining Order Fulfillment at CAV." Assume that you are part of an evaluation team formed to assess the success of CAV's development project and the new order fulfillment system it delivered.
   a. Describe any factors that you believe should be included in the project overview of your post-implementation evaluation report. Why should these factors be included?
   b. Given the information provided in the case, what objective measures can you employ to assess system quality, project management, and organizational relevance?
   c. Given the information provided in the case, what can CAV learn from this development project?

6. Reread the Chapter 5 opening case, "Process Thinking and Workflow Automation." Assume that you are part of an evaluation team formed to assess the success of TCB's development project and the new 401K administration system it delivered.
   a. Describe any factors that you believe should be included in the project overview of your post-implementation evaluation report. Why should these factors be included?
   b. Given the information provided in the case, what objective measures can be employed to assess system quality, project management, and organizational relevance?
   c. Given the information provided in the case, what can TCB learn from this development project?

◆ REFERENCES

Dublin, L. E. "Learn While You Work." *Computerworld*, August 30, 1993, pp. 81–82. See also G. Gery, *Electronic Performance Support Systems*. Boston: Weingarten Publications, 1991.

Gelinas, U. J., Jr., A. E. Oram, and W. P. Wiggins. *Accounting Information Systems*. Boston: PWS-Kent, 1990.

Griss, M. "Software Reuse: Objects and Frameworks Are Not Enough." *Object Magazine*, February 1995, pp. 77–79, 87.

Gulliver, F. R. "Special Report: Post-Project Appraisals Pay." *Harvard Business Review*, March/April 1987, pp. 128–132.

Jacobson, I., M. Ericsson, and A. Jacobson. *The Object Advantage: Business Process Reengineering with Object Technology*. Workingham, England: Addison-Wesley, 1995.

Rettig, M. "Testing Made Palatable." *Communications of the ACM* 34, no. 5 (May 1991), pp. 25–29.

Yourdon, E. *Object-Oriented Systems Design: An Integrated Approach*. Englewood Cliffs, NJ: Yourdon Press/Prentice-Hall, 1994. See especially Chapter 6 for a discussion of software reuse.

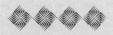

Final Construction of ETG's Order Processing System

This installment of the ETG case is brief because so many of the activities of final construction, testing, and installation of ETG's order processing system were illustrated in the plans presented in Chapter 12 and discussed in Chapter 13. Here, the case narrative provides a chronological view of these activities to help you visualize them.

FINAL CONSTRUCTION

Guided by the construction plan and the few interface changes suggested during the JAD-review-and-confirmation workshop, Victoria and Denny began final construction of ETG's new order processing system. Again Denny focused on the database, creating a data dictionary to document ETG's data elements and fine-tuning the physical database design to meet ETG's requirements. In the meantime, Victoria fine-tuned and unit tested the Access macro code needed to manipulate and validate the data and to generate reports. She also planned the training activities and arranged to rent several computer systems for a few days so that the ETG users would have hands-on experience learning the new system. Victoria also wrote her sections of the system documentation manual.

Susan Young, a sales clerks who was also a technical writing student, was assigned the task of creating the user guide. Working from Victoria's outline and occasionally assisted by Denny, Susan prepared a user-friendly, task-oriented document that clearly explained all the procedures clerks would have to perform. When the user guide was completed, Susan gave it to Victoria, who approved it and then made several copies so that each ETG user could refer to it during training.

Paul took responsibility for revising ETG's current job descriptions. He eliminated the inventory clerk position and modified the sales clerk job description to include checking rental tapes in and out, processing fines, and contacting rental customers who had overdue tapes or excessive unpaid fines. Paul also outlined the duties of two new positions: a systems manager responsible for the system's technical maintenance and trouble-shooting and a systems administrator responsible for maintaining the database, running reports, and so on. Paul hoped to convince Denny to sign on as the part-time systems administrator; Beto had already volunteered to fill the systems administrator position.

As final construction proceeded, ETG clerks began asking customers to complete the new membership application form. The clerks also used this opportunity to advertise the new system and to tell customers about the improved customer service it would provide. Using the updated membership data, Denny and Beto prepared a few of the new membership cards. They used the bar code printer to create a membership number bar code label for each card and then used the bar code reader to verify that each card's label could be read correctly. These activities served as a unit test of these system components. Denny also worked with Helen to prepare and to unit test the rental tape bar codes. Again, they verified the scanning hardware and software using several of the newly created bar-coded rental tapes.

SYSTEM TESTS

When the software, hardware, and data components of the rental order processing system had been constructed and the user guide written, Denny oversaw several ETG users as they performed test procedures to verify the system components. The test procedures first verified the tape and membership card scanning functions and then performed all the tasks required in each use case. The use case activity not only verified the database, user interfaces, and system behaviors but also verified the clarity and completeness of the user guide, which ETG testers referred to as they performed the use cases. Use case testing established the completeness and accuracy of the system.

Then Denny worked with Beto, Susan, and Paul to test the backup, security, and recovery procedures described in the operations manual. Beto was especially attentive during these tests because he was likely to be called upon to perform many of these procedures. His comments helped Denny to clarify several of the procedures descriptions. Finally, Victoria and Denny conducted the volume and stress tests and pronounced the system capable of serving ETG's order processing needs even if the customer and tape volume doubled.

It was time to move the system "out front" and into production.

SYSTEM INSTALLATION

The most time-consuming task facing the development team was converting ETG's manual records. Finalizing the physical database structures took Denny just a few hours. However, converting ETG's 1000 customer record notecards and its 2500 rental tape notecards to digital records would be far more time consuming. Consulting with Paul, Denny decided to enlist the help of off-duty ETG employees. Not only would this speed up data conversion, it would also provide valuable training and experience to the clerks who were to be the system's primary users.

First, Denny installed the order processing software on the five computers Victoria had rented for the training sessions. Then, he conducted a half-day training session for the clerks, explaining hardware and software fundamentals and allowing the clerks to practice entering data. Then Denny and any available clerks started entering the customer and tape records. Having multiple systems available for several days greatly increased the rate at which notecards were converted to database records. In just over a week, the master customer and tape files were complete.

Victoria and Denny also conducted training sessions for the clerks and Paul to demonstrate the normal processing and backup/recovery procedures. Victoria worked with Susan to create a user and system documentation library in ETG's back office. Beto and Helen took care of buying and storing the required system supplies: paper, ink cartridges, sales and rental order forms, blank diskettes, and any other supplies needed to "feed" the system.

All during this time, Paul took every opportunity to "sell" Denny on taking the systems manager position. Paul was impressed with Denny's technical skills and his ability to work so effectively with ETG employees. "You know, we both can benefit from your taking this position," he told Denny one day. "I get someone who already knows my business and system inside and out and is a proven commodity; you get system administration experience, which will look very good on your resume, and flexible hours with a steady source of income while you complete your last year of school." After talking with Victoria about the pros and cons, Denny agreed to take the position.

In the meantime, a construction crew worked early morning and late evening hours to remodel ETG's retail space. They installed additional tape display shelves and constructed a new sales counter to accommodate the computer system and scanning devices. They also installed the electronic security gate and built a partition to direct customers entering or leaving the premises through the security gate. Everyone monitored the construction team's progress with anticipation, knowing that the remodeling had to be completed on time if installation and conversion were to be completed on schedule.

With the facility complete, ETG closed for business on Wednesday so that Victoria, Denny, Paul, and three employees could perform the system installation and conversion. Moving the hardware out of the back office and installing it at the sales counter, they ran a few of the most critical test conditions again to verify that all components were functioning properly. Late that afternnon, the system was subjected to its final test: the user acceptance review. The ETG users—and most importantly, the user-sponsor, Paul—agreed that the system was every bit as good as they had expected. So Victoria, Denny, Paul, and all the ETG employees had a festive dinner to celebrate the launch of the new system. The next morning, when ETG opened its doors for business, its customers were greeted by a huge banner that read "ETG Enters the Information Age!"

GLOSSARY

acceptance criteria The system quality criteria that the system must achieve to gain user acceptance.

accuracy A condition of a database that contains only correct data; achieved by employing input validation routines to verify the format and range of each data element and to generate exception reports listing any records that fail the validation criteria.

adaptability A system quality criterion that is satisfied if the system's PPDSH components are loosely coupled, i.e., a change in one of the components necessitates few or no changes in the other components.

affinity diagram A matrix that shows the intersection of two dimensions of the organization, for example, activities and functional areas, or activities and data.

agenda An action plan that structures the activities of a meeting, indicating the approximate time devoted to each activity and the person(s) responsible for leading each activity.

application controls Manual procedures, organizational policies, and programmed procedures built into the system's application software; designed to validate system functions and to ensure accuracy.

application procedures Instructions that users follow to run an application in order to perform a business task.

application software Programs that automate a specific business function.

attribute A data item that characterizes an object.

balancing A DFD leveling technique in which all data flows related to the parent process are shown again in the child diagram.

bar graph A graphic technique in which each bar represents one data component, for example, the number of widgets sold in a particular month; especially effective for comparing figures for various time frames.

batch processing A processing technique in which transactions are accumulated and then processed as a batch at a later time.

benchmark Comparative throughput measure given a typical user workload processed on each vendor's hardware; used to evaluate alternative hardware solutions.

black hole A DFD process or data store that receives data that are never used again; a process or data store that has input data flows but no output data flows.

black-box testing strategy A testing strategy that treats the system as a box whose contents cannot be discerned; assumes that if, given certain inputs, the system generates the correct outputs, then the system's programs, data, interfaces and so on must be correct.

business area analysis Evaluation of the functional areas and/or management levels that will use an information system.

business area boundaries A component of project scope that defines which functional areas are to be studied within the business.

business functional areas Business areas of production, sales and marketing, finance and accounting, and human resources.

business objective An organization's measurable goals; includes both short- and long-term goals.

business objects People, places, things, and transactions about which an organization must maintain data and which perform functions to help an organization reach its goals.

business process reengineering (BPR) Fundamental rethinking and radical redesign of an entire business process to achieve dramatic improvements in critical measures of performance.

candidate class An object class identified early in analysis by studying workflow diagrams and other enterprise models.

cardinality The number of instances of one object class that can or must be related to one instance of another object class.

CASE (computer-aided systems engineering) A software package that enforces a systems development methodology and provides tools to support various techniques.

change management A process instituted to better manage system evolution; involves appointing a change review board to assess and approve requested changes to a production system.

child process (diagram) A DFD process that decomposes a higher-level process.

clarity A system quality criterion requiring that a system's functions be consistent and predictable.

class library See "object library."

class specification The object-oriented equivalent of a data dictionary; specifies the class name, relationships, attributes, and methods.

client A single-user desktop computer running user-friendly software with a graphical user interface; provides data entry, querying, and reporting capabilities.

client/server information architecture Network that integrates and distributes data and processing among multiple computers.

cohesiveness A characteristic of a design that specifies only one function per module or one function per method.

collaboration relationship An object relationship in which two objects must communicate to access data or to perform methods.

combined user-level workflow diagram A workflow diagram that models all the entities and workflows of a system.

command dialog A human-computer dialog that employs a command language defining the valid terms and syntax for interaction.

competitiveness Measure of an organization's ability to provide more value to its customers or to provide equal value at a lower price.

completeness A condition of a database in which all valid data are entered; achieved by using batch controls or hash totals to manage the number of records entered.

component-based application development A trend in software development that constructs applications by "snapping in" and customizing prebuilt modules.

composition relationship An object relationship in which one object (the component) is a part of another object (the composite).

computer A processing device that performs logical and arithmetic operations on data and controls the operations of peripherals.

constraints Management limitations on resources to be used to analyze, design, and implement the system; resources include time, money, and personnel.

construction plan A plan that indicates the tasks that must be performed to finalize the system, including who will perform these activities, when they will be performed, and any additional resources that will be needed.

control flow A flag or indicator that determines which of multiple program paths should be followed or that reports the status of the program.

control function Activity performed to verify the validity and accuracy of inputs and outputs and to ensure the integrity of stored data.

control procedures Instructions on how to back up data, verify input data, and restrict access to information resources.

conversion The point at which responsibility for the system shifts from the development team to the production users; i.e., when a system moves from the development phase into the production phase.

cost-benefit analysis Method used to evaluate the cost-effectiveness (economic feasibility) of a capital investment project.

coupling A characteristic of a design that minimizes the number of data and control flows passed between modules.

creeping requirements A term used to describe the fact that, on average, user requirements grow or change about 1 percent per month; a problem in systems development projects in which requirements are frozen early in the development process.

cross-platform development tool A rapid application development (RAD) tool that allows developers to generate the code for user interfaces running on multiple platforms.

CRUD The four data management activities: create, read, update, delete.

CSF (critical success factors) analysis A technique used to identify the few things an organization must do well in order to succeed in its environment.

data Raw facts collected, processed, and stored by an information system.

data dictionary A structured repository of data about data; defines each data structure in a database.

data element The smallest unit of data consisting of a combination of characters that describe one feature of an entity or object. Equivalent to an attribute in logical data modeling.

data entry screen A user interface used to enter data into a computer-based information system.

data flow The movement of data between processes, entities, and data stores.

data flow diagram (DFD) A graphical modeling technique that models the sources and destinations of data, the data inputs and outputs, and the data maintained by an information system.

data modeling A systems development activity in which an organization's data requirements are analyzed as the foundation for designing a database.

data staging An upsizing strategy that periodically downloads data from a mainframe to a LAN server.

data store A manual or computerized repository for data.

data-driven system perspective A technique for identifying candidate object classes that focuses on the data that the system must maintain; thinks of objects in terms of what they look like.

database A collection of related files.

database management systems (DBMS) Software that provides an interface between an organization's data and the programs that must use the data.

design specification report A report that documents the system data structure, behavior, and user interface designs and outlines plans to complete the project.

designer An information systems professional who analyzes an organization, identifies its processing and information requirements, and creates the blueprints of a new information system.

detailed design Design that specifies the chosen system's physical IPOSC functions in terms of the PPDSH components.

development costs The costs of analyzing, designing, and implementing an information system.

development phase System life cycle phase in which an information system is analyzed, designed, and implemented.

development/test environment The system environment in which an information system is designed, constructed, and tested.

device independence A system quality-portability criterion that requires hardware components to operate in a variety of environments.

dialog flow diagram A graphic technique used to model the command hierarchy; shows the major screens or windows of the system as labeled rectangles and indicates the flow of control between screens as directional arrows.

direct cutover An installation strategy that immediately replaces the old production system with the newly developed system.

direct manipulation dialog A human-computer dialog that uses a pointing device such as a mouse to manipulate screen objects that perform system functions.

documentation Description of the five PPDSH components to serve as a road map as the components are revised.

downsizing The trend of moving applications off the mainframe and onto smaller platforms.

economic feasibility Analysis of the anticipated benefits to be derived from the system; a system is economically feasible if its expected benefits are equal to or greater than its expected costs.

encapsulation Packaging of data and behavior into a single construct. Also called information hiding.

end-user User who utilizes the system to perform job activities.

enterprise analysis A study that investigates an organization's business objectives, structure, information needs, objects, and processes.

enterprise models Graphical representations of an organization's structure, information needs, objects, and processes.

enterprise object model A graphical model that identifies and groups all objects of interest to the organization into subjects.

entity A person, place, thing, or event about which data is collected and maintained.

entity-relationship diagram The logical data modeling technique most commonly used in traditional systems development.

event-driven system perspective A technique used to identify candidate classes by focusing on what an object does.

evolutionary prototyping A prototyping strategy in which the prototype becomes the production system; a full systems development methodology.

existence dependency An object relationship in which an instance of one object cannot exist if no instance of a related object exists.

external document All the tangible "pieces of paper" that are used to gather inputs to or that are generated as outputs from the system.

external entities In a workflow diagram, persons or organizations—external to the study organization—that provide inputs to or receive outputs from an information system; in a data flow diagram, persons or organizations—external to the information system—that provide inputs to or receive outputs from the system.

facilitator A business or IS professional responsible for planning, conducting, and summarizing a joint application development (JAD) workshop.

fall-back plan A plan that specifies how daily operations will be continued in the event of system failure.

feasibility study A report to the user-sponsor that analyzes the likelihood of achieving the system objectives within the project constraints; it evaluates the organizational, technological, operational, and economical feasibility of a systems development project.

field See "data element."

file A collection of related records.

file conversion The process of converting from manual to digital files or from digital files in one format or structure to digital files in another format or structure.

final construction The process of making "production-ready" the prototype system that evolved during iterative analysis and design systems development stage in which users are trained, hardware resources are obtained, documentation is written, and the production-quality database and programs are constructed.

final construction strategies The single-team versus the multiple-team approach and the single-phase versus the multiple-phase approach; choice of strategies depends on how much time and effort is required to transform the prototype into a production-grade system.

flexibility A system quality criterion that evaluates an information system's ability to adapt to changes in the organization's needs.

foreign key The primary key of a related record included as a field of another record.

form-filling dialog A human-computer dialog that replicates a source document and, as its name suggests, requires the user to "fill in the form."

fourth-generation language (4GL) A nonprocedural language that in some cases provides a database management system.

fourth-generation tool (4GT) Productivity tool that allows users to develop their own applications.

frontware A rapid application development (RAD) tool that allows developers to create graphical user interface front-ends to existing mainframe applications (also called screen scrapers).

functional decomposition Process of identifying the major activities of a system and then breaking each activity into its composite steps.

functional requirements The logical IPOSC functions that a system must perform to help an organization meet its goals.

functionality A system quality subgoal that defines the facilities, performance, and other factors that the user requires in the finished system.

Gantt chart A planning tool that combines textual and graphical elements to document what task will be performed by whom, using what resources over what time frame.

general controls Organizational policies and manual and automated standard operating procedures designed to oversee the way systems are developed and to protect the system from unauthorized use.

general design Broad sketch of the IPOSC requirements in one or more design alternatives.

glass-box testing strategy A testing strategy that verifies system components and functions by examining each line of code and data structure.

glasshouse information architecture A system configuration that uses dumb terminals running character-based screens to access data from mainframes and minicomputers running software programmed in a third-generation language.

graphical 4GL A programming language that supports rapid application development by combining many of the features of GUI generators, frontware, and RDBMS tools with object-oriented constructs.

group decision support system (GDSS) A computer-based, interactive system designed to help a group of decision makers solve unstructured problems.

GUI (graphical user interface) generator A tool that allows developers to create visual representations of user interfaces and then generate the underlying source code.

hard copy A printed report.

hardware Physical equipment used to enter, process, output, store, and transmit data.

HAS-A relationship See "composition relationship."

human-computer dialog The style of interaction between the system and its users; types of dialogs include command, menu, form-filling, and direct manipulation.

identifier An attribute that uniquely identifies each instance of an object class or entity.

implementer Information systems professional who implements system specifications, turning plans on paper into a functioning information system.

index A file that relates the value of one or more fields to the physical storage address where the related record is located.

information architecture Configuration of hardware, software, data, and telecommunications designed to meet an organization's information needs.

information system A system that accepts data from its environment (input) and transforms the data (processing) to produce information (output).

information system components (PPDSH) The "pieces and things" that comprise an information system; include people, procedures, data, software, and hardware.

information system functions (IPOSC) The functions performed by an information system; include input, processing, output, storage, and control.

information systems plan A forward-looking definition of an information architecture and information systems that are aligned with the organization's strategic plan.

inheritance A feature of object-oriented design in which instances of a subclass inherit all the properties (attributes and methods) of their superclass.

input data Data entered into an information system.

input function An information system function that accesses data for processing.

installation plan A plan that indicates the chosen installation strategy, schedules and assigns responsibility for all installation activities, and identifies any additional resources needed.

installation strategy A strategy for dismantling the old system and replacing it with the new system. See

"direct cutover," "pilot installation," "phased installation," and "parallel operation."

intangible benefits Benefits that are not readily quantified or assigned a dollar amount.

integrated performance support system (IPSS) A well-conceived blend of computer-based training programs, interactive tutorials, videotaped instruction, printed and on-line user documentation, and help-desk support designed to support and guide the user on a "just in time" basis.

integration test A test to verify the flow of control and data between software modules.

interface object Objects that provide a bridge between users in the real world and business objects in an automated system; captures and displays the system's data.

internal entity A person or functional area within an organization (workflow diagram) or one that performs system processes (data flow diagram).

interoperability The ability to integrate applications from various sources, including custom-developed programs and commercial packages from multiple vendors, and to run these applications on a variety of hardware platforms.

interorganizational information systems (IIS) An information system that spans organizational boundaries to automate the flow of information between an organization and its external entities.

IPOSC The functions of an information system: input, processing, output, storage, and control.

IS-A relationship See "specialization relationship."

iteration To perform the same behavior(s) repeatedly. The number of repetitions may be fixed or determined by a test condition.

JAD See "joint application development."

JAD roles Functions performed by JAD workshop participants.

JAD-analysis workshop A JAD workshop whose purpose is to analyze requirements in detail and to outline the design of the new system.

JAD-design workshop A JAD workshop whose purpose is to design procedures, reports, and screens for the new system.

JAD-review-and-confirmation workshop A JAD workshop whose purpose is to review the progress-to-date and to confirm changes made to the system; scheduled at any point in the development life cycle.

job-level system flowchart A system flowchart that documents the process detail of an information system, showing each program as a separate process block.

joint application development (JAD) Development technique in which information systems professionals and users work closely together to analyze, design, and construct an information system; strategy created to overcome the communications gap between users and designers and to reduce the time and effort devoted to documenting and approving requirements and design specifications.

JRP (joint requirements planning) workshop A JAD workshop whose purpose is to verify the developers' understanding and to identify the requirements of the new system.

kick-off meeting A half-day meeting prior to a JAD workshop hosted by the user-sponsor to "gear up" for high-level participation during workshops.

language independence The ability to run programs written in a standard language under different operating systems.

legacy system Application that was developed using older technologies and is past its prime but is so critical to the organization that it cannot be disrupted without impacting the organization.

Level 0 DFD The highest-level DFD, documenting the major processes of an information system.

leveled DFDs Multiple DFDs in which each successive level presents a more detailed view of a process.

line graph A graphic technique that represents data as points in time, where the x-axis is a time line and the y-axis gives the quantity of the item being measured (for example, dollar sales or units sold).

logical data modeling A technique used to specify object classes (entities), attributes, and relationships.

logical DFD A data flow diagram that models system processes without any indication of how they will be performed.

logical function A function independent of the technology used.

logical record A collection of related fields that describes one instance of an entity or object class.

magic process A DFD process that spontaneously creates data; a process whose outputs could not be generated, given its inputs.

maintainability A system quality subgoal that requires a system to be easy to understand, test, and modify when revisions are mandated.

management levels One view of an organization's structure; includes operational management, which oversees the day-to-day business operations; tactical management, which allocates resources and implements the organization's strategies; and strategic management, which sets long-term business goals.

maximum cardinality The number of instances of one object class that can be related to one instance of another object class.

menu dialog A human-computer dialog that lists several possible actions and requires the user to select an option.

menu-oriented documentation An approach to creating user documentation that organizes user guide content by describing the commands available in each menu.

message A request from one object to another object, signaling the receiving object to perform one of its methods.

metaphor An interface design technique that associates one concept or thing with another concept or thing; for example, a "window" or "desktop."

method A function an object can perform.

methodology Systematic description of the sequence of activities required to solve a problem.

middleware Software that connects an end-user's client PC to a wide variety of mainframe databases.

milestone Completion of a task that produces a measurable output of critical importance to meeting the project schedule.

minimum cardinality The number of instances of one object class that must be related to one instance of another object class.

model Simplified representation of some aspect of the real world; used to analyze real-world constructs and to communicate this understanding to others.

modularity A system quality-maintainability criterion that evaluates how loosely coupled a program's modules are so that a change in one module does not necessitate a change in other modules.

module A group of instructions that is executed to perform a program function; ideally, each module should represent only one function.

network operating system (NOS) Operating system that controls the functions of a telecommunications network.

Nominal Group Technique (NGT) A structured technique for conducting a group interview or brainstorming session whose goal is to maximize individual participation while building group consensus.

object class A set of people, places, things, or transactions that share common attributes and perform common methods.

object instance A member of an object class; a particular person, place, thing, or event described by specific values for its attributes.

object library Encyclopedia containing an organization's object classes whose purpose is to promote reusability.

object relationship diagram An expressive logical data modeling technique used to analyze and design object classes, attributes, methods, and relationships.

object structure and behavior analysis Process of decomposing an information system into objects.

object-oriented analysis and design A systems development methodology that analyzes, designs, and constructs a system's object classes, methods, and attributes.

online help system A user documentation component that replicates the user guide online and assists users in understanding and using system features and functions.

on-time criterion A project management criterion that measures the ability to deliver the required system within the time allocated by the project schedule.

open issue Issue raised during a JAD workshop that cannot be resolved in a reasonable time and that may impede progress toward completing the agenda.

open issues list A running record of action items to be investigated and reported on later in the JAD workshop or at a subsequent workshop.

operating system A collection of programs that control and manage the activities of a computer system.

operational feasibility Analysis of user acceptance, management support, and requirements of entities and factors in the organization's external environment.

operations manual A document that describes the procedures for starting and shutting down the system, performing routine data backup, recovering from system failure, and employing security and access controls (also called the *technical operations manual*).

organization chart Graphical model of an organization's structure, representing the reporting structure between the management levels and the functional areas.

organization-level workflow diagram A workflow diagram that collapses all internal entities into a single internal entity representing the system or organization, highlighting the workflows between the system and its external entities.

organizational boundaries A component of project scope that defines which business units, divisions, or branches of an organization are to be studied.

organizational context Internal system environment including data, people, organizational culture, structure, policies, and operating procedures.

organizational culture Commonly shared assumptions about the organization's purpose and the practices required to achieve that purpose.

organizational effectiveness Measure of how an organization allocates its resources to achieve its goals.

organizational efficiency Measure of productivity: time, money, and other resources required to produce an output.

organizational feasibility Analysis of the proposed system's contribution to organizational efficiency, effectiveness, and competitiveness.

organizational relevance A systems development goal that measures the ability of an information system to contribute to organizational success.

organizational structure Representation of an organization as a matrix of functional areas and management levels.

output data Data generated by an information system, including documents and reports.

output function An information system function that generates processed data.

"over the wall" thinking A problem in traditional organizations in which one functional area performs activities and then throws its output "over the wall" to the next functional area.

overview system flowchart A system flowchart that represents all the processes of an information system as a single process block, labeled with the name of the system.

parallel operation An installation strategy in which both the old production system and the new production system are operated concurrently until the user-sponsor has been assured of the new system's accuracy and reliability.

parent process (diagram) A DFD process that is decomposed in a lower-level DFD.

partition To segment a physical DFD into programs, i.e., each partition represents a program that will be executed to support a business process.

payback point The point at which an organization accumulates enough benefit dollars to "pay back" the costs of developing and operating an information system.

people An information system component that includes users, designers, and implementers.

performance requirements Factors such as response time, transaction volume, data volume, and so on relevant to evaluating hardware devices and telecommunications capabilities.

peripherals Equipment that is distinct from the central processing unit and that provides the system with outside communication, storage, and input/output capabilities.

phased development Strategy that partitions a large system into subsystems or data capabilities and performs the structured analysis and design stages iteratively until the full system is implemented.

phased installation An installation strategy in which conversion from the old production system to the new system occurs in phases, for example, by subsystem or geographic location.

physical data flow diagram A traditional process modeling technique used to specify how the IPOSC functions will be implemented in a new information system.

physical database design A design that specifies the file organization, physical records, and indexes for each file in a database.

physical function A function described in terms of the technology used to perform it.

pie chart A graphic technique that uses a "pie" sliced into various pieces, the size of the piece representing the percentage that each data component contributes to the whole.

pilot installation An installation strategy that uses the direct cutover strategy to install the new system at one location, division, or branch office; if the pilot is successful, the system is installed at other locations.

pointer A technique used to relate records in a database.

polymorphism The ability to hide different implementations behind a common interface, simplifying the communications among objects.

portability A system quality-flexibility criterion that requires an information system to operate in a variety of environments with a variety of hardware components.

post-implementation evaluation A study conducted weeks or months after conversion to determine how well the delivered system and the development process achieved the systems development goals.

PPDSH The components of an information system: people, procedures, data, software, and hardware.

preliminary construction The process of developing an operational system that implements the design specifications.

preliminary investigation First stage of the traditional systems development methodology during which the objectives, constraints, and scope of the system are identified.

presentation scribe A scribe who uses word processing, presentation, and desktop publishing software to record the minutes of a JAD workshop, to generate a summary report document, and to prepare presentation graphics.

primary key A data element assigned to a record during physical database design; uniquely identifies each record.

private method A method performed for the benefit of the containing object and not known to any other object.

problem definition Identification of the symptoms that indicate a problem with the existing information system and determination of the objectives, constraints, and scope of a development project.

procedural flexibility A system quality-flexibility criterion that requires loosely coupled systems adaptable to new uses.

procedures Sets of instructions that people in the organization follow to perform their tasks.

process A systematic sequence of operations to produce a specified result. A set of activities that produces an output.

process description label An active verb phrase (verb + data) that is used to name a process in a DFD.

process identification number The number assigned to a DFD process to individuate it from other processes and, in some instances, to indicate the sequence in which processes are performed.

process thinking A BPR requirement that the organization think in terms of processes, not activities or functional areas.

processing function An information system function that manipulates data to perform business functions and to produce information of value in management decision making.

production costs Costs incurred to operate and maintain an information system; costs incurred during the production stage of the system life cycle.

production environment The system environment in which an information system is used to perform the organization's daily operations.

production phase System life cycle phase during which an information system is used to perform business functions.

program structure chart A traditional design technique that employs functional decomposition to specify the structure and functions of an application program.

program-data independence A desirable information system characteristic in which a change in the data component does not require major revisions of the software component.

project management A systems development goal that evaluates the quality of the development process.

project risk A measurement of the likelihood that a proposed system will satisfy the systems development goals.

project risk evaluation form A technique used to evaluate and document the organizational, technical, and operational feasibility of a project.

project scope Specifications of what is or is not included in the study; limits the processes and business areas addressed by a systems development project.

prototyping A systems development technique that constructs and shows a working model to users to help them better understand the features and functions of the new system; iterative refinement of a working model of an information system.

prototyping tools Productivity software that allows developers to illustrate and/or mimic the functions and interfaces of an information system.

public method (or service) A method that "services" the needs of other objects; it is "public" in the sense that other objects know about its existence.

rapid application development (RAD) A systems development methodology that partitions a large system into subsystems or data capabilities and performs the analysis, design, and prototyping stages iteratively within a non-extendible time limit.

RDBMS (relational database management system) tools Tools that facilitate database development.

real-time processing A processing technique that receives input data, processes it, and returns results (output) fast enough to affect an ongoing process.

relationship A data modeling construct that models business policies stipulating how many instances of one object class can or must be related to one instance of another object class.

relationship types The three basic relationships, expressed as the maximum cardinality of each object in the relationship: 1:1 (one-to-one), 1:N (one-to-many), and N:M (many-to-many).

reliability A system quality-functionality criterion that requires PPDSH components to perform the system's functions completely and accurately.

report A user interface that summarizes and organizes data in a format that is meaningful to its intended users. See "hard copy" and "soft copy."

request for proposal A document used to solicit vendor responses when you know the functional requirements and features of the required software or hardware but have no specific product in mind.

request for quotation A document used to solicit vendor responses when you have already selected a product and need price quotations from several vendors.

requirements prototyping A prototyping strategy that uses a prototype to determine the functional requirements of a proposed system.

reusability The ability to reuse existing knowledge and program code as a new system is developed or an existing system is modified.

rules of operation A set of rules specifying the interaction of participants during a JAD workshop.

schema A description of a database's logical and physical structure as well as the validation rules, access authorization, and other aspects of the database.

screen scraping "First-step, quick fix" strategy that uses frontware to update the interface to a legacy application without modifying any application code.

scribes IS professionals, with skills in CASE, prototyping, and presentation tools, who capture the requirements and design specifications and who generate prototypes of reports, screens, and processes (i.e., program code) during a JAD workshop.

secondary index An index assigned to a non-key field.

selection A structured text construct that tests for one or more conditions, and depending on which condition is true, performs one set of statements or another.

selection criteria The software or hardware features and functions required or desirable to satisfy the system's functional requirements and other organizational needs; used to evaluate alternative software and hardware solutions.

sequence A structured text construct for specifying behaviors to be performed one after another.

server One or more multi-user computers that store data and/or programs to be shared by multiple users.

service See "public method."

service interface The "face" that an object presents to other objects; the public methods of an object class.

sociotechnical perspective A view of information systems that includes not only the technology but also the behavioral or social factors that affect the information system's ability to meet the needs of the organization as a whole.

soft copy A report displayed on screen.

software A collection of instructions that direct a computer system to perform a task.

software-oriented documentation An approach to creating user documentation that focuses on commands used to work with the software, organizing user guide content alphabetically by command name, and providing a definition of each command's purpose and syntax.

specialization relationship An object relationship in which one object (the subclass) is a special case of another object (the superclass); the mechanism that supports inheritance.

storage function Activity required to maintain system data.

stored data Data maintained in a manual file or on disk or tape.

strategic information systems Information systems used by an organization to implement one or more competitive strategies.

strategic pull A systems development catalyst in which a change in strategy "pulls" an organization into developing systems that support these strategies and help the organization stay competitive.

stress test A test that simulates hardware malfunctions, extreme data and transaction volumes, and other conditions in order to ensure that the system degrades gracefully under extreme conditions.

structured text A technique used in traditional systems development in which a quasi-formal language specifies system behaviors and business rules.

structured walkthrough A verification process to simulate program execution by "walking through" a program structure chart's processes and flows of data and control.

subclass (child) A specialization of a superclass; inherits the attributes and methods of its superclass.

subject A cohesive grouping of a subset of an organization's object classes.

superclass (parent) A generalization of a subclass.

SWAT (Skilled With Advanced Tools) team A small group, usually no more than five, of experienced, well-trained developers who can work together efficiently and effectively.

symptom Evidence that an existing information system is inefficient or ineffective.

system A set of related components that work together in a particular environment to perform functions in order to achieve an objective.

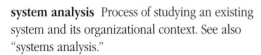

system analysis Process of studying an existing system and its organizational context. See also "systems analysis."

system behavior A response to a stimulus; the stimulus for a behavior can be satisfaction of a condition.

system behavior analysis Development activity that analyzes the functions a system must perform and the actors and documents involved in these functions.

system behavior design Development activity that specifies how system functions will be implemented using specific information technologies.

system boundary Definition of the aspects of the organization that a new information system will support; indicated on a combined user-level workflow diagram.

system data structure analysis Development activity that defines object classes, attributes, and relationships.

system data structure design Development activity that specifies how objects will be implemented as data structures.

system decomposition Taking the system apart to gain a full understanding of its parts.

system design Process of synthesizing or reassembling the components and functions identified during analysis. See also "systems design."

system development goals The criteria by which the systems development project and product are evaluated; these are the goals of a system developer.

system efficiency The ability of a system to execute its functions quickly and to minimize its use of people and hardware resources.

system environment Factors internal and external to the system that influence the operation of the system; includes the organizational context and external entities and factors.

system evolution The modification of system functions; a business-driven undertaking that requires significant user involvement and commitment.

system flowchart An analysis and design technique used to document the technological components (hardware, software, and digital data files) of an information system.

system implementation A systems development stage in which construction, testing, and installation of the new system are performed.

system life cycle Life of an information system which consists of two phases: development and production.

system maintenance The modification of one or more system components; largely a technology-driven undertaking that does not involve users.

system objective Description of the organization's goals for the system, i.e., the benefits the organization will obtain by developing the system.

system overview A design specification report section that provides easy-to-understand explanations of the final system design and relates aspects of this design to the functional requirements identified earlier in the project.

system procedure Instructions on how to operate hardware and how to start, shut down, and maintain the system.

system quality A systems development goal that evaluates the functionality, flexibility, and maintainability of an information system.

system software Software designed to control the operations of computer hardware, including not only the system unit but also all input, storage and output devices connected to the computer.

system test A test that simulates the production environment as closely as possible to verify that all components are integrated effectively and that the system performs its functions accurately, reliably, and efficiently.

system test and installation Development stage during which the system as a whole is tested to ensure that all its components work well together and then is placed into production.

systems analysis Development activity that seeks to understand the system's existing environment, document its functionality, and determine the new system's requirements. See also "system analysis."

systems approach A problem-solving method that breaks a problem into pieces, designs a solution for each piece, and then integrates the solutions into a complete system.

systems design Development activity that synthesizes the IPOSC requirements identified during the analysis stage into a new system blueprint. See also "system design."

tangible benefits Benefits that are readily quantified or assigned a dollar amount.

task analysis A user-interface analysis activity in which the procedures users employ to perform work tasks are identified, categorized, and defined.

task dependency A situation in which one activity provides outputs that are inputs to another activity and so must be completed before the second activity can begin.

task-oriented documentation An approach to creating user documentation that organizes content by task, describing system commands in terms of the tasks the user will perform to use the application.

technical documentation A document that specifies the system's design for future developers who will maintain and evolve the system (also called *system documentation*).

technical feasibility Analysis of the system in terms of software capability, reliability, and availability and the skills of the development team.

technical scribe A scribe who uses CASE and prototyping tools to document requirements and data and process definitions, to build models, and to generate prototypes.

technical specifications A design specification report section that provides final models of the system, including the physical DFDs, object

relationship or other data model, class specifications or physical database design, and so on, depending on the modeling techniques used to analyze and design the system's data structures and behaviors.

technique Method used to perform specific activities of a systems development methodology.

technology push A systems development catalyst in which a new technology that makes possible more effective and efficient ways of doing business prompts (or "pushes") an organization to fund a development project.

telecommunications devices Hardware components that allow computers to transmit data from one computer to another or from a computer to a remote peripheral device.

test data Sets of data used to perform unit and system tests; sources include data sets created by users or selected subsets of historical production data copied to the test environment.

test plan A plan that indicates the testing strategy to be employed, defines test scenarios, and assigns responsibility for testing activities to users and developers.

test specification A form used to outline the procedures for testing an information system; serves both to plan and to document the results of unit and system tests.

testing procedure Stipulates how test data will be created, what test cases will be run, who will perform each test, and how the results will be documented.

testing strategies See "black-box strategy" and "glass-box strategy."

timebox Nonextendible time limit placed on the prototyping phase in a rapid application development (RAD) project.

tool Software that supports one or more techniques.

top-down approach A system development approach that calls for the development of an integrated information system based on the business objectives.

traditional systems development Analysis of a system to identify the functions it must perform and the components from which it is constructed.

training plan A plan that outlines the training schedule, objectives, and materials; approved by the user-sponsor before training begins.

transaction analysis A program structure chart technique used to segment DFD processes into alternate flows of control depending on a condition or user selection.

transform analysis A program structure chart technique used to segment sequential DFD processes into input, processing, and output modules.

tutorial A user documentation component that instructs users in the system's basic functionality.

unit test A test to verify the correctness of each software module as it is constructed.

upsizing A system evolution strategy that involves connecting the mainframe to existing PC LANs.

usability test A test performed to ensure that system interfaces are easy to learn and use and that they support the desired level of user productivity; typically conducted by human-computer interface specialists to identify where users are most prone to make errors, to evaluate user reactions, and to assess productivity.

use case A sequence of transactions in a system whose task is to yield a result of measurable value to an individual actor of a system.

user A person who uses an information system to perform job tasks; typically a person who has attained a degree or developed skills in one of the business functional areas.

user acceptance review A final test to ensure that the system satisfies the users' acceptance criteria.

user commitment Degree to which the system's users and sponsors support the development project and are willing to use the system.

user demand A system development catalyst arising from problems that users have with the current system, including system errors, system inefficiency, system incompatibility, and the need for system enhancements.

user documentation The part of the user interface that describes how to use the system; includes the user guide, reference card, on-line help system, and tutorials.

user guide A user documentation component that describes all the manual procedures performed by users and relates each user interface to the procedure that uses it.

user interface The system aspects that are visible to users, allowing them to interact with the system's data, software, and hardware.

user review Demonstration of the system to the users, who may request changes in its design or identify additional requirements for the next iteration.

user's mental model The concepts a user develops to explain the system's behavior, giving the user expectations about the outcome of his actions.

user-level workflow diagram A workflow diagram that models the entities and workflows described by a single user.

user-manager User who supervises the work of end-users.

user-sponsor A high-ranking executive of the project who motivates users, including the user-manager, to participate in development activities; user who authorizes project initiation and approves funding for development.

validity A condition of a database that contains only authorized, genuine data; achieved by reviewing all records before file conversion.

volume test A test conducted to verify that the system meets the required response time, through-put, and demand levels set by users (also called a *capacity test*).

within-budget criterion Measures the ability to deliver the required system at the cost specified in the project budget.

workflow The transfer of data—typically a document—from one entity to another.

workflow diagram Diagram that traces the flow of data among internal and external entities.

CHECK YOUR UNDERSTANDING ANSWERS

CHECK YOUR UNDERSTANDING 1-1

1. d

2. e

3. a

4. c

5. b

CHECK YOUR UNDERSTANDING 1-2

1.
a. AA
b. DA
c. AA
d. DA
e. DA

2.
a. OOSD
b. TSD
c. TSD
d. OOSD
e. both

CHECK YOUR UNDERSTANDING 1-3

Catalysts for developing the mainframe system:

◆ User demand—system efficiency: The paper-intensive system required faxing the same documents three or four times between Hasbro's headquarters in Pawtucket, Rhode Island, Seattle, and Hong Kong.

Catalysts for developing the PC-LAN system:

◆ User demand—system efficiency: Users were frustrated by
   a. the four-hour turnaround time for printing reports from the mainframe-controlled data.
   b. the mainframe's cumbersome procedures and job queues.

◆ Technology push: The client/server PC-LAN was an attractive alternative to mainframe processing because
   a. it provided all the data access, analysis, and reporting capabilities that Hasbro needed.
   b. it would eliminate the users having to perform cumbersome procedures.

◆ Strategic pull—efficiency: Management decided that mainframe processing was too expensive given the tracking system's infrequent transaction processing activity.

CHECK YOUR UNDERSTANDING 1-4

SQ-Functionality: The mainframe-based import tracking system was *inefficient* in that it cost too much and had an unacceptable turnaround time (4 hours). The case does not provide any information about the system's *reliability*; however, given that it employed stable mainframe technology, we can assume that the hardware component was reliable. The system's "cumbersome" procedures may have been *unclear* or *inefficient*.

SQ-Flexibility: We can infer that the mainframe-based import tracking system was quite *portable* and *adaptable,* given the ease of porting the COBOL application program from the mainframe to a Windows environment.

SQ-Maintainability: Not specified.

CHECK YOUR UNDERSTANDING 1-5

OR-Efficiency: The client/server import tracking system improved Hasbro's efficiency by reducing turnaround time.

OR-Effectiveness: The client/server import tracking system improved Hasbro's effectiveness by providing better, more timely information about product status.

OR-Competitiveness: Not specified, but we could assume that gains in efficiency and effectiveness may have improved Hasbro's competitiveness.

CHECK YOUR UNDERSTANDING 2-1

Input functions:
◆ Scan resumes.
◆ Accept keywords to search.

Processing functions:
◆ Convert hard-copy resume into two computer-readable files.
◆ Process ASCII resume file to build a candidate profile.
◆ Match job requisition with candidates.
◆ Evaluate candidates.
◆ Perform keyword searches.

Output functions:
◆ Display resume image on screen.
◆ Generate letters of acknowledgement.

Storage functions:
◆ Maintain an image of each resume.
◆ Maintain an ASCII file of each resume.
◆ Maintain the candidate profile file.

◆ Maintain the job requisition file.

Control functions:

◆ Not specified.

CHECK YOUR UNDERSTANDING 2-2

People-User: A staff of 1,000 volunteers; hiring managers.

People-Designer: Computer TaskGroup, Inc.

People-Implementer: Computer TaskGroup, Inc.

Procedures-Application: Scan resumes, display resume image, perform keyword searches, and generate letters of acknowledgement.

Procedures-System: Not specified, but would include procedures for startup and shut-down of the system, using the OCR scanners, and so on.

Procedures-Control: Not specified.

CHECK YOUR UNDERSTANDING 2-3

Input data: Hard-copy resumes.

Stored data: Image of each resume, ASCII file of each resume, the candidate profile file, and the job requisition file.

Output data: Letters of acknowledgment.

CHECK YOUR UNDERSTANDING 2-4

System software: Novell network operating system, Sun Microsystems operating system (assumed), and optical character recognition software.

Application software: Resumix.

4GT: Not specified.

CHECK YOUR UNDERSTANDING 2-5

Input hardware devices: 3 OCR scanners, keyboards.

Processing hardware devices: 13 Sun Microsystems workstations, 20 personal computers.

Output hardware devices: Video display terminals, printers.

Storage hardware devices: Not specified but assume floppy and hard drives (i.e., DASD) because system needs to access records directly; could be CD-ROM for image files.

Telecommunications devices: Not specified, but assume cabling, router, hub, and so on, to connect computer systems dispersed among four floors.

CHECK YOUR UNDERSTANDING A-1

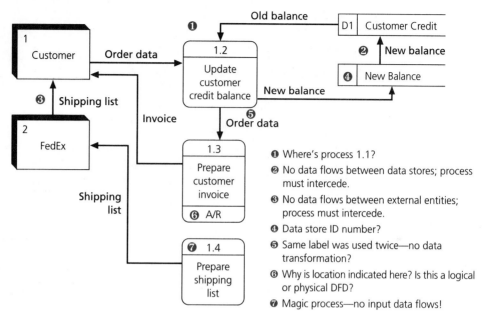

❶ Where's process 1.1?

❷ No data flows between data stores; process must intercede.

❸ No data flows between external entities; process must intercede.

❹ Data store ID number?

❺ Same label was used twice—no data transformation?

❻ Why is location indicated here? Is this a logical or physical DFD?

❼ Magic process—no input data flows!

Revised DFD

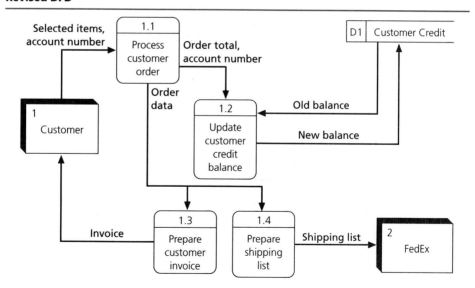

CHECK YOUR UNDERSTANDING A-2

Level 0 DFD

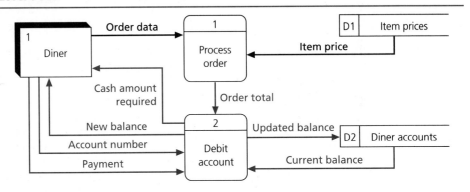

Level 1 DFD

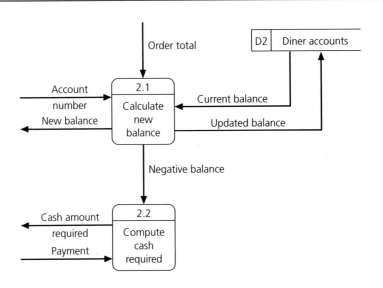

CHECK YOUR UNDERSTANDING A-3

Modified Level 0 DFD

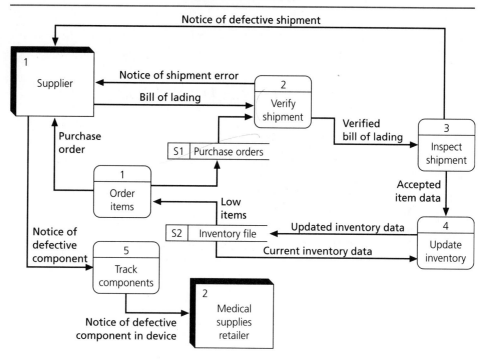

Level 1 DFD of Process 5.0

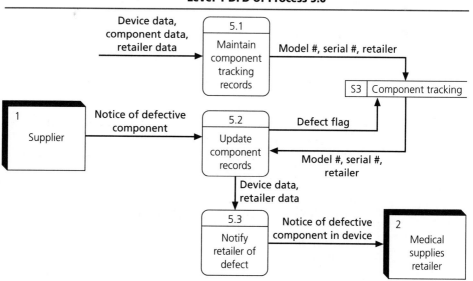

CHECK YOUR UNDERSTANDING 3-1

1. SA
2. PI
3. SA
4. SI
5. SD

6. PI
7. SD
8. SI
9. PI
10. SD

CHECK YOUR UNDERSTANDING 3-2

1. Both PD and RAD
2. Both PR and JAD
3. Primarily PD and RAD; but also JAD
4. JAD
5. Primarily PR; but also JAD
6. Primarily PR; but also JAD

CHECK YOUR UNDERSTANDING 3-3

1. DSD
2. STI
3. PI
4. PCR
5. PIA

6. BA
7. Any stage
8. FC
9. DSA or DSD
10. BD

CHECK YOUR UNDERSTANDING 4-1

1. a   organizational context
   c   operational management
   d   external entity
   e   organizational structure
   b   strategic management
2. a. Ford's accounts payable system supports the operational level of the accounts payable, receiving, and purchasing functions.
   b. Supplier: inputs provided are invoice and shipping document; outputs received are purchase order and payment.

CHECK YOUR UNDERSTANDING 4-2

1. value chain
2. process
3. process thinking, value-chain integration
4. "over the wall" thinking

CHECK YOUR UNDERSTANDING 4-3

1. T

2. P

3. O

4. O

5. P

6. O

7. T

CHECK YOUR UNDERSTANDING 4-4

To qualify as an an interorganizational system, Ford's new accounts payable system would have had to use, for example, EDI to link Ford with its suppliers. Creating an interorganizational system would have complicated Ford's project in that it would have required that the development team investigate the suppliers' requirements, thus broadening the scope and complexity of the project.

CHECK YOUR UNDERSTANDING 4-5

1. Generally F, but could be true of some legacy systems.

2. T

3. T

4. F

5. F

6. T

7. T

8. F

9. T

10. T

CHECK YOUR UNDERSTANDING C-1

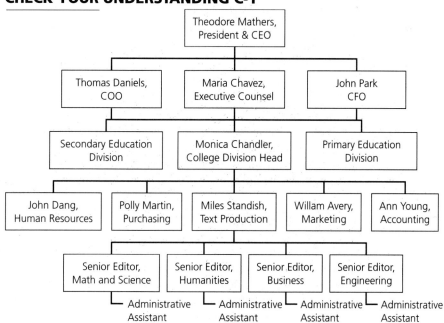

CHECK YOUR UNDERSTANDING C-2

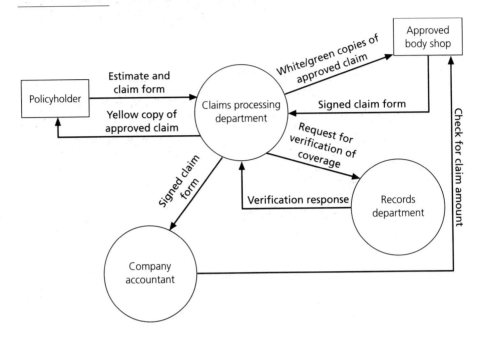

CHECK YOUR UNDERSTANDING 5-1

1. The three levels of analysis in the top-down approach are organizational (Enterprise Analysis), business area (Business Area Analysis), and process (Systems Analysis). In the Ryder project, the business areas were the key area of analysis, redesigning the order entry, sales, marketing, and inventory systems.
2. Ryder's critical success factors include excellent customer service, competitive rental rates, and unit usage maximization.
3. A temporal CSF prompting development of the RyderFirst system was the economic recession in the 1980s that caused business losses.
4. The business objectives of the system were to increase revenue-per-unit 20 percent and to decrease transfer expenses 15 percent.
5. Inventory management is critical to business unit success because Ryder must maximize the usage of its inventory (i.e., rental trucks) in order to maximize profits.

CHECK YOUR UNDERSTANDING 5-2

1. The activities addressed by the Ryder project included processing orders, managing inventory, and notifying dealers of rental rate changes and promotional campaigns.
2. The activities that use the Rental-Truck data include processing orders and managing inventory. Processing orders requires an instance of Rental-Truck data; managing inventory tracks the location and availability of each Rental-Truck .

CHECK YOUR UNDERSTANDING 6-1

1. S
2. C
3. O
4. C

5. C
6. S
7. O
8. C

CHECK YOUR UNDERSTANDING 6-2

1. a. DC
   b. DC, if done as part of development; PC, if done to maintain systems during production.
   c. DC
   d. IB

   e. PC
   f. TB
   g. TB
   h. PC
   i. IB
   j. PC

2. "Providing better customer service" could be quantified in terms of an increase in repeat business, which can be measured. "Improved management decision making" can be quantified in terms of more effective allocation of resources—lower inventory or personnel costs or fewer stockouts—and increased market share.

CHECK YOUR UNDERSTANDING 6-3

1. Op
2. T
3. Op
4. Or

5. Op
6. T
7. Or

CHECK YOUR UNDERSTANDING 7-1

1. a. GDSS
   b. facilitator
   c. NGT
   d. JAD design
   e. technical scribe

2. a. False
   b. True
   c. True
   d. False
   e. True

CHECK YOUR UNDERSTANDING 7-2

1. c
2. d
3. e
4. e
5. d

CHECK YOUR UNDERSTANDING 8-1

1. B
2. E
3. B
4. R
5. R

6. E
7. E
8. E
9. B
10. E

CHECK YOUR UNDERSTANDING 8-2

1. a. Evolutionary prototyping
   b. Evolutionary prototyping, phased development
   c. Phased development
   d. JAD

2. a. Software
   b. 4GL
   c. SWAT team
   d. Component-based application development

CHECK YOUR UNDERSTANDING D-1

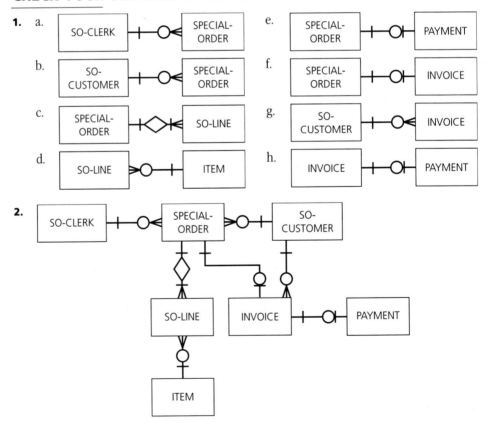

CHECK YOUR UNDERSTANDING D-2

The object classes in the Pet License Application form include OWNER, PET, DOG, CAT, and LICENSE. DOG and CAT are subclasses of PET (note that "Date of last feline leukemia vaccination" is tracked only for cats).

CHECK YOUR UNDERSTANDING D-3

Assumptions:

◆ Each pet is related to exactly one license; i.e., when the license is renewed, the existing license is updated.
◆ Each owner can own many pets and therefore be related to many licenses.
◆ The pet licensing system has "no knowledge" of an OWNER instance or a PET instance if they have never been recorded on a license.

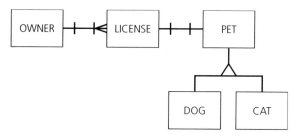

CHECK YOUR UNDERSTANDING D-4

Identifiers:

◆ OWNER = Name + Phone
◆ LICENSE = Number
◆ PET = no unique identifier; perhaps Name + Breed + RabiesVacc

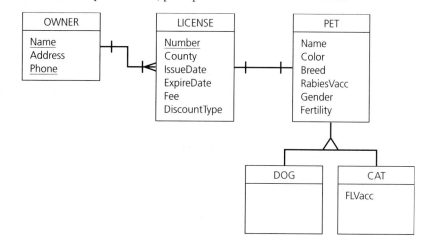

CHECK YOUR UNDERSTANDING 9-1

1.   e   field
      f   physical record
      b   file
      d   database
      a   primary key
      c   foreign key

2.   a.   Program-data dependence
      b.   Data inconsistency
      c.   Data redundancy
      d.   Interface
      e.   Any three of the following: high one-time startup costs, higher operating costs, greater complexity, increased vulnerability

CHECK YOUR UNDERSTANDING 9-2

1.   d
2.   b
3.   c
4.   d
5.   d

CHECK YOUR UNDERSTANDING 9-3

SUPPLIER (<u>SupplierID</u>, SupplierName, SupplierAddr, SupplierPhone)

PURCHASE-ORDER(<u>PONumber</u>, PODate, POTerms, POSubtotal, POSalesTax, POShipCharge, POTotal, *SupplierID, CustNumber*)

CUSTOMER (<u>CustNumber</u>, CustName, CustAddr, CustPhone, CustContact, ContactPhone)

PO-LINE (<u>*PONumber, ProdNumber*</u>, Quantity, ExtPrice)

PRODUCT (<u>ProdNumber</u>, ProdDesc, UnitOfMeasure, RecentPrice, DiscountQuantity)

CHECK YOUR UNDERSTANDING 10-1

1.   B   **5.**   B
2.   P   **6.**   P
3.   L   **7.**   B
4.   P   **8.**   P

CHECK YOUR UNDERSTANDING 10-2

Each Level 0 process is a separate partition because each performs a task at a different time. Each partition can be implemented using either batch processing or real-time processing. "Process 1.0—Bill customers" is a good candidate for batch processing because most of its input data are retrieved from files; sales order and shipping notices could be batched, their data entered into the system, and then invoices processed overnight. "Process 2.0—Manage accounts" and "Process 3.0—Process payment" are also good candidates for batch processing for the reasons just given.

The Level 1 processes 2.1 through 2.3 are grouped into one partition because all three relate to processing sales returns. The program automating these processes should be real-time if customers require immediate refunds for returned items; otherwise, it could be a batched process performed at regular intervals. "Process 2.4—Prepare bad debts journal voucher" requires a separate partition because its activity is not related to sales returns, but to nonpayment of invoices. Process 2.4 is an ideal candidate for batch processing because it is a task that can be performed at regular intervals and processes only stored data.

Thus, a total of four programs is required to automate these processes: one to invoice customers, one to process returns, one to process bad debts, and one to process payments.

CHECK YOUR UNDERSTANDING 10-3

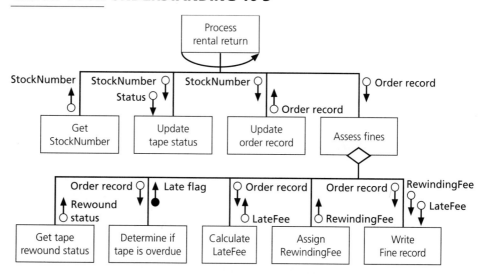

CHECK YOUR UNDERSTANDING 10-4

1. PRM
2. MS
3. E
4. PUM
5. M
6. P
7. PUM
8. E

CHECK YOUR UNDERSTANDING 10-5

1. The method reportStatus should be contained in ACCOUNT because ACCOUNT is the controlling class.
2. The method addAccount should be contained in CUSTOMER because CUSTOMER is the controlling class.
3. Neither LINE-ITEM nor PRODUCT contains all the attributes required to perform this method. Nonetheless, the method calculateExtPrice should be contained in LINE-ITEM because LINE-ITEM will require a method to get PRODUCT as part of its other responsibilities, thus giving it access to the Price attribute.

CHECK YOUR UNDERSTANDING 11-1

1. a. ED   e. R
    b. HCD   f. HCD
    c. R   g. ED
    d. DES   h. HCD

2. The Sales report in 1c should be printed because it will not fit on one or two screens. The Past Due Accounts report in 1e can be a screen report, assuming that it will fit on one or two screens and that only one user is responsible for calling delinquent customers. However, if several users call delinquent customers, thus requiring the report items to be parceled out to many users, it may be more effective to print the report.

CHECK YOUR UNDERSTANDING 11-2

1. d   5. a
2. e   6. d
3. d   7. e
4. e

CHECK YOUR UNDERSTANDING 11-3

1. F   6. T
2. T   7. T
3. F   8. T
4. T   9. F
5. T   10. T

CHECK YOUR UNDERSTANDING 12-1

1. SO   7. TS
2. TS   8. TS
3. SO   9. SO (nontechnical description), TS (technical description)
4. SO
5. SO   10. TS
6. TS

CHECK YOUR UNDERSTANDING 12-2

1. F
2. F
3. T
4. F

5. T
6. T
7. F

CHECK YOUR UNDERSTANDING 12-3

1. I
2. FC
3. T
4. FC
5. I

6. FC
7. all
8. FC
9. T
10. T

CHECK YOUR UNDERSTANDING 13-1

a. operations manual
b. integrated performance support system
c. file conversion
d. technical documentation

e. selection criteria
f. benchmarks
g. integration test
h. training plan

CHECK YOUR UNDERSTANDING 13-2

1. a. BB
   b. GB
   c. GB
   d. BB
   e BB

2. a. F
   b. T
   c. F
   d. T
   e. F

CHECK YOUR UNDERSTANDING 13-3

1. This system should be installed using the parallel operation strategy because it performs a critical task in monitoring a patient's vital signs. Both the old and the new system should operate concurrently until the users have been assured that the new system is reliable and accurate.

2. This system should be installed using either the phased or pilot installation strategy. Phasing installation by branch is appropriate because it allows bank management to determine the system's accuracy and reliability before installing it at other locations. Also the task of installing the system at all branches simultaneously would be costly and complex; phasing in the systems would allow the bank to spread the costs over a longer time period. The pilot installation strategy would also be appropriate. If the system does not function acceptably at the pilot location, management will be spared the cost and added detriment of having installed it at all branches, thus reducing risk.

3. A small system such as this is a good candidate for the direct cutover strategy. The "award-winning" package is probably accurate and reliable, so black-box testing should establish its compatibility with other system components, thus minimizing the risk of system failure. In addition, the hardware store management can devise a fall-back plan in the unlikely event of system failure.

4. An integrated system consisting of several modules, is ideal for phased installation. The system should be installed one module at a time; only after the installed module is functioning reliably and users have become accustomed to it should another module be installed.

INDEX